ETHICS IN PSYCHOLOGY

ETHICS IN PSYCHOLOGY

Professional Standards and Cases

Second Edition

GERALD P. KOOCHER
Harvard Medical School

PATRICIA KEITH-SPIEGEL
Ball State University

New York • Oxford

Oxford University Press

1998

Oxford University Press

Oxford   New York
Athens   Auckland   Bangkok   Bogota   Bombay   Buenos Aires
Calcutta   Cape Town   Dar es Salaam   Delhi   Florence   Hong Kong
Istanbul   Karachi   Kuala Lumpur   Madras   Madrid   Melbourne
Mexico City   Nairobi   Paris   Singapore   Taipei   Tokyo   Toronto   Warsaw

and associated companies in
Berlin   Ibadan

Published by Oxford University Press, Inc.
198 Madison Avenue, New York, New York 10016

Oxford is a registered trademark of Oxford University Press

Library of Congress Cataloging-in-Publication Data
Koocher, Gerald P.
   Ethics in psychology : professional standards and cases /
Gerald P. Koocher, Patricia Keith-Spiegel. — 2nd ed.
      p.   cm. — (Oxford textbooks in clinical psychology ; v. 3)
   Rev. ed. of: Ethics in psychology / Patricia Keith-Spiegel, Gerald
P. Koocher. 1st ed. c1985.
   Includes bibliographical references and index.
   ISBN 0-19-509201-5
   1. Psychologists—Professional ethics.   2. Psychology—Research—
Moral and ethical aspects.   3. Psychology—Study and teaching—
Moral and ethical aspects.   4. Psychology—Standards.
I. Koocher, Gerald P.   II. Keith-Spiegel, Patricia.   Ethics in
psychology.   III. Title.   IV. Series.
BF76.4.K46   1998
174'.915—dc21   97-28322

9 8 7 6 5 4 3

Printed in the United States of America
on acid-free paper

We dedicate this volume to Gleena, The Prince, Gritty, and the Snares.

—GPK and PCK-S

Preface

To be good is noble, but to teach others to be good is nobler and less trouble.

Mark Twain

When our first edition was published in 1985, the American Psychological Association (APA) had 60,000 members, and specific courses on professional and scientific ethics in psychology graduate programs were only just beginning to evolve. Today more than 151,000 psychologists and psychology students are affiliated with the APA, and every graduate training program accredited by the APA is expected to provide specific training in ethics for its students.

The changing scope of psychology is reflected in the substantially revised content of this volume. Psychologists continue to fill their traditional roles as teachers, researchers, diagnosticians, psychotherapists, measurement experts, curriculum designers, and so forth. However, increasing numbers of psychologists are managers, organizational and agency consultants, elected officials, public policy makers, foundation heads, and university presidents. In 1985 microcomputer technology was a novelty, no one had heard of the "electronic superhighway" or the Internet, and very few people had heard of HMOs. Professional liability insurance policy rates were low. Managed care and "telemedicine" were not yet on our event horizon, and ethical controversies of the day focused on issues such as psychologists in the broadcast media and advertising. Few openly questioned the notion that sexual intimacies between clients and psychotherapists should be prohibited for life.

Notwithstanding the changes in our field in both size and scope, psychologists have insisted on maintaining and enforcing a code of ethics applicable to all psychologists, especially those who are either members of the American Psychological Association or who are licensed by a state or provincial licensing board adopting the APA ethics code. Although the most recent version of the code, officially adopted by the American Psychological Association in 1992, is relatively brief and easy to read, its application in specific situations is often extremely difficult; thus many of the implicit and necessary ethical dilemmas are left for individual psychologists to resolve on their own.

PURPOSE AND GOALS
OF THE BOOK

Our primary purpose is to present the full range of contemporary ethical issues in psychology as not only relevant and intriguing, but also as integral and unavoidable aspects of the professional role of a psychologist. Regardless of one's training specialty or the work setting, ethical dilemmas will arise—probably with some regularity—and action decisions must be made. By providing an awareness of the ethical standards of the profession, and by revealing how they apply to specific situations, we hope to achieve a useful and practical guide.

After serving for many years on ethics committees and licensing boards, we began to realize that numerous people who are already functioning as fully trained psychologists are not as well attuned to the expectations for ethical conduct and how the profession monitors itself as they could be. We also observed that inquiries to ethics committees or calls for consultation on ethical matters often arrive after-the-fact and that the resolution primarily involves reactive or remedial, rather than preventative, steps. Consequently, this book sensitizes readers to the monitoring and redress mechanisms available when ethical violations occur, and it also provides information and decision-making strategies to assist in avoiding or preventing ethical misconduct.

Nonetheless, we cannot provide solutions to every conceivable ethical problem that might arise in psychology practice, research, or teaching. Many specific situations are, in fact, so complicated that no ethics code, policy guideline, or law can deftly point the way to a satisfactory and "correct" resolution. In some situations, for example, one ethical principle may seem to be pitted against another, or upholding an ethical principle may be at variance with a legal requirement, leaving the psychologist mired somewhere in the middle. Moreover, the discipline of psychology and our society in general are constantly evolving, causing profound ethical dilemmas that neither the ethics code nor the profession are fully equipped to handle. We do assume, however, that the more information and sensitization to issues made available to psychologists or psychologists in training, the better they will be able to sort out even the most complex ethical problems and make the best possible professional judgment.

AN EXPLANATION OF SOME
SPECIFIC FEATURES OF THIS BOOK

This book was revised using the most recent ethics code of the American Psychological Association (1992) as a starting point. The document, formally known as the *Ethical Principles of Psychologists and Code of Conduct* was a radical revision of its predecessor code (last overhauled substantially in 1981), driven almost as much by legal and regulatory forces as by psychological innovation. We are not entirely happy with the 1992 code, for reasons that are discussed throughout this book. As a result, the content goes well beyond the APA code and incorporates the input of many psychology ethics experts. Even as this book goes to press, a new task force formed to revise that version of the code has held its initial meeting. Yet, the 1992 code is in force, so we have cited it as relevant extensively throughout the text and have reprinted it as an appendix.

We have annotated the text of the book with reference to the APA ethics code throughout. When relevant, we cite the portions of the code that are aspirational (i.e., the Ethical Principles of Psychologists) with bracketed notations to the relevant principle, thus: [EP: A], to cite Ethical Principle A. When referring to the enforceable standards of the code (i.e., the Code of Conduct) we use the bracketed notation [ES] followed by the specific numerical location to identify the relevant ethical standard. We hope that this will make it easy for the reader to look up the exact wording of the code in Appendix A as relevant to the text discussion. We also reprint the *Rules and Procedures* (R&P) of the APA Ethics Committee for information as Appendix B. The R&P change much more frequently than the code, so readers may want to check with the APA Ethics Office for the current version from time to time.

Because ethical problems often overlap or cluster around several principles, it was difficult to create neat piles of material from which to develop discrete chapters. Whereas each chapter has a specific focus, some cross-referencing was necessary to inform readers where additional information may be found. Although we have attempted to be comprehensive, it was certainly not possible to cover, in a single volume, every conceivable ethical situation that psychologists might face. The omission of specific topics should not be taken to suggest that they are unimportant, and the neglect of some forms of questionable conduct does not mean that such behaviors are implicitly condoned.

We use case vignettes as a way to illustrate ethics. Our case examples are adapted from ethics committees' case files, licensing board decisions, case law, or from actual incidents known to us. Except for public information (e.g., news stories and case law), we have disguised the material in a variety of ways, such as through combining the details of one case with another, switching the sex of one or more principals, or altering contexts in which the activity occurred. It should also be noted that we often "trimmed" cases by focusing on only one aspect of the charge or violation. In fact, most cases brought to the attention of ethics committees involve charges of violating two or more ethical principles.

As in our last edition, we continue to avoid routine methods of designating the principal characters in our case material (e.g., "Dr. A." or "the client"). We also wanted to reduce the risk of using bogus names that might correspond to those of real people. Hence, most of our pseudonyms are highly contrived. Students report finding this approach more readable and memorable. In using clearly bogus names, it is *never* our intent to trivialize the seriousness of the content under discussion, but rather to enhance interest and recall of specific cases. Any resulting resemblance between the names of our characters and those of actual people is purely coincidental. The names used in particular cases do *not* even remotely resemble the names of the actual people involved. When actual names of the principals are used, the case material is accompanied in the text by citation of the relevant legal case or other public source.

ACKNOWLEDGMENTS

A book aspiring to provide appropriate guidance for ethical decisions and actions across a wide range of professional and scholarly activity carries a heavy responsibility. We felt obligated to submit our chapters to extensive external review by acknowledged experts in specific topic areas. We were also fortunate to have consultation from a number of students who reviewed chapters from their unique consumer's perspective. We are deeply indebted to our reviewers for their invaluable assistance in ensuring the accuracy and integrity our book. Among our psychologist colleagues, we wish to offer special thanks to Drs. Norman Abeles, Celia B. Fisher, Thomas G. Plante, and Michael Wiederman, who read the entire volume and offered extensive detailed comments. We also offer special applause to Marci Gaither of Ball State University who, as head of our student consulting group, also reviewed the complete manuscript making extensive helpful comments. We extend our appreciation to the following professional colleagues, a talented group of psychologists, ethicists, attorneys, physicians, students, and hybrids who also comprised our reviewing panel: Deborah Ware Balogh, Melvyn S. Berger, Bruce E. Bennett, Debra Borys, Patricia Bricklin, Laura S. Brown, James N. Butcher, Jessica Henderson Daniel, Elena J. Eisman, Lorraine D. Eyde, Glenn O. Gabbard, Michael C. Gottlieb, Leonard J. Haas, Eric Harris, Walter M. Haney, Shirley Higuchi, Samuel S. Hill, Stanley E. Jones, Karen S. Kitchener, James H. Korn, James L. McHugh, Wilbert J. McKeachie, Russell J. Newman, John C. Norcross, David V. Perkins, Kerri Pickel, Kenneth S. Pope, Richard Racimora, Gerald M. Rosen, Simon S. Rubin, Joan E. Sieber, Daniel E. Shapiro, David L. Shapiro, Janet L. Sonne, Donald E. Spiegel, George P. Taylor, Leon D. VandeCreek, Melba J. Vasquez, Kate M. Wachs, Bernard E. Whitley, Jr., Arno F. Wittig; and student editorial consultants: Rose Carano, Kim Carr, Jennifer Klimek, Robin Lett, and Darrell Leslie.

Boston, Massachusetts   G. P. K.
Muncie, Indiana   P. K.-S.
November 1997

Contents

ETHICS IN PSYCHOLOGY

OXFORD TEXTBOOKS IN CLINICAL PSYCHOLOGY

Editorial Board

Larry E. Beutler
James N. Butcher
Gerald P. Koocher
John C. Norcross
Diane J. Willis

Series Editor

Bruce Bongar

1

On Being an Ethical Psychologist

Always do right; this will gratify some people and
astonish the rest.

Mark Twain

A young client who has just received news of passing the bar exam bounces toward you with wide,
outstretched arms and puckered lips.

You arrive at your office complex anxious to meet
the new receptionist that the others in your group
practice hired while you were on vacation. There
at the desk sits a person who had been your client
for four years.

Your sister pleads with you to treat her oldest son.
He has been setting fires at school, and she insists
that he refuses to be counseled by anyone but you.

The client has a wild look in her eyes. She hisses,
"That creep is going to pay big time for what he
did, and tonight is the night." You are pretty sure
that she owns a gun.

The department chair expressed how very appre-
ciative he would be if you would teach the course
in personality theory next semester. You are up for
tenure and do not want to risk displeasing your
supervisor. But, you have only taken one course
in personality theory, and that was 11 years ago
as a junior in college.

INTRODUCTION

This book considers many of the ethical questions and dilemmas that psychologists encounter in their everyday practice, research, and
teaching. Most psychologists enter the profession with a desire to promote human welfare
and, directly or indirectly, to serve others. As
such, the majority of psychologists would never
intentionally harm their clients, students, or colleagues and others with whom they work. Unfortunately, good intentions are not enough to
ensure that wrongs will not occur, and psychologists often have no choice but to make ethically
ambiguous decisions. We acknowledge that
confusion, pressure, frustrations, anxiety, and
the tendency to rationalize or intellectualize are
common responses to ethical challenges. We
aim to provide insights and ideas for our readers
that will help recognize, constructively approach,
and reconcile ethical predicaments while, at
the same time, remaining compassionate and
concerned about the well-being of those with
whom you work.

Ethics is traditionally a branch of philosophy that deals with moral problems and moral judgments. White (1988) defines ethics as the evaluation of human actions. In doing so, we evaluate behavior as "right" or "wrong," "good" or "bad," "acceptable" or "unacceptable" according to the perspective of a moral principle or ethical guideline. In this book we approach professional ethics and standards from a practical perspective, applying some core ethical principles to situations presented in the course of the work that psychologists do. Ethics codes are almost as old as recorded history, with the Hippocratic oath (written about 400 B.C.) the first profession-generated code of ethics (Sinclair, Simon, & Pettifor, 1996). We apply the formal ethical guidelines and professional standards, primarily the ethics code of the American Psychological Association (APA, 1992), although we sometimes take issue with some of its provisions. The complete APA code can be found in appendix A. We cite it whenever we discuss a specific ethical principle (designated EP, followed by the appropriate letter) or ethical standard (designated ES, followed by the appropriate number). The reader may refer to the wording directly.

Ethics and Risk Management

A "risk management" approach to ethics has become popular in recent years as a result of the increasing number of complaints and lawsuits against psychologists. This approach involves taking as many steps as possible to avoid being placed in precarious ethical or legal circumstances. The focus of risk management is to assist practitioners in protecting themselves against the hazards of modern-day professional practice (see Bennett, Bryant, VandenBos, & Greenwood, 1990; Gottlieb, 1994; Stromberg et al., 1988). The key to effective risk management involves scrupulously upholding the tenets of relevant laws, policies, professional standards, and ethics codes.

Whereas the practice of defensive ethics makes good sense in a litigious society, it may also insidiously create the mind-set that consumers of services are always out to "get" psychologists. We take the position that the rationale for being an ethically aware and sensitive

psychologist is not solely for self-protection. Being ethical also ensures delivery of the best possible service to consumers and a personally gratifying career. Reaching for the highest standards emboldens us in the face of ethical uncertainty. Holding high ethical standards requires acting with benevolence and courage rather than donning protective armor and running for a safe place to hide.

Core Ethical Principles

Ethical perfection is beyond reach for most of us humans, even if we could completely agree on what is "ethically proper" in every situation. Furthermore, all psychologists will encounter ethical dilemmas, such as the ones presented at the beginning of this chapter, and not know exactly what to do. We recognize that situational factors, insufficient information, conflicting loyalties, and other conditions converge to challenge even the most principled among us, and these obstacles to ethical perfection also are more fully discussed.

The nine core ethical principles that we believe should guide the behavior of psychologists are adapted from several sources (Beauchamp & Childress, 1989; Frankena, 1973; Gilligan, 1982; Josephson, 1991; Kitchener, 1985; Ross, 1930).

1. *Doing no harm* (nonmaleficence). Through commission or omission, psychologists strive to benefit those with whom they work, at the same time taking care to ensure that the potential for damage is eliminated or minimized to the greatest extent possible.

2. *Respecting autonomy.* The rights of individuals to decide how to live their lives as long as their actions do not interfere with the welfare of others is accepted by psychologists as an ultimate goal for clients, students, research participants, and others with whom psychologists work. Members of our profession are often in the business of moving those with whom we work toward greater independence and self-reliance.

3. *Benefiting others.* All decisions that psychologists make should have the potential for a positive effect on others. Often, this principle must be balanced against doing no harm, respect for autonomy, available resources, and utility.

4. *Being just.* Actions should be fair and equitable. Others should be treated as psychologists would want to be treated under similar circumstances.

5. *Being faithful.* Issues of fidelity, loyalty, truthfulness, trust, promise keeping, and respect for those with whom psychologists work converge to form the delicate standards necessary in fiduciary relationships. When psychologists are straightforward, sincere, candid, and without intent to mislead or deceive anyone, ethical action is more likely.

6. *According dignity.* Psychologists view others as worthy of respect. This enhances the probability that decisions will be ethical.

7. *Treating others with caring and compassion.* Psychologists should be considerate and kind to those with whom they work, yet maintain professional boundaries.

8. *Pursuit of excellence.* Maintaining competence, doing one's best, and taking pride in one's work are important in ensuring high-quality professional services, as well as providing hedges against unprofessional and unethical actions.

9. *Accepting accountability.* Psychologists who act with a consideration of possible consequences, who accept responsibility for actions and inactions, and who avoid shifting blame or making excuses are acting with integrity. Putting principles over expediency is sometimes the longer and more arduous route, but in the long run it is the one that ensures self-respect.

What may strike you about the nine ethical principles is that some are unlikely to be practiced unless they are already embedded in the fabric of psychologists' characters. For example, is it possible to "act" with caring and compassion unless that is the kind of person one already is? Ideally, people behave ethically because they have virtuous characters. But, "principle ethics," defined for our purposes as acting according to the moral principles listed above, allows the possibility that ethical behavior can occur solely as the result of professional obligation and deliberate adherence to rules rather than moral commitment according to one's conscience and personally held standards. The reader interested in learning more about principle versus virtue ethics as they apply to psychology is referred to Meara, Schmidt, and Day (1996).

HOW ETHICAL PROBLEMS ARISE

Who Is Unethical?

The stereotype of the "unethical psychologist" is quite unsavory. "Greedy," "stupid," "psychopathic," "devious," and "immoral" are among the common descriptors according to our own informal polling of colleagues. Some psychologists do willfully, even maliciously, engage in acts they know to be in violation of the ethical and legal standards. How avarice, expediency, and other self-serving motives can blur judgments is illustrated throughout this book. The cases below illustrate the lurid, extreme range of unacceptable acts by mental health professionals. As with all of our cases, they are based on true incidents.

Case 1-1: A psychologist plotted against a former client who had accused him of professional misconduct. The psychologist hired a man to burglarize a business and place the stolen items in the ex-client's home and then to call the police with a tip that a person fitting the client's description was observed leaving the victim's business in a car with the ex-client's license number. Fortunately for the ex-client, the hired burglar repeated the story to others in a bar, leading to his quick arrest and disclosure of the psychologist's scheme.

Case 1-2: A jury found in favor of a client, and awarded her a large sum, after the woman made a compelling case that her therapist had sex with her regularly over a 10-year period while she was a client. In addition, the therapist had rented a home for her and employed her as his family's housekeeper. The defendant claimed that his conduct should be excused because the "sex was good" and the client was no more disabled currently than when she entered his care. His attempt to escape liability was not persuasive to the jury.

Psychologists count on consumers' trust to accomplish their most effective work; however, these cases reveal how that trust can be badly abused. But, are such drastic behaviors typical of psychologists who violate professional ethical standards? In our experience, the prevailing portrait of those crossing over the line is considerably more muted and complex and can include people of decency, intelligence, and emotional fitness caught up in circumstances that they did not evaluate or respond to appropriately.

Although rarely mutually exclusive, the underlying characteristics of psychologists who engage in questionable, unethical, or unprofessional behavior can be illustrated as falling into nine primary categories: Those who (1) are unaware or misinformed with regard to the ethical standards; (2) practice outside their realm of competence; (3) are insensitive to the needs of their clients or students or to the dynamics of a situation; (4) are exploitative; (5) behave irresponsibly; (6) seek vengeance against perceived harms to themselves by clients or other professional entities; (7) are fearful; (8) rationalize inappropriately; and (9) are usually competent and aware but "slip," lose sight of a goal, or become momentarily distracted. These categories are described more fully below.

1. *The Unaware or Misinformed Psychologist.* A substantial number of violators appear to be either naive or uneducated about the standards of their profession. Offenses of ignorance can be fairly minor and cause no one real harm (Keith-Spiegel, 1977).

Case 1-3: Recently licensed Stanley Unworldly,[1] Ph.D., accepted the offer of Trendy Cool, his brother-in-law, a marketing specialist, to help promote his fledgling private practice. A flashy advertisement in the local paper gave a misleading description of Unworldly's professional experience. For example, "trained at Memorial Hospital" referred to a year of volunteer work that Unworldly performed at the hospital as a high school student. Another psychologist in the building called Unworldly in for a chat and pointed out that Unworldly himself retained professional responsibility for such statements and was lax in allowing his relative to "run loose around the truth."

For the minor violators in this category, educative contacts are typically sufficient to ensure that the behavior will not recur. Often inexperienced, these psychologists are usually embar-

rassed on being informed of their obliviousness and frequently insist that such matters were never discussed during their formal training.

Sometimes, psychologists operate under the belief that they are fully aware of an ethical provision when, in fact, no such provision exists or what is stated in the ethics code is misunderstood.

Case 1-4: When questioned by an ethics committee about an affair that went awry with a client he had terminated only a month earlier, Romeo Quickie, Psy.D., replied that the APA ethics code specifically stated that sex with ex-clients was perfectly acceptable.

How the 1992 APA ethics code responds to sexual relationships with those who were previously clients is discussed fully in chapter 9 (see ES: 4.07), but we note here that Dr. Quickie's understanding was very confused. Ignorance, however, will not let Quickie off the hook.

For those violators who are more experienced but who have lost touch with their professional identity and commitment, remediation is considerably more difficult. Some of the most serious infractions are committed by psychologists in this group, suggesting that far more than simple ignorance is operating.

Case 1-5: Urie Upper, Ph.D., was contacted by an ethics panel regarding his alleged distribution of amphetamines during group therapy sessions. He responded that he was "under the distinct impression that psychologists had the same prescriptive privileges as physicians." He claimed to "have read about it somewhere." "And besides," he continued, "it makes the sessions much more lively."

2. *The Incompetent Psychologist.* The misconduct of psychologists in this category arises from an incapacity to competently perform the services being rendered. Sometimes, their training is inadequate, or some other factor, such as emotional disturbance, has blunted their ability to do competent work. Competence is not al-

---

1. We use improbable names throughout the text as a way to enhance interest and, because our cases are based on actual events, ensure that identities of all parties are not discernible. It is not our intention to trivialize the seriousness of the issues.

ways easy for psychologists to assess in themselves. Many who come to the attention of ethics committees or licensing boards have vastly miscalculated the level of their overall skills or of their ability to apply a specific technique or provide a particular service, such as a neuropsychological assessment or expert forensic testimony.

Case 1-6: A clinic supervisor eventually recognized that many clients were being misdiagnosed and provided with inappropriate treatment plans based on the reports of Remi Partway, Ph.D., the psychologist hired to do diagnostic assessments. When the supervisor asked Partway to detail her training and experience with several specific tests, Partway admitted she had virtually no training or experience but believed she was "picking up speed" on her own.

Partway's situation is, unfortunately, too common. Typical doctoral training programs cannot teach every skill a particular employer may require. We have even run across cases for which employers insist that services be provided anyway, even with full knowledge that the psychologist lacks the requisite training. Chapter 3 is devoted to fully exploring the ethical ramifications of incompetence.

Psychologists suffering from their own emotional difficulties, personal stressors, or burnout also account for a substantial number of violators of ethical standards. Their problems often lead to poor professional judgment and incompetent performance of services. Although this is a pitiable group, they can cause considerable harm to vulnerable consumers.

Case 1-7: Colleagues reported to the clinic manager that Melanie Gloom, Psy.D., was not coming to the office at all, nor was she calling to cancel her appointments. It took some of her clients almost an hour by bus to get to and from the clinic. A few quit coming at all, complaining to the receptionist that their therapist did not even care enough about them to show up for an appointment. It was then discovered that Gloom, herself, was so depressed that she could not always pull herself out of bed.

Case 1-8: Ed Bellevue, Ph.D., physically attacked a client with an umbrella, claiming that she was an agent of Zardac, the dark force that dwells behind the sun.

Psychologists are not immune to emotional disorders, including serious psychopathology. Obviously, the actual people we call Drs. Gloom and Bellevue were in need of treatment themselves (ES: 1.13).

3. *The Insensitive Psychologist.* Though an elusive category, psychologists often exceed the bounds of ethical propriety because they appear to have insufficient regard for the needs and feelings, and sometimes the rights and welfare, of clients, colleagues, and students. Reasons are varied and include lack of empathy, a need to exercise control, overzealousness regarding a specific approach, and prejudicial attitudes toward certain groups of people. Often, the insensitivity precludes the recognition that an ethical issue even exists.

Case 1-9: Justin Tyme, Ph.D. was often late for therapy sessions. When a female client complained, he responded, "You don't have a job, so what difference does it make?"

Case 1-10: After taking continuing education classes in hypnosis, Lila Spellbinder, Psy.D., wanted to use her newly acquired skill on every client, regardless of their reasons for consulting her. When a client expressed reticence, she told him that he was being very silly and stupid, and if he really wanted to improve he would do things her way.

Case 1-11: Fred Narrow, Ed.D., informed the international exchange students, who attempted to introduce information relevant to class discussion about their cultures, that their perspectives were not germane to the course content. Soon, these students were not participating in the discussions, and Narrow faulted them for being disinterested in his class. "You are here to learn our ways, and you can't do that by just sitting there like lumps."

4. *The Exploitative Psychologist.* Exploitation occurs when psychologists take advantage of consumers by abusing a position of trust, expertise, or authority. Psychologists who allow

their own needs to take precedence over those of consumers they serve, or who put the lure of financial gain above the welfare of consumers, best fit the common stereotype of the unethical psychologist.

Engaging in sexual activity with current clients, students, and supervisees is the most commonly discussed form of exploitation. Other forms of multiple role relationships entered into for the purpose of giving the psychologist some advantage or personal gratification are increasingly problematic and have been more openly discussed in recent years. Chapters 8 and 13 discuss these matters in detail, and the 1992 APA code has several references to issues of exploitation (see, especially, ES: 1.19). Here, we illustrate how subtle and largely undetectable such exploitation can be.

Case 1-12: Tom Stare, Ph.D., created a seating plan in his classroom that purposely placed Minny Monroe in the first row, directly in front of the lecture podium. He confided to a colleague that the entire seating scheme was done to position himself near an "adorable chick who wears short skirts and doesn't always pay attention to what she is doing with her legs." When the colleague suggested that his behavior was questionable, Stare countered that the colleague had "no sense of humor" and was "obviously getting old."

Professor Stare's attitude is quite typical of exploitative psychologists. He clearly has no insight into what his view of harmless gratification and how it might influence the quality of his teaching and the care and seriousness he brings to this class. He has also taken advantage of a student to whom he owes a professional responsibility.

The percentage of exploitative psychologists who could be described as avaricious, placing financial considerations ahead of professional standards, is probably low. Among those who could be described as greedy, many are what we term "green menaces," inexperienced or novice psychologists in a hurry to become wealthy or successful. They often try a misguided gimmick or overrate their services. Occasionally, someone calls them on it.

Case 1-13: Jacob Ladder, Psy.D., attempted to convince a client, who was a supporting actor in a long-running television series, to pass out Ladder's business cards on the set and attest to Ladder's "magical skills" as a therapist. When the client refused, Ladder expressed anger and disappointment. The disgusted client terminated Ladder's services and contacted a local ethics committee.

Some exploitative psychologists are recalcitrant and difficult to educate. Their infractions can be serious, such as defrauding insurance companies, accepting kickbacks, using elaborate bait-and-switch techniques, or making highly misleading claims about the effectiveness of their services.

5. *The Irresponsible Psychologist.* Ethical infractions based on irresponsible behavior arise in several forms, including lack of reliable execution of professional duties, shoddy or superficial professional work, and attempts to blame others or make excuses for mistakes.

Case 1-14: Janet Slow, Ph.D., agreed to support Job Hunter in his quest for employment. However, Mr. Hunter learned that Dr. Slow failed to return prospective employers' calls and that the promised letters of recommendation were never written. When Hunter expressed disappointment to Dr. Slow, she apologized, explaining that she had gotten so busy that she didn't even have time to take care of her own priorities.

Abandonment, a form of irresponsibility, occurs when psychologists fail to follow through with their duties in a way that then causes consumers of their services to become vulnerable or to feel discarded or rejected. Consumers may feel the psychologist's abdication of responsibilities leaves them resourceless or rejected. Many complaints from psychotherapy clients echo themes of abandonment.

Case 1-15: As Dee Compensating became increasingly ill, Lucia Panicky, Ph.D., did not want to continue treating her. Dr. Panicky informed Dee that she couldn't be her client any longer and Dee should find another therapist. When Dee asked for an explanation, Panicky only replied, "I have my reasons."

It is likely that all psychologists have found themselves in situations from which they wished to extricate themselves. In many such instances, they probably should disengage. Dr. Panicky may have been incompetent to continue treating her client. However, termination of services must be handled sensitively and with due regard for consumers' needs and welfare, as is discussed more fully in chapter 4.

6. *The Vengeful Psychologist.* Psychologists who actively seek revenge against a colleague or service consumer are few. However, occasionally psychologists become outraged and allow their emotions to supersede their professional judgment. Usually, the infraction involves an impulsive act, as opposed to a premeditated plot to retaliate against an antagonist. The behavior is often characterized by a childish quality.

Case 1-16: Edgar Touchy, Ph.D., became so angry at a client, who scoffed at his interpretation of the meaning of a past event, that he retorted with a barrage of profanity.

Often, vengeful psychologists feel remorseful and foolish later and frequently apologize for their loss of control. Unfortunately, permanent damage may already have been done because the impact of such outbursts cannot always be fully rectified. Rarely, acts of vengeance can be perilous.

Case 1-17: When Vinny Dictive, Psy.D., was laid off from his job at a mental health clinic, he waited in the parking lot and fired a shot at the medical director as she was getting into her car, wounding her in the hip.

7. *The Fearful Psychologist.* Psychologists sometimes attempt to cover fears of retribution or exposure for already committed acts (or observed acts of others) that would create embarrassment or serious consequences should they be openly disclosed. In doing so, they commit additional acts of commission or omission that are also unethical.

Case 1-18: Isaw Ewe, a graduate research assistant, confronted Ivan Trim, Ph.D., with his concerns that Trim had deleted some of the data collected as part of a large grant project on a treatment for adults with mental disabilities. These alterations resulted in attaining statistically significant results that suggested the treatment was effective. Dr. Trim denied the charges and, apparently out of fear of being discovered, started spreading rumors that Mr. Ewe was a pathological liar.

Fortunately for Mr. Ewe, a backup disk containing the original data was brought forward by another graduate student, thus vindicating Mr. Ewe.

Case 1-19: Lila Witness, Ph.D., caught a glimpse of her colleague Hulk Knockum, Ed.D., buttoning his pants as a female client left his office in their group counseling complex. She had suspected misbehavior, but never confronted Hulk because she found him intimidating. Several months later, the client contacted Dr. Witness. The client had noticed what Witness observed and asked if she would testify to it in a civil trial. Witness denied seeing anything and suggested the client drop the case.

Witness was not an active accomplice, nor was the client in her care. But, Knockum was her colleague, and she chose to lie to protect him. Like those who do nothing, and additionally cover up when they observe one family member abusing another, Witness is ethically tainted.

8. *The Psychologist Who Rationalizes.* We have been struck over the years by the dazzling array of defenses psychologists have used to justify behaviors that many others would judge as highly questionable. Here are two examples, one outrageous and the other more representative of what well-meaning psychologists might get themselves into without fully thinking a matter through.

Case 1-20: When asked why he admitted to having had sex with 17 clients even though he knew it was prohibited, Clouded Thot, Ph.D., replied, "It was my way of giving generously of myself to women who desperately needed love."

Sometimes, psychologists may have had very good intentions that blinded them to potential problems, as the next case illustrates.

Case 1-21: Rollie Blender, Psy.D., was surprised that a client threatened to contact an ethics committee. Blender had hired the client to be his gardener because the client was recently released from a mental hospital, had little work experience, and could not find a job. Blender thought he was doing the client a big favor, but the client complained that gardeners are supposed to earn more than minimum wage.

Rationalization often operates under subtle and seemingly harmless circumstances, sometimes to justify inaction or convenience. Psychologists need to remain alert because we are all vulnerable to talking ourselves in or out of doing something based on reasoning that is other than honest and clearheaded. The Josephson Institute of Ethics (Josephson, 1991) offers a list of rationalizations used to justify unethical behavior; the list includes "If it's necessary, it's ethical"; "If it's legal, it's proper"; "I'm just fighting fire with fire"; "It doesn't hurt anyone"; "It's OK if I don't gain personally"; "I can still be objective"; and, "I've got it coming to me" (p. 6). Pope and Vasquez (1991) offer a few more: "It's not unethical as long as you don't talk about ethics"; "It's not unethical as long as you can name at least five other psychologists who do the same thing"; "It's not unethical as long as none of your clients has ever complained about it"; and "It's not unethical as long as there's no intent to do harm" (pp. 14–15). We have encountered several cases for which the insidious rationalizations were "Just this once" and "This time it's different." These one-time-only rationalizations can have consequences, as the next case illustrates.

Case 1-22: Because Bill Receiver, Ph.D., was a friend and colleague with similar interests, Tom Tellit, Ph.D., shared some highly sensitive information about the staff problems in a company for which he was performing human factors assessments. Much later, Tellit had reason to believe that Receiver had leaked that information to the company's competitor.

Denial or perceptual distortion, prejudice, bias, and other rigid mental sets can have the same effect as rationalization. These processes also preclude objective judgment, which, in turn, greatly elevates the chances of making poor judgments.

9. *The Psychologist Who Slips.* Often related to the preceding category, a fairly substantial percentage of ethics violators appear to be psychologists whose *usual* conduct is ethical and competent and who are normally sensitive to ethical dilemmas. However, circumstances converge to displace usual awareness, perhaps due to inconvenience or distraction.

Case 1-23: Skid Greenspace, Ph.D., prided himself on using anything that had remaining function before recycling it. Dr. Greenspace was chagrined when a client pointed out that the scratch paper he left in the waiting room for children to draw on had confidential client treatment notes on the backside.

All psychologists are vulnerable to membership in this category, and it is the most difficult type to predict or prevent. For some reason, often based on immediate situational demands, psychologists commit acts that have unintended consequences.

Risky Situations

Carelessness, lack of awareness, inadequate knowledge or training, self-delusion, or some deficit in the psychologist's character are not the only conditions spawning ethically questionable actions. Alert, well-meaning, sensitive, mature, and adequately trained psychologists functioning within their bounds of competence will also encounter ethical dilemmas that can result in vulnerability to charges of misconduct or the need to make a difficult decision. Sieber (1982) outlined several common conditions that result in ethical problems; we have adapted and expanded them in the following list.

1. *Unforseen dilemmas.* Sometimes an ethical issue is simply not predictable. For example, a psychologist's published research findings could be applied inappropriately by another,

such as by distorting a result by taking it out of context to support "expert witness" testimony. Or, an agitated and abusive client could discover a psychologist's home address and unexpectedly show up at the front door, which was opened by the psychologist's 13-year-old daughter.

2. *Inadequate anticipation.* An ethical problem may be understood, but not expected to arise, in a given circumstance. Or, a psychologist might underestimate the magnitude of the problem or decide that safeguards were unnecessary or too costly. For example, a psychologist consulting a couple during a divorce may not be sufficiently alert to the possible confidentiality dilemmas that could develop if one parent later subpoenas the psychologist for testimony should a custody dispute ensue. Or, a psychologist may decide to save time by leaving identities on research questionnaires figuring that no one else would be seeing them anyway, even though the participants were informed that their names would be promptly removed. Potential ethical problems may never materialize, but, if they do, the psychologist will be faulted for not taking reasonable precautions.

3. *Unavoidable dilemmas.* An ethical problem may be foreseen, but there may be no apparent way to avoid it. A clinical psychologist, to protect the welfare of a client, may recognize no other course of action except to share information obtained in confidence. Or, when a psychologist intervenes on behalf of a client who claims to have been abused, other family members may be distraught or feel harmed. Others, as illustrated in chapter 2, may judge the psychologist's actions, after the fact, as to whether avoidance of the problem was possible.

4. *Unclear dilemmas.* In a variation of the anticipated ethical problem, ambiguity may cloud the choice of what action to take. We cannot always predict the consequences of available alternatives. The use of innovative or controversial research or therapeutic techniques, for example, is problematic because the risks, if any, are simply unknown or unpredictable.

5. *Inadequate sources of guidance.* An ethical problem may arise whenever relevant guidelines or laws are inadequate, nonexistent, ambiguous, or contradictory. The general or nonspecific nature of ethics codes and other regulations can create considerable confusion. The 1992 APA code, for example, often provides latitude for interpretation because of vagueness and ambiguity (Bersoff, 1994; Keith-Spiegel, 1994).

6. *Loyalty clashes.* An ethical problem may arise whenever psychologists are required to respond to the demands of a law, governmental policy, or ethical principle that simultaneously jeopardizes the welfare of people with whom they work. In individual situations, psychologists may feel torn among those who pay for the services, taxpayers or other third-party payers, colleagues, employers or employees, professional image, those whom one owes a favor, those who hold power, society, or even one's own conscience. These thorny dilemmas cause considerable distress because the psychologists must often choose from among legitimate loyalties. Someone or some entity may not be well served as a result.

Another critical dilemma arises when, in making ethical decisions, one moral principle conflicts with another. Which one takes precedence? Principle ethics does not guide us by putting them in any rank order. Principle clashes occur more regularly than you might think. For example, you might consider holding back a truthful response because the client would likely be harmed by it. Ethical decision making becomes a process that psychologists must master early in their careers.

PREVENTING AND AVOIDING UNETHICAL BEHAVIOR

It is not uncommon for psychologists to attempt to defend unethical acts with the argument that they were unaware of the relevant content of the ethics code. Similar to legal liability, however, ignorance is no excuse. A thorough familiarity with, and commitment to uphold, high standards of conduct are hedges against engaging in ethical misconduct. The 1992 APA ethics code includes a provision obliging psychologists to be familiar with its code, as well as other applicable ethics codes (ES: 8.01).

Ethics codes often do not deal adequately with many contradictions that can arise. For example, although most codes stress consumer welfare, it is not unusual for a circumstance to arise in which protecting a consumer may simultaneously place another person, group, or even the general community at risk. Psychologists incur ethical responsibilities to their clients, students, supervisees, research participants, employers, the law, and society in general, as well as to their profession and their colleagues. It is often difficult, if not impossible, to protect the rights and fulfill the legitimate needs of all of these constituencies simultaneously. (See chapter 2 for more discussion of ethics codes.)

Ethical Decision Making

A thorough knowledge of relevant professional codes, accompanied by a sincere motivation to follow them, will not completely insulate psychologists from questionable conduct. Ethics codes are composed primarily of general, prescriptive guideposts and have inherent contradictions and gaps that provide inadequate guidance when considering what action to take (Kitchener, 1984). Indeed, ethics codes were never intended to cover every conceivable event, and it is unlikely that such a comprehensive guideline could ever be created. Whereas ethics codes can give general guidance, it is the decision-making process for each ethics-related incident that will help fine-tune and shape appropriate responses. We have encountered the argument that being overly concerned with the proscriptions in ethics codes can be inhumane and compromise the effectiveness of the services we are rendering (Lazarus, 1994). Yet, as Gottleib (1994) responded, ethical decision making and good professional judgment are bound together and reciprocally influence each other.

Psychologists must develop some decision-making strategies to assist in coping with each ethical matter as it arises. We expect that such a process will maximize the chances of an ethi-

cally sound result, but we are also quick to note that this does not always happen. Some outcomes remain problematical no matter how much effort was expended in attempting to resolve them. But, the fact remains that those who can document a sustained, reasoned effort to deal with the dilemma will be in an advantageous position should their decision later be called into question.

It is important to stress at the outset that the application of ethical decision-making strategies does not actually *make* a decision. However, such strategies do permit a systematic examination of the situation and the factors that may well influence the final decision (Tymchuk, 1981).

A Suggested Ethical Decision-Making Process

A knee-jerk reaction on facing a complicated ethical dilemma is unlikely to be satisfactory. Taking the time to document, reflect, and consult will probably produce a better result. Whereas decision making should be done deliberately, the process can range from a few minutes to days or weeks. (Making swift decisions under emergency or other urgent conditions is discussed in the next section.) A procedure, adapted from Tymchuk (1981) and Haas and Malouf (1989), is presented here.

1. *Determine that the matter is an ethical one.* Ethical decision making will not occur unless the situation is recognized as involving an ethical dilemma or problem. People certainly differ in their ability to perceive that something they might do, or are doing, could directly or indirectly affect the welfare of others (Rest, 1982). As noted above, many violators of ethics codes did not initially judge a situation adequately, for reasons such as ignorance or denial, and thus failed to undertake any decision-making process before acting. And, we should note the distinction between the merely unorthodox or poor professional etiquette and unethical behavior is not always easy to discern when one is emotionally involved or feeling under attack.

It is helpful to locate the general moral or ethical principles applicable to the situation at hand. As we have already seen, overarching ethical principles such as respect for autonomy, nonmaleficence (doing no harm), justice, and according dignity and caring toward others are among those often cited as crucial for the evaluation of ethical concerns. Elements of all these principles are reflected in most ethics standards, though sometimes one will take precedence over another (e.g., autonomy is set below responsibility if a client is threatening to harm another party). It is possible, though not a foregone conclusion, that the ethical matter in question can be matched to a specific element of a relevant ethics code, policy, or law (see Bass et al., 1996; Gorlin, 1994).

2. *Consult the guidelines already available that might apply to a specific identification and possible mechanism for resolution.* Relevant information may be found in the APA ethics principles or some other code or guideline that represents the moral responsibilities of psychologists performing their professional roles. If the act is clearly described as a violation in the current APA code, the identification task is easy and straightforward. Unfortunately, the APA code is sometimes ambiguous, although the commentary interpreting the 1992 code (Canter, Bennett, Jones, & Nagy, 1994) often offers useful and more clear-cut advice.

Be prepared to do more homework. This book and others (e.g., Bersoff, 1995; Canter et al., 1994; Haas & Malouf, 1989; Pope & Vasquez, 1991) may help to clarify dilemmas. Codes from other relevant professional associations, policy statements issued by the APA or related professional organizations, federal law or policy (e.g., the Department of Health and Human Services' regulations regarding research procedures with human or animal participants), local and state laws (including those regulating the profession), research evidence (including clinical case studies that may apply to the particular situation), and general writings on value systems and ethical decision making are among the other materials that one might consult. We encourage readers to create a personal library of ethics-related materials.

The solution does not necessarily become clear at this point, and contradictions may be uncovered that cause more confusion than before this decision-making process started. Nevertheless, this is a critical step to take conscientiously because a disregard for extant policy or relevant ethical obligations may well have serious consequences.

Information from all relevant parties involved or from sources relevant to the matter should be collected early in the process. Sometimes, it will be discovered that a simple misunderstanding led to an improper interpretation, or the matter may be revealed as far more grave than first suspected. Confidentiality rights must be assessed and, if relevant, protected throughout the process.

3. *Consider, as best as possible, all sources that might influence the kind of decision you will make.* An extremely common reason for poor ethical decisions is the inability to see the situation objectively because prejudices, set attitudes, or personal needs distort the perception of the dilemma. We should try to introspect (a trusted colleague may be helpful with this process) to gain awareness of any mind-sets that could affect our judgment. We should also try to avoid being unduly influenced by irrelevant variables that could impair our judgment. In addition, we recommend searching out any financial ramifications and seeking to ensure that they are not blurring anyone's vision, including your own.

Except in those rare instances when the issues are clear-cut, salient, and specifically defined by established guidelines, psychologists are likely to have differing opinions regarding the "best" decision. The current APA ethics code (1992) contains considerable qualifying language that further encourages disparate interpretation (see chapter 2). In a survey requiring respondents to make ethical decisions on various treatment issues, Tymchuk et al. (1982) found that the inconsistencies among psychologists were greatest when the treatments described were novel or when no guidelines existed.

Other factors that lead to inconsistent interpretations of ethical situations include gender, years since achieving a terminal degree, type of degree, and employment setting (Haas, Malouf, & Mayerson, 1988; Kimmel, 1991; Morrison, Layton, & Newman, 1978). Decisions to take action could also reflect differences in beliefs about the reprehensibility of a particular act. Indeed, we have observed such discrepancies during actual ethics committee deliberations!

Personality styles and one's chosen guiding moral principles will significantly influence one's ethical decision-making process (Hogan, 1970). These personal characteristics might include criteria used to assign innocence, blame, and responsibility; personal needs and goals, including emotional involvement; a need to avoid censure; needs for control and power; and the level of risk one is willing to undertake. Multiple role relationship dilemmas are especially susceptible to self-delusion. Gottleib (1993) has created an ethical decision-making model tailored to multiple role relationship dilemmas; it focuses on the assessment of power (see chapter 8).

4. *Locate a trusted colleague with whom you can consult.* Because ethical decision making is a complicated procedure influenced by our perceptions, we can usually benefit immeasurably by input from others (see ES: 8.02). We suggest that those chosen for consultation be known in advance to have a strong commitment to the profession, be sensitive to ethical matters, and be a forthright individual over whom you have no advantaged status.

We have heard of consultants who gave flawed advice, even causing the person seeking it to commit an ethical infraction. For example, a colleague asked to comment on a request for counsel about whether to continue treating a borderline client, given that the therapist had no previous experience with this diagnostic group, replied, "Sure, how else are you going to learn?" If you personally do not know a suitable consultant, state psychological associations or the Ethics Office of the APA may be able to provide names of individuals with ethics-related problem-solving skills.

5. *Evaluate the rights, responsibilities, and vulnerability of all affected parties* (including, if relevant, an institution and the general public). It is not unusual to discover that a flawed decision resulted from the lack of awareness of a party's right to confidentiality, informed consent, or evaluative feedback.

6. *Generate alternative decisions.* This phase should be conducted without focusing on whether each option is ethical or feasible and may even include alternatives that might otherwise be considered useless, too risky, too expensive, or inappropriate. The decision not to make a

decision, or to do nothing, should also be included. Establishing an array of options allows the occasional finding that an option initially considered less attractive may be the best and most feasible choice after all.

7. *Enumerate the consequences of making each decision.* Whenever relevant, these consequences should include economic, psychological, and social costs; short-term, ongoing, and long-term effects; the time and effort necessary to effect each decision, including any resource limitations; any other risks, including the violation of individual rights; and any benefits. Present any evidence that the various consequences or benefits resulting from each decision will actually occur. The ability to document this phase may also be useful should the foundation of your final decision and corresponding action be questioned by others.

8. *Make the decision.* Rachels (1980) has observed that the right action is the one backed by the best reasons. If the above phases have been completed conscientiously, perhaps with the ongoing support of a consultant, a full informational display should now be available. The best course of action is sometimes very obvious.

Ideally, information should also be shared with everyone who is affected by the decision, or at least with some subset of representatives if a larger population is involved. If affected parties cannot be contacted, are unable to participate, or cannot give consent due either to age or to physical, mental, or other limitations (e.g., small children, prisoners, or developmentally disabled people), additional responsibilities are incurred to ensure that their welfare is protected. Special advocates or other safeguards may be required.

In some cases, your role will be limited to the information presentation because those affected have the right to make the final decision themselves. This might be experienced as a personal dilemma because, whereas psychologists are morally obligated to make decisions in the best interests of those with whom they work, clients, students, and other service consumers are often free to make the decisions that affect them even though we might find their decisions to be counterproductive or destructive (Battin, 1985).

Some decision options can be quickly dismissed because they involve flagrant violations of respectable governing policies or someone's rights or because the risks far outweigh the possible benefits. Sometimes, several decisions appear to be equally feasible or correct. Alternatively, the best decision may not be feasible due to various factors, such as resource limitations, that require consideration of a less preferable decision.

The best situation occurs when a decision can be made prior to taking a contemplated action that would have otherwise had untoward consequences. But, often enough, the decision is made in response to an already ongoing, problematic situation. Sometimes, the appropriate action is simply to cease and desist from a previous practice that, after a careful decision-making analysis, seems ethically risky even if no harm has yet been done. Acting on the decision sometimes involves a recognition that competence is lacking and that continuing education or additional supervision is necessary before proceeding. Often, the decision will involve the need to do something differently from now on and the attempt to alleviate any damage that might have already been caused. Remediation attempts can range from an apology to additional interventions or the provision of services or resources to those who were wronged. The decision may involve a recognition of the need for psychotherapy for psychologists themselves. Other times, the decision is to contact an ethics committee or licensing board on your behalf or to report a colleague to determine the appropriate resolution.

9. *Implement the decision.* It is at this point that the decision-making process comes to fruition, and the psychologist actually *does* something. According to Rest (1982), "executing and implementing a plan of action involves figuring out the sequence of concrete actions, working around impediments and unexpected difficulties, overcoming fatigue and frustration, resisting distractions and other allurements, and keeping sight of the eventual goal" (p. 34).

The implementation phase is also a point at which the entire process can easily become derailed. There is evidence that psychologists formulate what they should do, using formal ethics codes and legal guidelines. However, they are more likely to respond to their own values and practicalities when determining what they would actually do (Smith, McGuire, Abbott, & Blau, 1991), which is less than they know they should do (Bernard & Jara, 1986; Bernard, Murphy, & Little, 1987; Wilkins et al., 1990). Survey data have also revealed that clinical psychologists were most often willing to implement decisions that were less direct, less restrictive, and less consistent with APA guidelines, often acting from expedience and opportunism (Smith et al., 1991).

These are discouraging findings. The profession will remain strong and respected only to the extent that psychologists are willing to take appropriate actions in response to ethical dilemmas as they are encountered.

Ethical Decision Making Under Crisis Conditions

When ethical conflicts arise, the most appropriate resolution is far more likely to be satisfying if several other conditions simultaneously pertain. These conditions include the following: (1) sufficient time for the systematic collection of all pertinent information for considering strategies or planning for change, intervention, and follow-up; (2) the opportunity to involve all relevant parties; (3) proper identification of the person(s) or entity to whom primary allegiance is owed; (4) low stress and a mind-set that allows maximizing objectivity; and (5) the maintenance of an ongoing evaluation, which allows midcourse corrections or other changes to resolve satisfactorily the dilemma (adapted from Babad & Salomon, 1978). Fortunately, in most instances involving ethical dilemmas, decisions do not have to be rushed before the above conditions can be met. However, frantic phone calls in the night, or alarming revelations during a therapy session, are not rare occurrences among those who practice psychology.

Psychologists are among the few professionals vulnerable to ethical and legal requirements to make decisions and act under crisis conditions. Psychologists can be called on even when they are not directly involved in the emergency situation itself. Rubin (1975) vividly describes an instance in which he was summoned by the administrators of his university to manage a threatening and armed student. Time was of the essence. Even the determination of "client" could not be carefully considered. Was the client the violent student, the people he was menacing, the university, or society in general? The psychologist could hardly maintain "professional distance" because his own life was also in danger. Although this is an extreme case, most psychologists will face, at least once in their professional career, serious situations requiring ethical decision making under less-than-optimal conditions. The issues embedded in the following cases include confidentiality, client welfare, invasion of privacy, and endangerment of identifiable others or the public.

Case 1-24: A client, who had expressed considerable suicidal ideation and who had made numerous suicidal gestures, appeared uncommonly "flat" and resigned during a therapy session. The psychologist was aware that the stressors in the client's life were intense and was concerned that his apathy and apparent calm could indicate a commitment to kill himself rather than a sign of improvement. The psychologist questioned the man about his plans, but the answers were vague. Any intent to do himself harm was denied. The client stood up and calmly asked to be excused 15 minutes before the session was over.

Case 1-25: A female student burst into tears during the initial session at the counseling center, declaring that if she returned to her home her abusive and alcoholic boyfriend would kill her.

Case 1-26: A 10-year-old female client was brought to therapy by her mother because the child was behaving "in an uncommonly reserved and withdrawn manner." The mother could offer no explanation for this abrupt change in personality. The child revealed to the therapist that for the past 3 months her stepfather had been entering her room every night after everyone else was asleep. He touched her body and requested that she fondle his genitals. The stepfather had warned the girl not to tell the mother or her brothers because, if she did, she would be responsible for breaking up the family.

Case 1-27: An employee expressed considerable anger toward a boss, who had recently threatened to fire him. During a psychological assessment for promotion, the employee told the industrial/organizational psychologist that the boss was "an exploiter of the working class and deserved to be exterminated." The employee detailed a plan to perform the execution himself. The psychologist tried to convince the employee otherwise when the employee abruptly bolted from the room and disappeared down the hall.

As each of the above cases illustrates, crises with ethical implications occur most often when an element of immediate danger appears to be present. Psychologists are in the unenviable position of having to make a number of delicate decisions at a time they may also be experiencing marked emotional stress. Should confidentiality, from both legal and ethical perspectives, be maintained? If disclosure appears warranted, who should be drawn into the matter? A client's family? An emergency response team? The police? How much should they be told? There is no single formula that would apply to the array of possible actions under a given set of conditions.

Ethics codes are too general to offer much help in a crisis. The 1992 APA ethics code, for example, allows divulgence of information shared in confidence only as mandated or permitted by law (ES: 5.02). Case law in many states allows disclosure when a client or others require protection from harm. (See chapter 6 for a more detailed discussion of disclosure obligations.) The cases above appear to meet that standard. Yet, if a client says, "I can't stand my mother, and today I feel like wringing her neck," does that constitute a sufficient threat? Prediction of the actual level of immediate danger is not an exact science, but psychologists can and have been held accountable for their inaction and misjudgments.

The high incidence of child abuse suggests that most psychologists will have to face the dilemma of reporting it at some time. All states have some form of reporting laws for child abuse and maltreatment. Knowing what to expect and what to do alleviates the tension to some extent (see Committee on Professional Practice and Standards, 1995).

Suicidal statements and gestures are relatively common among therapy clients (Deutsch, 1984), and analyses of legal actions by suicide patients' families reveals no agreed-upon, clear-cut course of action required when clients threaten to harm themselves (Berman & Cohen-Sandler, 1983; Fine & Sansone, 1990; Litman, 1991; Slawson, Flinn, & Schwartz, 1974). Pope and Vasquez (1991) observe that "few responsibilities are so heavy and intimidating for therapists as carefully assessing and responding to their clients' suicidal risk" (p. 153). According to several surveys, nearly one quarter to one half of therapists sampled lost a client through suicide (e.g., Brown, 1987; Chemtob, Bauer, Hamada, Pelowski, & Muraoka, 1989; and Chemtob, Hamada, Bauer, Torigoe, & Kinney, 1988). With appropriate caveats, Pope and Vasquez (1991) have presented 20 factors associated with an increased risk of suicide that can serve as an aid during the assessment of an individual case. These are summarized as follows: (1) a direct verbal statement of intent; (2) a plan of action; (3) a history of past attempts; (4) indirect statements or behavioral signs such as giving away valued possessions; (5) depression; (6) feelings of hopelessness; (7) alcohol use; (8) certain clinical syndromes; (9) male gender; (10) older age, especially over 65 years; (11) Caucasian ethnicity; (12) Protestant religious affiliation; (13) living alone; (14) experiencing bereavement; (15) unemployment; (16) poor health; (17) impulsivity; (18) rigid thinking; (19) environmental stressors; and (20) recent hospitalization. Depending on the situation, some therapists may struggle with the ethics of suicide itself, as when a client is terminally ill and in pain. (See Heyd & Bloch, 1991, for an excellent, yet concise, analysis of the ethics of suicide. See also Bongar, 1991, 1992a, 1992b, and Jobes & Berman, 1993, for information regarding clinical practice with suicidal clients and Peruzzi, Canapary, & Bongar, 1996, for a review of the role of mental health professionals in assessing patient competency or decision-making ability for physician-assisted suicide.)

Another complicating factor during crisis situations is the level of involvement with the client and how it might, temporarily, be acceptably augmented. We argue consistently throughout this book that psychologists almost always serve the consumers of their services best when they hold firm to professional boundaries (see, especially, chapter 8). However, true crises may call for exceptions to the usual rules. The most ethical response under conditions of possible disaster—especially those involving matters of life and death—might conceivably involve going to clients' homes, ministering to distraught family members, being more patient or engaging in more than the usual nonerotic touching, or even actively searching for clients' or their significant others' whereabouts.

People sometimes wait until their situation reaches emergency proportions before consulting a mental health professional. In such instances, psychologists may be placed in positions of making critical judgments, with potentially momentous consequences, about people with whom they have not yet formed meaningful professional relationships (Tancredi, 1982) or gathered sufficient information. The next case illustrates how perplexing this predicament can be.

Case 1-28: During the first minute of the initial therapy session, a highly agitated father claimed that a neighbor was abusing his adult daughter by forcing her into "sexual slavery." He rambled on, detailing bizarre sex acts that the neighbor allegedly perpetrated on his daughter, and the father restated several times his conviction that her life was in immediate danger.

Is the father's story credible? Is the agitation based on what is actually happening to his daughter, or perhaps a misunderstanding of consenting adults' particular sexual proclivities? Could the father be in a state of delusion? Why isn't the daughter with him? Where is she now?

Although crisis techniques cannot be described in detail here, we propose some suggestions for preventive action that may be useful when making decisions under conditions of intense time constraint, crisis, or emergency.

1. Know the emergency resources available in your community. Keep the names, numbers,

and descriptions of these services in an easy-to-access location. The prudent psychologist will also check the quality of the resources as well. Sometimes promotional materials promise more than agencies actually deliver. Some are known to be slow or disorganized, ineffective, or even inhumane in actual crisis situations. This list should be updated at least once every couple of years because well-meaning and enthusiastic community support services are sometimes short-lived. Some lose their funding and disband, new ones are established, and some undergo reorganizations that improve or downgrade the quality of services. If such emergency resources are used during a crisis, follow up on the quality of their performance and carefully monitor the client's progress.

2. Form or join an alliance of colleagues in your community; each person agrees to be available for consultation when emergencies arise. Ideally, a mental health professional with experience in crisis care should be included. Keep these names and numbers in your easy-access emergency resource file.

3. Know the laws and policies in your state or locale relating to matters that are likely to accompany crisis events. These include state evidence codes (mandating the conditions under which information obtained in confidence must be reported) and commitment procedures. Any sections of the law or policies that are unclear should be clarified *before* it is necessary to fully understand them. Frantic searches through files or late night phone calls to colleagues or attorneys are poor substitutes for preexisting knowledge.

4. Locate an attorney in your community who is knowledgeable about matters that have legal implications relevant to the practice of psychology. Keep that phone number in the emergency resource file.

5. Actively seek out learning experiences that will sharpen your knowledge about the kinds of crises that may arise in professional practice. Take a continuing education class in crisis counseling if your formal training was deficient in this area.

6. Conscientiously define your own areas of competence, then practice only within these confines (Bongar, 1992a). Although competence is

an ethical issue in and of itself (see chapter 3), remaining within one's proper bounds provides additional advantages during emergencies. Psychologists' abilities to function properly during crises are often related to their level of expertise and experience with a particular clientele population or diagnostic group.

7. Carefully monitor the relationship between yourself and those with whom a close and trusting alliance has been built. The mishandling of transference by therapists has been traced as the cause of crises, including completed suicides (Skodol, Kass, & Charles, 1979; Stone, 1971).

8. Do not rely on your memory. Carefully document each crisis event, including the decisions you made and your rationale for making them. Keeping careful records will be of great assistance to you and, possibly, others should the event later require a formal review.

INFORMAL PEER MONITORING

We have discussed psychologists' obligations when faced with ethical problems. However, in addition, psychologists are responsible to watch out for each other. Unethical activity often can persist, totally unchecked, unless another professional takes notice and intervenes. Observing or learning of an ethically questionable act by a colleague constitutes the front-line opportunity for the corrective intervention of informal peer monitoring. Action can be taken directly by confronting the colleague or indirectly in the form of advising clients or others how to proceed with concerns about another psychologist's behavior.

Ironically, professionals themselves frequently divulge their ethical infractions to a peer, sometimes without an awareness of doing so.

Case 1-29: During a casual, private conversation at a professional meeting about unconventional therapy techniques, Herman Noclue, Ph.D., described an adult female client whom he would take across his knee and slap gently on the buttocks. He claimed that the technique was extremely useful in "facilitating transference" and, in a seeming gesture of helpfulness, encouraged the listener to try it.

The stunned listener did not comment on Dr. Noclue's "unconventional" technique at the time. The talk lingered in the listener's mind, and he struggled with what, if anything, to do about it. He did not know Dr. Noclue very well, and they lived a thousand miles apart.

Psychologists' Obligations to Intervene

What intervention should be taken on learning of an alleged unethical act by a colleague? Because less serious forms of unethical behavior may not be formally pursued (see chapter 2), informal peer monitoring creates the best chance to adjudicate questionable behavior of colleagues. Rationalizing the colleague's behavior as a minor or one-time mistake, believing that others who know of the behavior will take care of it, or trusting that "what goes around comes around" are inadequate excuses for shirking professional responsibility. Yet, too many psychologists may conclude that it is much easier, and therefore best, not to get involved. Rusch's (1981) survey reveals that the majority of the psychologists sampled indicated that they would take action after witnessing a serious ethical violation and that direct contact with the violator was the most preferred option. However, for a minor and less serious violation, the matter was likely to be ignored.

Conflicting feelings of a perceived duty to take some action toward unethical colleagues and a need to maintain a loyal and protective stance toward them are common sources of reticence to get involved. One of the very attractive features of informal peer monitoring, however, is that both goals can be met simultaneously. When you successfully intervene, you will have solved a problem *and* protected a colleague from having to interact with a more formal (and onerous) correctional forum.

The more recent versions of the APA ethics code (1981, 1990, 1992) actively deputize psychologists to monitor peer conduct, although in a somewhat cautious and protective manner. Earlier versions of the ethics code mandated that, as the first line of action, psychologists directly deal with ethics violations committed by colleagues. Only if an informal attempt proved unsuccessful should an ethics committee be contacted. Before 1981, it was not an uncommon occurrence for complaints pressed by APA members to be either returned to the complainants or tabled by the ethics committee until complaining psychologists had attempted to resolve the complaints by themselves.

It is likely that the earlier versions of the ethics code stifled the entire process of informal peer monitoring. Psychologists observing or suspecting ethical misconduct by peers were on their own, in waters that likely felt dangerous and cold, especially if the suspected violator was litigious or antisocial. We are aware of several instances of threatened physical harm, retaliation, or legal action for harassment and slander against psychologists who attempted to deal directly with the ethical misconduct of their colleagues.

Case 1-30: When Melba Goodtry, Ed.D., received complaints from several clients and other counselors about the "whiskey breath" of one of the psychologists in the same office complex, she approached him with her concerns. The psychologist yelled at Dr. Goodtry, accused her of being jealous of his wife and threatened to sue her if she repeated these "vicious allegations" to anyone else. Goodtry felt helpless and afraid. However, she had also noticed the heavy stench of liquor.

Currently, and partially because of reported incidents of harassment and intimidation, the 1992 APA ethics code gives psychologists the option of deciding the appropriateness of dealing with the matter directly. If an informal solution seems unlikely (for reasons left unspecified in the code), psychologists are mandated to take formal action—such as contacting a licensing board or ethics committee—so long as any confidentiality rights or conflicts can be resolved (ES: 8.05). The level of seriousness of the alleged behavior is not a stated consideration in the 1992 code, although Canter et al. (1994) advise against informal resolutions of complex violations such as evidence that serious sexual misconduct has occurred. Dr. Goodtry, under the present rules, would have had the option of reporting her colleague directly to an ethics committee, although psychologists in distress present special problems because they are more likely to be in denial. The psychologist who learned of Dr. Noclue's (Case 1-29) bizarre "transference inducement" technique might have expressed concern about it, on the spot, or initiated communication later. In the actual incident, the listener believed he did the best he could when, after a long phone conversation, Noclue agreed that his technique was not appropriate and stated that he would discontinue it.

Peer monitoring may often involve colleagues whose conduct and professional judgment are affected by stress, addiction, or physical or mental disability. According to a survey undertaken by the APA Task Force on Distressed Psychologists, almost 70% of the sample personally knew of psychologists experiencing serious emotional difficulties. However, only about a third made substantive attempts to help (reported in VandenBos & Duthie, 1986). We estimate, from our own experience on ethics committees, that almost half of those psychologists with complaints against them appear to have some personal problem that contributed to the alleged ethical violation. Although intervening with an impaired colleague may feel particularly onerous and even risky, we encourage such efforts because the potential for benefit for the colleague, as well as for the consumers of the colleague's services, is substantial. (Consult VandenBos & Duthie, 1986, for an excellent essay on confronting and supporting colleagues in distress.)

It is not uncommon to be told of an ethics violation by parties who then request assistance to deal with the alleged violator but insist that their identities be concealed. Often, these people are fearful of reprisal or feel inadequate to defend themselves. Occasionally, the problem is that yet another person, critical to the case, is unavailable or unwilling to become involved or to be identified. These situations pose extremely frustrating predicaments. Approaching colleagues with charges issued by "unseen accusers" violates the essence of due process. Further, alleged violators often know (or *think* they know) their accusers' identities anyway. When the alleged unethical behaviors are extremely

serious, possibly putting yet others in harm's way, and when the fearful but otherwise credible individuals making the charges are adamant about remaining anonymous, psychologists may not feel comfortable ignoring the situation altogether. However, there may be nothing else that can be done. Sometimes, the option to do nothing may not exist, as with adherence to a state's mandatory reporting laws (Canter et al., 1994). However, for other reporting situations not required by law, the current APA code leaves psychologists no options if confidentiality issues cannot be resolved.

Case 1-31: A tearful client told Ima Current, Ph.D., that he had a terrible experience with his previous therapist. He claimed that Dr. Aaron Brusque would sit for most of the hour saying nothing or browsing through a magazine while the client was talking. When Brusque did speak, the client claimed he simply barked orders, such as, "Just get out of that relationship" or "Why don't you kill yourself if you feel so worthless." Dr. Current was acquainted with Dr. Brusque and thought him to be very strange. She wanted to attempt to discuss the matter with Dr. Brusque, but when she offered to intervene, the client became hysterical and remained resolute in his refusal to be identified.

Dr. Current can consider approaching Dr. Brusque about his therapy style, but she must be very careful to do it in a way that will not betray the source of information. Given the description of Brusque's therapy demeanor, it is unlikely that the client was the only one to observe it, although the possibility that Brusque was attempting to apply some strategic or paradoxical principles to the particular client must be considered. Dr. Current can certainly help educate the client about the behavior expected of professionals and possibly help him gain strength to later follow through with a complaint if that becomes the client's wish.

We now explore in more detail how to confront a colleague suspected of engaging in unethical conduct and what biases and emotional resistances can get in the way of dealing with unethical peers.

Hints for Engaging in Informal
Peer Monitoring

1. The relevant ethical principle that applies to the suspected breach of professional ethics should first be identified. This may involve an overarching moral principle, or it may involve a specific prohibition in an ethics code or policy.

If nothing can be linked to the action, and no law or relevant policy or ethics code has been violated, then the matter may not be an ethical one. This conclusion is reached most often when a colleague has an offensive personal style or holds personal views that are generally unpopular or widely divergent from your own. You have the right, of course, to express your feelings to your colleague, but this should not be construed as engaging in a professional duty.

2. Assess the strength of the evidence that a violation has been committed. Ethical infractions, particularly the most serious ones, are seldom committed openly before a host of dispassionate witnesses. With few exceptions, such as plagiarism or inappropriate advertising of services, no tangible exhibits corroborate that an unethical event ever occurred.

A starting point involves categorizing the source of your information into one of five types:

a. clear, direct observation of a colleague engaging in unethical behavior;
b. knowing or unknowing disclosure by a colleague that he or she has committed an ethical violation;
c. direct observation of a colleague's suspicious, but not clearly interpretable, behavior;
d. receipt of a credible secondhand report of unethical conduct from someone seeking your assistance as a consultant or intervening party; or
e. casual gossip about a colleague's unethical behavior.

If you did not observe the actions directly, how credible is the source of information? Can you imagine an ethical reason why the person might have engaged in this action? That is, can you think of more than one reason why the person might have acted that way? If the information came by casual gossip, proceed with considerable caution. The motivations of those passing the story along, coupled with the exaggeration and distortion that always hangs heavy on "grapevines," could cause a colleague unfair damage. If there is no way to obtain any substantial, verifiable facts, you may choose to ignore the information or, as a professional courtesy to the colleague, inform your colleague of the "scuttlebutt." If the colleague is guilty of what the idle hearsay suggests, you may have a salutary effect. However, we recognize that this is risky business and may be effective only if the colleague is one whose reaction you can reasonably anticipate.

If the information is secondhand, and you are approached by a credible person who claims firsthand knowledge and is seeking assistance, we advise being as helpful as you can. Because we will often advise you to consult with colleagues before taking any action, it is only fitting that you should be receptive when others approach you for assistance in working through ethical issues. Often, you will be able to assist the person with a plan of action that will not include your direct involvement or offer a referral if the dilemma is not one about which you can confidently comment. If you do agree to become actively engaged, be sure that you have proper permission to reveal any relevant identities and that you have available all possible information.

3. Get in close touch with your own motivations to engage in (or to avoid) a confrontation with a colleague. Psychologists who are (or see themselves as being) directly victimized by the conduct of a colleague are probably more willing to get involved. In addition to any fears, anger, biases, or other emotional reactions, do you perceive that the colleague's alleged conduct—either as it stands or if it continues—may undermine the integrity of the profession or harm one or more of the consumers served by the colleague? If your answer is affirmative, then some form of proactive stance is warranted. However, if you recognize that your emotional involvement or vulnerability (e.g., the colleague is your supervisor) creates an extreme hazard that will likely preclude a satisfactory outcome, you may wish to consider passing the interven-

tion task to another party. In such cases, any confidentiality issues must first be settled.

4. Consultation with a trusted and experienced colleague who has demonstrated a sensitivity to ethical issues is strongly recommended at this point, even if only to assure yourself that you are on the right track. Identities should not be shared if confidentiality issues pertain.

5. Make your final decision about confronting the colleague and how to best do it. The decision-making scheme presented above may be helpful at this point. Even though you are not responsible for rectifying the unethical behavior of another person, the application of a decision-making model may facilitate a positive educational function.

You might well find yourself, at this point, tempted to engage in one of two covert activities as alternatives to confronting a colleague directly. The first is to pass the information along to other colleagues in an effort to warn them. Although informing others may provide a sense that duty has been fulfilled, it is far more likely that responsibility has only been diffused. Idle talk certainly cannot guarantee that an offending colleague or the public has been affected in any constructive way. Moreover, as noted above, to the extent that the conduct was misjudged, you could be responsible for an injustice to a colleague that is, in itself, unethical.

The second temptation is to engage in more direct, but anonymous, action, such as sending an unsigned note or relevant document (e.g., a copy of an ethics code with one or more sections circled in red). Constructive results, however, are hardly guaranteed. The recipient may not understand the intended message. Even if the information was absorbed, the reaction to an anonymous charge may be counterproductive, only assisting an offender in perfecting nondetection. Also, it may instill a certain amount of paranoia, which could result in additional negative consequences, such as adding suspiciousness to the colleague's character. Thus, although both of these covert actions feel proactive, we do not recommend either.

6. If you decide to go ahead with a direct meeting, schedule it in advance, although not in a menacing manner. For example, do not say,

"Something has come to my attention about you that causes me grave concern. What are you doing a week from next Thursday?" Rather, indicate to your colleague that you would like to speak privately and to schedule a face-to-face meeting at your colleague's earliest convenience. A business setting would normally be more appropriate than a home or restaurant, even if the colleague is a friend. Handling such matters on the phone is not recommended unless geographical barriers preclude a direct meeting. Letters create a record, but do not allow for back-and-forth interaction, which we believe to be conducive to a constructive exchange in matters of this sort. We do not recommend E-mail for the same reason, as well as the additional concern that electronic communications can be accessed by unauthorized others.

7. When entering the confrontation phase, remain calm and self-confident. The colleague is likely to display considerable emotion. Remain as nonthreatening as possible. Even though it may feel like a safe shield, avoid a rigidly moralistic demeanor. Most people find righteous indignation obnoxious. We suggest nonthreatening language, such as expressing confusion and seeking clarification. It might go something like this: "The data reported in your article are not quite the same as what you showed me earlier. I am confused about that and wonder if you could help me understand it. Is there a problem here?" Or, "I met a young woman who, on learning that I was a psychologist, told me that she was your client and that the two of you were going to start dating. I thought we should talk about it." Things are not always as they seem, and it would be wise at the onset to allow an explanation rather than provoke anxiety. For example, it is at least possible that the colleague might learn that the young woman was briefly a client years earlier. Such responses may not render the matters moot, but the discussion would likely proceed far differently than had the confronting colleague galloped into the meeting like Rambo.

8. Set the tone for a constructive and educative session. Your role is not that of accuser, judge, jury, and penance dispenser. The session will probably progress best if you see yourself

as having an alliance with the colleague—not in the usual sense of consensus and loyalty, but as those facing a problem together.

9. Describe your ethical obligations, noting the relevant moral or ethics code principles that prompted your intervention. Rather than equivocating, state your concerns directly and present the evidence on which they are based. Do not attempt to play detective by trying to trap your colleague through leading questions or withholding any relevant information that you are authorized to share. Such tactics lead only to defensiveness and resentment and diminish the possibility of a favorable outcome.

10. Allow the colleague ample time to explain and defend in as much detail as required. The colleague may be flustered and repetitive; be patient.

11. What is your relationship with the suspected colleague? This will affect both the approach taken and how you interpret the situation. Those who observe or learn of the possible unethical actions by other psychologists often know the alleged offenders personally. They could be good friends or disliked antagonists. They could be subordinates or supervisors. Reactions, depending on the relationships with those suspected of ethics violations, affect both the approach taken to deal with them and the attributes assigned to colleagues. Fear of reprisal can stifle action and enhance the rationalization for inaction. If the colleague is disliked, courage to act may come more from the thrill of revenge than from genuine bravery and conviction.

If the colleague is a friend or acquaintance with whom there have been no previous problematic interactions, the meeting usually goes easier. You can express to your friend that your interest and involvement are based on caring and concern for his or her professional standing. The danger, of course, is that you may feel that you are risking an established, positive relationship. If your friend can be educated effectively by you, however, you may well have protected him or her from embarrassment or more public forms of censure. Moreover, if you have lost respect for your friend after observing or learning of possible ethical misconduct, the relation-

ship has been altered anyway. Discomfort, to the extent that it ensues, may be temporary.

If the colleague is someone you do not know personally, the confrontation will be, by definition, more formal. An expression of concern and a willingness to work through the problem cooperatively may still be quite effective.

If the colleague is someone you do know but dislike, your dilemma is more pronounced. If the information is known to others (or can be appropriately shared with others), you might consider asking someone who has a better relationship with this person to intercede or to accompany you. If that is not feasible, and a careful assessment of your own motivations reveals that the possible misconduct clearly requires intervention on its own merits, then you should take some form of action. It may still be possible to approach this individual yourself and, if you maintain a professional attitude, it may work. We know of one psychologist who approached his long-standing nemesis with concern about her ethical conduct, and the two eventually became friends as a result of working through the matter together.

If you are intervening on behalf of another, you will first have to disclose why you are there and offer any other caveats. You might say something like, "I, myself, have no direct knowledge of what I want to discuss, but I have agreed to speak with you on behalf of two students." Your role in such instances may be to arrange another meeting with all of the parties present and possibly serve as mediator during such a meeting.

12. If the colleague becomes abusive or threatening, attempt to steer the person to a more constructive state. Although many people need a chance to vent feelings, they often settle down if the confronting person remains steady and refrains from becoming abusive in return. If the negative reaction continues, it may be appropriate to say something calming, such as, "I see you are very upset right now, and I regret that we cannot explore this matter together in a way that would be satisfactory to both of us. I would like you to think about what I have presented and, if you would reconsider talking more about it, please contact me within a week." If a return call is not forthcoming, other forms of

action must be considered. This could involve including another appropriate person or pressing formal charges to some duly constituted monitoring body. It is probably wise to have another consultation with a trusted colleague at this point. The suspected offender should be informed (in person or in a formal note) of your next step.

If you are ever the recipient of a colleague's inquiry, be grateful for the warning about how you have been perceived by others and strive to participate openly and honestly with the goal of settling the matter in a way that satisfies everyone involved without the necessity of a full review by outside evaluators. The next chapter carries us into the more formal mechanisms by which ethical standards are enforced.

References

American Psychological Association. (1981). Ethical standards of psychologists. *American Psychologist, 36,* 633–638.

American Psychological Association. (1990). Ethical principles of psychologists (amended June 2, 1989). *American Psychologist, 45,* 390–395.

American Psychological Association. (1992). Ethical principles of psychologists and code of conduct. *American Psychologist, 47,* 1597–1611.

Babad, E. Y., & Salomon, G. (1978). Professional dilemmas of the psychologist in an organizational emergency. *American Psychologist, 33,* 840–846.

Battin, M. P. (1985). Non-patient decision-making in medicine: The eclipse of altruism. *Journal of Medicine and Philosophy, 10,* 19–44.

Beauchamp, T. L., & Childress, J. F. (1989). *Principles of biomedical ethics.* New York: Oxford University Press.

Bennett, B. E., Bryant, B. K., VandenBos, G. R., & Greenwood, A. (1990). *Professional liability and risk management.* Washington, DC: American Psychological Association.

Berman, A. L., & Cohen-Sandler, R. (1983). Suicide and malpractice: Expert testimony and the standard of care. *Professional Psychology: Research, Theory and Practice, 14,* 6–19.

Bernard, J. L., & Jara, C. S. (1986). The failure of clinical psychology graduate students to apply understood ethical principles. *Professional Psychology: Research and Practice, 17,* 313–315.

Bernard, J. L., Murphy, M., & Little, M. (1987). The failure of clinical psychologists to apply understood ethical principles. *Professional Psychology: Research and Practice, 18,* 489–491.

Bersoff, D. N. (1994). Explicit ambiguity: The 1992 ethics code as oxymoron. *Professional Psychology: Research and Practice, 25,* 382–387.

Bersoff, D. N. (1995). *Contemporary conflicts in ethics for psychology.* Washington, DC: American Psychological Association.

Bongar, B. M. (1991). *The suicide patient.* Washington, DC: American Psychological Association.

Bongar, B. M. (1992a). The ethical issue of competence in working with the suicidal patient. *Ethics and Behavior, 2,* 75–89.

Bongar, B. M. (Ed.). (1992b). *Suicide: Guidelines for assessment, management, and treatment.* New York: Oxford University Press.

Brown, H. N. (1987). Patient suicide during residency training (I): Incidence, implications, and program response. *Journal of Psychiatric Education, 11,* 201–216.

Canter, M. B., Bennett, B. E., Jones, S. E., & Nagy, T. F. (1994). *Ethics for psychologists: A commentary on the APA ethics code.* Washington, DC: American Psychological Association.

Chemtob, C. M., Bauer, G. B., Hamada, R. S., Pelowski, S. R., & Muraoka, M. Y. (1989). Patient suicide: Occupational hazard for psychologists and psychiatrists. *Professional Psychology: Research and Practice, 20,* 294–300.

Chemtob, C. M., Hamada, R. S., Bauer, G., Torigoe, R. Y., & Kinney, B. (1988). Patient suicide: Frequency and impact on psychologists. *Professional Psychology: Research and Practice, 19,* 416–420.

Committee on Professional Practice and Standards, APA Board of Professional Affairs. (1995). *Professional Psychology: Research and Practice, 26,* 377–385.

Fine, M. A., & Sansone, R. A. (1990). Dilemmas in the management of suicidal behavior in individuals with borderline personality disorder. *American Journal of Psychotherapy, 44,* 160–171.

Frankena, W. K. (1973). *Ethics.* Englewood Cliffs, NJ: Prentice-Hall.

Gilligan, C. (1982). *In a different voice: Psychological theory and women's development.* Cambridge, MA: Harvard University Press.

Gorlin, R. A. (Ed.). (1994). *Codes of professional*

responsibility (3rd ed.). Washington, DC: BNA Books.

Gottlieb, M. C. (1993). Avoiding exploitative dual relationships: A decision-making model. *Psychotherapy, 30,* 41–48.

Gottlieb, M. C. (1994). Ethical decision making, boundaries, and treatment effectiveness: A reprise. *Ethics and Behavior, 4,* 287–293.

Haas, L. J., & Malouf, J. L. (1989). *Keeping up the good work: A practitioner's guide to mental health ethics.* Sarasota, FL: Professional Resource Exchange.

Haas, L. J., Malouf, J. L., & Mayerson, N. H. (1988). Personal and professional characteristics as factors in psychologists' ethical decision making. *Professional Psychology: Research, Theory and Practice, 19,* 35–42.

Heyd, D., & Bloch, S. (1991). The ethics of suicide. In S. Bloch & P. Chodoff (Eds.), *Psychiatric ethics* (2nd ed.) (pp. 185–202). New York: Oxford University Press.

Hogan, R. (1970). A dimension of moral judgment. *Journal of Consulting and Clinical Psychology, 35,* 205–212.

Jobes, D. A., & Berman, A. L. (1993). Suicide and malpractice liability: Assessing and revising policies, procedures, and practice in outpatient settings. *Professional Psychology: Research and Practice, 24,* 91–99.

Josephson, M. (1991). *Ethical values and decision making in business.* Marina Del Rey, CA: Josephson Institute of Ethics.

Keith-Spiegel, P. (1977). Violation of ethical principles due to ignorance or poor professional judgement versus willful disregard. *Professional Psychology, 8,* 288–296.

Keith-Spiegel, P. (1994). The 1992 ethics: Boon or bane? *Professional Psychology: Research and Practice, 25,* 315–316.

Kimmel, A. J. (1991). Predictable biases in the ethical decision making of American psychologists. *American Psychologist, 46,* 786–788.

Kitchener, K. S. (1984) Intuition, critical evaluation and ethical principles: The foundation for ethical decisions in counseling psychology. *Counseling Psychologist, 12,* 43–55.

Kitchener, K. S. (1985). *Ethical principles and ethical decisions in student affairs.* In H. J. Canon & R. D. Brown (Eds.), *Applied ethics in student services* (pp. 17–29). San Francisco: Jossey-Bass.

Lazarus, A. A. (1994). How certain boundaries and ethics diminish therapeutic effectiveness. *Ethics and Behavior, 4,* 253–261.

Litman, R. E. (1991). Predicting and preventing hospital and clinic suicides. Special issue: Assessment and prediction of suicide. *Suicide and Life Threatening Behavior, 21,* 56–73.

Morrison, J. K., Layton, D. B., & Newman, J. (1978). *Reported ethical conflict among mental health professionals in the community.* Paper presented at the American Psychological Association meeting, Toronto.

Peruzzi, N., Canapary, A., & Bongar, B. (1996). Physician-assisted suicide: The role of mental health professionals. *Ethics and Behavior, 6,* 353–366.

Pope, K. S., & Vasquez, M. J. T. (1991). *Ethics in psychotherapy and counseling: A practical guide for psychologists.* San Francisco: Jossey Bass.

Rachels, J. (1980, June). Can ethics provide the answers? *Hastings Center Report,* 32–41.

Rest, J. R. (1982). A psychologist looks at the teaching of ethics. *Hastings Center Report, 12,* 29–36.

Ross, W. D. (1930). *The right and the good.* Oxford, England: Clarendon Press.

Rubin, J. (1975). A psychologists dilemma: A real case of danger. *Professional Psychology: Research, Theory and Practice, 6,* 363–366.

Rusch, P. C. (1981). *An empirical study of the willingness of psychologists to report ethical violations.* Unpublished doctoral dissertation, University of Southern California, Los Angeles.

Sieber, J. E. (1982). Ethical dilemmas in social research. In J. E. Sieber (Ed.), *The ethics of social research: Surveys and experiments* (pp. 1–29). New York: Springer-Verlag.

Sinclair, C., Simon, N. P., & Pettifor, J. L. (1966). The history of ethical codes and licensure. In L. J. Bass, D. T. DeMers, J. R. Ogloff, C. Peterson, J. L. Pettifor, R. P. Reaves, T. Retfalvi, N. P. Simon, C. Sinclair, & R. M. Tipton (Eds.), *Professional conduct and discipline in psychology* (pp. 17–38). Washington, DC: American Psychological Association and Montgomery, AL: Association of State and Provincial Psychology Boards.

Skodol, A. F., Kass, F., & Charles, E. S. (1979). Crisis in psychotherapy: Principles of emergency consultation and intervention. *American Journal of Orthopsychiatry, 49,* 585–597.

Slawson, P. F., Flinn, D. E., & Schwartz, D. A.

(1974). Legal responsibility for suicide. *Psychiatric Quarterly, 48,* 50–64.

Smith, T. S., McGuire, J. M., Abbott, D. W., & Blau, B. I. (1991). Clinical ethical decision making: An investigation of the rationales used to justify doing less than one believes one should. *Professional Psychology: Research and Practice, 22,* 235–239.

Stone, A. (1971). Suicide precipitated by psychotherapy: A clinical contribution. *American Journal of Psychotherapy, 25,* 18–26.

Stromberg, C. D., Haggarty, D. J., Liebenluft, R. F., McMillan, M. M., Mishkin, B., Rubin, B. L., & Trilling, H. R. (1988). *The psychologist's legal handbook.* Washington, DC: Council for the National Register of Health Service Providers in Psychology.

Tancredi, L. R. (1982). Emergency psychiatry and crisis intervention: Some legal and ethical issues. *Psychiatric Annals, 23,* 799–802.

Tymchuk, A. J. (1981). Ethical decision making and psychological treatment. *Journal of Psychiatric Treatment and Evaluation, 3,* 507–513.

Tymchuk, A. J., Drapkin, R., Major-Kingsley, S., Ackerman, A. B., Coffman, E. W., & Baum, M. S. (1982). Ethical decision making and psychologist's attitudes toward training in ethics. *Professional Psychology: Research, Theory and Practice, 13,* 412–421.

VandenBos, G. R., & Duthie, R. F. (1986). Confronting and supporting colleagues in distress. In R. R. Kilburg, P. E. Nathan, & R. W. Thorenson (Eds.), *Professionals in distress* (pp. 211–231). Washington, DC: American Psychological Association.

White, T. I. (1988). *Right and wrong: A brief guide to understanding ethics.* Englewood Cliffs, NJ: Prentice-Hall.

Wilkins, M., McGuire, J., Abbott, D., & Blau, B. (1990). Willingness to apply understood ethical principles. *Journal of Clinical Psychology, 46,* 539–547.

2

Enforcement of Ethical Conduct

One cool judgement is worth a thousand hasty councils.

Thomas Woodrow Wilson

The degree to which the public can trust a profession is ultimately determined by its members' collective commitment to integrity. We outlined the importance of self-monitoring and psychologists' responsibility to educate each other about ethical matters in the first chapter. Unfortunately, informal self- and peer monitoring are insufficient to fully protect the public. Also, the public *expects* accountability. Stromberg puts it this way: "Today, people want to feel empowered. They demand to know what lies behind the professionals' decisions. And when clients or patients second-guess the professionals, they are willing to question not only their competence but also their ethics" (1990, p. 15).

Formalized rules and adjudication arenas exist to educate psychologists, to investigate complaints, and to issue sanctions when complaints against psychologists are upheld. In this chapter, we consider the role of ethics codes and the current (and possibly shaky) status of mechanisms for monitoring, processing, and sanctioning unethical conduct.

ETHICS CODES

Functions of Ethics Codes

As professions developed, the public began to expect that professional constituents would be trustworthy and competent. A code of ethical standards "professionalizes" an occupation by creating an implied social contract with the public that purports to balance professional privilege with responsibility and a commitment to consumer welfare (Sinclair, Simon, & Pettifor, 1996; Weinberger, 1988; Wilensky, 1964). Despite wide variations in length and specificity, the functions of most professional ethics codes echo similar themes: (1) to promote the welfare of consumers served, (2) to maintain competence, (3) to do no harm, (4) to protect confidentiality and privacy, (5) to act responsibly, (6) to avoid exploitation, and (7) to uphold the integrity of the profession through exemplary conduct. (See Gorlin, 1994, for a very useful compendium of professional

ethics codes and related documents and resources.)

Besides serving as a public pledge, ethics
codes of professional organizations attempt to
serve many other functions, probably too many.
They are impressive public relations documents.
They spell out which principles morally responsible members are expected to practice. They
attempt to clarify the proper use and misuse of
skills and expertise. They are general guides to
decision making. They help educate the next
generation of professionals. They are the rules
by which to judge those whose actions have
been called into question by ethics committees
and other regulating bodies. They are the basis
for weeding out the unethical among us (Keith-
Spiegel, 1994; Levy, 1974; Stromberg, 1990;
Talbutt, 1981; Van Hoose & Kottler, 1978; Winston & Dagley, 1985). Ethics codes may, however, create conceptual confusion in their attempt to be so much to so many (Clouser, 1975),
and they frequently contain contradictory and
ambiguous directives (Kitchener, 1984).

Not every organization with an ethics code
has an ethics committee to enforce it. Although
some may view unenforced codes as mere window dressing for the public, they still serve a
purpose by setting aspirations for members, educating the public about what they should be
able to expect from members of the profession,
reducing internal bickering about what is and
what is not proper conduct, and serving as tools
for licensure boards, civil litigants, and others
to use in sanctioning and defending members'
conduct.

Ethics codes may also serve to safeguard the
profession itself. Because they create protection
against outside regulation by attempting to preclude it, ethics codes are often as protective of
the profession as of the consumer and may omit
many issues of ethical concern (Kitchener, 1984)
or word the provisions in such a way that allows
loopholes and multiple interpretations (Bersoff,
1994b; Keith-Spiegel, 1994). Ethics codes also
represent the collective acumen of those within
the organization empowered to make decisions
about ethical matters and are, therefore, invariably the product of political compromise
(Bersoff & Koeppl, 1993).

The Ethics Codes of the American Psychological Association

Creating an ethics code for psychologists presents many complications because the dissimi-
lar specialties within psychology are practiced
in diverse settings serving consumer groups with
widely differing needs. It is difficult to be specific when creating ethical mandates that apply
to, say, a physiological psychologist conducting
research in a university primate laboratory, as
well as to a counseling psychologist working
with families in a community mental health
center. Although the American Psychological
Association (APA) established an ethics committee in 1938 to hear complaints on an informal
basis, it did not issue an ethics code until 1952.
The first code was developed in a quasi-empiri-
cal manner. The APA solicited input about ethics cases and dilemmas from its membership
and forged the first code using, as a database,
the more than 1,000 responses. The ethics code
has since undergone a number of minor, as
well as several major, revisions. (For more details about the historical development of the
APA ethics code, see Bass et al., 1996; Canter,
Bennett, Jones, & Nagy, 1994; Golann, 1969,
1970; Hobbes, 1948; Holtzman, 1979; and
Pope & Vetter, 1992).

The 1977 revision was created using another
unusual technique. Hundreds of previously decided cases were summarized, and the code was
crafted to ensure that the agreed-upon infractions could be adjudicated (that is to say, the
code could effectively speak to all of the summarized infractions). However, a decision also to
create an uplifting, positive document, accomplished primarily by mandating what psychologists *should* do rather than what they *should not*
do, was probably a miscalculation. A psychologist appealed a sanction by a licensure board
and received a favorable ruling on the grounds
that the APA code, which was adopted by the
state as a disciplinary standard, did not offer
sufficient guidance in some of the ethical principles to prohibit activities. Another major revision was issued in 1981, using a similar format
and much of the same content of the 1977
revision; minor changes, primarily dealing with

advertising issues, were introduced later in the decade.

The latest code, issued in 1992, appears in its entirety as appendix A. It presents an entirely new structure and involved a multistage revision process, though not a critical incident collection or analysis. A subcommittee of the APA Ethics Committee was appointed in 1986 (it later became a task force after the members' terms on the committee expired). The first draft was published in the *APA Monitor* in 1990, and commentary was invited. Consultants were hired by the APA to review the drafts from a legal perspective. The legal consultants, all members of the defense bar, were experienced in defending psychologists against malpractice charges. The failure to include attorneys whose primary specialty was public interest law has resulted in criticism (Koocher, 1994). In all, three drafts were published, and many alternatives were decided toward the end of the process by action of the APA Council of Representatives.

Many new and improved features were introduced in the "*Ethical Principles of Psychologists and Code of Conduct*" (APA, 1992). It has two major sections: aspirational principles and enforceable standards. The aspirational principles are noble statements expressing ideal moral behaviors to which all psychologists should aspire, even though they would be virtually impossible to enforce. The six topics are (1) competence, (2) integrity, (3) professional and scientific responsibility, (4) respect for people's rights and dignity, (5) concern for others' welfare, and (6) social responsibility.

The bulk of the 1992 APA code of conduct consists of enforceable standards, intended to be specific enough to use as compelling rules resulting in sanctions should they be broken. The eight section headings are (1) general standards (covering the relationship between the code and the law, competence boundaries, issues of respect and nondiscrimination, multiple relationships and other forms of exploitation, fees and records, third-party requests for services, and avoiding harm); (2) evaluation, assessment, and intervention; (3) advertising and other public statements; (4) therapy (including informed consent, couple and family relationships, issues surround-

ing sexual intimacies with current and former clients, and termination); (5) privacy and confidentiality issues (including disclosure and the limits of confidentiality and record preservation); (6) teaching, training, supervision, research, and publishing; (7) forensic activities; and (8) methods for resolving ethical conflicts. As we refer to specific sections of the 1992 code, we include its exact designation, using EP to refer to one of the aspirational ethical principles (e.g., EP: B) and ES to refer to a particular ethical standard (e.g., ES: 2.01). This will enable the reader to quickly locate the complete statement in appendix A.

The 1992 APA code deals with emerging issues not explicitly covered in previous versions of the code, such as forensic psychology, sex with previous clients, and bartering. Specific strengths include a heightened sensitivity to cultural diversity and respect for individual differences, more detail and a proscriptive orientation, more recognition of client involvement in therapy decisions, and more breadth and specificity (Bersoff, 1994a, 1994b; Canter et al., 1994; Keith-Spiegel, 1994).

The 1992 APA code, despite its strong points, has been criticized for its abstract and ambiguous wording, insufficient specificity for application to actual occurrences, and unclear meaning, which make the enforceable sections difficult to interpret (Bersoff, 1994a, 1994b). It contains many qualifiers (e.g., "reasonable precautions," "whenever feasible," and "attempts to"), which allows some flexibility in responding to different contexts. Given the diverse activities under a wide range of conditions that characterize the work of psychologists, it is often difficult to make clear mandates that apply to every situation. That is to say, the code emphasizes that psychologists can be held accountable only for what is feasible and reasonable in a given situation. The effect, however, could also be to narrow psychologists' liability by creating enough ambiguity and loopholes to wriggle out of charges of unethical misconduct (Bersoff, 1994b; Keith-Spiegel, 1994; Koocher, 1994). The current code will ultimately be judged by whether it allowed the discipline of behaviors the profession agrees are unethical. The APA is actively working on another major revision of its code, which will probably be finalized early in the 21st century (S. Jones, personal communication, December 10, 1996).[1]

The ethics code is not the sole publication concerned with ethical matters within the APA, although it is the only standard enforceable by the APA Ethics Committee. Other APA guidelines dealing, at least in part, with ethical matters include the *Guidelines for Providers of Psychological Services to Ethnic, Linguistic, and Culturally Diverse Populations* (APA, 1990), *Guidelines for Computer Based Tests and Interpretations* (APA, 1987b), *General Standards for Providers of Psychological Services* (APA, 1987a), *Guidelines for Ethical Conduct in the Care and Use of Animals* (1986), *Standards for Educational and Psychological Testing* (1985), and *Ethical Principles in the Conduct of Research with Human Participants* (1982, under revision). See also a discussion of guidelines related to raw test and assessment data, child custody, record keeping, and animal care in chapters 7, 15, and 17. Other major APA boards, committees, task forces, and divisions have been active in dealing with the ethical matters relevant to their mandates, often in cooperation with the ethics committee. Many of these documents can be viewed in their entirety on the Internet (http://www.apa.org/).

ENFORCEMENT OPTIONS

Various formal mechanisms have been established by law and within the profession itself to protect the public from unlawful, incompetent, and unethical actions perpetrated by psychologists. The five enforcement arenas listed below are adapted from Hess (1980).

1. Control is exerted through the general criminal and civil laws applicable to psychologists and all citizens.
2. Control is formally maintained by psychologists themselves, with ethics committees emerging as the primary peer control mechanism.
3. Profession-specific legal controls emanate from state licensing boards. Licensing boards also establish standards for entry into the profession, define the scope of practice, and delineate offenses and sanctions.
4. Additional controls are provided through civil litigation of malpractice complaints.
5. Controls are also imposed by or derived from federal laws and regulations, such as the policies issued on the protection of human participants in social and behavioral science research and the mandated establishment of peer standards review committees. Other state laws (such as involuntary psychiatric hospital admission statutes) and institutional regulations, such as rules promulgated by JCAHCO (Joint Commission on the Accreditation of Health Care Organizations), may provide additional sources of enforcement of professional standards.

The existence of several sources of control of the profession and protection of the public has both advantages and drawbacks. The primary asset is that each source has its own focus, which, ideally, allows an incident or issue to have a most appropriate forum for a hearing and resolution. For example, if a psychologist extorts money from a client, adjudication by criminal law would probably result in the most appropriate outcome. If an insurance company questions treatment applicability or claims, peer standards review committees could be particularly well-suited forums for evaluation. However, reviews undertaken by managed care organizations are driven chiefly by economic concerns (see chapter 10). When a psychologist is dangerous to the public, licensing boards may be the most appropriate first contact because they have the power to revoke a license to practice. Nevertheless, it is fairly easy to generate a list of reprehensible, objectionable, and blatantly unethical acts that are neither illegal nor in violation of any policy except an ethics code. In such cases, ethics committees may be the sole source of consumer redress.

Sometimes more than one arena is applica-

---

1. We do not examine the ethics code of the Canadian Psychological Association in this book. For more information about this interesting code, see Bass et al. (1996).

ble to a single incident. For example, an ethics committee of a professional association would probably want to investigate a complaint of criminal conduct against a member. In fact, it is theoretically possible for a single case to be investigated in all five arenas. Herein lies a primary liability associated with the existence of so many avenues of control. Efforts may be duplicated, resulting in unnecessary expense and confusion. Moreover, investigators within each source may expect that another arena is in control of the matter, resulting in diffusion of responsibility and an inadequate investigation. Territoriality, the need for confidentiality, and poor communication channels among sources of control can cause obfuscation and confusion. None of these arenas is known for its swiftness in responding to, investigating, and finalizing cases. It takes months to many years to resolve complaints, much to the consternation of *complainants* (the individual making the complaint) and *respondents* (the psychologist against whom the compliant is lodged). Enforcement is expensive. Almost $1 million was spent on the APA ethics program in 1995.

However, there are arguments to favor several different types of control. A single act can be relevant to one system but not another. For example, an act committed while performing in the role of a professional could be civilly actionable—allowing the party alleging harm the right to sue for monetary damages or some other remedy—but can sometimes fall outside the reach or concerns of professional ethics codes, malpractice standards, or licensing or criminal laws (Stromberg, 1988). An example might be breaching an HMO contract or failing to deliver a manuscript for which a monetary advance from the publisher was previously accepted.

The Relationship of Law and Ethics

General criminal and civil law do not adequately protect consumers from unethical conduct by psychologists. As Clouser (1973) noted, morality is external to law despite an apparent overlap. The illusory similarity results because morals and laws often have a similar purpose: to outline rules of conduct that assist in harmo-

nious living and facilitate the achievement of individual wants and goals in a socially acceptable manner. Laws have, however, been criticized, and even overturned, because they were immoral and unjust. In addition, a great many matters of morality and ethics cannot be sanctioned or enforced by laws. The result is that the correspondence between "legal" and "ethical," as well as between "illegal" and "unethical," is complicated and sometimes incongruent.

Often enough, conduct codified as unethical is civilly actionable or criminal. A psychologist found guilty of a felony can be both delicensed and expelled from state and national psychological associations as a result. However, conviction on a misdemeanor will not usually be handled in the same manner by ethics committees unless the offense also involved the violation of an ethical principle (Hare-Mustin & Hall, 1981). Differences among state legal statutes allow discrepancies in these cases. For example, engaging in sexual intimacies with psychotherapy clients is a criminal offense in some jurisdictions, but not in others (see chapter 9).

The more striking disparity between ethics and the law is the many instances of fully legal conduct (or, perhaps more correctly, conduct that ordinarily would not be in violation of any criminal or civil law) that are unethical according to the profession's ethics code. Examples from the APA ethics code (1992) might include participating in the misapplication of research findings, continuing to teach despite a serious emotional condition that compromises the ability to fulfill professional duties, being unfamiliar with the reliability and validity of assessment techniques that one is actively using, accepting as a client an individual with whom there has been previous sexual activity, and failing to inform clients that their therapist is an intern.

Psychologists may rarely be placed in a most unfortunate dilemma. On occasion, a psychologist might believe that it is in a client's best interest to resist responding to a legal reporting mandate. The requirement to report child abuse regardless of professional judgment or individual circumstances can create an especially serious ethical dilemma for psychologists (Pope & Bajt, 1988). Ambiguity of reporting thresholds and reporting discretions (see chapter 6) create confusion and room for interpretation according to one's professional judgment, although the psychologist may be held accountable, depending on the consequences. Ansell and Ross (1990) suggest that, because laws are not framed by psychologists and require impossible skills (e.g., accurate predictions of future violence), it is not surprising that even the behavior of scrupulously ethical psychologists is not always consistent with the law. The next case illustrates civil disobedience based on a matter of conscience.

Case 2-1: After many attempts at negotiation, a group of psychologists agreed to participate in a sit-in in the administrative office of Bozo Managed Care, Incorporated. The psychologists contended that the patients were being misled and were receiving incompetent treatment. The management at Bozo allegedly told them earlier that if they continued criticizing the organization, they would all be terminated as providers. The psychologists who participated in the sit-in felt so strongly about their concerns that they were willing to lose their provider status despite the fact that Bozo threatened to call the police and have them all arrested for trespassing. The police came, and the psychologists were arrested when they refused to leave.

Psychologists should generally obey the law. However, when law and ethical values seem to conflict, psychologists should attempt to resolve the dilemma or conflict through thoughtful consultation (ES: 1.02). The APA code sometimes explicitly bypasses the discrepancies between moral conscience and the law by exempting acts that are mandated by law. On the matter of confidentiality, for example, permission is given to allow the relevant state law to prevail. That is, the code stresses the importance of confidentiality in professional relationships, but only to the point at which the relevant state law demands disclosure (ES: 5.02). It is unlikely that a licensing board or ethics committee will ever fault a psychologist who obeyed a valid law, but civil disobedience can be a legitimate ethical or moral stance. Sanctions may follow, and psychologists are wise to be fully aware of

what the sanctions might be. (See chapter 13 for a discussion of whistle-blowers.)

Licensing Boards and Ethics

State licensing boards establish and monitor the entry-level qualifications required to offer psychological services to the public under the protected title of "psychologist." The relevance to the ethical principles of the professional organization is that well-functioning licensing boards are in a position to help ensure competence. State licensing boards also monitor the conduct of the psychologists they have licensed. In general, state boards adopt some or all of the APA ethics code; thus, the same misconduct may qualify for sanctioning at both state and national levels, although reasons specified for denial, revocation, or suspension of licensure can vary significantly among the states.

Licensing boards have come under attack for abuse of power and unfair or improper investigative procedures. Often enough, psychologists' complaints about state licensing boards are little more than self-righteous whining, but there are cases of well-documented abuses on record. In one case, a psychologist ultimately won a suit against a state licensing board, resulting in an apology and an award of $100,000 in damages. Consider these additional actual examples.

Case 2-2: A licensing board of Largely Rural State relied on a system that involved deputizing local psychologists to conduct investigations of cases far from the board's headquarters. In one situation, the ex-wife of a client treated by Ima Sucker, Psy.D., complained that the individual psychotherapy her former husband had received led to their divorce. The woman was never Dr. Sucker's client, and her ex-husband never signed a release of information to the licensing board. Nonetheless, the board asked a local psychologist to investigate. Not knowing any better, the local psychologist contacted Dr. Sucker. In an effort to cooperate fully, Dr. Sucker gave information without asking for a release. The case soon became a major embarrassment for the board when it realized that it had unintentionally led Dr. Sucker to breach the man's confidence.

Case 2-3: Mary Tripped-Up, Ph.D., was asked to undertake a child sexual abuse evaluation by a woman who was seeking a divorce because of domestic violence. Dr. Tripped-Up evaluated the child only, but found no signs of abuse. Nonetheless, she was subpoenaed to court by both parties in the divorce. In an informal meeting with both parties and their lawyers outside court, she was asked for "informal advice" on a child custody settlement. She made a variety of properly qualified recommendations, which were readily accepted by all concerned, and a court hearing was avoided. Months later, when the settlement broke down, the father filed a licensing board complaint. The board, in a hurry to resolve cases, did no careful investigation and offered Dr. Tripped-Up a consent decree by which, if she admitted giving improper advice, they would simply issue a reprimand. Tripped-Up's lawyer, who was unfamiliar with the issues and potential consequences, urged her to take the offer without seeking any expert advice. She accepted and was promptly sued by the father, who cited the consent agreement as evidence. Tripped-Up was then dropped from two managed care panels because of "disciplinary sanctions" by the board. Ironically, Dr. Tripped-Up had done nothing wrong except for obtaining poor legal advice and an inadequate defense.

Critics of the practice of licensing have asserted that this process does less to protect the public than to shield professions from competition. In his historical analysis, Gross described licensing as "a mystifying arrangement that promises protection of the public but that actually institutionalizes a lack of accountability to the public" (1979, p. 1009). He asserts that passing an exam may provide little more than an illusion of competence, restrict competition, and set prices. Further, Gross declares that licensing only provides a loosely woven safety net because licensing boards, with their few resources and low budgets, do an incompetent job of weeding out incompetents. The quality of licensing exams and statutes have also been called into question (e.g., Herbsled, Sales, & Overcast, 1985; Koocher, 1979).

Unlike ethics committees, however, licensing boards can prevent an unscrupulous and harmful individual from operating with the title of psychologist in the state. This is a tremendous power when one realizes that even successful criminal or civil litigation may not prevent a psychologist from practicing. In balance, the public is well served when a licensing body is functioning effectively and is focused on the primary function of protecting the public from unqualified and unethical practitioners. (For more information on licensing and malpractice, see chapter 3.)

ETHICS COMMITTEES

State regulatory boards governing the practice of psychology rarely have access to the resources or the inclination to deal with more minor violations of ethics codes or violations that may be extremely offensive to the profession but not necessarily harmful to the public, such as interprofessional disputes over publication credit. Furthermore, many psychologists are not required to be licensed (e.g., psychology professors or research psychologists). It is here also that the ethics committees of professional associations can fill the monitoring gap by dealing with members who commit less serious infractions and with psychologists who are not required to be licensed, but who are members of a professional association with a peer-monitoring system.

Ethics committees usually consist of psychologists—typically experienced and well regarded for their sensitivity to ethical matters—elected or appointed by the governing body of the professional association. (Some committees also include public members.) Committee members serve without pay and, at the state and local levels, usually without reimbursement for expenses. Serving on an ethics committee is not an easy duty. The dilemmas committee members face are often extremely difficult because the issues are intricate, the parties to the action are almost always distressed or vulnerable, and the facts of the case are not always discernible. The time commitment can be extensive, and the experience itself is often exhausting.

Most complaints are more complicated than a browse through the ethics code would suggest. Committee members must search the code to find the point of alignment with the specific complaints. This can create quite a challenge. Consider the task in the following actual complaint, all aspects of which were eventually substantiated.

Case 2-4: A client charged that Scat Shotgun, Ph.D., actually earned his doctoral degree in religious studies while representing himself as a doctoral-level psychologist. Shotgun told the client's friends personal information about him, loaned the client money at a high interest rate, foreclosed on his home when he could not keep up the payments, and attempted to induct him into an off-beat religious group, suggesting that he could not be cured with the "current stain on his soul."

Although most state psychological associations, as well as a few of the larger city or county associations, have ethics committees, some of these function solely as educative bodies. As ethical complaints have become more multifarious, the conclusions reached by ethics committees are increasingly appealed or challenged. Whereas ethics committees were originally intended to serve as the hallmark of a profession—namely, fulfilling an autonomous, self-monitoring function—accused psychologists today more often view the process as adversarial rather than collegial. Legal assistance and outside consultants, liability insurance, and associated clerical and duplicating services quickly drain the already modest budgets of most state and other smaller associations. As a result, a number of state associations, fearful of facing devastating ordeals, no longer investigate and adjudicate complaints. This may result in additional burdens for state licensing boards and the APA. There is currently some talk of curtailing the complaint processing role of the APA, which will reduce or eliminate a major option for consumers wishing to file complaints. (The American Psychological Society, the other psychological association at the national level, does not have an enforcement mechanism or its own ethics code, although it has issued a brief statement mandating its members to follow relevant ethics codes and federal regulations.)

It is unfortunate that state psychological associations appear to be moving away from hearing complaints because they have several advantages over the monitoring process at the national association level. Geographical proximity may allow smaller groups to meet more frequently and arrange face-to-face interviews with complainants and/or respondents. In comparison, the APA committee meets only in Washington, D.C., and operates almost entirely by reviewing written documents and correspondence, except for formal hearings provided only if the committee recommends that the respondent be expelled. State associations may be the preferred level of processing when peer pressure or monitoring is likely to be most effective. Also, as Nagy (1996) has pointed out, state ethics committees are more familiar with local nuances in standards of practice and are in a better position to recommend and monitor effective remediation programs.

The Effectiveness of Ethics Committees

Although ethics committees are uniquely able to pick up some of the slack that other levels of control may be unwilling or unable to handle, whether professional association ethics committees are always a constructive and efficient means of peer control and public protection is debated. Specific criticisms of their effectiveness include the following: the assessment of "token penalties" that have no genuine impact on the respondent's pattern of professional behavior in academia and other nonclinical settings; conflict of interest or bias among committee members; lack of training and experience of members to function adequately in a quasi-judicial capacity; the potential for a "group-think" mentality, leading to flawed deliberation and recommendations; taking excessive time to adjudicate cases, resulting in possible harm to the public in the interim; insufficient investigatory and other resources to do the job properly; timid procedures as a result of fears of lawsuits; reactive rather than proactive procedures; the tendency to protect guild interests and due process rights of respondents over the welfare of the complainants; and (conversely) the tendency to take the complainants' sides while depriving the respondents of due process and an unbiased tribunal. (For more detailed criticisms of self-regulation in general and/or ethics committees in particular, see Chalk, Frankel, & Chafer, 1980; Clouser, 1975; Derbyshire, 1974; Hess, 1980; Hogan, 1979; Moore, 1978; Sinnett & Linford, 1982a, 1982b; Taylor & Torrey, 1972; Wallace & Howell, 1992; Wright, 1989; Zemlick, 1980).

Without denying that some of the criticisms are valid in some situations, we sustain a far more positive view of the effectiveness of peer monitoring by ethics committees. Some critics are unduly harsh, even inflammatory, and others single out ethics committees for shortcomings that exist, unfortunately, at any level of monitoring. For example, let us take a closer look at the charge of token penalties. A letter of reprimand may not seem like much to someone who has never received one, but any negative sanction can have a considerable emotional impact. As one teaching psychologist wrote, "I am embarrassed because an esteemed group of my peers has judged my behavior to be inappropriate. This will stay with me forever." Furthermore, the impact is no longer experienced solely as a personal, but otherwise private, blow. Findings of misconduct are now published in some professional newsletters and journals (Stromberg, 1990). Expulsions by the APA that result from actions begun after June 1, 1996, will be confirmed to any person who inquires about an expulsion. The Association of State and Provincial Psychology Boards (ASPPB) maintains an interstate registry of licensing board actions regarding serious cases and publishes a report that includes the names of those disciplined and capsule summaries of the disciplinary actions by state. The report is circulated to all member boards, which are represented in all 50 states, Washington, D.C., and the Canadian provinces. The APA Ethics Office receives copies and follows up on APA members whose licenses have been suspended or revoked.

Malpractice insurance applications, license renewal forms, insurance provider applications, and hospital staff membership applications ask whether any ethics charges have been sustained against the practitioner. Thus, even a reprimand would have to be reported and explained, with an attendant risk of nonrenewal or exclusion. In addition, professional job applications may require disclosure of any discipline for professional misconduct, which means that hospital or health maintenance organization (HMO) privileges could be denied, even for minor infractions.

Although respondents may not always appreciate it, there are advantages to well-functioning, readily available ethics committees. Frustrated complainants are increasingly rushing to lawyers or the media when sources of redress are inefficient or slow to act.

Case 2-5: Upsetta Grandee became impatient with the lengthy delay and interminable paperwork involved in submitting a complaint to a state licensing board. She had corroborating witnesses and some "incriminating" notes handwritten by the psychologist and took her evidence to the local newspaper. The paper carried a front-page story, which attracted the interest of the television station. A camera crew showed up, unannounced, at the psychologist's home. He yelled at them, charging harassment because he had not yet had his day in court. This outburst caught the attention of a popular "tabloid" television show producer, who ran the entire story on national, syndicated television.

The result of the media coverage was to greatly diminish the psychologist's practice and reputation as well as to humiliate the complainant, whose delicate private life was also exposed. Two of the charges against this psychologist—both involving poor judgment with this particular client—were eventually sustained, but we can only speculate whether the psychologist and the complainant would have been better served had the board been more responsive earlier.

When ethics committees are functioning well, they have advantages over other monitoring methods. The flexibility of ethics committee proceedings, compared with legal and administrative procedures, permits a wider range of data-gathering methods without forcing stringent evidence and examination requirements. Because many matters can be handled without an adversarial process, ethics committees can remain proconsumer without being antipsychology. An investment in protecting the profession does not eliminate a concern for the welfare of consumers and society because the reputation of a profession is based primarily on the public's image of it. Thus, it is in the profession's best interests to maintain high ethical standards and to police itself effectively.

Ethics Complaints Not Pursued

Generally speaking, ethics committees do not pursue complaints falling under any of seven conditions: (1) The nature of the complaint has no relevant provision in the ethics code; (2) the alleged infraction was not committed while the psychologist was functioning in his or her role as a psychologist; (3) an ethics committee is not the appropriate mediator in a specific case; (4) the respondent is not a member of the association; (5) the complaint is against a group, agency, corporation, or institution rather than an identifiable individual member; (6) the complaint is anonymous, and its essence is not in the public domain; (7) the complaint appears to be frivolous or improper; and, (8) the complaint is received after limitation statutes or rules have expired.

When There Is No Provision in the Code

An ethics code cannot cover every conceivable unethical act or poor judgment that psychologists might make. Indeed, the creators of ethics codes are faced with a dilemma. If they make the code very specific and detailed, then loopholes abound. But, if codes are composed of very general statements, complainants can always claim that their contentious act was not clearly addressed. Seeking a proper balance between specificity and generality is an ongoing challenge.

Case 2-6: Tim Nopenny, a graduate student, complained that Don Staunch, Ph.D., director of a clinical internship program, discriminated against him and any other applicants with limited financial resources living some distance from the facility. The program required applicants to appear for a personal interview. Tim claimed that he did not have enough money to make the trip and requested the facility pay for his travel expenses, the staff

director come to him, or the interview be conducted over the telephone. Dr. Staunch rejected these alternatives on the grounds that the budget was insufficient to pay for the applicants' travel expenses, the entire staff was involved with the evaluation process, and on-site applicant visits were critical to the determination of suitability for training.

Although an ethics committee might sympathize with Tim Nopenny's predicament, nothing in the ethics code prohibits a psychologist, acting in this case as an agent for an internship program, from administering selection policies that can be reasonably justified.

Case 2-7: Kitty Friend wrote a letter to an ethics committee charging that a psychologist she read about in the newspaper, who was doing research on evoked potentials in cat brains, was unethical, inhumane, and immoral.

The ethics committee would have pursued a complaint if it found that the animals were being subjected to unjustified discomfort, were poorly cared for, or endured surgical procedures without appropriate anesthesia, all of which are explicitly proscribed by the APA ethics code (ES: 6.20). However, it is not unethical, per se, to do research on cats or any other infrahuman species.

Infractions Not Committed in the Role of a Psychologist

Sometimes people unhappy with a psychologist's private behavior try to involve an ethics committee. The APA Ethics Committee only reviews complaints involving psychologists whose activities were part of their work activity or were psychological in nature (ES: 1.01). Thus, if the psychologist was functioning *clearly* outside a professional/psychological role when the alleged infraction occurred, even if the behavior was contemptuous, falling short of commiting a felony (see below), the psychologist is not subject to the ethics code. Ethics committees are rarely the appropriate recourse for mediation in such instances, as the next case illustrates.

Case 2-8: Bucky Newoff, a recently divorced man who worked in the same office building with Norman Onenite, Ph.D., complained to an ethics committee that the psychologist had exploited him and was responsible for his current high-anxiety state. The two had started dating and had spent the night together on several occasions. Then, he claimed, the psychologist abruptly broke off the relationship without adequate explanation.

After clarifying with the complainant that he was not now and never had been a client or supervisee of the psychologist, the ethics committee informed Newoff that it would not intervene in relationship failures between consenting adults functioning in their roles of private citizens.

Whether the role is a private or professional one, however, is not always that clear-cut, as in the next case.

Case 2-9: At a large wedding party, Yalom Tipsy, Ph.D., joined a raucous celebration in which everyone was kissing everybody else. When he unexpectedly came face-to-face with one of his clients, they happily embraced and kissed each other on the cheek. This incident was to be the basis of a later complaint.

The client claimed that Tipsy should have known that his act would leave her with uncomfortable feelings, regardless of the circumstance. Was Tipsy's explanation to an informal inquiry that he was at a private party, joining other consenting adults who had a little too much to drink, adequate? The client was uncomfortable enough to complain, although we do not have any information about additional dynamics. (See chapter 8 for a detailed discussion of socializing with clients.)

Even individuals who serve on ethics committees do not always agree that cases should be rejected when psychologists were acting as private citizens or in some other nonpsychologist role, especially if the misconduct was of an especially grave nature. The argument advanced is that when a person who happens to be a psychologist engages in extreme acts with serious consequences, that person's competence and fitness to be a psychologist should also

be called into question. A secondary argument holds that if the psychologist's private conduct is of an exceptionally menacing nature and becomes highly publicized, highlighting the person's identity as a psychologist, then the public trust in psychology and psychologists is reduced. A third argument holds that a person's persistent behavior, perhaps reflecting his or her underlying character, may preclude fitness to be a psychologist. To refrain from any action under these circumstances might reflect poorly on our profession. However, Stromberg (1990) notes that these arguments call for subjective judgments, and it is often difficult to prove that the consumers were, in fact, harmed by psychologists' private acts. Stromberg believes that ethics committees should, however, be empowered to consider any conduct that seems reasonably likely to impair professional functioning or "betrays the specific values that [the] profession is sworn to uphold" (p. 22).

The APA's Ethics Committee procedures do allow accelerated action when a member has been found guilty of a felony, regardless of the direct relevance of the crime to that person's professional identity. A "show cause" proceeding offers a short period of time for the psychologist/felon to explain why the APA should not expel him or her from the organization subject to appeal by the APA Board of Directors.

Case 2-10: Andrew Bumpoff, Ph.D., was convicted of the attempted murder of his wife when a young man he hired to do the killing confessed after questioning by the police. The man claimed that Dr. Bumpoff had taken out a large insurance policy on his wife's life and promised the man one quarter of the payoff if he would break into the house on a particular evening when the doctor was seeing clients, shoot the doctor's wife, and take a few expensive items to make it look like a robbery. The trial was widely publicized, and Dr. Bumpoff's profession was prominently woven into every story.

Other actual cases of private misconduct that resulted in expulsions, using a show cause procedure, include a psychologist who strangled his housekeeper to death, another who abused drugs with clients in group therapy sessions, and yet another who purposely set university buildings on fire. The same show cause process can be used for members who have had their licenses revoked or suspended by a state board or have been expelled or suspended by a state or local association (APA, 1996).

When an Ethics Committee Is Not the Appropriate Mediator

Sometimes an ethics committee refuses to process complaints when it becomes clear that the committee will be unable to make any reasonable contribution to the solution of the problem. This occurs most often under the following circumstances: (1) when two or more psychologists are involved in an intense interpersonal conflict that bubbled over into their professional relationship with each other; (2) when the infraction involves acts that might conceivably be unethical, but are virtually impossible for ethics committees to evaluate or investigate; (3) when the issues are related to nonethical aspects regarding standards of practice or interprofessional political disputes; or (4) when other sources of redress are clearly more appropriate.

Case 2-11: Edgar Potshot, Ed.D., who had a long-standing and intense dislike for a colleague, complained that the colleague engaged in unprofessional conduct when he told a department secretary that the complainant had "crap for brains." When the committee asked the colleague about the incident, he countercharged that Dr. Potshot had been making horrendous remarks about him to others for years.

The committee realized that it was not going to resolve the ethical issues or the intense and ingrained interpersonal difficulties between the two men. A duplicate letter informed both psychologists that the committee was withdrawing from the case and pointed out that this was a no-win situation for all concerned. The letter stressed the professional responsibilities of both parties and urged them to embark on some course of action that would lead to a neutralization of the destructive nature of their working relationship.

Case 2-12: A student complained that a psychology professor gave her a B in a course when she believed she deserved an A.

Some complaints, including most involving grading disputes, are virtually impossible for ethics committees to assess adequately (see chapter 16). The student in the above case was encouraged to speak with the professor about the matter and, if she was not satisfied, to seek appropriate redress within the university. Some cases are far better handled through established channels closer to the source.

Other complaints reaching ethics committees involve disputes over acceptable standards of practice or intraprofessional disagreements. Unless incompetence or malicious intent are clearly involved, committees typically send the parties back to their respective arenas to resolve the matters among themselves.

Case 2-13: A Ph.D. psychologist complained that another psychologist hired an M.A.-level person as an agency counselor. The Ph.D.-level psychologist had applied for the job and felt that he should have gotten it because of his more advanced degree.

Degree status, per se, cannot be conclusively designated as the marker of competency or fitness for a particular job. Unless a prospective employee could demonstrate that he or she was the victim of discriminatory hiring practices, an ethics committee would have no place in evaluating the matter. And, even if hiring practices were discriminatory, other agencies (e.g., the Equal Employment Opportunity Commission) would be more likely to remedy the problem.

Case 2-14: A psychologist complained that other members of the board of directors of a local psychological association criticized him during an executive session for the low quality of performance of his duties as a task force chair.

The ethics code does not automatically support psychologists who have received negative evaluations by peers unless such evaluations were unfairly biased.

Ethics committees may inform complainants that other sources of redress are more appropriate and suggest that these be pursued. In such instances, the committee takes the role of facilitator by serving as a resource and/or referral agent.

Case 2-15: An ethics committee received a charge against the complainant's psychologist-cousin alleging that Rob Filch, Ph.D., had bilked the complainant's mentally incompetent daughter out of a large inheritance when Filch was a staff psychologist at a psychiatric facility in which the daughter was being treated. Dr. Filch responded that the money was a gift from the complainant's daughter. The complainant provided documentation that indicated that her daughter was seriously impaired and had been institutionalized on a number of occasions. She contended that the young woman neither possessed the capacity to give such a gift in a fully voluntary and informed manner nor had the capacity to pursue a complaint independently.

An ethics committee does not have the necessary resources to fully explore such a complaint, nor does it have the authority to make appropriate restitution, should that be warranted. The complainant was advised to seek legal counsel.

When Respondents Are Not Association Members

Professional psychological associations are voluntary membership organizations, and the jurisdiction of their ethics committees extends only to current members. It is not uncommon for complaints to be filed against psychologists who are not members of the association to which the complaint is sent. Such complaints cannot be processed, although information can be offered to the complainant about alternative sources of redress with jurisdiction. On occasion, the complainant believes the offender to be a psychologist when he or she is actually a psychiatrist, social worker, or marriage and family counselor. In these instances, the complainant is usually provided with the name and address of the appropriate organization representing the discipline.

Complaints against licensed psychologists can be referred to state boards when the psychol-ogist does not hold a membership in a professional organization with an ethics committee. However, as we noted above, there is considerable variability in the responsiveness of many of these regulating bodies, except in those fairly rare instances when the alleged infraction poses imminent harm to the public. One of our colleagues told us the story of bringing a complaint against a colleague (who was not an APA member) to the state licensing board for refusal to return research data owned by our colleague after the psychologist volunteered to help analyze it. After 4 years of inaction, the board finally informed our frustrated colleague that "the case is so low on the priority list that it is unlikely to ever surface." As a result, our hapless colleague's research project, which had already taken 2 years of work on her part, had to be scuttled.

Case 2-16: A group of students presented evidence from their own "sting operation" to support the allegation that Sam Scam, Psy.D., who owned a consulting firm, was supplying letters of reference for a $100 dollar fee to students he had never even met in support of their applications to graduate school.

Dr. Scam was not a member of any professional association nor was he licensed. Scam is difficult to restrain because, despite the extreme impropriety of the service he performs, its illegality is not clear-cut.

Unfortunately, some of the most serious or bizarre complaints have been leveled against psychologists (or untrained persons holding themselves out to the public as psychologists or using unprotected titles such as "personal consultants" or "counselors") who are not members of any professional association, hold no license or certification, and are self-employed. The next case provides an example.

Case 2-17: A client and her attorney gathered considerable evidence to substantiate that Ransom Fleece, "Ph.D." (later identified as unlicensed and holding a "doctorate" supplied by a mail-order diploma mill), was extorting large sums of money to buy her silence. Fleece told the woman that he would inform her influential and wealthy husband of her many affairs and follies as revealed to him during the course of "psychotherapy" unless she complied with his demands for payment.

"Dr." Fleece's actions are clearly illegal and could be pursued in a court of law if the client so desired. But, he is outside the reach of professional association monitoring and state licensing boards.

Professional association membership does not, of course, guarantee competence or virtuous qualities, nor does nonmembership in professional organizations suggest incompetence or impoverished character. However, consumers do have additional protection when the psychologists providing services for them voluntarily agree to ethical scrutiny by virtue of their membership in organizations with peer control mechanisms.

When Complaints Are Against Groups, Agencies, Corporations, or Institutions

Whereas a complainant can name more than one person in a single complaint, each respondent must be known to the committee by name, and the involvement of each in the dispute must be specified. Ethics committee mechanisms are not set up to deal with an organization or a corporation, as is possible in the courts. Even a cursory reading of ethics codes reveals a focus on ethical responsibilities of individuals. Thus, when complaints are received against the U.S. Army, a state psychology examining committee, an entire psychology department, or a mental health clinic, the material is returned to the complainant with a request that the conduct of individual psychologists be described separately. Unless the specific behavior of such individuals can be linked to ethical violations, the case cannot be processed by an ethics committee.

When Complaints Are Anonymous

Occasionally, an ethics committee receives an unsigned complaint. Usually, the reason for anonymity is noted, and it is typically fear of retribution. Ethics committees are often concerned, especially when a letter is well documented and the alleged infraction is grievous. But, the rules

and procedures of ethics committees allow the respondent the right to know his or her accuser. Thus, unless the complaint contains information that can be substantiated in some other way (e.g., processed *sua sponte*, as illustrated in Cases 2-23 and 2-24), the committee cannot pursue the case.

Related to the anonymous complainant are those who do reveal their identities, but insist that the committee not disclose this information to the respondents. In such cases, the committee is able to explain the procedures—including what safeguards the committee can extend—and defend the requirement for making identities known to respondents. Some then agree to pursue the case according to the necessary procedures, while others choose to withdraw their complaints.

When the Complaints Are Improper

Occasionally, ethics committees receive complaints that are judged, from the available evidence, to be frivolous and intended to harm or harass a psychologist rather than protect the public. In such cases, formal ethics committee inquiries may be unwarranted. When the complainant is not a member of the professional association, an allegation that appears to be harassing, speculative, or internally inconsistent will be disregarded (APA, 1996). When the complainant is a psychologist, he or she may receive an unwelcome surprise. As we mentioned above, it is an ethics violation in and of itself to issue complaints that are deemed "frivolous and are intended to harm the respondent rather than to protect the public" (ES: 8.07).

Case 2-18: Nute Rankled, Ph.D., wrote to an ethics committee complaining that Charlton Rebuff, Ph.D., had promised to refer clients to him, but failed to follow through with his offer.

Rankled may be disappointed that his colleague did not measure up to expectations, but there is nothing in this scenario that should involve an ethics committee. It appears that Rankled is attempting to use an ethics committee to aggravate Rebuff.

When Complaints Arrive Beyond the Statute of Limitations

Ethics committees expect that complaints should be filed within specified periods of time after the alleged violation occurred or came to the complainee's attention. The APA rules and procedures allow an elapsed time of 3 years when the complaint is issued by an APA member (APA, 1996). For nonmembers and students, the time is extended to 5 years. The reason for the discrepancy favoring the nonmember is that members are expected to be more aware of the ethics code and redress procedures and to act promptly. Nonmembers, on the other hand, usually do not possess such knowledge, and it may not become available to them for some period of time. In addition, other factors could interfere with punctual reporting. In some cases, the nonmembers suffered emotionally in ways that were immobilizing for an extended period, and they were incapable of pursuing their complaints until the trauma had been worked through or had dissipated. Students may wish to wait until after graduation. Under certain conditions involving more serious situations, these limits can be extended further (APA, 1996).

The next case was heard by an ethics committee, even though 8 years had passed since the alarming episode occurred.

Case 2-19: Arthur Stunned agreed, as requested, to disrobe and turn his back to Frank Bigshock, Ph.D. Stunned charged that Bigshock then, without warning, shoved his thumb into Stunned's anus. Bigshock then declared that Stunned would now never feel fear again, that he had been "set free."

Stunned was so traumatized by this "therapy" technique that he left treatment and did not confide to anyone about his ordeal for 7 years. He did eventually correspond with Dr. Bigshock and saved the response letter from Bigshock describing the technique and why it was designed to be beneficial. Stunned, with the support of his new therapist, brought ethics charges to the APA against Bigshock. The ethics committee agreed to hear the case.

WHO COMPLAINS AGAINST PSYCHOLOGISTS?

Over the years, we have arrived at some solid impressions about the characteristics of people who press ethics complaints against psychologists. The majority of complaints, at least 60% in our estimation, comes from persons who are (or were) psychotherapy clients or family members of psychotherapy clients and who were dissatisfied with the conduct, therapy techniques, competence, or payment policies of the psychotherapist. A substantial minority of complaints, perhaps 25%, comes from other psychologists or closely allied professionals concerned about the conduct of their colleagues. The small remainder is divided almost equally among students, supervisees, and other private citizens dissatisfied with psychologists' nontherapeutic services, such as teaching methods and performance evaluations, business consultations, or research procedures.

The majority of complaints have had direct, personal interactions with the psychologists against whom they are charging ethical misconduct. However, a minority of the cases (perhaps 10%) involves complaints against psychologists by persons the complainant does not know personally. In such instances, the complainants are usually other psychologists or allied professionals. For example, psychologists may mail in newspaper accounts of misconduct or lawbreaking by other psychologists and suggest that the ethics committee undertake an investigation if they have not already done so. Most cases of plagiarism are discovered by other psychologists or by students in the course of their literature searches. Sometimes, psychologists will assist a client in pressing charges against the client's previous therapist, teacher, or employer.

People who complain to ethics committees appear to share several common characteristics. They tend to be knowledgeable about redress procedures, capable of clearly describing the situation as they see it, and sufficiently motivated to sustain themselves through the various, and sometimes arduous, stages of the formal ethics inquiry process. Anger is prevalent among complainants who were personally involved with the accused psychologists. Often, such feelings are explicitly described (e.g., "I have never felt such intense rage before in my life"), while at other times they are easily inferred (e.g., "Dr. Slovenly is a destructive, moronic ass"). An extremely disgruntled complainant sent us (and scores of other psychologists) volumes of materials by fax, including confidential file material and pleas to intervene on her behalf and requests for stiffer penalties from the state licensing board, interspersed with vindictive commentary about the psychologist/respondent.

Ethics committees, then, tend to hear from complainants who are resourceful, articulate, rankled, and persevering. They may well comprise a highly selective group. Consumers who may have legitimate grievances against psychologists, but who are frightened, debilitated by hurt, unassertive, unresourceful, inarticulate, or lack knowledge about how to pursue a complaint may never bring the complaints to the attention of ethics committees or any other redress mechanism.

Psychologists and students often question us about the prevalence of complaints from people who are highly disturbed or delusional, believing their rate to be quite high. In fact, very few complainants could be characterized, solely on the basis of the correspondence, as seriously impaired. When committees receive complaints such as the ones illustrated below, the most common recourse is to ask for more specific details and evidence or to contact the psychologists for their impressions of what took place.

Case 2-20: A woman complained that her psychologist had claimed the souls of her cat, two dogs, and the canary.

Case 2-21: A retired military officer charged two Veteran Administration psychologists with attempting to brainwash him to "kill small boys, homosex [sic], overthrow the British Empire, and bomb Los Angeles."

Case 2-22: A secretary wrote a long and rambling letter charging her psychologist with following her everywhere she went, tapping into her home telephone, stealing small items from her apartment, and hiring someone to drive by her place on a motorcycle at all hours of the day and night.

Ethics committees do not simply dismiss such complaints without finding out more about the situation. At the very least, an attempt is made to ensure that the psychologists did their utmost to protect these individuals' welfare.

Occasionally, ethics committees press charges *sua sponte.* That is, on the basis of information in the public domain (e.g., newspaper articles, local television news stories, service advertisements, or court records), the committee initiates the investigation on its own.

Case 2-23: A large envelope was sent to an ethics office with no identifying information about the sender. The contents consisted of a 1989 journal article describing the results of a survey on teenage runaways and a microfilm copy of a 1995 doctoral dissertation, authored by someone else, that contained the same data and most of the text as it appeared in the earlier journal article.

Although ethics committees do not normally pursue anonymous complaints, this was an exception because the evidence was objective and publicly available. The committee charged the psychologist with a plagiarism violation for the dissertation.

Case 2-24: The evening news carried a story about five students who were charging a psychologist working in the counseling center of the local college with sexual misconduct. A psychologist who viewed the news report wrote down the information and called to inform the state ethics committee of the incident.

The viewer did not have to put herself in the position of being a formal complainant. The story was in the public domain, and the ethics committee was in a position to make its own inquiry.

The Perils of Being a Complainant

Complainants must be willing to have their identities and the nature of their complaint shared with the accused psychologist. They must also sign a waiver allowing the respondent to share information relevant to the case. Often, this material was originally shared in confidence (i.e., therapy notes, diagnoses, or psychological assessment records) and will now be shared with complete strangers (committee members). The complainants may be especially uncomfortable because their earlier disclosures to psychologists might now be used by the psychologists' to defend themselves against the charges.

Case 2-25: On receiving an inquiry letter from an ethics committee, Sanford Assail, Ph.D., responded, "This woman is totally bonkers. You cannot believe anything she says."

Ethics committee members will not dismiss a case simply because a psychologist claims that the complainant is not credible. They respect the vulnerability of complainants and will look further into the matter before making a final decision. Further, Dr. Assail made a poor impression on the committee because of his offhanded description of a client.

Sometimes, the respondent does not offer a defense and agrees that the ethical violation occurred precisely as the complainant described it. Occasionally, in an attempt to create a defense, the respondent will, unwittingly, offer additional incriminating data.

Case 2-26: Shuin Mouth, Psy.D., responded to an ethics inquiry that the reason she sat in her client's lap and allowed him to stroke her hair during their therapy sessions was because the client insisted on it. She wrote, "I pride myself in responding to the wishes of all of my clients, whatever the wishes might be."

Some frivolous or contrived complaints may be reconsidered when complainants realize that pursuing an ethics charge is a serious and complicated business. However, the reasons for backing off can never be known. Unfortunately, some sincere complainants may decide that they are unwilling to endure the process. Those who persist, as most do, have agreed to have their identities known to the respondent and relevant matters about themselves shared with the committee from the perspective of the psychologist they have accused of misconduct.

Then, the complainants must wait. Cases often take more than a year to adjudicate. This may be distressing to the complainant (and the respondent as well) because the act of pressing a charge, as well as being on the receiving end of one, sets up a persistent, uncomfortable anticipation while awaiting resolution. When the investigation is complete and the decision has been reached, the complainant will be informed. But, feedback about the details are likely to be very scanty compared with what most complainants would like to know.

Counter-Complaints

When the complainant is also a psychologist, the respondent sometimes files a countercomplaint against the complainant-psychologist. This sometimes appears to be for no purpose other than to harass the psychologist making the original charge, as the next case illustrates.

Case 2-27: Terry Push, Ed.D., complained to an ethics committee that Hunker Downe, Ph.D., had refused, after three requests, to supply information about an ex-client that Push was currently seeing even though the client had signed a release waiver. Downe issued a countercomplaint, insisting that that Dr. Push was rude and therefore "not a worthy recipient of a professional courtesy."

Committees become uneasy when thrust into the role of "weapon" and attempt to minimize being used for this purpose. Although proving such a motivation might be remotely possible, the act of making a frivolous charge judged to be for the sole purpose of harassing a psychologist is itself unethical (ES: 8.07). Dr. Hunker should have released the information that the client and the new therapist requested shortly after receiving the initial request. Even if the new therapist, Dr. Push, had a rude manner (which might be understandable after multiple requests for information), that does not absolve Downe from not fulfilling a professional responsiblity. Downe's countercomplaint appears to be an attempt to evade responsibility and shift blame to Push.

Earlier APA procedure did not allow adjudicating a charge and a countercharge simultaneously. The APA Ethics Committee attempted to ascertain what led to the first complaint, but did not act on the second complaint until the first one was resolved. The current preferred procedure remains the same, but, with a two-thirds vote of the ethics committee, simultaneous charges can be reviewed in exceptional circumstances.

The Perils of Being a Respondent and How to Respond if Charged

On receiving the charge letter, some respondents are outraged that anyone would dare to question their judgment or their method of practice. As Steger reports, "They see harassment by the committee as a frontal attack, berating the committee or the complainant and rejecting any decision by the committee that does not agree with theirs. Yet another type of colleague showers the committee with paper and attempts to bog it down, often with the aid of attorneys, with legalistic interrogatories and objections" (1983, p. 3).

What psychologists who are charged with an ethical infraction must keep foremost in their minds is that "beating the system" is not the appropriate goal. Psychologists have previously agreed—voluntarily and with full consent—to be on the inside of a profession that has obligated itself to formal peer monitoring. All of us, as well as the public, receive advantages from this system. Were ethics committees to be discontinued, the profession would be at the mercy of outsiders' control.

We have seen other reactions from respondents. Some respondents are so stressed and upset that they appear to jeopardize their own health. Many are able to retain a dignified approach to the charge, but all are anxious to get to resolve the matter as soon as possible. Receiving an inquiry or charge letter from any professional monitoring agent is not, of course, going to make anyone's day. However, we offer some advice to consider if you ever find yourself in such a situation.

1. Know who you are dealing with and understand the nature of the complaint and the potential consequences *before* responding.
   a. Are you dealing with a statutory authority or a professional association?
   b. Are you dealing with nonclinician investigators or professional colleagues?
   c. Is the contact an informal inquiry or a formal charge? Sometimes licensing boards and ethics committees approach less serious allegations by asking the psychologist to respond before they decide to make formal charges. In such instances, however, "informal" does *not* mean "casual." Rather, such inquiries may be a sign that the panel has not yet concluded that the alleged conduct was serious enough to warrant drastic action or meets their definition for issuing a formal charge. The correct response should be thoughtful and cautious.
   d. Do you have a detailed and comprehensible rendition of the complaint made against you?
   e. Do you have copies of the rules, procedures, or policies under which the panel operates?
2. Do not do anything impulsive. Knee-jerk actions are more likely than not to be counterproductive.
3. Do not contact the complainant directly or indirectly. The matter is no longer subject to informal resolution. Any contact initiated by you may be viewed as coercion or harassment.
4. If appropriate, confide in a colleague who will be emotionally supportive through the process. We must strongly suggest, however, that you refrain from discussing the charges against you with many others. It will increase your own tension, likely produce an adverse impact as more and more individuals become aware of your situation, and possibly raise additional problems regarding confidentiality issues. In no instance should you identify the complainant to others, aside from the board making the inquiry.
5. If the complainant is a client, be sure that the authorities have obtained and provided you with a signed waiver authorizing you to disclose confidential information before responding to the charges. We know of instances of licensing boards asking psy-

chologists to obtain consent from their own clients. Such requests are inappropriate because they put the psychologist in the uncomfortable and awkward position of asking someone to surrender their confidentiality to serve the needs of another.

6. Assess the credibility of the charge. Compile and organize your records and the relevant chronology of events. Respectfully respond fully to the committee's questions within the allotted time frame. Failure to cooperate with the APA Ethics Committee is, itself, an ethical violation (ES: 8.06). Limit the scope of your response to the content areas and issues that directly relate to the complaint. If you need more time, ask for it. Be sure to retain copies of everything you send.

7. Do not take the position that the best defense is a thundering offense. This will polarize the proceedings and lower the chances for a collegial solution.

8. If you believe that you have been mischarged, state your case clearly and provide any appropriate documentation.

9. If the complaint accurately represents the events, but does not accurately interpret them, provide your account with as much documentation as you can.

10. If you have committed the offense, document the events and start appropriate remediation actions immediately. Present any mitigating circumstances. It would probably also be wise to seek legal counsel at this point, if you have not already done so.

11. Be patient. It is likely that you will have to wait for what will seem like a long while before the matter is resolved. It is acceptable to respectfully question the status of the matter from time to time.

12. Take active, constructive steps to minimize your own anxiety and stress levels. If this matter is interfering with your ability to function, you might benefit from a professional counseling relationship in a privileged context.

13. Consultation with a lawyer is advised, especially if the matter involves an alleged legal offense, the ethics committee is not following the rules and procedures you consented to follow by virtue of your membership in the organization, or if the action might lead to public disciplinary action. The information distributed from the APA Ethics Office to respondents explains that the APA staff is available to discuss questions about procedure, but encourages consultation to determine the need for further legal services. However, except for expulsion hearings or formal license revocation, respondents are expected to respond personally to the inquiry. A letter from your attorney alone is not sufficient and will probably also be regarded as inappropriate. If a charge is sustained and you are asked to accept disciplinary measures without a formal hearing, you may want to consider reviewing the potential consequences of the measures with an attorney before making a decision.

14. Know your rights of appeal.

DISPOSITIONS AND LEVELS OF SANCTIONS AVAILABLE TO ETHICS COMMITTEES

The atmosphere of "collegial exploration," in which psychologists who had complaints lodged against them engaged in a back-and-forth communication process with fairly simple ground rules, is being increasingly replaced by tightly drawn, legalistic rules and procedures. As ethics committees and their codes and decisions came under increasing assault by unhappy respondents and complainants, the face of the adjudication process was forced to change. Our discussion of ethics committee deliberations is based on the 1996 version of the *"Rules and Procedures"* of the American Psychological Association, which is presented in its entirety as appendix B. This document is everchanging in the face of new challenges. We refer to it in general terms, but this complicated 20-page document requiries careful scrutiny in its own right to fully appreciate the ethics committee procedures.

When a complaint of alleged unethical conduct is received by the APA, it is evaluated to determine its appropriateness before being presented to the full committee. Some cases never get to the full APA Ethics Committee for reasons noted in the section presenting complaints not pursued. But, other complaints can remain unconsidered if the alleged violation is very minor and no further action would be required if the problem has already been adequately addressed in another way, or if a reasonable basis exists to support a conclusion that the alleged violation could not be proven by a preponderance of the evidence (APA, 1996). If a case is opened, the respondent receives a charge letter, and a formal mechanism is set into motion. Also, at that time, the APA Membership Office is directed not to allow the complainant to resign. Several resolutions are available: a request for further investigation by the APA Ethics Office ("remand"), dismissal of the charges, an educative letter, a recommendation for a reprimand, a recommendation for a censure, a recommendation for expulsion, and a recommendation for a stipulated resignation (APA, 1996). Membership can also be voided if it was obtained by false or fraudulent means.

Dismissal of Charges

No Violation

When a preliminary review or a full committee hearing reveals no evidence of wrongdoing as charged, the respondent and complainant are so informed, and the case is closed. In such instances, the complainant often misunderstood the psychologist's conduct or did not understand the psychologist's responsibilities in certain difficult situations. At other times, the psychologist's conduct (and often that of the complainant as well) could hardly be characterized as exemplary, but was judged to be inside the arena of tolerable expression of emotion or behavior given the situational context. Three cases illustrate the typical conditions for which the decision to dismiss the charges is appropriate.

Case 2-28: Mazy Pickle complained that she was tricked into committing herself to expensive psychotherapy through a "bait-and-switch" technique. She claimed that she was seeing a therapist at no charge because her company agreed to pay for her sessions. But, during the 10th session the psychologist announced that the fee would now be $40 per hour. Mazy suspected that he was collecting from both the company and from her.

The psychologist explained, and the company's personnel director corroborated, that he was part of a referral network for the company, which agreed to pay for the first 10 sessions for their employees. Afterward, if the psychologist and the client wished to continue the therapy process, fees would be charged based on the employee's ability to pay. This arrangement was fully described in the company's benefits brochure and, according to the psychologist, discussed briefly during the initial session. On inquiry, the client remained confused but did remember "something about 10 sessions but then didn't think any more about it."

Case 2-29: Jen Frantic complained that her psychologist, Leslie Concerned, Ph.D., called the paramedics and police and told them she was suicidal when she claimed she was, in fact, only a "little agitated" and only wanted to "get the psychologist's attention." Ms. Frantic claimed she suffered extreme embarrassment, and her landlord asked that she move because of the commotion caused by this incident. She also complained that the psychologist violated his duty to keep information shared between them confidential.

Dr. Concerned responded that the answering service called him at 3:00 A.M., informing him that Frantic claimed to have taken "lots of pills" and that he should go over to her place right away. Because he feared for her safety and did not know what kind of pills or how many were ingested, he decided that other forms of assistance should also be marshalled. When he arrived, the police (called by the paramedics) were already there, and the client was throwing things at them. A hospital report indicated that the woman had not taken any pills. The psychologist's careful account of the evening and some of the other dynamics between the two persuaded the committee that he exercised appropriate professional judgment given the apparent emergency.

Case 2-30: Billy Blunt, an employee at a state mental facility, complained that a psychologist had called him "inept" in front of patients and other staff, thus jeopardizing his employment status.

The psychologist admitted that she was extremely angry at the employee, but that his behavior deserved a sharp reaction. She was able to document that Mr. Blunt had just struck a severely regressed schizophrenic in the face because the man had ignored orders to go to the day room.

Insufficient Evidence

When it is decided that a complaint, if valid, would consitute a breach of ethics, the ethics committee may still be unable to move to a cause for action (i.e., open a formal case) when sufficient evidence cannot be gathered during a preliminary investigation. So, unless additional credible witnesses or supporting documents can be produced, it usually becomes the complainant's word against the respondent's. Impressions of credibility do factor in, but are not always persuasive one way or the other. Both the complainant and respondent may be informed that definitive evidence is lacking, and that any additional evidence or information that either may possess should be shared with the committee. But, often, the alleged infraction occurred in private, and no evidence beyond hearsay or opinion is available to either party or the ethics committee.

Closing the matter without further action is frustrating both to the individual who made a valid complaint and to an innocent psychologist who was complained against. The complainant who was indeed wronged by the respondent no doubt experiences further stress when an ethics committee is unable to substantiate the charge. In these unfortunate cases, consumers suffer an additional insult when the profession seemingly lets psychologist-offenders "off the hook." This perception on the part of consumers is understandable, though not entirely accurate. The records are not destroyed for a long period of time, and, should similar complaints arise against those same psychologists in the future, the initial complaints may be retrieved and reviewed. In addition, ethics committee members are hopeful that in such instances the investigation process had a salutary effect on psychologists who were, in fact, guilty of an ethical violation. Even though lack of evidence may have allowed escape this time, sensitization to the issues and the noxious experience of undergoing an ethics inquiry by their peers may preclude a reoccurrence of such infractions.

As for the unjustly accused psychologist who could not substantiate his or her innocence, a lingering feeling of unrest may persist despite the fact that no violation was found and hence no sanction was imposed. It is unfortunate that an innocent psychologist, who committed no infraction, would have to undergo an inquiry by peers, who close the case in doubt.

Certainly, ethics committee members themselves are also disappointed when cases are shut because of insufficient evidence. The committee members are aware that someone was not served well, but they could not determine who that someone was.

Educative Letters

Ethics committees take every opportunity to educate psychologists who appear before them. Even when the charges are dismissed, the respondent may receive an educative letter. For example, Mazy Pickle's therapist (Case 2-28 above) was found innocent of perpetrating bait-and-switch fee-setting. However, the letter from the ethics office closing the matter offered the therapist some ideas for assuring that no such misunderstandings resurfaced in the future. The psychologist who called a hospital aid inept (Case 2-30 above) also received an educative letter, even though no charges were sustained against her, because of the circumstances under which the outburst occurred.

Sustained Charges, Sanctions, and Directives

Psychologists who have been found to have violated the ethics code may receive an educative letter, and/or one of several other sanctions and directives may be imposed. It is generally useful to consider the degree of seriousness of an infraction as a criterion for determination of sanctions, although, as we illustrate below, other factors may mitigate or aggravate the determination of which penalty is ultimately imposed.

As is clear on even a cursory reading of the APA or most any other professional ethics code, the violation of some principles causes far more harm than the violation of others. A scheme to aid in understanding the seriousness of infractions is presented in Table 2-1 (Koocher, Keith-Spiegel, & Klebanoff, 1981) and remains in general agreement with rules and procedures (APA, 1996). It allows a consideration of the appropriateness of sanctions and other mediating factors.

Level I deals essentially with *malum prohibitum* offenses; that is, behavior that is wrong primarily because it is proscribed in a code of ethics, in contrast to behavior that is inherently immoral (*in mala se*). *Level IA* involves behavior that might be in poor taste, involve an arguable point, or simply be stupid in light of prevailing standards. No malicious intent can be ascribed to the psychologist in question, and an ethics committee could respond by educating the individual or suggesting better ways of handling such matters in the future.

Level IB carries IA a step further, addressing behavior that is unquestionably inappropriate and somewhat offensive. Still, the committee may have the sense that the violation is a relatively minor one, that the individual in question did not fully realize the nature of the problem, and that an educative stance, rather than a punitive one, would be most effective and helpful in the long run. Such cases might include advertising infractions, inappropriate public statements, or mild uncollegiality. An ethics committee may request that the psychologist cease the actvity or behavior, noting that a more serious finding could result if the practice continued.

Level II (and *Level III*) involves *malum in se* offenses, that is to say, behavior that is unethical in itself in the view of the professional/scientific community. This category is reached when an ethics committee finds that a substantive violation did, indeed, occur. For *Level II* offenses, the

Table 2-1 Levels of Ethical Violations and Possible Directives or Sanctions

Level IA	A finding that a behavior or practice was not clearly unethical, but in poor taste or insufficiently cautious. An educational letter may be sent to the complainant offering suggestions or advice.
Level IB	A finding that a minor infraction occurred, but the potential for harm was unlikely. The psychologist may have been unsufficiently cautious, though not necessarily intentionally. An educational warning letter or a directive to cease and desist might be issued.
Level IIA	A finding of clearly unethical misconduct although unlikely to harm the public or profession substantially. The psychologist should have known better, although the consequences of the action (or inaction) were minor. The appropriate sanction may be a letter of reprimand. A directive might include requiring the psychologist to complete an educational program in ethics or some other area to remediate a deficiency in competence.
Level IIB	Deliberate or persistent behavior that could potentially lead to substantial harm to the client or public, although little harm may have actually occurred. The appropriate sanction may be a censure. Additional directives might include supervision or other corrective actions within the purview of the association.
Level IIIA	Continuing or dramatic misconduct producing a genuine hazard to clients, the public, and the profession. Motivation to change or to demonstrate concern for the behavior is unclear. A possible sanction is expulsion or a stipulated resignation with a directive for mandated supervision.
Level IIIB	Individual clients or others with whom one worked are substantially injured, and there are serious questions about the potential rehabilitation of the psychologist. The probable sanction is expulsion.

Source: Adapted from Koocher, Keith-Spiegel, and Klebanoff, 1981, and APA, 1996.

psychologist clearly should have known better, although the action or inaction did not result in any harm beyond remedy.

When it has been determined by an ethics committee that a violation of the ethics code has occurred, but that a recommendation of loss of membership does not appear warranted because the violation itself was unlikely to cause harm to another or to substantially tarnish the profession, the respondent may receive a letter of reprimand. If the violation was more likely to cause harm, but not gravely serious harm, to another or to the profession, the member may be censured.

Remedial directives assigned by an ethics committee might include mandated supervision, probation, referral for psychotherapy, enrollment in a continuing education course, or other appropriate corrective action. Ethics committees cannot order monetary payments to complainants, but, occasionally, respondents offer to return money to dissatisfied clients or consumers on their own as part of a good faith effort to resolve the problem.

Level III is reached when substantial harm accrues to others or to the profession as a result of the respondent's unethical behavior. The respondent may seem resistant to or ill-suited for rehabilitation and poses a threat to the public. In some cases, resignations with stipulations are permitted, while in other cases the individual is expelled from the organization.

Case 2-31: Seymour Fraud, Ph.D., who was found guilty of cheating Medicare out of thousands of dollars, was being investigated by a state regulatory agency and an ethics committee. During the period when both investigations were actively open, a major insurance company made new charges that Dr. Fraud had billed for over 50 client sessions that had never taken place.

Case 2-32: Harlan Stud, Ph.D., was charged by several women with sexual exploitation. Dr. Stud admitted engaging in sexual relations with them, but denied that it was exploitative. He claimed that they all needed special types of sexual activity in order to function as effective women. He attempted to elucidate a theoretical justification as to why he was the appropriate one to provide these

experiences. Despite claims by the clients that he forced his sexual attentions on them, Dr. Stud continued to deny wrongdoing or poor professional judgment. The only issue on which he would agree was that his form of therapy "did not work on these four women, but," he added, "it has worked beautifully on scores of others."

The two cases above are illustrative of cases resulting in the ethics committee recommendation of expulsion from the professional organization. Both psychologist appeared to be unsuitable candidates for rehabilitaion because neither revealed insight into the problematic nature of their behavior nor any indication that their views and practices would change.

Stipulated resignations, a less formidable sanction, can be offered by the committee, contingent on the approval of the board of directors. The agreement may include various provisos. This sanction is most likely to be offered when respondents admit to an ethical violation or the act that prompted a show cause action. The violator is offered an opportunity to resign from the association for a negotiated period of time. At the end of this period, the psychologist may reapply, and the committee will reexamine the case to see if the psychologist can demonstrate that major steps, either those stipulated or those taken on their initiative, have been taken to ensure that the nature of the difficulties have been ameliorated and are unlikely to resurface. At its option, the committee can act to restore the psychologist to membership in good standing if the psychologist reapplies for membership.

Mitigating Factors and Exposure

The system we described above provides a helpful framework to assist in curbing capricious punishment or excessive leniency relative to the specific violation. It must be recognized, however, that violations that appear identical may be decided differently for a variety of reasons. Common mitigating factors that might lead to different sanctions for similar violations include (1) the motivation or intent of the respondent, (2) actual or potential harm caused as a result of the infraction, (3) number of prior complaints against the respondent, (4) degree of experience in the field, (5) the willingness of the respondent to accept responsibility for his or her actions, and (6) the respondent's self-initiated attempts at remediation. For example, ethics committees may show lenience (e.g., apply an educative approach) to a first offender who is not malevolent, but who committed a relatively minor offense due to inexperience. If the same offense were committed by a recalcitrant, experienced psychologist, however, a more severe sanction would be considered.

Most of the sanctions imposed are made known only to the respondent and, sometimes, to the complainant. Sanctions have an immediate impact to the extent that the respondents have been educated, sensitized, embarrassed, or shamed into shaping up their behavior. Other more tangible consequences noted earlier may also accrue. Expulsion from the APA does result in the dissemination of the violator's identity and the general nature of the offense to all members of the APA as a part of the annual membership dues statement package. A recent alteration also allows the APA Ethics Office to inform any person who inquires in writing that a former member lost APA membership because of a sustained ethics charge or show cause action if the process occurred after June 1, 1996. (Stipulated resignations are excluded unless such disclosure was part of the stipulation.)

The APA cannot, on its own, delicense psychologists. It can, however, inform licensing and certification boards when an APA member is expelled. The recipients of the information may then take some action of their own. At its discretion, the APA may also inform other parties if it is determined that additional sharing of information would be in the best interests of the public or the profession. The APA has not yet proactively disclosed serious violators to the public, as have some other professional organizations. The California chapter of the professional association representing marriage and family counselors, for example, describes in its bimonthly magazine sustained charges that led to licensure revocation or suspension of marriage and family counselors *and* psychologists by the respective boards in California. Identities and location of practice are disclosed. The de-

scriptions are in such detail that we have been able to adapt a number of the cases described in this book from them.

Does the Profession Weed Out Enough?

Critics have noted that, because so few expulsions based on ethics committee actions occur each year at both national and state levels, the truly morally defective and incompetent among us are left mostly untouched. However, critics rarely discuss one important factor that may account for why many psychologists who violated the ethics code are not ejected from their professional associations. Ethics committees can determine that, despite the seriousness of the offense, evidence suggests that the respondent may be amenable to education or rehabilitation. In these instances, it would be a disservice to the public and perhaps even irresponsible to expel the member. Once a member is dropped, the association no longer has any monitoring control over that individual. Unless another regulatory body intervenes (and this eventuality cannot be guaranteed), the violator is likely to continue to function as a psychologist.

By keeping a respondent with rehabilitation potential in the ranks, the association can issue the kinds of directives (e.g., careful supervision at the psychologist's own expense for an extended time with periodic supervisor feedback, ethics courses, or tutorials) to help ensure that the member regains fitness. For those offenders willing to undergo remediation as recommended by an ethics committee, a lesser sanction than expulsion may be in everyone's best interests. The next two cases illustrate the rationale for the decision to keep serious violators in the ranks.

Case 2-33: Rocky Stumble, Psy.D., initiated contact with an ethics committee, confessing sexual intimacies with a client. The psychologist expressed considerable remorse. He noted that he became swept away with the affectionate nature of the client and, due to personal turmoil in his marriage, allowed sexual intimacies to transpire on two occasions. Realizing what he had done, he terminated the client and made several referrals available to her. He admitted his errors to her and informed her that he was no longer an appropriate therapist for her. Dr. Stumble then initiated his own psychotherapy and confessed in an effort to deal with his conscience. Stumble's therapist confirmed that the psychologist was highly motivated to ensure that this conduct would never resurface.

In this instance, the case investigation was tabled for 1 year, while Dr. Stumble continued treatment and his therapist provided quarterly reports to the ethics committee. At the end of the year, the therapist's report was favorable. Dr. Stumble's insight into his problems appeared to be considerable, and he was making good progress toward resolving the problems. A violation was ultimately found, but rather than offering Stumble a stipulated resignation or an expulsion, he was censured and was allowed to remain a member of the organization.

Case 2-34: Alan Jumbled, Ph.D., was discovered by an insurance company to have overbilled clients. Dr. Jumbled admitted the wrongdoing, but also provided documentary evidence that he had underbilled many other clients. He explained that he had been extremely agitated due to personal matters, which revealed itself in several ways, including erroneous record keeping. He had reimbursed the insurance company for the $1,000 in overcharges. His pastor and many other community members sent letters attesting to how highly regarded he was in the community and documented his record of volunteer community service.

Whereas insurance fraud is a very serious offense, the ethics committee carefully considered the other factors and entered a reprimand letter into his files. The portrait of an individual trying to make "fast money" by dishonest means simply did not emerge. The committee requested that Dr. Jumbled begin treatment on his own to work out his personal problems and mandated supervision of his work (including billing records and procedures) for 1 year. At the end of this period, considerable progress had been made in psychotherapy, and the supervisor attested to his high-level skills and moral character. In the meantime, Jumbled had joined and

was functioning effectively in a group practice and was able to relinquish the billing procedures to a bookkeeper hired by the group.

WHO TUMBLES THROUGH THE CRACKS?

As we stated above, licensure and professional association membership do not ensure that a given psychologist is competent and ethical. However, consumers are afforded protection and redress channels when psychologists providing services to them voluntarily agree to ethical scrutiny by virtue of their membership in organizations with peer control mechanisms. Psychologists who have earned credentials that qualify them for licensure or membership in a professional association with a monitoring mechanism, but who seek neither, are subject only to criminal or civil law or, if not self-employed, to the quality control mechanisms at their place of employment.

Most medium- to large-size communities have at least one individual offering services that appear to strongly resemble those of psychologists and related regulated professionals, but these individuals have neither suitable formal training nor the credentials to qualify them for licensure or membership in a professional association. Some have purchased impressive-looking credentials from "diploma mills" to hang on their walls. These individuals may sport unprotected titles that sound legitimate, but are unregulated by the state, such as "personal counselor," "relationship expert," or "motivational consultant." (Protected titles are professional designations that only state-licensed individuals can use legally to identity their practice to the public. "Psychologist" is a protected title. See chapter 3 more more information on fake institutions.)

Bogus professionals are slippery when pursued because, whenever a complaint appears imminent, they usually pick up stakes and relocate. In some states, the display of imitation or fraudulent diplomas can be investigated by authorities if a complainant was reasonably led to believe that the individual was licensed. But, generally speaking, the public is not well protected from these phony practitioners.

References

American Psychological Association. (1982). *Ethical principles in the conduct of research with human participants*. Washington, DC: Author.

American Psychological Association. (1985). *Standards for educational and psychological testing*. Washington, DC: Author.

American Psychological Association. (1986). *Guidelines for ethical conduct in the care and use of animals*. Washington, DC: Author.

American Psychological Association. (1987a). *General guidelines for providers of psychological services*. Washington, DC: Author.

American Psychological Association. (1987b). *Guidelines for computer based tests and interpretations*. Washington, DC: Author.

American Psychological Association. (1990). *Guidelines for providers of psychological services to ethnic, linguistic, and culturally diverse populations*. Washington, DC: Author.

American Psychological Association. (1992). Ethical principles of psychologists and code of conduct. *American Psychologist, 47*, 1597–1611.

American Psychological Association. (1996). Rules and procedures. *American Psychological Association, 51*, 529–548.

Ansell, C., & Ross, H. L. (1990). When laws and values conflict: A reply to Pope and Bajt. *American Psychologist, 45*, 399.

Bass, L. J., DeMers, S. T., Ogloff, J. R., Peterson, C., Pettifor, J. L., Reaves, R. P., Retfalvi, T., Simon, N. P., Sinclair, C., & Tipton, R. M. (1996). *Professional conduct and discipline in psychology*. Washington, DC: American Psychological Association and Montgomery, AL: Association of State and Provincial Psychology Boards.

Bersoff, D. N., & Koeppl, P. M. (1993). The relation between ethical codes and moral principles. *Ethics and Behavior, 3*, 345–357.

Bersoff, D. N. (1994a). *Ethical conflicts in psychology*. Washington, DC: American Psychological Association.

Bersoff, D. N. (1994b). Explicit ambiguity: The 1992 ethics code as oxymoron. *Professional Psychology: Research and Practice, 25*, 382–387.

Canter, M. B., Bennett, B. E., Jones, S. E., & Nagy, T. F. (1994). *Ethics for psychologists: A commentary on the APA ethics code*. Washington, DC: American Psychological Association.

Chalk, R., Frankel, M. S., & Chafer, S. B. (1980). *AAAS Professional Ethics Project*. Washington, DC: American Association for the Advancement of Science.

Clouser, K. D. (1973). Some things medical ethics is not. *Journal of the American Medical Association, 223*, 787–789.

Clouser, K. D. (1975). Medical ethics: Some uses, abuses, and limitations. *New England Journal of Medicine, 297*, 384–387.

Derbyshire, R. C. (1974). Medical ethics and discipline. *Journal of the American Medical Association, 228*, 59–62.

Golann, S. E. (1969). Emerging areas of ethical concern. *American Psychologist, 33*, 1009–1016.

Golann, S. E. (1970). Ethical standards for psychology: Development and revision, 1938–1968. *Annals of the New York Academy of Sciences, 169*, 398–405.

Gorlin, R. A. (Ed.). (1994). *Codes of professional responsibility* (3rd ed.). Washington, DC: BNA Books.

Gross, S. (1979). The myth of professional licensing. *American Psychologist, 33*, 1009–1016.

Hare-Mustin, R. T., & Hall, J. E. (1981). Procedures for responding to ethics complaints against psychologists. *American Psychologist, 36*, 1494–1505.

Herbsled, J. D., Sales, B. D., & Overcast, T. D. (1985). Challenging licensure and certification. *American Psychologist, 40*, 1165–1178.

Hess, H. F. (1980). Enforcement: Procedures, problems, and prospects. *Professional Practice of Psychology, 1*, 1–10.

Hobbes, N. (1948). The development of a code of ethical standards for psychology. *American Psychologist, 3*, 80–84.

Hogan, D. (1979). *Regulation of psychotherapists*. Cambridge, MA: Ballinger.

Holtzman, W. H. (1979). The IUPS project on professional ethics and conduct. *International Journal of Psychology, 34*, 696–702.

Keith-Spiegel, P. (Ed.). (1994). Special section. The 1992 ethics code: Boon or bane? *Professional Psychology: Research and Practice, 25*, 315–387.

Kitchener, K. S. (1984). Intuition, critical evaluation and ethical principles: The foundation for ethical decisions in counseling psychology. *Counseling Psychologist, 12,* 43–55.

Koocher, G. P. (1979). Credentialing in psychology: Close encounters with competence? *American Psychologist, 34,* 696–702.

Koocher, G. P. (1994). The commerce of professional psychology and the new ethics code. *Professional Psychology: Research and Practice, 25,* 315–387.

Koocher, G. P., Keith-Spiegel, P., & Klebanoff, L. (1981). *Levels and sanctions.* Unpublished report of the APA Task Force on Ethics System Procedures.

Levy, C. S. (1974). On the development of a code of ethics. *Social Work, 19,* 207–216.

Meara, N. M., Schmidt, L. D., & Day, J. D. (1996). Principles and virtues: A foundation for ethical decisions, policies, and character. *Counseling Psychologist, 24,* 4–77.

Moore, R. A. (1978). Ethics in the practice of psychiatry: Origins, functions, models, and enforcement. *American Journal of Psychiatry, 135,* 157–163.

Nagy, T. F. (1996, January/February). Ethics committees: Investigate or educate? *National Psychologist,* 15–16.

Pope, K. S., & Bajt, T. R. (1988). When laws and values conflict: A dilemma for psychologists. *American Psychologist, 43,* 828.

Pope, K. S., & Vetter, V. A. (1992). Ethical dilemmas encountered by members of the American Psychological Association: A national survey. *American Psychologist, 47,* 397–411.

Sinclair, C., Simon, N. P., & Pettifor, J. L. (1966). The history of ethical codes and licensure. In L. J. Bass, D. T. DeMers, J. R. Ogloff, C. Peterson, J. L. Pettifor, R. P. Reaves, T. Retfalvi, N. P. Simon, C. Sinclair, & R. M. Tipton, *Professional conduct and discipline in psychology* (pp. 17–38). Washington, DC: American Psychological Association and Montgomery, AL: Association of State and Provincial Psychology Boards.

Sinnett, E. R., & Linford, O. (1982a). Is there a crisis in professional self-regulation of the practice of psychology? *Professional Psychology, 13,* 332–333.

Sinnett, E. R., & Linford, O. (1982b). Processing of formal complaints against psychologists. *Psychological Reports, 50,* 535–544.

Steger, H. G. (1983, August). Reflections on two years as ethics chair. *Ohio Psychologist,* 3–5.

Stromberg, C. D. (1988). *The psychologist's legal handbook.* Washington, DC: Council for the National Register.

Stromberg, C. D. (1990). Key legal issues in professional ethics. In *Reflections on ethics: A compilation of articles inspired by the May, 1990 ASHA Ethics Colloquium* (pp. 15–38). Rockville, MD: American Speech-Language-Hearing Association.

Talbutt, L. C. (1981, October). Ethical standards: Assets and limitations. *Personnel and Guidance Journal,* 110–112.

Taylor, R. L., & Torrey, E. F. (1972). The pseudoregulation of American psychiatry. *American Journal of Psychiatry, 129,* 658–663.

Van Hoose, W. H., & Kottler, J. (1978). *Ethical and legal issues in counseling and psychotherapy.* San Francisco: Jossey-Bass.

Wallace, R. E., & Howell, R. J. (1992). Due process: American Psychological Association: When worlds collide: Law and ethics in conflict. *Forensic Reports, 5,* 189–210.

Weinberger, A. (1988). Ethics: Code value and application. *Canadian Psychology, 29,* 77–85.

Wilensky, H. L. (1964). The professionalization of everyone? *American Journal of Sociology, 70,* 137–158.

Winston, R. B., & Dagley, J. C. (1985). Ethical standard statements: Uses and limitations. In U. Delworth & G. R. Hansen (Eds.), *New directions for student services* (No. 30, 49–65). San Francisco: Jossey-Bass.

Wright, R. (1989). On ethics committees: Happiness and the pursuit of life and liberty. *Psychotherapy in Private Practice, 7,* 1–18.

Zemlick, M. J. (1980). Ethical standards: Cosmetics for the face of the profession of psychology. *Psychotherapy, Theory, Research and Practice, 17,* 448–453.

3

Knowing Thyself: Competence and Credentials

There is nothing more dangerous than ignorance in action.

Johann Wolfgang von Goethe

The quotation from *Faust* stands as a warning to colleagues who believe that they have mastered all there is to know about their specialized field. This chapter is about knowing one's limitations and how this knowledge should guide a psychologist's ethical behavior. Truly competent psychologists recognize their limitations and weaknesses, as well as their strengths and skills. When psychologists become blind to their areas of weakness or inadequacy, clients may be hurt and the public put at risk. The ability to explore one's motives and relationships insightfully is not easily taught and never perfected, yet these skills are among the most critical to effective professional ethical functioning.

Before exploring the problems of the incompetent or troubled psychologist, it is important to understand basic ethical problems associated with training, credentialing, maintaining competence at the postgraduate level, and, finally, recognizing problem relationships when they develop. While standards and credentials in psychology are topics of some controversy, it is critical that psychologists recognize the boundaries of their competence and the limitations of their techniques (Abeles, 1994).

CONCEPTUAL ISSUES

Pope and Brown (1996) have described two types of personal competencies needed for high-quality professional practice: intellectual competence and emotional competence. *Intellectual competence* refers to the acquisition of knowledge based on empirical research and sound clinical scholarship regarding practice with a particular population. Intellectual competence may also refer to a clinician's general ability to assess, conceptualize, and plan appropriate treatment for a particular client or problem. Most important, possessing intellectual competence means recognizing what one does not know. For example, vast experience in treating middle-class Caucasian clients does not necessarily translate into the special competence needed to treat some clients of other racial identities (e.g., see the discussion of ethnicity and psychotherapy in chapter 4). This does not mean that clinicians should only assess or treat members of their own racial or ethnic groups, but rather that the clinician must be able to recognize all relevant individual differences and strive to acquire any incremental knowledge needed to treat the client appropriately.

Emotional competence refers to psychotherapists' ability to emotionally contain and tolerate the clinical material that emerges in treatment, their willingness to detect and skill at detecting the intrusion of personal biases into the clinical work, and their capacity for self-care in the context of the difficult work that is psychotherapy (Pope & Brown, 1996). Not all therapists can work with all clients or all kinds of problems. Recognizing and acknowledging this fact is not a sign of weakness. But, unfortunately, many clinicians may feel personal, social, or economic pressures to see whomever comes to their office.

The American Psychological Association (APA) and other organized groups of psychologists have long struggled with the problem of defining professional competence and incompetence. These efforts have taken many forms, including development of ethical codes, standards of practice or practice guidelines, third-party-payer quality assurance programs, state licensing or certification boards, and other types of credentialing bodies, such as the American Boards of Professional Psychology and the American Psychological Association College of Professional Psychology. Despite these efforts, however, none of the extant structures have been able to effectively detect and then act in response to incompetent professional behavior, or even routinely to enforce sanctions against those deemed incompetent.

Only the most egregious instances of incompetence, those that lead to filing formal complaints, ever come to the attention of licensing boards and ethics committees, as discussed in chapter 2. Part of the difficulty is related to a general presumption of competence, much akin to the dictum that one is "innocent until proven guilty." Obtaining a consensus on a definition of competence also has been elusive (Claiborn, 1982). In addition, incompetence is often difficult to prove, especially when one is bound by

the constraints of due process and the need to accumulate substantial evidence in each case.

Standards of Practice

The APA has historically promulgated documents that represent significant and comprehensive attempts to codify general standards of practice in psychology (APA, 1977, 1981). In part, these were designed to define minimum levels of competent professional practices and procedures, both generally and within specific specialty areas. Although worthy efforts, these documents were seldom cited, largely unenforced, and, in some cases, subsequently "withdrawn" following discussions with the Federal Trade Commission (see chapter 11).

Part of the confusion regarding determination of competence involves controversy about what constitutes a specialty, subspecialty, proficiency, or particular area of expertise in the practice of psychology. Clinical, counseling, industrial/organizational, and school psychology have traditionally been recognized as specialties, but there are certainly many special areas of expertise within each of these headings. For example, an industrial psychologist competent in human-factors engineering may not be qualified to consult on personnel selection, a clinical psychologist well trained in psychotherapy and assessment may lack the forensic knowledge to evaluate a defendant's competence to stand trial, and a counseling psychologist with many years experience as a psychotherapist to adults may be untrained in work with children. What constitutes the basic qualification needed to practice personnel consultation, forensic evaluations, or child psychotherapy? Are these specialties or subspecialties, or simply special types of competence, proficiencies, or skills? American psychology has often lacked clear consensus on these matters. Consider the following examples:

Case 3-1: Charlotte Hasty, Ph.D., had practiced individual psychoanalytically oriented psychotherapy with adult clients for 10 years. After attending a continuing education program (half-day workshop) on family therapy, Dr. Hasty began to conduct, while reading books in the field during her spare time, family therapy sessions for some of her clients.

Case 3-2: Carl Klutzkind, Psy.D., had no forensic experience and had been treating a woman with many adjustment problems in the wake of a separation and impending divorce. After Dr. Klutzkind worked with the woman for 6 months, her attorney asked if he would testify in support of her having custody of her 7-year-old child. Dr. Klutzkind agreed and from the witness stand offered many opinions about the adjustment of the woman and her child. An ethical complaint was subsequently filed against him, noting that he was not trained in child work, he never actually interviewed the child, and he was generally negligent in offering an opinion. It seems that the child was in treatment with another psychologist, and Klutzkind had also never sought information from that colleague or the child's father. It was clear that Klutzkind knew little about child custody work or clinical assessment of children.

Case 3-3: Sarah Bellum, Ed.D., completed her graduate training in the 1970s, before clinical neuropsychology evolved as a clinical specialty. She was trained to "assess organicity" using the first edition of the Wechsler Adult Intelligence Scale (WAIS), House-Tree-Person drawings, and the Bender Motor Gestalt Test. She has never studied neuroanatomy and has no knowledge of newer assessment tools designed for use in neuropsychological assessment. Her current practice is chiefly psychotherapy. An attorney contacted Dr. Bellum about assessing a client who had suffered a closed head injury and was experiencing language, memory, and perceptual sequella. She accepted the referral and tested the client using the "tried and true" techniques she learned nearly three decades earlier.

In these three cases, the psychologists have failed to recognize the boundaries of their respective formal training. While it must be acknowledged that no clear professional standards now exist to define expertise in family therapy or child custody work, it is reasonably clear that more expertise than either Drs. Hasty or Klutzkind had is required. In Hasty's case, we cannot say for certain whether anyone was actually hurt or helped, nor would the lack of training be

discovered under normal circumstances (i.e., unless a formal complaint were filed). Dr. Hasty does not see anything wrong with applying this new *technique* because she is an "experienced therapist." Dr. Klutzkind failed to prepare adequately for the role he agreed to perform, but for which he was not equipped by training to undertake. Perhaps his concern for his client, his desire to expound his views in court, or simple ignorance led him into trouble. His behavior clearly had a potentially hurtful impact on all the parties in the case and is in clear violation of extant professional standards, of which he seems unaware (APA, 1994).

Dr. Bellum, who trained in an era that predated most of what is considered current neuropsychological assessment science, has made no effort to keep current with that part of her training. There was nothing wrong with her professional choices until she agreed to take on a case for which her skills were no longer current or adequate. It is not clear that Dr. Bellum is even aware of the evolution in the field since her doctoral training ended. Both Drs. Bellum and Klutzkind also appear ignorant of ethical constraints on psychologists' functioning as expert witnesses (see chapter 15 for a full discussion).

When no formal standards exist for given practices or techniques, it is incumbent on the practitioner to be prudent and conservative in assessing whether additional training is required prior to using them. In such circumstances, it is best to consult colleagues widely regarded as experts on the particular matters at hand for their guidance regarding adequacy of training or of practice standards.

There are relatively few published papers exploring conceptualizations of competent psychological practice, and those few are limited in scope. One author argues that specific competencies cannot be used to adequately describe the fundamentals of psychotherapy (Whyte, 1994). Others have underscored competence in professional practice skills (Berven & Scofield, 1987) and have claimed to document therapist competence validly and reliably within a particular therapeutic framework (Svartberg, 1989; Svartberg & Stiles, 1992). A critical incident survey of 27 psychoanalytically oriented psychotherapists revealed that they felt most competent when they were able to address a client's resistance and countertransference constructively (Sandell, Ronnas, & Schubert, 1992). Another study reported a relationship between therapist-trainees' sense of competence and fee levels, with those in a high-fee condition rating themselves as more competent than those in a low-fee condition (Glennon & Karlovac, 1988).

A particularly useful study by Peterson and Bry (1980) reviewed appraisals of 126 Doctor of Psychology students by 102 faculty and field supervisors. After rating students with whom they had worked, faculty and supervisors were asked to describe the dominant characteristics of "outstanding" and "incompetent" trainees. The quality most frequently mentioned for outstanding students was "high intelligence," while the most common characteristic for incompetent trainees was "lack of knowledge." When a rating scale composed of the 28 most commonly used terms was used by supervisors to rate students the subsequent year, four factors emerged as central to the conceptualization of competence: (1) professional responsibility, (2) interpersonal warmth, (3) intelligence, and (4) experience. The data also suggested that behaviorally oriented supervisors gave somewhat less weight to warmth in evaluating competence than did eclectic or psychodynamically oriented supervisors.

It will become evident that competence-related issues pervade many chapters in this book. Competence issues related to psychodiagnostic assessment and testing are specifically addressed in chapter 6. Similarly, issues related to competence as a psychotherapist are implied in the details of chapters 4 and 5. The purpose of this chapter is to discuss matters of competence and weakness more generally, especially as they relate to the psychologist's personal development and professional behavior.

Detecting Incompetence

Ethics codes enjoin psychologists to avoid practicing beyond their areas of competence; however, such codes are very general in nature and give too few specifics to permit one to easily identify incompetent practice. Periodic formal reports by the APA Ethics Committee, usually published in the June or December issues of the *American Psychologist*, attempt to illustrate incompetence and other unethical behavior through case examples. Detection of incompetence must rely on observation and, ultimately, complaints by someone. When such cases come under the scrutiny of ethics committees, the most severe punishment available is expulsion from the organization. While this is not a minor penalty, because colleagues and the public may be notified of the action, this will not necessarily interrupt the practice of the offender. Offenders may simply practice without association membership. If a licensing board acts on an incompetence complaint and revokes the practitioner's license, the individual may continue to practice under an unregulated title such as "psychotherapist" or "counselor." Incompetence can be a basis for malpractice litigation; however, one must first be able to establish that damages have occurred (as discussed in chapter 15).

Another problem to keep in mind in conceptualizing and detecting competence is the range or variability of skill among psychologists, whether they are practitioners, academics, or consultants to industry. The point is well summarized by Hogan (1977), who notes, with respect to the regulation of psychotherapy, that there is a substantial difference between adequate and superior competence. Within each pool of credentialed practitioners, for example, there will be some who barely passed the admission criteria and some who "topped the pool." By definition, not everyone can be "above average." It is certainly desirable to be exceptionally competent, but it is not unethical to practice in an area in which one's competence is simply "adequate," assuming we know what adequate means (ES: 1.04–1.05) and are correct in setting that threshold.

TRAINING ISSUES

A variety of controversies have evolved regarding the training of psychological practitioners. These controversies have involved questions about just how psychological practitioners ought to be trained and how psychologists not trained as practitioners ought to go about being retrained if they wish to become human service providers. A variety of training conferences have been held, often referred to by the meeting's geographic site, yielding the Boulder or Vail (Colorado) training models or the Virginia Beach (Watson, Caddy, Johnson, & Rimm, 1981) recommendations. We do not intend to explore the question of whether a scientist-practitioner training model is ideal or whether a professional school program is most appropriate for modern practitioners. Rather, we are concerned about ethical issues in the conduct of training. Are psychologists adequately trained for the jobs they intend to perform? Are the techniques used to train them ethically defensible? Are students evaluated in an ethically appropriate manner? Is the institution providing the training competent to do so? These are the substantive ethical problems linked to psychologists' training.

Competence by Degrees?

Unlike the fields of law and medicine, for which the entry-level practice degrees in the United States are recognizable (i.e., as the J.D. and M.D., respectively), psychology has historically been more diverse. In addition to the Ph.D., Ed.D., Psy.D., M.A., and M.S. degrees, psychologists have listed the following earned degrees in reporting their qualifications for recognition as psychological health service providers (Wellner, 1978):

C.A.G.S.	D.S.Sc.	M.L.H.	M.Sc.
D.A.G.S.	Ed.S.	M.P.A.	P.D.
D.M.H.	J.D.	M.P.H.	Th.D.
D.M.S.P.	M.C.P.	M.P.S.	
D.Min.	M.Ed.	M.S.Ed.	
D.P.A.	M.L.	M.S.S.W.	

In addition to departments of psychology, the following academic departments were listed by applicants as granting "closely related degrees" as they sought recognition as psychologists (Wellner, 1978): American civilization, anthropology, child study, divinity, education, educational research and measurement, general studies, guidance counseling, health and physical education, home and family life, law, philosophy, political science, rehabilitation, religion,

social and human relations, special education, and speech pathology.

The major fields within these departments in which degrees were granted are even more diverse. In part, this variety sprang from the fact that many state licensing laws at one time recognized degrees in psychology "or a closely related field" as a qualification for psychology licensing. Over the past decade, highly successful efforts on a state-by-state level have resulted in elimination of most of the closely related field options for would-be psychologists. Many who were accepted for licensing up to the mid-1980s, however, were approved on the basis of their seniority at the time legislation was passed (such regulations are often termed *grandparenting* provisions).

The Doctoral Versus Master's Degrees

The doctoral degree has been well established as the entry-level practice credential in psychology (Fox, 1994; Robiner, Arbisi, & Edwall, 1994), although approximately 8,000 master's degrees are awarded each year in psychology, leading to potential identity crises for those who do not continue study to the doctoral level (Centor & Stang, 1976; Moses, 1990). Unlike doctoral programs, master's programs are not accredited by the APA or any other national psychological organization. It is also clear by examination of course content and curriculum duration that master's and doctoral training in psychology are not equivalent (Robiner et al., 1994). In states where master's-level psychologists are allowed to sit for the national licensing exam administered under the auspices of the Association of State and Provincial Psychology Boards (i.e., the Examination for the Professional Practice of Psychology, EPPP), they are consistently outscored by doctoral-level licensing candidates (Robiner et al., 1994).

Does all this mean that holders of doctoral degrees are always more competent at specific professional tasks than holders of master's degrees? Of course, it does not. Rather, the data suggest that, on the whole, a person trained at the doctoral level will have acquired a more substantial foundation in terms of both required course work and supervised experience (Stevens, Yock, & Perlman, 1979). From an ethical perspective, the key issues, independent of the degree held, are accurate representations of one's training and credentials, practice within the scope of such training, and adherence to the regulations applicable to psychologists in one's practice jurisdiction (e.g., not holding oneself out as a psychologist in a state where one's degree does not qualify for use of that title).

Psy.D. Versus Ph.D.

Some psychologists have argued that a Ph.D. degree is too generic a scholarly credential for determination of who ought to be recognized as a health service provider in psychology (Shapiro & Wiggins, 1994). They suggest that a Doctor of Psychology (or Psy.D. degree) should identify the doctoral-level health service provider in psychology and go so far as to recommend that Psy.D. degrees be awarded retroactively, in much the same manner as the J.D. degree was awarded to attorneys who had earned LL.B. degrees prior to the mid-1960s. Although the APA Council of Representatives was not receptive to such arguments, leading to abandonment of the effort in 1996, there is a strong sentiment that professional psychology needs a single, comprehensive definition that can be readily understood by the public (Fox, 1994).

In a survey of training directors of APA-approved clinical psychology programs (Mayne, Norcross, & Sayette, 1994), Psy.D. applicants were 4 times more likely to gain admission, but 6 times less likely to receive full financial assistance than applicants to research-oriented Ph.D. programs. In general, admission rates to Psy.D. programs were 23% (standard deviation = 16), whereas practice-oriented and scientist-practitioner-oriented Ph.D. programs admitted 9–10% of applicants (standard deviation = 4). These data are interesting, but convey little about the competence of graduates.

Ingredients of the Doctoral Program

Recognizing that psychologists who act as human service practitioners take on great responsibility, the APA has developed a thoughtful and detailed accreditation system (Office of Program Consultation and Accreditation, 1996). This system provides a means for evaluating academic and internship programs purporting to train psychological practitioners. Curricula must address biological, cognitive-affective, and social bases of behavior; history and systems of psychology; psychological measurement; research methods; techniques of data analysis; scientific foundations of practice; assessment and diagnosis; and cultural and individual diversity. However, there is considerable latitude permitted within categories. For example, it is possible for a program fully approved by the APA in clinical psychology to graduate doctoral students who have never treated a child, worked with a geriatric client, or learned projective testing. Some programs send students on an internship with experience in several practica and dozens of client assessments behind them, whereas faculty of other programs believe that students who may have seen fewer than a dozen assessment and treatment cases in practica are "ready to go" on their internship.

One area of noteworthy historical omissions across many graduate programs is training for serving people of various races and ethnic origins. Mintz, Bartels, and Rideout (1995) surveyed 268 psychology interns regarding their perceptions of training received on ethnic minority issues and availability of resources during graduate training. Only 40% had graduate-level course work in counseling ethnic minorities, and these issues were not often incorporated in core courses. Of those responding to the survey, 67% reported the presence of at least one faculty member with expertise in such issues. By the turn of the millennium, the United States will be a fully multiracial, multilingual, multicultural country (Sue, 1991). Despite increasing attention to multicultural issues in psychology and within the APA, graduate students still experience relatively little exposure to multicultural issues in course work, supervision, and workshops (Pope-Davis, Reynolds, Dings, & Nielson, 1995). We agree that treatment of culturally distinct persons by those not competent to work with them should be considered unethical (Casas, Ponterotto, & Gutierrez, 1986) and stress the need to improve training on that score.

Another problem with many graduate programs involves perceived heterosexual bias. A survey of gay and lesbian graduate students in professional psychology (Pilkington & Cantor, 1996) revealed that many trainees experienced general discouragement, pejorative comments, difficulty finding supervisors, warnings about adverse career consequences, and other problems related to sexual orientation. Examples of inappropriate incidents, including pathologizing, stereotyping, ridiculing, or discussing "curing" homosexuality, are detailed in the survey report.

The variability across different programs is not necessarily bad, as long as graduates are aware of their competence and limitations. The recent graduate of a doctoral program who recognizes a training inadequacy can remedy it in many ways, including postdoctoral fellowships, continuing education programs, and proficiency development programs. More substantial difficulties face the psychologist who wishes to change specialties, such as a social, experimental, or developmental psychology graduate who wishes to become a health services provider. Such shifts are occasionally permitted by generic state licensing laws, as discussed in the following section.

The APA policy adopted by the Council of Representatives holds that an internship or applied training as such is insufficient for the professional "retread," as those who wish to convert to clinical work are sometimes called. The policy holds that such individuals must also complete course work that would be equivalent to the desired degree but is missing from their academic records. It is preferable that this course work be taken in a programmatic, sequential, and carefully monitored program, as opposed to a loose collection of casually collected courses. Some universities offer special 1- or 2-year programs aimed at retraining such individuals. Psychologists sometimes choose a "back door" route, seeking internships or training in applied settings without accompanying course work. The APA can attempt to discipline approved training sites that accept such individuals, but licensing or credentialing bodies are not bound, or necessarily influenced, by APA criteria. Training may also occur in settings that are not APA approved. Consider these examples that describe specialized services to children:

Case 3-4: George Grownup, Ph.D., completed a degree in clinical psychology from a program fully accredited by the APA. He took all of his practica, field work, and internship training at settings treating adults (i.e., a college counseling center and Veterans Administration Hospital). Although he has not taken courses in child development or child psychopathology, he now wants to do clinical work with children. He begins to add child clients to his practice after reading a half dozen books about developmental psychology and child treatment.

Case 3-5: Dee Vella Pmental, Ph.D., completed her degree in human development within a psychology department. She then worked for 2 years as a researcher interviewing victims of family violence and assessing the cognitive development of infants with Down's syndrome. She has decided that she would like to be able to do more clinical forms of work, including personality assessment and psychotherapy, with the types of patients she has been studying. Dr. Pmental volunteers more than a dozen hours per week for 3 years at a local teaching hospital with an APA-approved internship program. She sees patients under close supervision, while also attending didactic seminars and taking courses in personality assessment at a local university.

Dr. Grownup is a well-trained adult clinician, whose attempt to prepare himself to work with children is glaringly superficial. He is certainly exceeding his trained competencies, although he does not seem to realize it. Dr. Pmental is certainly better trained to work with children than Dr. Grownup, but technically she has not sought formal retreading. She has gone further and is considerably more cautious than Dr. Grownup in attempting to ensure her competence in the activities she hopes to practice. Although her behavior may technically violate an APA policy or professional standard, it is not necessarily unethical. As long as she limits her ultimate practice to the areas in which she is well trained, her behavior would be considered ethically appropriate.

The Student in Transition

Students in psychology are obligated to abide by ethical principles, just as are other psychologists. At times, however, some advanced students find themselves caught in an interesting bind as they attempt a professional transition. Consider the following case example:

Case 3-6: Karen Quandary, M.S.W., has 4 years of experience as a clinical social worker and is licensed as an "independent clinical social worker" in her state. She decides to enter the Applied Institute of Professional Psychology, in its fully accredited and approved program in clinical psychology.

Ms. Quandary acknowledges that she is not licensed as a psychologist, although technically she is a "psychology student," and has identified herself as a psychologist by joining a professional association. At the same time, she is trained in psychotherapy through a social work program. She is licensed to practice as a social worker and has been doing so legally. While she is not qualified for licensing as a psychologist, and thus cannot practice as a psychologist (e.g., undertake psychodiagnostic testing without supervision), there is no reason to believe that she is not competent to practice as a social worker.

A person with two valid professional identities is not required to surrender one while developing the second. As long as Ms. Quandary is not leading the public or her clients to believe that she is a psychologist, and as long as she practices within her areas of social work competency, she is not behaving unethically. Technically, Ms. Quandary cannot consider herself a psychologist or announce herself one to the public until she meets appropriate professional and statutory standards for the profession. One must, however, discriminate between professional titles and professional functions for which one has appropriate training. To the extent that social work ethics and psychology ethics differ in specificity, Ms. Quandary should always hold herself to the more stringent standard. In addition, she would be wise to check with her faculty about any special limitations imposed on a stu-

dent above and beyond the literal meaning of the ethics code.

Student Evaluations

The APA's *Guidelines and Principles for Accreditation of Programs in Professional Psychology* (Office of Program Consultation and Accreditation, 1996) points out the special responsibility of faculty to assess the progress of each student continually and to keep the students advised of these assessments. Students who exhibit long-term serious problems or who do not function effectively in academic and/or interpersonal spheres should be counseled early. If necessary, they should be made aware of career alternatives or, after appropriate due process procedures, dropped from the program. Each program should have specific procedures to routinely assess the progress and competence of students, advise them of the outcome, and delineate appropriate sequences of action and alternative outcomes. These procedures should be explicit, written, and available to all students and faculty. Graduate students terminated from degree programs represent an occasional source of ethics complaints against faculty, which raises competence issues.

Case 3-7: Michael Mello left his urban West Coast home to attend graduate school at a rural midwestern university. At the end of his third semester, he received a written notice that he was being terminated as "personally unsuited" to continue in the school's counseling psychology doctoral program. Mello filed ethics complaints against the director of training and department chair, complaining that he had never previously been advised of problems, his grades were excellent, and he had been denied due process.

Case 3-8: Liz Militant also traveled across the country to attend graduate school in psychology. After 3 years in the program with satisfactory grades, she took her comprehensive examinations and failed. In a hurry to take an internship for which she had been accepted, Ms. Militant again attempted the exams and failed. As a result of failing twice, she was terminated as a degree candidate in accordance with department regulations. Ms.

Militant filed an ethics complaint against several faculty members, noting that the grading of the exams she failed was highly subjective, and other psychologists to whom she had shown her answers thought they were well done. She went on to claim that her strong feminist views and ethnic heritage had been a source of friction between herself and some faculty for her 3 years at the school, and she attributed her failures to contamination by these factors in the subjective grading of her exams.

These two cases had several elements in common when they came before an ethics committee at approximately the same time. They involved students with cultural values different from the majority of the faculty and community within which they were training. On inquiry by the ethics committee, it became clear that both schools lacked formal procedures for student grievances, and that both students were "surprised" by the efforts to dismiss them. Mello claimed to have had no warning that he was deemed to have serious problems prior to the written notice. There was reason to believe that, while he had been given a variety of ambiguous messages, he had never been counseled or warned that dismissal was within the realm of possibility. Militant had sensed friction with some faculty members, but had received good evaluations from her field placement supervisors and satisfactory or better grades in all courses. While she had known about the rule that two failures terminated candidacy, she had expected to pass and felt, in any case, that she was entitled to an appeal.

While the universities and students involved each had valid reasons for criticizing the other's behavior, it was also evident that the students were the more vulnerable parties and had been, at the very least, subjected to some communication problems. Mediation by the ethics committee led to Mello's being awarded a master's degree for work completed, and he was able to transfer to another university. Militant's university agreed to ask a panel of psychologists, suggested by the ethics committee, from universities in neighboring states to evaluate her exam answers independently and to be guided by their judgment. Much of the acrimony generated in these episodes might have been prevented had

the universities involved developed more specific procedures for monitoring the progress of students and given them timely feedback about their competence.

The problem of the impaired psychologist or "sick doctor" is addressed at the end of this chapter. Many of the issues discussed under that heading can also apply to students, and it seems appropriate to highlight the impaired student at this point. The students mentioned in Cases 3-7 and 3-8 were not clearly impaired. Consider the following cases from psychology and medical graduate schools:

Case 3-9: In 1975, Jane Doe entered New York University's Medical School. Prior to her admission, she had a long history of emotional problems, including numerous involuntary hospitalizations, which were never revealed to the school. During her first year, her condition "flared up" again, and she began behaving in a "bizarre and self-destructive manner," including at least one alleged suicide attempt in a laboratory on campus. She was later encouraged to take a leave of absence; she sought voluntary hospitalization and was released with a "guarded" prognosis. The medical school later denied her readmission after an examining psychiatrist deemed her emotionally "unfit to resume her medical education" (see *Doe v. New York University*, 1981).

Case 3-10: Irwin Flamer was enrolled as a graduate student in clinical psychology at Middle State University. After a series of 12 arson fires in the psychology building, Flamer was discovered as the culprit and sentenced to a term in prison. Following his parole, he reapplied to complete his degree. He was a "straight A" student and had nearly completed a master's degree prior to his arrest.

Case 3-11: Emma Petuous was enrolled as a graduate student at the Manhattan School of Professional Psychology, where she earned respectable, but not outstanding, grades. Some of the practica supervisors noted that she tended to be impulsive and somewhat "emotionally immature," although she was also able to function quite well in a number of professional circumstances. After receiving an unsatisfactory "C" grade in her statistics course, Ms. Petuous prepared a batch of handbills characterizing the instructor as "sexist and idiotic, with an anal personality and a perverse intellectual" and a variety of other unflattering terms. She placed the handbills on bulletin boards around the school building and inserted them in student and faculty mailboxes.

As the citations indicate, the Jane Doe case is drawn directly from case law. A New York federal court issued a preliminary injunction ordering the medical school to readmit Ms. Doe as an "otherwise qualified" person under federal antidiscrimination legislation. The court found that she would "more likely than not" be able to complete her education, despite her psychiatric history, based in part on the fact that she had earned a master's degree in public health at Harvard and had held down a stressful job without deterioration during the years of litigation. Mr. Flamer and Ms. Petuous represent disguised cases of variable pathology. They presented focal symptoms that must be considered in light of the emotional context, their other behavior, and their professional goals. One cannot say without more information whether the behavior cited is grounds for termination from the program, as opposed to some less drastic and more rehabilitative approach. The most difficult case is that of the student who seems personally unsuited to the field for which he or she is pursuing a psychology degree, but whose problems are more diffuse and less easily documented.

The key point is that psychologists who operate training programs hold a dual responsibility, one toward the public and potential clients and the other toward the student. Considerable time and careful due process are required to advise students of any perceived difficulties, to suggest remedies, and to assist them in exploring other alternatives. Nonetheless, these are responsibilities that must be assumed by psychologists who direct academic and field training programs. The consequences for psychology programs and faculty for failure in ethical obligations can be both serious and expensive, as illustrated in the following case:

Case 3-12: In 1992, Susan A. Stepakoff was expelled from the clinical-community doctoral psychology program at the University of Maryland.

Stepakoff had complained within the psychology department about racist and sexist remarks made by faculty members and about other alleged faculty misconduct. In one of many examples provided to the court, Stepakoff alleged that during one class, when students watched a group therapy session through a one-way window, a professor remarked that he was "imagining the clients naked." He reportedly added that he found the thought of viewing one large woman naked "really disgusting" (Shen, 1996). Stepakoff also complained that some professors were having sex with students. Department and university officials failed to respond to her requests for action. Instead, some faculty made a variety of allegations about Ms. Stepakoff and succeeded in having her expelled after she had been admitted to doctoral candidacy. These were not, however, sufficient allegations to convince a court of law. In June 1996, a Prince Georges County jury found that Stepakoff's free speech rights had been violated and awarded her $600,000 in compensatory and punitive damages. In November 1966, the state settled with Stepakoff for $550,000 rather than appeal the case (Shen, 1996; "State Agrees,", 1996; *Stepakoff v. University of Maryland* et al., 1996).

One of the authors of this book (GPK) served as an expert witness for Ms. Stepakoff. All facts reported here, however, are drawn solely from public sources, as cited.

The Incompetent Institution

While many people are aware that it is possible to purchase phony diplomas by mail, few realize that the diploma mill industry flourishes in this country and abroad. Certificates or transcripts based on flimsy correspondence courses or no course work at all can easily be used to mislead and defraud the uninformed consumer (Daly & Keith-Spiegel, 1982). Often, such incompetent institutions provide diplomas that are larger and more impressively decorated than those from accredited schools. Such institutions often attempt to cover any liability by stating in their advertisements that the diplomas are "novelty items." The names of these diploma mills can sound quite impressive (e.g., Lawford State University, the Royal Academy of Science and Art,

Sussex College of Technology, Atlantic Southern University, Oxford Institute for Applied Research, and Brownell University). Sometimes, the names of legitimate institutions of higher learning are used as well.

In one announcement from Addison State University, the mail order inquirer is informed: "[We are] . . . an institution which has no formal or rigid academic requirements, no rigorous courses of study, and no examinations as we are not an institution of higher learning. The sole qualification for a degree is completion of the application form attached, and payment of the required fee ($34.95)." In another advertisement, a novelty company offers a "make your own diploma kit" for $25, offering degrees "at all levels" in 15 fields from such nonexistent institutions as "North American University, Pacific Cascade University, Great Lakes University, Benson University, and the Carnegie Institute of Engineering."

The rules and regulations relative to awarding degrees vary from state to state, and there are few regulations with any impact on the sale of such "credentials" through the mail. Thus, there are many opportunities for deception. There are also no national standards for accreditation, and a school that may be state accredited in California might not be recognized in New York (Bear, 1980). The watchword in determining a degree's professional validity is *regional accreditation*. The following commonly used terms do not equal accreditation: licensed, recognized, authorized, approved, or chartered. These terms may differ in legal meaning from state to state and may have no relevant meaning at all. Many poor quality schools or bogus degree programs will claim accreditation, but often by a spurious or unrecognized body. The U.S. Office of Education and its Council on Post-Secondary Accreditation (COPA) are the bodies that recognize accrediting associations; for colleges or universities, there are only six regional accrediting associations, the Middle States, North Central, Northwest, Southeastern, Western, and New England Association of Schools and Colleges (Bear, 1980).

Only earned degrees from regionally accredited universities and colleges may be cited by APA members when discussing their credentials

(see chapter 11). While it is not unethical to purchase or hold a phony degree, any misleading or deceptive use of the degree as a psychologist would be unethical. This includes hanging or posting the degree in a location where a client or member of the public might be mistakenly influenced by it.

CREDENTIALING ISSUES

Credentials presumably exist as a tangible indicator of accomplishment in a given field, with implications for gauging the competence of the holder. In psychology, there are at least three levels of credentials, distinguished by their intrinsic characteristics and the data on the basis of which they are awarded. These have been referred to as primary, secondary, and tertiary credentials (Koocher, 1979). As one moves from the primary toward the tertiary level, one moves further and further away from the data most relevant for predicting potential competence. The need to develop valid measures of entry-level and continued professional competence is widely acknowledged, but the predictive validity of current levels of credentials is highly variable (Bernstein & Lecomte, 1981).

Primary credentials are those that are earned over time by direct contact with trained instructors. They are based on longitudinal samples of the practitioner's behavior, with person-to-person supervision and direct observation by senior colleagues. Objective and subjective evaluations of progress are made by multiple evaluators as training progresses in a stepwise fashion. Examples of such credentials include graduate training programs, supervised practica, internships, and specialized postdoctoral training. The credential is not a generic one, but rather reflects expertise in the particular matters and activities studied.

Secondary credentials use primary credentials as prerequisites, but also incorporate other elements in determining qualifications. Such credentials include statutory licensing and certification, as well as recognition by specialized certification boards (e.g., American Boards of Professional Psychology). One must first complete the appropriate training and degree programs (i.e., have the appropriate primary credentials) to be considered for a secondary-level credential. Next, some sample of the psychologist's professional behavior is sought. The sample is usually cross-sectional in nature and may consist of a multiple choice, essay, or oral examination; submission of a work sample; direct observation of a session with a client; or a combination of these. Some of the examination models used may be extensive and well representative of the practice domain the psychologist intends to enter, but others are notoriously inappropriate (Carsten, 1978; Greenberg, 1978). An example of the inappropriate type would include using a multiple choice pencil-and-paper instrument to predict competence in delivery of psychotherapy, even though no validity data exist to justify such predictions. Another example involved an attempt by the Association of State and Provincial Psychology Boards to ignore errors in the EPPP (Examination for the Professional Practice of Psychology) and then to block public revelation of their behavior (Koocher, 1989a, 1989b).

In the absence of detailed knowledge of the candidate's background and behavior over time, the grantors of secondary credentials usually require the approval or endorsement by colleagues chosen by the candidate. In general, secondary credentials place heavy reliance on the honor system, and the credential granted is often generic in nature. Psychologists are supposed to recognize, acknowledge, and abide by their limitations; there is little exploration of these undertaken by the grantor of the credential (Hogan, 1977; Koocher, 1979).

Tertiary credentials in psychology are distinguished from the other two types by virtue of requiring no behavioral sample, first-person contact, or substantial individual scrutiny intrinsic to the credential itself. Rather, they are based solely on evidence that primary and secondary credentials have been obtained. In a sense, they simply attest to the fact that the psychologist holds primary and secondary credentials. Membership in certain APA divisions or listing in the *National Register of Health Service Providers in Psychology* are examples of tertiary credentials.

In chapter 11, we discuss the listing of various credentials in advertising or presentations of oneself in a professional manner to the public. We also cite preliminary data that suggest that the public may not necessarily understand the meaning or underpinnings of certain credentials, and that these credentials may sound more impressive than is justified. Certainly, in terms of content validity, criterion-related validity, or predictive validity for which professional competence is at issue, tertiary credentials are relatively worthless, and secondary credentials may be suspect for reasons discussed in the following pages. Primary credentials are the most likely to provide predictive validity regarding a practitioner's competence, as long as they are accurately represented and understood by the holder. How does this become an ethics issue? Consider the following case:

Case 3-13: Narcissa Schmit, Ed.D., served as a field placement supervisor for the Central States School of Professional Psychology and as such was appointed an adjunct assistant professor at the school. Her role consisted of volunteering 2 hours per week of supervision. She was also listed in the *National Register of Health Service Providers in Psychology* by virtue of her degree, state license, and 2 years experience working in a health care setting. Next to her diplomas and licenses in her waiting room were framed copies of a letter confirming her "faculty" status and a "certificate of inclusion" in the register. She also chose to list those credentials in a published announcement of her practice.

Dr. Schmit's behavior falls in that gray area between the unethical and the acceptable in professional behavior. The uninformed member of the general public has no idea what the *Register* listing signifies and could misinterpret it as an additional credential or a testimony to Dr. Schmidt's competence. The reference to faculty status could also be misleading and represent a deceptive attempt to boost her prestige by implication of a university affiliation that has little or no bearing on her practice. Depending on how these affiliations are presented, Schmit could be behaving unethically should the misrepresentation be deemed substantive. It would be better not to present these accomplishments and affiliations as credentials, because they are not.

LICENSING

Licensing of the professions has rarely been sought by the public. More often, licensing has been sought by professionals as a legal means to obtain recognition by the state, although protection of the public is generally cited as the paramount rationale (Gross, 1978; Shimberg, 1981). The relationship between licensing and the competence of practitioners is at best speculative and is based on unverified assumptions (Bernstein & Lacomte, 1981; Gross, 1978; Hogan, 1979; Koocher, 1979). In fact, some evidence tends to refute the claim that licensing protects the public and suggests it may have some potential adverse effects (Danish & Smyer, 1981; Gross, 1978).

Aside from questions of the validity of the examinations on which licensure is based, as noted above (Bernstein & Lecomte, 1981; Carsten, 1978; Greenberg, 1978), Hogan's (1977) classic treatise demonstrating how, in the case of psychotherapy, licensure has failed to protect the public adequately has gone effectively unchallenged. Except for the most populous states, licensing boards are often so overworked and underfunded that disciplinary enforcement in nearly impossible except in the most flagrant cases of abuse or misconduct. Given the time-consuming task of investigating complaints with due process for the accused, while also screening applications, conducting examinations, drafting regulations, and attending to the other duties of the board, little time remains to worry about such idealistic matters as checking the competence of practitioners about whom no complaints have been received.

In most states, the psychology license is a generic one. That is, one is licensed as a psychologist—period. In the application, the candidate may have been asked to specify and document areas of expertise (e.g., clinical psychology, school psychology, industrial consultation, etc.), but there is seldom any monitoring of this specialization after licensing unless a complaint is filed or suspicions are aroused.

Generic licensure creates a public information problem because many people tend to assume that *licensed psychologist* is synonymous with *clinical psychologist* (Greenberg, 1982). Greenberg (1982) argues for strict regulation of title use and public education to help overcome this problem. The assumption of the ethics code is that this could be unnecessary because the psychologist should recognize his or her limitations and act in a responsible, informing manner toward the public. Wiens and Menne (1981) dismiss the need for specialized licensure with a medical analogy: any physician is qualified to make an initial evaluation or appraisal and follow it with an appropriate referral. Unfortunately, in our experience, there are many psychologists who do not seem to know their competence limits or when to make a referral to another professional.

Perhaps the greatest single problem with licensing statutes for psychology is their variability from state to state. Even states that use the same examination procedure may employ different cutoff scores. An individual who is deemed qualified to sit for the licensing examination in one state may be denied entry to the examination in a neighboring state.

MAINTAINING PERSONAL COMPETENCE

It has been estimated that the half-life of a doctoral degree in psychology, as a measure of competence, is about 10–12 years (Dubin, 1972). That is, using the analogy of radioactive decay, about a decade after receipt of the doctorate, half of the knowledge that went into that training is obsolete. In other fields such as medicine and law, the turnover may be even more rapid (Jensen, 1979) because of advances in the basic sciences and changing legal decisions, respectively. Jensen (1979) posed the interesting question of how one can retain any modicum of professional competence over a career that spans more than 30 years. He also noted that rapidly advancing technology in many fields can also reduce the half-life dramatically. The 1941 engineering graduate's training had a half-life of 12 years, but by 1971 the new graduate could expect only a 5-year half-life. Similarly, it is not surprising to find analogies in psychology considering the impact on psychological practice and research of the introduction of personal computers in such areas as automated testing, improved actuarial prediction, biofeedback, artificial intelligence, and all manner of simulation programs.

A variety of strategies have been advanced to ensure that professionals strive to maintain competence. These include mandated continuing education, recertification requirements, and professional development models. Many states now require practitioners to complete certain amounts and types of continuing education course work to maintain a professional license. No states or certifying bodies, however, have deemed it appropriate to require formal reexamination or recertification of license holders or diploma holders.

Part of the difficulty in implementing plans to monitor practitioner competence over time is a definitional problem. What constitutes a meritorious step toward maintaining one's competence? Is attending a workshop commensurate with teaching one? Is writing an article for a refereed journal a sign of continuing competence? Will taking or retaking a multiple choice examination prove anything? Before we can address a means of maintaining professional capabilities, we must arrive at criteria that are linked to continuing competence (Jensen, 1979). Professional skills, competently executed on a daily basis, will certainly enhance competence. But, experience per se does not immunize one against error. It seems unlikely that a comprehensive solution to the problem of maintaining competence over time will be found in the near term. The most appropriate course of action for a psychologist is to strive for a constant awareness of her or his limitations, recognize that these can increase over time after formal training has ended, and seek constructive remedies by both formal and informal means to keep skills current.

Case 3-14: Nardell Slo, Ed.D., conducted a cognitive evaluation of an adult client using the WAIS-R a full 2 years after the revised form (WAIS-III) had been published. When questioned on this point, he noted, "They're about the same, and the new kit is too expensive."

Case 3-15: I. P. Freely, Psy.D., continued to recommend long-term individual psychotherapy for child clients with secondary reactive enuresis, despite substantial evidence that certain behavioral treatments for this problem can be highly effective in a relatively brief time. When this was called to his attention, he seemed surprised and sought information in the professional literature.

Drs. Slo and Freely are in the same category as the college professor who has not bothered to update course notes in several years (see chapter 16 for additional material on this topic). Both are delivering substandard service to their clients. Slo does so with some disturbing and inaccurate rationalizations, while Freely is simply ignorant of treatment innovations. At least Freely seems willing to attempt to find out about his area of ignorance, although the apparent apathy (implied by the fact that he did not do so sooner) is worrisome. Slo's resistance suggests a more serious problem, blending ignorance with arrogance. Clients who rely on the expertise of these practitioners will not receive the most efficient and effective treatments. Even if some new technique (e.g., the behavioral treatment for enuresis) presents problems from Freely's professional and theoretical perspective, he has a responsibility to be aware of the development and to advise clients of alternative treatments and choices when discussing his recommendations with them.

NEW PRACTICE DOMAINS

Beyond Competence

There are times when it is reasonable for psychologists to stretch in extending their areas of competence, even if doing so demands special arrangements and breaking down old taboos. One such occasion might be termed the *compassionate exemption,* a term occasionally used in drug trials when treatment with an experimental protocol is authorized for a patient in extreme or unique need. Clinicians in rural areas know this problem well (Hargrove, 1986).

Case 3-16: Frederick Focus, Ph.D., was trained primarily in short-term treatment models. When he and his family moved to a small town in a mountain community, one they found very much suited to their ideal lifestyle, Dr. Focus was not prepared for the severity of problems that a few of his clients presented. Some of these people could clearly benefit from longer term psychotherapy, but the nearest practitioners trained in such models lived almost 200 miles away.

Is counseling from a therapist who lacks sufficient background in treating certain problems better than no treatment at all? There is no single correct answer to cover all such possible cases, but the undisputed facts are that not all people are helped by therapy and that some are actually harmed by it. Dr. Focus must ensure that he causes no harm. One strategy might be to engage in a three-step process. First, Dr. Focus must ensure that he fully understands every possible referral resource available in his community. If no appropriate resources exist, Dr. Focus might consider a second step: treating particular clients with ongoing, supportive consultation by telephone with a colleague who does have the proper competencies. We would quickly underscore that psychologists should not stretch too far using this second step, and the consulting colleague can help determine the reasonableness of the approach. Finally, if the discrepancy between the client's needs and the therapist's competence is too disparate, then the therapist risks causing more harm than good and should not undertake treatment.

Prescription Privileges

Perhaps no single issue has stirred more controversy among psychologists in the 1990s than the notion of granting some of our colleagues prescription privileges. Arguments reported in favor of the practice include the following: (1) The majority of psychiatric care is already delivered by nonpsychiatrist providers; (2) psychologists practice in many communities lacking psychiatrists; (3) improved care of elderly overmedicated patients in nursing homes would be possible; (4) psychologists are already very well equipped to assess behavioral and cognitive changes in a scientific manner; (5) some other providers, such as podiatrists and nurse practitioners, already have prescription privileges; and (6) psychologists are at least as well trained in human psychopathology as psychiatrists.

Arguments reported opposing extending prescription privileges to psychologists include these: (1) Psychiatrists use all their training to function as a physician for the whole patient, and psychologists would need full medical training to do so; (2) the nonphysician providers who currently do prescribe already have medical backgrounds; (3) if we do that, we will become just like those we despise (Adams & Bieliauskas, 1994); (4) we will forget how to do psychotherapy; and (5) psychologists who have more ready access to psychoactive drugs may experience an increased incidence of substance abuse.

The most compelling arguments in favor of psychologists' entry into this new practice domain have been social necessity and effective demonstration projects conduced under military auspices (DeLeon, Sammons, & Sexton, 1995). The objections raised are largely speculative and can be effectively addressed by focusing on restricting practice in the new arena to those who are at any point in time legally authorized and clinically competent to do so. Buelow and Chafetz (1996) propose more elaborate ethical practice guidelines for clinical psychopharmacology. They advocate for specially trained clinical psychopharmacologists, specify assessment as a critical precursor to prescription, note that drug intervention alone is insufficient for most patients, cite risk-to-benefit ratios, encourage avoiding polypharmacy, encourage special attention to the unique needs of the medically ill, and urge avoiding the medical model in which every physician can prescribe any drug. We agree that this new practice arena carries new risks; however, we also agree that competently trained and ethically sensitive psychologists will be able to rise to the challenges.

THE SICK DOCTOR

When personal problems begin to interfere with professional activities, the psychologist becomes a serious danger to clients. Much more has been written about the impaired physician than the impaired psychologist, but perhaps that is because physicians' access to drugs makes them more visible foci of concern. There are many facets to the problem of the sick doctor, including consideration of some types of psychological practice as "high-risk" or "burnout prone" occupations (Freudenberger & Robbins, 1979; Jenkins & Maslach, 1994; Koocher, 1980; Maslach, 1993). Another facet is a psychologist's failure to recognize when a client is not improving or is deteriorating while in the psychologist's care. Most dramatic, however, are the instances when the psychologist, by virtue of addiction, emotional disturbance, or other problem-induced inadequacy, begins to harm clients and presents a danger to the public.

These cases can be especially painful for members of ethics committees because the ethics inquiry itself often places additional stress on the troubled colleague. When the case is severe in terms of public impact, the ultimate sanction available to such a committee is expulsion from the professional organization. At the same time, however, expelling a member puts that person beyond the rehabilitative influence of the committee. While physicians have long had programs to assist and monitor impaired colleagues (Green, Carroll, & Buxton, 1978), formal rehabilitation programs for the impaired psychologist are rare, although not unheard of (Laliotis & Grayson, 1985; Larson, 1981), and increasing attention is being devoted to this problem (Mearns & Allen, 1991; Sadoff & Sadoff, 1994). The difficulty in handling impaired practitioners is well summarized by Annas (1978). He notes that a conference of physicians agreed that an emotionally impaired airline pilot should be grounded immediately and, before being permitted to fly again, required to submit to carefully monitored treatment until beneficial results are documented. Not surprisingly, a group of pilots believed that impaired physicians should immediately cease practicing and abstain from practicing permanently unless successfully treated and rehabilitated. Some pilots argued that at least they have copilots present in the cockpit. Needless to say, some physicians find this sort of turnabout unfair play.

Burnout

Burnout has generally been described as a kind of emotional exhaustion resulting from excessive demands on energy, strength, and personal resources in the work setting (Freudenberger, 1975). It may involve a loss of concern for the people with whom one is working, as well as a loss of positive feelings, sympathy, and respect for one's clients (Maslach, 1993). Another major component, however, is that of aversion to the client, at times mixed with elements of genuine malice (Maltsberger & Buie, 1974). Important client factors related to staff burnout include the client's prognosis, the degree of personal relevance the client's problems have for the psychologist, and the client's reactions to the psychologist (Maslach, 1993).

Helplessness and emotional loss have long been recognized as causal components of depression (Seligman, 1975) and as powerful components of countertransference stress (Adler, 1972; Maltsberger & Buie, 1974). These stresses can arouse substantial anger in the therapist. The anger appears to have two distinct components: aversion and malice. Societal and professional values mediate against direct expressions of malice or sadism toward one's clients. The aversion component of countertransference stress may be more subtle and, as a result, more insidious. The psychotherapist may experience aversion in relation to the client both directly and unconsciously. A schedule suddenly becomes "too crowded for an appointment this week." A troubled client who gripes, "I don't need any help," is permitted to withdraw emotionally instead of being engaged in dialogue.

These events are especially likely when the therapist is feeling helpless with guilt because the client is not progressing satisfactorily or is continuing to manifest signs of difficulty (e.g., suicidal ideation, addiction problems, or life-threatening illness). If efforts to assert control over one's emotional issues and a client's distress fail, perceived helplessness may result (Seligman, 1975). People experiencing this reaction no longer believe that their actions are related to their outcomes. Both patient and therapist may come to feel that they will suffer regardless of their behavior. In such circumstances, a therapist may defend against experiencing strong emotion by using detachment (Maslach, 1993). While some in medicine have traditionally suggested that a style of "detached concern" is an appropriate means of relating to clients (Lief & Fox, 1963), clear dangers are inherent in this response. Clients may experience such detachment as a lack of concern or unresponsiveness.

Case 3-17: George Sarcoma, Ph.D., worked as a clinical psychologist at a cancer treatment facility. This was his full-time job for several years. He was a caring and sensitive clinician who made himself available "on call" for extended service hours. Following both the death of a client with whom he had been particularly close and a disruption in his marriage, Dr. Sarcoma's performance began to fall off. He failed to respond to messages from colleagues and clients, occasionally missed appointments without notice, and became somewhat aloof and detached from his clients. Ultimately, he was fired from his job but went on to perform well at another setting.

Case 3-18: Susan Skipper, Ed.D., was an educational psychologist in a large urban public school system. She was overworked and unappreciated by clients and administrators, who often made unreasonable demands on her time. Dr. Skipper was not able to set limits on her work situation and began to dread going to work each day. She applied for a job in another part of the country and resigned her position to take the new job, giving less than adequate notice and leaving behind several uncompleted student evaluations.

Drs. Sarcoma and Skipper were both burned out. This occurred as a result of an interaction of their jobs, personal life events, the stressful client problems they dealt with regularly, and a variety of other factors. Any psychologist who spends most of his or her day listening to the problems of others is a potential victim. Both Sarcoma and Skipper became victims of learned helplessness and depression, and both hurt their clients as a result. Sarcoma's avoidance and detachment may not have yielded identifiable injury to clients; however, it is likely that some

suffered as a result. While Dr. Skipper's abrupt departure has elements of vengeful retaliation against her ungrateful employer, it may well have hurt a number of her clients, whose reports went unfinished or who had to await her replacement.

As with many potential ethical problems, the best way to deal with burnout is through prevention. Employers need to be aware of impending problems among their employees, and psychologists who begin to see symptoms of burnout in colleagues or sense it in themselves should take steps toward early intervention (Koocher, 1980). Warning signs of burnout include (1) uncharacteristic angry outbursts, (2) apathy, (3) chronic frustration, (4) a sense of depersonalization, (5) depression, (6) emotional and physical exhaustion, (7) hostility, (8) feelings of malice or aversion toward patients, and (9) reduced productivity or lowered effectiveness at work.

A substantial body of research (for example, Dupree, 1995; Jenkins & Maslach, 1994; Koeske & Kelly, 1995; Koocher, 1980; Lee & Ashforth, 1996; Maslach, 1993; and Mc-Knight & Glass, 1995) has identified many factors that can predispose a person to professional burnout, including (1) role ambiguity at work, including vague or inconsistent demands and expectations; (2) conflict and tension in the workplace; (3) a high level of discrepancy between ideal and real job functions; (4) unrealistic preemployment expectations; (5) lack of social support at work; (6) a perfectionistic personality with a strong sense of being externally controlled; (7) losses through death or divorce in the family; (8) chronic helplessness; (9) permeable emotional boundaries; (10) substance abuse; and (11) overly high expectations for oneself, such as a savior complex.

Conversely, factors that can help insulate a person from burnout include (1) role clarity, (2) positive feedback, (3) an enhanced sense of autonomy at work, (4) opportunities for rehabilitation from stress at work, (5) social support in the workplace, (6) personal accomplishment, (7) realistic criteria for client outcome, (8) an accurate awareness of personal strengths and weaknesses, along with a good sense of internal control.

The Troubled Psychologist

Whether the troubled psychologist works in research, teaching, or clinical practice does not seem to matter so far as incidence of pathology is concerned. While the variety of resulting ethical infractions seems endless, many people, including the psychologist involved, are hurt in the end. Consider these examples.

Case 3-19: Martha Ottenbee, Ph.D., was charged with overbilling clients. It turned out that she is extremely disorganized, an absent-minded psychologist. Her records were often incomprehensible. She was totally inept at managing her practice, although she seemed basically good hearted. She was slightly frantic and easily distracted when asked to explain her behavior to the ethics committee.

Case 3-20: Kurt Mores, Psy.D., was convicted in state court of "fornication" after a female client complained that she had been emotionally harmed as a result of having sex with him. At an ethics committee hearing, Dr. Mores admitted having had sexual intercourse with a dozen of his female clients over the past few years. He added that extreme pressure within his marriage had caused considerable anxiety, loss of self-esteem, and feelings of sexual inadequacy. He told the committee, referring to his sexual activity with clients, "It was good for them, it was good for me, and I didn't charge them for that part of the session." He also expressed the belief that, "It's okay to ignore the ethical code as long as you think about it carefully first and talk it over with clients."

Case 3-21: Paul Pious, Ph.D., is a nationally known psychologist and author in the field of moral development. He is at work on a major teaching program for application in public schools, when his life begins to become unglued. He is involved in a stressful divorce and is publicly listed in a newspaper as a "tax delinquent." He finds himself becoming increasingly suspicious about the motives of people with which he works. When a schoolteacher raises objections to the teaching program, Dr. Pious calls the school superintendent and reports that the teacher, a member of the gay community, is engaged in sexual relationships with high school students. An investigation reveals no support for the allegations, and Dr. Pious acknowledges lying to protect his project. He is subsequently admitted to a mental hospital for treatment.

Case 3-22: Lester Lapse, Ed.D., came before an ethics committee following a complaint that he had plagiarized an entire article from a professional journal and submitted it to another journal, listing himself as the sole author. At the committee hearing, Dr. Lapse appeared despondent. He described many pressures in his life and admitted that he must have plagiarized the article, although he had no conscious memory of having done so. He actually believed that he had conducted the study himself, even though there was no evidence that he had done so, and the article he submitted was identical, down to four decimal places in the tabular data reported, to the prior publication by another psychologist.

Dr. Ottenby's incompetence in the business end of her practice causes one to wonder what she is like as a clinician. Dr. Mores seems to have a unique moral outlook, with minimum insight into problems caused by his conduct, and few, if any, regrets. Dr. Pious finds himself in a desperate situation and adopts a distorted moral standard that permits him to lie and nearly ruin the career of an innocent party. Dr. Lapse, like Dr. Pious, seems to have a mental illness defense for his admittedly unethical conduct.

Sometimes, the cases that present competence problems are especially frightening.

Case 3-23: Two clients had almost died while in treatment with Flip Grando, Ph.D. At an ethics hearing looking into the case, Dr. Grando explained these unfortunate occurrences as the result of "insufficient faith" on the part of the clients. Dr. Grando's therapy technique involved locking the client in an airtight box for an extended period of time because, Grando explained, he had been given the special power to convert the client's own carbon dioxide into a healing force for all psychological and physical ailments. Dr. Grando's whole demeanor suggested a serious emotional disorder.

Case 3-24: Willis C. Driscoll, Ph.D., was a well-regarded psychologist in central Ohio. One day in 1991, he left Columbus in a hurry, never returning from lunch to retrieve files or say goodbye. He left behind two daughters and three sons, relocating to his mother's home in North Carolina. In May 1996, his sister telephoned local North Carolina police from her home in Florida. She was concerned that Dr. Driscoll would not allow her to talk to her mother on the telephone. After obtaining a search warrant, police located the skeletal remains of 96-year-old Mrs. Driscoll behind her locked bedroom door, on the floor, surrounded by trash and rodent droppings. Dr. Driscoll was sent to the Dorothea Dix Hospital in Raleigh for evaluation (Stephens & Somerson, 1996).

How should each of these cases be addressed? Certainly, there is no single remedy or rehabilitation for all of these cases. Should one even bother to try to rehabilitate the psychologists mentioned? Is mental illness a proper defense against a charge of ethical misconduct? Will Dr. Mores's arrogant attitude justify a harsher sanction than that dealt to Drs. Lapse and Pious, who each acknowledge their weaknesses? Should the committee investigating Dr. Ottenby's slipshod business practices seek to investigate her clinical skills, although they have not been specifically addressed in the complaint? Will Dr. Grando eventually cause a person's death? If Dr. Driscoll ever resumes practice, will clients who know his history feel comfortable with him?

These are complex questions that demand additional data before they can be adequately addressed, but such is the nature of these complaints. In general, we would reply that rehabilitation ought to be the paramount goal, except when the behavior itself is sufficiently objectionable to warrant more strictly punitive action. Mental illness is certainly an issue that psychologists will want to consider, but it does not justify ethical misconduct. Many psychologists with serious emotional problems are able to seek treatment without committing ethical misconduct. An interesting paper on the claim of mental illness as a defense by lawyers brought before

the bar association on charges of misconduct (Skoler & Klein, 1979) suggests similar reasoning. The authors conclude that, while bar association discipline committees and courts will consider mental illness as a mitigating factor, it will seldom be a fully adequate protection.

We have observed that the impaired psychologist is most typically an individual who is professionally isolated. This fact suggests that those psychologists who strive to maintain regular professional interactions with colleagues may be less susceptible to burnout and decompensation or may simply have such problems called to their attention constructively prior to committing serious ethical infractions.

The psychologist who recognizes problems with his or her behavior and seems committed to address them constructively certainly appears more likely to be rehabilitated than one who does not. At the same time, one must be careful about broadening an ethics inquiry to include aspects of a psychologist's professional life that are not in question. However, if personal impairment or mental illness is suspected, a broad inquiry may be necessary in the public interest. This is especially true if the psychologist claims emotional problems as a defense. Such a claim implies that the psychologist would be willing to cooperate in a comprehensive rehabilitative plan.

It is not often that a psychologist will spontaneously recognize the fact that personal distress is impairing his or her judgment. It is still more infrequent that the psychologist will be willing to make these judgment errors public. A rare and sensitive paper by Kovacs (1974) traces such events and their consequences for him and one particular client. It is certainly worth reading for anyone who would like to see the subtle encroachments of poor judgment in eroding a therapeutic relationship.

An important potential remedy for the troubled colleague might involve the formation of support networks through professional associations at the state and local levels. Such groups might offer supportive consultation and referral to colleagues willing to treat disturbed peers. Mutual support groups for psychologists working in particularly stressful settings are another possibility, as are the checklists or guides to the warning signs of professional burnout presented above.

The Client Who Does Not Improve

The APA ethical code clearly indicates that a psychologist should seek to terminate a relationship with a client when it is evident that the client is not benefitting from it. This may involve transferring the client to another practitioner, who may be able to treat the client more effectively, or it may mean simply advising the client that services are no longer needed. Consider the following cases.

Case 3-25: Ida Demeaner had been in psychotherapy with Manny Continua, Psy.D., weekly for 6 years. Ida had successfully dealt with the issues that first brought her to treatment, but had become very dependent on her sessions with Dr. Continua. While there had been no real change in Ms. Demeaner's emotional status for at least 4 years (aside from the increasing attachment to him), Dr. Continua made little effort to move toward termination. His philosophy is, "If the client thinks she needs to see me, then she does."

Case 3-26: Nemo Creep initially entered psychotherapy with Harold Narrow, Ph.D., for treatment of his growing anger at his employer. It became evident to Dr. Narrow that Mr. Creep was becoming increasingly paranoid and troubled. Narrow tried to suggest hospitalization to Creep several times, but each time Creep refused to consider the idea. Narrow continued to treat him and ultimately became the object of Creep's paranoid anger.

Case 3-27: Ivan Snidely, Ph.D., is an industrial/organizational psychologist hired to assist a major corporation improve employee morale and reduce product defects in a large factory. According to effectiveness data Snidely collected himself, it was evident that his efforts were not meeting with success. Nonetheless, he chose to ignore the data, tell the company that a longer trial period was needed, and continue to supply the ineffective services at a high fee for several additional months before the company canceled its contract with him.

Dr. Continua has a conceptualization of psychotherapy that suggests the potential for end-less psychotherapy. While it is not possible to state categorically that diminishing returns begin at a certain point, or that all treatment beyond "X" sessions is useless, Continua may well be mistreating his client. He may have fostered her dependency and actually be perpetuating her "need" for treatment. Ideally, he should evaluate his work with her critically from time to time and refer her for a consultation with another therapist if he has doubts about the necessity for continued treatment. This assumes that he does not have an emotional blind spot that prevents him from recognizing her situation.

Dr. Narrow has failed to recognize that a case is beyond his capability to treat. When it became clear that Mr. Creep needed more intensive (i.e., inpatient care) treatment, but was refusing to consider it, Dr. Narrow could have taken a number of steps to help Creep. One such step would have been to decline to treat Creep anymore unless Creep would seek appropriate care for himself. If Creep's behavior presented a danger or warranted a commitment for involuntary hospitalization, Dr. Narrow would be responsible for considering those options.

Dr. Snidely may be greedy or simply blind to his own inadequacy for the task at hand, but there is no excuse for his ignoring the data. If he had no alternative plan, he should not have continued to provide services that he knew to be ineffective. The failure to reassess treatment plans in the face of continued client problems or the failure of the intervention are inexcusable.

PSYCHOLOGISTS AS TEACHERS AND RESEARCHERS

The focus of this chapter has been on psychologists who perform clinical and related services. This is because the discipline has almost exclusively confined its attention to competence evaluation in these areas. State laws do not require specific training or licensing for teaching psychology or conducting research, despite the fact that most who engage in such work have earned advanced degrees or are in the process of earning them. Our relative neglect of the competence issues surrounding teaching and research activities does not imply that profound ethical problems are irrelevant or rare. In chapters 16 and 17, many of the case examples involve competency deficits that have harmed students and research participants.

SUMMARY GUIDELINES

1. Official APA documents describing standards of practice or guidelines of various sorts do not carry the weight or enforcement mandate of the ethics code, but they can be useful in guiding competent practice behaviors. It is important to be aware of such documents as they may be cited as indices of failure to follow professional standards should an ethics complaint or malpractice lawsuit arise.

2. Many subareas, specialty interests, or unusual techniques require expertise for which no generally accepted practice criteria exist. In those situations, psychologists should consult with experienced practitioners in that subarea, specialty, or technique to assess appropriate levels of training before using such interventions.

3. There is no comprehensive consensus on course work or training ingredients for all types of degrees in psychology; the holders of many types of psychology degrees (i.e., Ph.D., Ed.D., or Psy.D.) may be equally well qualified to perform certain tasks. Ultimately, however, it is each psychologist's personal responsibility to ensure that she or he is practicing within the range of activity appropriate to her or his training.

4. Psychologists administering training programs should recognize and balance dual sets of responsibilities, one set to their students and another set to the public that will be studied, counseled, or otherwise served by the students.

5. Students in psychology training programs should expect timely evaluations of their developing competence and status. Each program should have a formal evaluation system with routine means of feedback, progress assessment, and appeal.

6. Many institutions or organizations exist that grant degrees of a questionable or totally bogus nature. Psychologists should not associate themselves with such institutions and should not behave in any way that implies that the credentials granted by such programs suggest competence in the field.

7. Generic licensing laws and the variety of valid earned degrees held by people licensed as psychologists in various states present the potential for considerable ambiguity. Psychologists should behave in ways that make the nature of their training and credentials explicit, recognizing that some credentials have little relationship to competence or present an ambiguous meaning to the public at large. Consumer questions should be answered frankly, honestly, and with appropriate factual information.

8. Students or master's-level psychologists may well be competent to perform a number of sophisticated psychological functions, but they must abide by all appropriate statutes and professional standards. When practitioners from a different field (e.g., social workers, nurses, or subdoctoral counselors) aspire to train as psychologists, they are expected to adhere to standards for psychologists.

9. Psychologists should be mindful of the potential for burnout or exhaustion in certain types of job settings. They should counsel colleagues who are distressed or seek help themselves as needed to avoid causing distress, inconvenience, or harm to the clients they serve.

10. When a client does not show progress or seems to be worsening despite a psychologist's interventions, consultation and/or appropriate means to terminate the ineffective relationship should be sought.

11. The distressed or impaired psychologist should refrain from practicing to the extent that his or her impairment bears on ability to perform work with competence and responsibility. If in doubt, the psychologist should consult with colleagues familiar with her or his skills and problems.

References

Abeles, N. (1994). Competence. In R. J. Corsini (Ed.), *Encyclopedia of Psychology* (Vol. 1, pp. 275–276). New York: Wiley.

Adams, K. M., & Bieliauskas, L. A. (1994). On perhaps becoming what you had previously despised: Psychologists as prescribers of medication. *Journal of Clinical Psychology in Medical Settings, 1,* 189–198.

Adler, G. (1972). Helplessness in the helpers. *British Journal of Psychology, 45,* 315–326.

American Psychological Association. (1977). *General guidelines for providers of psychological services.* Washington, DC: Author.

American Psychological Association. (1981). Specialty guidelines for the delivery of services. *American Psychologist, 36,* 640–681.

American Psychological Association. (1977). *Standards for providers of psychological services.* Washington, DC: Author.

American Psychological Association. (1994). Guidelines for child custody evaluations in divorce proceedings. *American Psychologist, 49,* 677–680.

Annas, G. (1978, December). Who to call when the doctor is sick. *Hastings Center Report,* 18–20.

Bear, J. B. (1980). *The alternative guide to college degrees and non-traditional higher education.* New York: Stonesong Press.

Bernstein, B. L., & Lecomte, C. (1981). Licensure in psychology: Alternative directions. *Professional Psychology, 12,* 200–208.

Berven, N. L., & Scofield, M. E. (1987). Ethical responsibility in establishing and maintaining professional competence. *Journal of Applied Rehabilitation Counseling, 18,* 41–44.

Buelow, G. D., & Chafetz, M. D. (1996). Proposed ethical practice guidelines for clinical pharmacopsychology: Sharpening a new focus in psychology. *Professional Psychology: Research and Practice, 27,* 53–58.

Carsten, A. A. (1978). A public perspective on scoring the licensing exam. *Professional Psychology, 9,* 531–532.

Casas, J. M., Ponterotto, J. G., & Gutierrez, J. M. (1986). An ethical indictment of counseling research and training: The cross-cultural perspective. *Journal of Counseling and Development, 64,* 347–349.

Centor, A., & Stang, D. (1976). Masters level programs in areas of clinical psychology. In *Council of Representatives Agenda* (Item No. 16S-1). Washington, DC: American Psychological Association.

Claiborn, W. L. (1982). The problem of professional incompetence. *Professional Psychology, 13,* 153–158.

Daly, J., & Keith-Spiegel, P. (1982). *Diploma mills and consumer awareness: or, "Where did your psychologist go to school?"* Paper presented to the Western Psychological Association, Sacramento.

Danish, S. J., & Smyer, M. A. (1981). Unintended consequences of requiring a license to help. *American Psychologist, 36,* 13–21.

DeLeon, P. H., Sammons, M. T., & Sexton, J. L. (1995). Focusing on society's real needs: Responsibility and prescription privileges? *American Psychologist, 50,* 1022–1032.

Doe v. New York University, No. 77 Civ.6285 (GLG) (S.D. N.Y. Sept. 25, 1981).

Dubin, S. S. (1972). Obsolescence or lifelong education: A choice for the professional. *American Psychologist, 27,* 486–496.

Dupree, P. I. (1995). Psychotherapists' job satisfaction and job burnout as a function of work setting and percentage of managed care clients. *Psychotherapy in Private Practice, 14,* 77–93.

Ellis, H. C. (1992). Graduate education in psychology: Past, present, and future. *American Psychologist, 47,* 570–576.

Fox, R. E. (1994). Training professional psychologists for the 21st century. *American Psychologist, 49,* 200–206.

Freudenberger, H. J. (1975). The staff burn-out syndrome in alternative institutions. *Psychotherapy: Theory, Research, and Practice, 12,* 73–81.

Freudenberger, H. J., & Robbins, R. (1979). The hazards of being a psychoanalyst. *Psychoanalytic Review, 66,* 275–296.

Glennon, T. M., & Karlovac, M. (1988). The effect of fee level on therapists' perceptions of competence and nonpossessive warmth. *Journal of Contemporary Psychotherapy, 18,* 249–258.

Green, R. C., Carroll, C. J., & Buxton, W. D. (1978). *The care and management of the sick and incompetent physician.* Springfield, IL.: C. C. Thomas.

Greenberg, M. D. (1978). The examination of professional practice in psychology (EPPP). *American Psychologist, 33,* 88–89.

Greenberg, M. D. (1982). "Specialty" licenses in psychology. *American Psychologist, 37,* 102.

Gross, J. S. (1978). The myth of professional licensing. *American Psychologist, 33,* 1009–1016.

Hargrove, D. S. (1986). Ethical issues in rural mental health practice. *Professional Psychology: Research and Practice, 17,* 20–23.

Hogan, D. B. (1977). *The regulation of psychotherapists* (Vol. 1–4). Cambridge, MA: Ballinger.

Jenkins, S., & Maslach, C. (1994). Psychological health and involvement in interpersonally demanding occupations: A longitudinal perspective. *Journal of Organizational Behavior, 15,* 101–127.

Jensen, R. E. (1979). Competent professional service in psychology: The real issue behind continuing education. *Professional Psychology, 10,* 381–389.

Koeske, G. F., & Kelly, T. (1995). The impact of over involvement on burnout and job satisfaction. *American Journal of Orthopsychiatry, 65,* 282–292.

Koocher, G. P. (1979). Credentialing in psychology: Close encounters with competence? *American Psychologist, 34,* 696–702.

Koocher, G. P. (1980). Pediatric cancer: Psychosocial problems and the high costs of helping. *Journal of Clinical Child Psychology, 9,* 2–5.

Koocher, G. P. (1989a). Confirming content validity in the dark. *Professional Psychology: Research and Practice, 40,* 275.

Koocher, G. P. (1989b). Screening licensing examinations for accuracy. *Professional Psychology: Research and Practice, 40,* 269–271.

Kovacs, A. L. (1974). The valley of the shadow . . . *Psychotherapy: Theory, Research and Practice, 11,* 376–382.

Laliotis, D. A., & Grayson, J. H. (1985). Psychologist heal thyself: What is available for the impaired psychologist? *American Psychologist, 40,* 84–96.

Larson, C. (1981, August/September). Psychologists ponder ways to help troubled colleagues. *APA Monitor,* pp. 16, 50.

Lee, R. T., & Ashforth, B. E. (1996). A meta-analytic examination of the correlates of the three dimensions of job burnout. *Journal of Applied Psychology, 81,* 123–133.

Lief, H. I., & Fox, R. C. (1963). Training for "detached concern" in medical students. In H. I.

Lief, V. F. Lief, & N. R. Lief (Eds.), *The psychological basis of medical practice.* New York: Harper & Row.

Maltsberger, T., & Buie, D. H. (1974). Countertransference hate in the treatment of suicidal patients. *Archives of General Psychiatry, 30,* 625–633.

Maslach, C. (1993). *Burnout: A multidimensional perspective.* Washington, DC: Taylor & Francis, 1993.

Mayne, T. J., Norcross, J. C., & Sayette, M. A. (1994). Admission requirements, acceptance rates, and financial assistance in clinical psychology programs: Diversity across the practice-research community. *American Psychologist, 49,* 806–811.

McKnight, J. D., & Glass, D. C. (1995). Perceptions of control, burnout, and depressive symptomatology: A replication and extension. *Journal of Consulting and Clinical Psychology, 63,* 490–494.

Mearns, J., & Allen, G. J. (1991). Graduate students' experiences in dealing with impaired peers, compared with faculty predictions: An exploratory study. *Ethics and Behavior, 1,* 191–202.

Mintz, L. B., Bartels, K. M., & Rideout, C. A. (1995). Training in counseling ethnic minorities and race-based availability of graduate school resources. *Professional Psychology: Research and Practice, 26,* 316–321.

Moses, S. (1990). Master's graduates suffer identity crisis. *APA Monitor, 21,* 28–29.

Office of Program Consultation and Accreditation, Education Directorate, American Psychological Association. (1996). *Guidelines and principles for accreditation of programs in professional psychology.* Washington, DC: American Psychological Association.

Pilkington, N. W., & Cantor, J. M. (1996). Perceptions of heterosexual bias in professional psychology programs: A survey of graduate students. *Professional Psychology: Research and Practice, 27,* 604–612.

Peterson, D. R., & Bry, B. H. (1980). Dimensions of perceived competence in professional psychology. *Professional Psychology, 11,* 965–971.

Pope, K. S., & Brown, L. S. (1996). *Recovered memories of abuse: Assessment, therapy, forensics.* Washington, DC: American Psychological Association.

Pope-Davis, D. B., Reynolds, A. L., Dings, J. G., &

Nielson, D. (1995). *Professional Psychology: Research and Practice, 26*, 322–329.

Robiner, W. N., Arbisi, P., & Edwall, G. E. (1994). The basis of the doctoral degree for psychology licensure. *Clinical Psychology Review, 14*, 227–254.

Sadoff, R. L., & Sadoff, J. B. (1994). *The impaired health professional: Legal and ethical issues.* New York: John Wiley & Sons.

Sandell, R., Ronnas, P. A., & Schubert, J. (1992). Feeling like a good therapist—or a bad one: Critical incidents in psychotherapists' experiences. *Psychoanalytic Psychotherapy, 6*, 213–229.

Seligman, M. E. P. (1975). *Helplessness: On depression, development, and death.* San Francisco: W. H. Freeman.

Shapiro, A. E., & Wiggins, J. G. (1994). A Psy.D. degree for every practitioner: Truth in labeling. *American Psychologist, 49*, 207–210.

Shen, F. (1996, June 8). Woman awarded $600,000 by jury: Expelled student objected to U-Md. professors' actions. *The Washington Post*, p. B1.

Shimberg, B. (1981). Testing for licensure and certification. *American Psychologist, 10*, 1138–1146.

Skoler, D. L., & Klein, R. (1979). Mentally troubled lawyers: Client protection and bar discipline. *Mental Disability Law Reporter, 2*, 131–143.

State agrees to pay $550,000 to woman expelled from U-Md. (1996, November 28). *The Washington Post*, p. C5.

Susan A. Stepakoff v. University of Maryland at College Park, Robert Brown, Robert Dies, Raymond Lorion, and Barry Smith. Cir. Prince Georges County, Cal. 92-17117 (filed June 6, 1996).

Stephens, S., & Somerson, M. D. (1996, May 21). Police say psychologist lived with dead mom. *Columbus Dispatch*.

Stevens, J., Yock, T., & Perlman, B. (1979). Comparing master's clinical training with professional responsibilities in community mental health centers. *Professional Psychology, 10*, 20–27.

Sue, D. W. (1991). A model for cultural diversity training. *Journal of Counseling and Development, 70*, 90–105.

Svartberg, M. (1989). Manualization and competence monitoring of short-term anxiety-provoking psychotherapy. *Psychotherapy, 26*, 564–571.

Svartberg, M., & Stiles, T. C. (1992). Predicting patient change from therapist competence and patient-therapist complementarity in short-term anxiety-provoking psychotherapy: A pilot study. *Journal of Consulting and Clinical Psychology, 60*, 304–307.

Watson, N., Caddy, G. R., Johnson, J. H., & Rimm, D. C. (1981). Standards in the education of professional psychologists: The resolutions of the conference at Virginia Beach. *American Psychologist, 5*, 514–519.

Wellner, A. M. (1978, May). *Education and credentialing in psychology.* Washington, DC: American Psychological Association.

Whyte, C. (1994). Competencies. *British Journal of Psychotherapy, 10*, 568–569.

Wiens, A. N., & Menne, J. W. (1981). On disposing of "straw people": Or an attempt to clarify statutory recognition and educational requirements for psychologists. *American Psychologist, 36*, 390–395.

4

Ethical Obligations in Psychotherapy

Neurotic means he is not as sensible as I am, and psychotic means that he is even worse than my brother-in-law.

Karl Menninger

Ask psychotherapists about the ethics of their work, and they become philosophers. Writing on the ethics of their craft, psychotherapists have referred to the practice of therapy as a science (Karasu, 1980), an art (Bugenthal, 1987), the systematic use of a human relationship for therapeutic purposes (Strupp, 1992), a house of cards (Dawes, 1994), the purchase of friendship (Schofield, 1964), a means of social control (Hurvitz, 1973), a source of honest and nonjudgmental feedback (Kaschak, 1978), tradecraft (Blau, 1987), and even as a means of exploring one's "ultimate values" (Kanoti, 1971). The secretary for the proceedings of the historic Boulder conference on the training of psychologists satirically noted: "We have left therapy as an undefined technique which is applied to unspecified problems with a nonpredictable outcome. For this technique we recommend rigorous training" (Lehner, 1952, p. 547).

Debate about the worth of psychotherapy or the need to use trained experts to provide it has spanned more than three decades in the scientific literature (Eysenck, 1952; Freedheim,

1992; Garfield, 1981; Marshall, 1980). Objective assessment of the worth of psychotherapy has been challenged, beginning with Freud's assertion that psychoanalysis ought to be exempt from systematic study (Strupp, 1992). As Garfield noted in reviewing 100 years of development, "carrying out research on psychotherapy is a complex, difficult, and even controversial activity" (1992, p. 354). Still, despite controversy, the majority of clients apparently benefit from psychotherapy, while many professionals offer such services and train others to do so as well.

A national poll (Goode & Wagner, 1993) shows that 81% of Americans think that therapy for personal problems would be helpful "sometimes" or "all of the time." The same article suggested that more than 16 million Americans seek mental health treatment each year. More recently, a poll of *Consumer Reports* readers confirmed the benefits of psychotherapy in the eyes of the public and related increased benefits with longer duration of treatment and greater experience of the therapist (Seligman, 1995).

The matter of whether a placebo effect exists in psychotherapy is not at all in question. That is, there is good evidence that seemingly inert "agents" or "treatments" may be demonstrated to have psychotherapeutic effects (O'Leary & Borkovec, 1978; Shapiro & Struening, 1973). From the client's viewpoint, it may matter little whether improvement results from newly acquired insights, a caring relationship, restructured cognitions, modified behaviors, abandoned irrational beliefs, or a placebo effect. From the ethical standpoint, the central issue is client benefit. If the client improves as a result of the therapist's placebo value, so much the better. If, however, the client fails to improve, or his or her condition worsens while under a psychologist's care, the therapist is ethically obliged to take corrective action. When the client seems to be experiencing a deterioration in condition, consultation with more experienced colleagues in an effort to find alternative treatment approaches becomes more urgent. When the client is not benefitting, the appropriate step is to terminate the relationship and offer to help the consumer locate alternative sources of assistance.

When considering the psychotherapist's ethical obligations, it is not always easy to recognize when a problem occurs in the therapeutic relationship. It may also be difficult to deal with a sensitive problem when one is noticed. Recognizing, preventing, and remediating problems in the client-therapist relationship are the crux of ethical concern for client welfare in psychotherapy. We do not attempt to answer basic questions about the nature of psychotherapy: What is it? Does it work? If so, how? Can it make you worse? except to reply: Don't know . . . maybe . . . not sure . . . and . . . possibly.

ETHICAL OBLIGATIONS OF PSYCHOTHERAPISTS

In a rather angry and overly one-sided volume about the practice of psychotherapy (Dawes, 1994), which even the most favorable reviewers describe as showing questionable scholarship "owing to lack of completeness" (Miller, 1995, p. 132) and "occasionally offering firmer nega-

tive conclusions than the data warrant" (p. 131), Dawes criticized the authors of this book by purporting that our previous edition predicates the philosophy of ethics in psychology on the "one-up relationship between professional and client" (p. 255). Dawes claims that the authors of this book view the psychologist-client relationship as analogous to that of parent and child, with a resulting "paternalistic ethic" that allegedly "not only resolves problems raised by the professionals' ambivalent feelings toward their clients but advances the profession" (p. 256). Dawes also informs his readers, with a degree of self-righteousness, that he quit graduate school in clinical psychology in 1960 during his second year. He also reports serving for 2 years on the APA Ethics Committee in the mid-1980s, resigning after being outvoted 6 to 1 on a policy matter. We note that it is far easier to quit a difficult circumstance and criticize from afar than to persist and effect change collaboratively.

Our actual view of psychotherapists' ethical obligations is not based on parentalism. Rather, it is based on premises of trust and knowledge of intimate secrets. We do not, as Dawes apparently concludes, espouse the view that psychologists are one up on their clients as a matter of course. Rather, we believe that clients invest us with a significant degree of confidence when they come seeking help with their most personal concerns. This reliance demands particular safeguards. An airline pilot who takes people where they want to fly, an architect who designs a safe and attractive new home for clients, and the plumber who installs a new toilet in conformity with sanitary codes all exercise a degree of professional expertise to take care of our needs. We rely on these people and trust them to work on our behalf as professionals with special skills. Because the competent psychotherapist has special knowledge and expertise related to understanding human distress, psychopathology, and intervention strategies, a degree of authority is conferred and must be exercised thoughtfully and collaboratively with the client. We assert that psychotherapists have an exceptional responsibility to respect the rights of all clients and to advance their well-being as professional consultants or advisors in partnership with them.

This stance should be enabling in every respect, not paternalistic.

In this chapter, we discuss the nature of the treatment contract and the special obligations of the psychotherapist. In the next chapter, we discuss technique-oriented ethical problems, such as the special difficulties of multiple-client treatment (i.e., group, marital, and family therapy), sex therapy, hypnosis, behavioral approaches, and unproven or fringe therapies.

The Therapeutic Contract

If a client and psychologist are to form a therapeutic alliance, they must share some basic goals and understandings about their work together. In warning psychotherapists about how not to fail their clients, Strupp (1975) noted three major functions of the psychologist. First is the *healing function* or the alleviation of emotional suffering through understanding, support, and reassurance. Second is an *educational function*, which includes promoting growth, insight, and maturation. Finally, there is a *technological function*, by which various techniques may be applied to change or modify behavior. He noted "the client has a right to know what he [sic] is buying, and the therapist, like the manufacturer of a product or seller of a service, has a responsibility to be explicit on this subject" (p. 39).

The notion of a client-therapist contract is not new, although attempts to define the parameters of such contracts began only within the past two decades (Everstine et al., 1980; Hare-Mustin et al., 1979; Liss-Levinson et al., 1980). The most recent APA ethics code (APA, 1992) and a number of state laws now make it clear that the psychologist must inform clients of a number of aspects of the professional relationship at the outset of their work together (ES: 5.01). This is not to say that therapists and clients should necessarily have formal or written documents outlining their relationship in great detail. Rather, it suggests that the therapist should assume responsibility to provide clients with the information they need to make decisions about therapy. The therapist should be willing to treat the client as any consumer of services has a right to expect. This may include responding to clients' questions about training and experience, attempting to resolve clients' complaints, and even using formal written contracts when indicated (Hare-Mustin et al., 1979). Essential elements of any client-therapist treatment agreement are summarized in Box 4-1.

Recently, state laws have begun to mandate various types of consent to treatment procedures as part of a therapeutic contract. In one attempt to assess the impact of such a law, Handelsman and his colleagues (1995) found that psychotherapists in Colorado were obeying the law, but were not necessarily providing ethically desirable data in usable form. For example, fewer than 40% of the forms reviewed gave specific details when discussing limits of confidentiality, and fewer than 5% discussed goals of therapy. The average readability of the consent forms they reviewed was at grade level 15.7 (i.e., upper-level college), whereas 64% of the forms reached a readability grade of 17+.

The Client's Frame of Reference

Implicit in the contracting process is the assumption that the therapist will be able to take the client's unique frame of reference and personal psychosocial ecology into account when

---

Box 4-1. Key Elements of a Therapuetic Contract

Setting the goals of treatment
   What will we be working toward?
Discussing the process of therapy
How will we work together?
   What are the client's rights?
   What are the therapist's responsibilities?
   What risks may accompany treatment?
Addressing the process of therapy
What should both of us expect regarding:
   Fees, methods of payment, and covered services
   Techniques to be used, therapist availability
   Limits of confidentiality

deciding whether and how to organize treatment. Therapists unfamiliar with the social, economic, and cultural pressures confronting women, minority group members, and the poor may fail to recognize the contribution of such stresses in creating or exacerbating psychological problems. Conventional psychotherapy training often emphasizes clients' contributions to their problems, at times neglecting to consider the external forces that help to shape the client's behavior. The counseling of clients of culturally diverse backgrounds by psychologists who are not trained to work with such groups has been cited as unethical behavior (APA, 1993). Many subgroups of society, including women, children, the elderly, people living in institutional care, and certain disadvantaged minorities, are socialized in a manner that may accustom them to having their individual rights to self-determination denied (Liss-Levinson et al., 1980). The therapist must be sensitive to these issues and the general reluctance that an emotionally troubled client may have in asking important questions or raising certain needs or concerns. In such cases, the therapist must assess the client's circumstances carefully and elicit basic information needed to conclude a meaningful treatment contract.

Brown (1994) has introduced the notion of "empowered consent" as a means of framing what would constitute a genuine and competent informed consent process essential to a therapeutic contract. To provide empowered consent (as opposed to simply informed consent), the therapist considers the quality of information and the manner in which it is presented to maximize the client's optimal capacity to consent freely and knowingly to all aspects of the therapy relationship without feeling in any way coerced. The goal of such a process is to reduce the risk that a therapist might unilaterally impose a risky or unwanted intervention on an unwitting client. Consider these illustrations:

Case 4-1: Marsha Young, a recent business school graduate, was hired by a prestigious advertising agency. The office was highly competitive, and she soon developed anxiety attacks and insomnia. At times, she felt as though she were the "token woman" in the organization, and she feared that her work was being scrutinized far more critically than that of recently hired males with an M.B.A. She sought a consultation with Jack Chauvinist, Ph.D. Dr. Chauvinist soon concluded that Ms. Young suffered from "penis envy" and was afraid of heterosexual intimacy. He advised her that it was critical for her to address these matters in therapy if she ever hoped to be able to be married and bear a child, thus fulfilling herself as a woman.

Case 4-2: Yochi Tanaka was the eldest son of a proud Japanese family, who was sent off to attend college in the United States at age 17. He had some difficulty adjusting at the large state university and failed midterm exams in three subjects. Mr. Tanaka sought help at the college counseling center and was seen by Hasty Focus, M.A., a psychology intern. Mr. Focus was deceived by Tanaka's excellent command of English, Western-style fashion consciousness, and tendency to nod in seeming assent whenever Focus offered a suggestion or interpretation. Focus failed to recognize the subtle, but stressful, acculturation problem or to detect the growing sense of depression and failure Tanaka was experiencing. Tanaka was apparently unwilling to assert his concerns over the interpretations of the "expert" in an unseemly fashion. After 5 sessions and 6 weeks, fearing failure on his final exams and disgrace in the eyes of his family, Tanaka committed suicide.

Case 4-3: Inda Closet had always felt attracted to other women, but had dated men from time to time because it was what her parents and society seemed to expect of her. Concerned about sexuality, fearful of social rejection, and wondering about how to explore her sexual feelings, Ms. Closet built up the courage to consult a psychotherapist and made an appointment with Heda Knowsitall, Ph.D. After taking a brief history Dr. Knowsitall informed Ms. Closet that she was "definitely heterosexual" because "she had a history of dating men and, therefore, instinctual drives toward heterosexuality." Closet was advised to enter behavior therapy to unlearn her attraction to women.

All three of these cases suggest some incompetence on the part of the psychologist, but our intent here is to show that a more central problem was ultimate failure to adequately detect and incorporate the client's psychosocial needs into the treatment plan. Dr. Chauvinist seems to have ignored some very real life stresses in Ms. Young's psychological and social ecology. He had little sense of her possible career goals, professional interests, or the pressures she might be feeling. Instead, Chauvinist seemed to be relying on a stereotypic interpretation of her complaint, which may have little relevance to her immediate needs or symptoms. Likewise, Mr. Focus was unaware of the cultural pressures his client feels and the impact of these with respect to the current problem. Focus was deceived in part by Tanaka's head nodding, a cultural response intended as a common courtesy, interpreted by Focus as license to pursue irrelevant goals. Dr. Knowsitall manifested little understanding of lesbian sexuality and was far too glib in offering her unfounded opinions as the primary basis for directing therapy. None of these therapists showed much interest in eliciting specific goals or therapeutic direction from the client, although all would probably claim to be doing so.

Another sort of dilemma related to the client's frame of reference and goals is a tactic known as the "bait and switch" in psychotherapy (Williams, 1985). This term refers to the unethical tactic sometimes used in retail sales. A department store may advertise a product at substantial savings to lure customers into the store. Once on the scene, a salesperson will attempt to make the specific item on sale seem inferior and encourage the client to purchase a more expensive model. Williams draws the analogy between this practice and certain types of long-term psychotherapy. He presents the following comments from one of his clients, describing a previous therapist:

> My physician was concerned that there might be a psychological cause for my high blood pressure, so he sent me to see a psychotherapist. I was eager to go because I had become desperate for some kind of relief, and the medicine I took had too many bad side-effects. Psychotherapy was an approach I hadn't even considered. I walked into the therapist's office for my first session. He greeted me and asked me to sit down, and we sat there looking at each other for a while. Finally, he asked me

about my sex life, which I said was fine. We looked at each other some more, then he told me that the time was up. He expected to see me the following week, but I never went back. (Williams, 1985)

In this case, the client had consulted a therapist for help in managing hypertension. The next thing he knew, the topic of discussion was his sex life. In the client's view, the therapist had a certain agenda different from his own and expected the client to buy it without serious questions. If the client explicitly chose to discuss his sex life or any other issues on his own, or if the therapist indicated some connection might exist between the topic and the presenting symptom, there would have been no "switch" and no ethical problem. If the client decided to seek personal growth and exploration through treatment, there would also be no problem. Instead, however, the story implies that the pursuit of this other issue was a unilateral and undiscussed decision of the therapist, possibly intended to extend the duration of contact with the client. Perhaps this particular approach was therapeutically indicated and perhaps not. Regardless, the rationale should have been discussed with the client.

Williams (1985) notes that diverse psychotherapy systems, including psychoanalysis and Gestalt therapy, incorporate rationales for such bait-and-switch tactics (e.g., "the problem is really unconscious, and the patient is unaware of the real meanings," or "anybody who goes to a therapist has something up his sleeve"). A theoretical rationale does not make use of the technique ethical. It is clearly possible to retain one's theoretical integrity in any psychotherapy system and still call on the client for active participation in setting goals and doing the work of treatment.

Case 4-4: Mary Slick, Ph.D., advertised a special "assessment package" and low-cost "short-term treatment option" for children with behavior problems at a relatively inexpensive rate. One consumer complained that, when she took her child for the appointment, she was encouraged to purchase a more expensive "complete assessment battery" rather than the less costly one advertised.

This case is more obviously unethical than the situation described by Williams (1985). Dr. Slick advertised an attractive price and then attempted to switch the client to a more expensive arrangement after arrival at the office. Slick's inclusion of a treatment option as part of an assessment package also sounds suspiciously as though she has preordained the existence of a problem requiring treatment.

Conflicting Values in Psychotherapy

What about the situation in which the goals and values of the client and therapist are at variance or the result of treatment may be more than the client bargained for? One of the most fundamental dilemmas related to therapy goals is whether to encourage a client to rebel against a repressive environment or attempt to adjust to it (Karasu, 1980). Issues related to abortion choice, sexual preference, religion, and family values are among the potential conflict areas. The therapist must be responsible for avoiding the imposition of his or her own values on the client.

Case 4-5: Arnold Polite, age 14, is referred to Frank Facilit, Psy.D., out of concern that he is becoming increasingly depressed and socially withdrawn. Dr. Facilit finds Arnold to be somewhat inhibited by the close, and at times intrusive, ministrations of his parents while Arnold struggles to develop a sense of adolescent autonomy. Over several months, Facilit sees good progress in his work with Arnold, but then he begins to get telephone calls from Mr. and Mrs. Polite, who express concern that Arnold is becoming too assertive and too interested in people and activities apart from the family. They express the fear that Facilit's work with Arnold will alienate him from the family.

In this instance, the progress of the client alters his relationship with his parents, and they may not care for the new behavior. As we discuss below (see Case 4-13), the best interests of one client may well be antithetical to the best interests of a co-client or close family member. Perhaps Dr. Facilit can work toward some accommodation by means of a family conference or

similar approach, but the possibility exists that this will not be satisfactory.

Case 4-6: Sam Escape, age 23, moved from Boston to Chicago and entered psychotherapy with Sidney Silento, Ph.D. Shortly thereafter, Mr. Escape terminated contacts with his family in Boston. His parents and uncle, a psychiatrist, contacted an ethics committee to complain that Dr. Silento would not respond to inquiries about the location or welfare of the young man. Because Mr. Escape was an adult, the committee was reluctant to become involved; however, it seemed to the committee members that the family was at least entitled to a response to their unanswered letters and phone calls. Dr. Silento ignored three letters from the committee and was then sent a letter from the committee's legal counsel threatening him with sanctions for failure to respond to a duly constituted ethics panel. At this point, Dr. Silento replied apologetically, noting that he was preoccupied with his day-to-day therapeutic efforts and had a poor correspondence filing system. He reported that Mr. Escape was attempting to establish himself as an autonomous adult in Chicago and did not wish to contact his family or to authorize contacts by Dr. Silento.

In this situation, Dr. Silento was not unethical for failing to give information to the family, although he certainly could have responded to them with that fact rather than simply ignoring their calls and letters. His excuse for failing to respond to the committee over several months was another matter. His procrastination only dragged out the case and exacerbated the family's considerable anxiety, while costing the psychological association a substantial sum in staff time and legal fees needed to evoke a simple explanation. It was unclear to what extent the treatment with Dr. Silento led to Escape's decision to avoid family contacts, although he was well within his rights to do so, and Dr. Silento was obligated to respect that decision, even if he felt sympathy for the family. (See discussion on failure to respond to ethics committees in chapter 2 and ES: 8.06).

Case 4-7: Helena Sistine, Ed.D., is a psychologist and a Catholic who holds deep traditional values.

She works in the counseling center of a state university. Carl Quandary comes in for an initial appointment and wants to discuss the anxiety he is experiencing over several homosexual contacts he has had during the prior 6 months. Mr. Quandary reports, "I don't know what I'm supposed to be. I want to try and figure it out." Dr. Sistine realizes that her own feelings of opposition to homosexuality would make it difficult for her to work with Quandary objectively, especially if he should decide to continue having sexual relationships with other men. She listens carefully to his concerns and explains that she plans to refer him to a colleague at the counseling service who has had particular experience helping clients with similar issues.

Dr. Sistine has recognized her potential value conflict with Quandary's need to make important life decisions according to his own values. In addition, she realizes that she is unfamiliar with the life experiences and issues with which he is struggling. She also recognizes that Quandary is in a highly vulnerable emotional state, so she does not expose her value system to him and does not attempt to engage him in a therapeutic dialogue. Instead, she collects the information needed to make an appropriate referral and presents the referral to the client in a positive manner to minimize the risk of his feeling rejected or abandoned.

Ethnic and Cultural Diversity

Hays (1995) notes that clinical literature on multiculturalism in psychology tends to focus almost entirely on ethnicity. Perhaps this is the direct result of psychologists' attention being drawn to racism and the relative absence of ethnic minorities in their field. Whatever the reason, this state of affairs ignores many minority populations facing special cultural issues and related needs, for example, elderly people, urban teenagers, gay men, lesbians, religious minorities, people with sensory or mobility disabilities, those who are HIV seropositive, and people with serious illness such as AIDS. Hays suggests a model to conceptualize individual differences; she has assigned the model the acronym ADDRESSING; meaning *a*ge or generational *d*ifferences, *d*isability, *r*eligion, *e*thnicity,

social status, *s*exual orientation, *i*ndigenous heritage, *n*ationality, and *g*ender (1995, p. 310).

Hays (1995) believes that cognitive-behavioral therapies lend themselves to multiculturally sensitive application because of their emphasis on the uniqueness of the individual, focus on client empowerment, attention to both conscious processes and specific behaviors, and integration of assessment over the full course of therapy. However, one potential drawback of the cognitive behavioral approach is its presentation as a "value-neutral" approach. The fact is that there are no value-neutral psychotherapies. For example, some therapies may pay relatively little attention to a client's history, including upbringing and life experiences. Others may rely on stereotypes or formulas of how certain elements of a person's history always dictate a particular intervention. Still others may focus on rational thinking and scientific method in a manner that flies in the face of people with culture and world views more spiritually oriented or focused on the importance of consensus building and cooperation. For example, in Chinese culture, the individual is supposed to forgo the self in favor of the family or larger society. In some circumstances, this might make it difficult for a person to accept interventions oriented toward increasing personal autonomy and assertiveness.

Despite the egalitarian appeal of the ADDRESSING concept, we must not lose sight of how critical race and ethnicity are in the United States. Given that fewer than 7% of all psychologists are people of color, most individuals of color who seek psychotherapy will of necessity be treated by Euro-Americans. Although programs accredited by the APA must incorporate teaching on matters of diversity, accomplishing this in a sensitive and effective manner is extremely difficult. An excellent discussion by Tatum (1992) illustrates the problems inherent in teaching about racism. With her training as a clinical psychologist and her considerable expertise at teaching such emotionally loaded material, she is able to describe and delineate the extent of guilt, anger, and distress involved in confronting issues of racism, even in a supportive setting.

The next set of case illustrations is based on

reports by clients to a subsequent therapist (J. H. Daniel, personal communication, December 1995).

Case 4-8: Nan Turner, a 28-year-old African American woman, reported that during her first appointment with Darla Dense, Ph.D., she was questioned about which part of the urban ghetto she had been raised. Turner explained that she grew up in the same suburban community as Dr. Dense, but the psychologist's perceptions of the town were quite different from Ms. Turner's. Dense therefore concluded that Turner was either misrepresenting her past due to shame or had poor reality testing abilities.

Case 4-9: When Henry Jackson, an African American college student over 6-feet tall, went to the University Counseling Center for help in dealing with difficulties he was experiencing on campus, he was assigned to Biff Jerko, Psy.D. In an effort to "forge an early alliance," Dr. Jerko attempted to greet Mr. Jackson with a "high five" instead of a more traditional handshake. During the course of the session, Dr. Jerko continued his "attempt to connect" by using profanity and slang that he regarded as emulating ghetto talk. Mr. Jackson wanted to talk about the fact that his imposing stature and dark skin seemed to make people uncomfortable. Dr. Jerko quickly attempted to reassure Mr. Jackson that he would be judged only by his character and studies on campus and resisted exploring the impact of prejudice that may accrue to tall black males. Neither the hand greeting nor slang use were a part of Mr. Jackson's background, and both were perceived as alienating. Adding insult to injury, Dr. Jerko asked Mr. Jackson whether he planned to try out for the college basketball team. Jackson did not have the energy or assertiveness to attempt reeducation of the therapist, and he never returned for another appointment.

Case 4-10: Carlotta Hernandez, a Latino woman in her early 20s, was struggling with issues involving her relationship with her mother when she sought consultation with Carl Cutter, Ph.D. Ms. Hernandez was the first college-educated person in her extended family and was torn between traditional obligations to family and her newly experienced social mobility. Dr. Cutter praised her academic achievement and encouraged her to sever or minimize contact with her family, which continued to reside in a poor inner-city neighborhood. He did not understand the importance of balancing family connections with individual achievement manifested in many Latino cultures. Ms. Hernandez needed to pursue options of how to stay connected in an emotionally healthy way. The more Dr. Cutter pressed her to disconnect, the more depressed she became.

Case 4-11: Pam Passer, a very fair-skinned African American, was concerned about just how "black" she was, given that she could "pass" as White. Robert Blinders, Psy.D., her therapist, dismissed such concerns, stating that she should just see herself "as an American." Passing for White might give her greater social and professional mobility, but the price would be disconnection from her family and the community in which she was raised. Dr. Blinders could not hear the implications of the disconnections for her as these were not his values.

These case examples illustrate a range of inappropriate and unethical behaviors with a common theme: insensitivity or inadequate attention to the individualized needs of clients who are different because of race or social class. Dr. Dense made damaging assumptions regarding her client and could not entertain the concept that the client's reality of living in the same town might be different from her own. Dr. Jerko based his feeble attempt at establishing rapport on caricature stereotypes and could not recognize or acknowledge the impact of being a large Black man on Mr. Jackson's day-to-day existence in a biased society. Drs. Cutter and Blinders could not grasp the struggle for acceptance and accomplishment balanced with the need to value family connections that is very much a part of life for many ethnic minorities. Being uninformed, unwilling to learn, unable to hear, and relying on stereotypes as reality remain major ethical problems to which too many psychotherapists are inadequately attentive.

Just as it is not reasonable to expect that one therapist will be able to meet the treatment needs of every client, it is also unreasonable to expect that the ideal therapist (i.e., in terms of ethnicity, culture, etc.) for any given client will be readily available in every community. In recognition of this reality, the APA has assembled a series of guidelines to assist therapists in enhancing their sensitivity and understanding of diverse client needs. These APA guidelines address sex bias (1975); psychotherapy with women (1978); work with gay or lesbian clients (1991); and intervention with ethnically, culturally, or linguistically diverse client populations (1993). In unusual situations, one can often learn much simply by asking direct questions.

Case 4-12: Annie Pueblo was a 5-year-old Native American who had been relocated along with her mother from her home on a reservation to a major urban center by the Federal Indian Health Service. Annie was in critical need of an organ transplant and was "on standby" at a large medical center. A nurse became concerned after overhearing a partial conversation in which Annie and her mother were talking about communicating with the dead. The nurse expressed her concern to the consulting psychologist on the organ transplant team: "Conversations about such things are certain to depress the child." The psychologist met with the child, who told him of a dream: "Dead people are trying to give me food, but I'm not gonna take it!" The child's mental status and behavior were normal aside from these unusual remarks, so the psychologist sought out the child's mother and asked for her help by noting, "I'm not familiar with the ways of your people. Do you have any ideas about why Annie is saying this?" The mother laughed and explained that Annie had reported dreaming of an old woman in distinctive costume who offered her food. The mother explained that she did not know who it could be, so she telephoned her own mother on the reservation. Annie's grandmother listened to the report of the dream and immediately recognized the spirit of her own mother. The dream spirit was Annie's long-deceased great-great-grandmother, come to watch over her. This was a good and protective omen; however, it is also very important that one not accept food from spirits of the dead. Doing so requires that you join them. It was important that Annie know how to accept the protection, but decline the food (e.g., pretend you don't hear the offer or politely say, "Thank you, but I'm not hungry.").

By seeking information, the psychologist picked up valuable data that could be used to assure the nursing staff that Annie was in no way depressed or being put at risk. In fact, Annie had been given culturally appropriate information that helped her to feel cross-generational social support in a way that the local health care team could not provide. By recognizing that this family was culturally different, and by respectfully seeking information about those differences, the psychologist was able to defuse misunderstandings and educate others on the hospital staff. For an excellent commentary on cultural diversity issues in the treatment of children, readers are directed to Tharp (1991).

Consent for Treatment and the Right to Refuse

The matters of informed consent and the right to refuse are discussed at many points in this book, especially in relation to confidentiality (chapter 6) and participation in research (chapter 17). The section on the client's frame of reference, however, has implied that consent issues may be rather different in the context of psychotherapy. Psychotherapy unavoidably affects important belief systems and social relationships. This is well illustrated in a case study of Mary, a Christian Scientist with a socially reinforced obsessive disorder (Cohen & Smith, 1976). In a discussion of the ethics of informed consent in this case, it is clear that Mary experienced some sense of divided loyalties related to her religious practices as a result of psychotherapy. Coyne notes "even the simplest intervention may have important repercussions for the client's belief system and social relationships" (1976, p. 1015).

The consent-getting process for psychotherapists will generally involve a discussion of goals, expectations, procedures, and potential risks with clients (Everstine et al., 1980; Hare-Mustin et al., 1979; Noll, 1976, 1981). The need to disclose the limits of confidentiality in particular is discussed in chapter 5. Clients might also reasonably expect to be warned about other foreseeable indirect effects of treatment. Obviously, no psychotherapist can anticipate every potential indirect effect of treatment, but a client who presents with marital complaints, for example, should be cautioned that therapy might lead to behavior or decisions that could drastically alter the dynamics of the relationship for the worse. Likewise, a client who presents with job-related complaints could be cautioned that he or she might choose to resign from work as a result of therapy. Such cautions are especially warranted when the therapist notes that the client has many issues that are being inadequately addressed and suspects that uncovering these issues (e.g., long-repressed anger) might lead to distressing feelings.

Consider the married adult who enters individual psychotherapy hoping to overcome individual and interpersonal problems and to enhance the marriage. What if the result is eventual harm to the marriage and a decision to dissolve it?

Case 4-13: Tanya Wifely enters psychotherapy with Nina Peutic, Ph.D., complaining of depression, feelings of inadequacy, and an unsatisfactory sexual relationship with her spouse. As treatment progresses, Ms. Wifely becomes more self-assured, less depressed, and more active in initiating sexual activity at home. Her husband is ambivalent regarding the changes and the increased sense of autonomy he sees in his wife. He begins to feel that she is observing and evaluating him during sexual relations, which leads him to become uncomfortable and increasingly frustrated. He begins to pressure his wife to terminate therapy and complains to an ethics committee when she, instead, decides to separate from him.

We certainly do not have sufficient information to elucidate all of the psychodynamics operating in this couple's relationship, but treatment did change it. Perhaps Ms. Wifely experiences the change as one for the better. She certainly has the right to choose to separate from her spouse and continue in treatment. On the basis of these facts, we cannot conclude that Dr. Peutic did anything unethical. However, we do not know whether Dr. Peutic ever informed Ms. Wifely that her obligation as a psychotherapist was to Wifely's mental and emotional health, not to the marriage. We must wonder whether the outcome might have been different

had Dr. Peutic warned Ms. Wifely that changes could occur in the marriage as a result of her individual therapy.

A client who does not like the specifications and risk/benefit statement offered by the therapist can generally decide not to seek treatment or to seek alternative care, but some clients do not have such a choice. These clients include patients confined in mental hospitals and minors brought for treatment by their parents or guardians. Some ethical issues related to special settings (e.g., schools, the military, and correctional institutions) are discussed in chapter 12. It is important to recognize the rights and vulnerabilities of the hospitalized patient with respect to ethics and psychotherapy.

In the landmark case of *O'Connor v. Donaldson* (1975), the U.S. Supreme Court recognized for the first time a constitutional basis for a "right to treatment" for the nondangerous mentally ill patient. This ruling essentially said that the state could not confine such patients unless treatment was provided, but what if the patient does not want the treatment? A host of lawsuits asserting the right of mental patients to refuse treatment, especially those that involve physical interventions (e.g., drugs, psychosurgery, and electroconvulsive shock therapy), have highlighted special ethical problems (Appelbaum & Gutheil, 1980; White & White, 1981). In particular, the right of the patient to refuse medication has been described ironically as the "psychiatrist's double bind" (Ford, 1980) and dramatically as the "right to rot" (Appelbaum & Gutheil, 1980).

As nonphysicians, psychologists historically have not been trained to use somatic therapies and have therefore not yet been the object of such suits. In August 1995, the APA Council of Representatives approved steps in that direction by developing curricula necessary to train psychologists to prescribe psychopharmacologic agents. The Department of Defense has a highly successful program for psychologists in the military medical corps who are interested in learning to prescribe psychotropic medications (Jones, Cohen, Munsat, Doris, & Berson, 1996). Such developments will create new opportunities, but would also open a whole new set of professional obligations and hazards. Some additional ethical problems that may accompany prescribing privileges were discussed in chapter 3.

One development predicted on the basis of cases finding a right to refuse medication and other somatic treatments is an increased demand for nonmedical treatment of psychological disorders and hence a greater role for psychologists (White & White, 1981). There are instances in which institutionalized clients have asserted a right to refuse psychological treatment, but these have generally been technique related (e.g., behavior modification) and are discussed in the next chapter.

Obtaining consent for treatment from a minor presents another set of issues (Koocher & Keith-Spiegel, 1990; Melton, Koocher, & Saks, 1983). Although a small number of states (e.g., the Commonwealth of Virginia) permit minors to consent to psychotherapy independently of their parents, such authority is an exception to the norm. In some states, such services could conceivably be provided as adjuncts to a minor's right to seek, without parental consent, birth control, or treatment for sexually transmitted diseases or substance abuse. Usually, however, a parent's permission would be needed to undertake psychotherapy with a minor client. When a child wishes to refuse treatment authorized by a parent, there is, under many circumstances, no legal recourse for the child even if the proposed treatment involves inpatient confinement (Melton et al., 1983, Weithorn, 1987). The courts have tended to assume that the mental health professional called on to hospitalize or treat the child at the parent's behest is an unbiased third party who can adequately assess what is best for the child. Some psychologists have argued that the best interests of parents are not necessarily those of children, and that mental health professionals are not always able to function in the idealized unbiased third-party role imagined by the court (Koocher, 1983; Melton et al., 1983; Weithorn, 1987).

Case 4-14: Jackie Fled, age 13, walks into the Downtown Mental Health Center and asks to talk to someone. Jackie is seen by Amos Goodheart, Ph.D., and tells him of many personal and family problems, including severe physical abuse at home. Jackie asks Dr. Goodheart not to discuss the case with "anyone, especially my folks." Dr. Goodheart discusses his options with Jackie, explaining that he cannot offer treatment to anyone under 18 years of age without parental consent. Goodheart also discusses his duty to report suspected child abuse to the state's Department of Child Welfare. Jackie feels betrayed.

Decisions are sometimes too difficult to expect children to make independently. While it is clear that some children under age 18 may be competent to consent to treatment in the intellectual and emotional sense, it is also evident that many are not (Grisso & Vierling, 1978). Dr. Goodheart recognized two important legal obligations and an additional ethical obligation. First, he recognized that he could not legally accept Jackie's request as a competent informed consent for treatment with all that it implies (including responsibility to pay for services), although it did not occur to him to warn Jackie about the limits of confidentiality from the start of their session. Second, he recognized his obligation to report the case to authorities duly constituted to handle child abuse complaints. This is a statutory obligation in all states, although it certainly would have been less than professionally responsible had he sent Jackie home to additional potential abuse and done nothing. Finally, he recognized Jackie's rights as a person and a client, taking the time to discuss his intended course of action with Jackie, thereby showing considerable respect for the child.

SPECIAL OBLIGATIONS OF THE THERAPIST

At this point, it may seem that we have already discussed many obligations of the psychotherapist to the client. However, there are three special types of obligation that deserve highlighting. These include (1) respect for the client, even the difficult or obnoxious client; (2) duties owed to clients who make threats; and (3) the obligation to terminate a relationship when it is clear that the client is not benefitting. These are common factors related to ethical complaints. That is, few clients complain to ethics committees about a psychologist's failure to obtain treatment consent or adequately consider their cultural value system. However, many complaints grow out of cases related to particularly difficult clients or the failure to terminate a nonbeneficial relationship or treatment that has "gone wrong" (ES: 4.09b).

The Exceptionally Difficult Client

The definition of the exceptionally difficult type of client is a relative one since the client who may prove difficult for one therapist could be another's forte. There are some types of clients, however, who would be considered difficult by virtually any therapist. These include the client who makes frequent suicidal threats, who is intimidating or dangerous, who fails to show for appointments and/or fails to pay bills, who is actively decompensating and acting out, who is overdependent and telephones with urgent concerns at all hours of the day and night, or who harasses the therapist's family.

Case 4-15: Robert Bumble, Ph.D., began treating a troubled young woman in an office at his home. Dr. Bumble failed to recognize signs of increasing paranoid decompensation in his client until she began to act out destructively in his office. At that point, he attempted to refer her elsewhere, but she reacted with increased paranoia and rage. Dr. Bumble terminated the relationship, or so he thought. The ex-client took an apartment across the street from his home to spy on him, telephoned him at all hours of the day and night with an assortment of complaints and explicit threats, and filed ethical complaints against him.

Case 4-16: An ethics committee received a long, handwritten letter from Anna Crock, an anguished client of a public agency, complaining that ira Brash, Ph.D., the supervisor of her therapist, had treated her in an unprofessional manner, creating considerable stress and depression. The therapist was a psychology intern who was apparently having severe difficulties with Ms. Crock and had asked her to attend a joint meeting with Dr. Brash. Crock had seen the intern for 14 sessions, but had never met the supervisor. She complained that during the joint session Dr. Brash was extremely con-

frontational. The committee wrote to Dr. Brash asking for his account of these events. Brash gave a clinical description of Ms. Crock's "negative transference" to the intern. Ms. Crock allegedly treated the intern in a hostile manner, calling him "stupid" and "a know-nothing." He indicated that the joint meeting was an attempt to "work through" the problem. He stated that the use of confrontational tactics was an effort to get Ms. Crock to release some feelings. He stated that he had to leave the joint meeting early and alleged that after his departure the intern berated Ms. Crock for her abusive behavior during the joint meeting and abruptly terminated her. Dr. Brash attempted to remedy this later in another meeting with Ms. Crock, in which, by her account, "He was a completely different person." However, she was still quite angry.

In both of these cases, the psychologists seem to have made some serious miscalculations in dealing with their troubling clients. Dr. Bumble failed to realize that his client was beyond his ability to treat until matters had seriously deteriorated. When he finally recognized that the case had gone awry, there was little he could do. Although many of the client's bizarre accusations were unfounded, it was evident to the committee that Bumble had been practicing beyond his level of competence and, as a result, had contributed to the client's problems. Bumble ultimately had to seek police protection and obtain a court restraining order in an effort to stop his ex-client's intrusive harassment.

The case of Ms. Crock, Dr. Brash, and the intern is problematic from a number of viewpoints. To begin, Ms. Crock had thought that treatment was going well for 14 weeks, while the intern and his supervisor believed that treatment was progressing poorly. Brash's attempt to handle a complicated clinical problem in a single session, which he had to leave prematurely, showed questionable judgment. His use of a confrontational style with Crock in the absence of a therapeutic contract, alliance, or even minimal rapport was also questionable in the ethics committee's view. The committee also chastised Dr. Brash for attempting to shift some of the responsibility for the premature termination to the intern. As the supervisor, Brash could not escape ultimate responsibility. Poor communication, a difficult client, an attempt to move too quickly in therapy, and a botched termination all combined in a manner that left the client feeling angry and hurt.

In working with difficult clients, it is essential that psychologists remain cognizant of their professional and personal limitations. This means knowing enough not to take on clients that one is not adequately prepared to treat or knowing enough to help clients in need of different services to find them early in the relationship rather than waiting until problems develop. Some types of clients seem especially likely to evoke troubling feelings in the therapist. The client who is verbally abusive, sarcastic, or does not speak very much during the session can certainly generate a number of unpleasant feelings on the therapist's part. Substance abusers, pedophiles, individuals with borderline personality styles, and mentally retarded clients will occasionally be referred elsewhere by some therapists.

There is nothing unethical about refusing to treat a client who stirs up troubling feelings or anger in the therapist. In fact, it is probably more appropriate to refer such clients than to try to treat them while struggling with strong countertransference. On the other hand, it is important to minimize the risk and discomfort to all clients. One should therefore learn to identify those sorts of clients one cannot or should not work with and refer them appropriately and quickly without causing them personal discomfort or stress.

Case 4-17: Jack Fury was an angry 15-year-old referred to Harold Packing, Ph.D., for displaying antisocial behavior, including school vandalism. After the fourth session, Dr. Packing was in an appointment with another client when they smelled smoke and discovered that a fire had been set in the waiting room. The fire was put out, and Dr. Packing called Jack and his parents in for a meeting. Jack acknowledged setting the fire. When Packing expressed concern that he could have been killed in the blaze, Jack replied, "Everybody's got to go sometime." Dr. Packing was understandably angry and informed the Fury family that he was no longer willing to treat Jack.

Case 4-18: Serena Still contacted Patience Mc-Graw, Ph.D., seeking psychotherapy as a means to overcome her shyness and difficulty in establishing new relationships. The sessions were characterized by long periods of silence. Dr. McGraw found herself unable to draw Ms. Still into conversation aside from the most superficial pleasantries. She tried several different approaches, including asking Ms. Still to write down her thoughts about events between sessions, but Ms. Still remained quite taciturn and uncommunicative. After four such sessions, Dr. McGraw suggested that perhaps she should attempt to help Ms. Still find a therapist with whom she could communicate better or that they should discontinue sessions until Ms. Still had some issues she wished to discuss.

In both of the cases above, the therapists were clearly uncomfortable with the client's behavior. Dr. Packing was so angry at Jack Fury's fire setting and subsequent indifference that he was unwilling to continue treating him. Presumably, he would be willing to refer the family elsewhere, giving the new therapist an appropriate warning about Jack's behavior. Whereas some therapists might have been willing to continue working with Jack, Dr. Packing was not. He recognized these feelings and dealt with them promptly.

Dr. McGraw had a somewhat different problem. Her client's stated problem was shyness, and this is the manifest symptom the client has not been able to address in treatment sessions. Dr. McGraw's best efforts to engage the client have been fruitless, and she feels somewhat frustrated. Certainly, she should raise the problem directly with Ms. Still and explore alternatives (e.g., a different therapist or a break in the treatment program), but she should do this as gently as possible given the likelihood that this is a source of probable anxiety for the client. We address the matter of the client who is not benefitting from treatment in a separate section below. We raise the problem of Ms. Still to underscore therapists' common tendency to become angry by a client's lack of participation, resulting in a failure to be fully sensitive to the client's fears.

Still another type of difficult client is the one whose behavior or problems tend to interact with the psychological conflicts of the therapist to cause special countertransference situations.

Case 4-19: Barbara Storm sought a consultation from Michael Splitz, Psy.D., shortly following her divorce. Splitz was also recently divorced, although he did not mention this to Ms. Storm. Her presenting complaint was that she had difficulty controlling her rage toward her ex-spouse. As Dr. Splitz listened to her vindictive attacks on her ex-husband, he found himself tensing considerably and continually biting his lip. Minutes later, Ms. Storm screamed and fled out of the office. She wrote to an ethics committee, complaining that Dr. Splitz was a vampire. The committee feared that they were dealing with a very disturbed complainant, but contacted Dr. Splitz, asking if he could provide any explanation for her perception. Dr. Splitz recounted essentially the same story, noting he had unconsciously bitten his lip to the point that it began to bleed. He had not realized it until after Ms. Storm had left, when he looked in a mirror and saw the trickle of blood that ran from his lip to his shirt collar.

Aside from the unfortunate stress the incident caused Ms. Storm, the scene might have been laughable. The point here is that psychologists must strive for sufficient self-awareness to recognize their anger toward clients and make every effort to avoid acting out or otherwise harming the client unnecessarily. There are many appropriate ways to handle anger toward a client, ranging from direct overt expression (e.g., "I am annoyed that you kicked that hole in my office wall and am going to charge you the cost of repairing it") to silent self-exploration (e.g., the client who stirs up countertransference feelings because of similarities to some "significant other" in the therapist's life). The client is always to be considered vulnerable to harm relative to the therapist, and the psychologist is obligated not to use the power position inherent in the therapist role to the client's detriment. If such problems occur more than rarely in a psychologist's career, it is likely that one is practicing beyond his or her competence or has a personal problem that needs attention.

The most difficult sort of client a psychotherapist can encounter is the person who not only presents a clinical challenge, but who also presents issues that are emotionally loaded for the therapist.

Case 4-20: Ralph Redneck is a 15-year-old high school sophomore who has sought treatment in response to feelings of inadequacy and embarrassment about his lack of athletic ability and late pubertal development. A good therapeutic alliance has been formed, and Ralph is working effectively on these sensitive issues. As he has felt more comfortable in therapy, Ralph has begun to evidence a considerable amount of racial and ethnic prejudice. He often criticizes some of his classmates as "niggers" or "Jew bastards." Ralph is unaware that his White therapist is Jewish and is married to a person of color.

The case of Ralph Redneck focuses clearly on the clash of client and therapist values. Should the therapist offer self-disclosure in an effort to provoke some enlightened attitude change on Ralph's part? It is clear that Ralph did not seek psychotherapy to improve his race relations. In such cases, the therapist should make every effort to maintain clear personal boundaries and focus treatment on the issues raised by the client. Should Ralph discover that his prejudices apply to the therapist, it would then be appropriate to discuss them as one would any aspect of the therapeutic relationship. Self-disclosure and initiation of such a discussion by the therapist, however, would constitute an inappropriate intrusion into Ralph's ongoing treatment because Ralph does not (at least initially) experience his biases as problems. Attempting to call his attention to these prejudices could place additional emotional stress on Ralph, while not addressing the problems he presented in requesting help.

A more difficult question is whether Ralph's therapist can maintain an adequately empathic relationship or whether negative countertransference and conscious anger will begin to compromise treatment. This is a question that therapists must ask themselves frequently when conflicting values unrelated to the foci of treatment are raised by clients. In such circumstances, it is most appropriate for the therapist to seek guidance or perhaps therapeutic consultation from a colleague to assess the legitimate therapeutic needs of the client as distinct from their own. The therapist's issues should never become the client's problems.

Case 4-21: Two weeks prior to his scheduled appearance before the state parole board, Mickey Malevolent telephoned Charlene Choice, Ph.D., from prison. Mr. Malevolent explained that he was in the 8th year of a 20-year criminal sentence for child rape and ritualized sexual abuse of children and was now eligible to apply for an early release from prison. He explained that his case before the parole board would be helped if he could line up a psychotherapist to work with him after release. Mr. Malevolent noted that he was innocent of all wrongdoing, despite his conviction, but had been "framed" and "railroaded" by the parents of several "oversexed kids" and a legal system biased against his satanic religious beliefs. He went on to say that he really did not need therapy, but just wanted to show the authorities that he knew "how to play their game." When Dr. Choice declined to take him as a client, Mr. Malevolent filed an ethics complaint, claiming that Dr. Choice had unreasonably discriminated against him by not accepting him as a potential client or offering him a referral to another practitioner.

Dr. Choice was confronted with a self-referral from an individual whose conduct she found despicable. She has no ethical obligation to take any particular new client who calls for an appointment. She is free to turn down any such referral without giving a reason. In addition, she has ample reason to believe that Mr. Malevolent is not truly seeking treatment, but rather is seeking to manipulate the parole system. By his own statements, Mr. Malevolent presents himself as an individual who is unlikely to make appropriate use of psychotherapy and may be at high risk to offend again. In addition, she has no ethical or professional obligation to Mr. Malevolent and need not assist him locating another therapist. In fact, she would be doing a disservice to colleagues were she to pass their names on to Mr. Malevolent, who might mistakenly assume that the referral was a recommendation from her that they agree to work with him.

When a Client Threatens

The worst thing the therapist can do when a client becomes threatening is nothing. Do not assume that the threats will stop or go away spontaneously. All threats or acts of violence by clients should be taken seriously. This is a time to reassess the patient, the diagnosis, and the treatment plan. Violence may escalate over time, and verbal threats may progress to actions. Pay special attention to the client's history with respect to violence or acting out, but remember, although prior violence may be a predictor of future violence, there is always a first time. Make it clear to patients who verbally abuse or threaten that such behavior is unacceptable and could lead to termination of the relationship. Document all threats, your responses, and the rationales for your responses in your clinical record. Duties to warn and protect third parties are discussed in chapter 5, but the same action principles apply whether the threat is made to the therapist or others.

Clients who threaten are often overwhelmed by personal or family distress. Many have serious mental illness in addition to difficulty with impulse control, problems with anger control, or a history of antisocial behavior. Be mindful of the potential danger when taking on such clients, and be certain you are reasonably qualified to handle what may come up (Blau, 1987; Botkin & Nietzel, 1987). When conducting intake interviews with new or prospective clients, be sure to ask about difficulties in these areas. Consider asking, What is the most violent or destructive thing you have ever done?

When threats occur, obtain consultation on the case as soon as practical from your attorney and senior colleagues. Do not wait until an event occurs to hunt for such consultants. Draw up a list of names and telephone numbers of potential consultants and keep it available. State psychological associations can often be especially helpful in referring colleagues to attorneys in their geographic area who are familiar with psychological practice issues. Review your treatment plan and revise it to take into account the new developments. Consider a hierarchy of responses from least intrusive to more confrontational, keeping the safety of yourself and others in mind. Be certain that you are not alone in the office area or at a remote location when meeting with the client. If working in an institution, notify security personnel. When threats or actions occur outside the office, contact police. If work with the client is to continue, set clear rules regarding threatening behavior and consider increasing the frequency of sessions with a focus on rage and fear themes (Blau, 1987). Clinical competence, good diagnostic skills, an understanding of the confidentiality issues involved (see chapter 6), and careful advance planning are the best preventive measures.

Sometimes, there is simply not very much that a therapist can do to avoid becoming the victim of an angry client:

Case 4-22: Bertha Blitz had intermittently failed to keep or cancel several appointments with her psychotherapist, Vic Tem, Psy.D. After several warnings, Dr. Tem informed Ms. Blitz that he would have to begin charging a fee for missed sessions not properly canceled in advance. Blitz missed the next session without canceling, and at the subsequent kept appointment Dr. Tem reminded her that there would be a fee for the missed appointment. Ms. Blitz said that she had used the time to go to a smoking cessation group as Dr. Tem had urged her to do. Dr. Tem replied that her participation in the group was good, but did not make up for her failure to cancel their appointment. Ms. Blitz became angry, asked how much she owed for the missed session, wrote out a check, slammed it on the therapist's desk, and stormed out of the office. When Dr. Tem left the office 2 hours later, he found over 100 hammer dents in the hood and roof of his car. He had no proof that Ms. Blitz was responsible, but was strongly suspicious.

In this instance, there is little that Dr. Tem can do without evidence. At the same time, however, it appears that he may have missed an opportunity to deal with Ms. Blitz's anger in the office. We will never know whether direct efforts to engage her in conversation about her feelings of not being treated fairly might have prevented the mysterious automobile damage.

Failure to Terminate a Client Who Is Not Benefitting

This important obligation of the psychologist to the client, termination when treatment is no longer beneficial, was discussed in chapter 3, but warrants some special comment with respect to psychotherapy. Ethical problems related to the duration of treatment fall in this category. In the previous case examples, we discussed premature termination. But, what of the client who, by virtue of fostered dependency or other means, is encouraged to remain "in treatment" past the point of actual benefit? Such judgments are complicated by varying theoretical orientations. Some therapists would argue: "If you think you need therapy, then you probably do." Others might argue: "If you are sure you don't need it, then you definitely do."

We recognize such biases in many of our colleagues and could choose two of them on opposite ends of the continuum for a test. A person might be selected at random and sent to each for a consultation. One would probably find the person basically well adjusted, whereas the other would probably find the same person in need of treatment. One might presume that one or the other is unethical, either for suggesting treatment when none is needed or for dismissing a person prematurely who is in need of help, but neither is necessarily the case. If the psychologist presents the client with the reasons why treatment is or is not needed and proposes a specific goal-directed plan (Hare-Mustin et al., 1979), the client is in a position to make an informed choice. The therapist who sees emotional health may do so in the absence of symptoms, while the therapist recommending treatment may sense some unconscious issues or potential for improved functioning. These views can and ought to be shared with the client.

Ethical problems arise if the psychologist attempts to use the client's fears, insecurities, or dependency as a means of treatment when it is not needed. Consider these examples.

Case 4-23: Justin Funk has been quarreling with his spouse about relationships with in-laws and decides to consult a psychologist, Tyrone Mull,

Ph.D. A half-dozen sessions later, Mr. Funk believes that he has acquired some new insights into matters that upset him and some new ways of handling them. He is arguing less with his wife, thanks to Dr. Mull, and states his intent to terminate treatment. Mull acknowledges that progress has been made, but reminds Funk of many sources of stress in his past that have "not been fully worked through," hinting darkly that problems may recur.

Case 4-24: Brenda Schmooze has been in psychotherapy with Vivian Vain, Psy.D., for nearly 5 years. At the beginning of treatment, Ms. Schmooze was very unhappy with the hostile-dependent relationship she had developed with her intrusive mother. Schmooze had long since resolved those problems and was living independently, working in an office, and coping well in a general sense, although she remained an emotionally needy and lonely person. Her therapy sessions with Dr. Vain have generally entailed discussions of her activities, mixed with praise for Dr. Vain's help. There has been little change in Schmooze's social or emotional status for nearly 2 years.

Mr. Funk believes that he has gotten something out of psychotherapy but Dr. Mull's remark suddenly leaves him feeling somewhat anxious. Has he really made progress? Will he experience a "pathological regression" if he drops treatment now? Will his marriage deteriorate? Dr. Mull seems to be using his powerful position (i.e., as an expert) to hint that additional treatment is needed. This seems at variance with Funk's desires, but instead of outlining the basis of his impression and suggesting an alternative contract, Mull stirs Funk's insecurities in a diffuse and unethical manner.

Ms. Schmooze and Dr. Vain seem to have established a symbiotic relationship. Schmooze has acquired an attentive ear and Vain an admiring client. Some might say: "What's wrong with that, if it's what Schmooze wants? She's an adult and free to make her own choice." Unfortunately, it seems that Dr. Vain may have replaced Ms. Schmooze's mother as a dependency object. Schmooze may not be able to recognize this, but Dr. Vain ought to be sensitive to the problem. It might be that the relationship with Dr. Vain is preventing Ms. Schmooze from

forming more adaptive friendships outside treatment, for which she would not be paying. If Vain does not find treatment issues to raise and work on with Ms. Schmooze, she is ethically obligated to help the client work toward termination.

From time to time, legitimate doubts will arise as to a client's therapeutic needs. When this occurs, client and therapist should discuss the issues, and the client should probably be referred for a consultation with another practitioner. This procedure is also often useful when a client and therapist disagree on other major treatment issues.

Case 4-25: Ernest Angst had been in treatment with Donald Duration, Ed.D., intermittently over a 3-year period. Angst had many long-standing neurotic conflicts which he struggled with ambivalently. He began to wonder aloud in his sessions with Dr. Duration if therapy was doing him any good at all. Angst acknowledged that he wanted to work on his conflicts, but had mixed feelings about them. He expressed the thought that perhaps someone else could be of more help to him than Duration. Dr. Duration interpreted these comments as a means of avoiding other issues in treatment, but suggested that Angst should get a second opinion. He provided Angst with the names of several well-trained professionals in the community. Angst selected one and saw him for two sessions, following which both client and consultant decided that he should continue trying to address the difficult conflicts he felt with Dr. Duration, who knew him well and could help focus the work better than a new therapist could.

In this case, the client raised a legitimate issue, and the therapist had a contrary opinion. The therapist suggested a consultation in a nondefensive manner and assisted the client in obtaining it. In the end, the client returned to treatment with renewed motivation and reassured trust in his therapist.

SUMMARY GUIDELINES

1. Psychotherapists should strive to reach explicit understandings with their clients regarding the terms of the treatment contract,

whether formal or informal. This includes some mutual discussion about the goals of treatment and the means to achieve these goals.

2. Psychotherapists are obliged to consider carefully the unique needs and perspective of each client in formulating therapeutic plans. This includes special attention to issues of diversity, particularly race and social class issues relevant to the client.

3. A psychotherapist's personal beliefs, values, and attributes may limit his or her ability to treat certain types of clients. Therapists should strive for awareness of such characteristics and limit their practices appropriately.

4. In certain circumstances, clients have specific legal rights either to receive or to refuse treatment. Psychologists should be aware of these rights and respect the underlying principles, even when no specific laws are in force.

5. Therapists should strive to recognize their feelings with respect to each client, as well as the degree to which these feelings may interfere with therapy. When the client does not seem to be benefitting or the client's behavior is provocative, the therapist should promptly consider alternative courses of action.

References

American Psychological Association. (1975). Report of the Task Force on Sex Bias and Sex-Role Stereotyping in Psychotherapeutic Practice. *American Psychologist*, 30, 1169–1175.

American Psychological Association. (1978). Guidelines for therapy with women. *American Psychologist*, 33, 1222–1223.

American Psychological Association. (1991). *APA policy statements on lesbian and gay issues.* Washington, DC: Author.

American Psychological Association. (1992). Ethical principles of psychologists and code of conduct. *American Psychologist*, 47, 1597–1611.

American Psychological Association. (1993). Guidelines for providers of psychological services to ethnic, linguistic, and culturally diverse populations. *American Psychologist*, 48, 45–48.

Appelbaum, P. S., & Gutheil, T. G. (1980). Drug refusal: A study of psychiatric inpatients. *American Journal of Psychiatry*, 137, 340–345.

Blau, T. H. (1987). *Psychotherapy tradecraft.* New York: Bruner/Mazel.

Botkin, D., & Nietzel, M. (1987). How therapists manage potentially dangerous clients. *Professional Psychology: Research and Practice*, 18, 84–86.

Brown, L. S. (1994). *Subversive dialogues: Theory in feminist therapy.* New York: Basic Books.

Bugenthal, J. F. T. (1987). *The art of the psychotherapist.* New York: W. W. Norton.

Cohen, R. J., & Smith, F. J. (1976). Socially reinforced obsessing: Etiology of a disorder in a Christian Scientist. *Journal of Consulting and Clinical Psychology*, 44, 142–144.

Coyne, J. C. (1976). The place of informed consent in ethical dilemmas. *Journal of Consulting and Clinical Psychology*, 44, 1015–1017.

Dawes, R. M. (1994). *House of cards: Psychology and psychotherapy based on myth.* New York: Free Press.

Everstine, L., Everstine, D. S., Heymann, G. M., True, R. H., Frey, D. H., Johnson, H. G., & Seiden, R. H. (1980). Privacy and confidentiality in psychotherapy. *American Psychologist*, 35, 828–840.

Eysenck, H. J. (1952). The effects of psychotherapy: An evaluation. *Journal of Consulting Psychology*, 16, 319–324.

Ford, M. D. (1980). The psychiatrist's double bind: The right to refuse medication. *American Journal of Psychiatry*, 137, 332–339.

Freedheim, D. K. (Ed.). (1992). *History of psychotherapy: A century of change.* Washington, DC: American Psychological Association.

Garfield, S. L. (1981). Psychotherapy: A 40-year appraisal. *American Psychologist*, 36, 174–183.

Garfield, S. L. (1992). Major issues in psychotherapy research. In D. K. Freedheim (Ed.), *History of psychotherapy: A century of change* (pp. 335–359). Washington, DC: American Psychological Association.

Goode, E. E., & Wagner, B. (1993, May 24). *U.S. News & World Report*, pp. 56–65.

Grisso, T., & Vierling, L. (1978). Minors' consent to treatment: A developmental perspective. *Professional Psychology*, 9, 412–427.

Handelsman, M. M., Martinez, A., Geisendorfer,

S., & Jordan, L. (1995). Does legally mandated consent to psychotherapy ensure ethical appropriateness? The Colorado experience. *Ethics and Behavior, 5,* 119–129.

Hare-Mustin, R. T., Marecek, J., Kaplan, A. G., & Liss-Levenson, N. (1979). Rights of clients, responsibilities of therapists. *American Psychologist, 34,* 3–16.

Hays, P. A. (1995). Multicultural applications of cognitive-behavior therapy. *Professional Psychology: Research and Practice, 26,* 309–315.

Hurvitz, N. (1973). Psychotherapy as a means of social control. *Journal of Consulting and Clinical Psychology, 40,* 232–239.

Jones, C. B., Cohen, S. A., Munsat, P. E., Doris, J. F., & Berson, B. S. (1996). *Cost-effectiveness and feasibility of the DoD Psychopharmacology Demonstration Project: Final report.* Arlington, VA: Vector Research.

Kanoti, G. A. (1971). Ethical implications in psychotherapy. *Journal of Religion and Health, 10,* 180–191.

Karasu, T. B. (1980). The ethics of psychotherapy. *American Journal of Psychiatry, 137,* 1502–1512.

Kaschak, E. (1978). Therapist and client: Two views of the process and outcome of psychotherapy. *Professional Psychology, 9,* 271–278.

Koocher, G. P. (1983). Consent to psychotherapy. In G. B. Mellon, G. P. Koocher, & M. Saks (Eds.), *Children's competence to consent.* New York: Plenum.

Koocher, G. P., & Keith-Spiegel, P. C. (1990). *Children, ethics, and the law: Professional issues and cases.* Lincoln, NE: University of Nebraska Press.

Lehner, G. F. J. (1952). Defining Psychotherapy. *American Psychologist, 7,* 547.

Liss-Levenson, N., Hare-Mustin, R. T., Marecek, J., & Kaplan, A. G. (1980). The therapist's role in assuring client rights. *Advocacy Now,* March, 16–20.

Marshall, E. (1980). Psychotherapy faces test of worth. *Science, 207,* 35–36.

Melton, G. B., Koocher, G. P., & Saks, M. (Eds.). (1983). *Children's competence to consent.* New York: Plenum.

Miller, G. A. (1995). Strong medicine. *Psychological Science, 6,* 129–132.

Noll, J. O. (1976). The psychologist and informed consent. *American Journal of Psychiatry, 133,* 1451–1453.

Noll, J. O. (1981). Material risks and informed consent to psychotherapy. *American Psychologist, 36,* 916–918.

O'Connor v. Donaldson, 422 U.S. 575 (1975).

O'Leary, K. D., & Borkovec, T. D. (1978). Conceptual, methodological, and ethical problems of placebo groups in psychotherapy research. *American Psychologist, 33,* 821–830.

Schofield, W. (1964). *Psychotherapy: The purchase of friendship.* Englewood Cliffs, NJ: Prentice-Hall.

Seligman, M. E. P. (1995). The effectiveness of psychotherapy: The *Consumer Reports* study. *American Psychologist, 50,* 965–974.

Shapiro, A. K., & Struening, E. L. (1973). The use of placebos: A study of ethics and physicians' attitudes. *Psychiatry in Medicine, 4,* 17–29.

Strupp, H. H. (1975). On failing one's patient. *Psychotherapy: Theory, Research and Practice, 12,* 39–41.

Strupp, H. H. (1992). Overview: Psychotherapy research. In D. K. Freedheim (Ed.), *History of psychotherapy: A century of change* (pp. 309–310). Washington, DC: American Psychological Association.

Tatum, B. D. (1992). Talking about race, learning about racism: The application of racial identity development theory in the classroom. *Harvard Educational Review, 62,* 1–24.

Tharp, R. G. (1991). Cultural diversity and treatment of children. *Journal of Consulting and Clinical Psychology, 59,* 799–812.

Weithorn, L. A. (Ed.). (1987). *Psychology and child custody determinations: Knowledge, roles, & expertise.* Lincoln, NE: University of Nebraska Press.

White, M. D., & White, C. A. (1981). Involuntarily committed patients' constitutional right to refuse treatment: A challenge to psychology. *American Psychologist, 36,* 953–962.

Williams, M. H. (1985). The bait-and-switch tactic in psychotherapy. *Psychotherapy: Theory, Research and Practice, 22,* 110–113.

5

Ethics in Psychotherapy
Techniques

Some remedies are worse than the diseases.

Publilius Syrus

Just as chapter 4 focused on the basic obligations of psychotherapists to all clients, this chapter addresses technique-oriented issues in psychotherapeutic practice. The strategies and tactics of therapists differ widely across a range of psychological problems and client populations. Some approaches to psychological treatment demand highly specialized training and competencies and ethical considerations beyond basic doctoral-level skills. Certain special client circumstances may also require modification of a therapist's standard operating procedures. Thinking through the ethical dilemmas posed by such variations requires thoughtful planning, creativity, and ethical sensitivity.

THERAPIES INVOLVING MULTIPLE CLIENTS

In marital, family, and group therapies, the psychologist has more than one client in the session simultaneously. It is most unlikely that the best interests of every client in the treatment room will fully coincide with those of another. Especially in marital and family work, it is more often the case that the needs or wishes of one member are quite different from those of another. Competence in conducting group therapies also requires different techniques and training than individual psychotherapies (Lakin, 1994). Such therapies raise a host of other ethical issues, including matters of confidentiality and social coercion. In this section, we attempt to highlight some of the most common ethical dilemmas associated with multiple-client therapies.

Marital and Family Therapy

Ethical guidelines dealing with a therapist's responsibility to clients, confidentiality, informed consent, and client rights are certainly ambiguous at times when considering the interaction between one psychologist and one client. When a couple or multiple family members are involved in treatment, matters become even more complicated. Treatment will often involve a therapeutic obligation to several individuals with conflicting needs (Hare-Mustin, 1980; Hines & Hare-Mustin, 1978). Margolin (1982) cites several illustrations of such conflicts. She describes the mother who seeks treatment for her child so that he will be better behaved, which may ease pressure on the mother while not helping her child. Margolin (1982, p. 789) also cites the case of the wife whose goal is to surmount fears of terminating her marriage, whereas her husband's goal is to maintain the status quo. A therapist in such situations must strive to ensure that improvement in the status of one family member does not occur at the expense of another. When such an outcome may be unavoidable (e.g., in the case of the couple whose treatment may result in the decision of one or both partners to seek a divorce), the psychologist should advise the couple of that potential outcome early in the course of treatment. In this type of situation, the therapist's personal values and theoretical orientation are of critical importance (Hare-Mustin, 1978, 1980; Hines & Hare-Mustin, 1978; L'Abate, 1982; Margolin, 1982) (see chapter 4).

Case 5-1: Hugo Home, Psy.D., likes to consider himself a "gentleman of the old school" who holds the door open for women, tips his hat when passing them on the street, and is generally quite deferential to the "fair sex." In conducting family therapy, however, Dr. Home has a clear bias, favoring the view of women in the wife-mother role. He believes that mothers of children under 12 should not work outside the home and frequently asks his female clients who seem depressed or irritable whether it is their "time of the month again." Dr. Home does not recognize how these biases might adversely affect the female partner in marital counseling.

Case 5-2: Ramona Church, Ed.D., is a family therapist and a devout member of a religious group that eschews divorce under any circumstances. She continues to encourage her clients in marital therapy to work with her, "grow up," and "cease acting out immature fantasies," even when both partners express some serious consideration of divorce. She will often tell clients who have worked with her for several months that they will have

failed in treatment and that she will have no more to do with them if they choose divorce.

Both Drs. Home and Church have clear biases and seem either oblivious to their impact or self-righteously assertive of them. They fail to recognize fully the power and influence they wield as psychotherapists and their responsibility to clients as a result. Neither should be treating couples in marital therapy, at least not without a clear warning from the outset about their biases. Dr. Church's threat to abandon any of her clients who stray from the personal values she prescribes is particularly dangerous. The vulnerable and insecure client, especially, will be prone to harm at the hands of such therapists. Hines and Hare-Mustin (1978) highlight the "myth of valueless thinking" and enjoin therapists to carefully attend to the impact that their own values and stereotypes may have on their work.

Two decades ago, the APA Task Force on Sex Bias and Sex-Role Stereotyping (1975) found that family therapists are particularly vulnerable to certain biases. These included the assumption that remaining in a marriage represents the better adjustment for a woman and a tendency to defer to the husband's needs over those of the wife. The same report noted the tendency to demonstrate less interest in or sensitivity to a woman's career as opposed to a man's and the perpetuation of the belief that child rearing and children's problems are primarily in the woman's domain. The report also cited that therapists tended to hold a double standard in response to the extramarital affairs of a wife versus those of a husband. Although we believe that conditions have improved significantly since the report was issued, it is important that psychologists be aware of the historical problem as an illustration of the need for sensitivity to such issues.

Several authors have noted that the prevailing "therapeutic ideology" holds that all persons can and should benefit from therapy (Hines & Hare-Mustin, 1978). Some family therapists also insist that all members of the family must participate in treatment (Hare-Mustin, 1980; Hines & Hare-Mustin, 1978; Margolin, 1982). What does this do to a person's right to decline treatment? Must the reluctant adolescent or adult be pressured into attending sessions at the behest of the psychotherapist? Data suggest children as young as 14 are as competent as adults in making decisions about treatment (Grisso & Vierling, 1978), yet it is unclear how often such family members are offered a truly voluntary choice.

Case 5-3: Ronald McRigid, Ph.D., a family psychologist, was consulted by Harold and Anita Hassol. The Hassols had three children ranging in age from 12 to 18. The youngest child had been acting out and was recently arrested for destroying school property. The juvenile court judge recommended family counseling. The Hassol's oldest child had no interest in participating, but both parents and the two younger children (including the identified client) were willing to attend sessions. Dr. McRigid informed the Hassols that he would not treat them unless everyone attended every session.

Coercion of any reluctant family member to participate in treatment would be unethical. This does not preclude a therapist's urging that the resistant family member attend at least one trial session or attempting to address the underlying reasons for the refusal. The therapist who strongly believes that the whole family must be seen should not use coercion to drag in the reluctant member, nor should such therapists permit that reluctant member to deny treatment to the family members who wish to have it. In such cases, the therapist should be willing to provide the names of other professionals in the community who might be willing to treat the group desiring treatment. When the client in question is a minor child, the therapist has a special duty to consider that client's needs as distinct from those of the parents (Koocher, 1976, 1983; Simmonds, 1976).

Still another issue that complicates marital and family therapy is the matter of confidentiality. Should a therapist tolerate secret keeping or participate in it? Should parents be able to sign away a child's right to confidentiality (Hare-Mustin, 1980)? The concept and conditions of confidentiality are somewhat different in the family context than as discussed in chapter 6. Often, couples may have difficulty in establishing boundaries and privacy with respect to their own lives and those of their children (Hines & Hare-Mustin, 1978; Margolin, 1982). Adult clients can, and should, be able to assert some privacy with respect to their marriage and to avoid burdening their children with information that is frightening, provocative, or simply beyond their ability to comprehend adequately. On the other hand, there are many attempts to maintain secrets that are manipulative and do not serve the general goals of treatment.

The most reasonable way to handle this matter ethically is to formulate a policy based on therapeutic goals and define the policy to all concerned at the outset of treatment. Some therapists may state at the beginning of therapy that they will keep no secrets. Others may be willing to accept information shared in confidence to help the person offering it determine whether or not it is appropriate for discussion in the whole group. Still another option would be to discuss the resistance to sharing the information with the member in question, with the goal of helping that person to share the information with the family, if indicated. Secret keeping presents the added burden of recalling which secret came from whom, not to mention the need to recall what was "secret" and what was not. The therapist who does not consider these matters in advance and does not discuss them early with family clients is asking for serious ethical dilemmas within a very short time.

Group Therapy

Psychotherapists may treat unrelated clients in groups for a variety of reasons, ranging from simple economy to specialized treatment plans. For example, a group may consist of people with similar problems, such as recently hospitalized mental patients, divorced males, women with eating disorders, bereaved parents, or children with handicaps. In such groups, the identified clients gather to address similar emotional or social problems in a common supportive context. Other groups may focus on enhancing personal growth or self-awareness, as opposed to addressing personal psychodynamics or psychopathology. Rogers (1970) offered a sample listing of group types, including so called "T-groups," encounter groups, sensitivity groups, task-oriented groups, sensory awareness or body awareness groups, organizational development groups, team-building groups, victim groups, perpetrator groups, and Gestalt groups.

Group treatment has considerable potential for both good and harm. The influence and support of peers in the treatment process may facilitate gains that would be slow or unlikely in individual treatment. The group may also become a special therapeutic ecology within which special insights and awareness may develop. At the same time, however, there are significant hazards to group members when the group leader is not properly trained or is unable to adequately monitor the experience for all members. Pressures toward cohesion and emotional expressiveness common in group therapy can be inappropriate for some clients (Lakin, 1994). The group therapist has much less control over the content and direction of the session than does the individual therapist. As a result, there is greater potential for individuals in the group to have unfavorable or adverse experiences. Problems might include stresses resulting from confrontation, criticism, threats to confidentiality, or even development of dependency on the group. In many ways, the risk of harm to individual clients is greater in group than individual therapies (Corey, Williams, & Moline, 1995).

Our discussion here focuses on two sets of related issues, the first regarding groups intended as psychotherapy experiences and then on that subset of group programs intended as growth experiences. The last term is used in reference to short-term group experiences in which individual development or growth, rather than psychopathology, is the focus. We shall use the term *group therapy* to generally discuss treatment for people seeking help in response to specific emotional or psychological symptoms; the treatment is usually over a period of months or years rather than days or weeks as in the growth experience programs.

The somewhat dated APA "Guidelines for Psychologists Conducting Growth Groups" (1973) make several important points that can be categorized as mandates for the psychologist leader to provide informed consent, ensure that participation is fully voluntary, conduct proper screening of participants, and carefully differentiate roles based on whether the group is intended to be therapeutic or educational. These guidelines make it evident that the responsibility for these obligations rests on the psychologist leading the group.

Case 5-4: The president of a small manufacturing company was so excited about the insights he acquired in a weekend marathon therapy session conducted by Grover Grouper, Ed.D., that he hired Grouper to run such a session for his executive staff and ordered them all to participate.

Case 5-5: Lena Lonely was a socially isolated freshman at a large state college. She joined an 8-week "encounter group" run by Vivian Speedo, Ph.D., at the college counseling center. Ms. Lonely hoped that the group experience would help to remedy her social isolation. When the group sessions ended 8 weeks later, Lonely was disillusioned by her lack of accomplishment and despaired over what she perceived as her inadequacies. She dropped out of school.

Case 5-6: Fernando Frank, Psy.D., is a strong proponent of the "tell it like it is" school of therapy. In the first meeting of a new group, Dr. Frank focused attention on Jack Small, encouraging Small to reveal some intimate detail of his life to the group. Mr. Small shared such a detail, only to have Frank and the other group members focus on it and highlight the personal inadequacies it implied. Small never returned to the group and was admitted to a mental hospital 2 weeks later, experiencing severe depression.

All three of these cases suggest inadequacies in preparation, screening, orientation, and follow-through by the psychologist in question. Dr. Grouper, for example, in agreeing to conduct the group, seems to have overlooked the coercion involved in demanding that the staff attend. Both the nature and goals of the group are unclear. If it is intended as therapy, then the failure to screen potential participants for appropriateness and the enforced participation (or even voluntary participation) of people who work together raises serious questions with regard to individual privacy and therapeutic merit. If the goals of the group are educative, it still behooved Grouper to screen participants carefully and ensure that no coercion, however subtle, was involved in their decisions. Parker (1976) reports the somewhat radical views of Schultz (1971) that each person in the group is solely responsible for himself. "You have your choice. If you want to bow to pressure or resist it, go crazy, get physically injured, stay or leave or whatever, it's up to you." Parker rightly recognizes this philosophy as one that leads to high-risk groups and a dangerous laissez-faire leadership style. However trendy or attractive this may seem, it is dangerous and presents the potential of serious harm to clients.

Lieberman, Yalom, and Miles (1973) list many participant vulnerability factors therapists must consider in constructing and conducting groups. The factors include vulnerability to aggression, fragile self-esteem, excessive dependency needs, intense fears of rejection, withdrawal, transference to the group leader, internal conflicts aroused by group discussions, unreal expectations, and guardedness. In many ways, the group therapist's ethical burden is far greater than that of the individual therapist because the psychologist conducting group therapy must consider the psychological ecology of the therapy or program as it affects a variety of different participants. An excellent overview of the clinical issues and ethical nuances in conducting group psychotherapy presented across professional associations is provided by Corey et al. (1995).

The matters of confidentiality and privileged communication in group psychotherapy are also an important issue. Although these are generally discussed in chapter 6, the group context adds a new variable to the equation since, by definition, more than two people are in a position to disclose a confidence learned in the session (i.e., the therapist and at least one other client). After reviewing chapter 6, the reader will recognize the differences between privilege and confidentiality. In most jurisdictions, no statutory privilege extends to material disclosed in group sessions to client members of the group (Slovenko, 1977). The therapist should therefore advise clients in two ways early in the group treatment process. First, the clients must be cautioned about the lack of legal protections (i.e., privilege) regarding information disclosed. Second, the therapist should encourage recognition of the importance to all group members of a mutually respectful duty of confidentiality so far as what each member says in the course of treatment.

Slovenko (1977) notes that therapists tend to be far more concerned about issues of confidentiality than are members of the group. One wonders whether clients in group treatment should reasonably be aware that gossip about sensitive material revealed in sessions may be communicated to others outside the group by their peers. As a result, clients might be expected to censor material about which they are particularly sensitive. Even so, the pressures toward self-disclosure in group therapy or even experiential growth programs may be very intense, and therapists should have these issues in mind as the group sessions proceed.

SPECIAL TECHNIQUES AND ISSUES

Under the general heading of psychotherapy, there are a number of special issues or techniques that have attracted sufficient numbers of ethics inquiries over time to warrant specific discussion. These include the issue of triage and intake procedures, as well as techniques associated with sex therapy, behavior modification, the use of psychological devices, so-called coercive treatment techniques, and electronic media. The reasons why such matters attract special ethical concerns are in part a function of the sensational nature of the context or style within which they are applied and in part a function of the special social concerns associated with the treatment issue (e.g., sexual practices and sex therapy or civil rights and coercive treatment programs).

Triage and Intake

Triage is a concept, frequently applied in medical emergency situations, referring to a priority assignment to certain patients waiting to be seen. For example, a patient who has stopped breathing or who is hemorrhaging will be seen immediately, even if other less severely injured patients must wait for an extended period in pain and discomfort. Likewise, a clinic with a long psychotherapy waiting list might move a suicidal client to the head of the line for treatment because of the urgent nature of the problem. At times, however, clients are not informed of such priorities, even if reasonable, with the result that the client may suffer needlessly rather than seeking an alternative treatment. In some instances, the system of priorities or intake procedures themselves may be ethically questionable.

Case 5-7: Midtown Psychological Associates, Incorporated, is a private group practice consisting of several licensed psychologists. To keep all available appointment times filled, the secretary is instructed to keep a waiting list of at least 8 to 10 clients. Potential clients seeking an intake appointment are told that they are being put on a short waiting list and will be called for an appointment soon, even if there are no openings in the foreseeable future.

Case 5-8: The Central City Community Mental Health Center (CMHC) had a 4-week backlog for intake assessments and a policy that only emergency cases could be taken out of order. Nicholas Bluster, the mayor of Central City, telephoned the psychologist who directed the CMHC seeking an immediate appointment for his adolescent son, who had been "mouthing off at home." The psychologist placed Junior Bluster at the head of the list.

Both of these cases demonstrate unethical setting of priorities, which is detrimental to some clients. In the case of Psychological Associates, the people waiting for appointments should be advised of the potential duration of their wait and offered the opportunity to be referred elsewhere. An indefinite hold on the waiting list could be reasonable if the potential client were advised of the details and chose to wait, but the situation described above is misleading. The director of the CMHC was clearly responding to political expedience. Perhaps Junior Bluster is in need of services and entitled to them; however, moving him ahead of others on the list is

unethical unless it is clear that an emergency intervention is required. The director could have met the political social demands of the situation in many appropriate ways, such as offering a referral elsewhere or making time available personally to assist the Blusters, while not delaying services to others in need.

Sex Therapy

The very use of the word *sex* immediately captures the attention of an adult audience, and when the term *sex therapy* is used, most mental health professionals think only of the most common presenting symptoms (e.g., erectile dysfunction, premature ejaculation, anorgasmia, dyspareunia, vaginismus, and loss of interest in sexual activity). There are, however, a variety of other problems that might become the focus of sex therapy. These include hysterical conversion reactions with a sexual focus, paraphilias (e.g., exhibitionism, pedophilia, and voyeurism), gender dysphoria syndromes (e.g., transsexualism), physical developmental disorders (e.g., hypospadias), disease-related disorders, and problems resulting from medical side effects, surgery, or traumatic injury to the sex organs (Meyer, 1976; Rosen & Leiblum, 1995a, 1995b). Some clients may also present with varying degrees of concern about sexual functioning and homosexuality.

The American Association of Sex Educators, Counselors, and Therapists (AASECT, 1980) and the Association of Sexual and Marital Therapists (ASMT, 1986) have published codes of ethics and training guidelines for individuals practicing in this specialized field. These codes and other writings on sex therapies (e.g., Brown & Field, 1988; Crowe, 1995; Hill, 1992; Rosen & Leiblum, 1995a, 1995b) highlight the complexity of the social, psychological, anatomic, and physiological factors that may be involved in sexual problems. As these complexities illustrate, special skills and ethical sensitivities are required in this field of practice. Often, the style and substance of clinically appropriate sex therapy will differ dramatically from other therapeutic activities. For example, Lowery and Lowery claim that the most ethical sex therapy is that "which cures the symptom and improves the marital relationship in the briefest time and at the least cost" (1975, p. 229). They also specify that neither insight-oriented treatment nor sex with the client satisfy these criteria. Clearly, special credentials are in order for any practitioners who desire to provide treatment for sexual dysfunction (ASMT, 1986; Bancroft, 1991; Brown & Field, 1988).

Emotional reactions linked to the nature of the problems treated are not limited to the general public. A fascinating debate began in the professional literature with the publication of a study describing highly specific behaviorally oriented masturbation procedures for anorgasmic women (Zeiss, Rosen, & Zeiss, 1977). This was followed by a critique entitled "Psychotherapy or Massage Parlor Technology?" (Bailey, 1978), which invoked ethical, moral, and philosophical (as well as social psychological) reasoning. This was followed by a comment describing Bailey's critique as "antiscientific" (Wagner, 1978), followed subsequently by a reasoned critique noting that value-free therapy does not exist and enjoining the therapist to involve the client fully in goal setting while conducting the least intrusive treatment (Wilson, 1978).

Therapists may also find themselves caught between members of a couple with very different sexual goals and expectations. For example, Wylie, Crowe, and Boddington (1995) report on the ethical problems that arose when a couple presented for sex therapy to address the wife's sexual reluctance, particularly in relation to conflicts over the husband's demands for anal sex.

Perhaps the most dramatic focus of concern in the evolution of practice in sex therapy involves the use of sexual surrogates—sexual partners used by some mental health professionals to assist certain clients by engaging in a variety of social and sexual activities for a fee. The use of surrogates is far more than a prescription for prostitution (Jacobs, Thompson, & Truxaw, 1975). Although initially used by Masters and Johnson with some single clients, the actual use of sex surrogates is today a more rare and atypical technique, with more attention being paid to a host of other issues and techniques (Masters & Johnson, 1976; Rosen & Leiblum, 1995a, 1995b). Still, some therapists may be tempted to use surrogates from time to time, although this may lead to substantial ethical and legal complications.

In some states, a mental health professional who refers a client to a sex surrogate may be liable for criminal prosecution. Some state laws could lead to prosecution under prostitution statutes and antifornication laws, or even under rape charges, should some aspect of the relationship go wrong or come to the attention of a zealous district attorney. A variety of potential civil liabilities or tort actions are possible if one spouse objects to the other's use of a surrogate or if the client contracts a sexually transmitted disease from or transmits one to the surrogate. In such cases, the referring practitioner may have a vicarious liability and will generally find his or her liability insurer unwilling to cover the resulting claim. In the case of the AIDS virus, the costs of this type of "treatment" can be especially high.

Case 5-9: Lorna Loose worked as a receptionist and secretary to Cecil Thud, Ph.D. Dr. Thud approached her about acting as a sexual surrogate for some of his male clients. Ms. Loose agreed and allegedly enjoyed the work sufficiently that she began to offer such services on a freelance basis in addition to her work with Thud's clients. Subsequently, her ex-spouse sued for custody of their two children, citing her work as "a prostitute" in court. Loose allegedly sought emotional and documentary support from Thud and later claimed that he seduced her.

Case 5-10: George Trotter, Psy.D., employed one male and three female assistants with masters degrees in counseling fields to work in his clinic. His specialization was sex therapy, and he would occasionally refer some of his clients to one of the assistants, who was to act as a sexual surrogate. Trotter reasoned that he was behaving appropriately since the surrogates were trained in counseling and were not the therapists of the specific clients in question. Ultimately, Dr. Trotter was prosecuted on prostitution charges, and fraud charges were filed by an insurance company, which claimed that Trotter had billed the sex sessions with his assistants as psychotherapy.

These dramatic cases are illustrative of the blurring of roles and values that often seems to occur when sexual surrogates are being employed, as well as some of the complex problems that may develop. Dr. Thud denied ever having had sex with Ms. Loose, although he did acknowledge recruiting her as a sex surrogate and admitted that this role later caused her considerable personal difficulty. It caused him difficulty as well when she sued him and won a substantial award in a highly publicized trial. Dr. Trotter was at best ethically insensitive and careless in his conclusion that the use of his assistants, however willing, was not a conflict-ridden situation. His decision to bill these visits as compensable services, when he had been given clear information that they were not covered by the insurance company, constituted strong evidence of fraud. Although the prostitution charges were ultimately dropped, a substantial amount of harmful publicity deeply troubled the more appropriate and conservative sex therapists in the community.

Sexual behavior is an emotionally charged, value-laden aspect of human life, and therapists working actively at altering such behavior must be appropriately cautious and sensitive to both community and professional standards. In such areas of practice, haphazard ethical practices and indiscretions are much more likely to lead to major problems for the client and practitioner than in almost any other realm.

Behavior Modification

As in the case of sex therapy, the application of behavioral techniques such as operant conditioning, classical conditioning, aversive therapies, and other types of physical interventions (e.g., physiological monitoring, biofeedback, stress management, etc.) require specialized training of an interdisciplinary nature (Martin & Pear, 1996). This may include training in anatomy and physiology, as well as the analysis of behavior and application of learning theory. In addition, a keen awareness of one's limitations

is also needed, as illustrated by knowing when a medical consultation is indicated or when a certain instrumental procedure may edge toward the violation of a client's rights.

The application of behavioral techniques usually involves the assumption of a substantial degree of control over the client's environment. Generally, this takes place with the active involvement and consent of the client (Martin & Pear, 1996). In some instances, however, the client may be technically or literally incompetent to consent, as in the case of mentally retarded or severely psychotic clients. When the client is incompetent to fully consent and powerful environmental controls are enforced, special substituted judgment procedures using independent advocates may be needed (Koocher, 1976, 1983).

From time to time, there have been outcries in the mass media about the application of behavioral techniques in schools, prisons, and other settings. Many have called for, produced, or rebutted the need for specialized guidelines to be used in applying behavioral techniques (Davidson & Stuart, 1975; Geller, Johnson, Hamlin, & Kennedy, 1977; Stolz, 1977; Thaw, Thorne, & Benjamin, 1978; Turkat & Forehand, 1980). We find that behavioral therapies are no more or less in need of regulation per se than other forms of treatment also subject to abuse. As Stolz notes, behavioral clinicians, like other therapists, should be governed by the ethics code of their professions; also, the ethics of all intervention programs should be evaluated in terms of a number of critical issues (ES: 1.07, 1.23, 2.02).

Specific complaints regarding behavior therapies commonly encountered by ethics committees are illustrated by these cases:

Case 5-11: Gordon Convert, Ed.D., agreed to treat Billy Prissy, age 5, whose parents were concerned about his "effeminate" behaviors. Dr. Convert devised a behavioral program for implementation in the office and at home involving the differential reinforcement of toy choice, dress-up play, and a variety of other activities of a stereotyped sex-role nature. When reports of this project were published in professional journals, a storm of protest resulted.

Case 5-12: Seymour Diversion, Ph.D., worked in a state hospital for children with emotional problems. He designed a specialized program that applied aversive stimulation (e.g., brief application of an electric shock rod) to interrupt self-injurious behavior in a head-banging child. The child had caused permanent damage to one eye and was in danger of losing the other as well. Less drastic means of interrupting the behavior had failed. A nurse at the hospital was outraged and informed local newspapers of how Dr. Diversion was "torturing" the child.

Case 5-13: Thelma Splatter, Psy.D., designed an aversive treatment program to deal with severely retarded residents of a state school, who were toileting in public on the grounds of the school or in corridors. The program involved an operant reward system, as well as a spray of ice water in the face, administered from a small squirting bottle. Some of the attendants were inadequately trained in the rationale and application of the technique. One evening, an attendant caught a male resident of the school smearing feces and pushed the man's face into a toilet bowl, while flushing it several times. He reported that he did not have the spray bottle with him.

The case of Dr. Convert is typical of those complaints that revolve around the matter of client choice and goal setting in therapy. It is not possible to tell from the brief information we have given here just how appropriate or inappropriate the program was. The context and nature of decision making and treatment goal setting are critical (Stolz, 1978). In this case, Billy's viewpoint demands just as much consideration as the preferences expressed by his parents. These issues are well illustrated in a series of comments to a manuscript on alternatives to pain medication (Cook, 1975; Goodstein, 1975; Karoly, 1975). The original report focused on a 65-year-old man admitted to a psychiatric ward with symptoms of chronic abdominal pain and a self-induced drug habit to control the pain (Levendusky & Pankratz, 1975). He was successfully withdrawn from the drug using a treatment procedure that involved some deception and lacked fully informed consent. The ethical dilemma here is the matter of client involvement

in making choices, rather than the technique itself.

Dr. Diversion was asked to respond to an ethics committee and did so with openness and in detail. Several less invasive attempts to prevent the child from destroying his remaining eye by head banging had been unsuccessful. A special panel had been asked to review the case and approve the trial of aversive techniques independently of Dr. Diversion and the hospital. Diversion managed the program personally and noted that he had been prepared to discontinue the use of aversive stimuli promptly if no benefit was resulting for the child. The committee agreed that every appropriate precaution had been taken, and that Diversion had behaved appropriately, given the severe nature of the child's self-injury.

Dr. Splatter's program may have been adequately conceptualized, but it was poorly implemented. The attendant clearly did not discriminate between the intended shock value of the ice-water spray and the sadistic and punitive act of holding a person's face in the toilet. The unethical behavior here was chiefly Splatter's failure to adequately supervise the people charged with executing her treatment program. If she were unable to adequately supervise all of those participating in the program she designed, then she should have limited the scope of the program to those she could adequately supervise. Although the attendant was responsible for his own behavior, Dr. Splatter may have inadvertently provided a context within which the act seemed appropriate to him.

During a conversation hour at an APA meeting several years ago, the late B. F. Skinner was talking bemusedly about the controversy that seemed to focus on labels as opposed to practice. He noted that a school board had promulgated a threat to fire any personnel who used behavior modification. He then wondered aloud what would happen the next payday when the "reinforcements" were handed out in the form of paychecks. This illustrated once again that it is not the technique itself that presents the ethical problem, but the manner in which it is applied and labeled.

Unfortunately, not all psychologists who attempt to employ behavioral techniques are well trained in underlying learning theory. Confusion on the distinction between the concepts of "punishment" and "negative reinforcement" is one example of a common problem. In other instances, aversive treatment protocols have occasionally been introduced without first trying less restrictive techniques.

It is especially important that psychologists show careful concern for ethical problems inherent in the use of aversive stimuli with relatively powerless clients. This would include, for example, institutionalized, incarcerated, or incompetent individuals, as well as children or other people not fully able to assert their rights.

Case 5-14: Marquis deSique, Ph.D., operated a private residential facility for emotionally disturbed and delinquent children. The parents of a 10-year-old boy filed ethics charges when they discovered multiple bruises and lacerations all over their son's body during a visit. Dr. deSique explained that the boy required several beating sessions each week to "break his strong will" and permit more appropriate behavior to emerge. It was later discovered that all of the residents were routinely subjected to such sessions, conducted in a specially equipped punishment room. In addition, Dr. deSique would also take nude photographs of them following the beatings.

This sort of case causes sensitive, objective, and competent behavioral psychologists outrage because Dr. deSique's "treatments" do not conform to standards of professional practice or ethics. The practices also have no basis in empirical data or learning theory. It seems more likely that deSique was satisfying some peculiar needs of his own at the expense of his vulnerable wards.

Psychological Devices

The report of the APA Task Force on Psychologists' Use of Physical Interventions (1981) lists more than a score of instruments and devices used by psychologists for clinical assessment and psychotherapy. These include a variety of electrodes and monitors used in biofeedback training, as well as an assortment of color vision testers, dynamometers, audiometers, restraints,

and even vibrators. Some of these devices are regulated by the U.S. Food and Drug Administration, and most require specialized training. Detailed suggestions for the use of such devices have been published by R. L. Schwitzgebel (1970) and R. K. Schwitzgebel (1978) and Fuller (1978). Psychotherapists have also been involved in discussing problems associated with the use of lie detectors (Lykken, 1974; Szucko & Kleinmuntz, 1981) and suicide prevention by means of computer-mediated therapy (Barnett, 1982).

The use of technology in the future of psychotherapy is likely to increase and along with it ethical complaints of a related nature. Skip ahead to the case of Dr. Anna Sthesia (Case 15-19) for an example of technology-related negligence. The basic caveat is that psychologists should recognize the boundaries of their competence, especially when attempting to make use of new technologies. They must avoid using unsafe or unproven devices, not to mention those that might prove dangerous to clients through electric shock or other hazards. Psychologists must also be mindful that they are not physicians and should never attempt treatment of problems with possible organic causes without a collaborative relationship with a qualified physician. In addition, federal law may govern the licensing and use of some instruments, and psychologists are obligated to keep themselves abreast of these statutes and resulting duties.

Coercive Therapies

As noted first section of in this chapter, psychotherapy has sometimes been considered a means of social control (Hurvitz, 1973) and has been compared in some ways with brainwashing (Dolliver, 1971; Gaylin, 1974). The use of "coercive persuasion," "deprogramming," and hypnotic suggestion techniques (Fromm, 1980; Kline, 1976) have all been discussed from the viewpoint of client manipulation. That is, to what extent do certain psychological techniques permit the psychotherapist to manipulate or control the client by force or threat? In chapter 4, we discussed the right to refuse treatment, and we cite these issues here as examples of techniques that from time to time have been the object of complaints.

In general, it is unethical for a psychotherapist to coerce a client into treatment or to force certain goals or outcomes against the client's wishes. In chapter 14, we discuss some special problem situations along these lines (e.g., clients who are in the military or are involuntarily confined in institutions such as prisons). The subtler aspects of coercion are the most difficult to be sensitive to: group pressure, guilt induction, introduction of cognitive dissonance, attempts at total environmental control, and the establishment of a trusting relationship with the goal of effecting change in another person (Dolliver, 1971). It is critical that the psychotherapist attempt to remain aware of potentially coercive influences and avoid any that do not offer full participation, discussion, and choice by the client. The constant critical reexamination of the strategies and goals of treatment involving both client and therapist is the best means to this end.

Psychotherapy and Electronic Media

With the advent of the "electronic superhighway," telecommunications technology has taken us to the point at which new media are being used to deliver services intended to be psychotherapeutic in nature. We reserve judgment as to whether these modes of delivery will come to be accepted as psychotherapy.

Would you pay as much as $180 for 45 minutes of psychotherapy by telephone? That is what it can cost according to one press account (Carton, 1994). Several such services now operate using either 1-900, pay-by-the-minute lines, or toll-free numbers that require callers to provide a valid credit card number before they are connected to a therapist.

In April 1993, the APA Ethics Committee (1993) issued a policy statement about psychotherapy by telephone. The APA ethics code is not specific regarding that practice, and there are no rules prohibiting such telephone services or the use of 1-900 numbers. The APA Ethics Committee noted that any complaints received about such services would be handled on a case-by-case basis. The committee also noted that telephone contact can be an important and beneficial tool, citing the well-established success of suicide hot lines, brief crisis and referral services, or provision of educational messages by telephone. However, the committee noted that the use of the telephone for ongoing psychotherapy is an emerging area, not to be confused with "media psychology." As such, psychologists participating in such services would be expected to observe all applicable professional standards (for example, EP: A, C; ES: 1.04, 1.14, 1.20, 1.23, 4.04, 5). In addition, psychologists would need to consider issues of confidentiality and any state regulations that might apply. In essence, the APA Ethics Committee avoided the opportunity to initiate standards that could influence psychologists proactively.

Insurance companies have not waited for guidance from the APA. They will generally not cover the cost of such services, and many legal and ethical questions about them remain unresolved. For example, there is no clear regulatory authority for services. Consider the possibilities from this case example:

Case 5-15: Neuro Transmitter, Psy.D., works in Paramus, New Jersey, and provides services through a service known as 1-900-SHRINK-ME of Dallas, Texas. One afternoon he is connected by phone with a new caller to the service. She is Ann Hedonia of Simi Valley, California. After 20 minutes of the session, Dr. Transmitter recognizes that Ms. Hedonia is seriously depressed with suicidal ideation and is feeling at the edge of her ability to cope. He gently suggests that perhaps she ought to think about hospitalization near her home. Ms. Hedonia replies, "Even you don't care about me! That's it. I'm going to do it!" and slams down the telephone receiver.

How does one conduct an adequate assessment over the telephone to enable formulation of an adequate treatment plan? How does one intervene in the event of suicidal or homicidal ideation? How does one ensure privacy from electronic eavesdropping or simple monitoring by someone over an extension phone? Suppose Ms. Hedonia has a complaint about Dr. Transmitter. From whom can she seek a remedy? Which state's law applies for professional practice, confidentiality, or licensing qualifications? Must Dr. Transmitter even be licensed to offer this service? Arguably, such therapy is interstate commerce, so no single state's laws (and licensing board) may have clear authority. What remedies does an aggrieved client have?

Similar issues apply to a plethora of new services being offered on the Internet and World Wide Web. One service invites people to submit questions, which will be answered privately within 48 hours "by a person with at least a master's degree in counseling." That service charges according to the byte size of the reply, possibly inviting the longest replies the consultant can generate. Another service offers to answer individual questions for a flat $20 fee and provides a listing of half a dozen doctoral-level clinicians who will field the items submitted. Still a third services invites participants to a private real-time dialogue with a therapist via a computerized bulletin board "chat line" service. All invite payment by credit card, and all raise the same questions as the pay-per-minute telephone service, plus a few more.

Case 5-16: Following his disconnect from Ann Hedonia, Dr. Transmitter checks in with PSYCH-AUTIX, Incorporated, an E-mail network for mental health practitioners. He finds a private posting from one of his clients, Art Tonomy, who sent the message by Internet from his workstation at the accounting firm of Dewey, Cheatem, and Howe. Mr. Tonomy is feeling somewhat guilty about a secret extramarital affair he is having with the wife of one of the senior partners. He is looking for some confidential help. Mr. Tonomy is unaware that the accounting firm has established an "echo capture system" that records all incoming and outgoing messages as redundant protection against loss. In reviewing the external E-mail traffic next week, the head of computer security will find Mr. Tonomy's message and call it to the senior partner's attention. There is nothing illegal about doing so.

In this situation, Dr. Transmitter could not provide warnings about this limitation on privacy or confidentiality because he had no idea of the system from which the message came.

Telehealth is a term now being used in medicine for a variety of models for providing professional services via telephone and videoconferencing. Radiology and cardiology are just two of many medical specialties that have been regularly using these techniques for consultation. In recognition of the increasing involvement of psychologists in such services, the APA Ethics Committee updated its 1993 statement on telephone therapy with a new statement, *Services by Telephone, Teleconferencing, and Internet* (APA Ethics Committee, 1995). The statement pointed out that many of the current ethical standards apply to such work by psychologists, including sections on assessment (ES: 2.01–2.10), psychotherapy (ES: 4.01–4.09, especially 4.01 and 4.02 on structuring the relationship and informed consent, respectively), and confidentiality (ES: 5.01–5.11). General standards addressing the professional and scientific relationship also apply, including (ES: 1.03), boundaries of competence (ES: 1.04a–1.04c), basis of scientific and professional relationship (ES: 1.06), description of services (ES: 1.07a), avoiding harm (ES: 1.14), financial arrangements (ES: 1.25), and advertising (ES: 3.01–3.03).

Although the idea of bringing psychological consultation swiftly and efficiently to people who might not find their way to the psychotherapist's office is appealing, a headlong rush into new technological approaches without thoughtful and accountable professionalism invites disaster. Psychotherapy is challenging enough when a client presents in one's office. In addition to the lack of nonverbal communication typical of a telephone conversation, E-mail services also remove voice, pitch, tone, and other verbal cues as clinical data. This can only increase the potential for errors and problems. Perhaps we will be more sanguine when real-time videophone technology is widely available and licensing issues are clarified, but for the moment we are very concerned about the total lack of consumer-oriented regulation.

Sexual Orientation Conversion Therapy

Sexual orientation conversion therapies were considered the treatment of choice when homosexuality was considered to be an illness. For over a century, medical, psychotherapeutic, and religious practitioners have sought to reverse unwanted homosexual orientation through a variety of methods, including psychoanalysis, prayer, electric shock, nausea-inducing drugs, hormone therapy, surgery, and a variety of behavioral treatments, including masturbatory reconditioning, visits to prostitutes, and excessive bicycle riding (Murphy, 1992). The American Psychiatric Association's 1973 decision to remove homosexuality from its *Diagnostic and Statistical Manual of Mental Disorders* marked the official passing of the illness model of homosexuality. Despite this now-complete official depathologizing of homosexuality, efforts by both mental health professionals and pastoral care providers to convert lesbians and gay men to heterosexuality have persisted (Haldeman, 1991, 1994). Such efforts span a variety of treatment modalities and are generally referred to as *conversion therapy*. There are two major concerns about the so-called rehabilitation of gay men and lesbians. First, conversion therapies have long been regarded as ethically questionable. These ethical concerns involve the extent to which conversion treatments are in keeping with the issues of therapist responsibility and consumer welfare. Second, empirical studies fail to show any evidence that conversion therapies do what they purport to do: change sexual orientation. Haldeman's work (1991, 1994) reviews conversion methods, focusing on scientific validity issues, and demonstrates that such therapies are unethical and professionally irresponsible, as well as being based on inadequate and questionable science.

Haldeman (1994) notes that sexual orientation conversion therapy was the treatment of choice when homosexuality was thought to be an illness. He examines the construct of sexual orientation, as well as what constitutes its change. The literature in psychotherapeutic and religious conversion therapies is reviewed, showing no evidence indicating that such treatments are effective in their intended purpose. A need for empirical data on the potentially harmful effects of such treatments is established. Ethical considerations relative to the ongoing stigmatizing effects of conversion therapies are presented. The need to develop more complex models for con-

ceptualizing sexual orientation is discussed, as well as the need to provide treatments to gay men and lesbians that are consonant with the client's wishes and a nonpathologizing stance on homosexuality.

UNTESTED OR FRINGE THERAPIES

From time to time, ethics complaints will develop in response to a new or unusual form of psychotherapy or allegedly therapeutic technique. Often, these so-called treatments are of questionable merit or frankly dangerous. There must be room for appropriate innovation and the development of new treatment strategies in any scientific field, but rigorous standards must be applied to avoid misleading, or actually harming, potential clients. No program of psychotherapy should be undertaken without a firm theoretical foundation and scientific basis for anticipating client benefits. New approaches to psychotherapy should be labeled as experimental with appropriate informed consent when that is the case and should be discontinued at the first indication that any harm is accruing to the clients.

This is Therapy?

Examples of some questionable schools of psychotherapeutic thought include past lives therapy, rage weekends, rebirthing therapy, and harassment therapy. Some consider Scientology a type of fringe or unproven therapy as well. The work of Wilhelm Reich, which reportedly occasionally involved physical stimulation of clients to the point of orgasm (Reich, 1948), and the body invasion technique of Rolfing (Leland, 1976) are examples of therapeutic ideas at the outer limit of acceptability. The difficulty, of course, is that we have hardly reached the state of psychological science in which precise evaluation of therapeutic outcome is possible. Still, some clear ethical problems do arise.

Case 5-17: Millard Brute, Ph.D., prepared an audiotape for experimental use in implosive desensitization of child abusers. The tape described with vivid imagery the successively escalating physical assault on a child, culminating in the dismember-ment and cannibalization of the corpse. The tape was played for a professional audience, and one outraged participant filed an ethics complaint.

Case 5-18: Renee Roper, Psy.D., is a proponent of "harassment therapy." This sometimes involved extended verbal attacks on particular clients, and in other situations involved tying clients up and forcing them to struggle to get loose. When an ethics complaint was filed, Dr. Roper explained her belief that it was necessary to be "harsh" on "the whimpering dependent types."

Case 5-19: Gwendolyn Strange, Ed.D., required her individual therapy clients to participate in group therapy sessions at her home on a biweekly basis. They were required to sit in a circle on floor pillows, while Dr. Strange perched above them on a stool, clothed in a black leotard, and read to them from a book manuscript she was writing.

Case 5-20: Tanya Teton, Ph.D., is a proponent of "radical reparenting" therapy and strongly believes that she must help her clients to "recover from defective early nurturance" by fostering "regres-sion and renurturing." Early in treatment, she asks her adult clients to sit in her lap and drink from a baby bottle. At times, clients are instructed to wear a diaper, and Dr. Teton powders their behinds. As treatment intensifies, she has occasionally invited these clients to nurse from her bare breast.

Dr. Brute informed the ethics committee that the tape was not an actual treatment tool, but rather an experimental project he used for illustrative purposes with audiences composed of professionals only. Nonetheless, the commit-tee noted the sensitive nature of the tape and advised Dr. Brute to be more considerate of his audience's sensitivities in the future. Certainly, the intense nature of the implosive therapy regi-men would need thorough discussion with any client prior to implementation. Some might question whether adequate data exist on which to predicate such treatment.

The theoretical rationales of Drs. Roper and Strange are vague and questionable at best. It is difficult to imagine that either one has advised the clients in question of the potential risks in-volved in the so-called treatments. Have any of

their clients been objectively apprised of more conventional and better proven treatments for their problems? Dr. Teton was surprised by the "empathic failure" of the client who com-plained about her to an ethics committee. The male client was experiencing confusing feelings of sexual arousal during the nursing experience, but Dr. Teton discounted this in her response to the ethics panel, noting that there was "nothing sexual about it" so far as she was concerned. Often, it is the most egocentric and least compe-tent practitioners who come to the attention of ethics committees via this sort of complaint.

Proprietary Psychotherapy

From time to time, proprietary systems of psy-chotherapy have been developed and marketed as unique approaches to dealing with human problems. Characteristics of such systems usu-ally include requirements that specialized train-ing, for which substantial fees are paid, be ob-tained only from designated instructors. The usual justification involves maintaining quality control or monitoring the purity of the interven-tion. As a result, there is often an aura of secrecy and lack of scientific scrutiny surrounding such approaches to treatment. Two examples that have become well known to the public and professional communities are Eye Movement Desensitization and Reprocessing (EMDR) and Erhard Seminars Training (est).

The EMDR technique was developed by Francine Shapiro (1995) and is described as a comprehensive method for treating disturbing experiences such as trauma associated with sex-ual abuse, violence, combat, grief, or phobias. The 8-phase treatment approach features having clients focus on a traumatic memory while mov-ing their eyes rapidly from side to side or using other left-right stimulation. This approach is de-scribed as leading to a rapid integration of the traumatic memories, which leads to the elimina-tion of associated symptoms (Greenwald, 1994). Some reviews have reported marginal benefits (Os-walt, Anderson, Hagstrom, & Berkowitz, 1993), others note poor methodology in case studies and research reports claiming to show efficacy of the technique (Acierno, Hersen, Van Hasselt, & Tremont, 1994). Other studies have shown good results with specific symptoms using a randomized clinical trial model (Wilson, Becker, & Tinker, 1995). Although EMDR has clearly been beneficial for some types of clients, the marketing, restrictions on teaching the technique, and aura of secretiveness that result have contributed to a sense of mystique and controversy.

Werner Erhard, developer of est, was a skilled salesman with no professional training as a psychotherapist. His programs have evolved to become the "Forum" seminars (Efran, Lukens, & Lukens, 1986; Wistlow, 1986). The basic approach focused on challenging participants' sense of psychological identity or, as one commentator noted, systematic escalation and discounting of each participant's "adapted child," eventually forcing the participant into their "free child" state, thereby releasing a large amount of "bound energy" (Klein, 1983, p. 178). Other articles have described est as "brainwashing" (Moss & Hosford, 1983), and there was reported that a patient suffered a psychotic episode following his participation in an est program (Higgitt & Murray, 1983). One of the few careful attempts to study Erhard's techniques in a rigorous fashion showed no long-term treatment effects and concluded that claims of far-reaching effects for programs of the Forum were found to be exaggerated (Fisher, Silver, Chinsky, & Goff, 1989).

From an ethical perspective, EMDR, although controversial, has been shown to have reasonably documented effectiveness with certain clinical populations (Wilson et al., 1995), far more than can be said in favor of Erhard's est or Forum. These are only two of many "new modalities" of psychological intervention that have been introduced to the public with greater fanfare than substance. The central message from an ethical perspective is the obligation of psychologists to have a sound scientific foundation for their psychotherapeutic work. Proof of efficacy should precede mass marketing of new techniques to the public or to colleagues.

SUMMARY GUIDELINES

1. When the psychologist is treating more than one client at a time, as in group or family therapy, the rights of all the clients must be respected and balanced. Therapists should also be sensitive to their own values with respect to the family or group and attempt to facilitate the growth of all concerned within their own value systems.

2. Psychologists conducting group treatment or educational programs should carefully define and articulate the goals, methods, and purposes of each group for each participant in such a manner as to permit each potential client a fully informed choice about participation.

3. In the application of special therapeutic techniques that require unique training, including (but not limited to) sex therapy, behavior modification, hypnosis, and the use of psychological devices, psychologists must be certain that their training is adequate to use the technique in question. Any mechanical or electrical devices (e.g., biofeedback equipment) should be free from defects and appropriately sanitized.

4. When some symptoms or technique raise special emotional or public policy questions, psychologists should be sensitive to the issues and discuss them and their implications with the client. Psychologists are also obliged to keep abreast of evolving standards and regulations governing the use of specialized techniques and devices.

5. Coercion is not an appropriate part of a psychotherapeutic program. To the extent that subtle coercive pressures enter into a therapeutic relationship, a psychologist should attempt to ensure that these are not used to the detriment of the client.

6. Only empirically validated or clinically proven approaches to treatment should be presented to clients as established treatment. Experimental procedures must be described as such, and, to minimize client risk, extreme caution should be used in the development of new modalities of treatment.

References

Acierno, R., Hersen, M., Van Hasselt, V. B., & Tremont, G. (1994). Review of the validation and dissemination of eye movement desensitization

and reprocessing: A scientific and ethical dilemma. *Clinical Psychology Review, 14,* 287–
299.

Association of Sexual and Marital Therapists. (1986).
Association of Sexual and Marital Therapists
Code of Ethics. *Sexual & Marital Therapy, 1,*
109.

American Association of Sex Educators, Counselors,
and Therapists. (1980). *Code of Ethics AASECT.*
Washington, DC: Author.

American Psychological Association. (1973). Guidelines for psychologists conducting growth groups.
American Psychologist, 28, 933.

American Psychological Association. (1975). Report
of the Task Force on Sex Bias and Sex-Role Stereotyping in Psychotherapeutic Practice. *American
Psychologist, 30,* 1169–1175.

American Psychological Association. (1981). *Task
Force Report on Psychologists' Use of Physical
Interventions.* Washington, DC: Author.

American Psychological Association Ethics Committee. (1993, April 18). *Psychotherapy by telephone.* Washington, DC: Author.

American Psychological Association Ethics Committee. (1995, July 6). *Services by telephone, teleconferencing, and Internet.* Washington, DC:
Author.

Bailey, K. G. (1978). Psychotherapy or massage parlor
technology? Comments on the Zeiss, Rosen,
and Zeiss treatment procedure. *Journal of
Consulting and Clinical Psychology, 46,* 1502–
1506.

Bancroft, J. (1991). Ethical aspects of sexuality and
sex therapy. In S. Bloch & P. Chodoff (Eds.),
Psychiatric ethics (2nd ed., pp. 215–242). Oxford, England: Oxford University Press.

Barnett, D. C. (1982). A suicide prevention incident
involving use of the computer. *Professional Psychology, 13,* 565–570.

Brown, R. A., & Field, J. R. (Eds). (1988). *Treatment
of sexual problems in individual and couples therapy.* Costa Mesa, CA: PMA.

Carton, B. (1994, February 7). Dialing for therapy:
Telephone psychology finds adherents, skeptics.
Boston Globe, 245, pp. 1, 7.

Cook, S. W. (1975). Comments on ethical considerations in "self-control" techniques as an alternative to pain medication. *Journal of Abnormal
Psychology, 84,* 169–171.

Corey, G., Williams, G. T., & Moline, M. E. (1995).

Ethical and legal issues in group counseling.
Ethics and Behavior, 5, 161–183.

Crowe, M. (1995). Couple therapy and sexual dysfunction. *International Review of Psychiatry, 7,*
195–204.

Davidson, G. C., & Stuart, R. B. (1975). Behavior
therapy and civil liberties. *American Psychologist, 30,* 755–763.

Dolliver, R. H. (1971). Concerning the potential parallels between psychotherapy and brainwashing.
*Psychotherapy: Theory, Research, and Practice,
8,* 170–173.

Efran, J. S., Lukens, M. D., & Lukens, R. J. (1986).
It's all done with mirrors. *Family Therapy Networker, 10,* 41–49.

Fisher, J. D., Silver, R. C., Chinsky, J. M., & Goff,
B. (1989). Psychological effects of participation
in a large group awareness training. *Journal of
Consulting and Clinical Psychology, 57,* 747–
755.

Fromm, E. (1980). Values in hypnotherapy. *Psychotherapy: Theory, Research and Practice, 17,* 425–
430.

Fuller, G. D. (1978). Current status of biofeedback
in clinical practice. *American Psychologist, 33,*
30–48.

Gaylin, W. (1974). On the borders of persuasion: A
psychoanalytic look at coercion. *Psychiatry, 37,*
1–9.

Geller, E. S., Johnson, D. F., Hamlin, P. H., &
Kennedy, T. D. (1977). Behavior modification
in a prison: Issues, problems, and compromises.
Criminal Justice and Behavior, 4, 11–43.

Goodstein, L. D. (1975). Self-control and therapist-
control: The medical model in behavioral clothing. *Journal of Abnormal Psychology, 84,* 178–
180.

Greenwald, R. (1994). Eye movement desensitization
and reprocessing (EMDR): An overview. *Journal
of Contemporary Psychotherapy, 24,* 15–34.

Grisso, T., & Vierling, L. (1978). Minors' consent to
treatment: A developmental perspective. *Professional Psychology, 9,* 412–427.

Haldeman, D. (1994). The practice and ethics of
sexual orientation conversion therapy. Special
section: Mental health of lesbians and gay men.
*Journal of Consulting and Clinical Psychology,
62,* 221–227.

Haldeman, D. C. (1991). Sexual orientation conversion therapy for gay men and lesbians: A scien-

tific examination. In J. C. Gonsiorek & J. D. Weinrich (Eds.), *Homosexuality: Research implications for public policy* (pp. 149–160). Newbury Park, CA: Sage.

Hare-Mustin, R. T. (1978). A feminist approach to family therapy. *Family Process, 17,* 181–194.

Hare-Mustin, R. T. (1980). Family therapy may be dangerous for your health. *Professional Psychology, 11,* 935–938.

Higgitt, A. C., & Murray, R. M. (1983). A psychotic episode following Erhard Seminars Training. *Acta Psychiatrica Scandinavica, 67,* 436–439.

Hill, D. (1992). Ethical issues in marital and sexual counseling. *British Journal of Guidance and Counseling, 20,* 75–89.

Hines, P. M., & Hare-Mustin, R. T. (1978). Ethical concerns in family therapy. *Professional Psychology, 9,* 165–171.

Hurvitz, N. (1967). Psychotherapy as a means of social control. *Journal of Consulting and Clinical Psychology, 40,* 232–239.

Hurvitz, N. (1973). Marital problems following psychotherapy with one spouse. *Journal of Consulting Psychology, 31,* 38–47.

Jacobs, M., Thompson, L. A., & Truxaw, P. (1975). The use of sexual surrogates in counseling. *Counseling Psychologist, 5,* 73–76.

Karoly, P. (1975). Ethical considerations in the application of self-control techniques. *Journal of Abnormal Psychology, 84,* 175–177.

Klein, M. (1983). How EST works. *Transactional Analysis Journal, 13,* 178–180.

Kline, M. V. (1976). Dangerous aspects of the practice of hypnosis and the need for legislative regulation. *Clinical Psychologist, 29,* 2–5.

Koocher, G. P. (1976). A bill of rights for children in psychotherapy. In G. P. Koocher (Ed.), *Children's rights and the mental health professions* (pp. 23–32). New York: Wiley.

Koocher, G. P. (1983). Consent to psychotherapy. In G. B. Melton, G. P. Koocher, & M. Saks (Eds.), *Children's competence to consent* (pp. 111–128). New York: Plenum.

L'Abate, L. (1982). *Values, ethics, legalities and the family therapist.* Rockville, MD: Aspen Systems.

Lakin, M. (1994). Morality in group and family therapies: Multi-person therapies and the 1992 ethics code. *Professional Psychology: Research and Practice, 25,* 344–348.

Leland, J. (1976). "Invasion" of the body? *Psychotherapy: Theory, Research and Practice, 13,* 214–218.

Levendusky, P., & Pankratz, L. (1975). Self-control techniques as an alternative to pain medication. *Journal of Abnormal Psychology, 84,* 165–168.

Lieberman, M. A., Yalom, I. D., & Miles, M. B. (1973). *Encounter groups: First facts.* New York: Basic Books.

Lowery, T. S., & Lowery, T. P. (1975). Ethical considerations in sex therapy. *Journal of Marriage and Family Counseling, 1,* 229–236.

Lykken, D. T. (1974). Psychology and the lie detector industry. *American Psychologist, 29,* 725–739.

Margolin, G. (1982). Ethical and legal considerations in marital and family therapy. *American Psychologist, 37,* 788–801.

Martin, G., & Pear, J. (1996). *Behavior modification: What it is and how to do it.* Upper Saddle River, NJ: Prentice-Hall.

Masters, W. H., & Johnson, V. E. (1976). Principles of the new sex therapy. *American Journal of Psychiatry, 133,* 548–554.

Meyer, J. K. (1976). Training and accreditation for the treatment of sexual disorders. *American Journal of Psychiatry, 133,* 389–394.

Moss, C. S., & Hosford, R. E. (1983). Reflections on EST training from the viewpoint of two correctional psychologists. *International Journal of Eclectic Psychotherapy, 2,* 18–39.

Murphy, T. (1992). Redirecting sexual orientation: Techniques and justifications. *Journal of Sex Research, 29,* 501–523.

Oswalt, R., Anderson, M., Hagstrom, K., & Berkowitz, B. (1993). Evaluation of the one-session eye-movement desensitization reprocessing procedure for eliminating traumatic memories. *Psychological Reports, 73,* 99–104.

Parker, R. S. (1976). Ethical and professional considerations concerning high risk groups. *Journal of Clinical Issues in Psychology, 7,* 4–19.

Reich, W. (1948). *The discovery of the orgasm. Volume 1: The function of the orgasm.* New York: Orgone Institute Press.

Rogers, C. (1970). *Carl Rogers on encounter groups.* New York: Harper & Row.

Rosen, R. C., & Leiblum, S. R. (Eds.). (1995a). *Case studies in sex therapy.* New York: Guilford Press.

Rosen, R. C., & Leiblum, S. R. (1995b). Treatment

of sexual disorders in the 1990s: An integrated approach. *Journal of Consulting and Clinical Psychology, 63,* 877–890.

Schultz, W. C. (1971). *Here comes everybody.* New York: Harper & Row.

Schwitzgebel, R. K. (1978). Suggestions for the uses of psychological devices in accord with legal and ethical standards. *Professional Psychology, 9,* 478–488.

Schwitzgebel, R. L. (1970). Behavior instrumentation and social technology. *American Psychologist, 25,* 491–499.

Shapiro, F. (1995). *Eye movement desensitization and reprocessing: Basic principles, protocols, and procedures.* New York: Guilford Press.

Simmonds, D. W. (1976). Children's rights and family dysfunction: "Daddy, why do I have to be the crazy one?" In G. P. Koocher (Ed.), *Children's Rights and the Mental Health Professions* (pp. 33–39). New York: Wiley.

Slovenko, R. (1977). Group psychotherapy: Privileged communication and confidentiality. *Journal of Psychiatry and the Law, 5,* 405–466.

Stolz, S. B. (1977). Why no guidelines for behavior modification? *Journal of Applied Behavior Analysis, 10,* 541–547.

Stolz, S. B. (1978). Ethics of social and educational interventions: Historical context and behavioral analysis. In A. C. Catania & T. A. Brigham (Eds.), *Handbook of applied behavior analysis* (pp. 222–235). New York: Irvington.

Szucko, J. J., & Kleinmuntz, B. (1981). Statistical versus clinical lie detection. *American Psychologist, 36,* 488–496.

Thaw, J., Thorne, G. D., & Benjamin, E. (1978). Human rights, behavior modification, and the development of state policy. *Administration in Mental Health, 5,* 112–119.

Turkat, I. D., & Forehand, R. (1980). Critical issues in behavior therapy. *Behavior Modification, 4,* 445–464.

Wagner, N. N. (1978). Is masturbation still wrong? Comments on Bailey's comments. *Journal of Consulting and Clinical Psychology, 46,* 1507–1509.

Wilson, G. T. (1978). Ethical and professional issues in sex therapy: Comments on Bailey's "Psychotherapy of massage parlor technology?" *Journal of Consulting and Clinical Psychology, 46,* 1510–1514.

Wilson, S. A., Becker, L. A., & Tinker, R. H. (1995). Eye movement desensitization and reprocessing (EMDR) treatment for psychologically traumatized individuals. *Journal of Consulting and Clinical Psychology, 63,* 928–937.

Wistlow, F. (1986). Being there. *Family Therapy Networker, 10,* 20–29.

Wylie, K. R., Crowe, M. J., & Boddington, D. (1995). How can the therapist deal with a couple with male demands for anal sex? *Sexual and Marital Therapy, 10,* 95–98.

Zeiss, A. M., Rosen, G. M., & Zeiss, R. A. (1977). Orgasm during intercourse: A treatment strategy for women. *Journal of Consulting and Clinical Psychology, 45,* 891–895.

6

Privacy, Confidentiality, and Record Keeping

Three may keep a secret, if two of them are dead.

Benjamin Franklin

The confidential relationship between psychologist and client has long been regarded as a cornerstone of the helping relationship. The trust conveyed through assurance of confidentiality is deemed so critical that some have gone so far as to argue that psychotherapy may be worthless without it (Epstein, Steingarten, Weinstein, & Nashel, 1977). Without assurance of confidentiality, many potential clients might never seek psychological services. Once services are sought, the lack of confidentiality might lead to concealment of information, resulting in potentially ineffectual treatment or compromised consultative opinions (DeKraai & Sales, 1982). The changing nature of societal values has led to a variety of concerns about the traditional meaning of confidentiality in psychological practice, and this in turn raises many questions regarding the nature and degree of confidentiality obligations across a variety of situations.

Recent American history provides ample public examples of how breaches in confidentiality of mental health data have had major implications for both the clients and society. Thomas Eagleton, a U.S. Senator from Missouri, was dropped as George McGovern's vice presidential running mate in 1968 when it was disclosed that he had previously been hospitalized for the treatment of depression. Dr. Lewis J. Fielding, better known as "Daniel Ellsberg's psychiatrist," certainly did not suspect that the break-in at his office on September 3, 1971, might ultimately lead to the conviction of several high officials in the Nixon White House and contribute to the only resignation of an American president (Morganthau, Lindsay, Michael, & Givens, 1982). Martin Orne's release of audiotapes from his therapy sessions with then-deceased Pulitzer-Prize-winning poet Anne Sexton to her authorized biographer caused considerable debate within the profession, despite authorization of the release by her daughter, the executrix of her literary estate (Burke, 1995; Chodoff, 1992; Goldstein, 1992; Joseph, 1992; Rosenbaum, 1994). Disclosures of confidential information received by psychotherapists also played prominently in the press during the murder trials of the Menendez brothers and O. J. Simpson. A psychotherapist who had briefly treated Nicole Simpson drew national attention when the psychotherapist felt the need to "go public" shortly after the homicide with content from the therapy sessions. Subsequently, that same therapist drew disciplinary sanctions from the California licensing board because of that confidentiality violation.

The special sensitivity of information gleaned by psychologists in the routine performance of their work, whether it be assessment, psychotherapy, consultation, or research, cannot be ignored. Unfortunately, the complexity of the issues related to the general theme of confidentiality often seem to defy easy analysis. Bersoff writes of confidentiality that, "no ethical duty [is] more misunderstood or honored by its breach rather than by its fulfillment" (1995, p. 143).

Modern telecommunications and computers have substantially complicated matters. Massive electronic databases of sensitive personal information can easily be created, searched, cross tabulated, and transmitted around the world at the speed of light. Even prior to the Internet and the World Wide Web, psychologists were concerned about the threats posed to individual privacy and confidentiality by computerized data systems (Sawyer & Schechter, 1968).

Psychologists are ethically obligated to keep records of various sorts (e.g., interactions with clients and research participants, test scores, research data, and even patient accounts) and must safeguard these files. Increasingly, people are seeking all types of medical and psychological information about others and about themselves. This leads to an entirely new subset of problems on the matter of records: What is in them? Who should keep them? How long should they be kept? Who has access? Is this a legal matter or a professional standard? How do these policies have an impact on the ethical principle of confidentiality? What about the rights of psychologists' students and research subjects? These are all matters addressed in this chapter.

THE PROBLEM OF DEFINITIONS

The area of confidentiality related ethical problems is complicated by common misunderstandings about these frequently used terms: pri-

vacy, confidentiality, and privilege. At least part of the confusion is related to the fact that in particular situations these terms may have narrow legal meanings quite distinct from broader traditional meanings attached by psychologists or other mental health practitioners. Many difficulties are related to a failure on the part of psychologists to discriminate among the different terms and meanings. Still other difficulties grow out of the fact, discussed in chapter 1, that legal obligations are not always fully congruent with ethical responsibilities.

Privacy

The concept of privacy is often considered a basic right granted by the Fourth, Fifth, and Fifteenth Amendments to the U.S. Constitution. It is basically the right of individuals to decide how much of their thoughts, feelings, or personal data should be shared with others. Privacy has often been considered essential to ensure human dignity and freedom of self-determination.

The concepts of both confidentiality and privilege grow out of the concept of an individual's right to privacy, which is clearly a much broader topic. Concern about electronic surveillance, the use of a lie detector, and a variety of other observational or data-gathering activities fall under the heading of privacy issues. The issues involved in public policy decisions regarding the violation of privacy rights parallel concerns expressed by psychologists regarding confidentiality violations (Smith-Bell & Winslade, 1994). In general, psychologists' privacy rights may be subject to violation when their behavior seriously violates the norms of society or somehow endangers others. An example would be the issuance of a search warrant based on "probable cause" that a crime has been or is about to be committed. These principles are discussed in greater detail from the psychological perspective in the pages that follow. However, psychologists must also give consideration to the concept of privacy as a basic human right due all people and not simply limited to their clients.

Confidentiality

Confidentiality refers to a general standard of professional conduct that obliges a professional not to discuss information about a client with anyone. Confidentiality may also be based in statutes (i.e., laws enacted by legislatures) or case law (i.e., interpretations of laws by courts). But, when cited as an ethical principle, confidentiality implies an explicit contract or promise not to reveal anything about a client except under certain circumstances agreed to by both parties (Smith-Bell & Winslade, 1994). Although the roots of the concept are in professional ethics rather than in law, the nature of the psychologist-client relationship does have legal recognition (Bersoff, 1995; DeKraai & Sales, 1982). It is conceivable, for example, that a client whose confidence was violated could sue a psychologist in a civil action for breach of confidentiality and even seek specific criminal penalties if available under state law. For example, a New York appeals court ruled that a patient may bring a tort action against a psychiatrist who allegedly disclosed confidential information to the patient's spouse, allowing him to seek damages for mental distress, loss of employment, and the deterioration of his marriage ("Disclosure of Confidential Information," 1982; *MacDonald v. Clinger*, 1982).

The degree to which one should, if ever, violate a client's confidentiality has been a matter of some controversy (Siegel, 1979), despite uniform agreement on one point: The client has a right to know the limits on confidentiality in a professional relationship. The initial interview with any client (individual or organizational) should include a direct and candid discussion of limits that may exist with respect to any confidences communicated in the relationship. Interviews with our colleagues, occasional surveys, and other anecdotal reports indicate that far too few practitioners actually do this early in a professional relationship. Failure to provide such information early is not only unethical, but may also lead to problems later. The information may be given orally or as "new client information" in a pamphlet or written statement. Every psychologist should give sufficient thought to this matter and formulate a policy for his or her practice. This policy should be based on applicable law, ethical standards, and personal conviction, integrated as meaningfully as possible given the legal precedents and case examples discussed in the following pages.

Privilege

Privilege and confidentiality are often-confused concepts, and the distinction between them is critical for understanding a variety of ethical problems. *Privilege* (or privileged communication) is a legal term describing certain specific types of relationships that enjoy protection from disclosure in legal proceedings. Privilege is granted by law and belongs to the client in the relationship. Normal court rules provide that anything relative and material to the issue at hand can and should be admitted as evidence. When privilege exists, however, the client is protected from having the covered communications revealed without explicit permission. If the client waives this privilege, the psychologist may be compelled to testify on the nature and specifics of the material discussed. The client is usually not permitted to waive privilege selectively. In most courts, once a waiver is given, it covers all of the relevant privileged material.

Traditionally, such privilege has been extended to attorney-client, husband-wife, physician-patient, and priest-penitent relationships. Some jurisdictions now extend privilege to psychologist-client or psychotherapist-client relationships, but the actual laws vary widely, and it is incumbent on each psychologist to know the statutes in force for her or his practice. In one survey of legislation and key case law affecting the primary mental health professions (i.e., psychologists, psychiatrists, social workers, and psychiatric nurses) in all 50 states, DeKraai and Sales (1982) noted that nurses were hardly ever mentioned, and physicians in general were frequently mentioned, with respect to privileged communication. The same authors also note that there are no federally created privileges for any mental health profession; the federal courts generally look to applicable state laws. In 1996 the U.S. Supreme Court took up this issue based on conflicting rulings in different federal appellate court districts in the case of *Jaffe v. Redmond* (1996).

Case 6-1: Mary Lu Redmond was a police officer in a suburban Chicago neighborhood. In 1991, she shot and killed Ricky Allen while responding to a "fight in progress" call. After the shooting, Officer Redmond sought counseling from a licensed clinical social worker. Later, Jaffe, acting as administrator of Mr. Allen's estate, sued Redmond, citing U.S. civil rights statutes and Illinois tort law. Jaffe wanted access to the social worker's notes and sought to compel the therapist to give oral testimony about the therapy. Redmond and her therapist refused. The trial judge instructed the jury that refusing to provide such information could be held against Officer Redmond. The jury awarded damages based on both the federal civil rights and state laws.

On June 13, 1996, the Supreme Court overturned the lower court decision, upholding the existence of a privilege under Federal Rules of Evidence to patients of licensed psychotherapists by a vote of 7–2. In a decision written by Justice John Paul Stevens, the Court noted that this privilege is "rooted in the imperative need for confidence and trust," and that "the mere possibility of disclosure may impede development of the confidential relationship necessary for successful treatment" (*Jaffe v. Redmond*, 1996, 4492–4493). Writing for himself and Justice Renquist, Justice Scalia dissented, arguing that psychotherapy should not be protected by judicially created privilege and that social workers were not clearly expert in psychotherapy and did not warrant such a privilege (Smith, 1996). Nonetheless, this case has set a new national standard that affords privilege protections across jurisdictions.

LIMITATIONS AND EXCEPTIONS

Almost all of the statutes addressing confidentiality or providing privileges expressly require licensing, certification, or registration of psychologists under state law, although some states extend privilege when the client reasonably believes the alleged psychologist to be licensed (DeKraai & Sales, 1982). In general, students (including psychology interns, unlicensed postdoctoral fellows, or supervisees) are not specifically covered by privilege statutes. In some circumstances, trainees may be covered by privilege accorded to communication with a licensed supervisor, but state laws vary widely, and this cannot be assumed.

Some jurisdictions permit a judge's discretion to overrule privilege between psychologist and client on determination that the interests of justice outweigh the interests of confidentiality. Some jurisdictions limit privilege exclusively to civil actions, whereas others may include criminal proceedings, except when homicide is involved. In many circumstances, designated practitioners are mandated by law to breach confidentiality and report certain information to authorities. Just as some physicians are compelled under some state laws to report gunshot wounds or certain communicable diseases, psychologists may be obligated to report certain cases, such as those involving child abuse, to state authorities. These restrictions could certainly affect a therapeutic relationship adversely, but the client has a right to know any limitations in advance, and the psychologist has the responsibility both to know the relevant facts and to inform the client as indicated.

Other circumstances, such as a suit alleging malpractice, may constitute a waiver of privilege and confidentiality. In some circumstances, a client may waive some confidentiality or privilege rights without fully realizing the extent of potential risk. In certain dramatic circumstances, a psychologist may also face the dilemma of violating a confidence to prevent some imminent harm or danger from occurring. These matters are not without controversy, but it is important for the psychologist to be aware of the issues and think prospectively about how one ought to handle such problems.

When law and ethical standards diverge (e.g., when a confidential communication is not privileged in the eyes of the law), the situation becomes extremely complex, but it would be difficult to fault a psychologist ethically for divulging confidential material if ordered to do so by a court of competent authority. On the other hand, one might ask whether it is appropriate to violate the law if one believes that doing so is necessary to behave ethically. Consider, for example, the psychologist who is required by state law or court order to disclose some information learned about a client during the course of a professional relationship. If the psychologist claims that the law and ethical principles are in conflict, then by definition the ethical principles in question are illegal. The psychologist may choose civil disobedience as one course of action, but does so at his or her own peril in terms of the legal consequences. The 1992 version of the American Psychological Association (APA) ethics code offers little useful guidance on this point, instructing psychologists to resolve such conflicts "in a responsible manner" (APA, 1992; ES: 1.02).

Students of ethical philosophy will immediately recognize a modern psychological version in the controversy developed in the writings of Immanuel Kant and John Stuart Mill. Is it the intention of the actor that should be the basis for judgment, or solely the final outcome of the behavior that matters? For example, if a competent psychologist, intending to help a client, initiates an intervention that causes some unanticipated harm, is the act ethical (because the intentions were good) or unethical (because harm resulted)? Clearly, the answer will not be found in these pages. Each situation is different, but the most appropriate approach to evaluate a case would be to consider the potential impact of each alternative course of action and choose with regard to the outcomes one might reasonably expect. Perhaps the best guidepost that can be offered is a kind of balancing test in that the psychologist attempts to weigh the relative risks and vulnerabilities of the parties involved. Several of the cases discussed in this chapter highlight these difficult decisions.

Statutory Obligations

As noted above, in some circumstances the law specifically dictates a duty to notify certain public authorities of information that might be acquired in the context of a psychologist-client relationship. The general rationale on which such laws are predicated holds that certain individual rights must give way to the greater good of society or to the rights of a more vulnerable individual (e.g., in child abuse or child custody cases; see Kalichman, 1993). Statutes in some states address the waiver of privilege relative to clients exposed to criminal activity either as the perpetrator, victim, or third party. One might presume that violation of a confidence by obeying one's legal duty to report such matters (in the

states where such duties exists) could certainly hinder the psychologist-client relationship, yet the data on this point are mixed (DeKraai & Sales, 1982; Kalichman, Brosig, & Kalichman, 1994; Nowell & Sprull, 1993; Woods & McNamara, 1980). Some commentators have argued that the therapeutic relationship can survive a mandated breach in confidentiality so long as a measure of trust is maintained (Brosig & Kalichman, 1992; Watson & Levine, 1989). At times, state laws can be confusing and complicated.

Case 6-2: Euthan Asia was full of remorse when he came to his initial appointment with Oliver Oops, Ph.D. After asking and receiving assurance that their conversations would be confidential, Mr. Asia disclosed that, two months earlier, he had murdered his wife of 50 years out of compassion for her discomfort. Mrs. Asia was 73 years old and suffered from advanced Alzheimer's disease. Mr. Asia could not stand to see the woman he loved in such a state, so he gave his wife sleeping pills and staged a bathtub drowning that resulted in a ruling of accidental death by the medical examiner.

In most jurisdictions, Dr. Oops would be obligated to respect Mr. Asia's confidentiality because few states require reporting of past felonies that do not involve child abuse. If the conversation took place in Massachusetts, however, Dr. Oops would be required by law to report Mr. Asia twice. First, Dr. Oops would have to notify the Department of Elder Affairs that Mr. Asia had caused the death of a person he was caring for over the age of 60. Next, he would be obligated to report to another state agency that Mr. Asia had caused the death of a handicapped person. Although every American state and Canadian province has a mandatory "child abuse" reporting law (Kalichman, 1993), not all have "elder abuse" or "handicapped person abuse" reporting requirements. As a result, psychologists are ethically obliged to know all applicable exceptions for the jurisdiction in which they practice and provide full information on these limits to their clients.

Psychologists have also been concerned about the potential obligation to disclose "future crimes" (i.e., a client's stated intent to commit a crime at some future date). Shah (1969) has argued that, in most cases, this type of behavior is essentially help seeking rather than an actual intent to commit a crime. Siegel (1979) also argued that interventions short of violating a confidence are invariably possible and more desirable, although he acknowledged that one must obey any applicable laws. No jurisdictions currently mandate psychologists to disclose such information. When a particular client may be a danger to self or others creates a special circumstance; this is discussed below as the "duty to warn."

Malpractice and Waivers

Although not all states have specifically enacted laws making malpractice actions an exception to privilege, it is unreasonable not to allow psychologists to defend themselves by revealing communications from clients during sessions. Likewise, no ethics licensing board or professional association ethics committee could investigate a claim against a psychologist unless the complainant were willing to waive any duty of confidentiality that the psychologist might owe to him or her. In such instances, the waiver by the client of the psychologist's duty of confidentiality or legal privilege is a prerequisite for full discussion of the case. While some might fear that the threat to reveal an embarrassing confidence would deter clients from reporting or seeking redress from offender-psychologists, this can easily be dealt with procedurally. Ethics committees, for example, generally conduct all proceedings in confidence and may offer assurances to the client who wishes to complain about a psychologist. Sensitive testimony in a malpractice case could be held *in camera* (i.e., a proceeding in which all spectators are excluded from court, and records are sealed from the public).

In other circumstances, when a client is willing to waive his or her privilege or confidentiality, the psychologist may wish to advise against it or warn the client of potential problems.

Case 6-3: Barbara Bash, age 23, suffered a concussion in an automobile accident, experiencing memory loss and a variety of neurological sequelae. Her condition improved gradually, although she developed symptoms of depression and anxiety as she worried about whether she would fully recover. She sought a consultation from Martha Muzzle, Ph.D., to assess her cognitive and emotional state, subsequently entering psychotherapy with Dr. Muzzle to deal with her anxiety and depression. Ms. Bash informed Dr. Muzzle that she had previously sought psychotherapy at age 18 to assist her in overcoming anxiety and depression linked to a variety of family problems. Some 10 months after the accident, Bash is still being treated by Muzzle and has made much progress. A lawsuit is pending against the other driver in the accident, and Bash's attorney wonders whether to call Dr. Muzzle as an expert witness at the trial to document the emotional pain Ms. Bash suffered, thus securing a better financial settlement.

If consulted, the psychologist should remind Ms. Bash's attorney and inform Ms. Bash that, if called to testify on Ms. Bash's behalf, she would have to waive her privilege rights. Under cross examination, the psychologist might then be asked about preexisting emotional problems, prior treatment, and a variety of other personal matters that Ms. Bash might prefer not to have brought out in court. The danger is always that such testimony might damage the client's credibility. In this case, the legal strategy involved documenting Bash's damages, with the intent of forcing an out-of-court settlement, but the client ought to know the risks of disclosure should courtroom testimony be required.

Pressures of various sorts may be applied by employers, schools, clinics, or other agencies for clients to sign waivers of privilege or confidentiality. Often the client may actually not wish to sign the form, but may simply be complying with the wishes of an authority figure or be fearful that requested help would otherwise be turned down (Rosen, 1977). If a psychologist has doubts about the wisdom or validity of a client's waiver in such circumstances, the best course of action is to consult with the client about the reservations prior to supplying the requested information.

The Duty to Warn or Protect Third Parties

No discussion of confidentiality in the mental health arena can be complete without reference to the *Tarasoff* case (i.e., *Tarasoff v. Board of Regents of the University of California*, 1976) and a family of other cases that have followed in its wake (see Knapp & VandeCreek, 1982; VandeCreek & Knapp, 1993). Detailed analyses of the legal case are provided by Stone (1976) and Everstine et al. (1980), but a brief summary follows for those unfamiliar with the facts.

Case 6-4: In the fall of 1969, Prosenjit Poddar, a citizen of India and naval architecture student at the University of California's Berkeley campus, shot and stabbed to death Tatiana Tarasoff, a young woman who had spurned his affections. Poddar had been in psychotherapy with Dr. Moore, psychologist at the university's student health facility, and Dr. Moore had concluded that Poddar was quite dangerous. This conclusion stemmed from an assessment of Poddar's pathological attachment to Tarasoff and evidence that he intended to purchase a gun. After consultation with appropriate colleagues at the student health facility, the psychologist notified police both orally and in writing that Poddar was dangerous. He requested that Poddar be taken to a facility to be evaluated for civil commitment under California's civil commitment statutes. The police allegedly interrogated Poddar and found him rational. They concluded that he was not really dangerous and secured a promise that he would stay away from Ms. Tarasoff. After his release by the police, Poddar understandably never returned for further psychotherapy, and 2 months later stabbed Ms. Tarasoff to death.

Subsequently, Ms. Tarasoff's parents attempted to sue the regents of the University of California, the student health center staff members involved, and the police. Both trial and appeals courts dismissed the complaint, holding that, despite the tragedy, there was no legal basis in California law for the claim. The Tarasoff family appealed to the Supreme Court of California, asserting that the defendants had a duty to warn Ms. Tarasoff or her family of the danger, and that they should have persisted to ultimately ensure his confinement. In a 1974 ruling, the court held that the therapists, indeed, did have a duty to warn Ms. Tarasoff. When the defendants and several *amici* (i.e., organizations trying to advise the court by filing *amicus curiae*, or "friend of the court," briefs) petitioned for a rehearing, the court took the unusual step of granting one. In their second ruling (*Tarasoff v. Board of Regents*, 1976), the court released the police from liability without explanation and more broadly formulated the obligations of therapists, imposing a duty to use reasonable care to protect third parties against dangers posed by a patient.

Although the impact outside California of this decision was not immediately clear, the issue of whether psychologists must be police or protectors or otherwise have a "duty to protect" rapidly became a national concern (see, e.g., Bersoff, 1976; Leonard, 1977; Paul, 1977). A former president of the APA (Siegel, 1979) took the view that, if Poddar's psychologist had accepted the absolute and inviolate confidentiality position, Poddar could have been kept in psychotherapy and the life of Tatiana Tarasoff might have been saved. Siegel believed the therapist "betrayed" his client and observed that, if the psychologist had not considered Poddar "dangerous," he could not have been held liable for "failure to warn." This may be a valid position; however, many psychologists would argue the need to protect the public welfare with direct action. From both legal and ethical perspectives, the key test of responsibility is whether the psychologist *knew or should have known* (in a professional capacity) of the client's dangerousness. There may be no single ethically correct answer in such cases, but the psychologist must also consider his or her potential obligations.

Perhaps the ultimate irony of the *Tarasoff* case in terms of outcome is what happened to Poddar. His original conviction for second degree murder was reversed because the judge had failed to give adequate instructions to the jury concerning the defense of "diminished capacity" (*People v. Poddar*, 1974). He was convicted of voluntary manslaughter and confined to the Vacaville medical facility in California. He has since been released from confinement and "has returned to India, and by his own account is now happily married" (Stone, 1976, p. 358).

A variety of decisions outside California since *Tarasoff* have dealt with the duty of psychotherapists to warn and/or protect potential victims of violence at the hands of their patients (Knapp & VandeCreek, 1982; Truscott, 1993; VandeCreek & Knapp, 1993). The cases are both fascinating and troubling from the ethical standpoint.

Cases 6-3–6-6 are not disguised or synthesized examples; they are drawn from legal records and form a portion of the growing case law on the duty to warn. The cases themselves do not necessarily bespeak ethical misconduct. Rather, they are cited here to guide the reader regarding legal cases that interface with the general principle of confidentiality.

Case 6-5: Dr. Shaw, a dentist, was in group therapy with Mr. and Mrs. Billian. Shaw became romantically involved with Mrs. Billian, only to be discovered one morning at 2:00 A.M. in bed with her by Mr. Billian, who had broken into Shaw's apartment. On finding his wife in bed nude with Dr. Shaw, Mr. Billian shot at Shaw five times, but did not kill him.

Dr. Shaw sued the psychiatric team in charge of the group therapy program because of the team's alleged negligence in not warning him that Mr. Billian's "unstable and violent condition" presented a "foreseeable and immediate danger" to him (*Shaw v. Glickman*, 1980). In this case, the Maryland courts held that, although the therapists knew Mr. Billian carried a handgun, they could not necessarily have inferred that Billian might have had a propensity to invoke the "old Solon law" (i.e., a law stating that shooting the wife's lover could be considered justifiable homicide) and may not even have known that Billian harbored any animosity toward Dr. Shaw. The court also noted, however, that, even if the team had this information, they would have violated Maryland law had they disclosed it.

Case 6-6: Lee Morgenstein, age 15, was in psychotherapy with a New Jersey psychiatrist, Dr. Milano, for 2 years. Morgenstein was involved with drugs and discussed fantasies of using a knife to threaten people. He also told Dr. Milano of sexual experiences and emotional involvement with Kimberly McIntosch, a neighbor 5 years his senior. Morgenstein frequently expressed anxiety and jealousy when Ms. McIntosch dated other men, and he reported to Dr. Milano that he once fired a BB gun at a car in which she was riding. One day, Morgenstein stole a prescription blank from Dr. Milano and attempted to purchase 30 Seconal tablets with it. The pharmacist became suspicious and called Dr. Milano, who advised the pharmacist to send the boy home. Morgenstein obtained a gun after leaving the pharmacy and later that day shot Kimberly McIntosch to death.

Dr. Milano had reportedly tried to reach his client by phone to talk about the stolen prescription blank, but was too late to prevent the shooting. Ms. McIntosch's father, a physician who was familiar with the *Tarasoff* decision, and his wife ultimately filed a civil damage suit against Dr. Milano for the wrongful death of their daughter, asserting that Milano should have warned Kimberly or taken reasonable steps to protect her.

Dr. Milano sought to dismiss, the suit claiming that the *Tarasoff* principle should not be applied in New Jersey for four reasons. First, to do so would impose an unworkable duty because the prediction of dangerousness is unreliable. Second, violating the client's confidentiality would have interfered with effective treatment. Third, assertion of the *Tarasoff* principle could deter therapists from treating potentially violent patients. Finally, Milano claimed that all of this might lead to an increase in unnecessary commitments to institutions. The court rejected each of these arguments and denied the motion to dismiss the case (*McIntosch v. Milano*, 1979). The court noted that the duty to warn was a valid concept, and, despite the fact that therapists cannot be 100% accurate in predictions, they should be able to weigh the relationships of the parties. An analogy was drawn that compared the situation with warning communities and individuals about carriers of a contagious disease. The court stated that confidentiality is not absolute and must yield to the greater welfare of the community, especially in the case of imminent danger.

Case 6-7: James, a juvenile, was incarcerated for 18 months at a county facility. During the course of his confinement, James threatened to murder a child in the neighborhood if released, although no particular individual was mentioned. James was paroled and did indeed kill a child shortly thereafter.

In the litigation that resulted from this case (*Thompson v. County of Alameda*, 1980), the chief concern was whether the county had a duty to warn the local police, neighborhood parents, or James' mother of his threat. While recognizing the duty of the county to protect its citizens, the California Supreme Court declined to extend the *Tarasoff* doctrine to this case, noting that it would be impractical and negate rehabilitative efforts to give out general public warnings of nonspecific threats for each person paroled. Warning the custodial parent was also deemed futile because one would not expect her to provide constant supervision ("*Tarasoff* Duty," 1980).

After many years of state court decisions clarifying the *Tarasoff* doctrines, a 1991 Florida decision (*Boynton v. Burglass*, 1991) complicated matters still further.

Case 6-8: The Florida state appeals court declined to adopt a duty to warn and held that a psychiatrist who knew or should have known that a patient presented a threat of violence did not have a duty to warn the intended victim. The case was brought against Dr. Burglass, a psychiatrist who had treated Lawrence Blaylock. Mr. Blaylock shot and killed Wayne Boynton, and Boynton's parents alleged that Burglass should have known about the danger to their son and should have warned him. The trial court dismissed the case for failure to state a cause of action. The appeals court declined to follow the *Tarasoff* case, ruling instead that such a duty is "neither reasonable nor workable and is potentially fatal to effective patient-therapist relationships." The court cited the inexact nature of psychiatry and considered it virtually impossible to foresee a patient's dangerousness. The court also noted a common law rule that one person has no duty to control the conduct of another. Although a "special circumstance" may create such an obligation in some cases, this was not deemed true in Blaylock's case because he was a voluntary outpatient.

The bottom line for psychotherapists is this: consult a lawyer familiar with the standards that apply in your particular jurisdiction. Such consultation proved very helpful to the two practitioners who treated Billy Gene Viviano:

Case 6-9: In March 1985, a jury awarded Billy Gene Viviano $1 million for injuries he had received at work. Much to Mr. Viviano's dismay, Judge Veronica Wicker overturned the verdict and ordered a new trial. During the next several months, Mr. Viviano became depressed and sought treatment from psychiatrist Dudley Stewart and psychologist Charles Moan. During the course of his treatment, Mr. Viviano voiced threats toward Judge Wicker and other people connected with his lawsuit. Drs. Stewart and Moan informed the judge of these threats, and Mr. Viviano was arrested, pleaded guilty to contempt of court, and agreed to a voluntary psychiatric hospitalization. Viviano and his family sued the two doctors for negligence, malpractice, and invasion of privacy, but the jury found that the doctors had acted appropriately. Viviano appealed, but lost again (*In re Viviano*, 1994).

In ruling for Drs. Stewart and Moan, the Louisiana Court of Appeals cited the *Tarasoff* case, noted that Dr. Stewart repeatedly consulted an attorney prior to disclosing the threats, and cited testimony by both doctors that Mr. Viviano's threats had become increasingly intense, to the point at which both believed he would attempt to carry them out. After weighing these factors, the appellate court reasoned that the applicable standard of care in warning third parties had been followed.

HIV and AIDS

Psychotherapists who work with clients infected with the human immunodeficiency virus (HIV) or who have developed acquired immunodeficiency syndrome (AIDS) must consider additional issues with respect to confidentiality and reporting obligations. McGuire, Nieri, Abbott, Sheridan, and Fisher (1995) studied the relationship between therapist's beliefs and ethical decision making when working with clients who are HIV positive and who refuse to warn sexual partners or use safe sex practices. Psychologists licensed in Florida were the focus of the survey because of a state law mandating HIV-AIDS education. Although homophobia was low among psychologists sampled, increases in homophobia were significantly related to the likelihood of breaching confidentiality in AIDS-related cases. This finding suggests that some degree of prejudice may drive behavior in these circumstances.

Therapists should remain current regarding medical data on transmission risks and interventions. They also should be aware of state laws regarding professional interactions with HIV patients. Therapists should speak openly and directly with clients about risks of "dangerous" behaviors. Individuals who are putting others at risk typically have emotional conflicts about this behavior and may be grateful for a therapist's attention to the issue (Knapp & VandeCreek, 1990; VandeCreek & Knapp, 1993). If the client continues to resist informing partners or using safe practices, clinical judgment is a key issue in the duty to protect. If all other options are exhausted, the therapist may have to breach confidentiality to warn identified partners; however, one should first notify the client, explain the decision, and seek permission. The client may agree to go along with the notification. Once again, such case patterns should be an occasion to consult colleagues and attorneys and to be sure that one is not acting because of prejudice.

Imminent Danger and Confidentiality

At one time, the APA's "Ethical Principles of Psychologists" (APA, 1981) authorized the disclosure of confidential material without the client's consent only "in those unusual circumstances in which not to do so would result in clear danger to the person or others." Perhaps as a reflection of the legal developments reported

here, the current APA "Code of Conduct" simply notes: "Psychologists have a primary obligation to take reasonable precautions to respect the confidentiality rights of those with whom they work" (APA, 1992; ES: 5.02). Despite more permissive current language, we believe that one should only disclose information to the extent necessary to remove the danger. Consider these case examples:

Case 6-10: Bernard Bizzie, Ed.D., was about to leave for the weekend when he received an emergency call from a client, who claimed to have taken a number of pills in an attempt to kill herself. Bizzie told her to contact her physician and come in to see him at 9:00 A.M. on Monday morning. He made no other attempts to intervene. The client died later that evening without making any other calls for assistance.

Case 6-11: Mitchell Morose, age 21, was being treated by Ned Novice, a psychology intern at a university counseling center. Morose had been increasingly depressed and anxious about academic failure and dependency issues with respect to his family. During one session, Morose told Novice that he was contemplating suicide, had formulated a plan to carry it out, and was working on a note that he would leave "to teach my parents a lesson." Novice attempted to convince Morose to enter a psychiatric hospital for treatment in view of these feelings, but Morose accused Novice of "acting like my parents" and left the office. Novice immediately called George Graybeard, Psy.D., his supervisor, for advice. Graybeard agreed with Novice about the risk of suicide, and, acting under a provision of their state's commitment law, they contacted Morose's parents, who could legally seek an emergency involuntary hospitalization as his next of kin. The parents were told only that their son was in treatment, that he was having suicidal ideation, and that he was refusing care. The parents then assisted in having Morose committed for treatment. Following discharge, Morose filed an ethical complaint against Novice and Graybeard for violating his confidentiality, especially by communicating with his parents.

Dr. Bizzie was clearly unethical in his negligence by not attending more directly to his client's needs. Even those rare psychologists who have previously asserted in print that one should never disclose confidential information without the informed consent of the client would not counsel inaction in the face of such a risk (Dubey, 1974; Siegel, 1979). There are many steps Bizzie could have taken short of violating the client's confidentiality. Most obviously, he should have attempted (at the very least) to learn her location and assure himself that help would reach her if he were unable to do so. While there are certainly times when suicidal threats or gestures are manipulative and do not represent a genuine risk, it is a foolish and insensitive colleague who ignores them or attempts to pass them off glibly to another.

The case involving Mr. Morose represents a variation on the same theme. Novice certainly had reason to be concerned and to discuss the matter with his supervisor. (As an aside, we must assume that, early in their work together, Novice had explained his "intern" status to Morose, including the fact that the case would routinely be discussed with his supervisor.) Novice had attempted to ensure the safety of his client through voluntary hospitalization, but the client declined. Because the state laws, well known to Dr. Graybeard, provided a mechanism that called for the involvement of next of kin, the decision to contact the parents was not inappropriate, despite the client's wishes. Morose had provided ample reason to consider him at risk, and the responsible parties disclosed only those matters deemed absolutely necessary to ensure his safety (i.e., that he was at risk for suicide and refusing treatment). The parents were not given details or other confidential material. In the end, Morose's confidence was indeed violated, and he was angry. Under the circumstances, however, Novice and Graybeard behaved in an ethically appropriate fashion.

If there are means to anticipate and avoid such dilemmas in one's practice, three separate issues are probably involved. First, each psychologist should clearly advise every client at the start of their professional relationship of limits on confidentiality. Second, psychologists should think through and come to terms with the circumstances under which they will breach confidentiality or privilege. Consultation with an attorney about the law in the jurisdiction in which

the psychologist practices is crucial because of diverse case law decisions and variable statutes. Finally, should an actual circumstance arise bearing on these issues, consultation with colleagues is appropriate to sort out alternatives that may not have come to mind initially. These steps will not solve all such problems, but can help reduce their likelihood.

ACCESS TO RECORDS

Psychologists keep records of their work and clients for a variety of reasons—legal obligation, reluctance to rely on memory, communication to other professionals, ready availability of important data, and documentation of services provided, to name a few. By definition, such records will often contain confidential material, and, as long as they exist, someone other than the psychologist who collected the material may seek access to them. In addressing this issue, we must first consider the process of securing a client's informed consent for the release of information. We must then consider the claims and circumstances under which various parties might seek access, as well as the nature of the information being sought. Finally, we consider the use of client records for teaching or research purposes, including the use of recordings and photographic materials.

Informed Consent for the Release of Records

The existence of transferable records can be of great assistance or substantial detriment to clients, depending on what is contained in them and how they are used. Often, the process of consent getting is so hurried or perfunctory that clients may not fully understand what they are authorizing or why. Some may even sign release-of-information forms against their wishes because of a variety of subtle and obvious pressures or because no alternatives were offered (Rosen, 1977). The psychologist has an important role in educating and helping to safeguard the client's interests in such cases.

A consent or release-of-information form should contain several key elements, including

(1) the name of the person to whom the records are to be released, (2) which specific records are to be sent, (3) the purpose or intended use, (4) the date the form was signed, (5) an expiration date, (6) any limitations on the data to be provided, (7) the name and signature of the person authorizing the release, and (8) that person's relationship to the client (if not the client) and the signature of a witness (if signed outside the psychologist's presence). If a psychologist receives a release or request for information that does not seem valid or might present some hazard to the client, it would be appropriate to contact the client directly and seek confirmation prior to releasing any material.

Whenever a consent form is signed, the client should be given a copy, and the psychologist should make the original a part of that client's files. The psychologist should also keep a record of which materials were sent, to whom, and when. The materials should be appropriately marked as confidential, and the recipient should be aware of any limitations on their use. One should also exercise caution to see that only material appropriate to the need is sent. Consider this example:

Case 6-12: Kurt Files, Psy.D., had evaluated 8-year-old Sheldon Sputter at his family's request because of school problems. The evaluation included taking a developmental and family history, meeting with both parents, reviewing school progress reports, and administering cognitive and personality tests. Dr. Files discovered that Sheldon had a mild perceptual learning disability and was also reacting to a variety of family stresses, including his mother's reaction to paternal infidelity, his father's recent discovery that Sheldon was not his child, and a host of other family secrets that had recently come to light. He recommended appropriate psychotherapeutic intervention, and the family followed through. Several weeks later, Dr. Files received a signed release form from the school Sheldon attended asking for "any" information he had on Sheldon's problem. Files responded with a letter describing the cognitive test results and referring in general terms to "emotional stresses in the family that are being attended to."

In this situation, the psychologist recognized the school's valid need to know information that could help better serve Sheldon. At the same time, Dr. Files recognized that some of the material was not relevant to the school's role, and he made the appropriate discrimination despite the vague and broad request for any information.

Client Access to Records

Clients' access to their mental health records remains a matter of some controversy, although the issues vary somewhat as a function of the precise type of records involved. The three general types of records are (1) institutional (e.g., hospital, clinic, school, government agency), (2) private practitioners' office records, and (3) so-called working notes. Access to institutional records is often governed by institutional policy and statute. The federal Freedom of Information Act of 1966 and state patients' rights laws often specify a right of access to institutional, agency, or medical records in general. Although mental health records were occasionally excepted in the past, this trend has been rapidly reversing. Records kept by practitioners in the private, as well as institutional, offices may also be covered by specific legislation. Psychologists should assume that any patient may someday ask to see his or her records and that all who persist will ultimately be able to obtain copies, whether the clinician agrees this is a good idea or not. Some portions of psychologists' office records might include material that ought to be safeguarded from disclosure to nonprofessionals (e.g., copies of intelligence test protocols or other such materials that could compromise test security by their release). Disclosure of psychological test data raises special issues (Committee on Psychological Tests and Assessments, 1996); these are discussed in detail in chapter 7. Generally, however, it is the category of records we have termed *working notes* that causes the most concern.

By working notes, we refer to those impressions, hypotheses, and half-formed ideas that a psychologist or trainee may jot down to assist in formulating more comprehensive reports or recommendations later. Often, these notes are reworked into a report, used for discussion with a supervisor, or simply discarded as new data are considered. Because of the speculative and impressionistic nature of such working notes, they may not be meaningful or useful to anyone except the person who made them. Such notes are definitely not the sort of material one would want released to anyone. They should be temporary documents that are occasionally reworked into more formal office or institutional records and subsequently destroyed. Psychologists should be aware that there is always at least some risk that any written materials might someday be disclosed in public through a court proceeding. A regular pattern of reviewing and consolidating detailed working notes into less sensitive summaries should be the rule for all cases. This avoids the danger of an accusation that a case file has been selectively edited simply because court action was pending. The reasons for this suggestion are made clear in the following pages.

One fact should remain uppermost in the reader's mind as the discussion of record access continues. The records do not belong to the client, but rather are the property of the institution or private practitioner, as their generator and keeper, depending on the setting involved. While clients may have a right to copies of, or access to, their records, and certainly an interest in them, the records themselves do not belong to the client unless expressly transferred to the client for some reason. Clients may from time to time assert the claim to a record "because I paid for that report" or "those therapy sessions." In fact, the client paid for services rendered, or perhaps a copy of a report, but not for the actual original records (e.g., case notes, process notes, or test protocols) unless that was a specific part of the agreement.

Opponents of free client access to records generally make two types of claims. First, they assert that, to be properly creative, one must be free to speculate and jot down any thought or comments. Some of these will invariably be erroneous or misleading if taken out of context. Second, opponents of open access might claim that harm may be done by sharing technical psychological information with clients who are not equipped to understand or deal with it (Strassburger, 1975). Consider the case of *Godkin v. Miller* (1975):

Case 6-13: On several occasions between 1962 and 1970, Janet Godkin had been a voluntary mental patient at three different New York hospitals. She and her husband decided to write a book about her experiences and sought access to her records, wishing to verify some of the material. The requests were refused, which led to a lawsuit against the New York State Commissioner of Mental Hygiene and the directors of the hospitals involved ("Doctor and the Law," 1975).

The judge in the case agreed with the refusal to provide the records when the hospitals expressed a preference for releasing the records to another professional rather than the client herself. The rationales presented by hospital staff included that the records would be unintelligible to the layperson; certain of the information might prove detrimental to the individual's current well-being; and the records could contain references to other individuals, who might be harmed by disclosure (Roth, Wolford, & Meisel, 1980). The judge also noted that records are the property of the practitioner or the hospital and that a client consults the practitioner for services, not for records ("Doctor and the Law," 1975). More recently, the New York Supreme Court granted Matthew C. Fox, a former patient of the Binghamton Psychiatric Center, full access to his medical records despite the center's contention that such access would be antitherapeutic (*Fox v. Namani*, 1994). Fox was suing the center for malpractice and acting as his own attorney. Changing views about clients' right of access over the intervening two decades since the *Godkin* case has also contributed to the shift toward releasing records.

Those advocating more open access to records cite the legitimate interest of the client in such materials and regard such access as a means to actually help clients and to improve their rights as consumers (Roth et al., 1980). Other arguments in favor of this position include the notion that providing such records to clients can improve the efficiency of service delivery by avoiding delays when the client is able to share the records directly with other practitioners. Studies performed at the University of Vermont and Pittsburgh's Western Psychiatric Institute suggest that a more open access policy may yield clients who are more cooperative, less anxious, and generally relieved. No adverse effects were documented (Roth et al., 1980). Other psychologists have argued against the assumptions that "professionals know best," "clients are fragile" (Brodsky, 1972), or that secrecy might actually help the client in some way (Fischer, 1972).

The point is often made that, ultimately, clients may well get hold of their records with or without the psychologist's full cooperation. If that is the case, records should be kept and written with that possibility in mind, and the psychologist should be willing to share the material, along with an explanation of terms and answers to other questions that the client may have. In a study conducted in an inpatient psychiatric unit, the effects of client access to records were clearly positive. The clients reported feeling better informed and more involved in their treatment, and the staff became more thoughtful about their notes in the charts (Stein, Furedy, Simonton, & Neuffer, 1979).

We generally favor full client access to their mental health records. However, there may be circumstances, such as notes on group therapy sessions or records collected on behalf of a corporate client regarding many individuals, when full access to records could violate the privacy and confidentiality of another party. There also may be a few rare instances when access to some recorded data might cause substantial and concrete detriment to an individual client.

Case 6-14: During an acute psychotic episode, Tyrone Propper penned a series of bizarre, sexually explicit notes to his psychotherapist. Because the notes seemed clinically relevant at the time, they were kept in the therapist's private case files. Mr. Propper later recovered fully and returned to his job as a bank officer. He visited the therapist for a follow-up session and asked to review the case file to help gain perspective on what had happened to him. Propper had few memories from the psychotic period.

Case 6-15: Barry Icarus had been raised by his aunt and uncle because his parents died when he was 1 year old. He had suffered a reactive depression since his uncle's death from a heart attack on his 16th birthday. Six months of psychotherapy had helped him to deal with the loss successfully and go on to college away from home. A few years later, Barry's aunt died, and he returned to have a few sessions with the same psychologist who had helped him earlier. Barry expressed some interest in reviewing his records with respect to his prior treatment. In the psychologist's file was a developmental history given by the aunt and uncle when Barry was 16. This included the fact, still unknown to Barry, that his mother had been shot to death by his father, who later committed suicide.

In these cases, it would be appropriate for the practitioners in question to delete material (e.g., the sexually explicit notes and the circumstances of the parents' deaths) from the files prior to reviewing them with the clients. The notes could prove embarrassing to the recovered client. Revelation of them would serve no useful purpose and might possibly increase emotional distress. The information on Barry's parents is irrelevant to his reason for seeking treatment now, as at age 16, but was part of a thorough developmental history needed at the time. Providing him with this material now could add stress without an immediate constructive purpose.

When situations of this sort occur, it should be possible to supply the client with the sought-after information minus those sections that might violate the rights of others. In the case of the detrimental material, the residual content could be shared directly with the client. A decision about the actual degree of detriment, however, ought first be made by a professional in a position to offer an unbiased consultation on the matter. If records are appropriately kept in a factual manner, with a minimum of speculation, written in clear language, and well documented, there should be little need to fear client access.

Psychologists who do choose to make records available to clients should give serious consideration to the manner in which this will be done. Do you insist on being present? Do you charge for your time, or is it considered part of your service? Do you make your policy on such matters clear to clients before therapy (or other service delivery) starts? We believe that it is desirable to let clients know policies early in the course of the professional relationship. We also believe that it is desirable for the psychologist to be present during the record review to offer elaboration, explain technical terms, or deal with the client's feelings related to the material. If a significant amount of time is involved, it is appropriate to charge for this service; however, this should be tempered with an understanding of the client's financial situation, balanced with his or her needs and rights of access in a particular situation. The client who has terminated treatment for lack of funds, for example, should not be barred from a file review for inability to pay.

Access by Family Members

Occasionally, a concerned family member will seek access to a client's records. When the client is a child or has been deemed legally incompetent, parents or guardians may actually be entitled to legal access. Psychologists should recognize the unique problems that arise when working with minors or families and should be sensitive to each individual's right to privacy and confidentiality in such circumstances. From the outset of any such relationship, all parties should be informed about the specific nature of the confidential relationship. A discussion about what sorts of information might be shared and with whom should be raised early. This is not a difficult or burdensome process when done as a routine practice (Koocher & Keith-Spiegel, 1990).

Case 6-16: Cynthia Childs, Psy.D., has been treating 7-year-old Max Bashem for about a month. Max was referred for treatment because of secondary enuresis and acting-out behaviors of recent onset. The birth of a new sibling in the Bashem family several weeks ago seems to have been a precipitant. Near the end of the fifth therapy session, Max expresses some anger about his new sibling and tells Dr. Childs, "Tonight after my parents go to bed, I'm gonna kill that little weasel!"

Case 6-17: Donna Rhea, age 15, was also in psychotherapy with Dr. Childs. Donna feels alienated from her parents and is sexually active. Her parents

discovered that she has contracted genital herpes, and, in a moment of emotional distress after they learn this fact, she accused them of not being as "understanding as Dr. Childs." The parents were furious that the psychologist knew their daughter was sexually active and did not tell them. They demanded a full briefing from Dr. Childs, or they would pull their daughter out of treatment. They also threatened to file an ethics complaint.

These two cases illustrate some difficult, but not insoluble, problems (Taylor & Adelman, 1989). In the case of Max, Dr. Childs must consider several factors, not the least of which is the seriousness of Max's threat. Does Max have a history of violence toward others? Is he exaggerating his anger in the context of therapy for emphasis? Certainly, Dr. Childs will want to explore this issue with Max before ending the session, but suppose she does feel that there is some risk to the sibling? Suppose that Max cannot commit himself to leave the baby unharmed in the coming week between sessions. Childs could express her concern and discuss with Max the need to help keep him from doing something he might later regret. She could talk with him about alternatives and explore a variety of them, one being a family conference in which Max could be encouraged to share some of his angry feelings more directly. If all else fails and Childs believes that she cannot otherwise stop Max from hurting his sibling, she must discuss the matter with his parents as a duty to protect issue. Not to do so would constitute malpractice. While such a circumstance would be rare indeed, Childs should at least be certain to discuss with Max, before doing it, her need to violate the confidence for his ultimate benefit.

In the case of Donna, the problem is more complex. Dr. Childs almost certainly would have lost the trust of her client had she chosen to violate Donna's confidence. At the same time, providing a value-free climate in psychotherapy may have the net result of unintentionally condoning Donna's sexual behavior (Baumrind, 1990). The parents may be jealous of the trust and respect their daughter seems to have in the psychologist, while being angry and disappointed at her sexual activity and infection. A conference per se is not inappropriate, but would probably be best conducted as a family meeting with Donna present. Dr. Childs could attempt to be supportive and therapeutic in such a session without necessarily breaking a confidence. It is unclear what sort of information the parents are seeking. Better still would have been a pretreatment family conference with a discussion of the psychotherapy relationship and any attendant limitations. An outright refusal to meet with the parents in this circumstance would not serve the interests of any of the parties. Many state laws do permit minors to obtain treatment for venereal disease or birth control information without parental consent and in confidence. Dr. Childs' behavior does not seem to have been unethical per se. Other helpful suggestions for dealing with confidentiality issues with child clients may be found in Taylor and Adelman's 1989 paper.

When access to records is sought by family members of an adult, it should generally be denied unless there is some special reason to consider the request. Special reasons might include the imminent danger test discussed above, or the legally adjudicated incapacity of the client.

Case 6-18: Marla Noma was a cancer patient for many years, and during that period she occasionally consulted Michael Tact, Ph.D., about her fears and concerns related to the illness. During a surgical procedure, Marla was left comatose and was being kept alive on life support equipment, although there was little chance of any recovery. Members of her family planned to seek court authorization to discontinue mechanical life-support equipment and wondered whether any of Tact's records or conversations with Marla might provide some guidance to them and the court about her wishes.

In such a case, when the client cannot speak for herself, it probably would not be unethical for Dr. Tact to respond openly to a duly authorized request for information from the next of kin. The surviving line of consent generally recognized by courts is as follows. First in line to grant consent is the spouse (even if living apart from the client, as long as they are not divorced). Second are the children of legal age, with each

such child having equal voice. Next are parents or grandparents, followed by siblings, each having equal voice. If none of the above survive, courts will occasionally designate the next nearest relative or closest friend.

Court Access to Records

The concept of privileged communication discussed in the first part in this chapter is actually rather narrow, focusing on what material is protected from disclosure in court. Despite privilege, however, some courts or litigants may still seek access to protected information, as well as other confidential material. While psychologists must certainly respect appropriate requests emanating from the courts, they must also reasonably safeguard material from inappropriate release. Personal working notes are generally not subject to disclosure in court, especially in civil cases. In criminal cases, however, it is not unusual for a *subpoena duces tecum* to be issued, demanding that the psychologist appear in court bringing "any and all, files, documents, reports, papers, recordings, and notes" regarding the case in question.

It is important to understand the differences between a subpoena and a court order. A subpoena simply compels a response and in some jurisdictions can be issued simply by an attorney's request to a clerk of courts. The response need not be what is demanded in the subpoena document. If the papers seek documents or testimony that may be privileged, the psychologist should seek clarification from the client's attorney or the court. A court order, on the other hand, is based on a hearing before a judge and compels a disclosure unless the order is appealed to a higher court. In the end, the court must decide what is protected and what is not.

The first thing that a psychologist should do when a subpoena is served is simply nothing. That is, nothing should be surrendered to the person serving the subpoena no matter how aggressive the request. The subpoena document should be accepted, and the psychologist should then consult legal counsel regarding applicable law and resulting obligations. If it is ultimately determined that the call for the records has been appropriately issued by a court of competent authority, a psychologist may be placed in a very awkward position, especially if the client does not wish to have the material disclosed.

If a subpoena arrives from a client's attorney and no release form is included, check with your client, not the attorney, before releasing the documents. If a signed release form is included, but the clinician believes that the material may be clinically or legally damaging, discuss it with the client. Psychologists concerned about releasing actual notes offer to prepare a prompt report or summary. In a technical sense, a request from a client's attorney is legally the same as a request from the client; however, it is not unreasonable for the clinician to personally confirm the client's wishes, especially if the content of the records is sensitive in nature.

On occasion, a subpoena generated by an attorney opposing the psychologist's client or representing another person may arrive at a clinician's office. Under such circumstances, it is reasonable to contact the attorney who issued the subpoena and say: "I cannot disclose whether or not the person noted in the subpoena is now or ever was my client. If the person were my client, I could not provide any information without a signed release from that individual or a valid court order." Next, contact your client, explain the situation, and ask for permission to talk with his or her attorney. Ask the patient's attorney to work out privilege issues with the opposing attorney or move to quash the subpoena. These steps will ensure that the person to whom you owe prime obligations (i.e., your client) is protected to the full extent allowed by law. When in doubt, consult your attorney for advice, but never simply ignore a subpoena. An excellent and detailed discussion on coping with subpoenas for raw test data has been prepared by APA's Committee on Legal Issues (1996). This includes a detailed flow chart, reproduced here as Figure 1. Although the general principles illustrated in Figure 1 also apply to subpoenas intended to compel testimony, a detailed discussion of those issues appears in chapter 15.

Clinical psychologist Polly Rost learned the hard way about the importance of consulting an attorney in response to a subpoena for records. The Pennsylvania Board of Psychology

issued a formal reprimand to Rost for failing to seek legal advice in dealing with a subpoena. The parents of a child client were suing the York Jewish Community Center because their child suffered headaches after a fall there. Rost released the records of the child to the parents' attorney, and later to the Community Center's attorney, in response to a subpoena. The Pennsylvania licensing board ruled that Rost should have sought the advice of counsel before releasing records in response to the subpoena, and the courts upheld that ruling (*Rost v. Pennsylvania Board of Psychology*, 1995).

When it is appropriate to release materials from your case files, offer a notarized copy rather than the originals. If the court specifies that you must provide the originals, be certain to retain a notarized copy of the records for yourself or have your attorney do so. It is not unusual for documents to be lost or misplaced as they travel through the legal system.

Case 6-19: Arnold and Anita Abuser were being treated in marital therapy by Samuel Silent, Ed.D., when their child died of apparently inflicted injuries. Dr. Silent was subpoenaed to appear before a grand jury investigating the child's death and questioned about the content of his sessions with the Abusers as the district attorney sought incriminating evidence about the couple. There was no privileged communication statute in Dr. Silent's state, and a judge ordered him to testify or be held in jail for contempt of court. The Abusers did not wish Dr. Silent to discuss in court any material from their sessions.

Dr. Silent is in a particularly difficult situation. If he bows to the court order, he may be seen as violating his clients' confidentiality (ethical violation). If the Abusers are guilty and the psychologist's silence precludes prosecution, he may be protecting his clients to the detriment of society as a whole. In addition, if the Abusers had given Dr. Silent information about the abuse, he would have had a legal obligation to notify the state authorities under the mandated child abuse reporting statutes operating in all 50 states. If he knew of abuse and did not report it, he could be prosecuted.

If Dr. Silent does not comply with a judge's order to testify, he can be fined or jailed for

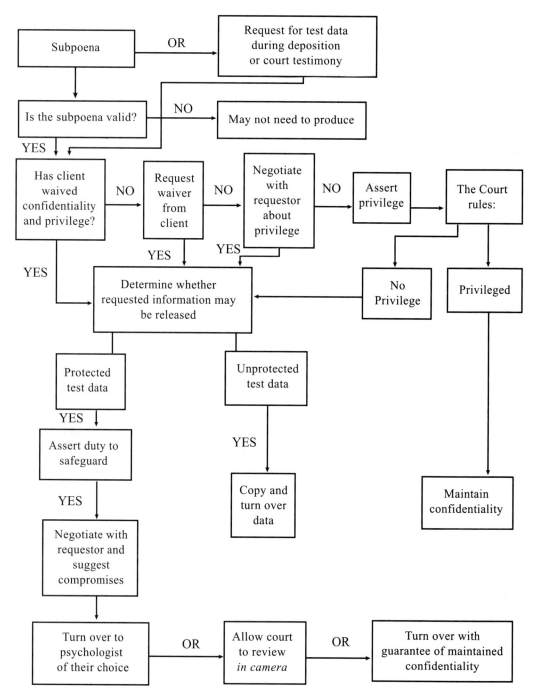

Figure 6-1 Coping with subpoenas: Disclosure Issues Diagram, used with permission from the Committee on Legal Issues, American Psychological Association, 1996.

contempt of court and may be accused of breaking the law (also an ethical violation). This situation is a prime example of a point at which ethical behavior may be at variance with legal requirements. If Dr. Silent believes he should not testify, the best advice would be to resist disclosure of confidential material using all legitimate legal avenues. When such avenues are exhausted, and if they fail, Dr. Silent would probably not be faulted for ultimately disclosing the confidential material. On the other hand, if he chooses to go to jail on a matter of principle rather than disclose the confidential material, it also seems unlikely that he would be found to have violated professional ethics solely because of a resulting contempt citation (ES: 1.02).

If Silent knew of abuse and chose to disclose details from the outset under mandated reporting laws, he would also not be considered unethical. If Silent had known of abuse and had failed to report it, he could possibly decline to testify, citing his Fifth Amendment right under the U.S. Constitution against self-incrimination, although such a claim is no protection from the ethical impropriety of not reporting the abuse.

Case 6-20: John Spleen, Ph.D., filed for divorce from his wife Sandra under circumstances that were less than amicable. John is a psychologist, and Sandra believed that he was lying about his income in the process of reaching a negotiated financial settlement. She sought a court order for her spouse to disclose the names, addresses, and billing records of his clients so that she and her attorney could verify the actual income from his practice.

Dr. Spleen is in a difficult position, even assuming that he has nothing to hide in a personal sense. Disclosing the names and addresses of his clients could certainly prove embarrassing and stressful to the clients. Perhaps there are ways for his records to be audited in confidence by a bonded professional, without the need to contact clients individually or otherwise disclose their names. In any event, the Spleens' dispute is a civil matter, and courts are less likely to pursue disclosure for civil matters than they are in a criminal or malpractice action. In a similar case, a California appellate court protected the confidentiality of the psychologist's records from the spouse, noting that public disclosure of client status itself might prove harmful to a client.

Case 6-21: Cindy Weisbeck was treated by James Hess, Ph.D., from November 1986 until June 1987 at South Dakota's Mountain Plains Counseling Center. In September 1987, he hired her as a part-time secretary at the center, of which he was the sole owner. Some 20 months after he stopped counseling Ms. Weisbeck, Dr. Hess allegedly initiated a sexual relationship with her. Cindy's husband, James Weisbeck, sued. In seeking to show that Hess had a history of taking advantage of vulnerable female clients, Mr. Weisbeck sought access to a list of Hess's patients going back 7 years and the right to depose Hess's personal therapist, a social worker named Tom Terry (*Weisbeck v. Hess*, 1994).

In the case involving Dr. Hess, the state supreme court denied the request for access to client records and the right to depose Hess's therapist, although privacy of the clients was not cited as the primary rationale. Rather, the court noted that the APA ethics code operating at the time did not establish Hess's behavior as a harmful act.

These examples clearly illustrate the importance of the recommendation, made in the section on client access to records, that personal notes containing speculation, hypotheses, and other tentative jottings be purged or synthesized frequently into more permanent and factual records. The best defense against harm caused by informal-type notes is to limit their life span. Files should be routinely culled of obsolete material, especially of the informal sort.

Computer Records and Cyberconfidentiality

The tremendous increase during the past few years in use of computers to store, retrieve, and transmit text and data (including patient records) raises many new types of confidentiality concerns. Vast amounts of information can now be stored in small magnetic or optical packages that can be easily used, misused, or misplaced. Use of on-line electronic communication services (e.g., America Online, Prodigy, and CompuServe) provides great convenience, as well as considerable unresolved confusion and controversy related to rights and obligations of users (Rosenoer, 1995). Psychologists making use of new technology must remain thoughtful and cautious about the hazards to confidentiality that result.

Case 6-22: Lydia Laptop, Psy.D., was busy typing on her portable computer as she flew home from a professional meeting. She had nearly finished the treatment summary on a new client when a familiar message came over the public address system: "In preparation for landing, please return your seatbacks to the upright position and stow any items you removed for use during the flight." Dr. Laptop saved the file to a diskette and placed the diskette in the seat pocket in front of her as she packed up her computer. The aircraft experienced a bit of turbulence as she zipped up the travel bag and slipped it under the seat. She lost her train of thought for a moment. Dr. Laptop walked off the plane 10 minutes later, leaving the diskette full of confidential client information in the seat pocket. As soon as she got home, she realized what had happened and called the airline. The diskette was never recovered.

Case 6-23: Hugh-Jim Bissel, Ed.D., received a faxed release of information form from a psychologist in another city. One of Bissel's former clients had relocated and was seeking treatment in his new locale. The new therapist was seeking information on the previous work done with Dr. Bissel. Bissel noted the E-mail address listed on the new therapist's letterhead and went on line to transmit the requested note. Unfortunately, Bissel was chatting on the phone as he attempted this task, and he lapsed into an oft-repeated pattern of keystrokes, accidentally transmitting the confidential material to 3,500 subscribers to International Poodle Fanciers On-Line list server.

If Dr. Laptop and her client were lucky, the diskette ended up in the trash as the airline cleaning crew went through the cabin. Dr. Bissel and his client were not so fortunate. The extent of these and other horror stories on "virtual" privacy violations is limited only by one's

imagination. Any psychologist planning to make use of new technology should carefully consider confidentiality issues in the implementation process. If Dr. Laptop were using commonly available encryption software for her confidential files, the loss of the disk would mean only lost work because any curious finder of her diskette would be unable to access its contents. Before transmitting any confidential material by E-mail, fax, or other electronic means, Dr. Bissel should have ascertained that the intended recipient address was appropriately secure and accurate. Technology will continue to evolve, but the ethical principle remains constant: Psychologists are ultimately responsible for safeguarding the privacy of material entrusted to them in confidence. If you are not certain that a particular new technology will be adequately secure, stick with the safer mode of communication to protect the client's welfare (see chapter 12).

Third-Party Access: Insurers and Managed Care

The role of so-called third parties is touched on in chapter 10 from the financial perspective. The point to be made here is that clients may sometimes authorize the release of information to third parties without fully understanding the implications. When clients decide to submit a claim for mental health benefits to an insurance company (or authorize a clinician to do so on their behalf), they may not realize that, in so doing, the provider of services is being authorized to share certain information (e.g., diagnosis, type of service offered, dates services were rendered, duration of treatment, etc.). In some circumstances, insurers or companies designated to manage mental health benefits may be authorized to seek detailed information from case files, including a client's current symptom status, details of a treatment plan, or other sensitive material. Once information leaves a psychologist's office, it is beyond his or her control, and insurance companies may not exercise the same caution and responsibility as the individual practitioner. Some insurance companies, for example, participate in rating bureaus or similar reporting services that may be accessible to other companies at some future date. A recent press account illustrated the problem with a description of the case of a business executive who was denied an individual disability insurance policy because he sought psychotherapy for family and work-related stresses. Disability underwriters described this denial as a nearly universal practice, and some insurers use a history of therapy as an exclusionary criterion for individual health or life insurance policies (Bass, 1995).

It is not always clear to clients that they are authorizing such a release when they turn over an insurance policy number or sign a claim form, although a specific general release statement is invariably there (usually in small print near the signature line), just as it is whenever someone applies for life insurance coverage. This yields an interesting problem when it comes to informing clients about the implications of their using insurance coverage to pay for psychological services.

Case 6-24: Victor Vigilant, Ph.D., routinely informs his clients about the issue of disclosure to insurance companies in the following manner. He tells clients who have coverage, "If you choose to use your coverage, I shall have to file a form with the company telling them when our appointments were and what services I performed (i.e., psychotherapy, consultation, or evaluation). I will also have to formulate a diagnosis and advise the company of that. The company claims to keep this information confidential, although I have no control over the information once it leaves this office. If you have questions about this, you may wish to check with the company providing the coverage. You may certainly choose to pay for my services out of pocket and avoid the use of insurance altogether, if you wish."

The client is in a difficult situation. Refusing to authorize release of information will result in the insurer refusing to pay the claim. Some clients may not care about the issue. A parent whose child is being seen for an assessment of perceptually based learning disabilities, for example, may be unconcerned. On the other hand, a client holding a sensitive public office might very well wish to avoid informing any third party that a psychologist was being con-

sulted. In some cases, the matter is further complicated by the fact that an employer may be self-insured, and claim forms may be sent back through company headquarters or be accessible to management. This may not constitute a significant threat, but for certain clients and some diagnoses, it might be best to avoid any type of disclosure without first checking on the channels through which the information will flow.

Peer review groups, such as professional association ethics committees, constitute a different type of third party with which the matter of disclosing confidential material occasionally becomes an issue. Psychologists are obligated to respond to inquiries from such duly constituted bodies, although they are obligated to first observe the basic principle of confidentiality. When asked by such a committee to respond, the psychologist should first determine whether an appropriate waiver of confidentiality has been obtained. No ethics committee can press an inquiry about a client unless it first obtains a signed release from the client regarding the psychologist's obligation of confidentiality. The same is true of complaints to licensing boards or other regulatory bodies. The principle here is the same as the one involved in malpractice litigation. The psychologist cannot defend his or her case unless the freedom to discuss the content of the relationship in question is granted.

Case 6-25: Roger Control filed an ethics complaint against a psychologist who allegedly "made my problems worse instead of better." Mr. Control complained about one session in particular that "caused me strong mental anguish and insomnia for several weeks." Mr. Control asserted that the dozen prior sessions with the psychologist were irrelevant and would only agree to let the psychologist talk about the one traumatic session he had cited. The ethics committee, noting that this limitation would not permit a sufficient response by the psychologist to their inquiry, declined to investigate the case without a broader authorization.

Suggestions for how to deal with licensing board and ethics committee complaints in general were discussed in greater detail in chapter 2.

TAKING ADVANTAGE OF CONFIDENTIAL INFORMATION

Occasionally, psychotherapists have an opportunity to gain personally as a result of information received in confidence. One such case involved Manhattan psychiatrist, Robert Willis.

Case 6-26: Robert Willis, M.D., was treating Mrs. Joan Weill, wife of the board chair of Primerica Corporation. In the course of treatment, Willis learned of business events in the life of his client and her spouse that were likely to affect the value of Primerica stock. The information communicated during treatment was not public knowledge. Dr. Willis made strategic investment decisions based on the information and earned more than $27,000 as a result. In a widely reported turn of events, Dr. Willis was caught, prosecuted, and fined by the Securities and Exchange Commission for "insider trading" (Rosenbaum, 1994).

It is impossible to know how often psychotherapists may benefit in some way from information that they receive in the course of work with clients. The use of such information is not intrinsically unethical. For example, a client who reports distress about an unreliable automobile mechanic may lead the therapist to avoid using that business. However, that is the sort of information generally available to many people by word of mouth and would not lead to personal gain at the expense of others, as was the case with Dr. Willis.

CONFIDENTIAL MATERIAL IN THE CLASSROOM AND LABORATORY

Ethical issues related to the classroom and psychological research laboratories are addressed in chapters 16 and 17; however, it is important to note at least a few special issues related to confidential material in such settings. The first point to be made involves confidential materials adapted for teaching purposes, and the second focuses on confidentiality problems involving research data.

Classroom Materials

Ideally, any materials prepared for teaching that use sensitive or confidential material involve the full informed consent of the client. When videotapes or audiotapes, detailed summaries of case material, or other accounts of psychological material not otherwise in the public domain are adapted, the client or client's guardian should have consented to the use of the material for teaching purposes. This is especially true when the nature of the material (e.g., visual reproductions or recognizable facts) might make it possible to recognize the client(s). Formal consent may not be necessary if the material is disguised sufficiently to make recognition of the client impossible. Below, we present appropriate examples. Some of the cases cited here involve actual legal decisions in the public domain and are cited as such, but others are disguised or synthesized versions of actual situations or case material. These are presented in a general manner so no real people are recognizable, except perhaps to themselves.

Case 6-27: Emily Barrassed entered psychotherapy with Will U. Tell, Psy.D., and was seen several times per week for nearly 2 years. During the course of these sessions, Ms. Barrassed shared a number of intimate and sensitive fantasies and life events with Dr. Tell. At the end of their work together, both felt that impressive progress had been made. Dr. Tell asked if Ms. Barrassed might permit him to mention some details of their work together in a book he was writing, provided he disguised the material so that she could not be recognized. She agreed and signed a release form he had prepared. Several years later, Dr. Tell's book became a best-seller, and Ms. Barrassed discovered, to her shock, that she was easily recognized in the book by those who knew her. Dr. Tell had changed some details, such as the name, city, and so on, but described her family, upbringing, occupation, and one-eyed amputee spouse without disguise.

Case 6-28: Irwin Klunk, Ph.D., shared the test data obtained in an evaluation of a disturbed child with his graduate psychology class. He passed around copies of drawings, test protocols, and interpretations. All of the sheets bore the child's full name and other identifying information. One of the students in the class was a friend of the boy's mother and told her. The mother filed an ethics complaint against the professor for violating her son's confidentiality. The professor responded that, because the testee was a minor and because the students were at a graduate level, he had not believed it necessary to remove identifying data.

The chances of having a relative, friend, acquaintance, or colleague of a client in the audience is not as small as one might imagine, and the consequences of revealing a confidence or sharing intimate details of a client's personal life in recognizable fashion may be devastating. There are times when this is unlikely, such as a classroom discussion of a response to the Rorschach inkblots in which the client is identified only by age and sex or the use of a case history that has been thoroughly blinded. Actual individual consent may not be needed for such material. When in doubt, however, the material should be reviewed with a colleague to be certain that some identifying facts have not inadvertently been included. Likewise, any superfluous facts that might help to identify the client, while not adding meaningful detail to the example, should be omitted.

Research Data

Perhaps the best example of the difficulties resulting with respect to confidential research data is the case of Samuel Popkin.

Case 6-29: On November 21, 1972, Samuel L. Popkin, an assistant professor of government at Harvard University, was imprisoned under a U.S. District Court order for refusing to answer several questions before a federal grand jury investigating the publication of the "Pentagon Papers." Popkin asserted a First Amendment right to refuse to provide the information collected as part of his scholarly research on Vietnam and U.S. involvement in that country. For failing to testify, he was subjected to confinement for the duration of the grand jury's service. He was released from jail after 7 days when the grand jury was discharged, and the U.S.

Supreme Court later refused to review the order that led to his confinement (Carroll, 1973).

Popkin was a political scientist, but he might easily have been a psychologist conducting attitude research or interviews on the personality structure of paramilitary militias or urban street gangs. Despite the fact that such research might not be able to take place without some pledge of confidentiality to respondents, "national security interests" led the courts to overrule any claim of privilege or assertion of confidentiality. Consider the case that follows:

Case 6-30: Seb Terfuge, Ph.D., was conducting a field study of homosexual encounters in a public men's lavatory. Using a set of unobtrusive timing devices and a periscopic videotape apparatus, Dr. Terfuge concealed himself in a toilet stall and recorded a variety of casual homosexual encounters over a period of several months. When he published an account of his findings in a professional journal, the local district attorney attempted to subpoena his videotapes to prosecute the observed men under an "unnatural acts" statute.

Dr. Terfuge should have anticipated such difficulties, given the sensitive nature of the matters he was studying, and attempted to determine whether it was possible to collect the data in any other fashion. Assuming that it was not possible to do so, and assuming that the potential hazards to the people under study were not sufficient to warrant cancellation of the project, he should have taken steps to protect their anonymity. Dr. Terfuge was not simply conducting a field study, but was actually putting his intended subjects at some risk to themselves without their knowledge and consent. One could argue that a police officer might have made arrests, had one been present, but Terfuge was not a police officer and is obligated to consider the welfare of those he studies in the course of his research. There are additional problems with this research, such as the dubious benefits and privacy invasion (see chapter 17 for additional discussion).

Not all confidential data are so threatening, and, in fact, there are times when the revelation of sensitive or confidential research data prove to be of enormous social benefit (Gordis & Gold, 1980). Epidemiological research presents a good example. Whereas the National Research Act (United States Code, Public Law 93-348) and the Privacy Act of 1974 (United States Code Public Law 93-579) specify many complex protective mechanisms, a variety of medical studies have illustrated the importance of being able to break the confidential code from time to time. The studies of diethylstilbestrol (DES) and its association with vaginal cancers one generation later, studies of occupational cancers with long dormancy intervals, and late-effects studies of long-term use of contraceptive pills are but three examples. In each type of study cited here, it would be necessary to locate and track an identifiable individual over time to establish data of meaningful long-term risk to clients as individuals and society as a whole (Gordis & Gold, 1980). The point is that some unexpected findings of legitimate interest to research participants may not be discovered until long after they had enrolled in a study with a promise of confidentiality.

Safeguards are indeed needed, but one must be prepared to seek advice and consultation from institutional review boards (IRBs) or other appropriate bodies when conducting such studies. Knerr (1982) and Boruch, Dennis, and Cecil (1996) offer considerable information and advice on what to do if one's data are ever subpoenaed. An attorney should also be consulted regarding the impact of laws such as the Freedom of Information Act. Above all, the rights of the individual participant in the research must be considered.

RECORD CONTENT RETENTION AND DISPOSITION

Content of Records

What should be in clinical case records? The APA adopted basic advisory guidelines in 1993 (APA, 1993), but we believe that more detailed recommendations regarding the prototype mental health record will be useful to readers. If a psychologist is sued or called to account by a peer review body, a high-quality clinical record is the best way to document rendering of appropriate care. Poor quality notes or inadequate history taking could be viewed as sloppy practice by a jury in a malpractice suit or by peers reviewing an ethics complaint (ES: 1.24). In a legal sense, if it was not written down, it did not happen. We suggest addressing the following points over the course of working with a client.

1. *Identifying Information.* Record the name, file number (if any), address, telephone number, sex, birth date, marital status, next of kin (or parent/guardian), school or employment status, and billing and financial information.

2. *First Contact.* Note the date of initial contact and referral source. Inform the client (i.e., orally, in writing, or both) about the limits of confidentiality and note in the record that this was done.

3. *Relevant History and Risk Factors.* Take a detailed social, medical, educational, and vocational history. This need not necessarily be done in the very first session and need not be exhaustive. The more serious the problem, the more history you should gather. Get enough information to formulate a diagnosis and initial treatment plan. Be sure to ask: "What is the most violent thing you have ever done?" and "Are you thinking of hurting yourself or anyone else now?" It is also wise to ask about the "most impulsive" thing a client has ever done. Seek records of past treatment based on the nature of the client's problems. Always ask for a signed release to contact prior therapists.

4. *Medical Status.* Collect information on the client's medical status (i.e., when his or her last physical exam was, if the client has a personal physician, if there are any current medical problems or conditions). This is especially important if the client has physical complaints or psychological problems that might be attributable to organic pathology.

5. *Medication Profile.* Collect information on all medications or drugs used, past and present, including licit (e.g., prescribed medications, alcohol, tobacco, and over-the-counter drugs) and illicit substances. Also note any con-

sideration, recommendation, or referrals for medication over the course of your work with the client and whether these were acted on.

6. *Why the Client Is in Your Office.* Include a full description of the nature of the client's condition, including the reason(s) for referral and presenting symptoms or problem. Be sure to ask clients what brought them for help at this point in time and note the reasons. Incorporate these in treatment planning, with subsequent revisions as needed.

7. *Current Status.* Include a comprehensive functional assessment (including a mental status examination). That is, describe how the client is functioning cognitively and emotionally and revise as needed.

8. *Diagnostic Impression.* Include a clinical impression and diagnostic formulation using the most current *DSM* (*Diagnostic and Statistical Manual of Mental Disorders*) or ICD (World Health Organization's International Classification of Diseases) model. Do not underdiagnose with the idea that this is protecting the patient. If you believe it is absolutely necessary to use a "nonstigmatizing" diagnosis, as opposed to some other label, use the r/o (rule out) notation to indicate the provisional nature of the diagnostic impression. The diagnosis must also be consistent with the case history and facts (e.g., do not use "adjustment reaction" for a hallucinating client with a history of prior psychiatric hospital admissions).

9. *Treatment Plan.* In consultation with the client, develop a treatment plan with specific long- and short-term goals and a proposed schedule of therapeutic activities. This should be updated every 4 to 6 months and modified as needed.

10. *Progress Notes.* Note progress toward achievement of therapeutic goals. Use clear, precise, observable facts (e.g., "I observed"; "the patient reported"; "the patient agreed that . . . "). As you write, fantasize the patient and his or her attorney looking over your shoulder. Avoid theoretical speculation or reports of unconscious content. Avoid being "cute" or sarcastic in your notes. Always portray yourself as a serious, dedicated professional. If you must keep theoretical or speculative notes, use a separate working notes format, but recognize that these may be subject to disclosure.

11. *Psychological Testing.* If any psychological testing has been done, copies of the results and a report or summary should be included.

12. *Client Homework.* If the therapy has included requests that the client produce homework or other written submissions such as diaries, anxiety attack logs, dietary records, or similar materials, copies should be included in the file.

13. *Service Documentation.* Include documentation of each visit, noting the client's response to treatment. Each entry should be dated and, in hospitals or institutional settings, signed or initialed by the therapist (and supervisor if the therapist is unlicensed for independent practice).

14. *Document Follow-up.* Include documentation for follow-up or missed appointments, especially with dangerous or seriously ill clients. Retain copies of all notices or correspondence sent to clients or others on a client's behalf and note substantive telephone conversations with, or regarding, clients.

15. *Obtain Consent.* Include signed consent forms for any information to be released to others. Ideally, the form should be specific, dated, witnessed by a third party, and renewed regularly if repeated releases are needed.

16. *Termination.* Include a discharge or termination summary note for all clients. In cases of planned termination, be certain that case notes prior to the end of care reflect planning and progress toward this end.

Record Retention

How long should one keep records? This question is difficult to answer easily because the number and type of records kept by psychologists, clinics, and other agencies vary widely in both content and purpose, as discussed above. The answer to this question will vary as a function of the type of record, nature of the client's need for documentation of prior services, probability of need for future services, validity of the data in the records, and the applicable state or federal regulations. In any given legal jurisdiction, for example, the responsibilities of a professional might vary widely, depending on whether the records in question are considered business files, medical records, school records, or research data. The two key factors a psychologist should consider in making a decision about retention or disposition of records are applicable legal obligations and client welfare.

Legal obligations are best determined by consulting with an attorney familiar with the statutes that apply to one's practice. Dramatic differences exist from location to location. Considering only "hospital records," Massachusetts permits the destruction of records 30 years following the discharge or final treatment of the patient. California requires retention of such hospital records for 7 years postdischarge or until the patient reaches age 21, but never less than 7 years. New York's statute is similar to the California requirement except that the time frame is 6 years. In Texas, the law specifies 10 years for general retention, whereas Pennsylvania specifies keeping the record itself for 15 years and keeping a permanent care file on each patient. Some states, such as South Dakota, specify that hospital records be kept permanently.

It should be no surprise that a somewhat dated survey by Noll and Hanlon (1976) demonstrated widespread disagreement and confusion among mental health center administrators on the matter of record retention, with usual responses ranging from "3 years" to "permanent" retention. Laws dealing with individual practitioners, as opposed to institutions or agencies, are generally less specific and often require shorter retention spans for client files. Many state laws do not specifically mention psychologists in laws governing case records. In general, the best recommendation we can offer is twofold. First, check your legal obligations based on state law with respect to any statute of limitations on business and medical records. Second, we note that the APA (1993) recommends a minimum of 3 years' retention for the full record and an additional 12 years for a summary of the record, except when the client is a minor the time frame should be extended until at least 3 years past the age of majority. We recommend the APA standard as a minimum, even if your state permits shorter periods. The retention

clock should start ticking at the end of the final professional service to the client.

The U.S. Internal Revenue Service (IRS) imposes yet another type of obligation on virtually all professionals with its 7-year record-keeping requirement. Although these obligations refer to business and financial records, some ability to access client names and payments is needed. A client being audited might have to seek confirmation of payments made to the psychologist, or the practitioner might have to document certain financial data regarding his or her practice to the IRS.

Client welfare concerns come up with respect to the matter of record retention in two ways. First, you must consider the client's need and the benefit to the client of such records. Second, you must consider the risks and hazards of such records to clients, especially when they contain obsolete or potentially harmful data and may pass beyond the originating psychologist's control. Records benefit the client in a variety of ways, including their potential to assist in the continuity of care across providers and over time. Even long after a client has improved and left the psychologist's care, a need might arise to document the fact that there had been a period of treatment, disability, treatment costs, and so forth. Records do, after all, have the potential to recall events better than, and outlive, the provider who prepared them. This last fact contributes to a potential hazard with respect to disposition of records, discussed below.

Potential problems with records, aside from the access issues mentioned in this chapter, often arise as the result of invalid or obsolete information. Determining what is "obsolete" can be a problem, however. One must resist the temptation, inherent in the psychologist's research training, to save any potentially analyzable data indefinitely. Attempt to balance this urge with an understanding of the reliability and validity of old data.

Case 6-31: A state agency serving children maintained its clinical files, including psychological test data, indefinitely. A request for information, validly executed, was received from a government agency, requesting copies of reports for purposes of security clearance on Warren Peace, a now 40-

year-old job applicant, who had been seen at the agency 30 years earlier. The question of whether I.Q. and other test or psychological information should be released is raised.

The agency may be obligated to release the information on Mr. Peace requested under the circumstances cited above, because the files exist and the authorization is valid. On the other hand, one should legitimately question whether full test data and detailed notes ought to be kept this long and thus be available for such requests. The IQ data obtained at age 10 will have no bearing on the Mr. Peace current employability, and any treatment or personality test data from that era are also of questionable value. If the records had been destroyed or purged of data no longer valuable to the agency, there would be little danger to the former client that such information could return from the past to be used against him or her. Likewise, facts of interest to treatment team members while a client is being seen may be mere gossip years later (e.g., "paternal aunt suffered from melancholia," "intense sibling rivalry is present," "parents have difficulty with sexual intimacy").

Disposition

When records or obsolete contents culled from records are to be disposed, this must be accomplished in a manner consistent with their confidential nature. Shredding, incineration, recycling, or other destructive action should be carried out or contracted, although actual responsibility for the proper destruction rests with the practitioner or agency head in charge of the material.

Case 6-32: Eurippides Upp, the administrator of a mental health agency planned to dispose of many clinical records that were several years old. The records were tied in plastic trash bags and inserted in an outdoor receptacle to await trash pickup. Neighborhood dogs, in quest of food scraps, tore several bags open, and the wind blew out many reports and notes bearing client names and other identifying material. Many of the clients whose records were strewn about still resided in the same community.

In this case, it is evident that Mr. Upp took little care to see that the sensitive material was properly disposed. The material should have been shredded or stored securely until it could be picked up by a responsible disposal agent.

The death of a psychologist can also raise a complex set of problems with respect to individual client records. In some cases, records have simply been destroyed by a surviving spouse or executor. In other cases, the records have been kept, but no arrangements were made available for the orderly processing and screening of requests to access information from them. The APA ethics code (ES: 4.08) addresses this issue. Although we know of no ethics complaints against dead psychologists, it is possible that this element of the code could be used as a basis for filing suit against a psychologist's estate. This is one reason why it is important for psychologists who have such files to specify disposition instructions in their wills. One alternative could be an arrangement with a professionally responsible colleague for the care and management of the records. Other alternatives would be to instruct one's spouse or executor how to seek advice from others on record management or to ask a professional association to assist in managing the files for a period of time after the death.

SUMMARY GUIDELINES

1. It is especially important for a psychologist to understand the distinctions between confidentiality (an ethical principle) and privilege (a legal concept) as they apply in his or her practice jurisdiction.
2. The psychologist should be aware of any exceptions and limitations, such as the so-called duty to warn, obligations to report child abuse, collection of bills, or other special conditions bearing on confidentiality and should discuss such exceptions with clients at the outset of the professional relationship.
3. Prior to the release of any records, the psychologist should secure written informed consent from the client and attempt to alert the client regarding any potential hazards to the release.

4. The psychologist should recognize the different types of formal and informal records that exist, consider the prototype record we suggest in collecting data, and attempt to ensure that the contents remain factual, appropriate, and current.

5. The increasing trend toward freer client access to records should be kept in mind when reports are prepared and files are maintained. Always write with the assumption that the record will ultimately be seen by the client.

6. When confidential material is properly released, the psychologist should carefully consider the need-to-know basis of the intended recipient and the manner in which the information is likely to be used.

7. Extra consideration must be given to the special rights of minors and legally incompetent individuals when considering requests for access to psychological files about them.

8. Psychologists should inform themselves about the proper response to subpoenas and other requests for records from courts or other third parties.

9. When using case materials for teaching purposes, care must be taken to secure proper permission and to disguise material sufficiently to protect the client.

10. In the conduct of psychological research, the welfare of those under study must be given careful consideration with respect to confidentiality.

11. Psychologists must take proper steps to ensure that the retention and disposition of records takes place within the context of clients' best interests.

References

American Psychological Association. (1981). Ethical principles of psychologists. *American Psychologist, 36*, 633–638.

American Psychological Association. (1992). Ethical principles of psychologists and code of conduct. *American Psychologist, 47*, 1597–1611.

American Psychological Association. (1993). Record keeping guidelines. *American Psychologist, 48*, 984–986.

Bass, A. (1995, April 13). Insurers spurn anyone in therapy. *Boston Globe*, pp. 25, 29.

Baumrind, D. (1990). Doing good well. In C. B. Fisher & W. W. Tryon (Eds.), *Ethics in applied developmental psychology: Emerging issues in an emerging field*. Norwood, NJ: Ablex.

Bersoff, D. N. (1976). Therapists as protectors and policemen: New roles as a result of *Tarasoff*. *Professional Psychology, 7*, 267–273.

Bersoff, D. N. (1995). *Ethical conflicts in psychology*. Washington, DC: American Psychological Association.

Boruch, R. F., Dennis, M., & Cecil, J. S. (1996). Fifty years of empirical research on privacy and confidentaility in research settings. In B. H. Stanley, J. E. Sieber, & G. B. Melton (Eds.), *Research ethics: A psychological approach* (pp. 129–173). Lincoln, NE: University of Nebraska Press.

Boynton v. Burglass, 590 So. 2d 466 (Fla. D. Ct. A.P. 1991).

Brodsky, S. L. (1972). Shared results and open files with the client. *Professional Psychology, 3*, 362–364.

Brosig, C. L., & Kalichman, S. C. (1992). Child abuse reporting decisions: Effects of statutory wording of reporting requirements. *Professional Psychology: Research and Practice, 23*, 486–492.

Burke, C. A. (1995). Until death do us part: An exploration into confidentiality following the death of a client. *Professional Psychology: Research and Practice, 26*, 278–280.

Carroll, J. D. (1973). Confidentiality of social science research sources and data: the Popkin case. *Political Science, 6*, unnumbered.

Chodoff, P. (1992). The Anne Sexton biography: The limits of confidentiality. *Journal of the American Academy of Psychoanalysis, 20*, 639–643.

Committee on Legal Issues, American Psychological Association. (1996). Strategies for private practitioners coping with subpoenas or compelled testimony for client records of test data. *Professional Psychology: Research and Practice, 27*, 245–251.

Committee on Psychological Tests and Assessments. (1996). Statement on the disclosure of test data. *American Psychologist, 51*, 644–648.

DeKraai, M. B., & Sales, B. D. (1982). Privileged communications of psychologists. *Professional Psychology, 13*, 372–388.

Disclosure of confidential information gives rise to tort action against psychiatrist. (1982). *Mental Disability Law Reporter, 6,* 79.

Doctor and the law: On patient's right to read own medical records. (1975, February 10). *Medical World News.*

Dubey, J. (1974). Confidentiality as a requirement of the therapist: Technical necessities for absolute privilege in psychotherapy. *American Journal of Psychiatry, 131,* 1093–1096.

Epstein, G. N., Steingarten, J., Weinstein, H. D., & Nashel, H. M. (1977). Panel report: Impact of law on the practice of psychotherapy. *Journal of Psychiatry and Law, 5,* 7–40.

Everstine, L., Everstine, D. S., Heymann, G. M., True, R. H., Frey, D. H., Johnson, H. G., & Seiden, R. H. (1980). Privacy and confidentiality in psychotherapy. *American Psychologist, 35,* 828–840.

Fischer, C. T. (1972). Paradigm changes which allow sharing of results. *Professional Psychology, 3,* 364–369.

Fox v. Namani, 622 N.Y.S.2d 842 (N.Y. Sup. Ct. 1994).

Godkin v. Miller, 379 F Supp. 859 (ED N.Y. 1974), aff'd, 514 F 2d 123 (2d Cir. 1975).

Goldstein, R. L. (1992). Psychiatric poetic license? Post-mortem disclosure of confidential information in the Anne Sexton case. *Psychiatric Annals, 22,* 341–348.

Gordis, L., & Gold, E. (1980, January 11). Privacy, confidentiality, and the use of medical records in research. *Science, 207,* 153–156.

In re Viviano, 645 So. 2d 1301 (La. Ct. A.P. 1994).

Jaffe v. Redmond, 116 S.Ct. 95-266, 64L.W. 4490 (June 13, 1996).

Joseph, D. I. (1992). Discussion: Anne Sexton and the ethics of psychotherapy. *Journal of the American Academy of Psychoanalysis, 20,* 665–669.

Kalichman, S. C. (1993). *Mandated reporting of suspected child abuse: Ethics, law, and policy.* Washington, DC: American Psychological Association.

Kalichman, S. C., Brosig, C. L., & Kalichman, M. O. (1994). *Journal of Offender Rehabilitation, 21,* 27–43.

Knapp, S., & VandeCreek, L. (1982). *Tarasoff:* Five years later. *Professional Psychology, 13,* 511–516.

Knapp, S., & VandeCreek, L. (1990). Application of the duty to protect HIV-positive patients. *Professional Psychology: Research and Practice, 21,* 161–166.

Knerr, C. R. (1982). What to do before and after a subpoena of data arrives. In J. E. Sieber (Ed.), *The ethics of social research. Surveys and Experiments.* New York: Springer-Verlag.

Koocher, G. P., & Keith-Spiegel, P. C. (1990). *Children, ethics, and the law: Professional issues and cases.* Lincoln, NE: University of Nebraska Press.

Leonard, J. B. (1977). A therapist's duty to warn potential victims: A nonthreatening view of *Tarasoff. Law and Human Behavior, 1,* 309–318.

MacDonald v. Clinger, No. 991/1981 (N.Y. A.P. Div. January 22, 1982).

McGuire, J., Nieri, D., Abbott, D., Sheridan, K., & Fisher, R. (1995). Do *Tarasoff* principles apply in AIDS-related psychotherapy? Ethical decision making and the role of therapist homophobia and perceived client dangerousness. *Professional Psychology: Research and Practice, 26,* 608–611.

McIntosch v. Milano, 403 A. 2d 500 (N.J. Super. Ct. 1979).

Morgenthau, T., Lindsay, J. J., Michael, R., & Givens, R. (1982). The unanswered questions. *Newsweek, 99,* 40.

Noll, J. O., & Hanlon, M. J. (1976). Patient privacy and confidentiality at mental health centers. *American Journal of Psychiatry, 133,* 1286–1289.

Nowell, D., & Sprull, J. (1993). If it's not absolutely confidential, will information be disclosed? *Professional Psychology: Research and Practice, 24,* 367–369.

Paul, R. E. (1977). *Tarasoff* and the duty to warn: Toward a standard of conduct that balances the rights of client against the rights of third parties. *Professional Psychology, 8,* 125–128.

People v. Poddar, 10 Ca. 3d 750, 518, P.2d 342, 111 Cal. Rptr. 910 (1974).

Rosen, C. E. (1977). Why clients relinquish their rights to privacy under sign-away pressures. *Professional Psychology, 8,* 17–24.

Rosenbaum, M. (1994). The travails of Martin Orne: On privacy, public disclosure, and confidentiality in psychotherapy. *Journal of Contemporary Psychotherapy, 24,* 159–167.

Rosenoer, J. (1995). Problems on the Internet: A lawyer's perspective. *Ethics and Behavior, 5,* 107–110.

Rost v. Pennsylvania Board of Psychology, 659 A.2d 626 (Pa. Commw. Ct. 1995).

Roth, L. H., Wolford, J., & Meisel, A. (1980). Patient access to records: Tonic or toxin? *American Journal of Psychiatry, 137,* 592–596.

Sawyer, J., & Schechter, H. (1968). Computers, privacy, and the national data center: The responsibility of social scientists. *American Psychologist, 23,* 810–818.

Shah, S. (1969). Privileged communications, confidentiality, and privacy: Privileged communications. *Professional Psychology, 1,* 56–59.

Shaw v. Glickman, 415A. 2d 625 (Md. Ct. Spec. A.P. 1980).

Siegel, M. (1979). Privacy, ethics, and confidentiality. *Professional Psychology, 10,* 249–258.

Smith, S. R. (1996). U.S. Supreme Court adopts psychotherapist-patient privilege. *Bulletin of the American Academy of Forensic Psychology, 17,* 1–15.

Smith-Bell, M., & Winslade, W. J. (1994). Privacy, confidentiality, and privilege in psychotherapeutic relationships. *American Journal of Orthopsychiatry, 64,* 180–193.

Stein, E. J., Furedy, R. L., Simonton, M. J., & Neuffer, C. H. (1979). Patient access to medical records on a psychiatric inpatient unit. *American Journal of Psychiatry, 136,* 327–329.

Stone, A. A. (1976). The *Tarasoff* decisions: Suing psychotherapists to safeguard society. *Harvard Law Review, 90,* 358–378.

Strassburger, F. (1975). Problems surrounding "informed voluntary consent" and patient access to records. *Psychiatric Opinion, 12,* 30–34.

Tarasoff v. Board of Regents of the University of California, 551 P. 2d 334 (Cal. Sup. Ct. 1976).

Tarasoff duty to warn discussed in three cases; no such duty found in Maryland. (1980). *Mental Disability Law Reporter, 4,* 313–315.

Taylor, L., & Adelman, H. S. (1989). Reframing the confidentiality dilemma to work in children's best interests. *Professional Psychology: Research and Practice, 20,* 79–83.

Thompson v. County of Alameda, 614 P. 2d 728 (Cal. Sup. Ct. 1980).

Truscott, D. (1993). The psychotherapist's duty to protect: An annotated bibliography. *Journal of Psychiatry and Law, 21,* 221–244.

VandeCreek, L., & Knapp, S. (1993). *Tarasoff and beyond: Legal and clinical considerations in the treatment of life-endangering patients.* Sarasota, FL: Professional Resource Exchange.

Watson, H., & Levine, M. (1989). Psychotherapy and mandated reporting of child abuse. *American Journal of Orthopsychiatry, 59,* 246–256.

Weisbeck v. Hess, 524 N.W. 2d 363 (S.D. Sup. Ct. 1994).

Woods, K. M., & McNamara, J. R. (1980). Confidentiality: Its effect on interviewee behavior. *Professional Psychology, 11,* 714–721.

7

Psychological Assessment
Testing Tribulations

One gets the impression that the major purpose
. . . was not to beat a dead horse but to administer
massive doses of statistics in the effort to bring the
unfortunate animal back to life.

Ann Anastasi, 1975, p. 356

Many professions have studied human behavior and capabilities, but in the realm of psychodiagnostic assessment or testing, the contributions of psychology are unique. The use of small samples of human behavior, collected in standardized fashion and scientifically evaluated to categorize, diagnose, evaluate, or predict behavior, is certainly one of the most noteworthy accomplishments by behavioral scientists in this century. At times, such tests are powerful tools for advancing human welfare, but, occasionally, great concern about the real, imagined, or potential misuses of tests have become public policy issues. At other times, misunderstanding of technical subtleties, such as those critiqued by Anastasi in the opening quotation for this chapter, give the false impression that the ability to quantify human behavior imparts some sort of intrinsic truth or merit.

One of the earliest and most striking public commentaries reflective of such misconceptions came from a 24-year-old journalist named Walter Lippman in a series of six articles on "The Mental Age of Americans" and "Mr. Binet's

Test," published between October 25 and November 29, 1922, in *The New Republic*. Lippman stressed the potential misunderstanding and "great mischief" that might follow if parents and school authorities became confused about the nature and validity of the assessment techniques devised by Binet in France and later revised by Terman in the United States, noting:

> If, for example, the impression takes root that these tests really measure intelligence, that they constitute a sort of last judgement on the child's capacity, that they reveal "scientifically" his pre-destined ability, then it would be a thousand times better if all the intelligence testers and all their questionnaires were sunk without warning in the Sargasso Sea. (Lippmann, 1922, p. 297)

One cannot underestimate the political and social significance psychological testing has come to have in America, and the converse impact of public attitudes to the field of psychometrics. Haney (1981) traced debates over the meaning of IQ, the social functions that tests serve, and the appropriate use of personality tests; Haney began with Terman's development of the Stanford-Binet scales in 1916 and the Army Alpha test during World War I. He makes a strong case for how social attitudes and values affect even professional writings on testing and affect issues that appear to be strictly technical on the surface. In the same vein, an excellent chapter by Laosa (1984) documented the historic misuse of psychological assessment in forging social policies against immigrants and people of color.

The ethical problems growing out of the use and potential misuse of psychological tests and assessment techniques are as varied as the many different types of instruments, users of them, purposes to which they are put, and consequences to those who are tested. For purposes of general definition, we consider a *psychological test* to be any questionnaire, examination, or similar sample of behavior collected in a prescribed or standardized fashion for the purposes of describing, classifying, diagnosing, evaluating, or predicting behavior. We must add the additional caveat that we are referring only to those techniques devised and routinely employed by psychologists in the course of their professional work. This is intended to exclude, for example, scientific anthropological or sociological survey and measurement techniques, as well as astral charts, tea leaf readings, biorhythms, or fondling the viscera of certain animals as a means to predict future events.

VARIETIES OF TESTS

Test instruments can be classified across a number of dimensions, including the purpose for which they are designed, the population for which they are standardized, the nature of their administration, the mode of interpretation, and their psychometric properties. Types of tests, listed according to intended use, include (1) personnel selection, promotion, or classification; (2) professional licensure or certification; (3) educational admission and placement; (4) certification testing in elementary and secondary schools; (5) ability and achievement testing in schools; (6) special education testing (including instruments designed for use with the blind, hearing impaired, and other people with disabilities); (7) clinical assessment (including cognitive, neuropsychological, and personality testing); (8) counseling and guidance (including vocational interest inventories); and (9) specialized instruments designed for program evaluation and programmatic decision making. Within each of these general categories, still more specific types of tests could be specified by intended function.

In terms of standardization samples, some tests are designed only for use with literate, English-speaking adults. Others are intended for children under age 7 or individuals with advanced typing skills. Without specific knowledge of the population for whom the test is intended and on whom the norms are based, test scores may be meaningless. This assumes, of course, both that the test does have norms available and that it is properly validated, as we discuss below.

Tests may be administered in large groups or individually, with one examiner and one client. They may be timed or untimed, involve paper and pencil or oral administration, require forced-choice or open-ended responses. Some tests require a skilled administrator, whereas others may be self-administered or monitored by a person without psychological training. Some tests are administered, scored, and partially interpreted solely based on the client's interaction with a computer terminal.

Similarly, test interpretation or data use may also vary widely. Some tests may be administered, scored, and interpreted quite simply by a person with little or no formal psychological training (e.g., tests of typing speed and accuracy). Other tests may not require skilled administrators, but demand sophisticated clinical training for proper interpretation (e.g., paper-and-pencil inventories or card-sort tasks). Still other tests may require high levels of psychological skill and detailed knowledge for proper administration and interpretation (e.g., projective personality assessment techniques such as the Rorschach inkblots).

KEY CONCEPTS IN TESTS
AND MEASUREMENTS

There are many important technical concepts necessary to understand the proper use of psychological tests for the purpose of psychological assessment (Matarazzo, 1990). While this chapter is not intended as a substitute for formal course work in test construction and measurement statistics, we summarize those key terms that are important to understand in ethical test use. Portions of this chapter may seem rather basic to some psychologists, especially those who are thoroughly familiar with concepts related to tests and measurements. Unfortunately, however, it is just such basics that are too often at the heart of ethical complaints related to testing or assessment. These include the concepts of reliability, validity, sources of error, and standard error of measurement.

Reliability is the property of repeatable results. That is, will the test dependably measure whatever it measures over time and across populations? Tests of relatively stable phenomena, for example, should have high test-retest reliability. If a person earns a certain score on a mathematics achievement test on Monday, that same person should earn a similar score on readministration of the same test several days later, assuming no special studying or additional teaching occurred during the interval. Likewise, the test should yield similar scores for people of relatively equal ability when these people are tested under similar conditions, whether or not the people differ on the basis of other extraneous characteristics (e.g., age, sex, race, etc.). If the test does not measure something reliably, it is useless because we would never know whether differences in score were related to the skill or trait being measured or to the unreliability of the instrument.

Validity refers to the concept of whether a reliable test actually measures what it is supposed to measure. A test cannot possibly be a valid measure of anything unless it is reliable. At the same time, a test may yield reliable scores yet not be a valid indicator of what it purports to measure. It is the ethical responsibility of test developers to demonstrate that a given test is appropriately valid for its recommended applications.

Content and *construct validity* refer to whether the test samples behavior representative of the skill, trait, or other characteristic to be measured. Content validity indicates the degree to which the items in the test are drawn from the domain of behavior that is of interest. This addresses the question: Are the test tasks related to the performance ability we wish to gauge? The degree to which test scores may be used to infer how well any given construct describes individual differences is the key factor in construct validity (Green, 1981; Guion, 1974). Cronbach claimed, "All validation is one, and in a sense all is construct validation" (1980, p. 99), and the latest version of joint technical standards (Joint Committee on the Standards for Educational and Psychological Testing, in preparation) stresses the centrality of construct validation. The existence or operational definitions of many hypothetical constructs (e.g., ego-strength, trait-anxiety, or even intelligence) may be controversial, with the result that tests predicated on these constructs are subject to question. For example, a test predicated on psychoanalytic concepts (e.g., the Blacky test, in which a dog named Blacky is shown acting out or witnessing scenes depicting various Freudian concepts such as oral gratification, anal rage, or castration anxiety) would be laughingly discounted by a behaviorally inclined clinician who is unwilling to consider constructs not directly observable in behavior. Similarly, the behaviorally oriented clinician who argues that nonobservable intrapsychic events do not exist or lack clinical significance would be seen as naive by most experienced clinicians. The responsibility for establishing whether the test measures the construct or reflects the content of interest is the burden of both the developers and the publishers.

Criterion-related validity deals with whether a given test's outcome is related to other criteria in predictive or concurrent fashion. For example, graduate departments of psychology have long been interested in what data will best predict success in graduate school. Test scores, undergraduate grades, references, and other data are collected to predict (and thereby select) those applicants who have the highest likelihood to do well in, and successfully complete, the program. Adequate demonstration of this type of relationship is also the responsibility of the test developers and publishers. Individual test users also have a responsibility to use test data in ways that reflect well-established predictive or criterion-related relationships or to sample a particular content domain.

Test scores are subject to many *sources of error*. One person may be more motivated to try on one occasion than another. A second person may be a good guesser relative to peers. Still a third might be feeling ill, hungry, or anxious or have greater familiarity with specific test items on one form of an instrument. The importance of any particular source of error depends on the specific use of the test in the context of the specific individual who took it. The goal of reliability studies is to estimate the magnitude of the errors of measurement from assorted sources. Any given test has many standard errors, and the user is responsible for being familiar with these and considering the appropriate one(s), depending on the comparisons to be made. A *standard error* of measurement is a score interval that, given certain assumptions, has a given probability of including any individual's true score.

Consider some cases related to these concepts as ethical issues:

Case 7-1: Norma Skew, Ph.D., develops a detailed interview schedule that is scorable in objective fashion, yielding a set of numbers she describes as a "leadership quotient," a "motivation index," and a "likelihood of success rating." The items were selected from a variety of existing personality assessment tools and questionnaires. Dr. Skew proceeds to advertise this instrument for use in "selecting executive talent," although as yet she has collected no validity data and simply presumes reliability "because the items are all based on questions asked in other reliable instruments."

Case 7-2: Marge N. O'Vera, Psy.D., retested a child who had been given the Wechsler Intelligence Scale for Children—Third Edition (WISC-III) by another examiner a few months earlier. The youngster, who was mildly mentally retarded, earned IQ scores 3 to 5 points higher when O'Vera tested him, and O'Vera told the child's parents, "This is a sign that he could be making some real intellectual progress."

Case 7-3: Tanya Shallow, Ed.D., is a school psychologist charged with selecting a few dozen intellectually talented youngsters from the Plainville Regional School District to be offered access to a special summer enrichment program. She decides that the simplest way to select candidates is to group administer a standardized paper-and-pencil IQ test and select students from among the high scorers.

Psychologists trained to use tests or who are familiar with assessment and measurement theory will no doubt wince at the prospect that any practitioner could behave as Drs. Skew, O'Vera, and Shallow have, but these types of problems are all too common.

Dr. Skew may be "creative" and "innovative" in designing her assessment instrument, but she has not bothered to validate it. We give her the benefit of the doubt and assume that she has secured permission to use any copyrighted material. The fact that she has used items of known validity related to other instruments, however, does not mean that these items are valid for the uses she ascribes to them in this new context. On the other hand, unless she has specific validity data to show that her items measure the constructs of leadership, motivation, and likelihood of success and that the scores her instruments yield are related to some meaningful predictive criterion of success in selecting talented executives, she is misusing psychological tests.

Dr. O'Vera is one of the most frightening kinds of practitioners because she is offering illusory grains of hope to the family of a child with a disability, perhaps with the result of promoting unfortunate expectations. The "new scores" are within the standard error of the differences for each, as described in detail in the WISC-III test manual. This means that the upward shift is most likely related to some chance variable or other trivial factor rather than a sign of intellectual gain. O'Vera's naiveté about mental retardation and the proper use of the test manual data hints strongly at incompetence.

Dr. Shallow's choice of a group-administered paper-and-pencil measure of intelligence as the sole selection criterion is an error. To begin with, many intellectually talented youngsters may not score well on such tests. One child, for example, may have been distracted by spitballs from a classmate, another might be preoccupied by family stresses, and still another might have an insufficient grasp of written English to do well on the test. Instead of using multiple criteria suited to the nature of the program and the type of students sought, Dr. Shallow appears to have sought a solution requiring the least effort on her part. She is using an instrument designed chiefly for another purpose and is ignoring potential drawbacks of the instrument as a valid indicator of the one variable she is actually measuring (i.e., the ability to do well on a group-administered paper-and-pencil task). At the very least, she should not rely on a single data source.

PRIMARY REFERENCE SOURCES

Three major reference works are important sources of information for anyone with a substantial interest in the proper use of psychological tests. The first two are *Test Critiques* (Keyser & Sweetland, 1994) and the *Mental Measurements Yearbook*, the definitive source. The most recent *Mental Measurements Yearbook* (11th edition, Kramer & Conoley, 1992) was published in two volumes and contains information on 1,200 tests, with reviews of tests and books on testing, as well as more than 18,000 references on the construction, use, and validity of specific tests. A supplement was published in 1994 (Conoley & Impara, 1994) and a 12th edition is scheduled to appear in print by 1998.

The third major reference work is the book titled: *Standards for Educational and Psychological Tests*. Published jointly by the American Psychological Association (APA), the American Educational Research Association (AERA), and the National Council on Measurement in Education (NCME) for more than 50 years, it contains a comprehensive set of standards addressing test development, and test use and special issues related to linguistic and cultural differences, testing the handicapped, testing the aged, and computerized adaptive testing. Currently under revision, the newest edition is to be published in 2000. The APA's casebook, *Responsible Test Use* (Eyde et al., 1993), provides an excellent supplement, including 78 case studies carefully indexed by topics and fully cross-referenced.

An additional reference work of interest to many readers is the special issue of the *American Psychologist*, "Testing: Concepts, Policy, Practice, and Research" (October 1981). It contains 20 invited articles, including overviews and discussion of then-current controversies, and represents an excellent collection of basic concepts, historical information, and opinions from psychologists with expertise in assessment. Although somewhat dated, most of the papers have significant conceptual value.

TEST ADEQUACY

As should be evident, the question of whether any given psychological assessment instrument is a "good test" or a "bad test" is quite complex. A test that is reliable, valid, and quite useful for one purpose may be useless or inappropriate for another. An instrument that is adequate for its intended use in the hands of a trained examiner could be subject to substantial misuse in the hands of less qualified users. The next section of this chapter focuses solely on the adequacy of particular instruments themselves and the factors that contribute to, or detract from, the appropriateness of the test.

Before moving ahead, however, it is important to note that techniques used in some forms of psychological assessment at times come to masquerade as psychological tests. The best example of this phenomenon is the use of anatomically detailed dolls (occasionally referred to inaccurately as "anatomically correct dolls") in the assessment of children thought to be victims of sexual abuse. In a comprehensive overview of the scientific basis for using such dolls, Koocher and his colleagues (1995) note that the assumption that such dolls constitute some form of psychological test (i.e., with demonstrated potential for detecting child sexual abuse or for stating with a degree of certainty that sexual abuse occurred) is unfounded and dangerous.

As noted above, psychological tests provide standardized procedures for the presentation of common stimuli, rules for recording responses, and rules for then assigning quantitative features (i.e., a score) to the elicited responses. Anatomically detailed dolls do not meet any of these requirements as yet (Skinner & Berry, 1993). At present, such dolls are not standardized as stimulus materials and appear in many shapes, sizes, and colors, even with varying genital and related characteristics that may affect a child's precepts and responses. No uniform sets of questions to elicit responses, method of presentation, or quantifiable means of evaluating responses have been proffered. Although many suggested protocols for use of anatomically detailed dolls have been published (see, e.g., American Professional Society on the Abuse of Children, 1990; Boat & Everson, 1986; Friedemann & Morgan, 1985; Levy, Kalinowski, Markovic, Pittman, & Ahart, 1991; White, Strom, Santilli, & Halpin, 1986), there is no uniform acceptance of such suggestions. In addition, there is no documentation of the validity of such dolls or of these suggested protocols for forensic purposes. Some may assume that such dolls are appropriately labeled if called a projective test or projective instrument. However, even projective techniques have a standard set of stimulus materials and specific rules of inquiry, and most have a set of scoring criteria. Anatomically detailed dolls have none of these attributes and do not properly fit any validated projective hypotheses (see, e.g., Chandler, 1990).

If not a test, what are anatomically detailed dolls? Koocher and his colleagues (1995) note that such dolls are best considered a diverse set of stimuli that can function as communication and memory aids to children and other individuals who have immature language, cognitive, or emotional development or who have impaired communication skills. They are simply intended to assist in the communication process, allowing children and others to demonstrate acts for which they have limited verbal descriptions, with which they have limited familiarity in life, or about which they are too embarrassed to speak. Unfortunately, they are readily available to police, child protective service workers, and even to some psychologists who do not understand the appropriate use or limitations. In fact, significant ethical complaints have grown out of evaluations conducted with such dolls. In some cases, for example, clinicians have too quickly assigned diagnoses of PTSD (post-traumatic stress disorder), "validating" child sexual abuse on the basis of observing repetitive anatomical doll play. Such presumed indications of PTSD may actually result from repeated investigatory interviews by law enforcement or child protection investigators (see Fisher, 1995, and Fisher, 1996).

The Test Manual

Each psychological assessment instrument should have a test manual that contains detailed information for potential users, including (1) the development and purpose of the test, (2) information on the standard administration and scoring conditions, (3) data on the sample used to standardize the test, (4) information on its reliability and measurement error, (5) documentation of its validation, and (6) any other information needed to enable a qualified user or reviewer to evaluate its appropriateness and adequacy for its intended use. The manual may have supplemental sections addressing particular issues or audiences (e.g., a technical measurement section or a section written in lay terms to help test takers understand the meaning of their scores). Optional versus mandatory components of a test manual will vary as a function of the intended applications of the tool. The key point is that the manual must be sufficiently detailed to permit the psychologist to determine the test's appropriateness for a specific population and assessment goal. The manual should also include references for all relevant published research on the instrument. Publication or distribution of a test without the availability of such documentation is unethical, as doing so omits critical information, violates accepted professional standards, and invites misuse.

Test manuals should also include data on potential biases, along with cautions to users regarding improper or unvalidated test applications. In advertising the test to professional or public audiences, the publisher must take care to avoid any suggestion that the instrument is more useful or valid than the existing research base warrants. Implying that any given test satisfies federal guidelines or requirements, for example, would not be appropriate since even tests that have some type of official recognition or approval are limited to certain specific contexts (Bersoff, 1981; Novick, 1981).

Case 7-4: Guy Grand, Ed.D., developed a personnel selection instrument that proved to have some validity for selecting middle-level managers of a large consumer goods manufacturing company. In that context, the use of the test was later deemed appropriate by the Equal Employment Opportunity Commission and the U.S. Department of Labor. These rulings were touted in advertising for the test sent to personnel officers of several other large corporations.

Case 7-5: The manual for the Omnibus Achievement Tests gives the numbers, grade levels, and ages of the school children on whom it was standardized. It fails to mention, however, primary language, ethnic/racial composition, geographic diversity, socioeconomic status, or similar demographic variables of the research samples.

Case 7-6: Joyce Nerd, Ph.D., is the primary author of the National Nonsequitor Personality Inventory-R (NNPI), which has been widely used as a personality screening tool for many years. In revising the test manual, Dr. Nerd omits references to several articles published in peer-reviewed journals that are critical of the NNPI's stated uses and validity studies. She reasons that the "overwhelming body of data" documents the utility of the test, whereas the "few polemic studies" critical of the test are not worthy of mention.

The point of all three cases cited above is that they involve tests that may be useful or valid, although all are presented or dealt with in a potentially unethical fashion. Dr. Grand's advertising may lead to unwarranted generalization regarding the "governmental approval" of his test. The recipients of his announcements most likely will be individuals who will not have sufficient knowledge of tests and measurements to conceptualize the issues needed to evaluate

his claims intelligently or to discriminate between the "recognized" and potential unrecognized uses of the test.

The Omnibus Achievement Tests severely handicaps any potential user by omitting crucial demographic data on the basic population sampled. This omission effectively vitiates any potential application of the test, valid and reliable though it might be, because there is no basis for any user to conclude that the population to be tested resembles the population for which norms exist. By omitting such critical data from the manual, users of this test would employ it at their peril because generalizable conclusions cannot be drawn. Marketing such a test with an incomplete manual is an unethical act because it might lead an unsophisticated potential user to think that it has some appropriate application.

Dr. Nerd may be letting her personal bias and investment in her work cloud her competence. She should not intentionally delete questions about the instrument raised in scholarly publications. These should be cited so that the informed test user can make an independent decision. It is reasonable for Nerd to rebut such citations in her manual, but the conscious omission of this information represents an act of deception and misrepresentation, regardless of Nerd's rationalization.

Test Administration

One of the important scientific values of a psychological assessment technique grows from the fact that it provides a means for assessing a standard sample of behavior. This implies a specific test ecology, adherence to administration rules, and specific scoring criteria. Consider these examples of variations in administration of certain tests.

Case 7-7: Erika, age 6, is having trouble academically in first grade. Her parents call Mr. Blitz, the school principal, to request a conference regarding their daughter's progress. In a hurry to get some data before the conference, Mr. Blitz has Erika sent to a third-grade classroom one morning, without prior notice, to take paper-and-pencil intelligence and achievement tests being administered to the third graders. When her scores are compared to first-grade norms, they are low, so Blitz concludes that the data prove her basic abilities are limited.

When Mr. Blitz removed Erika without warning from her first-grade class and put her in with a strange group of older children to take a test that was not explained to her, he put her at a substantial emotional disadvantage. Even if we assume that the tests were valid for the intended purpose, it would be inappropriate to base a conclusion about the child's ability solely on paper-and-pencil tests without considering such other factors as teacher reports, individual stresses on the child, and so on. The chief point to be made for this case, however, is the error of altering the child's ecology during the sampling of her behavior while not making any effort to assist her adjustment. It would have been much more appropriate to provide the child with an explanation and to schedule testing with a group of peers or with an individual examiner who could establish rapport with Erika and make individual observations of her work during the test.

Case 7-8: Sidney Mute is a deaf, nonverbal adult arrested as a suspect in a crime. There is some question as to whether he is mentally retarded or psychotic. Psychological testing is sought. Alice Stanine, Ph.D., is asked to do a psychological assessment, and she discovers that Mr. Mute can read and write at an elementary school level. She administers a test battery using intelligence and personality tests intended for hearing/speaking clients by providing Mr. Mute with specially prepared cards on which the test questions or instructions have been written. Her behavioral observations note that "Mr. Mute engaged in considerable hand-waving and finger-twitching ticlike behaviors suggestive of psychosis."

Dr. Stanine certainly attempted a creative approach in her evaluation of Mr. Mute. She is deviating from the test administration condition prescribed in the manual and must note that in any report of results. More important, she is using a test on an individual for whom it has not been validated. Some of the data she collects may be useful, although clearly not in the same fashion as when the client is able to hear and

speak. More troubling, however, is the fact that Dr. Stanine did not attempt to use one or more of the specific tests designed for use with the hearing impaired (e.g., the Hiskey-Nebraska Test of Learning Aptitude). She apparently did not consult anyone knowledgeable about assessing deaf clients and seems to have overlooked attempts by Mr. Mute to use sign language, misinterpreting these as suggestive of psychopathology. While this case has major implications regarding Dr. Stanine's competence, it also illustrates the problem of applying a standardized test instrument in a nonstandard fashion.

Case 7-9: A state psychology board scheduled a nationally administered, multiple-choice licensing examination. Candidates were told to arrive promptly at 8:00 A.M.; however, disorganized operations at the testing site resulted in delays of 2½ to 3 hours before people were seated for the test. The test was scheduled for a roped-off section of corridor in the lobby of a large state office building. During the course of the examination period, considerable pedestrian traffic passed through the lobby and corridor; people waited for elevators, the bells of which rang when the doors opened; and food aromas permeated the air from a cafeteria 100 feet from the roped-off area. When complaints were filed against the psychologist-members of the state licensing board, the board replied that the testing sites are assigned by a different branch of state government over which they had no control.

The state licensing board is also ignoring important aspects of test ecology. The examination was clearly administered in a setting and under conditions that could be expected to hinder concentration and potentiate the stress on the candidates taking it. Since the board is legally responsible for the licensing process, members cannot absolve themselves of responsibility for unsatisfactory testing conditions by deferring responsibility. If the board cannot ensure that the examination is given under the circumstances for which it was intended (e.g., a quiet, reasonably comfortable setting without extraneous distractions), they should postpone or defer testing until proper facilities are arranged. To do otherwise is a violation of proper test administration requirements and hence is unethical.

Also attracting some attention is the related issue of supervising clients taking multiple-choice instruments. In April 1993, the APA Ethics Committee (1993) issued a policy statement in response to an inquiry about whether it is a per se ethics violation to send a Minnesota Multiphasic Personality Inventory (MMPI) home with a client for completion. The committee noted that each such circumstance should be treated on a case-by-case basis and would involve any similar types of assessment, not simply the MMPI. The committee noted that violations have been found in the past when psychologists have sent test booklets and answer sheets home with clients (ES: 2.02a, 2.10). Such findings were based on violations of test security, failure to supervise the testing adequately (with resulting potential validity problems), and impairment of client welfare. Debate ensued as to whether there are ever any appropriate circumstances for which it might be reasonable and appropriate to allow administration of such a test away from a professional setting. In such cases, the psychologist would bear the burden of justifying why the client's welfare or other extenuating circumstances necessitated unmonitored administration. The clinician would need to ensure that test security was maintained and that the correct person completed the test. In addition, any reports resulting from data collected in a nonstandard manner should address that issue in terms of reliability and validity of the results under nonstandard conditions.

Finally, it is particularly important to confirm scoring accuracy, even when using the clear-cut criteria of so-called objective test instruments. In one study, for example, scoring errors were detected in 53% of personality inventories that had been hand scored by trained clinic personnel at an "unnamed metropolitan outpatient mental health clinic" (Allard, Butler, Faust, & Shea, 1995). Fully 19% of the hand-scored test protocols in question contained errors sufficient to alter clinical diagnoses. The same tests scored by computer program were free of errors.

Test Bias

The problem of test bias has received intense scientific and public scrutiny over the years, generating considerable scholarly and public debate. Even the definition of the term *test bias* consists of many quite disparate facets (Flaugher, 1978). Bias may manifest itself as a function of the skill or trait being tested, as a statistical phenomenon, as a selection model, as test content problems, as an overinterpretation issue, as the use of wrong criteria, or even as test atmosphere or test ecology issues. When discussing ethical problems related to the matter of test bias, it therefore is critical to consider what sort of definition and which cluster of issues one has in mind.

Fredricksen (1984) notes there is increasing evidence that economical multiple-choice tests have driven other testing procedures out of school evaluation programs, to the detriment of students. He argues that such testing in education has led to teacher and student behavior changes less conducive to practice with feedback and the development of higher level cognitive skills. He terms the adverse influence of testing on teaching and learning the "real bias" in psychological testing programs. Cole (1981) presents an excellent overview of the scholarly research on test bias and includes analyses of subtle differences in the content of test items to which individuals react differently. She argues that the basic issue in the matter of test bias is actually one of validity. She makes a careful distinction between whether a test is valid for some use and whether it should be used (even if valid). The point is that tests have often served as a kind of lightning rod or focal point of anger related to difficult social policy questions (Laosa, 1984).

Cole (1981) cites several examples of social policy problems. In selecting for employment or promotion, what is the best way to meet current employer needs while compensating for past wrongs and current individual rights? What role should selective admissions play in higher education, and how should broad opportunities be provided? What form should education for handicapped children take? How should we deal with people for whom English is not a native language? We agree with Cole's assertion that the bias issues are fundamentally questions of validity. The ethical problems are more clearly linked to the test developers and test users, who hold ultimate responsibility for remaining sensitive to the proper and improper application of the instruments they devise and employ, respectively. Psychologists should certainly speak out on major public policy issues, both as individual citizens and as scientists who may have data to assist in resolving problems beneficially, but the solution to complex social policy problems will rarely be found through a psychological test.

Case 7-10: Sara Slava was orphaned in Bosnia and relocated in the United States, where she was adopted at age 16 by an American couple. Shortly after arriving in the United States, she was referred for psychological evaluation and tested, using, among other instruments, the Wechsler Adult Intelligence Scale-Revised (WAIS-III) and the Rorschach inkblots. On the basis of IQ scores in the 60–70 range and unelaborated "explosion" or "fire" responses on the Rorschach, Sara was described by the psychologist who saw her as "most likely mildly retarded and prone to violent acting out."

Once again, the issue is not clear cut in terms of testing problems. One could argue, as in the case of Dr. Stanine (Case 7-8), that a question of user competence is involved. It is also evident that a test standardized on and designed for adult, English-speaking Americans is not the instrument to use for ability testing of a recent immigrant whose contact with English was limited. In fact, Sara proved to be a very bright youngster whose receptive and expressive language skills were limited in English. She was socialized not to complain and to be compliant, so she did not ask for clarification or protest her lack of understanding of instructions and test questions. All of Sara's family had been killed during a rocket attack on their village, and she still suffered nightmares of that episode. In that context, her "explosion" responses to the Rorschach seem less subject to the usual interpretation. If the psychologist who saw Sara had given careful thought to these issues, or at least had included adequate cautionary statements in discussing the test data, the use of the tests might have been at least partially justified. In the context of Sara's situation, the evaluation and tests were certainly culturally and linguistically biased, and this was unethically ignored.

The importance of both linguistic *and* cultural sensitivity in testing are critical. For example, the English word *peach* (i.e., a fruit) has two common translations in Spanish. *Durazno* is the word children from Mexico would use to name the fruit, whereas children from Puerto Rico would call it *melocoton*. A vocabulary test in Spanish would be flawed unless both uses were scored as correct. Similarly, in teaching reading comprehension, programs in the United States stress the concept of the main idea. Schools in Israel, on the other hand, stress the moral lesson of a given story. It is easy to see how tests keyed with one emphasis or the other could seriously underrate a person from a different cultural or linguistic background.

Subgroup Norming

During the 1980s, the U.S. Employment Service (USES) determined that an aptitude test used for referring job applicants to employers was having an adverse impact on the candidacy of members of ethnic minority groups, especially African Americans and Hispanics (Brown, 1994). In an effort to reduce the adverse impact of such testing on these groups, the USES made a decision to use within-group scoring, also known as subgroup norming. This practice resulted in percentile scores based on ethnic group membership. The practice has been controversial among psychologists, civil rights activists, and legislators. In the context of so-called reverse discrimination, matters culminated with passage of the Civil Rights Act of 1991, by which the 102nd Congress banned any form of score adjustment predicated on race, color, religion, sex, or national origin (Public Law 102-166, Section 106).

A special section of the *American Psychologist* focused on this issue (Brown, 1994; Gottfredson, 1994; Sackett & Wilk, 1994). The papers trace the agony of behavioral scientists and psychometricians who find themselves drawn into public policy debates that alternately cast them as social advocates and as threats to the compromise of personnel selection science. From our perspective, however, this debate is not a matter of test bias so much as an attempt to use psychological assessment methods to resolve social and political problems. Some would argue that testing contributed to the origin of the problem, but one need look only to Matarazzo's (1990) distinction between psychological testing and psychological assessment to understand that the problem is not the tests. Rather, the difficulty lies with users who focus on easily gathered test scores instead of comprehensive assessments. As is too often the case, society would like inexpensive and easy solutions to complex assessment problems and will find those willing to deliver services that fit the demand.

Key Litigation

Since major litigation has revolved about the issue of test bias, it seems reasonable to summarize some of the key cases here. We focus on two major cases in which issues of test bias were raised.

The first case is *Griggs v. Duke Power Company* (1971). This case was the first major challenge to employment tests (Bersoff, 1981) and grew out of an objection to the legality of using general ability tests to hire and promote employees in a private company. Employees of African American ancestry cited the 1964 Civil Rights Act, claiming that the practice of test usage constituted a form of racial discrimination. While the employer acknowledged that few people of color were employed or promoted and that the test may have had a prejudicial impact, the company claimed no intent to discriminate. A unanimous Supreme Court decision held that discriminatory practices were actionable regardless of whether the form is fair as long as the result is discriminatory. When statistical data were produced showing the disproportionate impact on Black workers, the court faulted the company for using broad and general testing devices (Bersoff, 1981). The court introduced the concept of "job relatedness" as critical to the valid use of personnel testing (Zedeck & Cascio, 1984). That is, the human attributes measured by the test must be clearly relevant to the duties performed in the particular job.

In another important case, *Larry P. v. Riles* (1979), the federal courts prohibited the use of standardized intelligence tests as a means of identifying educable mentally retarded (EMR) Black children or for placing such children in

EMR classes. The genesis of this case were the facts that Black children were disproportionately overrepresented in such classes and the primary basis for such placement in California (at that time) was such tests (Lambert, 1981). Attorneys for the children argued that the test items were drawn from White, middle-class culture, that Whites had more advantages and opportunities than children of color, and that language used by Black or Latino children may not correspond to that used in the test. In addition, they noted that the motivation of some ethnic minority children to perform on the tests may have been adversely influenced by the race of the examiners, who were mostly White, and that the number of children of color in the standardization sample was very low.

The type of problem demonstrated in the *Larry P.* case is essentially a validity issue. That is, the test was being used for making a type of discrimination or judgment for which it was neither intended nor validated. Use of a single psychometric instrument as the sole or primary criterion in making critical educational or other life decisions fails to consider each individual as a whole being in a specific life context. Such lack of comprehensive assessment is a frequent type of test misuse (Moreland et al., 1995).

In the case of *PASE v. Hannon* (1980), a federal court in Illinois reached the opposite decision from its West Coast counterpart in the *Larry P.* case. Continued use of psychological tests in educational decision making was permitted. This contrast is of interest because many of the same psychological experts testified in both cases, both cases were under active judicial review simultaneously, and the outcomes were quite different. One might be tempted to read these cases as contrast or contradiction in the legal system. We believe the contrasting opinions are best viewed as context specific. That is, the court was most likely convinced that use of the psychometric tools in Illinois was more appropriate to the context than was the use of the same instruments by the psychologists in the San Francisco school district. The fact that two different judges and sets of facts were involved, however, makes a definitive conclusion on the legal merits impossible. The point is that the clinician who becomes involved in testing to be used for critical decision making bears an especially heavy ethical burden to ensure the data are applied in an appropriate scientific context that does not unfairly discriminate against any individual being assessed.

As an aside, it is somewhat ironic that the judge in the *PASE* case permitted the standard questions and keyed answers to the intelligence tests used to become a part of the public record of the trial. The court clearly had little concern for the matter of test security.

The use of psychological tests for the educational classification and tracking of children in cases such as these was unethical in our judgment for three reasons: (1) the tests were not well suited for the sort of fair differentiation needed, (2) scores were being used inappropriately as paramount criteria for complex decisions affecting the lives of people, and (3) psychologists were not sufficiently sensitive to the flaws in their instruments and the manner in which these flaws could adversely affect the lives of others. There was little recognition of the tests' contribution to broader repressive social policies. It is incumbent on the psychologist who uses intelligence tests to be sensitive to these issues and take steps to ensure that his or her assessment work is not used to the detriment of the person tested.

USER COMPETENCE

Although we have thus far focused chiefly on basic concepts in testing and issues in test adequacy, many of the examples we have cited raise issues of test user competency or, more accurately, incompetency on the part of some test users. It also should be evident that there is much more involved in appropriate utilization of psychological tests than simply recording responses and totaling the score. Moreland and his colleagues (1995) describe 86 test user competencies and 7 factors accounting for most test misuse. The competence issues, discussed in chapter 3, are generally related to this point; however, testing also involves a special subset of competence problems. Many standardized psychological instruments are deceptively easy to administer and score, requiring little or no

formal training. However, the accurate interpretation and application of these instruments is another matter entirely. In addition to training issues, there are also special ethical problems related to diagnosis, test security, and sale of tests to unqualified users.

Training Issues

How much and what types of training ought to be required as a prerequisite for designation as a "qualified" user of psychological tests? The answer is complicated and is based on the type of test, the use to which it is put, and the setting in which it is applied. It is possible, for example, for a psychologist to graduate from an APA-approved doctoral program in clinical psychology without ever having administered a projective personality assessment technique (e.g., the Rorschach inkblots or Thematic Apperception Test). Some would argue that courses in statistics, individual differences, personality theory, abnormal psychology, and cognitive processes ought to be mandatory prior to undertaking comprehensive psychological assessments. If the evaluator intends to practice in organizational or industrial settings, course work in organizational behavior, personnel law, and similar fields might be needed. If a school setting is to be the primary workplace, a psychologist may need course work in curriculum planning and educational theory prior to undertaking assessments. There are few standards to specify the minimum competence needed to perform each assessment task adequately, and psychologists are generally left to address this matter on the basis of their own awareness of their competencies and limitations. Sometimes, this is an effective means of control, but at other times it is not.

Case 7-11: Dinah Saur, Psy.D., hired Mary Smurf to work in her private practice. Ms. Smurf had a B.A. degree in psychology, and Dr. Saur gave her a few hours training in the administration of the Wechsler tests, Thematic Apperception Test, and Rorschach inkblots. Saur would interview referred clients for about 10 minutes and then send them to Ms. Smurf, who would administer the tests she prescribed. Dr. Saur would then prepare and sign evaluation reports based on the data Smurf collected.

Dr. Saur has provided only minimal supervision and training to her relatively unqualified assistant. She then bases her reports on a superficial interview and data collected by a person not sufficiently trained to administer complex tests or to note the subtler aspects of meaningful variations in test behavior. The reactions of the client to certain test stimuli may go unrecorded; the nuance of a response, which may tend to suggest one meaning or interpretation over another, could be lost; and there seems to be no effort to ensure quality control of the process. In some ways, Dr. Saur is actually offering an impersonal service and giving the impression that she has conducted an evaluation, when she has actually had only minimal direct contact with the client.

Case 7-12: Sandra Toddler, Ph.D., had been trained in clinical child psychology, although her course work and practica had always involved school-age children and their families. When she began to receive referrals for assessment of developmentally delayed infants and children under age 4, she ordered copies of several developmental instruments (e.g., Bayley Scales of Infant Development, etc.), read the manuals, and began using them in her practice.

Dr. Toddler may be bright and sensitive enough to learn the administration of new instruments from their manuals rather quickly. Is she qualified, however, to assess the meaning of the data and integrate it with other information to produce a valid and useful assessment? We really cannot tell from the information provided. If Toddler were more attentive to her ethical responsibilities, she probably would have sought some consultation, supervision, training, or any combination of these from a colleague with expertise in infant assessment. Toddler could then, with a meaningful basis of comparison, be able to gauge her own competence and weakness on the tasks at hand.

Case 4-13: Norris Nemo, Ph.D., was trained in counseling psychology, and his doctoral program included supervised course work in the use of in-

telligence, personality, and vocational guidance assessment tools. He approached several large companies to offer "placement and exit counseling" services to their personnel offices.

Dr. Nemo seems rather naive. We are not sure what he means by placement and exit counseling, and it is not clear that he has any background in personnel assessment or organizational consultation. He may not even recognize that he is offering to provide services beyond his qualifications. On the other hand, he may be competent to offer the services he proposes, but these might not be what the potential client-company needs. Perhaps Nemo mistakenly assumes that vocational preference and IQ are the most important factors in successful job functioning. All we know for certain is that Nemo seems to be reaching out to offer assessment in areas for which his training has not adequately prepared him.

Each of the three cases cited above demonstrates a lack of awareness of adequate or necessary training for a variety of assessment activities. Although we would like to believe that there are few grounds for concern of this sort in day-to-day practice, a recent study by Smith and Dumont (1995) provides little reassurance. They found a group of psychologists all too willing to offer interpretive statements based on casual use of a poorly validated instrument for which they had little or no training. The clinicians tended to use the data at hand to find support for initial diagnoses (i.e., confirmatory bias) with an embarrassing lack of scientific rigor.

Diagnosis

Assigning a diagnostic label can have very serious consequences for a client. This issue is detailed in our discussion of confidentiality (chapter 6), but nowhere is the point better illustrated than in Hobbs's (1975) source books on issues in the classification of children, in which issues such as the adverse consequences of labeling and self-fulfilling prophecies are discussed. Szasz (1970) and Goffman (1961) highlight the labeling problem for mentally ill adults, whereas Mercer (1973) documents similar adverse consequences for those labeled mentally retarded.

Since psychological test data are at least occasionally the basis for applying diagnostic labels, it is critical that those using tests for that purpose be appropriately cautious and sensitive to potential alternatives.

Case 7-14: Kevin Bartley, age 15, was brought to a psychiatric facility by his mother, who demanded that he be hospitalized. She was overwhelmed by her life situation, including a divorce in progress and other young children at home. Kevin's truancy and problem behavior at home was too much for her. Because Kevin was a minor, he was admitted to the hospital over his objections and in the process was assigned a psychiatric diagnosis. Several months later, the courts ordered Kevin's discharge (*Bartley v. Kremens*, 1975). Some time after his 18th birthday, Kevin was denied a municipal job because of his "history of psychiatric illness."

The case of Kevin Bartley is important because his hospitalization was as much a function of his family situation as it was of any psychopathology he may have had. He was "diagnosed," and that diagnosis had very real adverse consequences for him when he later sought employment. This occurred in spite of a court decision, which suggested that he ought not to have been hospitalized in the first place.

Case 7-15: Carla Split sought the services of Jack Label, Ph.D., to assist her in coping more effectively with a variety of emotional issues. Dr. Label asked her to complete some paper-and-pencil personality inventories and then offered her his diagnostic impression. Ms. Split was, according to Dr. Label, "a psychopath from the waist down and schizoid from the waist up." Ms. Split was very upset by these rather unusual diagnoses. She had never heard of them, could not find reference to them in books she consulted, and began to believe that she was particularly disturbed in view of the "serious diagnoses."

Dr. Label appears to be a proponent of the creative school of diagnostic psychopathology. It appears that he offered a rather rapid diagnosis of Ms. Split, but failed to explain it adequately. In addition, he used an idiosyncratic, jargon-laden term that was more frightening than helpful to his client. Even when a diagnosis is based on a legitimate classification system properly applied, the terms should not be tossed off lightly to clients. In Dr. Label's case, one wonders how much thought he gave to the actual assessment, as well as to the capricious and demeaning terminology.

Case 7-16: Ivan Meek, age 7, transferred to the Rocky Coast School when his family moved to town from another part of the country. Ivan was shy and socially withdrawn and was not able to establish much rapport with Helen Brash, Ed.D., the school psychologist asked to assist in placing him in the proper class. Dr. Brash was very busy with the start of the new school year and recommended that Ivan be placed in a special education class on the basis of a 15-minute interview, during which she administered some "screening tests." Ivan spent 3 years in classes with mildly to moderately retarded youngsters before he was fully evaluated and found to be of average intellectual ability. During the 3 years, no effort was made to assess his potential or investigate the emotional issues that contributed to his shyness and withdrawal because most of the personnel simply assumed he was retarded by virtue of the placement Dr. Brash had suggested.

The situation in the case of Ivan Meek and Dr. Brash illustrated two major problems with labels and diagnoses. Both can be applied easily or by inference, and they may stick for a long time, much to the client's detriment. If we assume that Dr. Brash was overworked, we might excuse some initial haste and misjudgment. Apparently, however, she forgot about Ivan, failed to check with his prior school, did not order any follow-up evaluation, and did not apply any of a number of standardized assessment tools that might have proven more accurate than her quick judgment. Teachers and parents will often defer to professional judgment, and in Ivan's case it took 3 years for meaningful recognition of his needs and correction of the initial misclassification.

Cases 7-7, 7-8, and 7-10 can all be used as additional examples of the risks of misdiagnosis based on psychological test data. Discussion of actuarial prediction and automated test scoring programs below illustrate an extension of this hazard. This type of problem is most likely to occur when assessment fails to consider all relevant evidence, including nontest data. Certainly, any psychologist who intends to use psychological test instruments for psychodiagnostic purposes should have completed formal studies related to these issues.

Strange as it may seem, there are some circumstances when a diagnostic label may be desirable or even sought by a particular client. For example, a learning disabilities diagnosis might result in the ability to obtain special educational services or unique consideration at college examination time. In some court-related circumstances, certain diagnoses may suggest a lack of criminal responsibility or mitigating factors, leading to a reduced sentence. Some diagnoses might result in the ability to obtain disability insurance payments, while other diagnoses would not. Regardless of the client's preference, a psychologist should never offer a diagnostic assessment without adequate supporting data. The value of psychological assessment is a function of the examiners' integrity, as well as their clinical skills.

Test Security

Psychological measures that are well drafted and carefully standardized require considerable development and expense. Many such instruments could be compromised if their security were violated. Some tests also have substantial potential for abuse in the hands of untrained individuals and therefore should be made available only to individuals trained in their use and application. This security is not always easy to maintain, and any persistent person can obtain substantial "secure" test information by accessing journals or textbooks in major university libraries. There is ample documentation that a moderately clever nonprofessional can obtain copies of such test materials with ease (Oles & Davis, 1977). So-called truth in testing statutes enacted during the 1980s in some states mandated public access to certain types of group-administered educational placement, achievement, and admissions tests (e.g., Scholastic Aptitude Tests [SATs] and Graduate Record Exami-

nations [GREs]), along with the correct answers. Consider some cases for which the security of specialized clinical instruments was violated.

Case 7-17: A reporter working on a story about IQ testing sought an interview with Harlan Simp, Ph.D. During the course of the interview, Dr. Simp showed the reporter a test manual and many items from the WAIS-III. Subsequently, the reporter wrote an article for a national magazine, "How to Score High on IQ Tests." In the article, the reporter revealed 70–80% of the verbal questions on the test, along with practice hints and other clues linked to the items he had seen.

Dr. Simp was outraged and embarrassed when he saw the reporter's article, but there was little he could do. In attempting to be "open and candid with a member of the press," he had inappropriately shared material he should have treated as confidential. The impact of the article in terms of inflated and invalid scores is obviously unknown.

Case 7-18: Adolph Snitler, Ed.D., wrote a book popular with the public about notorious criminals; the book included reduced black-and-white reproductions of the Rorschach inkblots, along with lists of common responses to the same stimuli.

For his book on notorious criminals, the psychologist Dr. Snitler had sought and been given permission by the publisher to reprint copies of the Rorschach plates in achromatic reduced format. Many clinicians would assert that in doing so and listing common responses represents a serious unethical act. Others would note that more detailed Rorschach textbooks are available in many public libraries and suggest that the impact of reading such a book on potential test takers' subsequent performance is questionable. While a psychologically well-adjusted individual of sophisticated ability might be able to fake a disturbed Rorschach protocol, it is unlikely that a troubled client could muster the psychological resources to simulate a psychologically sound protocol no matter what information was available in the public domain. Again, the impact of this disclosure remains unknown, although the author certainly used questionable professional judgment.

Case 7-19: An executive of a large corporation was one of a group of candidates for promotion to a major position in that organization. All candidates were to take some psychological tests administered by a psychologist as part of the selection process. The executive consulted Seb Vert, Ph.D., a psychologist with training in personnel selection, to help him prepare for the tests, and Dr. Vert discussed a number of the potential test instruments. Dr. Vert even suggested response styles that might help the executive to seem most appealing in the final data.

Dr. Vert regards himself as being helpful to his client, the executive. While consulting on the general matter of how to "look good" in a specific type of interview situation is not necessarily unethical, Vert could be considered unethical to the extent that he reveals confidential test items, obtained in his role as a psychologist, to the client. In so doing, he is invalidating an instrument in secret, with the intent of undermining the objective work of a colleague.

Wetter and Corrigan (1995) surveyed a group of lawyers and law students and found nearly half of attorneys and fully a third of law students believed that clients referred for testing should be informed about the existence of validity scales for some psychological tests. Some lawyers also believe that it is appropriate to coach clients prior to such testing. Cooperation with such coaching by a psychologist would clearly be unethical as such conduct would undermine the validity of the instrument. At the same time, it is not inappropriate for a psychologist to advise an assessment client that some test scales may reveal atypical responses, unusual defensiveness, or other such response styles.

THE TESTING INDUSTRY

Psychological testing is big business. Here, we do not refer to psychologists using testing in their practices as part of the testing industry. In fact, because many managed mental health benefit programs require special approval before agreeing to pay for testing, psychologists are doing less of it. Rather, we refer to the test publishers and other companies offering automated scoring systems or national testing programs. Kohn (1975) noted that American school systems spent in excess of $24 million annually in the early 1970s on testing secondary and elementary school children. Although many publishers are secretive about income related directly to their testing services, Kohn uncovered some interesting figures. He reports that in 1974 Houghton Mifflin's measurement and guidance division had sales in excess of $5.5 million. The same year, related services sold by Harcourt Brace Jovanovich surpassed $20.8 million, the American College Testing Program netted nearly $11.3 million, and the Educational Testing Service (ETS) reported its annual income as $53.9 million. More recently, Haney and his colleagues (Haney, Madaus, & Lyons, 1993) estimated gross revenues of several major testing companies for 1987–1988 as follows: ETS, $226 million; National Computer Systems, $242 million; The Psychological Corporation (a division of Harcourt General), $50–55 million; and the American College Testing Program, $53 million.

The spread of consumerism in America has seen increasing assaults on the testing industry (Haney et al., 1993; Kaplan, 1982) and well-reasoned papers on test ethics from within the industry itself (Eyde, Kowal, & Fishburne, 1991; Messick, 1980). Most of the ethical complaints leveled at the larger companies fall into the categories of marketing, sales to unauthorized users, and the problem of so-called impersonal services. Publishers claim that they do make good-faith efforts to police sales so that only qualified users obtain tests. They note that they cannot control the behavior of individuals in institutions to which tests are sent, and one could argue that documented episodes of improper sales (e.g., Oles & Davis, 1977) involved at least a modicum of deception. Since test publishers must advertise in the media provided by organized psychology to influence their prime market, most major firms are also especially responsive to letters of concern from psychologists and committees of the APA. The use of automated testing services, however, raised a number of potential ethical issues that lead to frequent inquiries.

Automated Testing Services

The advent of the computer age made possible the bulk scoring and analysis of test data, creation of new profile systems, and even generation by computer of reports that spring from the electronic printer untouched by human hand or comment. As this period dawned, psychologists argued about the advantages of clinical versus actuarial prediction (Holt, 1970; Meehl, 1954). That is, can a computer-generated, statistically driven, actuarial diagnosis or prediction be more accurate and useful than predictions by clinicians in practice? We do not take sides in that debate, but simply note more recent developments (ES: 2.08).

Several large testing corporations (and even the subsidiary of a pharmaceutical company) now offer test scoring by mail. The user may ask for a "score report only" or for an "interpretive report." In the latter, the computer is programmed to score the test instrument and print out narrative paragraphs or simple statements describing the client diagnostically in terms of personality traits, vocational interests, or any of a number of other declarative or predictive ways. Several companies are willing to rent or sell terminals for the psychologist's office, which may be used to administer the test in automated fashion, with questions appearing on a screen and the client responding with a keyboard stroke or two.

Commenting on the ready availability of computerized personality assessment packages, Lanyon (1984) notes that the overwhelming problem is a lack of demonstrated validity for the printed interpretations they generate. His phone calls to several companies offering such services were "met with self-serving statements or papers that did not directly address validity" (p. 690). Lanyon suggests that perhaps the time has come for federal regulation of the testing industry as a consumer protection measure. Eyde and her colleagues (1991) describe a

methodology for studying the validity of the output of CBTI (computer-based test interpretation) systems. Their study involved a comparative analysis of the accuracy, relevancy, and usefulness of the output of seven CBTI systems for patients in a military hospital, which draws its patients from a wide geographical area. Although focused on the MMPI, their methodology is designed so that it may be adapted to CBTIs for other tests or self-report inventories.

One obvious hazard is the lazy or incompetent practitioner who relies on artificial intelligence and programmers' skills. A recent mailing brought us news of a new office system available to psychologists who wish to find "improved patient care, increased interaction time, and cost efficiency" by administering and interpreting some 20 different scales, indices, checklists, surveys, inventories, and schedules. Areas covered include intelligence, child development, personality, vocational preference, somatic problems, symptoms, and a measure of "depression and hopelessness." All of these instruments are intended for use by competent practitioners as adjuncts to first-hand clinical contact (Bersoff & Hofer, 1995).

Another hazard is potential misuse by untrained or poorly trained individuals and the need to have a qualified professional evaluate the accuracy of such reports. Can a commercial enterprise ignore a marketplace expansion opportunity for the sake of ethics, even if it is unregulated by government? Consider the following cases:

Case 7-20: A firm providing computer-generated MMPI and MMPI-II interpretive reports runs an advertisement in the *APA Monitor* promoting a "sample kit" and everything one needs to use their service for a $25 trial offer. The coupon states that one must be a qualified user, but does not specify what this means and seeks no evidence from responders. Subsequently, the same company solicits psychiatrists in a direct-mail invitation to use the service.

Case 7-21: Ann O. Vation, M.S.W., licensed social worker, makes use of computer-generated vocational guidance interest reports to offer career counseling to her clients in an effort to expand her practice.

Both of these cases illustrate the reach of the automated testing services to professionals outside psychology, as well as an emphasis on attracting new clients with little attention to the nuance of qualifications. The companies would argue that this is a clinician-to-clinician service, and the practitioner is responsible for how the material is used. Representatives of such companies would also note that the reports are replete with cautions and warnings about the use of data. They might also argue that psychiatrists (or other physicians) and social workers, as independent professionals, have a right to such services. On the other hand, given that so many psychologists are not fully trained to use complex psychometric tools, we must wonder how many nonpsychologist mental health service providers understand the complexities and proper use of these instruments. Such sales represent a serious ethical problem.

Case 7-22: An urban police department was planning a civil service examination for new recruits and was sensitive to the need for screening out psychologically troubled individuals. Because they could not provide in-depth interviews for several hundred candidates, the department decided to use a computer-scored personality inventory as a sieve. Those candidates with deviant scores would be selected for personal screening interviews.

This case represents a fairly appropriate use of the instrument, but something interesting happened. A substantial portion of the applicants obtained "grossly deviant" scores. It seems that the 566 true-false items on the personality inventory came at the end of a day-long exam. Many of the candidates were exhausted and found the items "silly" or "stupid." The purpose of the test was not explained by the civil service clerks administering the examination, so many candidates left most of the items blank, responded randomly, or "checked off the weird answers to gross out" the administrators of the program.

Tyranny in the Marketplace

When a commercial testing company dominates a niche of the marketplace, a degree of tyrany can occasionally lead to abuses of the consumer. The fact that the companies involved were founded and are managed by psychologists may offer little reassurance. The following case examples use the actual names of the testing companies involved.

Case 7-23: A high school student takes the SAT on two separate occasions. The student's scores improve significantly between the two administrations, but the ETS, which owns and administers the SAT, refuses to release the newer, higher score to colleges to which the student is applying. The ETS personnel express the belief that the student cheated, citing mysterious statistical analyses they decline to make public. When the student threatens litigation and produces expert psychometric support, ETS offers a substantial settlement without admitting wrongdoing and the student promises to keep the terms of the settlement confidential (see Haney, 1993a, 1993b).

Case 7-24: The Professional Examination Service (PES) in collaboration with the Association of State and Provincial Psychology Boards (ASPPB) produce and administer the Examination for the Professional Practice of Psychology (EPPP), a multiple-choice examination used nationally in the licensing of psychologists. When state licensing board members previewing a draft copy of the EPPP discovered errors on several questions and notified PES, the testing company declined to make appropriate corrections and included three erroneous items in the next version of the EPPP administered nationally. The members of one state licensing board, who knew of the errors, granted licenses to three candidates who had "failed" the exam by making an "error" on one of the faulty questions, and one member of the licensing board wrote a journal article describing the entire incident. When leaders of PES and ASPPB were offered the opportunity to reply to the manuscript, they attempted unsuccessfully to block publication and ceased allowing state licensing boards to preview the draft examinations. Representatives of ASPPB subsequently wrote a response that ignored the key issues and avoided mentioning their attempt to stifle publication of the information (see Koocher, 1989a, 1989b, and Rosen, Reaves, & Hill, 1989).

These cases illustrate that professional ethical codes do not necessarily ensure that psychologically sophisticated testing companies will act in the best interests of individual consumers, especially when the company holds a complete monopoly (as in the case of PES and ASPPB with respect to psychologists' licensing examinations) or dominates the marketplace (as ETS does with respect to college admissions testing).

Some have suggested that "testing police" should monitor, arbitrate, and enforce the use, administration, and interpretation of all types of psychological testing (Azar, 1994). Such recommendations grow from a sense that there is little recourse for people who feel wronged by testing, testers, or test results. The existing standards were developed to clarify proper usage, but many nonprofessionals use the tests, and the behavior of nonmembers of professional associations cannot easily be influenced. The APA and other kindred organizations, such as the AERA and NCME, are not prepared to become testing police according to senior APA staff (Azar, 1994).

USE OF TEST RESULTS

From the above discussion, it is evident that a "good test" may be ill used, either by inappropriate application or by misuses of the resulting scores. In this final section, we raise special questions about access to test results and the potential use or misuse that can result.

Problems of Consent

The issue of informed consent is raised several times in this book and is probably important in all decision-making behavior by clients of psychologists. Insofar as assessment is concerned, clients have a right to know the purpose of the evaluation and the use that will be made of the results. They are also entitled to know

who is likely to have access to the information they are providing to the evaluator. Such use and consent problems often arise when the psychologist who conducts the assessment does so as an agent of an institution or organization.

Chapter 14 includes a detailed discussion of ethical dilemmas in special work settings, such as prisons, schools, and industry. Consent as an issue is also discussed in the chapters on psychotherapy, confidentiality, and research (chapters 4, 6, and 17, respectively). The reason for raising it here is to illustrate some of the special consent problems associated with psychological testing. Consent implies three separate aspects: knowledge, voluntariness, and capacity (Bersoff, 1983, 1995). That is, the person seeking the consent must disclose sufficient information for the person granting consent to understand fully what is being asked. It is not necessary to disclose every potential aspect of the situation, only those facts a reasonable person might need to formulate a decision. Voluntariness refers to the absence of coercion, duress, misrepresentation, or undue inducement (Bersoff, 1983, 1995). Capacity refers to legal competence to give consent. Although all adults are deemed competent to grant consent unless they are found to be incompetent in a court proceeding, children are presumed to be incompetent to grant consent under the law.

Case 7-25: Sean Battery, Ed.D., was hired to consult with the Central City Fire Department. He put together a series of tests, including the MMPI, Rorschach inkblots, Thematic Apperception Test, Draw-a-Person, and a sentence completion series (i.e., all personality assessment tools) to be administered to potential firefighters along with the civil service examination. Several of the firefighters protested that such tests would be an invasion of their privacy.

Case 7-26: Patricia Popquiz, Psy.D., is a school psychologist for the Central City School Department. She scheduled and supervised the administration of standardized achievement testing and IQ testing for all students in Grades 3, 5, 7, and 9, as has routinely been done over the years. She is shocked when several parents complain that their children have been tested without their consent and responds: "But it was only routine testing!"

Case 7-27: As part of an evaluation to determine whether he is competent to stand trial for murder, Roger Slugo agrees to cooperate in a psychological assessment by Arnold Transfer, Ph.D. Mr. Slugo is found fit to be tried and is convicted of murder. During the subsequent penalty phase of the trial, the prosecutor attempts to use portions of Dr. Transfer's assessment of Slugo as a basis for seeking imposition of the death penalty.

These situations all involve consent issues relative to assessment. In the case of the fire department applicants, the complaint is quite appropriate. It may be considered an invasion of privacy to ask an applicant to reveal personal information that is not clearly relevant to the job in question (London & Bray, 1980). The APA Ethics Committee was once asked whether it is ethical to require potential employees to submit to a battery of tests (including personality tests) as a condition of employment if the tests have not been validated for the tasks involved in the job. The APA Ethics Committee unanimously agreed that such selection procedures are unethical (B. D. Gurel, memorandum on telephone ballot of APA's Committee on Scientific and Professional Ethics and Conduct, June 29, 1977, Note 1). Unless Dr. Battery has some basis for documenting the validity of the personality assessment techniques as firefighter selection tools, he is behaving unethically.

Dr. Popquiz sees no problem in continuing what has been the routine practice of the school system for many years. The fact that no one has complained previously does not immunize Popquiz from her responsibility to solicit appropriate consent and to remove from the routine testing program any child whose parents or guardians refuse to give consent (Bersoff, 1983, 1995; Pryzwansky & Bersoff, 1978). Permission may not be required for some systemwide achievement testing related to specific school curricula, but it certainly is for intelligence testing. Even routinely collected intelligence test data can have a lasting impact on a child's education and life (Hobbs, 1975). If parents do not

know that their child has been tested, they might never know that the scores exist. Inappropriate or erroneous data could not be challenged. While courts have ruled that the right of parents to veto testing is not absolute (Pryzwansky & Bersoff, 1978), failing to notify them at all is unquestionably unethical. Seeking cooperative consent is certainly good psychological practice, even if inconvenient.

The case of Mr. Slugo seems to pose the rare situation for which psychological test data can have life or death implications. Whatever the outcome, it is clear that Slugo was never informed that the test data might be used in this manner. He certainly might have declined to cooperate had he known of this risk. If Transfer routinely does evaluations of this sort, he should have been aware of the potential use of his report and so advised Slugo. If Transfer had not done such work before, he was practicing beyond his realm of competence by not first informing himself of the full implications of the report he had agreed to prepare.

Obsolete Scores

It is important to consider the problem of obsolete or outdated test files, how to manage them, and how to determine obsolescence.

Case 7-28: Helen Duration began working for General Tool and Power Company eight years ago. She had been given some paper-and-pencil general ability tests during the hiring period. She has recently applied for a higher level opening within the company, but the personnel department is not seriously considering her because the test scores of 8 years earlier are below those required for the new position.

The case of Helen Duration illustrates the problem of obsolescence. Test scores should be maintained in a client's file only as long as they serve a valid and useful purpose and continue to reflect the status of that client (London & Bray, 1980). Occasionally, some instruments do yield data that may be valid predictors some 8 or more years after they were collected (Bray, Campbell, & Grant, 1974), but that is a rare exception. The consulting psychologist who supervised the testing program at General Tool and Power Company should have cautioned the personnel department that Ms. Duration's scores should not be a basis for promotion decisions years later. In fact, efforts should have been made to ensure the obsolete test data were removed from her file.

One survey of professional psychologists (Berndt, 1984) was a "good news–bad news story." The good news is that most of the psychologists surveyed seemed to manage their testing practices in keeping with established ethical principles. They also seemed willing to give appropriate feedback on test results to clients. The bad news was that few of those surveyed had taken any steps to deal with the problem of obsolete data. The results also suggested that 76% expressed a willingness to release old test information to agencies with the consent of the client. This implied little recognition that such old records might be inaccurate or harmful.

It is difficult to formulate firm rules as to when a given set of data is no longer useful; however, the APA "Record Keeping Guidelines" (1993) offer general guidance, and the *Standards for Educational and Psychological Testing* (APA, AERA, & NCME, 1985, 1998) give some helpful examples. Broad test scores used for initial employment screening have little usefulness if more detailed evaluation follows and are certainly of no value after a year or more of employment. Likewise, college placement test scores have little value after the college course work is completed. Retention of such data (particularly low scores) could have a long-term stigmatizing effect. It is certainly possible to code data for use in long-term archival research, when indicated, while removing all traces of the same data from individual files.

Access to Test Data

Fairly uniform agreement among professionals holds that clients have the right of access to information about themselves and that parents have similar access to information about their minor children. The specific nature of the information has sometimes been raised as a question. While this topic is addressed in chapter 5, test data present some special difficulties because they seldom stand alone for interpretation. That is, the test scores themselves may well be meaningless or misinterpreted by a layperson. One way of handling this is to frame reports in plain language, keeping in mind that the reports are likely to be read by the people about whom they are written. Likewise, psychologists who work with children must frame their reports with the parents' right of access in mind.

Tranel (1994) notes that psychologists are often asked to provide raw data (i.e., scores, test stimuli, client responses) to non-experts, especially in legal proceedings, in response to court orders or in the face of a subpoena. Although ethics codes have traditionally discouraged release of raw data to unqualified persons (ES: 2.02b), little guidance is provided on how to deal with this conflict. In general, the best strategy in such circumstances is preventive (see chapter 6 for a discussion of responding to subpoenas). Records should be kept with the understanding that they may ultimately be released to the client or to a court. It is wisest to write test reports with a directness and clarity that makes it possible to give copies of the report to the client. Ideally, the psychologist will review the report together with the client and address any questions that come up. If asked for test manuals, printed record forms, or other copyrighted material, the psychologist may decline to provide them and refer those making the request to the published source. Actually, much of the material is readily available in the public domain. If asked to provide raw data to the court, the psychologist should explain the rationale for not doing so to lawyers and the court. Some experts (e.g., Shapiro, 1991) argue that one should release raw test data only to another qualified individual, noting, "courts have essentially recognized the legitimacy of this demand" (p. 236). The current APA ethics code (1992) suggests that a psychologist take "reasonable steps" to prevent misuse and to "refrain from releasing" raw data to nonqualified users (ES: 2.02b, 2.06–2.10).

Case 7-29: As part of a diagnostic evaluation, Dr. Ira Median administered intellectual and personality assessment tools to Victor Vector, age 8. Victor's parents were dissatisfied with Dr. Median's evaluation and recommendation that Victor was in need of psychotherapy. They demanded a copy of all the tests and the answers that Victor gave, along with a copy of Dr. Median's report, as they prepared to seek a second opinion.

If Victor Vector's test protocols, for example, include themes of "murderous rage," "Oedipal anger," or similar psychodynamic concepts, one would hope that Dr. Median will deal with the meaning or basic issues, as opposed to something like "Victor told stories in which a murderous boy kills evil father figures." Rather, Dr. Median might write: "Victor's test data suggest that he has difficulty dealing with angry feelings, especially in his relationship with his father." This sort of writing can convey all appropriate meaning, while avoiding jargon, which may be misunderstood or upsetting to the client.

At the same time, however, Dr. Median would be correct in refusing to supply copies of the actual test material and protocols (i.e., raw data) to the parents since they are not trained to use it. Dr. Median should be willing to discuss the results of the evaluation with the parents (or any adult client) and to prepare a report for them if that was a part of the agreed-upon service. However, he should refuse supplying the raw data, while expressing a willingness to send it to another psychologist trained to use it should they wish to have a second opinion (Abeles, 1992). An exception might occur in states where right of access to all records is granted as a matter of law. In such cases, the same steps should be followed, although the parents might have the statutory right to insist on the raw data.

Case 7-30: The Detroit Edison Company posted notice of six vacancies for the job classification "Instrument Man B" at a new power plant. All 10 employees who applied for the openings failed to achieve the acceptable cutoff score the company had set on a battery of psychological aptitude tests, so the vacancies were filled by promoting employees with less seniority who had scored at or above the recommended cutoffs. A union grievance was filed, and the union sought copies of the tests, employees' answer sheets, scores, and other related data, claiming that this was essential for arbitration (Eberlein, 1980).

The case involving Detroit Edison is one that went to the Supreme Court, with the APA filing an amicus (friend of the court) brief in support of withholding the requested information (*Detroit Edison Co. v. National Labor Relations Board*, 1979). The implications are discussed in detail elsewhere (Eberlein, 1980; London & Bray, 1980), but the Supreme Court rulings generally supported the company. By a 5–4 vote, the Court agreed that the "undisputed and important interests in test secrecy" justified refusing to turn over the tests and answer sheets directly to the union. The court noted that retaining test security represented a greater benefit to the public than would open disclosure of the test contents. By a 6–3 vote, the Court also ruled that the union's need for information was not so great as to require breach of the promise of confidentiality to the examinees or breach of the psychologists' code of ethics and resulting potential embarrassment to the examinees.

Psychological testing is at the very heart of our professional history. Along with significant diagnostic and predictive power, use of these tools demands special skill and ethical integrity. The need for caution in the use of testing is well illustrated by the list of elements of competent test use as provided by Eyde and her colleagues (1993, pp. 213–215; Moreland et al., 1995). These articles describe the results of research that can be applied to improving testing practices, including (1) 86 test user competencies and 7 factors accounting for much test misuse, (2) a test classification system based on critical incidents of test misuse, and (3) empirically based test purchaser qualification forms.

SUMMARY GUIDELINES

1. Although many different varieties of tests exist, each should adhere to the *Standards for Educational and Psychological Testing* (APA, AERA, & NCME, 1998) insofar as they present facts through a user's manual. Psychologists should also adhere to these standards when making use of tests.

2. Different types of technical test data exist, including reliability and validity findings. Any test user should be familiar with these

data for any instrument used and should be aware of limitations on the appropriate use of the instrument.

3. Test users should exercise great caution in the selection and interpretation of assessment techniques to ensure that each is valid for the intended purpose and specific situation in question.

4. Those developing new instruments bear a heavy scientific responsibility to ensure that potential users have the information necessary to use the test properly.

5. Those administering psychological tests are responsible for ensuring that the tests are given and scored according to standardized instructions.

6. Test users should also be aware of potential test bias or client characteristics that might reduce the validity of the instrument for that client in that context. Specific cautions should be reported along with test data in any situations in which bias or other problems with validity are suspected.

7. No psychologist is competent to use every standardized assessment tool. It is important to be self-critical and not attempt to use instruments without proper training. Nor should one employ assistants to administer tests unless the assistants are appropriately trained and supervised with those instruments.

8. The validity and confidence of test results often relies on the security of certain test information or items. This secure information should be protected carefully.

9. Automated testing services create a hazard to the extent that they may generate inaccurate data (Eyde et al., 1991) or produce valid results that are subsequently misused by individuals not fully knowledgeable regarding the instruments in use. Psychologists operating or using such services should observe the same stringent safeguards required with manually administered testing.

10. Automated testing services are appropriate only as a professional to professional service, and should never be offered directly to a client as an impersonal service.

11. A client who is to be tested should be informed in understandable terms of the purpose and intended use of the tests and test data.

12. A client has a right to know the results of an evaluation and a right to have test data kept confidential within the limits promised when consent is obtained.

References

Abeles, N. (1992). An ethical dilemma: Disclosure of test items to parents. *Psychotherapy in Private Practice, 10,* 23–26.

Allard, G., Butler, J., Faust, D., & Shea, M. T. (1995). Errors in hand scoring objective personality tests: The case of the Personality Diagnostic Questionnaire-Revised (PDQ-R). *Professional Psychology: Research and Practice, 26,* 304–308.

American Professional Society on the Abuse of Children. (1990). *Guidelines for psychosocial evaluation of suspected sexual abuse in young children.* Unpublished manuscript.

American Psychological Association. (1992). Ethical principles of psychologists and code of conduct. *American Psychologist, 47,* 1597–1611.

American Psychological Association. (1993). Record keeping guidelines. *American Psychologist, 48,* 308–310.

American Psychological Association, American Educational Research Association, & National Council on Measurement in Education. (1985). *Standards for educational and psychological testing.* Washington, DC: Author.

American Psychological Association, American Educational Research Association, & National Council on Measurement in Education. (1998). *Standards for educational and psychological testing.* Washington, DC: Author.

American Psychological Association Ethics Committee. (1993, April 18). *Policy statement of the APA Ethics Committee regarding "take home" tests.* Washington, DC: Author.

Anastasi, A. (1975). Harassing a dead horse (Review of D. R. Green, Ed., *The aptitude-achievement distinction: Proceedings of the second CTB/McGraw-Hill Conference on Issues in Educational Measurement). Review of Education, 1,* 356–362.

Azar, B. (1994, June). Could "policing" test use improve assessments? *APA Monitor,* p. 16.

Bartley v. Kremens, 402 F. Supp. 1039 (E.D. Pa. 1975).

Berndt, D. J. (1984). Ethical and professional considerations in psychological assessment. *Professional Psychology: Research and Practice, 14,* 580–587.

Bersoff, D. N. (1981). Testing and the law. *American Psychologist, 36,* 1047–1056.

Bersoff, D. N. (1983). Children as participants in educational assessments. In G. B. Melton, G. P. Koocher, & M. Saks (Eds.), *Children's competence to consent* (149–178). New York: Plenum.

Bersoff, D. N. (Ed.). (1995). *Ethical conflicts in psychology.* Washington, DC: American Psychological Association.

Bersoff, D. N., & Hofer, P. J. (1995). Legal issues in computerized psychological testing. In D. N. Bersoff (Ed.), *Ethical conflicts in psychology* (pp. 291–294). Washington, DC: American Psychological Association.

Boat, B. W., & Everson, M. (1986). *Using anatomical dolls: Guidelines for interviewing young children in sexual abuse investigations.* Chapel Hill, NC: University of North Carolina.

Bray, D. W., Campbell, R. J., & Grant, D. L. (1974). *Formative years in business.* New York: Wiley.

Brown, D. C. (1994). Subgroup norming: Legitimate testing practice or reverse discrimination? *American Psychologist, 49,* 927–928.

Chandler, L. A. (1990). The projective hypothesis and the development of projective techniques for children. In C. R. Reynolds & R. W. Kamphaus (Eds.), *Handbook of psychological and educational assessment of children, Vol. 2, Personality, behavior, and context.* New York: Guilford.

Cole, N. S. (1981). Bias in testing. *American Psychologist, 36,* 1067–1077.

Conoley, J. C., & Impara, J. C. (Eds.). (1994). *Supplement to the 11th Mental Measurements Yearbook.* Lincoln, NE: University of Nebraska Press.

Cronbach, L. (1980). Validity on parole: How can we go straight? In W. Schrader (Ed.), *New directions for testing and measurement: Measuring achievement progress over a decade* (Vol. 5). San Francisco: Jossey-Bass.

Detroit Edison Company v. National Labor Relations Board, 99 S. Ct. 1123, 1132 (1979).

Eberlein, L. (1980). Confidentiality of industrial psychology tests. *Professional Psychology: Research and Practice, 11,* 749–754.

Eyde, L. D., Kowal, D. M., & Fishburne, F. J. (1991). The validity of computer-based test interpretations of the MMPI. In T. B. Gutkin & S. L. Wise (Eds.), *The computer and the decision-making process. Buros-Nebraska Symposium on Measurement and Testing* (Vol. 4, pp. 75–123). Hillsdale, NJ: Lawrence Erlbaum.

Eyde, L. D., Robertson, G. J., Krug, S. E., Moreland, K. L., Robertson, A. G., Shewan, C. M., Harrison, P. L., Proch, B. E., Hammer, A. L., & Primoff, E. S. (1993). *Responsible test use: Case studies for assessing human behavior.* Washington, DC: American Psychological Association.

Fisher, C. B. (1995). American Psychological Association's (1992) ethics code and the validation of sexual abuse in day-care settings. *Psychology, Public Policy, and Law, 1,* 461–478.

Fisher, C. B. (1996). The (mis)use of posttraumatic stress disorder to validate child sexual abuse. *Register Report, 22,* 8–10. (Newsletter of the National Register of Health Service Providers in Psychology, Washington, DC)

Flaugher, R. L. (1978). The many definitions of test bias. *American Psychologist, 33,* 671–679.

Frederiksen, N. (1984). The real test bias: Influences of testing on teaching and learning. *American Psychologist, 39,* 193–202.

Friedemann, V., & Morgan, M. (1985). *Interviewing sexual abuse victims using anatomical dolls: The professional's guidebook.* Eugene, OR: Shamrock Press.

Goffman, E. (1961). *Asylums.* Garden City, NY: Anchor Books.

Gottfredson, L. S. (1994). The science and politics of race-norming. *American Psychologist, 49,* 955–963.

Green, B. F. (1981). A primer of testing. *American Psychologist, 36,* 1001–1011.

Griggs v. Duke Power Company, 401 U.S. 424 (1971).

Guion, R. M. (1974). Open a new window: Validities and values in psychological measurement. *American Psychologist, 28,* 287–296.

Haney, W. (1981). Validity, vaudeville, and values: A short history of social concerns over standardized testing. *American Psychologist, 36,* 1021–1034.

Haney, W. (1993a, April 15). *Cheating and escheat-*

ing on standardized tests. Paper presented at the annual meeting of the American Educational Research Association, Atlanta, GA.

Haney, W. (1993b, September 29). Preventing cheating on standardized tests. *Chronicle of Higher Education,* p. B3.

Haney, W. M., Madaus, G. F., & Lyons, R. (1993). *The fractured marketplace for standardized testing.* Norwell, MA: Kluwer Academic Publishers.

Hobbs, N. (Ed.). (1975). *Issues in the classification of children* (Vols. 1 & 2). San Francisco: Jossey-Bass.

Holt, R. R. (1970). Yet another look at clinical and statistical prediction: Or, is clinical psychology worthwhile? *American Psychologist, 25,* 337–349.

Joint Committee on Educational Psychological Tests (in preparation). *Standards for Educational and Psychological Tests* (5th edition). Washington, DC: APA.

Kaplan, R. M. (1982). Nader's raid on the testing industry: Is it in the best interests of the consumers? *American Psychologist, 37,* 15–23.

Keyser, D. J., & Sweetland, R. C. (1994). *Test critiques (Vol. 10).* Austin, TX: Pro-Ed.

Kohn, S. D. (1975, July–August). The numbers game: How the testing industry operates. *National Elementary Principal,* 11–23.

Koocher, G. P. (1989a). Confirming content validity in the dark. *Professional Psychology: Research and Practice, 40,* 275.

Koocher, G. P. (1989b). Screening licensing examinations for accuracy. *Professional Psychology: Research and Practice, 40,* 4, 269–271.

Koocher, G. P., Goodman, G. S., White, S., Friedrich, W. N., Sivan, A. B., & Reynolds, C. R. (1995). Psychological science and the use of anatomically detailed dolls in child sexual abuse assessments. *Psychological Bulletin, 118,* 199–222.

Kramer, J. J., & Conoley, J. C. (Eds.). (1992). *Mental measurements yearbook* (11th ed.). Lincoln, NE: University of Nebraska Press.

Lambert, N. M. (1981). Psychological evidence in *Larry P. v. Wilson Riles. American Psychologist, 36,* 937–952.

Lanyon, R. I. (1984). Personality assessment. *Annual Review of Psychology, 35,* 667–701.

Laosa, L. (1984). Social policies toward children of diverse ethnic, racial, and language groups in the United States. In H. W. Stevenson & A. E. Siegel (Eds.), *Child development research and social policy* (Vol. 1, pp. 1–109). Chicago: University of Chicago Press.

Larry P. v. Riles, 343 F. Supp. 1306 (N.D. Cal. 1972) (preliminary injunction), *aff'd,* 502 F. 2d 963 (9th Cir. 1974), opinion issued No. C-71-2270 RFP (N.D. Cal. October 16, 1979).

Levy, H., Kalinowski, N., Markovic, J., Pittman, M., & Ahart, S. (1991). *Victim-sensitive interviewing in child sexual abuse: A developmental approach to interviewing and consideration of the use of anatomically detailed dolls.* Chicago: Mount Sinai Hospital Medical Center, Department of Pediatrics.

Lippman, W. (1922). The abuse of tests. *The New Republic, 32,* 9–10, 213–215, 246–248, 275–277, 297–298, 328–330.

London, M., & Bray, D. W. (1980). Ethical issues in testing and evaluation for personnel decisions. *American Psychologist, 35,* 890–901.

Matarazzo, J. D. (1990). Psychological assessment versus psychological testing: Validation from Bitnet to the school, clinic, and courtroom. *American Psychologist, 45,* 999–1016.

Meehl, P. E. (1954). *Clinical versus statistical prediction.* Minneapolis: University of Minnesota Press.

Mercer, J. R. (1973). *Labeling the mentally retarded: Clinical and social system perspective on mental retardation.* Berkeley: University of California Press.

Messick, S. (1980). Test validity and the ethics of assessment. *American Psychologist, 35,* 1012, 1027.

Moreland, K. L., Eyde, L. D., Robertson, G. J., Primoff, E. S., et al. (1995). Assessment of test user qualifications: A research-based measurement procedure. *American Psychologist, 50,* 14–23.

Novick, M. R. (1981). Federal guidelines and professional standards. *American Psychologist, 36,* 1035–1046.

Oles, H. J., & Davis, G. D. (1977). Publishers violate APA standards on test distribution. *Psychological Reports, 41,* 713–714.

PASE v. Hannon, 506 F. Supp. 831 (N.D. Ill. 1980).

Pryzwansky, W. B., & Bersoff, D. N. (1978). Parental consent for psychological evaluations: Legal, ethical, and practical consideration. *Journal of School Psychology, 16,* 274–281.

Rosen, G. A., Reaves, R. P., & Hill, D. S. (1989). Reliability and validity of psychology licensing examinations: Multiple roles and redundant systems in development and screening. *Professional Psychology: Research and Practice, 20,* 272–274.

Sackett, P. R., & Wilk, S. L. (1994). Within group norming and other forms of score adjustment in preemployment testing. *American Psychologist, 49,* 929–954.

Shapiro, D. L. (1991). *Forensic psychological assessment.* Boston: Allyn & Bacon.

Skinner, L., & Berry, K. (1993). Anatomically detailed dolls and the evaluation of child sexual abuse allegations: Psychometric considerations. *Law and Human Behavior, 17,* 399–422.

Smith, D., & Dumont, F. (1995). A cautionary study: Unwarranted interpretations of the Draw-A-Person Test. *Professional Psychology: Research and Practice, 26,* 298–303.

Szasz, T. S. (1970). *The manufacture of madness.* New York: Harper & Row.

Tranel, D. (1994). The release of psychological data to nonexperts: Ethical and legal considerations. *Professional Psychology: Research and Practice, 25,* 33–38.

Wetter, M. W., & Corrigan, S. K. (1995). Providing information to clients about psychological tests: A survey of attorneys' and law students' attitudes. *Professional Psychology: Research and Practice, 26,* 474–477.

White, S., Strom, G. A., Santilli, G., & Halpin, B. M. (1986). Interviewing young sexual abuse victims with anatomically correct dolls. *Child Abuse and Neglect, 10,* 519–529.

Zedeck, S., & Cascio, W. F. (1984). Psychological issues in personnel decisions. *Annual Review of Psychology, 35,* 461–518.

8

Multiple Role Relationships and Conflicts of Interest

The worst deluded are the self-deluded.

Christian Nestell Bovee

Arthur Kovacs, in a revealing article describing his personal struggle to maintain professional boundaries with a particular client, offered a thought-provoking conclusion as to why therapists may be drawn toward complicated and complicating relationships with their clients:

> The style of the calling of a psychotherapist cannot be separated from the great themes of his own existence. We delude ourselves often that our task consists of our merely executing a set of well learned techniques in the service of our patients' needs. I now know that this information is nonsense. What we do with our patients—whether we do so deviously and cunningly or overtly and brashly—is to affirm our own identities in the struggle with their struggles. (1974, p. 376)

Multiple role relationships can be defined as "situations in which the psychologist functions in more than one professional relationship, as well as those in which the psychologist functions in a professional role and another definitive and intended role, as opposed to a limited

and inconsequential role growing out of and limited to a chance encounter" (Sonne, 1994, p. 376). Multiple roles may be concurrent, as when a therapist hires a client to be a housekeeper. Or they may be consecutive, as when a therapist and a client go into business together on termination of the therapy relationship. Harms and conflicts of interest are most likely to occur when roles are blended concurrently (Sonne, 1994). This chapter explores issues arising from the extension or compounding of relationships beyond the delivery of professional services to clients or other consumers. The focus is confined to multilayered relationships not involving sexual activity or attraction. Chapter 9 is devoted to romantic and sexual dual-role relationships.

We know far more about multiple role relationships than we did even a decade ago. Bennett, Bricklin, and VandeCreek note, "The more we have learned about the effective treatment of mental or emotional disorders, the more we have come to respect the fact that certain types of interactions between a therapist and client may be harmful to the individual's treatment" (1994, p. 263). In the first edition of this book (Keith-Spiegel & Koocher, 1985), we included a section on nonsexual dual-role relationships despite the fact that we had essentially no data-based references beyond our own undergraduate student's unpublished work (Tallman, 1981), now considered to be the first empirical study of therapists socializing with clients. However, for this revision we had plenty of published work and ethics cases from which to choose.

THE BATTLE OVER BOUNDARIES

Kovacs's (1974) words remind us that human beings do not operate as a collection of isolated functions. The type of work that psychologists do is conducive to leaky role boundaries because so much of it occurs in the context of relating, very often about intimate matters, with those we serve. It is the psychologist who is responsible for keeping the therapy process focused. As Gabbard concludes, "Because the needs of the psychotherapist often get in the way of the therapy, the mental health professionals have established guidelines . . . that are designed to minimize the opportunity for therapists to use their patients for their own gratification" (1994, p. 283).

Whereas today it is highly unusual to hear psychologists condone sexual intimacies with clients and others over whom they have direct supervisory or evaluative authority, the debate still rages regarding blending of nonsexual roles between psychologists and those with whom they work in a professional capacity. Some mental health professionals decry the concept of professional boundaries, asserting that they are harmful to the natural process of psychotherapy and have been improperly inserted into ethics codes, training programs, and licensing and malpractice litigation (Hedges, 1993; Lazarus, 1994). Rather, being a fully human therapist or teacher is the most constructive way to enhance personal connectedness and honesty in therapeutic relationships (Hedges, 1993) and may actually improve professional judgment (Tomm, 1993). Lazarus stated: "Practitioners who hide behind rigid boundaries, whose sense of ethics is uncompromising, will, in my opinion, fail to really help many of the clients who are unfortunate enough to consult them" (1994, p. 253).

The critics of drawing firm professional boundaries further contend that blendings are inevitable and attempting to control them by invoking authority (e.g., ethics codes) oversimplifies the inevitable complexities inherent in psychotherapy processes (Bogrand, 1993; Ryder & Hepworth, 1990) and creates the practice of defensive therapy (Clarkson, 1994). The answer, they say, is to educate both clients and therapists about how to deal with unavoidable breaks and disruptions in boundaries and to educate psychologists that exploitation is always unethical, regardless of boundary issues.

Exploitation is, of course, to be avoided in its own right. However, we are convinced that lax professional boundaries are often a precursor of exploitation, confusion, and loss of objectivity. While reviewing the cases in this chapter, the reader will note the pervasive incidence of harm caused by psychologists who were, themselves, completely out of touch with the impact that their judgments were having on those with whom they are working. Ethics charges based on role blurring are increasing and account for almost half of all complaints to the American Psychological Association (Sonne, 1994), and *all* psychologists are harmed by those who play too loose with boundaries (Bennett et al., 1994).

Most of the reasons why multiple role boundaries should be avoided are not solely for the protection of psychologists, but for the welfare of clients and others who seek our services. Despite the charge that those who remain boundary vigilant are "therapy machines" or "cookbook therapists" incapable of relating as a caring human being to their clients, there is no reason consistent and clear boundaries need to have an impact on a psychotherapist's warmth or empathy (Borys, 1994). The task at hand is to match therapy style and technique to a given client's needs (Bennett et al., 1994). This requires a clear vision, unencumbered by the psychologist's personal agendas. (See Smith & Fitzpatrick, 1995, and Gutheil & Gabbard, 1993 for reviews of the boundary issue literature.)

EVALUATING MULTIPLE ROLE RELATIONSHIPS

While recognizing that it may not always be possible to avoid nonprofessional contact with people with whom psychologists have a professional relationship, the APA (American Psychological Association) ethics code (1992) requires vigilance, especially if harm could result.

> Psychologists must always be sensitive to the potential harmful effects of other contacts on their work and on those persons with whom they deal. A psychologist refrains from entering into or promising another personal, scientific, professional, financial, or other relationship with such persons if it appears likely that such a relationship reasonably might impair the psychologist's objectivity or otherwise interfere with the psychologist's effectively performing his or her functions as a psychologist, or might harm or exploit the other party. (ES: 1.17)

The code expects psychologists to make their judgments based on the likelihood that problems reasonably *might* occur (Canter, Bennett, Jones, & Nagy, 1994). Although we agree that careful consideration should be given prior to softening a strictly professional relationship, we are unconvinced that accurate prediction can be a simple exercise in judgment. For psychologists already predisposed to blend roles, rationalization processes are probably well under way, thus subverting the caliber of any risk assessment. We also contend that there is *never* any justification for entering into some types of multiple role relationships with persons who are being actively counseled, formally taught, or supervised. Sexual and business relationships, for example, are inherently risky regardless of who is involved. Neither can be defended as reasonable dimensions to impose on a therapy relationship.

We are in agreement with Pope's contention that, "the professional therapeutic relationship is secured within a reliable set of boundaries on which both therapist and patient can depend" (1991, p. 23) and that conflicts, which are more likely to arise as boundaries blur, compromise the disinterest (as opposed to lack of interest) prerequisite for sound professional judgment.

As Borys puts it, "For many, if not most, types of patient problems and populations, boundaries and the personal meaning of the therapeutic boundaries are an arena in which critical emotional issues are manifested and worked through. Clear, consistent boundaries provide a structure and safety for many patients that is a curative factor in itself" (1994, p. 267). Therapists, students, and other consumers of psychological services are often confused and vulnerable. That the therapy relationship becomes a sanctuary in which consumers can focus on themselves and their needs and thereby receive "clean" feedback and direction is a model worth rigorously upholding.

Kitchener (1988) helps assess the appropriateness of boundaries by providing three guidelines, based on role theory, to predict the amount of damage that role blending can create. First, as the expectations of clients and therapists become more incompatible, the potential for harm is increased. Second, as obligations associated with the roles become increasingly divergent, the risks of loss of objectivity and divided loyalties rise. Third, to the extent that the power and prestige of the psychologist is greater than that of the consumer, the potential for exploitation is heightened. Kitchener reasons that when role expectations are compatible and conflict of interest and power differentials are small, the potential for harm to clients is also lowered. So, for example, hiring a client as a salesperson for your on-the-side tool business would create a high discrepancy across all three of Kitchener's criteria. Sitting with your client (who is also a psychologist) on the same airplane on its way to an APA convention would have fewer disparities. Yet, even here, clinical judgment may still dictate that roles not be mixed. The client's emotional status may contraindicate even brief contact outside a professional setting.

Gottlieb's (1993) equally useful model for avoiding exploitative dual relations tracks the level of psychologists' power with the duration (or expected duration) of the professional relationship and the clarity of termination, defined as the likelihood that the consumer or the client will have further professional contact. Thus, performing a vocational psychological assessment involves a relatively low power differential, brief duration, and unlikely professional contact later. Assuming that the test interpretations were not biased, the applicant is not a likely candidate for professional exploitation should a relationship eventually ensue. For more traditional individual and family therapy, the power differential is greater, the professional relationship could continue for a long while, and the termination date is not predictable.

Brown (1994) adds two boundary violations that, if present, heighten risks of harm. First, objectification can occur, with the therapist using the client as an "it" for the purpose of providing entertainment, convenience, or education. Second, boundary violations usually arise from impulse rather than from careful, reasoned consideration of therapeutic indications. Thus, hugging a client is not unethical per se, but the act of hugging a client should have been preceded by an assessment of any negative indicators.

It is important to understand that not all boundary crossings are boundary violations (Gutheil, 1994). Our primary goal is to sensitize readers to the possible conflicts and potential damage of one's actions so that reasoned, professional judgment may be exercised prior to risking any blending of roles. As Brown has written, "the goal of an ethical decision is not to avoid any and all violations of boundaries, for this is impossible. Instead, the goal is to remain on the more innocuous end of the continuum, in the position where the abuse and exploitation of the power of the therapist are minimized" (1994, p. 279).

RISKS OF ROLE BLENDING AND CONFLICTS OF INTEREST

Loss of objectivity and exploitation are but two possible negative outcomes of role blending. Confusion, feelings of rejection and abandonment, and misinterpretations of communications that result in a distortion of the relationship are some of the other effects that can harm clients and, in addition, bring misery into the lives of therapists themselves.

Risky Therapists

All psychologists are at some risk for inappropriate role blending. Yet, those whose competence is underdeveloped or who are improperly trained, those whose own boundaries are not firm, and those with problems that render them needy for adoration, power, or social connections are more likely to venture beyond the realm of appropriately relating to clients, students, or others with whom they work. Unfortunately, psychotherapy provides an almost ideal environment for emotionally or morally precarious professionals to attempt to fulfill their personal needs. The settings are private and intimate. The relationship power is with the therapist. If things turn sour, the relationship can simply be "terminated."

Psychotherapists who engage in considerable self-disclosure with clients may be at greater risk for problematic relationships with clients. Relatively neutral illustrations from the psychologist's life may help make a point. Whereas well-considered, more intimate disclosures to some clients may be helpful, it comes down to a matter of clinical judgment. Gutheil (1994) notes, and our experience with ethics cases confirms, that considerable self-disclosure of personal information to clients is a common antecedent to sexual misconduct.

Clients may inquire about psychologists' personal lives, and we agree with Lazarus's contention that "there is something demeaning and hostile about having one's questions dismissed and answered by another question" (1994, p. 258). "Do you have children, Dr. Shell?" "Why did you ask me that, Maurice?" But, not all clients' questions should be answered, and it may be necessary to explore the intention of a client who seems too inquisitive. The skillful clinician can respond without demeaning the client in the process.

Some therapists practicing within certain types of therapeutic orientations are probably more vulnerable to charges of boundary violations. For example, Williams (1998) notes that humanistic therapy and "encounter group" philosophies are heavily based on tearing down interpersonal boundaries. Therapists often disclose a great deal about themselves, hug their clients, and insist on the use of first names. These therapists are, according to Williams, vulnerable to ethics charges even though they are practicing according to how they were trained.

Risky Career Periods

It is fairly common to find that therapists who engage in inappropriate role blending are relatively inexperienced. Many have recently come from graduate programs in which students, in the process of transcending into professional identities, developed complicated relationships with their educators and supervisors. The internship period often involves role blending, including social, evaluative, and business-related activities (Slimp & Burian, 1994; see also chapters 13 and 16). It may be that many psychologists, new to functioning independently, have had insufficient opportunity to observe and model professional roles with appropriate boundaries in place. Further, some psychologists have experienced appalling supervisory models, involving sexual advances and other inappropriate behaviors (Glaser & Thorpe, 1986; Pope, Levenson, & Schover, 1980).

The midcareer period can be risky for psychologists whose profession or life in general has not panned out as earlier envisioned. Divorce or other family-based stresses involving teenage children, onset of an illness, apprehension about aging, and unfulfilled dreams of success are among the midcareer difficulties that can impair professional judgments. It is estimated that the majority of psychologists who engage in sexual relationships with their clients are middle-aged (see chapter 9).

Another higher risk period occurs at the far end of the career cycle. Sometimes, senior therapists have, perhaps without recognizing it, come to see themselves as beyond questioning regardless of what they do. Pepper (1990) discusses the psychodynamics of charismatic, grandiose, authoritarian senior therapists who may harm clients by encouraging complicated multiple relationships. We have seen several ethics cases that fit this pattern.

Case 8-1: Gloria Vast, Ph. D., referred to herself as the "grand dame of psychology." She ran large encounter groups based on her long-standing, best-selling book, *Touch Yourself, Touch the Universe.* She hired her current clients to seat the guests and to assist her. Whenever client-workers became disaffected, they were berated by Vast and the other clients and sometimes banished. One client who was expelled from the circle pressed charges with the state licensing board against Dr. Vast.

Case 8-2: Alan Groupie, Ph.D., went into business with a famous movie star who was suffering from severe depression. Groupie eventually became his manager. Dr. Groupie moved in with the star and personally monitored all of the celebrity's activities. Groupie charged his usual fee of $150 an hour, 24 hours a day, 7 days a week. This arrangement lasted for over a year.

Some of these therapists emerged during a period in the 1960s and 1970s when "creative" therapeutic improvisation was in vogue in some circles. The thorny issues involving appropriate professional boundaries began to be actively considered at that time, but not every psychologist paid attention to them.

Professional or personal isolation can conspire to cloud psychologists' judgments. The next case involves an indignant response to a fading career, compounded by an absence of close ties with family or friends.

Case 8-3: A well-known and outspoken psychologist, Panacea Grandee, Ph.D., alienated the professional community over the last several years with his ruthless personal attacks, especially when anyone referred to the theoretical foundation of the therapy orientation he pioneered in the 1950s as outmoded and faulty. Grandee, a widower, continued to maintain a successful practice in his condominium in an upscale area of a large metropolitan area, and his clients became the focus of his life. He hosted frequent social events at his home and invited himself along on clients' vacations. Colleagues in the community became concerned that Grandee had developed a cult of sorts, made

up of high-paying, perennial clients who also provided him with adoration, loyalty, and "family."

Dr. Grandee might elicit some sympathy
were it not for his ill-conceived approach to
solving personal problems. His case also raises
the issue of appropriate work settings, which we
consider next.

Risky Work Settings

During an APA Ethics Committee meeting in
the early 1980s, we noted that the majority of
cases involving boundary blurring (including
sexual ones) occurred among therapists who
maintained individual practices, often in isolated offices away from other mental health professionals. Sometimes, the setting was the therapist's own home. The committee seriously
discussed the feasibility of declaring solo practices "unethical." Although we quickly recognized that such a mandate could neither be
enforced nor withstand legal scrutiny, it seemed
clear enough that something about therapists
either choosing to work in isolation, or the isolat-
ing conditions themselves, fostered the clouding
of professional standards of care. Or, perhaps
some psychologists have been rejected by their
colleagues, as Dr. Grandee (Case 8-3) appears
to have been, and then turned to inappropriate
substitutes for support and validation. Regardless of the reason, an insular practice with no
provisions for compensating professional contact on a regular basis diffuses professional identity. If a therapist has no one with whom to
bounce off ideas and consult about predicaments, the chances of making errors in judgment and using clients for the purpose of fulfilling personal needs appear to be substantially
elevated.

Conducting therapy in ones' home is not a
desirable situation in our opinion, but is not
inherently inappropriate if the therapy room is
a professional-looking office (ideally, with its
own entrance) rather than the therapist's personal living quarters. Some clients may find
therapy in such an intimate location confusing,
and their emotional status could be worsened by
the connotations attached to the setting. Others
could potentially become burdens on the family

or act out in more frightening ways. Unless the
home-office therapist has another location where
new clients can be screened for suitability, it
cannot be known in advance who is going to
walk through the front door.

Risky Clients

Leslie (1989) uses the phrase "the wrong patient" to describe clients who cannot tolerate
boundary crossings. Even Lazarus, who favors
flexible boundaries, allows that:

> With some clients, anything other than a formal
> and clearly delineated doctor-patient relationship
> is inadvisable and is likely to prove counterproduc-
> tive. It is usually inadvisable to disregard strict
> boundary limits in the presence of severe psycho-
> pathology; involving passive-aggressive, histrionic,
> or manipulative behaviors; borderline personality
> features; or manifestations of suspiciousness and
> undue hostility. (Lazarus, 1994, p. 257)

Clients who have been victims of violent
attacks or abuse, because of the difficult issues
of trust or ambivalence surrounding "caretakers," are also particularly well suited to clear
boundary settings, despite their frequent "tests"
of such boundaries (Borys, 1994). Patients with
self-esteem or individuation issues often depend
on the constant approval of others for confirmation. The therapist who weakens boundaries by
reassuring the client that he or she is special
because he or she is taken to lunch, given gifts,
or is the recipient of considerable self-disclosure
by the therapist may be unwittingly colluding
with the pattern and thereby reinforcing the
problem (Borys, 1994). Those who have suffered early deprivations, and have not fully
mourned the finality of the past, may still be
seeking to rectify it to earn favor with those who
were physically or emotionally unavailable. As
Borys observes, "Developing a relationship with
a . . . therapist often mobilizes tremendous
hopes that the therapist can somehow replace
what was lost and 're-parent' them" (1994,
p. 269). If the therapist responds as a rescuer,
a totally inappropriate cycle is established, and
the client will again experience the loss because
a therapist never can (and most never intend
to) replace a parent or the past. In this context,

we gain considerable insight into the psychodynamics behind the many charges of "abandonment" brought by clients involved in multiple role relationships with their therapists.

Positive limit setting is a technique that should be mastered by all psychologists. It involves placing restrictions when responding to the client's request while, at the same time, reframing the response in a way that meets a legitimate underlying need. The next two cases provide examples of positive limit setting.

Case 8-4: Timmy Vulnerable, age 10, was enrolled in psychotherapy with Carla Carefull, Psy.D., by a state welfare agency and foster parents with whom he had been placed following a significant physical beating by his substance-abusing mother. After several months, the agency began to plan for a reunification with the mother, who was graduating from a drug rehabilitation program. During a session, Timmy asked Dr. Carefull, "Where do you live?" When she inquired why he wanted to know, Timmy replied, "I thought maybe if my mom started hitting me again some night, I could run out of the house and come to your place." She told Timmy, "You're right! You do need a plan for what to do if things get bad at home. I'm not always home, so it will be better if we figure ways that you could get help anytime." Dr. Carefull then informed Timmy of emergency resources and how to reach them, including 911.

Dr. Carefull was deeply moved by Timmy's situation and his poignant analysis of her as a helper in times of crisis. She also recognized, however, that she could not meet these needs in the way the child was asking.

Case 8-5: Rita Repeata sought psychotherapy with Hy Pedestal, Ph.D., following a breakup with the man she had been dating for 2 months. She described a series of relationships with 3 different men in the past 12 months. All followed the same pattern: casual social contacts led to sexual intimacies by the second date and a breakup within a few weeks. Each time Rita said she "felt like ending it all." She began her second therapy session with Dr. Pedestal by telling him how helpful the first session had been and what an exceptional therapist he was. She then got out of her chair and sat

on the floor at his feet, looking up at him adoringly. When Pedestal asked what she was doing, Rita replied, "I feel more comfortable like this."

Dr. Pedestal acknowledged Rita's feelings, but noted that sitting on the floor in that manner would do little to help her break out of the pattern for which she was seeking help. Politely, but firmly, Dr. Pedestal asked her to sit in one of the office chairs, and he initiated a discussion of the importance to focusing on the issues that brought her into therapy.

TYPES OF MULTIPLE ROLE RELATIONSHIPS

Among the types of multiple roles or conflicts of interest that a psychologist might conceivably encounter with clients or other service consumers, the following have been selected for discussion: (1) entering into business relationships with clients; (2) service and product bartering; (3) delivery of professional services to close friends and family members; (4) entering into professional relationships with employees; (5) socializing with clients and students; (6) accepting clients' referrals of their close relations; (7) accepting acquaintances as clients; (8) encountering "small world" hazards, especially the role conflicts that inevitably arise in smaller communities; (9) accepting gifts and asking for favors; (10) giving gifts; and, (11) conducting therapy outside a professional setting. We also discuss unavoidable clashes—circumstances into which psychologists are thrust without much warning—into role conflicts the psychologists had no part in creating.

Entering into Business Relationships with Clients

That psychologists enter into risky business dealings with those to whom they owe a fiduciary duty never ceases to amaze us. Investments and partnerships in commercial ventures may be rationalized as "strictly business," but we think everyone would agree that such activities are a constant source of tension and are often highly emotionally charged, regardless of who the players are.

Case 8-6: C. D. Rom had been a client of Teki Grabbit, Psy.D., for almost 2 years. Dr. Grabbit was in awe of Rom's creative computer skills, so when Rom announced his intent to start an interactive software company and invited Dr. Grabbit to become an investor, she jumped at the chance and invested $50,000. The company was formed, but things moved very slowly. Rom quit therapy because, as he later stated in his complaint to a state licensing board, "During our sessions, Dr. Grabbit focused almost exclusively on how the company was going, demanded that I make certain changes in the business plan, and ignored the emotional problems that I needed to deal with. When I told her that I resented having to pay her to talk about the business, she yelled, 'You owe it to me. I entrusted my life savings to you.'"

Case 8-7: "You and I would make a great team," declared cosmetic surgeon Marcel Sculpt, M.D., to his counselor Barbie Duh, M.A. "My clients often need counseling, and some of your clients may be interested in my services. We could share an office suite and call ourselves something like, 'Beautiful Inside and Out.' I know I can get you lots of clients." Ms. Duh, whose own caseload was flagging, thought the idea a bit wacky. But, the more she thought about the potential benefits, the more attracted she became to trying "something a little different." Duh did insist that Dr. Sculpt go into therapy with someone else, figuring that would defuse any dual-role dilemmas. However, after setting up the business, the expected clientele did not materialize, and Ms. Duh's share of the lavish office expenses were far more than she could afford. Her relationship with Sculpt soured, and, when they argued, she brought up issues from his counseling. The partnership was dissolved, leaving Duh deeply in debt. Duh blamed Sculpt for cajoling her into such a ridiculous venture and is considering suing him.

Greed played a part in both Grabbit's and Duh's cases, even though neither would likely admit to that trait in themselves. As a result, they became enmeshed in business dealings to the detriment of their clients and ultimately to

themselves (see ES: 1.15). Ms. Duh seems to think that because her client instigated the partnership, she has no responsibility for what transpired. On the contrary, the responsibility rested exclusively with her, and she gave in to faulty judgment. Terminating a client for the purpose of going into business is also unacceptable professional practice, even if Duh did assist Sculpt in finding a new therapist. If Duh goes ahead with her lawsuit, she will probably be in for a surprise when the tables turn on her.

Case 8-8: Oscar Scatterbill, Ph. D., hired client Thomas Clerk as his personal secretary. The relationship seemed to be working out until Clerk asked for a raise. Dr. Scatterbill refused, saying that he was already paying Clerk a good wage. Clerk countered by reciting Scatterbill's monthly income and comparing it to his own. Scatterbill allegedly laughed as he responded that a comparison between the two was hardly a meaningful one. An insulted Clerk quit his job and his therapy and wrote to an ethics committee claiming that Dr. Scatterbill had "ruined both his emotional and financial status."

Dr. Scatterbill should also have known better. Different roles call for different protocols, and the roles of therapist and "boss" require markedly different, and sometimes conflicting, styles of relating.

Even business dealings with clients motivated by genuine compassion can backfire. By becoming directly involved in a client's personal tragedies, the therapist in the next case unwittingly withdrew from his role as a safe, neutral haven.

Case 8-9: Barney Bigheart, Ph.D., was sympathetic when his client Bart Busted faced foreclosure on his home. Bigheart offered to loan Busted several thousand dollars to stave off the lender. Busted gratefully accepted, and an unsecured note was drawn up with a generously low interest rate. Busted's financial situation did not improve, however, and he failed to make his loan payments to Bigheart. Even though Bigheart exerted no pressure regarding the late payments, Busted expressed considerable guilt over "letting down the only person who ever gave a damn about me." Busted's depression deepened, and he became a serious suicide risk.

A more common situation involving students is more difficult to evaluate, perhaps because it usually satisfies everyone's needs.

Case 8-10: Professor Henry Hire lives in a small university town. Students often seek part-time employment, and he regularly hires them to do yard work, house repairs, and baby-sitting.

This practice is so prevalent that the attendant ethical issues are rarely considered. We recommend that students currently enrolled in one's classes never be employed to do nonprofessionally related work because an active dual role is present. Ethical issues are virtually defused altogether if student employees are not in the same departmental unit. Student employees should be selected for their competence and trustworthiness and paid a fair wage as ways of precluding complaints or entanglements. Expectations and agreements should be well-formulated in advance, including provisions for termination that are predicated on respect for the needs of students.

Case 8-11: To bring in extra income, Whatta Dump, Ph.D., and her husband fixed up their basement and rented it to a student in Dump's department. Within a few weeks, the student complained that the conditions were unbearable and that she wanted to leave. The student claimed that the basement stank and that she was lonely and wanted to live with other students. Dr. Dump reminded her that she had a lease that would have to be paid in full. The student went to the dean of students and the campus newspaper, sharing other details about the household, including the substance of the late night shouting matches between the Dumps.

It appears that this arrangement was poorly formulated from the beginning, to the ultimate detriment of both student and professor.

Bartering Services for Services

Agreements to exchange a service (e.g., psychotherapy) for a client's service (e.g., automobile maintenance), rather than paying for the services or copayments directly, are fraught with potential pitfalls having ethical relevance. Long frowned upon by the APA, the 1992 ethics code directly addressed the option of service bartering. After warning that psychologists should ordinarily refrain from accepting nonmonetary remuneration in return for psychological services because of the potential for exploitation and distortion of the professional relationship, the code adds, "psychologists may participate in bartering *only* if it is not clinically contraindicated, and the relationship is not exploitative" (ES: 1.18). A large national survey of psychologists has revealed that over half of the respondents believe that bartering is acceptable under some circumstances. Most psychologists (83%), however, have never accepted a service or product as payment for therapy, and those who have, do so rarely (Borys & Pope, 1989).

We acknowledge that entering into bartering agreements with clients can be a reasonable and even humanitarian gesture toward people who require mental health services but cannot afford them. We also acknowledge bartering arrangements that were highly satisfactory to both parties. A psychologist in a small farming community agreed to take fresh produce as payment for six sessions of couples counseling. Another counselor in a small town agreed to see a proud, but poverty-stricken, client in return for the client's carpentry work on a charitable home restoration project organized by a group that the psychologist actively supported. A third psychologist performed a child assessment in exchange for five trees from the parent-owner of a struggling nursery service. These were situations in which community resources were limited, as were the clients' assets, and exploitation was not at issue. Let us compare the above examples to another that appeared also to be going very well.

Case 8-12: A gifted seamstress was offered the job of making clothes for a psychologist in exchange for psychotherapy. The client was satisfied with the agreement because she needed therapy and had plenty of time available to sew. The therapist's elation was summarized by her giddy remark at a cocktail party, "I am most assuredly the best-dressed psychologist in town."

The potential for exploitation in this case is far more likely. Because the psychologist openly acknowledged, with delight, her dual relationship at a cocktail party, it is unlikely that she even recognizes the inherent risks of such arrangements. What will happen if an outfit does not fit properly or is not made to the therapist's satisfaction? What if the client becomes displeased with the therapy process and begins to feel like a one-woman sweatshop? What if the therapist remains so satisfied with this relationship that she creates within the client an unnecessary dependency to match her own? These "what ifs" are neither silly nor idle speculations when one considers incidents of bartering gone awry.

Case 8-13: Kurt Court, Esq., and Leonard Dump, Ph.D., met at a mutual friend's party. Mr. Court's law practice was suffering because of what he described as "mild depression." Dr. Dump was about to embark on what promised to be a bitter divorce. They hit on the idea of swapping professional services. Dr. Dump would see Mr. Court as a psychotherapy client, and Mr. Court would represent Dr. Dump in his divorce. Mr. Court proved to be far more depressed than Dr. Dump had anticipated. Furthermore, Court's representation of Dump was erratic, and the likelihood of a favorable outcome looked bleak. Yet, Mr. Court brought ethics charges against Dr. Dump. Court charged that the therapy he received was inferior and that Dump spent most of the time blaming him for not getting better faster.

Case 8-14: Decora Shod, Ph.D., had a client who owned a furniture manufacturing outlet. Dr. Shod mentioned that she was in the process of redecorating her home. The client offered to allow Dr. Shod to select furniture from his warehouse at his cost if Dr. Shod would see him at a greatly reduced rate. The client reasoned that they would both benefit because Dr. Shod would still be receiving more for far less than she could in retail outlets, and the client could also save money. Shod agreed to the proposal. During the therapy, Shod increasingly confronted the client in areas in which she felt the client was being self-destructive and defensive. The client reacted negatively to the therapeutic techniques and contacted an ethics committee, charging Dr. Shod with attempting to lock him into unnecessary treatment until her home was completely refurnished.

Case 8-15: Lex Icon, Ed.D., offered to tutor Trillion Typos, a student in the graduate department who was having trouble in one of her courses, in exchange for typing his book manuscript. Dr. Icon had taken Typos' report of her word-processing skill level at face value, but later found it to be unacceptable. Dr. Icon gave her a few tutoring sessions anyway, but terminated the other arrangement. Typos received an "F" in the course and pressed a grievance against Dr. Icon for failing to follow through with his agreement to help her and for allegedly telling her professor that she was incompetent, thus contributing to the failing grade.

These three cases illustrate not only the destructive results that can occur when the follow-through phase of bartering results in unhappy consumers, but also the vulnerable position in which psychologists are placed. Court's impatience, Shod's confrontations, and Icon's dissatisfaction may all have been appropriate under simpler circumstances. Because of the intertwining of nonprofessional issues in each situation, however, the actions of all three psychologists were experienced by others as retaliatory or self-serving.

Bartering psychologists are vulnerable to charges of exploitation if the value placed on the psychologists' time and skills are set at a higher rate than those of the clients.

Case 8-16: Elmo Brush agreed to paint several rooms in the home of Paul Peelpaint, Ph.D., in exchange for counseling for Brush's teenage daughter. Dr. Peelpaint saw the girl for six sessions and terminated the counseling. Brush complained that his end of the bargain would have brought $1200 in a conventional deal. Thus, it was as though he had paid $200 a session for the services costing Peelpaint's other full-paying clients $80 a session. Dr. Peelpaint argued that he had satisfactorily resolved the daughter's problems, and the deal was valid because task was traded for task, not dollar value for dollar value.

Trading a one-shot service with a known cost estimate, based on Brush's own professional experience, with a service that cannot be cost estimated in advance is problematic. Brush's daughter might have required 50 sessions, valued at $4,000, if Dr. Peelpaint was committed to doing a thorough job and had been collecting his usual fees, resulting in a substantial loss for the psychologist. Dr. Peelpaint's attitude also reveals little regard for fairness to Brush. Some of the ethical complexities of Dr. Peelpaint's case might have been avoided had he hired Brush outright, leaving Brush free to make a separate decision about engaging Peelpaint as his daughter's therapist after the painting job was finished.

Another risk exists because most professional liability insurance policies specifically exclude coverage involving business relationships with clients (Canter et al., 1994). What if Brush fell off his ladder, causing injury or damage? Many liability insurance carriers interpret bartering arrangements as business relationships and would decline to defend covered psychologists when bartering schemes go awry. These not-so-apparent risks need to be considered carefully in advance of bartering for services.

Case 8-17: X. Ploit, Ph.D., offered an unemployed landscaper, Sod Lawn, the opportunity to design and redo his grounds in return for psychotherapy. Dr. Ploit charged $80 an hour and credited Lawn at a rate of $6 an hour, which meant that Lawn worked over 13 hours for every therapy session received. Lawn complained to Dr. Ploit that the amount of time he was spending on the yard prevented him from entering into full-time employment. Dr. Ploit responded that Lawn could choose to terminate therapy and return when he could afford to pay the full fee.

Dr. Ploit's case is even more complicated and bothersome. Ploit figured the amount due for an ongoing service well below the going rate for a skilled landscape artist. The bartering contract probably did contribute to the client's difficulties. When the landscaper-client complained, the psychologist interrupted the agreement and abandoned the client.

Bartering Services for Goods

So far, we have been discussing strictly service bartering. Here, we explore more fully the exchange of psychologists' services for tangible objects. It has been suggested that this form of bartering is less problematic because a fair market price can be established (Canter et al., 1994). However, we know of such situations that were far from problem free.

Case 8-18: When Manifold Benz, Ph.D., learned that his financially strapped client was going to sell his classic automobiles to pay outstanding therapy and other bills, Benz expressed an interest in one of the cars. Dr. Benz said that he saw the same model on sale at a show for $19,000, and that he would be willing to credit the client with 200 hours of therapy in exchange for the car. The client was in arrears for about 100 hours.

Case 8-19: Flip Channel, Ph.D., allowed Penny Pinched to pay her past due therapy bill with a television set that Penny described as "near new." However, when Dr. Channel hooked it up, the colors were faded, and the picture flickered. He told Penny that the television was not as she represented it, and that she would have to take it back and figure out some other method of payment. Penny angrily retorted that Channel must have broken it because it was fine when she brought it to him. When Channel insisted that the TV was defective, Penny terminated therapy and filed ethics charges against him. She charged that he broke both a valid contractual agreement and her television set.

Benz is exploiting his client by committing him to a specific number of future therapy sessions that the client may not need. Further, we do not know if the amount Benz suggested is fair market value, and this may be difficult to determine accurately. (Allowing a client to "carry" 100 hours of therapy suggests other problems as well, described in chapter 10.) Dr. Channel found himself in a no-win situation as a result of the television fiasco, and a therapeutic relationship was destroyed in the process.

Case 8-20: Notta Rembrandt proposed that she paint a portrait of Gig Grump, Ph.D., in exchange for psychotherapy. Dr. Grump posed, and Rembrandt received therapy on an hour-for-hour basis. On the 11th session, Grump viewed the portrait and expressed dissatisfaction, calling it "hideous." An insulted Rembrandt insisted that the portrait was excellent and "captured Grump's soul." The conversation escalated into a fervent argument. Rembrandt grabbed her canvas, stomped out, and did not return. Dr. Grump sent Rembrandt a bill for 10 sessions. Rembrandt filed an ethics charge. Grump responded that the whole arrangement was the client's idea, and he was not responsible for the outcome.

Possible transference and countertransference issues notwithstanding, the arrangement between Rembrandt and Grump was shaky from the start, given the wide variability in artistic tastes. Rembrandt prevailed in her ethics complaint. Grump's attempt to fault the client was not a persuasive defense, and he did finally offer to withdraw his bill.

Because psychological services typically involve a combination of trust, sensitive evaluations, social influence, and the creation of some dependencies, the potential for untoward consequences are always present when bartering agreements are made. We are not convinced that psychologists considering a bartering arrangement are able to judge accurately the potential for exploitation and clinical contraindication. Further, by definition bartering involves a negotiation process. Is a client in psychological distress and in need of services in a position to barter on an equal footing with the therapist? After all, even psychologists are attracted to "a good deal." How does this pervasive human motive play itself out in a bartering situation with clients?

Finally, to complicate matters even further, additional questions about income tax evasion may arise should the monetary values of the bartered goods or services remain unreported. Given the potential for actual exploitation, appearance of exploitation, and unsatisfactory outcomes, despite the APA's countenance to bartering we strongly recommend against it. We advise use of the customary exchange system and the offering of referrals or other special arrangements (as discussed in chapter 10) for

clients who cannot afford a psychologist's services.

Delivery of Professional Services to Close Friends and Family Members

Psychologists, including those with no clinical training, come to expect frequent requests for advice and information from close friends and family members, with problems ranging from a child's acting out to a grandmother's memory lapses. When such inquiries require more than casual comment, psychologists may be tempted to enter into professional or quasi-professional relationships with good friends or family members. Psychologists may reason that they can provide especially good counsel to those with whom they have already established a close relationship because trust has already been established. They may be willing to see these "clients" at bargain rates or at no cost.

Despite the seeming advantages of giving counsel to friends or family members, sustained therapy relationships with them should be avoided. Friendships, family, and psychotherapy exist in the context of complex, intimate relationships. But, the differences in the function and process among these types of intimate relationships are striking. Successful personal relationships satisfy mutual needs, are not necessarily goal directed, and are emotionally involving for all parties. Professional relationships, on the other hand, serve the needs of the client and are directed toward specific therapeutic ends. Friendships and family relationships aspire to longevity, whereas professional relationships are designed to progress as rapidly as possible and terminate once the therapeutic goals have been achieved. When these two types of relationships are superimposed, the potential for adverse consequences to all concerned is substantially heightened. Expectations can clash, and trust can be broken.

The APA's ethics code states, "whenever feasible, a psychologist refrains from taking on professional or scientific obligations when preexisting relationships would create a risk of . . . harm" (ES: 117b). Because such predictions can prove faulty, we advise that accepting those with close preexisting relationships into a professional relationship should be avoided altogether, with the possible exception of short-term emergency support until a suitable referral can be located. The following cases illustrate how unexpected entanglements can occur, even when the therapists appear to have benevolent intent.

Case 8-21: Weight-reduction specialist, Stella Stern, Psy.D., agreed, after many requests, to work on a professional basis with her good friend Zoftig Bluto. Progress was slow, and most of Bluto's weight would return shortly after it was lost. Dr. Stern became impatient because Bluto did not seem to be taking the program seriously. Bluto became angry with Dr. Stern's irritation, as well as the lack of progress. She expressed disappointment in Dr. Stern, whom she believed would be able to help her lose weight quickly and effortlessly because, as Bluto put it, "I am one of her closest friends."

Case 8-22: An intellectual assessment of 9-year-old Billy was recommended by the boy's school. Billy's father, Paul Proud, asked his brother, Peter Proud, Ph.D., to perform it. The results revealed some low-performance areas and a full-scale IQ score of 93. Paul was very upset with his psychologist-brother for "finding only average intelligence and not making the boy look good to the school."

Case 8-23: Murray X. Plode, Ed.D., accepted his sister's 17-year-old daughter as a client. During the course of therapy, his niece revealed that she had been sexually abused by her father (the therapist's brother-in-law). Dr. Plode stormed over to the parents' home, threatened the father with police action in front of the entire family, and demanded that his brother-in-law pack his things and leave the house immediately. The father, who denied ever sexually molesting his daughter, complained to an ethics committee that Dr. Plode had violated his rights and destroyed his family. Plode responded that this was a personal family matter, and, therefore, nobody's business but his own.

These cases reveal how faulty expectations, mixed allegiances, role confusion, and misinterpretations of motives can lead to disappointment, anger, and sometimes a total collapse of the relationships. Dr. Stern's friend could not

embrace the obligations of the professional alliance, but expected results anyway. Dr. Proud's brother assumed that a close family member would be willing to fudge results. Dr. Plode could not separate his role as a legitimately upset uncle from that of a psychologist upholding the professional decorum and appropriate procedures with which such difficult matters must be handled.

Because psychologists are, by definition, emotionally involved with those with whom they have preexisting relationships, they may not even fully recognize extreme misuse of their own professional skills.

Case 8-24: Misty Resistant, the girlfriend of Lester Lovesick, Psy.D., rejected Dr. Lovesick's proposal of marriage because she could not yet commit to a relationship. Ms. Resistant was badly hurt in a previous marriage, and Lovesick was convinced that, if she worked out her issues, her attitude toward remarriage would change. He convinced her to take a battery of tests and to put aside an hour every other day for "formal counseling" with him.

Dr. Lovesick is desperately trying to manipulate his romantic interest into reciprocating his commitment to her. Whereas competent counseling is not what Ms. Resistant is receiving, she may not recognize Lovesick's ploy. Using assessment techniques under these circumstances is also extremely unprofessional. Lovesick is hardly in a position to interpret the tests objectively and, instead, is using them as tools to advance his own agenda. Dr. Lovesick's concern about Ms. Resistant's lack of reciprocity is not, in itself, unethical. Lovesick might suggest that they both enter counseling, on an equal footing, with another qualified professional (which is exactly what he finally did and how we came to know of this incident).

In summary, psychologists are free to be completely human in their friendship and family interactions and to experience all of the attendant joys and heartaches. Their psychological expertise might be used helpfully by offering emotional support, information, or suggestions. When the problems become more serious, however, the prudent course of action is to use one's professional expertise and contacts to refer family and close friends to other competent professionals.

Entering into Professional Relationships with Employees

We recognize that some amount of relationship overlapping occurs naturally in most work settings. People are not machines, and workers and their supervisors are often friendly, care about each other's welfare, and attend some of the same social events. However, this situation should not be further complicated by willfully appending yet another (and particularly sensitive) role when alternatives are almost always available to employees.

Case 8-25: Jan Typer worked as a records clerk for a large community mental health agency. She was directly supervised by Helmut Honcho, Ph.D. When Ms. Typer was experiencing personal problems and asked Dr. Honcho if she could be his client, he agreed. Ms. Typer later brought an ethics complaint against Honcho, charging him with blocking her promotion based on assessments of her as a client and not on her performance as an employee.

It may be impossible to unravel the true basis for any job-related decision making. Whether valid or not, the employee-client can always interpret any unpleasant reactions to what happens on the job as linked to therapy or vice-versa. When a client is also an employee, the consequences of a multiple role relationship gone awry can be especially devastating because of the potentially adverse economical ramifications for the employee-client.

Case 8-26: Renega Lease, Ph.D., owned an apartment building managed by William Wrench, who collected the rent and performed routine repairs. Wrench and his wife asked Dr. Lease to see them for couples counseling. Lease learned, during the second session, that Wrench was a heavy drinker. She fired him, thus forcing him and his wife to leave their home.

Information shared in one sector of a relationship influences the entire relationship. Whereas Lease cannot be faulted for wanting sober management of her apartment complex, she unethically used information shared in confidence against her client.

Socializing with Clients and Students

Critics of psychotherapy have referred to it as, among other things, "purchased friendship" (Schofield, 1964). We contend that it is precisely the differences between psychotherapy and friendship that account for its potential for effectiveness. Friendships should be formed from the beginning on an equal footing, with each party capable of voluntarily agreeing to the relationship. However, as Bogrand has put it, "When the therapist or teacher offers the client or student friendship, it is an offer that cannot be refused" (1993, p. 10). In the two sections below, we explore the ethical issues that emerge when psychology practitioners and teachers socialize outside a professional settings with their clients and students.

Becoming Friends with Clients

In the first empirically based inquiry into the practices of socialization with ongoing psychotherapy clients, Tallman (1981) reported that about one third of the 38 psychotherapist respondents stated that they had occasionally formed social relationships with selected clients, usually including their respective spouses. Interestingly, the socializing respondents were all male, even though half of the sample was female, revealing a sex difference that has since been replicated (e.g., Borys, 1988). Tallman's respondents justified role blending on various therapeutic grounds, such as providing additional support and facilitation of rapport. Some therapists offered no therapeutic justification, indicating simply that socializing occurred with clients whose company they enjoyed. In more than half of these instances, the friendships persisted after the professional relationship terminated.

Another third of Tallman's (1981) sample of psychologists, mostly women, indicated that they occasionally attended "special events" in clients' lives, such as a wedding or graduation ceremony. They noted that these were single and isolated episodes, attended for the meaning of their presence to the client rather than as a vehicle for two-way socializing. A more recent survey indicated that most psychologists do not see a problem with this, although few have actually done it (Borys & Pope, 1989). The final third of Tallman's sample held to a strict policy of no client contact outside professional settings. This group believed that risks, including ethical ones, were too likely. For example, new sets of needs may develop for both therapists and clients, and these may interfere with or contaminate the therapy process. Clients may be unsure of the boundaries of social relationships and experience anxiety or confusion. Concern was expressed that the therapists' capacity to function as objective parties may deteriorate. Dependencies may be reinforced. Roles are incongruent in the areas of power and trust. Finally, some of these respondents noted that, because people do not have to pay their friends to care and support them, the meaning of "friend" becomes warped in this instance.

The various complications that can arise when clients become friends are illustrated in the following cases. Readers might take note of the therapists' delayed awareness that anything was amiss.

Case 8-27: Soon after Patty Pal began counseling with Richard Chum, Ed.D., Patty asked Dr. Chum and his wife to spend the weekend at their family beach house. The outing was enjoyable for all. During therapy, however, Ms. Pal became increasingly reluctant to talk about her problems, insisting that things were going quite well. Other satisfactory social interactions among the foursome continued. Dr. Chum finally confronted Ms. Pal during a therapy session with his impression that "nothing was moving." She then admitted that she had been experiencing considerable distress, but feared that if she revealed more about her life during therapy sessions, Chum might choose to no longer socialize with her and her husband.

Patty Pal was put in a double bind. Regardless of what she does, she loses something. As Peterson (1992) observed about boundary violations in general, the client is always faced with a conflict of interest in that any direction in

which he or she moves, a problem presents itself.

Case 8-28: Jack Ace, Ph.D., and his client, King Draw, shared an affinity for poker. Ace accepted Draw's invitations to play with some of Draw's other friends on Wednesday nights. One evening, Dr. Ace was the big winner, and Draw was the big loser. After that evening, Draw began to cancel both appointments and games. A puzzled Dr. Ace confronted him. Draw admitted he no longer felt "right" about their relationship. He could not be specific, but did recognize that after Dr. Ace won several hundred dollars from him, he "saw him differently." Dr. Ace now seemed dangerous somehow, rather than helpful.

The above examples did not involve clients who pressed formal ethics charges against the psychologists, but such cases do exist. In these instances, the clients felt exploited or duped and abandoned.

Case 8-29: Buddy Flash had been treated by Will Crony, Psy.D., for 2 years. They had also invited each other to their homes. Flash gave especially elegant parties, and many influential community leaders were usually in attendance. During one event, Flash and Dr. Crony argued over what, to Crony, was a trivial matter. However, Flash terminated therapy and wrote to an ethics committee, complaining that Dr. Crony had kept him as a client for the purpose of capitalizing on his social status.

Case 8-30: Raphael Baroque, professional artist, complained to an ethics committee that Janis Face, Ph.D., did not follow through with her promises. Baroque had been Dr. Face's client for more than a year, during which time she praised his art work, accompanied him to art shows, and promised to introduce him to some of her gallery contacts. Baroque reported that he began to feel so self-assured that he terminated therapy with Face, fully expecting that their mutual interest in his career would continue. However, Dr. Face did not return his calls. Baroque became depressed, and his self-esteem dropped. When contacted by an ethics committee, Dr. Face explained that she was always "unconditionally supportive" to her clients. But, because Baroque was no longer a client, she had no further obligations to him.

Ethics committees found in favor of both Flash and Baroque. The therapists had intertwined their lives in ways that were confusing to the clients. Baroque, especially, was harmed by Dr. Face's faulty notions of supportive therapy.

Attending special events in the lives of clients deserves special mention. If not contraindicated for other reasons (e.g., transference issues), attending the symbolic portion of a client's special event (e.g., wedding, graduation, confirmation) is acceptable. Giving a card is both acceptable and sufficient. A gift is not required. But, if the psychologist decides to give one, it should be selected not for its material value, but for its thoughtful intent, which should be compatible with therapeutic goals. (Giving and accepting gifts are discussed in more detail in separate sections below.)

Becoming Friends with Students

Whereas psychologists and their clients must actively and willfully make specific arrangements to alter a professional relationship, professors and students often do not. Indeed, encouragement to attend simultaneously many activities outside the classroom is commonplace. Because the professor-student relationship does not involve quite the same type of trust and emotional intimacy characteristic of psychotherapy relationships, socializing on a casual basis does not typically raise concerns. Nonetheless, responsibilities toward students and the power of professors to influence them and their life opportunities are forceful enough to warrant caution.

Case 8-31: Marsha Scholar, Ph.D., was popular among students and socialized with many of them. She was shocked to learn that a grievance had been brought against her. The student claimed Scholar had given her a low grade because the student's husband had disagreed with Professor Scholar's husband at a party about the effectiveness of psychotherapy. Scholar responded that her husband never mentioned any such incident, and

that she had graded the student objectively and fairly.

Case 8-32: Several students complained to the department chair that Gregarious Bud, Ph.D., was nice to the students he liked and froze out the students he disliked. Professor Bud responded that he may have seemed friendlier to some students than to others because he knew some much better than others. In essence, he socialized with the more assertive students who sought out his company.

Drs. Scholar and Bud are apparently casualties of misperception. Professors are probably wise to limit their outside social contacts with classroom students to events associated with the university (such as departmental parties) until the student graduates. Teaching psychologists who wish to form closer relationships with current students should carefully assess the risks and be aware of the misunderstandings that might arise, including what meaning other students might place when observing a professor and one other student off by themselves. Teaching psychologists must also remember that students are extremely sensitive to issues of equity and believe that professors who operate (or appear to operate) on a tilted playing field are extremely unethical (Keith-Spiegel, Tabachnick, & Allen, 1992).

Professors must also carefully monitor their behavior whenever students are around, advice that Professor Plaster in the next case probably wished he had followed.

Case 8-33: The team won the game, and the victory party at the local pub was raucous. Plenty of beer was consumed, and Freddy Plaster, Ph.D., downed several. When a student vocally disagreed with Plaster's choice of the team's best player, he tossed a glass of beer in her face.

The actual case from which our beer-tossing case is adapted was widely publicized in the popular press. The professor (not a psychologist) was suspended for a semester ("Faculty Notes," 1995).

Becoming Friends After Therapy Termination or Graduation

When can more intimate social friendships be formed with people who used to be clients and students without the danger of multiple role complications? Regarding clients, as noted above, conservative critics say "never," even after the professional relationship has terminated. An ex-client may need to reenter therapy, and a clear pathway — including the beneficial effects of continuing transference — should be kept open for them.

If the friendship is disappointing or turns sour, elements of issues that were explored during therapy may resurface, raising new doubts in the client. The psychologists clients believed they knew so well may not completely resemble their professional personas in a nonprofessional context, as the next case illustrates.

Case 8-34: Sharon Joust, Ed.D., and her ex-client Marsha Nullify fully expected that they would get along exceptionally well as friends. However, Nullify found Joust to be excessively aggressive and controlling in social situations, and Nullify's other friends intensely disliked Joust's strident manner. Nullify began to doubt Joust's overall competence and distanced herself from the relationship. She also began to believe that the previous therapy was probably inept. She sought another therapist and pressed ethics charges of incompetence against Joust.

Nullify's charges against Dr. Joust were heard by an ethics committee, but not on the basis of the allegations that Nullify brought forward. Incompetence could not be conclusively proven, but what was clear to both a surprised respondent and the complainant was the upholding of a multiple role relationship violation. Toward the end of the therapy, Joust and Nullify had clearly planned their evolving relationship, and Joust had promised to continue to "take care of" Nullify, even though they would now "only be friends." Ironically, Joust herself provided these facts as a defense against Nullify's charges.

So, can psychologists ever be friends with ex-clients and students? Establishing purely social relationships with ex-clients has not received the same attention as has posttermination sexual relationships (discussed in the next chapter). The findings in a critical incident survey by Anderson and Kitchener (1996) suggest that nonsexual, nonromantic relationships occur with some regularity among therapists and their previous clients, but the judgments of the ethics of such relationships show little consensus.

The view that friendship for clients and students is always off limits may be too conservative and might deny opportunities for what could be productive, satisfying, long-term relationships. Gottlieb (1993, 1994), an expert in ethical decision making and a strong supporter of the maintenance of appropriate professional boundaries, believes that social relationships with some types of ex-clients may be acceptable.

Case 8-35: Mountain bike enthusiast Wilber Wheel consulted Spike Speedo, Ph.D., whom he had casually met at a biking exhibition. The therapeutic relationship went well and was terminated after 11 sessions. The two men found themselves in the same race a few months later and realized that they enjoyed knowing each other on a different basis. The friendship endured for 25 years, and Wheel delivered the eulogy at Speedo's funeral.

Whether this account represents a likely outcome is less relevant than the precautions that must be taken whenever a friendship with a person who was once a client is contemplated. Those who have been long-term clients, might be confused or harmed by changes in boundary points, or have difficulties that are likely to recur are best served by remaining available as an objective professional contact. If indicators appear to be favorable after a natural therapy termination (i.e., a therapeutic relationship should not end abruptly because the parties involved want to be friends), the risks should be discussed, and the agreement clearly understood that any future treatment would have to be with someone else. We must also caution psychologists that any attempt to deflect a role blending by promising or even hinting at the possibility of altering the roles between them and their therapy clients after therapy termination instantly alters the nature of the current relationship.

Students pose a somewhat different set of dynamics. Once they leave, the primary student-professor role is terminated forever. Some students become colleagues with whom teaching psychologists regularly interact, such as at professional meetings, for many years afterward. Continuing scholarly collaborations among teaching psychologists and those who were once their students is not uncommon. Professors often form extremely close relationships with those they are mentoring, usually graduate students collaborating in some way that is deeply absorbing for both parties. Relationships occurring toward the end of the training period sometimes last a lifetime.

The risk of forming close relationships with an advanced student or an ex-student is that things could go awry, in which case the student could lose a valuable resource forever. In that case, an employer may wonder why the psychologist did not list his or her dissertation supervisor or the program director as a reference. Both ex-students and their professors can cause each other continuing grief if their relationships disintegrate but they remain in the same circles (e.g., each can complain about how the other was as a student or professor). But, this is more a problem of interprofessional relationships than a conflict of roles (see chapter 13).

Accepting Clients' Referrals of Close Relations

Word of mouth is a primary means by which new clients are generated. Great care must be taken, however, when satisfied clients recommend you to their close friends or close relations. The potential for conflict of interest, unauthorized passing of information shared in confidence, and compromises in the quality of professional judgment are ever-present dangers.

Case 8-36: Dum Tweedle was pleased with his individual therapy progress and asked Janis Divide, Ph.D., to also counsel his fiancee Dee in individual therapy. Dum eventually pressed ethics charges against Dr. Divide for contributing to a

breakup, a process that began, Dum said, at the time Dee entered therapy. He contended that Dr. Divide encouraged Dee to change in ways that were detrimental to him and to their relationship. Dr. Divide contended that it was her responsibility to facilitate growth in each party as individuals, a responsibility she felt she had upheld.

Case 8-37: Tuff Juggle, Ed.D., accepted Jane Amiga as a client with full knowledge that she and Sandy Comrade, an ongoing client, were best friends and that aspects of the friendship were serious treatment issues for Sandy. He reasoned that he could compartmentalize them sufficiently, and that the women would benefit from the fact that he knew them both. One day, he slipped and shared with Sandy something that Jane had told him during a private session. Jane brought ethics charges against Juggle for breach of confidentiality.

Dr. Divide ignored the "third client"—namely, the relationship between the engaged couple—and attempted the improbable task of treating a duo as if they were unconnected entities. Although Dr. Juggle's situation involved a less engrossing relationship between two clients, that the friendship was an emotional issue should have provided sufficient front-end warning. Juggle's "slip" to the wrong party is an example of an ever-present risk when consulting people who know each other well enough to share some of the same material during individual sessions. Even the sharpest of memories may fail under such circumstances (see also discussion in chapter 3).

Problems can arise even when a referral is not specifically made by an ongoing client, as is illustrated in the following cases:

Case 8-38: Chance Encounter, Ed.D., ran into Possessia Grip, a client, and her friend at a bakery. Dr. Encounter pretended not to see them, but Grip came over to greet him. The friend had followed, so Grip introduced them. The friend asked Encounter what he did for a living, and Encounter divulged his occupation without revealing his relationship with Grip. Encounter quickly paid for his bread and exited the situation. The friend called Encounter 2 days later to make an appointment for counseling. When Grip arrived for her next appointment, she was furious. "How could you do this?" she screamed. "You are my therapist, and I don't want you to see her. Either that, or I am quitting. Well, what is it going to be?"

Some clients feel a sense of ownership toward their therapists. These issues need to be addressed in their own right. Nonetheless, Dr. Encounter is in a bind not entirely of his making. He does not even know if the friend knows that Grip is his client.

Business consultation clients differ from individual psychotherapy clients in many respects. It is still incumbent on the psychologist, however, to avoid even the appearance of "two-timing."

Case 8-39: During a business meeting luncheon, Buck Bank introduced his fierce competitor to Bart Mercantile, Ph.D., an industrial psychologist who consulted with Bank's firm on personnel management. The competitor later hired Mercantile to perform similar services for his firm. Bank brought legal action against Dr. Mercantile, charging that Mercantile used his inside knowledge to the detriment of Bank's operation, giving the competitor a substantial edge in the marketplace.

We are not suggesting that accepting all referrals from current clients is inappropriate. Psychologists must, however, assess as thoroughly as possible the relationship between the potential client and the referral sources, as well as the potential client and the context in which the established client and the referral know each other. If things feel potentially sticky, we advise referring the potential client to a suitable colleague.

Acquaintances as Clients

Another ready source of potential client contacts is found through psychologists' circles of acquaintances. A member of a psychologist's athletic club or church congregation may request professional services. Disallowing casual acquaintances to also be clients would, in general, be unacceptable to consumers as well as to psychologists. This section illustrates cautions that should be considered, however, before taking on clients who base their contact for services on the fact that they "know you slightly" from someplace else.

Case 8-40: Felina Breed, Ph.D., also raised pedigree cats. Many of her therapy clients were "cat people" she had met at shows. The small talk before and after the therapy sessions was usually devoted to discussions about cats. Clients also expressed interest in purchasing kittens from Dr. Breed, and she did sell them to her psychotherapy clients. This, however, came back to haunt Breed. When the therapy process was not proceeding as one client wished, the client accused Dr. Breed of "using" him as a way of selling high-priced kittens. In another instance, a woman client was upset because Dr. Breed sold her an animal that subsequently never won a single prize. The client assumed that if the therapist raised such defective cats, the trustworthiness of her therapy skills should be questioned as well.

The responsibility that Dr. Breed did not meet was the suppression of the acquaintance role while engaging in a professional role. This suppression can usually be accomplished without untoward consequences if the continuation of the former acquaintance role does not require more than minimal energy or contact and does not involve a conflict of interest. The risks and contingency plans for likely incidental contact with clients should be discussed during the initial session. In Dr. Breed's case, that would have meant refraining from extended discussions of cats before or after the psychotherapy session with any client she met at cat shows and certainly not selling cats to her therapy clients.

Distinguishing friends from acquaintances is not a clear-cut assessment process. We offer a few exercises to help distinguish between the two. If you are upset or in need of help, anyone in your social circle you would consider calling should be considered a friend. People with whom you have closely shared very meaningful events, such as traveling together, should probably be placed in the category of friends. Those you know and meet in the hallway or on the street and pause for a moment of idle chatter that never involves any intimate personal disclosure are probably acquaintances. Or, assume that you live in the same town as a person who was injured. If you would rush to the hospital shortly after hearing the news, the person should be designated as a friend. If you would send a card, the person is probably a friendly acquaintance. If you are planning a party to celebrate your wedding anniversary and can only invite 15 people outside the family, those 15 people should be classified as friends.

A twist on the acquaintance peril involves dealing appropriately with solicitations for services by someone who also holds some influence or advantage over you. Examples include requests from an admissions officer of the local college to which your daughter has applied to work with his own troubled son or a call for an appointment for marital counseling from the president of the bank that holds your mortgage. We encourage psychologists placed in this type of awkward position to explain the dilemma to prospective clients and offer to help find acceptable alternative resources.

A more delicate peril involves psychologists employed by colleges or universities who deliver private practice therapy services to students in the same institution. Here, an acquaintance role involves contact that may actively continue, and its nature could conceivably include evaluations and other responsibilities that extend a powerful influence on the students. In short, both facets of the dual-role relationship are (or could be) intense, and the potential dangers of role blurring could ensue. For example, the student, as a paying client, might expect special favors on campus, such as help getting into a needed class, a letter of recommendation, or some intervention on his or her behalf. Or, the psychologist may view and evaluate the student's academic performance differently based on what is learned about the student in therapy.

This dilemma can be greatly diminished by limiting student therapy clients to those who are not and are never likely to be in one's academic department and by discussing any "ground rules" in advance. Some university departments have policies on this matter and allow psychology faculty members to see psychology students in their private practices off campus, but require a stipulation between the two that the professor will not serve the student in any academic evalu-

ation capacity for the duration of the student's tenure at the university. Although this policy defuses the potential for dual-role conflicts, students may be disadvantaged by the restriction. We recommend the conservative course of action in the spirit of protection for all concerned, that is, refer students to the university's counseling center or to other practitioners in the community.

Small-World Hazards

Many hazards invariably present themselves to psychologists working in relatively small, isolated communities. Here, psychologists must adapt to the realities of bumping into clients or students outside a professional setting while coping as best they can with other perplexing role mixings. One psychologist, for example, relayed to us the special care taken to ensure that he and his client, the only sixth-grade teacher in town, could avoid difficulties that might arise due to the presence of the psychologist's rebellious 12-year-old son in her class. Another small-town psychologist shared the burden of scheduling neighbors to avoid unwanted face-to-face meetings in the waiting room. Yet another requested guidance from an ethics committee when a client's alcoholic and abusive husband yelled profanities at him at every opportunity—in the barbershop, bowling alley, restaurant, park, market, and even as they passed each other in their cars.

As anyone who has lived in a small town can attest, face-to-face contact with clients outside the office is inevitable. Several attributes of small communities also cause ethical dilemmas in the context of delivering therapy services. Information passes quickly through the community, and standards of confidentiality among professionals and community service agencies are often relaxed to the point that formal releases are not sought before information, originally shared in confidence, is released (Hargrove, 1986; Solomon, Heisberger, & Winer, 1981). Further, as Sleek notes, "Efforts to assure a patient complete confidentiality . . . can prove cumbersome against the intimate and often gossip-oriented nature of small communities" (1994, p. 26).

Residents of small communities are more hesitant to seek professional counseling and are not quick to trust outsiders, preferring to rely on their kinship ties, friends, and clergy for emotional support (Stockman, 1990). Because those who do seek therapy prefer someone known as a contributing member in the community, it may not be possible simply to commute from a neighboring town and expect to have much business. Ironically, then, to be accepted and trusted means putting oneself in the position of increasing complicated relationships (Stockman, 1990). Consider, for example, what might happen when a client is also a salesperson at the local car dealership. When the psychologist purchases a new car—and everyone will know of the purchase, what kind of car, and where it was bought—the client may be deeply offended if the psychologist purchased it from someone else.

Just because it is unlikely that psychologists in smaller communities can separate their lives entirely from those of their clients does not mean that professional boundaries become irrelevant. On the contrary, psychologists must make constant and deliberate efforts to minimize the confusion. For example, no matter how small the community, a therapist and a client would never need to socialize only with each other, such as meeting for lunch. Potentially risky acts over which psychologists always have complete control regardless of community size, such as giving gifts to clients, can still be easily avoided.

Small communities do not necessarily exist in geographical isolation. Close-knit military, religious, or ethnic communities existing within a larger community can pose the same kinds of dilemmas discussed above. Psychologists working in huge, metropolitan settings can experience what amounts to small-world hazards, often in unexpected ways. A psychologist might learn that his client is his wife's best friend's secret lover or that a client is his daughter's new boss. Such information may not be known in advance, as it would likely be in a smaller town. Such discoveries that may emerge during the course of psychotherapy can often be handled by staunchly maintaining the professional role without regard for the coincidences that link the therapist and client in other ways. Things

can, however, become more complicated; as illustrated next.

Case 8-41: Sid Fifer consulted Ron Wrung, Ph.D., after Fifer's offensive and antisocial behavior caused increasing trouble in his family and at work. Early in therapy, it was casually revealed that Fifer and the therapist's wife worked for the same large company, though in different locations and different departments. Several weeks later, Fifer was fired. He charged that Dr. Wrung must have told his wife about what he talked about in therapy, which she, in turn, shared with the company boss. Wrung vehemently denied sharing material about Fifer or any other client with his wife or anyone else.

Case 8-42: During the beginning of the second session, Kin Tribe, Ph.D., and his client Clip N. Split learned that Split had been briefly married years before to a distant cousin of Tribe. Split had deserted the cousin 2 weeks after the wedding and took all of their gifts and other possessions with him. The therapy sessions continued without any further discussion of the historical connection. Split, however, was to later complain that Tribe punished him for what he had done by being cold and abrupt and failing to provide competent services. Tribe was astonished by the ethics charge. He replied that he barely knew his cousin, and that she was not an issue at all. Rather, he focused on Split's current problems, which revealed continued flight from responsibility.

Dr. Wrung was apparently a casualty of the type of circumstances that could be neither easily predicted nor prevented. Dr. Tribe, however, encountered warnings early in the course of the professional relationship that should have been explored more thoroughly before proceeding with a professional alliance with Split.

Case 8-43: Ginger Nailbrain, the daughter of the divorced boyfriend of Linda Pleasemore, Ph.D., was encouraged to enroll in Dr. Pleasemore's section of an introductory psychology course. Pleasemore thought this experience would help solidify the relationship with the father. Halfway through the semester, however, the relationship between Pleasemore and Nailbrain's father dissolved. Nailbrain's final course grade was a "D." Nailbrain and her father filed complaints with the university and a state ethics committee charging that Dr. Pleasemore was seeking vengeance by assigning the daughter a poor grade.

Pleasemore's professional judgment was faulty on several grounds. She was not only agreeing to a multiple role relationship up front, but was also using a professional relationship as a vehicle for advancing a personal agenda. Even if the relationship had worked and the daughter had received a high mark, the ethical issues would remain unchanged, though they would not likely be contested.

Psychologists are more likely to be judged culpable when a small-world hazard was perceived in advance and alternatives were clearly available. The psychologists undertook a professional relationship anyway, which later resulted in charges of exploitation, prejudice, or harm.

Accepting Gifts and Asking for Favors

Psychologists who serve consumers as therapists, consultants, or teachers are often appreciated for jobs well done. Sometimes, gratitude is expressed beyond a verbal expression of thanks. Accepting small material tokens, such as homemade cookies or an inexpensive gift, typically poses no ethical problem. Some psychologists with whom we have talked refuse any gift as a matter of principle, but most believe that to refuse small gifts would constitute a rejection or insult, to the detriment of the client or student. Only a tiny minority of respondents in Borys' (Borys & Pope, 1989) large, national sample of psychologists believed that accepting gifts worth under $10 was unethical, and the majority of respondents had done it. There will be times, however, when even small gifts (e.g., a nude calendar, boxer shorts, a condom, or any other very personal or emotionally laden item) should be diplomatically refused.

When a gift is no longer "small," or when even a small gift constitutes a therapeutic issue or potential manipulation, problems of ethics and competent professional judgment arise. It is clear from several ethics cases that lines can

be crossed, and ethical or other adverse consequences can ensue.

Case 8-44: Wealthy Rich Porsche gave his recently licensed psychotherapist, Grad Freshly, Ph.D., a new car for Christmas; it was accompanied by a card stating, "To the only man who ever helped me." Dr. Freshly was flattered and excited. He convinced himself that his services were worth the bonus because Porsche had churned through many previous therapists, with disappointing results. As a more seasoned therapist might have predicted, Rich soon began to find fault with Dr. Freshly and sued him for "manipulating him into giving expensive gifts."

Case 8-45: On the last day of class, a student gave Bic Smoke, Ph.D., a silver lighter engraved with his initials. When the student got a "C" in the course, she was irate and complained to the professor. Smoke shared his grading procedure with her, but she remained dissatisfied and went to the department chair and the dean. Smoke wrote an ethics committee, describing what he now saw as a bribe attempt, and asked for guidance. He noted that he was uncomfortable with the present from the beginning, but because it was already engraved he did not know what else to do but to accept it.

Case 8-46: Fate L. Attraction brought Newton Callow, M.A., suggestive little gifts almost every session from the beginning of their counseling relationship. These gifts consisted of handkerchiefs hand-embroidered with tiny nude women, a T-shirt imprinted "Therapists Do It in Groups," original poems with double-entendres, and a fancy bottle with a label "Chemical that Makes Therapists Irresistible to Clients." Ms. Attraction ultimately pressed ethics charges against Mr. Callow for abruptly terminating and abandoning her after promising that he would "be there to make her better." During an ethics committee inquiry, Mr. Callow stated that he initially found Ms. Attraction to be a "fun client" whom he thought needed massive support to help boost her confidence. As therapy progressed, however, he became increasingly uneasy with her little offerings and flirtatious style. What was, at first, amusing and flattering turned "demanding and a little scary." She soon became more than he felt he could handle. When Callow suggested referring her to another therapist, she became livid and stalked out of the session, allegedly threatening him with reprisal for "leading her on."

These three cases illustrate naiveté and inexperience, which are fairly common denominators among psychologists who accept gifts and favors beyond the realm of small "one-time" or appropriate "special occasion" tokens. Regardless of any other dynamics or considerations, a very valuable gift should be refused. A person in a vulnerable situation, such as a client or student, can always charge exploitation later, and such a charge may well have substance despite the rationalizations of the recipients. Dr. Smoke's touchy situation, given the fact that the lighter was engraved and therefore inappropriate to give to someone else and unacceptable for a refund, might have been handled by asking the student to keep it until after she graduated and then give it to him if she still wanted to do so. Although this may not be the ideal resolution, it would at least defuse any attempt at manipulation. Callow was naive and probably coping with some unfulfilled needs of his own, which blurred his professional judgment substantially. A strong professional identity appears to be the key ingredient in dealing appropriately with offers of gifts and favors and the probable motivation behind them on a case-by-case basis. Until one reaches a level of professional comfort, a very conservative course of action may be in everyone's best interests.

Gifts and (usually) favors should never, of course, be requested from one's clients or students. Unfortunately, cases involving the direct solicitation of gifts and favors have been reported to ethics committees. One psychotherapist asked to borrow large sums of money from his wealthy clients, and then he went bankrupt, leaving them all unpaid. Another required members of her therapy groups to bring her gifts every session as symbols of their commitment.

When small, situational-based favors or requests by psychologists are involved, the picture grays a little. It may not be inappropriate for a professor to ask a student to return a book to the library or to drive him or her to the auto repair shop to pick up a car if the student will be passing that way anyway. A psychotherapist might reasonably request that a client change a regular appointment time to accommodate his or her own special need on occasion. However, the most prudent course of action is to avail oneself of alternatives whenever possible and to remain vigilant to cues that draw the line between reasonable and unreasonable. Psychologists must remember that a client or student may feel that he or she has no choice but to comply. Canter et al. (1994) offer the example of a bilingual dissertation advisee being asked to translate an article by her advisor. Dare she tell him that she is already so overwhelmed with her own workload that she is not getting enough sleep?

Even when no contraindications exist in a specific case, any favor requiring more than a trivial inconvenience to a client or student should not be requested except in rare instances of emergency. The psychologist who had a heart attack in the presence of his client in an otherwise deserted building, requiring the client to assume rather major responsibilities for a short time, is an example of the exceptional case.

Giving Gifts to Clients

Gifts have the power to please, control, manipulate, or symbolize love and caring of whatever type the recipient perceives. Many clients coming into therapy feel ignored, abandoned, violated, or uncared about and may misinterpret the motivation of therapists who give them gifts. Because of the potential complications and misunderstandings and the ever-present possibility that the therapists' own motives of benevolence are rationalizations for self-serving intentions, it is prudent to refrain from bestowing gifts on clients.

Case 8-47: Benny Nowalls, Ph.D., often gave many of his clients little trinkets and items he thought they would enjoy. The gifts ranged from silver spoons to fitness equipment. He also sent them cards when he was on vacation, hugged them often, worked out with them at the gym, and met them for lunch. Eventually, several clients complained about Dr. Nowalls for a variety of reasons, most dealing with abandonment issues.

Case 8-48: Herman Hustle, Ph.D., gave all of his clients, current and past, cheese baskets at Christmas holiday time. He confided to a colleague, "I want them to all to think about me as this good guy and maybe pass my name along to someone else."

Dr. Nowalls claimed to be shocked that he was being turned on by those to whom he had been "so kind and giving." He could never grasp how the multiple intrusions of his personal essence into his clients lives initiated dependencies he could not ultimately satisfy. Dr. Hustle wants to drum up business and is attempting to enlist clients as his sales force. This is unprofessional.

Gabbard (1994) offers an interesting perspective on gift giving. He notes that a goal of therapy is not to gratify clients so that they will like the therapist. There must be room for expressions of anger toward the therapist. Gabbard wonders if patients can truly feel free to deal with the negative feelings toward the therapist after receiving gifts.

Can psychologists ever give their clients gifts or do favors for them that have no relevance to therapy? Probably, with care, on occasion. A psychologist may offer a client a book believed to be therapeutically indicated, especially if the client is on a strict budget. Therapists may also go out of their way to help clients locate other needed resources relevant to improving their overall life situation. Small favors based on a situational need and common sense, such as giving a client a quarter for a parking meter, would obviously not raise concerns. In these acceptable cases, no ulterior motives pertain, and the scope is either related to the therapy or of a very specific and limited nature. A special situation can arise when the client is a child. Here, at times, it may be appropriate to give a small gift attending to the symbolic meaning that would advance the therapeutic function. For example, an anxious child about to leave for 3 weeks of summer camp might be soothed and emboldened by the gift of a flashlight.

Nontraditional Therapy Settings

Occasionally, therapeutic goals are better achieved outside an office or professional setting. Assessments can take place in a variety of nontraditional settings, including private homes. "Action-oriented" therapies, including crisis modalities, may involve ecological involvements with clients. A psychologist might accompany his "airplane phobia group" on a short flight. A stress reduction group might hold a special weekend at a serene lakeside lodge. A psychologist, as part of an established eating disorder clinic program, may go out to eat "real food," such as a pizza, with a client. Nevertheless, excursions beyond traditional professional settings require forethought to preclude charges of exploitation because of multiple role or conflict-of-interest overtones, confusion, or impairment of the psychologists' objectivity. Despite the atypical setting, it is important that the purpose is clearly understood as a professional activity.

Case 8-49: Homa Cloister feared crowds. Her therapist, Rip Vivo, Ph.D., suggested that they go out to dinner at busy, fancy restaurants after therapy sessions as a way of conditioning her to feel more comfortable around people. He did not charge an additional fee for the after-hour activity, but did require her to pay the dinner bill. The treatment proved to be ineffective and uncomfortable for this client. Homa later charged that Dr. Vivo exploited her by disguising a free meal ticket as psychotherapy.

Case 8-50: Several encounter group members charged that the therapist associated with the Touchie-Feelie Clinic conducted weekend retreats at a local hotel in a way that facilitated coercive and promiscuous behavior among the participants. They believed that various exercises encouraged and stimulated some members to become obnoxious and to pressure others into sexual activities after the formal evening activities concluded.

Case 8-51: Jake Sprint, Ed.D., suggested that he and Hal Jogger conduct their counseling sessions every Monday and Wednesday morning as they ran in the park. Later, Jogger complained to an ethics committee that he was not getting better because it was hard to concentrate, hear what his therapist was saying, respond, and run at the same time. Jogger believed that he was simply paying for Dr. Sprint's personal exercise regime.

Vivo's technique may have been acceptable, but he included the trappings of a social event and structured the financial aspect poorly. The Touchie-Feelie staff did an insufficient job of setting ground rules and monitoring compliance with the rules. Sprint's motives may not have been exactly as Jogger charged, but there was no acceptable rationale for jogging during therapy.

Such inimical results reveal that decisions to venture away from a strictly professional setting must be based on the following: (1) careful assessment of therapists' own motivations and needs; (2) a treatment plan for individual clients that clearly justifies the arrangement as the more effective setting for facilitating specific therapeutic goals; and (3) adequate client understanding of the proposed experience, setting and enforcing the rules of appropriate client and staff behavior, preparing for the experience, and obtaining fully informed consent from the clients to participate in it.

Other Role Conflicts

We have focused on multiple role relationships in which the psychologist directly occupied one of the roles. However, situations can arise that squeeze psychologists between two or more other forces. For example, demands of the agency employing a psychologist may conflict, in the psychologist's opinion, with the needs and welfare of the agency's clients. Government policy, legal requirements, or the welfare and safety of society in general may sometimes clash with the psychologist's judgments regarding what might be in the best interests of an individual with whom the psychologist is working. The identifications of priorities and loyalties can cause acute stress and conflict-of-interest dilemmas.

Often, psychologists are not in an objective position when acting under such conditions because the more powerful of the conflict sources, such as the law or the psychologist's employer,

may issue sanctions if the psychologist's actions do not favor the position of the more powerful party. Psychologists have sometimes been cited for contempt of court and have lost their jobs in such instances. Nevertheless, psychologists who comply with the more powerful of the conflict sources, despite a personal conviction that by so doing they caused the less powerful conflict source harm, may be left with feelings of self-disgust, guilt, and weakness. Throughout this book, these types of conflicts are illustrated in the context of specific settings and conditions under which they are likely to arise (see, especially, chapters 14 and 15 and the "whistle blower" discussion in chapter 12).

UNEXPECTED CONFLICTS AND OVERLAPS

Every psychologist is at the mercy of coincidence, and totally unexpected compounding of roles may occur in this way. The 1992 APA code states, "If a psychologist finds that, due to unforeseen factors, a potentially harmful multiple role relationship has arisen, the psychologist attempts to resolve it with due regard for the best interests of the affected person and maximal compliance with the Ethics Code" (ES: 1.17c). Although the appropriate response may be difficult to discern, psychologists must actively attempt to ameliorate the situation as best they can, trying to avoid devaluing or diminishing anyone in the process (Canter et al., 1994).

Whereas coincidences are more likely to occur in smaller communities, it must be remembered that unexpected collisions can happen anywhere. In fact, three of the four incidents described in the next cases occurred in large metropolitan areas.

Case 8-52: Mildred Suit, a client of Gina Squeezed, Ph.D., announced that she is suing a lawyer for rendering incompetent services during her child custody hearing. Suit informed Dr. Squeezed that she will be subpoenaed to testify about the mental anguish she suffered during that period. Suit also, for the first time, reveals the name of the lawyer she is suing. It is Orin Trial, another client of Dr. Squeezed. (Case adapted from Leslie, 1994.)

Case 8-53: Gilla Social gleefully announced to her psychologist husband that artist Pablo Miroklee agreed to speak at the art guild meeting. She wants to volunteer her home for the event and to entertain Miroklee for dinner afterward. The artist, who is extremely depressed and emotionally fragile, has been a long-term client of Social's husband.

Case 8-54: During a New Year's Eve event at a fashionable restaurant with some friends, Eva Close, Psy.D., spots one of her clients at a table across the room. This client is particularly sensitive about therapy and constantly worries about anyone finding out that she even knows a psychotherapist. Dr. Close and her husband had planned this evening for weeks and paid $200 in advance. Dr. Close thinks she may be able to stay in her corner of the dining area, but as people begin to drink they also move around the room to "make new friends." Dr. Close's husband and friends are also urging her to "get out there and dance up a storm."

Case 8-55: Fortuna Yikes, Ph.D., agreed to have dinner with her friends and a blind date that they had arranged for her. When she arrived at the restaurant and looked inside, she recognized the man sitting with her friends as one of her clients.

The psychologist's response, which must often be made quickly, depends on several factors. Confidentiality issues usually pertain. Unless the therapist and client have discussed what might be done should they bump into each other outside the office setting, the therapist will not know how to take the client's preferred option into account. The urgency of the situation is also a factor. Sometimes, it can be deflected, if there is time.

Dr. Squeezed may be able to extricate herself from the case by discouraging Suit from calling her to testify, but only if she sincerely believes that she has nothing useful to offer a hearing panel. In addition, Ms. Suit's attorney may concur because opening a discussion into her mental state could lead to far-ranging inquiries that might hurt her case. If Ms. Suit still plans to call Dr. Squeezed as a witness, her other client, Attorney Trial, will soon know of the relation-

ship. Dr. Squeezed will be on a list of potential witnesses, and Trial's own lawyer will most likely depose her. Ms. Suit, on the other hand, will not know of Dr. Squeezed's relationship to Mr. Trial unless he chooses to reveal it. In the deposition, Dr. Squeezed will most likely have to testify about Ms. Suit's psychological life under oath in front of both clients. In a technical sense, Dr. Squeezed could testify or prepare an affidavit (sworn written statement) regarding Ms. Suit's mental suffering without reference to Mr. Trial or even an acknowledgment of his status as a client. Obviously, he will have some feelings about this, as will Ms. Suit if she ever learns details after the fact. In addition, matters could becomes quite complicated if Mr. Trial's defense involved an attack on Dr. Squeezed's credibility or expertise.

The best advice to Dr. Squeezed would be to consult her attorney and, in the interim, avoid breaching the confidentiality of either client. Her attorney can ask Ms. Suit's lawyer whether and when Squeezed will be named on a potential witness list. When that occurs, she can discuss the fact of this listing (but no details of Suit's case) with Mr. Trial and discuss the implications for their continued work together. It may be that all parties will eventually permit the facts of her difficult conflict to be shared.

At first blush, the Socials' problem seems easiest enough to solve. If the client already knows about the art guild arrangement, Dr. Social should consider discussing the quandary with his client, if that seems appropriate, and some agreement could be reached. But, what does Dr. Social tell his wife? Spouses, after all, are not exempt from confidentiality mandates. We suggest that all psychologists reach an understanding with their partners and older children about the multiple role problems that might impinge on their lives on occasion. Close relations can be told that the nature of their profession may require changes in plans, possibly abrupt ones. Like many health service providers, sacrifices that also touch others may have to be made. Psychologists must ensure that their family members understand that no details can be given and no questions can be answered. Ms. Social's husband, if he has already reached an understanding with her, may simply say, "I'm sorry, the art guild meeting cannot take place here." She may be disappointed, but she would know that there is a good reason even if she will never know exactly what it is.

Dr. Close may have to figure out how to keep a low profile at the New Year's Eve event. She should not become intoxicated. Given the client's intense feelings, it would not have been inappropriate for Dr. Close to have earlier attempted to ensure that important events do not overlap with those of her client. In small communities, clients with such intense concerns about discovery might better be referred to someone in another city.

In the real story, Dr. Yikes was fortunately able to leave the restaurant before being seen by the people at the table. She paged her friends in the restaurant from her car phone, telling them that she had fallen ill. Because such twists of fate do actually happen and "quick exits" may not present themselves, we encourage psychologists to actively attempt to know in advance the identities of people with whom they will be interacting in any intimate social situation.

Incidental encounters with clients in public settings often result in feelings of surprise, uncertainly, and discomfort (Sharkin & Birky, 1992). We strongly encourage psychologists to raise the issue early of chance meetings with their clients outside therapy. Some clients may prefer they pretend that the two do not know each other. Others may favor acting as though they are acquaintances and okay the exchange of brief greetings.

We suggest that psychologists not be the ones to take the lead during such chance encounters, and that the clients understand in advance that the decision to interact with or ignore each other rests entirely with the clients. Clients should be assured that the psychologists will be comfortable either way. Our plan is recommended for application to all clients. That way, the therapist does not have to remember which "therapist reaction" each client prefers. There is no risk of being perceived as rejecting because the client will know always to take the lead when the two notice each other outside the office setting. With a preapproved plan well in place, common situations involving clients, such as finding oneself in the same line at the bank, can be handled

somewhat gracefully and without incurring more than minimal discomfort.

It must be noted, before concluding this section, that conflicts and role complications can occur in situations that are not face to face. An employer may call for a recommendation of an individual you know in the community who is (or was) also a client and about whom you would have reservations based on what transpired in therapy. In an actual case, a prominent psychologist was contacted by a state psychological association to approach a politician who had considerable power to affect the outcome of pending legislation favorable to psychologists. What the organization did not and could never know was that the psychologist had worked with the politician's family some years previously in regard to a sensitive problem of the sort that could ruin the politician's career. The psychologist felt torn between agreeing to set up some kind of meeting (even though he decided not to be present) and alienating his professional organization by refusing to do it. He decided to tell the organization staff that "family problems" precluded his involvement, leaving the staff to infer that the family to which he was referring was his own.

WATCHING FOR RED FLAGS

Psychologists can be helpful, caring, empathic human beings *and* maintain professional parameters within which they effectively relate to clients, students, or other service consumers. We again acknowledge the impossibility of setting firm boundaries appropriate for every consumer under every circumstance. We are concerned, however, that inappropriate crossings are often rationalized as benevolent or therapeutic. As Brown states, "In the many cases in which I have testified as an expert witness regarding abuses in psychotherapy and the standards of care, it is a very common experience for me to hear the accused therapist pleading the cause of greater humanity, and even love, as the rationale for having had sex with, breast fed, slow-danced with, gone into business with, moved in with, and so on with the complaining client" (1994, p. 276).

Neutralization processes even include blaming the client for untoward consequences. As a psychologist, who lost her license after it was verified that her life and that of a client became completely intertwined, told a news reporter, "Look what happened to me. I went out of my way to help him become a better person and he paid me back by destroying my career. I should have known. Once a snake, always a snake."

We conclude with some early warning signs of boundary crossings that could confuse or disadvantage consumers. These signals, some of which are found in Epstein and Simon (1990), include the following:

1. Actively seeking opportunities to be with a client outside the professional setting
2. Anticipating, with excitement, a certain client's visitation
3. Expecting that a client should volunteer to do favors for you (e.g., get you a better deal from his business)
4. Viewing a client as in a position to advance your own position and fantasizing as to how that would play out
5. Wishing that a client were not a client and, instead, in some other type of relationship with you (e.g., your best friend or business partner)
6. Disclosing considerable detail about your own life to a client and expecting interest or nurturing in return
7. Trying to influence a client's hobbies, political views, or other personal choices that have no direct therapeutic relevance
8. Allowing a client to take undue advantage without confrontation (e.g., missing many appointments)
9. Relying on a client's presence or praise to boost your self-esteem
10. Giving in to a client's requests and perspectives on issues from fear that he or she will otherwise leave therapy
11. Feeling entitled to most of the credit if a client improves, especially if marked achievement is attained while under your care
12. Viewing clients as the central people in your life

13. Greatly resisting terminating a client even though the indicators for it are clear
14. Believing that you are the only person who can help a particular client
15. Noticing that the pattern of interactions with a client is becoming increasingly irrelevant to the therapeutic goals

Perhaps the most difficult message to convey in writing is how "right" it might feel to slip into a multiple role. Our brief cases summarize what often takes weeks and even months to unfold. In the process, we may have failed to convey sufficiently the perceptions and rationalizations that are so often involved. So, perhaps the brightest red flag of all should appear any time you say to yourself, "This person will be different," or "This circumstance doesn't really qualify as a role conflict because . . ."

When one senses that the professional role is "leaking" into any area unrelated to the purpose of the professional relationship, immediate evaluation is warranted. Canter et al. (1994) suggest imagining the worst case scenario in terms of outcome should the present course continue and then seeking consultation with a peer. They further encourage choosing the colleague you think is the least likely to agree with your own assessment. We suggest favoring one with a known stance more conservative than your own to help ensure that all risks have been considered.

Sexual behavior between psychologists and their clients and students is the topic of the next chapter. We believe that it is important to note here that psychologists with blurry role margins do not necessarily stop with gift giving, conducting sessions in the park, and inviting clients out to dinner. Data from Borys' large national survey established a relationship between nonsexual and sexual boundary crossing (Borys, 1988; Borys & Pope, 1989). This association is not surprising because many forms of nonsexual multiple role behaviors are those also routinely associated with dating and courtship rituals. Male therapists are more likely to mix roles than are female therapists (Borys, 1988) and, as discussed in more detail in the next chapter, male therapists are also far more likely to engage in sexual relationships with their clients.

SUMMARY GUIDELINES

1. Psychologists should avoid multiple role relationships and conflict-of-interest situations with clients and students because the psychologists' role is so often characterized by attributed power, trust, influence, and knowledge of intimate secrets.

2. Psychologists should remain aware not only of the harm multiple role relationships may cause consumers of professional services, but to themselves as well. Psychologists have sometimes faced public and professional disapproval for even the appearance of conflict.

3. Sometimes, multiple role relationships are difficult to avoid, such as when psychologists work in small communities. When alternatives are very limited, psychologists should be especially sensitive to possible complications and attempt to minimize them.

4. Psychologists should avoid accepting gifts and favors from consumers of their services unless these are small tokens or appropriate gestures of appreciation, which by not accepting would be construed as offensive or countertherapeutic.

5. When venturing outside a traditional office setting to undertake an assessment or to conduct therapy, the plan should be conscientiously conceived, taking the needs and welfare of the client into consideration. The event should also be clearly defined and understood as a professional contact.

6. Psychologists must carefully monitor their own tendencies to use rationalizations when faced with multiple role conflicts and should seek another opinion before acting on any opportunity to mix roles.

References

American Psychological Association. (1992). Ethical principles of psychologists and code of conduct. *American Psychologist, 47,* 1597–1611.

Anderson, S. K., & Kitchener, K. S. (1996). Nonromantic, nonsexual posttherapy relationships between psychologists and former clients: An exploratory study of critical incidents. *Professional Psychology: Research and Practice, 27,* 59–66.

Bennett, B. E., Bricklin, P. M., & VandeCreek, L.

(1994). Response to Lazarus's "How certain boundaries and ethics diminish therapeutic effectiveness." *Ethics and Behavior, 4,* 263–266.

Bogrand, M. (1993, January–February). The duel over dual relationships. *The California Therapist,* 7–10, 12, 14, 16.

Borys, D. S. (1988). *Dual relationships between therapist and client: A national survey of clinicians' attitudes and practices.* Unpublished doctoral dissertation, University of California, Los Angeles.

Borys, D. S. (1994). Maintaining therapeutic boundaries: The motive is therapeutic effectiveness, not defensive practice. *Ethics and Behavior, 4,* 267–273.

Borys, D. S., & Pope, K. S. (1989). Dual relationships between therapist and client: A national study of psychologists, psychiatrists, and social workers. *Professional Psychology: Research and Practice, 20,* 283–293.

Brown, L. S. (1994). Concrete boundaries and the problem of literal-mindedness: A response to Lazarus. *Ethics and Behavior, 4,* 275–281.

Canter, M. B., Bennett, B. E., Jones, S. E., & Nagy, T. F. (1994). *Ethics for psychologists: A commentary on the APA ethics code.* Washington, DC: American Psychological Association.

Clarkson, P. (1994). In recognition of dual relationships. *Transactional Analysis Journal, 24,* 32–38.

Epstein, R. S., & Simon, R. L. (1990). The exploitation index: An early warning indicator of boundary violations in psychotherapy. *Bulletin of the Menninger Clinic, 54,* 450–465.

Faculty notes. (1995, April). *Chronicle of Higher Education,* p. A28.

Gabbard, G. O. (1994). Teetering on the precipice: A commentary on Lazarus's "How certain boundaries and ethics diminish therapeutic effectiveness." *Ethics and Behavior, 4,* 283–286.

Glaser, R. D., & Thorpe, J. S. (1986). Unethical intimacy: A survey of sexual contact and advances between psychology educators and female graduate students. *American Psychologist, 41,* 43–51.

Gottlieb, M. C. (1993). Avoiding exploitive dual relationships: A decision-making model. *Psychotherapy, 30,* 41–48.

Gottlieb, M. C. (1994). Ethical decision-making, boundaries, and treatment effectiveness: A reprise. *Ethics and Behavior, 4,* 287–293.

Gutheil, T. G. (1994). Discussion of Lazarus's "How certain boundaries and ethics diminish therapeutic effectiveness." *Ethics and Behavior, 4,* 295–298.

Gutheil, T. G., & Gabbard, G. O. (1993). The concept of boundaries in clinical practice: Theoretical and risk-management dimensions. *American Journal of Psychiatry, 150,* 188–196.

Hargrove, D. S. (1986). Ethical issues in rural mental health practice. *Professional Psychology: Research and Practice, 17,* 20–23.

Hedges, L. E. (1993, May–June). In praise of the dual relationship. *The California Therapist,* 46–49.

Keith-Spiegel, P., & Koocher, G. P. (1985). *Ethics in psychology: Standards and cases.* New York: Random House.

Keith-Spiegel, P., Tabachnick, B. G., & Allen, M. (1993). Ethics in academia: Students' views of professors' actions. *Ethics and Behavior, 3,* 149–162.

Kitchener, K. S. (1988). Dual role relationships: What makes them so problematic? *Journal of Counseling and Development, 67,* 217–221.

Kovacs, A. L. (1974). The valley of the shadow. *Psychotherapy: Theory, Research and Practice, 11,* 376–382.

Lazarus, A. A. (1994). How certain boundaries and ethics diminish therapeutic effectiveness. *Ethics and Behavior, 4,* 253–261.

Leslie, R. S. (1989, September–October). Dual relationships: The legal view. *The California Therapist,* 9–13.

Leslie, R. S. (1994, November–December). The unavoidable conflict. *The California Therapist,* 24–26.

Pepper, R. S. (1990). When transference isn't transference: Iatrogenesis of multiple role relations between practicing therapists. *Journal of Contemporary Psychotherapy, 20,* 141–153.

Peterson, M. R. (1992). *At personal risk: Boundary violations in professional-client relationships.* New York: W. W. Norton.

Pope, K. S. (1991). Dual relationships in psychotherapy. *Ethics and Behavior, 1,* 21–34.

Pope, K. S., Levenson, H., & Schover, L. R. (1980). Sexual behavior between clinical supervisors and trainees: Implications for professional standards. *Professional Psychology: Research, Theory and Practice, 11,* 157–162.

Ryder, R., & Hepworth, J. (1990). AAMFT Ethical Code: "Dual relationships." *Journal of Marital and Family Therapy, 16,* 127–132.

Schofield, W. (1964). *Psychotherapy: The purchase of friendship.* Englewood Cliffs, NJ: Prentice-Hall.

Sharkin, B. S., & Birky, I. (1992). Incidental encounters between therapists and their clients. *Professional Psychology: Research and Practice, 23,* 326–328.

Sleek, S. (1994, May–June). Ethical dilemmas plague rural practice. *APA Monitor, 25,* 26.

Slimp, P. A. O., & Burian, B. K. (1994). Multiple role relationships during internship: Consequences and recommendations. *Professional Psychology: Research and Practice, 25,* 39–45.

Smith, D., & Fitzpatrick, M. (1995). Patient-therapist boundary issues: An integrative review of theory and research. *Professional Psychology: Research and Practice, 26,* 499–506.

Solomon, G., Heisberger, J., & Winer, J. (1981). Confidentiality issues in rural community mental health. *Journal of Rural Community Psychology, 2,* 17–31.

Sonne, J. L. (1994). Multiple relationships: Does the new ethics code answer the right questions? *Professional Psychology: Research and Practice, 25,* 336–343.

Stockman, A. F. (1990). Dual relationships in rural mental health practice: An ethical dilemma. *Journal of Rural Community Psychology, 11,* 31–45.

Tabachnick, B. G., Keith-Spiegel, P., & Pope, K. S. (1991). Ethics of teaching: Beliefs and behaviors of psychologists as educators. *American Psychologist, 46,* 506–515.

Tallman, G. (1981). *Therapist-client social relationships.* Unpublished manuscript, California State University, Northridge.

Tomm, K. (1993, January–February). The ethics of dual relationships. *The California Therapist, 7,* 9, 11, 13–14.

Williams, M. H. (1998). Boundary violations: Do some contended standards fail to encompass commonplace procedures of humanistic, behavioral, and eclectic psychotherapies? *Psychotherapy, 34,* 238–249.

9

Attraction, Romance, and Sexual Intimacies

> Whatever houses I may visit, I will come for the
> benefit of the sick, remaining free of all intentional
> injustice, of all mischief, and in particular of sexual
> relations with both female and male persons, be
> they free or slaves.
>
> Hippocratic oath (ca. 400 B.C.)

The majority of psychologists perform their services in the context of close, trusting relationships. Successful therapy is most effective when psychologists and their clients collaborate to focus on the clients' personal growth, needs, and welfare. These alliances, however, have peculiar and significant features that sometimes require firm professional resolve. Twemlow and Gabbard state, "Every psychotherapist struggles with the temptation to seek personal gratification from the therapeutic situation" (1989, p. 71). Whereas the student-teacher or supervisee-supervisor roles may be inherently less intimate, they are often close to the point of being described as "very special." Based on surveys conducted over the last two decades, we feel confident in predicting that every psychologist will face, at some point in his or her career, erotized dilemmas in the context of professional duties.

Psychologists are human, and the allure of emotional pleasure can, unfortunately, be as strong or stronger than either financial gain or commitment to professional standards. This chapter focuses on the most powerful, the most frequently discussed, and often the most potentially damaging activities that can occur in a professional context: romantic dating and sexual activity. We also discuss sexual attraction, which can have serious ethical implications, depending on how it is managed. Finally, sexual intimacies between psychologists and previous clients or students, psychotherapy with former lovers, and a sexual relationship with a close relation of a client are explored.

Coerced sex is condemned in most societies. Forced sex involving psychologists and those with whom they have a professional relationship is apparently exceedingly rare. Psychologists do, however, usually hold an advantage of power (or at least perceived power) over the people with whom they work because psychologists often become privy to intimate secrets. Clients new to therapy do not know what to expect, and they trust the therapist to act in their best interests (Strasburger, Jorgenson, & Sutherland, 1992). Consumers of psychologists' services also assume that psychologists are experts, the ones with superior judgment and highly specialized skills. In addition, clients are also often vulnerable in some way. They are struggling with their own problems for which they have come for help, thus they are in a "one-down" position as they walk through the door. Students will be evaluated by their professors and supervisors in ways that can significantly affect their futures. The advantages of psychologists' personal power can be so strong as to interfere significantly with consumers' capacity to make decisions that, under a different set of circumstances, would be easy to make.

Some clients may not be so innocent, purposely seeking to seduce or manipulate their therapists. Yet, as we shall see, in such instances there is no excuse for other than a professional, self-controlled response.

Although data cannot be collected with the rigors demanded by the traditional scientific method, available evidence confirms that sexual activity with clients is very likely to be exploitative and harmful due to abuse of power, mishandling of the transference relationship, role confusion, and other factors. Ironically, psychologists can be seriously harmed as well. The extent of the devastation—which has often included loss of a job, license, spouse and family, financial security, and reputation—is typically far more pervasive than results from other types of professional ethical transgression.

ATTRACTION AND TOUCHING

As with most "normal" human courtship rituals, sexual relationships between psychotherapists and their clients often reveal the same stepping stone pathway: feelings of attraction, mild flirtation, some friendly touching on "safer" body areas, a coffee date, a switch of the client's schedule to the last appointment of the day, staying around for a while to talk afterward, hugging good-bye, and so on. The act of sexual intimacy is often the culmination of a process occurring over time, starting with vague, uneasy feelings of excitement, but progressing in tidy, rationalized steps.

Sexual Attraction to Clients

Sexual feelings require neither physical expression nor disclosure. They can remain one's own little secret and, most of the time, cause no harm. To have fleeting attraction feelings toward other people is part of being human. So, perhaps it surprised no one when Pope, Keith-Spiegel, and Tabachnick (1986) presented survey data indicating that psychologists who had never been attracted to any of their psychotherapy clients were in a distinct minority. However, of the 95% of the male therapists and 76% of the female therapists who admitted to having been attracted to at least one client, the majority felt guilty, anxious, or confused. (Older female therapists were less likely to report ever being attracted to a client, whereas the attraction rate for younger female therapists approached that of the male therapists.) Despite the high rates of attraction, however, a much lower percentage of psychologists (9.4% of the men and 2.5% of the women) reportedly allowed the attraction to escalate into sexual liaisons with their clients. Pope and Tabachnick (1993) reported that almost half of the therapists responding to their national survey had experienced sexual arousal during a therapy session. About a third believed that clients had been sexually aroused by them on occasion. So, even if you are not among the majority of psychologists who do become attracted to a clients, a client may become sexually attracted to you.

To whom do psychologists become attracted? Again, based on the Pope et al. (1986) survey, the overwhelming characteristic is "physical attractiveness" (offered by 296 of the 508 respondents who reported having been attracted to clients). "Positive mental/cognitive traits" (e.g., intelligent, well educated, articulate) and "sexual" were next (listed by 124 and 88 respondents, respectively). The fourth-place reason, "vulnerability" (needy, childlike, sensitive, fragile), was mentioned by 85 respondents. The "good personality" dimension was in fifth place, mentioned by 84 respondents. Of the respondents, 46 mentioned being attracted to clients who fulfilled their needs (e.g., boosted therapist's image, alleviated therapist's loneliness or pressures at home). Also, 30 reported that they became attracted because the clients were attracted to them, 12 found themselves attracted to clients who reminded them of someone else, and 8 admitted being attracted by the client's serious pathology. (Numbers of reasons for being attracted add to more than 508 because respondents were invited to list more than one.) We may debate whether some reasons are more acceptable or at least understandable than others. Nevertheless, it is obvious that some psychologists "use" their attraction to fulfill personal, nonprofessional needs, and, in some instances, the very vulnerable clients to whom they are attracted are likely placed at additional risk.

Under what conditions should the attraction be a cause for concern? How should such feelings be handled? If a psychologist finds attraction occurring often, should outside consultation be sought? (Similar issues arising in academic situations between psychologist educators and students are presented in the last section of the chapter.)

When therapists cannot bring their feelings under control or find that feelings toward clients interfere with normal functioning or have an impact on how clients are treated, a sensitive termination and referral are recommended as a way to protect all parties from possible complications, confusion, and harm. The therapist might say something like, "I would recommend that you work with someone more skilled than I in addressing the issues of concern to you."

Case 9-1: Lovitt Firstsite, Ph.D., knew after only a few minutes into the initial session with Meg Exquisite that he could not be her therapist. He felt like a schoolboy again, had trouble focusing on what Meg was saying, and became sexually aroused. He had difficulty finding his "therapist voice" and, after 10 minutes, he gently interrupted her to tell her that he was not the right therapist for her. Firstsite was honest with her about why. He offered to help her find another therapist.

Dr. Firstsite was forthright in recognizing that his initial intense feelings might not subside, were already blurring his judgments, and

that the less the client disclosed to him under the circumstances, the better. Unfortunately, in this real incident, Dr. Firstsite did not maintain a cautious stance. He married the woman within a matter of months, only to have the relationship dissolve shortly thereafter. The flattered "almost client" and the spellbound therapist soon realized that once the sparkle wore off, they had little in common and many areas of conflict. Some might argue that Firstsite was not unethical because the woman was not, strictly speaking, an "ex-client" since they "knew" each other for only 10 minutes. If the woman is defined as an ex-client, Dr. Firstsite would be guilty of a serious ethical infraction, even if the two had remained happily married forever after, because he did not heed the 2-year moratorium period (discussed below). Regardless, the fleeting therapeutic relationship was of sufficient intensity in terms of attributions and expectations to have warranted far more subsequent caution than Dr. Firstsite ultimately exercised.

Most instances of sexual attraction do not hit with such a strong initial force. More likely, a recognition that this person is pleasant to look at or intriguing in some way flickers, soon dissipating or remaining at a "safe" level as the therapist focuses on the demands of a purely professional relationship. Of course, attraction feelings can also escalate. Complicating the process may be the reaction some therapists have to their clients' idealization of them. These psychologists may come to believe that they are the only one who can rescue this client (Folman, 1991), which interjects a perilous "fairy tale" dimension, with the psychologist seeing himself or herself as the hero who will create the happy ending.

When a psychologist senses even a small attraction toward a client, it should not be ignored. Here are 10 "warning signs," any of which would indicate that the attraction feelings may be putting you at risk or that your services may not be objective and thereby may be incompetent. (See Pope, Sonne, & Holroyd, 1993, for additional discussion of clues to unacknowledged sexual feelings.)

1. Thinking often about the client while not in session.

2. Having recurring sexual thoughts or fantasies about the client, in or out of session.
3. Dressing or grooming in an uncustomarily
conscious fashion on the client's appointment day or looking forward to that client's
sessions above all others.
4. Attempting to elicit information from the
client to satisfy personal curiosities, as opposed to eliciting information that is required to achieve therapeutic goals.
5. Daydreaming about seeing the client socially as a "date."
6. Becoming mildly flirtatious or eliciting discussions of sexual material during therapy
when not therapeutically relevant.
7. Indulging in rescue fantasies or seeing
yourself as the only person who can heal
this person.
8. Believing that you could make up for all
of the past deficits, sadness, or disappointments in the client's life.
9. Becoming sexually aroused in the client's
presence.
10. Wanting to touch the client.

Psychologists may be surprised, even shocked,
to recognize in themselves sexual feelings toward a client (Pope et al., 1993). Whether attraction feelings should ever be discussed with clients is a matter of debate within the therapeutic
community. We recommend against it for the
following reasons: (1) the client may not be able
to deal with a frank admission of the therapist's
attraction and become confused, uncomfortable, and unclear about how to proceed; (2) it
would interject the therapist's own issues into
the client's life; and (3) the client may believe
that the discussion is an invitation to follow the
therapist's lead outside the office. We do believe
that the therapist should discuss lingering attraction feelings with someone, however, preferably
another therapist or a sensitive and experienced
colleague the psychologist trusts and respects.
Problems associated with sexual attraction are
that professional vision becomes blunted, and
excuses that seem valid flow all too easily. Another party can be helpful in clarifying the risk,
neutralizing any rationalizations, and offering
advice on how to proceed.

If a client is open and direct about erotic
feelings toward you, it is important to deal with
these impulses in a way that protects the client's
self-esteem. Leaping into heavy-handed interpretations may feel safe, but could be experienced as humiliating by the sincere client, who
mustered up considerable courage to disclose
innermost passions. Gabbard (personal communication, August 14, 1996) points out that the
client who expresses open and direct erotic feelings is not necessarily expecting to act on them.
A therapist's too-fast declaration that acting on
any such feelings would be unethical and unprofessional may be heard as an anxious overre-
action or as a misunderstanding of the client.
The better course of action is to explore the
clients feelings further. If a client becomes more
physically seductive, Gutheil and Gabbard (1992)
suggest a more unyielding approach: tell the
client that therapy is a "talking relationship,"
and they must sit down and discuss why the
client's action is inappropriate. We suggest that
therapists might, whenever a client makes a request that would be inappropriate to grant, ask
the client how the request would be of assistance
to him or her and discuss why granting the
request would not be helpful; thus, the focus
remains solely on a caretaking orientation.

Touching

Historically, the "laying on of hands" has been
an integral part of the healing process (Raimo,
1985). Modern-day science has repeatedly demonstrated the calming and attendant physical
benefits of supportive stroking during such procedures as childbirth (Kertay & Reviere, 1993).
What role does touching have in enhancing
the therapeutic process? What demarcates nonerotic touching from erotic or sexually intimate
contact? Does touching clients lead to sexual
intercourse? Whereas it is likely that students
in training will be taught to avoid sexual activity
with clients, clinical and ethical issues of touching do not seem to receive the attention they
deserve in graduate program curricula (Holub &
Lee, 1990) nor has sufficient research been conducted on the effects of touching in psychotherapy (Kertay & Reviere, 1993).

Earlier surveys revealed that the majority of psychologists and psychiatrists never or rarely engaged in nonerotic touching (Holroyd & Brodsky, 1977; Kardener, Fuller, & Mensh, 1973). Approximately half of the therapists responding to the Holroyd and Brodsky (1977) survey thought that nonerotic contact (such as hugging, kissing, or affectionate touching) could be beneficial to both male and female clients under certain conditions, but only 27% reported engaging in this type of contact. The emotionally or socially immature (e.g., children or schizophrenics) and the distressed or depressed were most frequently mentioned as the types of clients who might particularly benefit from receiving nonerotic touches. Circumstances most frequently mentioned for appropriate use of nonerotic touching included expressions of emotional support and reassurance and during the initial greeting or closing of sessions. A more recent survey (Stake & Oliver, 1991) reported reasonably high rates of nonerotic touching of the shoulder, arm, and hand and hugging by both male and female therapists with both male and female clients. Average rates were highest for women therapists and their female clients, and these touching behaviors were rarely viewed by the survey respondents as constituting misconduct. Similarly, the majority of respondents in the survey by Pope, Tabachnick, and Keith-Spiegel (1987) reported "sometimes" or "often" hugging clients or shaking their hands. The prevailing attitude was that both of these behaviors were ethical under most circumstances. Kissing clients on the lips or cheek was reported as occurring less often and was more likely to be viewed as unethical.

Wilson (1982) advises that the most acceptable parts of the body for nonerotic touching, when indicated, are the hand, back, and shoulder regions. She adds that the touch may be of very brief duration—only a few seconds—and still convey a caring or supportive message more powerfully than can any words. Wilson further suggests that the physical gesture be clarified and integrated with verbal communication to reduce any risk of misinterpretation.

Consider a dilemma that most therapists will face at some time:

Case 9-2: Ivan Holdme, a divorced father with custody of two difficult children experiencing trouble at school, had his car stolen the previous day. At the close of a dreary session, the father said to the therapist, "I really need a great big hug."

Although the nature of the already-established relationship will play a large role in the therapist's response, several questions will still come to mind (Scheller, 1993). Should I do it? How will it affect the therapy relationship? Could it possibly be misconstrued? What kind of a hug should it be: short, long, tight, limp?

According to Holub and Lee, "The decision to touch or not to touch clients may involve more than its effectiveness or the positive light that it casts on the therapist. The decision must also include deliberation over the correctness, perceptions, motives, and interpretations of the touch" (1990, p. 115). In their risk-management approach to touching, Bennett, Bryant, Vandenbos, and Greenwood (1990) also admonish psychologists to consider first how they think the client would react. The meaning and experience of touch may be interpreted incongruently. The intent of the initiator may not come through clearly to the recipient. The following case illustrates how differing perceptions of touch can lead to ethical problems.

Case 9-3: Janet Demure complained that her therapist, Ram Rush, Ph.D., behaved in a sexually provocative manner, which caused her considerable stress and embarrassment. He allegedly put his arm around her often, "massaged" her back and shoulders, and leered at her. Dr. Rush was "shocked" by the charges and vehemently denied any improper intentions. He claimed that he often put his hand briefly on his clients' backs and patted or moved his hand with the intention of communicating warmth and acceptance. His customary constant eye contact was his way to communicate that clients had his full attention. He admitted that Demure seemed uneasy, but expected this would "quickly pass as it did with several others who were not used to expressions of caring."

This case well illustrates the critical necessity of remaining aware of individual clients and their special needs and issues, a sensitivity that may well require an alteration in one's usual demeanor. Dr. Rush was trained in a "humanistic orientation," which is generally more favorably disposed to nonerotic touching of clients and supports arguments favoring the usefulness of touching (Holroyd & Brodsky, 1977).

Psychologists must assess their motivations as to whether a physical touch is appropriate in each instance, although some reasons may not be fully conscious. The therapist's level of comfort with touching and being touched will also come into play (Kertay & Reviere, 1993). For therapists who have already recognized a physical attraction within themselves toward a client, extra caution must be exercised. If the client has already indicated clear signs of sexual attraction toward the therapist, any physical contact is extremely risky.

Because therapists can be taken completely off guard, it is wise to have carefully considered these eventualities in advance. Not wanting to appear rejecting may overtake the moment, but a knee-jerk compliance with the request could, even if for only a small percentage of clients, have negative consequences. The next case is illustrative.

Case 9-4: Sarah Needy was afraid on finding herself alone in a new, large city. On entering the fifth session with Tim Startled, Ph.D., she embraced and held onto him tightly and did not let go. The astonished therapist put his arms lightly around her and nervously patted her on the back. Unfortunately, Needy interpreted Startled's willingness to be held for an extended period as a nonverbal admission that they were more than just therapist and client. When, after several minutes, Dr. Startled moved away and continued with usual mode of therapy, Needy became confused and angry. She walked out and later pressed ethics charges for "sexual misconduct."

Dr. Startled would have been far wiser had he ensured that Needy's unwelcome embrace was very short. Even if he had to take his client's arms and set them gently aside, a stance of caring and concern can be maintained without allowing physical contact to be prolonged. It must be pointed out, however, that touching

can be inappropriate in any form and under any circumstances for some clients.

Case 9-5: Conn Sole, Ph.D., and Jason Mourner had a long-standing therapy relationship that never involved any physical touching. On learning that Jason's father fell unexpectedly ill and died suddenly, Dr. Sole reached for Jason to give him a hug. Jason's body went rigid, and he did not return the gesture.

In an attempt at consolation, Dr. Sole miscalculated his client. Although he may not choose to discuss the ill-fated gesture during that particular session (allowing him to consider how he will approach it with his client), Sole should openly address it as soon as feasible, if only to apologize for unintentionally making the client feel uncomfortable.

Finally, we do admit that there is no touching policy to guide every situation. For example, it might seem that holding a patient's hand throughout a session would constitute a boundary violation. However, consider this case:

Case 9-6: Irving Flexible, Ph.D., was called to consult on the case of a 23-year-old woman with advanced lung disease secondary to cystic fibrosis. After introducing himself to the patient and sitting in the chair at her bedside, the psychologist asked how he could be helpful. The young woman, who was having great difficulty breathing despite wearing an oxygen mask, gripped his hand tightly and said, "Don't let go." Between attempts to catch her breath, she spoke of her terror at the thought of dying alone.

Occasionally, variations from the usual rules constitute the highest standard of care. Deviations, however, should be made only when the following question can be answered in the affirmative: "If my behavior was known to my colleagues, would they very likely agree that I was only serving the needs of my client?"

The general definition of *erotic contact* offered by Holroyd and Brodsky (1977, 1980) includes behavior primarily intended to arouse or satisfy sexual desires. Using this definition, such touching (excluding intercourse) was reported by 9% of male and 1% of female therapists sampled in their survey. The advantage of a definition that focuses not on the nature of the act but on the intent is that touching any part of the person is unethical if the intent was sexual gratification. The drawback is that accused therapists can always deny their intent, which may or may not be truthful. Or, their intentions may not be consciously recognized. Another definition focuses on what is touched. For example, *improper touch* has been defined as coming into contact with bare skin or through clothing of the breast of a female or the sexual organ, anus, groin, or buttocks of either sex (California Business and Professions Code, Section 728, 1989). The advantage of a list of what cannot be touched is that intent need not be proven. It also implicitly allows other forms of touching that should not necessarily raise concerns, such as shaking hands or a gentle and reassuring pat on the back. But, the list approach is problematic because humans can be "sexual" just about everywhere on their bodies. Therefore, if a forbidden touch site is not specifically noted, one might assume that touching it is acceptable. But, is it really okay to massage a man's breasts or nibble on clients' ears?

A fascinating letter written by Sigmund Freud in 1931 to his disciple, Sandor Ferenczi, reveals that the issue of sexual innuendo in therapy was brewing more than a half century ago. Ferenczi suggested that showing physical affection to patients might assist neutralizing early emotional deprivation. Freud responded:

> You have not made a secret of the fact that you kiss your patients and let them kiss you. . . . Now I am assuredly not one of those who from prudishness or from consideration of bourgeois convention would condemn little erotic gratifications of this kind. . . . But that does not alter the fact . . . that with us a kiss signifies a certain erotic intimacy. . . . Now picture what will be the result of publishing your technique. . . . A number of independent thinkers will say to themselves: Why stop at a kiss? Certainly one gets further when one adopts "pawing" as well, which after all doesn't make a baby. And then bolder ones will come along who will go further, to peeping and showing—and soon we shall have accepted in the technique of analysis the whole repertoire of demiviergerie and petting parties, resulting in an enormous interest in psychoanalysis among both analysts and patients. (Jones, 1957, pp. 163–164, cited in Marmor, 1972)

Are therapists who touch clients also more likely to have sexual relationships with clients? Holroyd and Brodsky (1980) found that those therapists who admitted having sexual relationships with their clients also advocated and engaged in more nonerotic touching of opposite-sex, but not same sex, clients. There was a group of subjects who engaged in erotic contact, but not intercourse, whose nonerotic contact was not confined to opposite-sex clients. These authors conclude, then, that nonerotic touching is predictive only when the therapist is selective about the gender touched. Regarding erotic touching, more male therapists than female therapists (10.9% v. 1.9%) reported having had engaged in such behavior, a sex difference similar to that involving sexual intercourse with patients in the early 1980s.

ROMANCING AND CASUALLY DATING CLIENTS

Although giving a client a dozen red roses, taking a client to dinner or for a drink at happy hour, or staying after hours in the office to chat while listening to music are not classified as "sexual intimacies," chapter 8 described how such activities would be instances of superimposing inappropriate activities into the therapy relationship. Casual social excursions outside the office are especially risky because they typically involve more intimate self-disclosure and other behaviors that could easily be perceived by clients or students as "courtship rituals." Even if therapists had no motivations beyond platonic pleasantries, clients are likely to be confused and possibly become as psychologically damaged as when boundary violations involve overt sexual activity (Simon, 1991).

Case 9-7: Norman Breakup, Ph.D., was lonely after a bitter divorce. He missed his teenage children and the companionship they provided. He began to single out several younger male and female clients on which to shower extra attention, alternating among them for one-on-one experiences. Sometimes, he would sit and talk for up to 3 hours after a session was over. He often took them out to lunch and sometimes shopping afterward for small gifts. Breakup was shocked when one of the women complained to a licensing board that he had "wined and dumped her."

Whereas we may empathize with Breakup's personal suffering, he exercised extremely poor judgment in using his clients as surrogate children and emotional bandages. Using one's client base as a population of convenient intimacy was both unprofessional and unethical.

The next case reveals a more common scenario.

Case 9-8: Simon Inchworm, Ph.D., was attracted to Selma Receptive, his client of several months. Selma readily accepted what Inchworm believed, at the time, to be a "professionally appropriate" invitation to attend a lecture on eating disorders because Selma's sister was anorexic. The lecture concluded at 5 P.M., so Inchworm invited Receptive to stop for a bite at a nearby deli. The next week, Inchworm accepted Receptive's gift of a book written by the speaker they had heard the previous week. The following week, Inchworm agreed to a "reciprocal" dinner at Receptive's place. Afterward, while enjoying a third glass of wine, they looked into each other's eyes, embraced, kissed for a while, and then retreated into the bedroom.

It does not take a rocket scientist to have predicted the outcome. Yet, it is amazing how highly educated male and female psychologists can allow themselves to put their clients and themselves in such precarious situations, which often cause great harm to both parties in the long run. In this actual case, an affair persisted for a few weeks. In the meantime, "Dr. Inchworm" met someone else of more interest to him and terminated the affair. When "Ms. Receptive" became upset, he also terminated the therapy relationship. The client sought and won a large damage award through a civil malpractice complaint.

SEXUALLY INTIMATE BEHAVIOR WITH PSYCHOTHERAPY CLIENTS

The express prohibition against sexual intimacies in the 2,500-year-old Hippocratic oath was not adopted by the American Psychological Association (APA), until 1977. The psychotherapy literature had previously acknowledged that feelings representational of earlier relationships manifesting themselves during psychotherapy (transference) could be very strong in both clients and therapists. Sexual contact between clients and therapists had, however, received little attention. Sex with clients had previously been viewed as poor professional practice, a dual-role relationship, and likely to be exploitative. Without an express prohibition, however, complaints were more difficult to adjudicate and were not always taken very seriously. Feminism, consumerism, and a growing admission and realization by psychologists that such contact does occur with unacceptable frequency were among the factors leading to a swell of concern about psychotherapists who would take sexual advantage of their clients. (The statement relevant to sex with current clients in the 1992 APA ethics code appears as ES: 4.05.)

Incidence

It is difficult to estimate accurately the actual frequency of sexual intimacies with psychotherapy clients. It is clear from self-report surveys, even if we assume that none of those who did not return their surveys had been sexually intimate with their clients, that far more therapists engage in sexual behavior than is reported to ethics committees and state licensing boards. It is also difficult to know whether the incidence of sexual activity between therapists and clients is declining. More recent self-report surveys offer hopeful signs that fewer numbers of psychologists are engaging in such behavior (Pope, 1993).

Forer's (1981) unpublished survey conducted in California in 1968 reported that 17% of his sample of male private practice therapists admitted having had sexual relationships with clients, compared with no such sexual experiences reported by female private practice therapists or male therapists working in institutional settings. For a long while, survey data indicated that an average of about 10% of male and 2% of female therapists reported having engaged in sexual intimacies with their clients. More recent national surveys, however, reveal the incidence falling to as low as 0.9% for male therapists and 0.2% for female therapists (Borys & Pope, 1989; Pope, 1990a), and no significant differences among psychiatry, social work, and psychology in the rates of self-reported sexual relationships with clients were found (Borys & Pope, 1989).

We can hope that the downward trend in self-report studies over the past decade reflects a true shift and mirrors the influence of the absolute condemnation of sexual misconduct by the helping professions as revealed in their ethical standards. However, that same impact may also result in underreporting (or a reduction in overreporting of the past?) on surveys because consumer complaints appear to be increasing (Gottlieb, Sell, & Schoenfeld, 1988), and psychologists may be more fearful of discovery. Yet another equally likely interpretation is that the increased awareness and avenues of redress have empowered more victims of sexual exploitation to come forward with complaints. Earlier, while the professional community was mostly ignoring the problem, clients may have felt too powerless to protest or, if they did, were discounted as delusional, subject to fantasy, and in a struggle with their transference neuroses (Barnhouse, 1978; Schwendinger & Schwendinger, 1974).

Who is Responsible?

Some clients, students, and supervisees actively and knowingly contribute to the creation of a sexually tempting predicament. Those with borderline or histrionic personality disorders have been especially singled out as potentially seductive (Gutheil, 1989; Notman & Nadelson, 1994). Psychologists, however, bear the responsibility to resist acting on their feelings of attraction and to focus, instead, on rendering professional services. Ethics committees and other hearing panels are not impressed when psychologists whine that they are the ones who were lured and snared, the victims of beguiling clients.

Case 9-9: Hap Bowlover, Ph.D., wrote a letter in response to an ethics committee inquiry; he insisted that he was systematically "worn down by a client who showed up for therapy sessions wearing dresses with the neckline and the hem almost meeting" and who "came at me every time she walked into the room." He declared that he was her victim, and that he was being used as a symbol for "all the men who had messed her up in the past." He likened the client to a black widow spider and claimed to have contacted a lawyer for the purposes of suing her.

Such excuses are not as rare as you might think. Some have even been sympathetic toward therapists, who, as Wright (1985) contends, are enticed and lured into lustful moments by unscrupulous clients seeking to exploit the vulnerability of psychologists to their own economic advantage. Many clients who appear to be encouraging a sexual relationship with their therapists, however, may be "repeating the eroticized behaviors that are sequelae of their childhood sexual abuse . . . and are not simply 'normal' individuals who find the therapist attractive or develop a rapid and intense erotic transference" and may become, as a result, revictimized by their therapists (Kluft, 1989, p. 485). Some clients may overwhelm the therapist incapable of managing erotic transference effectively, some falling into what Gabbard and Lester (1995) define as the "masochistic surrender" type. Here, the therapist may be attracted to difficult and demanding clients, pursuing humiliation and victimization in their personal and professional lives. The complex interactions with clients may lead them to accede to clients' demands, particularly those who are sadistic or psychopathic. Nevertheless, the bottom line is that shifting blame or responsibility to the client—even if the client is manipulative or seductive—is never an excuse for incompetent and unprofessional behavior. The obligation to uphold ethical, legal, and professional standards is not a duty that can ever be evaded or assigned to the client (Pope & Bouhoutsos, 1986).

Risks to Clients

When sex enters into therapy, a helping environment has been shattered (Kluft, 1989). Surveys of psychologists (Holroyd & Brodsky, 1977) and psychiatrists (Kardener et al., 1973) reveal that the majority of practitioners do not believe that erotic contact or sexual intercourse with clients could be beneficial. Such behavior has been compared to rape or incest (Barnhouse, 1978; Masters & Johnson, 1976), and it creates "therapeutic orphans" whose caretakers have failed in their role (Kardener, 1974). Harm may begin to accrue as soon as the sexual activity begins, or years can pass before the impact begins to consciously manifest itself.

The available data on harm to clients cannot be considered representative of all client-therapist sexual liaisons because they consist primarily of accounts by clients who brought complaints, who sought additional therapy or who responded to advertisements requesting information from those who had experienced sexual contact with their therapists. Some data are based on therapists' reports of clients who sought subsequent therapy after being abused by a previous therapist. For most clients assessed from these populations, the sexual experiences were damaging and harmful (e.g., Bates & Brodsky, 1989; Bouhoutsos, Holroyd, Lerman, Forer, & Greenburg, 1983; Feldman-Summers, 1989; Kluft, 1989; Pope, 1990b; Pope & Vetter, 1991; Taylor & Wagner, 1976). Psychiatric hospitalizations and suicides have traced the triggering incidents to sexual encounters with therapists.

Pope (1989a, 1994) describes a cluster of symptoms having some similarity to post-traumatic stress disorder (PTSD), which is seen in some clients who have had sexual relationships with their therapists. These symptoms include (1) ambivalence about the therapist, similar to that of incest victims who hold both love and negative feelings toward the family member; (2) feelings of guilt, as if the client were to blame for what happened; (3) feelings of isolation and emptiness; (4) cognitive dysfunction, particularly in the areas of attention and concentration;

(5) identity and boundary disturbances; (6) difficulties in trusting others, as well as themselves; (7) confusion about their sexuality; (8) lability of mood and feeling out of control; (9) suppressed rage; and (10) increased risk for suicide or other self-destructive reactions. Several poignant and absorbing personal accounts attest to the harm caused by sexualized therapy relationships (e.g., Bates & Brodsky, 1989; Freeman & Roy, 1976; Noel & Watterson, 1992; Plasil, 1985; Walker & Young, 1986).

Perhaps because of the serious professional, personal, and legal consequences that accompany sustained charges of sexual misconduct, the research on incidence and harmful impact on clients has been singled out for heavy criticism (e.g., Williams, 1992). There is no doubt that the self-report survey methodology has inherent limitations, and these are typically pointed out by the authors of many of the survey-based articles. Sampling, response, and experimenter biases are among the common faults found with such research. Others have criticized the assumption that harm automatically accrues as a result of having sex with a client, or that an adult client is incapable of consenting to having sex with whomever he or she chooses, or whether "transference" rather than "current reality" is always at issue (Slovenko, 1991). Although some may quibble about the quality of research, the extent of damage, and the generalizability of dynamics, such debates obscure the basic point: sex with clients is unethical and far outside accepted standards of care.

CHARACTERISTICS OF PSYCHOLOGISTS WHO ENGAGE IN SEXUAL RELATIONS WITH CLIENTS

General Characteristics

Sexually exploitative psychotherapists are often portrayed in the movies as dashing, debonair, and self-assured. These depictions hardly reflect the portrait that emerges from the available information about real therapists who sexually exploit their clients; these therapists more closely fit descriptions of impaired psychologists (see chapter 3).

Psychologists themselves may puzzle over how intelligent, educated men and women in a world permeated with carnal opportunity could be so stupid as to engage in behaviors blatantly unprofessional and dangerous to everyone concerned. However, therapists found guilty of sexual intimacies with clients are not confined to those who are poorly-trained, obtuse, or professionally isolated. Actual cases from our personal knowledge, as well as some listed by Sonne and Pope (1991) include a famous media psychologist, a past president of a state psychological association, a former member of a state licensing board, a professor at a major university who authored an article on professional ethics, a chair of a state psychological association ethics committee, and even an author of an article condemning sex with clients. Indeed, no psychologist is likely to be immune from temptation or exploitation because, as Twemlow and Gabbard remind us, despite the fact that psychotherapists are fond of thinking of their unethical colleagues as sick or different, a "subtle continuum exists in the area of deriving personal satisfaction from one's patients" (1989, p. 73). Gabbard and Lester (1995) describe the profoundly narcissistic professional who has risen to the top in his field and rationalizes his sexually exploitative behavior as acceptable because he is in a different, superior category from all others.

Although, again, data cannot be collected with the rigor demanded by the traditional scientific method, available findings indicate that psychotherapists who engage in sexual intimacies with clients have one or more personal problems, including the following: (1) general feelings of vulnerability; (2) fear of intimacy; (3) crises in their own personal sex, love, or family relationships; (4) feelings of failure as professionals or as individuals; (5) high needs for love or affection, positive regard, or power; (6) poor impulse control; (7) social isolation; (8) overvaluation of abilities to heal; (9) isolation from peer support; (10) depression or bipolar disorders; and (11) narcissistic, sadistic, and other character or predatory psychopathologies (Butler & Zelen, 1977; Dahlberg, 1970; Gabbard & Lester, 1995; Marmor, 1972; Olarte, 1991; Pope, 1990a; Solursh & Solursh, 1993). Offending therapists also tend to deny that their behav-

ior has any adverse impact on clients (Holroyd & Bouhoutsos, 1985).

The most common offender is a male in his 40s or 50s (Brodsky, 1989; Butler & Zelen, 1977; Chesler, 1972; Dahlberg, 1970; Notman & Nadelson, 1994; Sonne & Pope, 1991). The middle-aged therapist going through a divorce or having other problems in a primary relationship should remain alert because the risk of overinvolvement with clients is especially high (Twemlow & Gabbard, 1989). Clients exploited by their therapists are mostly younger women. Perhaps as many as 5% are minors at the time the sexual activity began, and almost a third have been victims of incest or physical abuse as children (Pope & Vetter, 1991).

A homosexual client of either sex with the same-sex therapist is the next most frequent category, although a distant second (Brodsky, 1989). Female psychologists have a much lower rate of engaging in sex with clients than do male therapists. Why women are less likely to engage in sexual intimacies with clients than their male counterparts has been debated in the absence of solid data. Perhaps female sex roles have allowed women to learn and practice a spectrum of techniques that do not involve sexuality for communicating love and nurturance. Maybe traditional cultural conditioning of women to refrain from taking the sexual initiative has also taught them better control of sexual impulses, as well as techniques for resisting sexual advances (Marmor, 1972). We had no cases of a male client bringing an ethics charge of sexual exploitation against his female therapist to describe in the first edition of this book (Keith-Spiegel & Koocher, 1985) because none had come to our attention.

We still know virtually nothing about how male clients are affected by sexual experiences with their female therapists, or why, if any are psychologically harmed, they do not choose to complain to ethics committees. Slovenko (1991) suggests that it never occurs to the male client, even in these litigious times, to sue a woman for having had sex with him. However, a psychologist, who has treated several male clients in the aftermath of harm caused by engaging in sexual relations with previous female therapists, told us that men do not make formal complaints because they fear a response of ridicule rather than compassion and concern.

When female therapists are respondents in ethics hearings or civil suits, the complainant will likely be a wife or a family member of the man with whom the psychologist is having an alleged sexual relationship. When it is the client who complains about a female therapist, that client is likely to be a woman.

Sexual Offender Scenarios

A topology of 9 common scenarios presented by Pope and Bouhoutsos (1986) reasonably categorizes a great many actual cases we have reviewed, although the frequency across categories varies considerably. A brief description of each scenario with sample cases appears below.

Role Trading

Here the therapist and the client trade roles with the therapist becoming the recipient of services. Professional boundaries collapse as the therapist focuses on his or her own needs.

Case 9-10: Ben Strippem, Psy.D., asked his young, female client to remove her clothes so he can measure her "vitals," which, he claimed, was necessary to help her give up smoking.

Dr. Strippem seems to have devised a way, albeit a highly unethical and unprofessional one, to satisfy a need for a quick gratification. The next case is the more common scenario, involving an attempt by a psychologist to remediate deficits in his own life.

Case 9-11: Samuel Sorry, Ph.D., a psychologist in his late 40s, explained to an ethics committee that his sexual relationship with a 26-year-old client was prompted primarily by a series of rapidly accelerating crises in his personal life. His wife of 25 years had left him for a woman, his son abused drugs, and his father had recently died. He was feeling abandoned and saw himself as a failure. His young client was trusting and complimentary, and, in his exact words, "She was the only thing [sic] in my life that I looked forward to."

That most of the clients who become involved in sexual intimacies with male therapists tend to be younger females suggests that sexually exploitative male psychologists may view such women as easy sources of "as if" intimacy or as a means to recapture waning youth and virility. However, other pairings have occurred.

Case 9-12: Lila Reclusive, Ph.D., was becoming more physically frail and increasingly isolated after her husband of 45 years passed away. Her children were grown and living in another state. A middle-aged male client willingly complied with requests by Reclusive for favors, which at first were small, helpful acts such as walking with her to her car after dark. Requests and enthusiastic compliance escalated, and soon the man was living in her home, and they were speaking of marriage. Without a full understanding of the professional aspect of their relationship and its possible legal ramifications, Reclusive's children brought civil charges against the client for extortion. But, the charges were dismissed when the ongoing roles of client and therapist were revealed.

Svengali

The Svengali type of psychologist deftly creates and then manipulates clients' dependencies. Clients may stay "in treatment" longer than appropriate, and sexual activity may also take place.

Case 9-13: Sam Svelt, Psy.D., always behaved as the perfect gentleman, a rock in a sea of turmoil. Sandra Moosh saw him as her only source of stability and became increasingly isolated except for her sessions with him. When Svelt suggested that they have an affair, it did not occur to her that she had a choice. She would do anything he asked of her. Only years later was she able to discuss this incident with anyone.

Unfortunately, it is likely that clients who succumb to Svengalis are unlikely to be assertive enough to complain. Thus, it is difficult to ascertain the prevalence of this pattern.

Rape

Clients have complained that they were attacked, without provocation or warning, by their therapists. The offender profile of rape is extremely rare.

Case 9-14: A client testified that during her second therapy session, Mel Sprint, Psy.D., bolted from his chair and started ripping at her clothing.

Sprint's behavior constituted attempted rape, and he was tried in a court of law and jailed for 6 months. He lost his license to practice psychology.

Sex Therapy

Sometimes, offenders have attempted to justify their involvement with clients on various therapeutic grounds, claiming that the sexual experience will somehow help clients with their intimacy or other problems.

Case 9-15: Flash Johnson, Ph.D., admitted in court that he stripped in front of his female clients as an integral part of his therapeutic technique, by which he intended to prove to them that there is no shame in nudity.

Case 9-16: John Bestman, Ed.D., convinced Marcia Willing that a psychotherapist was the perfect person with whom to have a sexual affair because no one else could better understand her needs or could be as trusted. When Marcia found Bestman a mediocre lover and felt the psychotherapy was now confusing and somewhat frightening, she contacted an ethics committee.

Case 9-17: As part of "reparenting therapy," Gloria Kanz, Ph.D., has her clients of both sexes "nurse" at her breast while she coos loving messages of devotion. One of her clients, Jeb Startle, became more "melancholy and strange" according to his friends, who insisted that he see another therapist for a consultation.

These "therapeutic interventions" are unprofessional and unethical. However, therapists in this category often manage to actually convince themselves that they are genuinely charitable by giving clients something special to make up for past deprivations and loneliness. Rescue fantasies are also common (Notman & Nadelson, 1994). Such therapists often have little insight into the self-serving nature of their actions.

Drug Use

Thankfully a rare category, a therapist occasionally uses drugs or alcohol to enhance the treatment-seduction process.

Case 9-18: Snow White, who had been switched to the position of last client of the evening by Cokie Snort, Ph.D., agreed to start staying a while later to help Dr. Snort "relax" after a long day. Snort started serving wine, but one evening produced some cocaine. Sex soon became an integral part of the after-hour ritual.

This case, adapted from one with a high profile, revealed a therapist who had no concept of boundaries in any area of his practice. He was eventually sued by several parties and lost his license to practice psychology.

"It Just Got Out of Hand"

The most prevalent offender group in our experience is composed of psychologists who fail to appropriately and respectfully monitor the intense emotional closeness that often develops between therapist and client. The sexualization of these therapy relationships typically started tentatively and involved some back-and-forth attraction signals in the form of nonerotic hugging, mildly flirtatious remarks, or suggestive joking, and then "it just got out of hand."

Case 9-19: Tim Scare, Ph.D., became concerned when a client, with whom he had intercourse on several occasions, started calling him at home "just to say hello." He had not predicted the increasing informality in the relationship nor did he welcome it. He suggested to his client that therapy should be terminated. She asked if that meant that they would then be "just lovers." When he responded that this was not his desire either, the client became furious and contacted an ethics committee.

Case 9-20: Willa Nip, Ph.D., realized too late that her outwardly affectionate and sometimes erotic kissing and touching of a client similarly attracted to her was not acceptable professional behavior. However, when she discontinued the behavior, the client felt that she no longer cared about her. Nip tried to assure her that this was not so, but the client contacted an ethics committee, charging that Dr. Nip's rejection and cold manner had worsened her mental state.

The first common sign of deterioration after the relationship becomes more actively sexualized usually occurs when the client expresses to the therapist a wish to extend the relationship and deepen the commitment between the two of them. At this point, most therapists (especially those who are married or in another committed relationship) react with some form of distancing. Whether a response to fear, guilt, delayed moralistic stirrings, disinterest, or a belated recognition that serious therapeutic errors have been committed, such withdrawal is experienced by the clients as rejection and abandonment. At this point, the angry clients may seek redress.

Hold Me

A client who may be lonely or sad and who desires contact comfort ("hold me"), is exploited by the therapist, whose touching turns erotic. Or, the therapist takes advantage of a client who is confused or unclear about the difference between erotic and nonerotic contact.

Case 9-21: Adam Octopus, Ph.D., had always found the delicate and petite Wilma Wilt enticing. Wilt would fall into his arms and sob every time they discussed her drug-addicted 12-year-old child. Octopus began to massage and fondle her during these episodes, eventually making sexual moves to which she did not object at the time. Wilt soon realized, however, that what she needed and what she was getting were hardly one and the same. She told her subsequent therapist about Octopus' behavior, and the new therapist encouraged Wilt to press charges.

"True" Love

Often enough, psychologists who enter sexually intimate relationships with clients excuse their sexual involvement because it is based on what they experience as true love of their clients. Gartrell, Herman, Olarte, Feldstein, and Localio (1986, 1989) report that 65% of offenders stated that they were "in love" with their patients.

Case 9-22: Elmer Smitten, Ph.D., was attracted to Luna Fond from the first therapy session. He recalled wanting to reach out and hold her, to take care of her. He thought about Fond constantly and anxiously anticipated the sessions with her. If Fond canceled an appointment, he was disappointed and depressed all day. The first social meeting occurred under conditions similar to the type that lovesick adolescents contrive. He would call to ask if she would mind changing her 10:00 A.M. appointment to 11:00 A.M. At the end of the session, he would then mention that he had not eaten all day and would casually ask Fond to join him at the little cafe across the street for a salad. He noted that he should have realized the pending danger when he found himself mentally rehearsing the lunch invitation many times. They had lunch. There were more lunches, then dinners, and finally sexual activity. Smitten maintained that if he were free, he would have committed himself fully to this woman. Soon, the guilt about having an affair with a married man began to gnaw at Fond. Dr. Smitten began to feel pressured, and frequent spats occurred. Fond terminated both the therapy and the personal relationship, consulted another psychologist, and contacted an ethics committee. In the meantime, Smitten continued writing her love letters, even after an ethics committee investigation had been initiated.

This type of offender may evoke some pity as compared with others, perhaps because the theme of "star-crossed lovers" seems tragic rather than malevolent. Loving a client, however, does not excuse a psychologist from professional responsibility. Twemlow and Gabbard (1989) and Gabbard and Lester (1995) describe the lovesick therapist far less sympathetically, as a narcissistic, emotionally dependent individual who enters an altered state of conscience when in the presence of the special client, which then impairs judgment in that case, but not for others. The state of lovesickness may reduce guilt because the therapist is convinced he or she will provide the client with quality parenting that will heal the clients's pain and torment. Such therapists lack insight into the destructive nature of their behavior and the harm they are causing their clients.

As If . . .

Therapists using an "as if" process believe that transference feelings are not a result of the therapy dynamics but, rather, emanate from genuine attraction to them as persons. That is, they convince themselves that the clients would have the same reaction to them had they met casually in another setting under a different set of circumstance. This scenario is more difficult to illustrate with a case and probably manifests itself to some extent in many of the other categories. Below is a more obvious example of a therapist who has deluded himself in an "as if" process.

Case 9-23: Iam Allthat, Ph.D., came to believe that he was an extraordinary therapist because, as a colleague put it, "He would often tell us during case conferences that, because his clients were always so complimentary and grateful, he never had any problems to bring to the table." He started writing his memoirs, tentatively titled, "Secrets from the #1 Psychologist." His colleagues thought him rather arrogant, but were surprised when two of the clinic's clients brought charges against him for sexual misconduct. Dr. Allthat vigorously defended himself by saying that they were crazy about him, and both had been trying to seduce him for a long time. The only reason they got upset, he claimed, is because he refused to commit to a long-term relationship with either of them.

Of course, not every case fits neatly into the categories presented above. We have reviewed a few cases that seem to be driven by mean-spirited, premeditated exploitation in the extreme, such as the psychologist who hypnotized clients for the purpose of getting them to masturbate in his presence, or the psychologist who had sexual relationships with 3 of the most intriguing of his dissociative client's 26 personalities. Many situations are combinations of two or more categories, such as the lonely therapist who encourages personal closeness in her needy clients (hold me) and believes that, because the client needs and cares about her as an individual (as if . . .), the client can also help her feel cared about (role trading).

RISKS TO THERAPISTS

Whereas consequences to clients as the result of engaging in sexual intimacies with their therapists can be shattering, many psychologists have not fared any better. Some people erroneously assume that psychologists who engage in sexual intimacies with clients are risking very little because psychotherapy is conducted in the absence of witnesses. If a client complains, one can simply deny the accusation, citing "fantasy," "delusion," or "transference" as the basis for the charges. Does this work? In one sense, it does. Perhaps half of the sexual intimacy cases result in the "he said, she said" type because the differing stories cannot be substantiated by either party. Ethics committees usually cannot sustain such charges. But, the psychologist is not exonerated because the victory is by default. If another charge is subsequently filed against the same psychologist, the scale becomes tipped against the psychologist because ethics committees do not destroy files containing serious charges when the psychologist was not explicitly judged innocent. Any case may be reopened if new evidence suggests that an earlier conclusion could have been reached in error. Malpractice insurance carriers no longer pay the plaintiffs' award damages in sexual impropriety cases. This means that defendants may need to bear the total cost, and they can be substantial. For this reason, it is rare that a psychologist is sued solely for sexual misbehavior. Typically, the grounds are "improper treatment."

Clients have a number of options for redress in addition to ethics committees. These include criminal law statutes (in some states), tort actions (including malpractice), and licensing board complaints. Clients also have additional support systems available to them, possibly including expert witnesses, subsequent therapists who are prepared to testify regarding the damage that the previous sexual activity caused, and the ethics code of the APA, which is a favorite "witness" for the prosecution.

Several states have criminalized sexual activities with psychotherapy clients, a seemingly fitting solution to the problem of intractable offenders. Criminal penalties might be the only hook that can influence the behavior of some therapists, whose perceptions of less serious consequences are apparently perceived as non-threatening. However, there may be unintended repercussions. When punishments are draconian, clients and colleagues may be less inclined to report offenders, not wanting the responsibility for putting another person in jail. Any motivation for sexually exploitative psychologists to confess evaporates. Clients who have suffered and could benefit from an award of damages in a civil procedure are not afforded that advantage in a criminal proceeding. The statutes also assume that psychotherapy clients are incapable of voluntary consent, an assumption that infantilizes and stigmatizes adult clients and has other inherent additional legal problems (see Deaton, Illingworth, & Bursztajn, 1992; Strasburger, Jorgenson, & Randles, 1991). (Reporting a client's previous therapist of sexual misconduct when the client objects is discussed in chapter 1.)

A few states have mandatory reporting statutes by which all licensed health providers are required to relate any instance of sexual misconduct, even if the information is disclosed in a confidential relationship or if they have reason to believe that a colleague has been sexually involved with a client (Gartrell, Herman, Olarte, Feldstein, & Localio, 1988). Although future exploitation by the previous therapist may be averted, one concern is that mandatory reporting may have a negative effect on the current therapy relationship (Strasburger et al., 1987). (Therapists may be exempted from mandatory reporting when their client is a therapist who has engaged in sexual misconduct.)

One would think that enforceable ethics codes, licensing regulations, civil law, mandatory reporting, and other legal reforms should deter even the most recalcitrant offenders. The effectiveness of these sanctions in discouraging or impeding sexual misconduct, however, is unclear. Complaints continue to be pressed, even in states where sexual misconduct with clients is a criminal offense.

Prevention, Education, Sanctions, and Rehabilitation

The first line of prevention for sexual activity with clients is sensitive and competent training. Graduate programs have been slow to incorporate the full range of sexually oriented issues into their curricula. Whereas most contemporary students are receiving the clear message that sex with clients is a serious ethical violation and a therapeutic error, instruction about sex bias in therapy, touching, sex with students and supervisees, and ways to understand and manage one's own erotic feelings and attractions toward clients requires far more attention (Anderson, 1986; Borys & Pope, 1989; Hall, 1987; Pope & Tabachnick, 1993; Strasburger et al., 1992). Students and trainees must feel comfortable speaking frankly with their educators and supervisors, an impossible situation if the training psychologists are uncomfortable or uninformed about the issues. Worse yet, some educators and supervisors provide appalling models to their students because they, themselves, are sexual predators (Glaser & Thorpe, 1986; Pope, Levenson, & Schover, 1979).

Because most practicing psychologists have not had adequate training in the array of sexualized dilemmas and approaches for managing them, continuing education lectures and workshops should be made available by psychology associations and educational institutions. Institutions employing therapists can also be held liable (under the legal theory of *respondeat superior*, or negligent hiring, supervision, and retention), so it behooves hospitals, clinics, and other mental health organizations to ensure that education about sexual misconduct is offered in-house (Strasburger et al., 1992).

The public has been more consistently advised in recent years that the seductive practitioner is not to be tolerated, and that sexualization of psychotherapy runs counter to their own best interests. Evidence suggests that lack of knowledge, rather than low motivation, prevents women from reporting sexually abusive therapists (Vinson, 1987).

It has been found that people can become quickly knowledgeable after reading an informational brochure (Thorn, Shealy, & Briggs, 1993). The APA distributes a pamphlet called *If Sex Enters into the Therapy Relationship*. Transference and ethical issues are described, as well as how sexuality can be inappropriately interjected into therapy. Readers are informed about what they can do if they feel uncomfortable or if they want to report their therapist. (See the full text in the article by the Committee on Women in Psychology, 1989.) Displaying these brochures in the waiting room area is an easy and convenient way not only to educate clients, but also to help draw boundaries for them. In California, psychologists are mandated to give a brochure, *Professional Therapy Never Includes Sex*, to any client who alleges sexual contact with a previous therapist. Failure to comply would, itself, constitute professional misconduct (California Business and Professions Code, Section 728, 1989). A recent case in California put a psychologist on 3-years probation because she did not offer a client the brochure ("Disciplinary Actions," 1997).

Some practitioners make written contracts with their new clients (see also chapter 4). A section on clients' rights might read, "Clients have the right to a therapeutic experience that is free from sexual harassment or sexual behavior of any kind." Whereas it would be awkward and perhaps even alarming to discuss this matter during an initial session, putting this "right" in writing makes the expectations of both parties clear from the onset.

Intervention programs for offenders is a critical issue because a substantial proportion of sexually abusing therapists abuse multiple victims (Bates & Brodsky, 1989; Strasburger, Jorgenson, & Randles, 1990). But, should rehabilitation programs for therapists, who either enter counseling voluntarily or are mandated to do so to continue practicing, be made readily available? Attitudes differ as to whether offenders should ever be allowed to practice again, if counseling for this population is effective, and if putting public resources into this population

is a worthy priority (see Gartrell et al., 1988; Pope, 1987, 1989b, 1994; Schoener, Milgrom, Gonsiorek, Leupker, & Conroe, 1989). In the absence of adequately validated rehabilitation interventions, clients of sexually exploitative therapists could still unknowingly be put at higher risk despite the therapists having completed some rehabilitative procedure.

Rehabilitation potential is probably strongly related to the type of offender. Those who suffer from antisocial or psychopathic personality disorders are not likely to be successful candidates, whereas those who become aware of their improprieties, experience remorse, show a willingness to cease their sexual acting out, and show a desire to explore their motives may be more amenable to change. Butler and Zelen (1977) reported discouraging data. Despite the fears, conflicts, and guilt reported by 95% of their offender sample, most continued their sexual acting out. Psychotherapy was sought by only 40% of their sample. These data, however, were collected before the APA ethics code was revised in 1977 to explicitly exclude sexual intimacies. Raised consciousness and pressure from within the profession may have resulted in increased motivation among offenders to rehabilitate.

Ethics committees sometimes include supervision or referral for therapy among their sanctions. The penalty for violating the code by engaging in sexual intimacies with clients often includes either expulsion from the APA or a forced resignation, with the stipulation that membership may be reinstated, usually after 5 years, if the psychologist can give evidence of rehabilitation. At this time, however, professional associations have not provided clear guidelines or developed programs to assist the psychologists in proving themselves ethically restored.

The question as to whether any psychologist, even those who actively undergo counseling, should ever be allowed to return to a work setting that involves direct services to clients is worth pondering. A judge caught taking a bribe or a preschool teacher convicted of molesting a child will "pay their debts to society" and possibly emerge as better people after rehabilitation, but neither would ever be allowed to resume their previous career (Pope, 1994; Pope

& Vetter, 1991). It is difficult to create solid arguments to justify returning psychotherapists who sexually exploited clients to their former status, especially when supervision during one-on-one therapy sessions is impossible.

The False Allegation

Some psychologists are fearful that they may have to deal with a bogus charge by a client who misunderstood what was said or done. Some clients, as we have already seen, are sensitive to a fault. Gutheil and Gabbard (1993) describe a client who brought charges against a psychologist for conducting therapy with the top two buttons of his shirt undone. The next case also reveals how misunderstandings can result.

Case 9-24: Prudence Pureheart sought treatment with Carl Quizitor, Psy.D., for a severe anxiety disorder. During the course of taking a diagnostic history, Quizitor asked Ms. Pureheart about situations that made her anxious. She mentioned "pressures" from her husband and quickly changed the subject. Dr. Quizitor asked for additional details. Ms. Pureheart haltingly reported sexual acts demanded by her husband. Dr. Quizitor asked a few clarifying questions intended to assist in developing intervention strategies. Ms. Pureheart subsequently complained to a licensing board that he had needlessly embarrassed her by forcing her to discuss these sensitive matters.

Some clients who press bogus ethics charges may be angry, vengeful, antisocial, or severely narcissistic. It is difficult to acknowledge that anyone would unjustly risk destroying a psychologist's professional and personal life with a false accusation of sexual contact, but it has happened in an estimated small percentage of cases (Pope & Vetter, 1991; Schoener et al., 1989). How can psychologists protect themselves against unwarranted claims of sexual impropriety? The following precautions might be considered:

1. Before engaging in any form of nonerotic touching or paying a compliment that could be interpreted as flirtatious or suggestive, thoroughly know your client's psychological functioning and history. As noted above, some clients may remain unsuited to these types of displays for the duration of therapy.

2. If uneasy feelings involving sexual attraction are perceived as emanating from a client, consult a trusted, sensitive, and preferably experienced counselor or colleague to help you work through the proper course of action.

3. Boundary violations of a nonsexual nature (such as taking a client to lunch, giving a client a gift, writing an "affectionate" note) are often taken by professional ethics committees and state licensing boards as presumptive evidence to corroborate allegations of sexual misconduct (Gutheil & Gabbard, 1992). Thus, it is recommended that any act that could conceivably be misconstrued at some later point be entered into one's notes (e.g., "sent flowers for husband's funeral").

4. Avoid offering therapy sessions or seeing clients in other than a professional setting. An office complex in which others are around most of the time is preferable.

5. Avoid a solo practice if at all possible. This suggestion is offered not only because the setting itself is secluded, but also because informal evidence indicates that psychologists in practice by themselves are more likely to feel emotionally isolated and may more easily loosen professional boundaries. (See also the list of "red flags" in chapter 8.)

The reader cannot help but be struck by a sense of frustration at this point. How can one be a caring, helping professional and also avoid any behavior that could be misconstrued or interpreted by someone else as unprofessional or unethical? Slovenko (1991) suggests that one of the consequences of the current climate is a "depersonalization" of therapy, with the therapist sitting defensively behind a desk and no longer coming across as a fellow human being. We believe, however, that competence, sensitivity, and a habit of regularly monitoring each client's treatment needs, as well as one's own responses to each client, will help preclude problems and still allow numerous avenues of expression for caring and compassion.

POSTTERMINATION SEXUAL RELATIONSHIPS WITH CLIENTS

Taken together, available survey data indicate that around 10% of the respondents have entered into sexual relationships with former clients (e.g., Borys & Pope, 1989; Pope et al., 1987, as cited in Pope, 1993). Less than half of the psychologists in Akamatsu's (1988) survey judged sex with ex-clients as a serious ethical problem. After terminating therapy, should two people who are no longer in a professional relationship be "ethically free" to commence a sexual relationship? Are not consenting adults in a democratic society accorded the autonomy to decide with whom they wish to consort? Was client autonomy not a primary goal of the therapy? As Bersoff notes, "Society in general and our professional association in particular should be committed to . . . respecting each individual's right to choose his or her own fate, even if the choices the individual makes do not serve . . . what the majority would consider to be in the individual's best interest" (1994, p. 382). Or, do other issues lurk indefinitely that preclude ever commencing a sexual relationship with an ex-client?

Before 1992, the APA ethics code was silent on the question of posttermination sex with clients, as were most state boards and ethics committees (Sell, Gottlieb, & Schoenfeld, 1986). (Several states—California, Florida, Illinois, Wisconsin, and Minnesota—had, however, formal criminal or civil laws regarding posttermination sex with clients.) Ethics committees did pursue charges prior to 1992 when a complainant made a compelling argument that therapy was terminated irresponsibly and harmful consequences ensued. However, substantiating botched terminations was difficult at best. The next two cases are among those that ethics committees did accept, even before the ethics code did not specifically prohibit posttermination sex with clients.

Case 9-25: Tom Anxious, Ph.D., was sexually attracted to his client Sam Reciprocale. The vibes indicated that Sam felt the same way toward him. Although Sam's treatment issues were far from resolved, Dr. Anxious terminated him without recommending further treatment. Their sexual relationship began shortly after termination. It was brief and unsatisfying to both.

Case 9-26: John Trick, Psy.D., provided counseling services for 7 months to Ashly Swinger, a high-priced call girl. Two weeks after he told Ms. Swinger that she needed no further therapy, he showed up at her door asking to be her client.

Both clients brought ethics charges against their ex-therapists. Reciprocale charged that Anxious maneuvered him into a sexual liaison, and then abandoned him when their relationship did not meet his expectations, leaving Reciprocale considerably more troubled than he had ever been. Ms. Swinger (working in a state where prostitution is legal) argued that she had been pressured to quit therapy and was already upset about that. Then, when Dr. Trick wanted to reverse roles, the issues of self-worth that brought her into therapy were exacerbated. This case is similar to another involving a psychiatric intern who, after treating a patient for alcohol and drug abuse, initiated a posttreatment relationship with the patient. They smoked marijuana and drank alcohol together, and their sexual activity resulted in the ex-patient's becoming pregnant. The court found that the intern's behavior constituted malpractice and intentional infliction of emotional distress because the client's specific vulnerabilities were exploited (*Noto v. St. Vincent's' Hospital and Medical Center of New York*, described in Appelbaum & Jorgenson, 1991).

The 1992 APA ethics code revision team considered the issue of posttermination sex directly. After lengthy debate about how to frame a prohibition, a 2-year posttermination moratorium clause was created, thus placing clear limitations in the short run, but opening the opportunity for sexual relations between ex-therapists and ex-clients without professional repercussion at some point in the future. The standard reads, "Psychologists do not engage in sexual intimacies with a former therapy patient or client for at least 2 years after cessation or termination of professional services" (ES: 4.07a).

While the 1992 APA code was under development, a revision task force argued strongly in favor of prohibiting sex with ex-clients altogether, noting that sometimes sacrifices were necessary to uphold the highest standards of the profession (Vasquez, 1991). Although the APA Council of Representatives failed to issue a lifelong ban on sexual intimacies with former clients, the new code could hardly be said to condone eventual liaisons with clients. An additional standard reads:

> Because sexual intimacies with a former therapy patient or client are so frequently harmful to the patient or client, and because such intimacies undermine public confidence in the psychology profession and thereby deter the public's use of needed services, psychologists do not engage in sexual intimacies with former therapy patients and clients even after a two year interval except in the most unusual circumstances. The psychologist . . . bears the burden of demonstrating that there has been no exploitation. (ES: 4.07b)

The 1992 APA code also includes lists of considerations that should be carefully weighed before embarking on sex with an ex-client. Time passage since termination is the hallmark for the APA code, and psychologists also agree that this is the major consideration, with a longer delay creating less ethical risk (Akamatsu, 1988). Other considerations include the client's current mental status and degree of autonomy, the length and type of therapy, how termination was handled, and what risks may still present themselves were a sexual relationship to commence (ES: 4.07b). Thus, the following complaint would likely be heard by an ethics committee, despite the fact that 2 years had already passed before sexual activity occurred.

Case 9-27: On termination of 9 years of psychotherapy, Mattie Stringalong, Ph.D., suggested that she and Lenny Endure "keep in touch." They exchanged intimate cards and letters, spoke on the phone almost every week, and occasionally met for lunch. After 20 months, Dr. Stringalong informed Endure that their relationship could become intimate soon if he were interested. They eventually married. Endure asked for a divorce a year later, also complaining to a state licensing

board that Dr. Stringalong had been "laying in wait" for him so that she could get her hands on the substantial family fortune.

The sexual activity occurred in the "correct time frame," but the therapist kept an uninterrupted relationship afloat. Even if Dr. Stringalong were not guilty of plotting to gain financially, her active perpetuation of an emotionally charged relationship was unethical.

The 1992 APA code also defines as unethical any statements or actions on the part of the therapist, while therapy was active, that suggested or invited the possibility of an eventual relationship with a client (ES: 4.07b). Had this code been in effect earlier, both Drs. Anxious and Trick (Cases 9-25 and 9-26) would have been guilty of an ethics violation primae facie, without the necessity of forcing complainants to convince anyone that the termination was improper. The next case illustrates a comment just after termination that would also be problematic.

Case 9-28: When Geraldo Futura, Ed.D., and his client Cecelia Sanguine tentatively acknowledged a mutual attraction, Futura allegedly told her that, because of professional ethics, they would not start an affair because he would get into "big trouble." However, during the last session, Futura whispered, "Give me a call in a couple of years."

An ethics committee would not be likely to view this sort of termination as appropriate either. So, what kind of posttermination relationship might be acceptable to an ethics committee? The next case, revealing a chance meeting years later, is an example of the kind of situation that may not be cause for concern to an ethics committee.

Case 9-29: Vasti Maloo signed up with Slim Downe, Ph.D., for a weight reduction program that used behavioral techniques. Ms. Maloo lost her goal of 7 pounds in 3 weeks, and the sessions were terminated by preagreement. After 6 years, Maloo and Dr. Downe found themselves face to face at a party. Maloo had to remind Downe who she was. They talked for a while, learned that each was free to date, and started seeing each other regularly.

It is impossible to predict exactly how an ethics committee would respond to any charge of posttermination sex, even after 2 years have passed. Members of the cohort of APA Council of Representatives who were responsible for approving the 2-year moratorium on sex with former clients held widely divergent opinions about the appropriateness of eventual sexual liaisons as described in the above vignettes, although the majority would have found Case 9-29 to constitute an acceptable liaison (Keith-Spiegel & Lett, 1997).

Anyone who has been extremely attracted to another person knows that passions cannot be effectively put on ice for very long. Data suggest that well over half of the posttermination sexual liaisons between therapists and their clients began quickly, within the first 6 months (Gartrell et al., 1986). If being together is not possible, however, both parties would typically go their own way. Taking human nature into account, those following the provisions of the APA ethics code are unlikely to ever consummate another kind of relationship.

However, serious concerns have been raised about the prudence of instituting the 2-year "cool-off" moratorium for other reasons. The APA stand on posttermination sex may alter the therapy relationship from the onset (Gabbard, 1994; Gabbard & Pope, 1989). If clients are attracted to their therapists (a common occurrence) and aspire to a different kind of relationship down the line, how likely are they to do or say anything that will put them in an unbecoming light? Would what went on during the sessions be psychotherapy or an investment in the future? As Vasquez stated, "The verbal disclosures, behaviors, attitudes, and feelings with a potential lover are quite different from those with a therapist who is clearly and solely a therapist" (1991, p. 48). The therapist's ability to be objective with a client toward whom a strong attraction is felt is also compromised. Even in the absence of any attraction, the possibility that clients could become lovers may contaminate the therapy process in subtle, yet detrimental, ways (Brown, 1988).

Transference and power differentials do not simply evaporate once clients are no longer in active therapy (Brown, 1988). From a psychodynamic perspective, an "internalized therapist" continues to assist a client in coping and integrating processes (Gabbard, 1994; Vasquez, 1991) and in facilitating responses to new situations (Appelbaum & Jorgenson, 1991). Strong transference may persist in some clients for a very long time (Gabbard & Pope, 1989). Such dynamics may well harm clients should they become, even years later, their previous therapists' lovers. Although transference was originally a psychoanalytic term, even therapists using cognitive, behavioral, or other approaches to treatment would often agree that the therapist is imbued by the client with special attributes that convey a kind of emotional authority or influence.

Psychologists' professional responsibilities are not concluded with termination. Continuing client rights to privacy, confidentiality, and privilege remain unaffected by therapy termination. The possibility of record subpoena and resulting court appearances also exists (Gabbard & Pope, 1989). As a result, clients could be severely disadvantaged should they have need of professional services from a therapist who is also a lover (or ex-lover). Psychologists must remain prepared for the responsibility of these continuing duties and carry them out in a context free from conflict and role confusion.

Secondary harm to other than the parties involved can be caused by posttermination sexual relationships. Brown (1988) offered the example of the negative feelings of other therapy group members in a lesbian community when the therapist began dating someone who had once been in the group. Clients in any close-knit or smaller community setting could be vulnerable to the negative feelings of resentment, envy, or heartache when their therapist picks out someone else with whom to form a "special" relationship.

Perhaps what is most controversial about the 2-year moratorium provision is that it suggests to the public that the ethics code for psychologists states that sex with one's psychologist is a viable possibility. The American Psychiatric Association, on the other hand, issued a clear message to the public, voting in 1992 to declare sex with former clients always unethical (American Psychiatric Association, 1992).

TREATING SEXUAL ABUSE BY PREVIOUS THERAPISTS

A harm that befalls clients who have been sexually exploited by previous therapists is the possibility that they may never receive help for the reasons they entered therapy or for the complications caused by the abusing therapists. When trust is broken by one member of a "class," all other members become suspect. It is estimated that a practicing psychologist's chances of encountering at least one client who claims abuse by a previous therapist to be about 50%, and that only a small percentage will be false allegations (Pope, 1994; Pope & Vetter, 1991).

Sonne and Pope (1991) present an array of reactions that psychologists may experience when treating clients who report having been sexually exploited by previous therapists. These include (1) disbelief and denial that a well-trained colleague could have done such a thing and an attendant suspicion that this "disturbed" client could be exaggerating or even lying; (2) a tendency to minimize the amount of harm done, perhaps as a reaction to denial or as a way of protecting a member of one's profession; (3) blaming the victim; (4) experiencing sexual arousal toward the victim; (5) worrying about the possibility that the client will bring charges against the previous therapist and what that will mean in terms of disruptions of one's own work and privacy (e.g., possible interactions with aggressive attorneys, record subpoenas, future interaction with the therapist); (6) having trouble keeping the previous therapist's identity a secret, especially when it is now believed that this still-practicing individual is harmful to the public; (7) taking over decision-making rights by encouraging the client to actively seek (or not seek) redress from an ethics committee, licensing board, or the courts; (8) experiencing vicarious helplessness when a pursued action against the previous therapist meets with stone walls, delays, and seemingly uncaring responses from licensing boards or ethics committees; and (9) serving

as an object of rage, neediness, or ambivalence while the client attempts to sort out feelings about what happened with the previous therapist. All these reactions have critical ethical implications. Consider the next case, based on a collage of actual cases (adapted from Sonne & Pope, 1991).

Case 9-30: A 19 year-old developmentally disabled man sought therapy with Kantbe So, Ph.D., claiming that a previous male therapist had raped him when he was 12 years old as his unsuspecting mother sat in the waiting room. The man claimed that the previous therapist had also undressed him and taken photographs on several occasions. He wanted to "make sure that this does not happen to other boys like him" and declared his interest in pursuing some form of action. The accused therapist was a well-known figure in the community, who had recently served as treasurer of the local psychological association and was seemingly happily married with three teenagers of his own. Furthermore, the accused therapist earned his degree from a highly rated clinical psychology program.

Put yourself in Dr. So's place, and you should be able to identify with many of the reactions to clients abused by a previous therapist. Sonne and Pope conclude that remaining open and sensitive to these common reactions can serve as an information source and as "a stimulus for reflection and consultation" (1991, p. 185). It may help if Dr. So keeps in mind the fact that the acts of the previous therapist, if true, represent a serious ethical, and probably legal, violation regardless of who committed them. Dr. So is obligated to work with her client, although it is probably always best to refer the client to appropriate legal advocates rather than attempt to take on a complaint process alone. Depending on where Dr. So is practicing, she may even be mandated to report the incident to some state agency (see chapter 2).

DELIVERING PSYCHOTHERAPY SERVICES TO FORMER LOVERS

We know virtually nothing about the incidence of accepting former lovers as psychotherapy clients. However, the 1992 APA ethics code prohibits a client-therapist relationship between psychologists and anyone with whom they have previously engaged in any sexually intimate behavior (ES: 4.07).

Case 9-31: Sonja Ex, Psy.D., agreed to see Dennis Didit as a client, even though 4 years previously they had an intense romantic relationship that lasted for several months. Despite Dr. Ex's revelation that she was happily married, Didit started recalling lustful moments from their past and making suggestive remarks to her during the therapy sessions. Dr. Ex terminated Didit because, as she told him, "You are not taking therapy seriously." Didit wrote to an ethics committee, complaining that Dr. Ex "took me for $450 before tossing me out as revenge for having dumped her 4 years ago."

Dr. Ex declared that she only agreed to see Didit because he seemed so sad and claimed that he had nowhere else to turn. She vigorously denied any interest in revenge. Accepting him as a client in the first place, however, was a serious and imprudent error in professional judgment. A sexually intimate background is not a foundation on which an objective therapeutic alliance can be built. Dr. Ex could have assisted Didit by making appropriate referrals.

SEXUAL RELATIONSHIPS WITH "SIGNIFICANT OTHERS" OF PSYCHOTHERAPY CLIENTS

Little has been written specifically about sexual involvement with the sisters, brothers, adult children, parents, or very close friends of current psychotherapy clients, and the 1992 APA ethics code does not address the matter specifically. These types of cases, which we might compare to the movie plot of *The Prince of Tides*, are becoming increasingly frequent.

Case 9-32: A client abruptly terminated therapy and complained to the state licensing board on learning that Rob Cradle, Psy.D., was "sleeping with my baby girl." Although the daughter was 25 years old, the parent-client felt betrayed by Cradle.

The client assumed that Cradle was sharing everything she said in therapy with her daughter and maybe they were even laughing about her after they made love.

In this case, the psychologist did know when the relationship began that his current lover was the daughter of a client, but reasoned that because the daughter was not his client and because the two were consenting adults, no ethical matter was at issue. However, it should have been obvious to Dr. Cradle that the ethic admonishing psychologists to refrain from entering into relationships "if it appears likely that such a relationship reasonably might impair the psychologist's objectivity or otherwise interfere with the psychologist's effectively performing his or her functions as a psychologist" (ES: 1.17) applied to him and this situation.

Case 9-33: Wadya Wannado, Ph.D., a clinical child psychologist, treated Billy Boyster on an outpatient basis. Billy, age 7, was showing signs of an adjustment disorder in reaction to his parents' deteriorating marriage. Dr. Wannado saw Billy individually on a weekly basis for several months and met jointly and individually with his parents on three or four occasions to provide "parent guidance" in dealing with Billy's problems. Soon after Billy's therapy was terminated, the relationship with Billy's mother became sexually intimate. The father filed an ethics complaint against Dr. Wannado, who responded that he was doing nothing wrong because he was no longer seeing Billy and the mother was never a client.

When the client is a child, it is therapeutically and ethically critical to consider the family as the unit of treatment. Although Dr. Wannado's clinical attention was focused on Billy, it was the parents who legally contracted with him for professional services. In addition, meeting with the parents in any professional capacity, whether termed "child guidance" or simply consultation, constitutes a psychologist-client relationship. Dr. Wannado owes ethical obligations to Billy and both parents equally just as though each were individual therapy clients. The fact that Dr. Wannado had ended treatment with Billy does not end the professional obligations to the boy. Even after divorce, children harbor fantasies of parental reunion. It is likely that Billy will feel ambivalent, if not outright betrayed, by the invasion of the therapist into the relationship between his parents. Dr. Wannado's conduct is particularly reprehensible as it intrudes adversely into the relationships of three people undergoing a difficult transition, who were all owed duties as clients.

RISKS TO STUDENTS AND THEIR PROFESSORS AND SUPERVISORS

Professors engaging in sexual liaisons with their young, nubile students are as durable an academic stereotype as are ivy, football, tower clocks, caps and gowns, and founder statues in the quad. Aristides describes the allure of the professor as "the man with the most knowledge in the room where knowledge is the only business of the hour, a figure of authority, confidence, intellectual grace—an object, if he does his work even half-well, of love" (1975, p. 361). Professors are surrounded by a perpetual bevy of attractive young people who treat them with respect, deference, and even a touch of awe. The academic environment is one in which some students and some professors will be tempted to enter into romantic relationships based on a variety of motivations, which run the gambit from gaining some future advantage or sexual fulfillment to true love. Indeed, most of us know professors who married one of their students.

However, times have changed, and institutions of higher education have been taking more vigorous stands to discourage educators from dating students. This stems neither from prudishness nor pressure from feminists. Rather, the increase in sexual harassment charges against professors, sometimes resulting in lawsuits (and sometimes countersuits by the accused professors) have created an economic motivation to deter such relationships. (Sexual harassment, not necessarily involving actual sexual intimacies, is examined in chapter 13.)

The ethical issues are about abuse of power and conflict of interest more than about sex per se. Whereas policies across the country fall short of an outright ban on all student-professor dating, most campuses have rules that prohibit, restrict, or strongly discourage professors from dating students over whom they have the power of evaluation, such as the students in one's class, advisees for a thesis or dissertation, and clinical supervisees. Although male professors and female students remain the prevalent pairing, as more women enter higher education as educators, as more older people return to the classroom as students, and as scattered cases of gay and lesbian student-faculty relationships surface, a discussion of dating students can no longer be exclusively confined to male professors and 18- to 22-year-old female students.

Whereas opponents to the ban on sexual relationships with psychotherapy clients are no longer to be found—at least not out in the open—vocal critics of bans on romantic and sexual relationships among faculty and students remain highly visible. A group called Consenting Academics for Sexual Equity argues that prohibitions against student-professor sex infantalizes students and creates an atmosphere of paranoia that will cause professors to be less accessible to students (Gibbs, 1995). Others have declared that those who have reached their 18th birthdays can be with whomever they please on their own time. It must be noted, however, that restrictions designed to prevent conflict of interest in the workplace may legitimately extend to university settings and thereby not infringe on constitutionally guaranteed privacy rights (Mooney, 1993).

Regardless of the debate, we doubt that anyone would openly approve of clearly coerced sexual activity, such as the case below illustrates.

Case 9-34: Cloris Push, Ed.D., made numerous suggestive remarks to her student, Sam Shun, and implied that the closer their personal relationship was the more likely Shun's path to successful completion of his degree program. Although Shun was not particularly attracted to Professor Push, he believed that rejecting her advances would endanger his grade.

Prohibitions against sexual encounters between professors or supervisors and their students or trainees were not explicitly included in the APA code until 1992. Such relationships are now recognized as "likely to be exploitative and to impair judgment" (ES: 1.19b). Previously, student complaints could be activated, but it was the responsibility of the complainant to convince the committee members that she (or, very rarely, he) had been disadvantaged, harmed, or sexually harassed. However, if the psychologist being charged has (or had at the time of the incident) evaluative or direct authority over the student, that burden of proof is no longer required.

A now-classic nationwide survey of psychologists by Pope et al. (1979) revealed that 10% of the respondents reported having had sexual contact, as students, with their educators, and 13% reported entering into sexual relationships, as educators, with their students. Gender differences were significant, mirroring both a traditional academic image and the difference trends in client-therapist sexual encounters; that is, 16.5% of the women and 3% of the men reported sexual contact with their educators when they were students, and 19% of the men, compared with 8% of the women, reported sexual contact with their students. Moreover, when these students became psychotherapists, 12% of the males and 3% of the females reported sexual contact with their clients, which was a slightly higher percentage for both sexes than revealed from other surveys of therapists taken during that era. In addition, student-educator sexual relationships appeared to be on the increase. Of the recent female graduates, 25% reported having had sexual contact with their educators, compared with 5% of those who had earned their degrees more than 21 years before the survey was conducted.

Other research has replicated both the extent of sexual relationships with psychologist educators or supervisors, as well as the later judgment that such involvement was detrimental to them. In Robinson and Reid's (1985) survey, 96% of their female respondents who had experienced sexual contact or sexual harassment as students believed that the relationship was harmful to one or both parties. Glaser and Thorpe (1986) found that 17% of their respondents had sexual contact with their psychology educators as students, a little over a third of these with clinical

supervisors. Interestingly, whereas only 28% of the respondents felt coerced at the time, their attitudes about the relationships became far more negative in retrospect.

How serious are the ramifications of consensual sexual relationships between educators and their students or supervisees? On the surface, it may appear that those who are concerned about sexual relationships between educators and their adult students are paternalistic moralists intruding in matters that are simply none of their business. On the other hand, it should be recognized that students and educators may not be in touch with their own highly vulnerable positions when their relationships become sexual. Further, as Bartell and Rubin observe, "mutuality is not a license for unethical behavior" (1990, p. 445).

The question has been raised as to whether students can give consent to persons who have, or are believed to have, authority, evaluative, or other power over them. Many say that because of the unequal status, coupled with the potential for negative consequences should the more powerful educator decide to exercise it, completely voluntary consent is not possible (Quatrella & Wentworth, 1995; Zalk, Paludi, & Dederick, 1990). We know of a case in which a student felt coerced to stay in a relationship with a professor even though he was not in any direct line of authority over her. She saw him chatting and laughing casually in the halls with other professors who taught courses she was currently taking. She assumed that if the professor she was dating became upset, he might harm her status by saying negative things about her to his colleagues, who would, in turn, use the information against her.

When the affairs of students and their educators go awry, the effects must be reckoned with in both the private and professional realms. Emotional fallout can include grief, embarrassment, fear, bitterness, and a desire for vengeance. When these feelings are superimposed on the academic role, serious consequences for students, professors, or both can ensue. In the extreme, professors who see themselves as perpetually powerful and entitled to enjoying students in whatever way is satisfying can, almost overnight, be reduced to the target of snide gossip and administrative or legal sanctions. Professors are far more vulnerable than therapists in the sense that psychotherapy clients are usually without access to other clients' identities and have trouble corroborating the offender's behavior pattern. Students, on the other hand, have ready access to each other, leaving the exploitative educator open to "group charges," with a considerably greater probability for exposure and ultimate censure. Also, students do not have to contact off-campus licensing boards or ethics committees. On most campuses, mechanisms for redress are readily available within walking distance. Other mechanisms remain available if the student is not satisfied with the campus response.

Case 9-35: After an affair between Gary Goferit, Ph.D., and Paula Jettison had ended, Jettison filed charges against Goferit for sexual harassment and exploitation. She also contacted the local papers, who ran the story. She was joined by several other students, who claimed that they, too, had been harassed and exploited by Goferit. Ultimately, Dr. Goferit lost his wife and job.

The contemporary popular press relishes stories like this, and even sophisticated academic publications, such as the *Chronicle of Higher Education*, feature them regularly. We collected scores of articles from the popular press, several involving psychology educators, from which to adapt our cases for this chapter.

Students are also more vulnerable than they may appreciate. At the time, some may see their relationship with professors as exciting and putting them on the fast rungs up the career ladder, only to later find themselves discarded and frozen out.

Case 9-36: Dexter Jerky, Ph.D., had been having frequent sexual liaisons with one of his graduate assistants, Mary Switch, for almost a year. Then, Switch met a young man she wished to date exclusively. When she told Professor Jerky that their affair was over, he allegedly became furious and expressed his intention to punish her. She was abruptly relieved of her assistantship. She heard rumors that Dr. Jerky was telling other faculty members that she was fired for gross incompetence

and was not "graduate school material." When Switch confronted Jerky, he allegedly told her that this was only the beginning. He had status and clout in the field, and if she chose to stay in psychology, she would find it very uncomfortable.

Students may believe professors to be wise and so mature that a vicious retaliation would not be in their repertoire. However, Dr. Jerky is not an isolated case. Scorned lovers, regardless of their IQ or position, may respond with every means at their disposal. Other students may feel too intimidated to complain because of their inherently weaker position. They may fear risking their professional futures, as in the case involving the vengeful Professor Jerky. Although a psychotherapy client could be harmed by a therapist, the client's career would rarely also be at stake. Students risk damage to themselves in both personal and longer term career terms.

The next case illustrates another unfortunate pattern.

Case 9-37: Selma Long, a serious graduate student with high professional aspirations, greatly admired psychology professor Irving Idol, Ph.D. She took every advantage of opportunities to interact with him. Although she did not aspire to having an affair at first, he began to insist on more intimate liaisons. However, as the relationship evolved, Long fell in love with Dr. Idol. She envisioned a life with him both as coworker and love partner. When she verbalized her fantasies, Dr. Idol turned cold. He told her that she had misunderstood his motives, and he had no long-range intentions. He suggested that, due to their mismatched needs, they should no longer work together. Long was so abashed that she could not face him at school. She dropped out of the degree program and never returned to complete her education.

Long represents a potentially larger group of students about whom we know very little. It takes a certain assertiveness that Long lacked to make a formal complaint, and she simply disappeared. She bore some responsibility in that she did have options, but a prized student who was not of sexual interest to Dr. Idol would never have to face such a conflict. Long's story is similar to several that have come to our attention over the years. In the actual case, "Dr. Idol" quickly moved on to his next student collaborator, unaware of the life he had disrupted so extensively, although even had he known of Long's fate it is not clear that he would have cared.

Academia provides the environment in which the faculty and supervisors are supposed to facilitate the intellectual, career, ethical, and personal development of students and supervisees. The intrusion of sexuality—which is always potentially volatile—into this fundamentally vital process is diametrically opposed to the mission of higher education. Even when relationships work out better (or end more gently) than the ones we have presented above, serious concerns still persist. First, we must ask the question, What are these students learning? It seems to us that they are learning that it is acceptable for psychologists to gratify their needs under whatever circumstances they choose, with minimal regard for maintaining objectivity and clarity in professional relationships with those over whom they have substantial power, influence, and responsibility.

Sexual relationships also compromise the process of assigning unbiased and valid evaluations. Thus, sexual intimacies with students undermine the obligation to evaluate students fairly and accurately (Blevins-Knabe, 1992; Keith-Spiegel, Tabachnick, & Allen, 1993; Pope, Schover, & Levenson, 1980; Slimp & Burian, 1994). Further, students may alter their academic behavior in ways that will inhibit or distort their learning. For example, a supervisee may not feel free to discuss sexual feelings toward clients for fear that a supervisor will interpret that line of discussion as a "come-on" (Bartell & Rubin, 1990; Pope et al., 1986).

The impact on the other students, which also affects departmental morale, needs to be considered when dating any student in the same department or graduate program. Regardless of any safeguards taken, the perception among other students will likely be that favoritism is somehow operating.

Case 9-38: Robbie Open, Ph.D., and graduate student Chuck Out could not conceal their relationship with each other in the small college town.

Despite their attempts to be discreet, the other students in the department suspected that Out was receiving a great many advantages besides being Open's lover. They believed that Out would be getting outstanding letters of recommendation and considerable help finding a job. In addition, Professor Open would surely attempt to influence his professional contacts to ensure that Out had the best opportunities.

Other students may overestimate what a single faculty member can do to convince colleagues to support a particular student, but the perception that Open may go overboard in advocating Out's future may well be accurate. Students greatly resent a "tilted playing field" when it comes to academic evaluation and opportunity and believe such biases to be among the most unethical acts that professors can commit (Keith-Spiegel, Tabachnick, et al., 1993).

The awkward status of the graduate teaching assistant (GTA) also deserves mention. When still a student, and yet also an instructor, what rules apply? Can the GTA date any "fellow" students? Can the GTA date "colleagues?" Or, is the GTA off limits to both populations? Again, casual observation reveals that graduate teaching assistants often date individuals from both groups. However, because many of the problems we have presented thus far apply to graduate assistants, we urge that, as an employee of an institution, the graduate teaching assistant follow the same policy expected of faculty: to refrain from dating anyone over whom you have evaluative authority or who has authority over you, thus defusing even an appearance of favoritism or conflict of interest. Otherwise, things can get messy.

Case 9-39: Caleb Grayplace, a graduate teaching assistant, was attracted to an undergraduate student in his introductory psychology course. He reasoned that because they were both students, openly dating each other was acceptable. He did inform her that she was not doing that well in the class, and that he would have to give her the grade she earned; he assumed that would take care of any possible misunderstanding. However, other students saw the two together often and began to made snide remarks to the young woman. When the student got a C in the class, she complained to Grayplace, who reminded her of his earlier warning. She screamed at him in the halls, complaining that he had damaged her reputation, as well as her GPA, causing a scene that was the topic of campus conversation for weeks.

Grayplace's supervisor and other faculty members informed him that he used very poor judgment in dating the student. Although Grayplace surely learned a lesson, it is likely that the letters of recommendation for future employment from the faculty in his department may be somewhat cautious or dampened. We would also note that the department and institution deserve some criticism as well. There was no indication that Grayplace had received proper orientation to his new position, which should have included discussions of multiple role conflicts.

We have often heard the remark that one's undergraduate students should be off limits for dating, but graduate students are acceptable and fair game. Survey data reveal that professor and graduate student liaisons are perceived as more ethically acceptable (Quatrella & Wentworth, 1995; Skinner et al., 1995). These beliefs are likely based on the assumed higher maturity level of graduate students. The fact is, however, that graduate students are likely put at greater risk than are undergraduates (Blevins-Knabe, 1992). Undergraduate students, even if exploited and scorned, have the option of moving to a new campus for graduate training. Undergraduates may have lost a good reference if an affair goes awry, but letters from other professors could make up for that. Graduate students often do not have many options. Because advanced programs typically have fewer teaching faculty in a given graduate specialty area (e.g., cognitive therapy), a highly desirable reference letter for jobs or continued training, funding decisions, and research opportunities (which are necessary to compete for jobs in academia) could be unavailable should the relationship go stale or end badly. Even if the relationship persists, the animosity other students might feel could have longer term implications. For example, peers in graduate school often become valuable contacts later on, though not for resented classmates. Finally, in the worst case scenario, if the sexual

liaison is with the student's major professor, there would be no place to turn should the relationship sour.

The 1992 APA code is also silent on whether professors in the same department can date students they will never likely teach or evaluate. The wording seems to imply that liaisons outside of the line of authority or evaluation could be acceptable. How far the concept of evaluation and authority extends is also not made clear in the APA ethics code. It could be interpreted as very encompassing, including all department chairs and any faculty member who sits on awards or other departmental or school committees that create policy or make decisions that could have an impact on the student.

Finally, can ex-students and teaching or supervising psychologists link as romantic partners in a way that is ethically acceptable? The APA code is silent about former students, and casual observation on any campus reveals that some students and their educators do eventually get together and sometimes commit to long-term relationships. The dynamics of therapy and student-supervisory relationships are somewhat different, with the latter typically being less intense and, when concluded, ushering the absolute closing of an era. Indeed, the ex-student and ex-professor roles often begin to overlap and even reverse with time, as when our former professors actively seek us out for help or even to teach them something! Nevertheless, under some circumstances educators who date their former students may still need to be sensitive to lingering fallout that continues to reverberate within the department. The next case (adapted from Keith-Spiegel, Wittig, Perkins, Balogh, & Whitley, 1993) illustrates the kind of problem that can materialize.

Case 9-40: Will Waite graduated with a B.A. degree and entered the Counseling Psychology master's program in the same department. Carrie Free, Ph.D., started dating Mr. Waite. As a physiological psychologist, she would be having no further direct line of authority over Waite. However, Waite would accompany Dr. Free to department faculty parties and other social events that included Waite's teachers. The members of the counseling faculty were uncomfortable with Waite's presence, figuring they had to watch everything they said, and they did not dare relax and have a good time.

Dr. Free should have been more sensitive to the relevant issues, at least as long as Waite remained a student in the department. Psychologists should always assess the impact that such liaisons will have on other students and colleagues besides themselves.

SUMMARY GUIDELINES

1. Whereas sexual attractions to clients and students appear to be, in and of themselves, a common occurrence, professional and ethical responsibilities require careful assessment, possible consultation, and restraint from acting on such attractions.
2. Psychologists should be aware of their vulnerabilities when it comes to sexual attraction. They should be able to recognize when these feelings are manifesting themselves in a professional relationship and seek consultation.
3. The kindness, passivity, adoration, and vulnerability of clients must never be exploited for personal gratification. Similarly, transference or therapist idealization should be recognized and never manipulated to fulfill the therapist's personal needs for power, love, or respect.
4. Touching clients is not necessarily unethical and may even be helpful in some circumstances. However, psychologists must carefully assess the appropriateness of touching clients, recognizing that there are considerable individual differences and varying perceptions about the meaning of touching and being touched. Some clients may remain unsuited for touching under any circumstance.
5. Touching intended for erotic gratification of the client or therapist is unethical.
6. Sexual intercourse and other sexually intimate acts with ongoing clients are unprofessional and constitute a serious ethical (and possibly legal) violation.
7. Just because a client (or student or supervisee) initiated a romantic or sexual element into the professional relationship does not in any way absolve the therapist (or teacher or supervisor) from maintaining professional standards.
8. Sexual relationships with ex-clients have such a high potential for a number of risks to manifest themselves that they are strongly discouraged despite the option included in the APA ethics code.
9. Psychologists should take preventive steps to avoid misunderstandings and erotically risky situations. These can include sharing, at the onset of therapy, consumer guides regarding sexually intimate behavior with clients and ensuring that the therapeutic environment is physically comfortable but businesslike.
10. Psychologists who treat clients who have been sexually exploited by previous therapists should fully understand the dynamics and reactions that will likely arise and be prepared to keep the client's best interests paramount.
11. Psychologists should not become therapists for their ex-lovers or others with whom they have had close relationships because objectivity has already been compromised.
12. Sexual intimacies with students over whom one has (or may have) evaluative responsibilities are unethical. Unsuccessful relationship outcomes are likely and have resulted in serious consequences for students, supervisees, and psychologists.
13. Teaching psychologists and supervisors should ensure that the students receive sufficient course work in the areas of sexual attraction and sexual intimacies with clients. Attraction feelings should not be interpreted as a therapeutic error, thus chilling the climate for discussing these feelings during supervision.

References

Akamatsu, T. J. (1988). Intimate relationships with former clients: National survey of attitudes and behavior among practitioners. *Professional Psychology: Research and Practice, 19,* 454–458.

American Psychiatric Association. (1992, December 4). Assembly takes strong stance on patient-doctor sex. *Psychiatric News, 1,* 20.

American Psychological Association. (1992). Ethical principles of psychologists and code of conduct. *American Psychologist, 47,* 1597–1611.

Anderson, W. (1986). Stages of comfort with sexual concerns of clients. *Professional Psychology: Research and Practice, 17,* 352–356.

Appelbaum, P. S., & Jorgenson, J. D. (1991). Psychotherapist-patient sexual contact after termination of treatment: An analysis and a proposal. *American Journal of Psychiatry, 148,* 1466–1473.

Aristides. (1975). Life and letters: Sex and the professors. *American Scholar, 44,* 357–363.

Barnhouse, R. T. (1978). Sex between patient and therapist. *Journal of the American Academy of Psychoanalysis, 6,* 533–546.

Bartell, P. A., & Rubin, L. J. (1990). Dangerous liaisons: Sexual intimacies in supervision. *Professional Psychology: Research and Practice, 21,* 442–450.

Bates, C. M., & Brodsky, A. M. (1989). *Sex in the therapy hour: A case of professional incest.* New York: Guilford.

Bennett, B. E., Bryant, B. K., Vandenbos, G. R., & Greenwood, A. (1990). *Professional liability and risk management.* Washington, DC: American Psychological Association.

Bersoff, D. N. (1994). Explicit ambiguity: The 1992 ethics code as an oxymoron. *Professional Psychology: Research and Practice, 25,* 382–387.

Blevins-Knabe, B. (1992). The ethics of dual relationships in higher education. *Ethics and Behavior, 2,* 151–163.

Borys, D., & Pope, K. S. (1989). Dual relationships between therapist and client: A national study of psychologists, psychiatry, and social workers. *Professional Psychology: Research and Practice, 20,* 283–293.

Bouhoutsos, J., Holroyd, J., Lerman, H., Forer, B., & Greenburg, M. (1983). Sexual intimacy between psychotherapists and patients. *Professional Psychology: Research, Theory and Practice, 14,* 185–196.

Brodsky, A. M. (1989). Sex between patient and therapist: Psychology's data and response. In G. O. Gabbard (Ed.), *Sexual exploitation in professional relationships* (pp. 15–25). Washington, DC: American Psychiatric Press.

Brown, L. S. (1988). Harmful effects of posttermination sexual and romantic relationships between therapists and their former clients. *Psychotherapy, 25,* 249–255.

Butler, S., & Zelen, S. L. (1977). Sexual intimacies between therapists and patients. *Psychotherapy: Theory, Research and Practice, 14,* 139–145.

Chesler, P. (1972). *Women and madness.* New York: Doubleday.

Committee on Women in Psychology. (1989). If sex enters into the psychotherapy relationship. *Professional Psychology: Research and Practice, 20,* 112–115.

Dahlberg, C. C. (1970). Sexual contact between patient and therapist. *Contemporary Psychoanalysis, 6,* 107–124.

Deaton, R. J., Illingworth, P. M., & Bursztajn, H. J. (1992). Unanswered questions about the criminalization of therapist-patient sex. *American Journal of Psychotherapy, 46,* 526–531.

Disciplinary actions. (1997, Jan.–Feb.). *The California Therapist,* 33.

Feldman-Summers, S. (1989). Sexual contact in fiduciary relationships. In G. O. Gabbard (Ed.), *Sexual exploitation in professional relationships* (pp. 193–209). Washington, DC: American Psychiatric Press.

Folman, R. Z. (1991). Therapist-patient sex: Attraction and boundary problems. *Psychotherapy, 28,* 168–185.

Forer, B. R. (1981, August). *Sources of distortion in the therapeutic relationship.* Paper presented at the annual meeting of the American Psychological Association, Los Angeles.

Freeman, L., & Roy, J. (1976). *Betrayal.* New York: Stein & Day.

Gabbard, G. O. (1994). Reconsidering the American Psychological Association's policy on sex with former patients: Is it justifiable? *Professional Psychology: Research and Practice, 25,* 329–335.

Gabbard, G. O., & Lester, E. P. (1995). *Boundaries and boundary violations in psychoanalysis.* New York: Basic Books.

Gabbard, G. O., & Pope, K. S. (1989). Sexual intimacies after termination: clinical, ethical, and legal aspects. In G. O. Gabbard (Ed.), *Sexual exploitation in professional relationships* (pp. 116–127). Washington, DC: American Psychiatric Press.

Gartrell, N., Herman, J., Olarte, S., Feldstein, M., & Localio, R. (1986). Psychiatrist-patient sexual contact: Results of a national survey, I: prevalence. *American Journal of Psychiatry, 143,* 1126–1130.

Gartrell, N., Herman, J., Olarte, S., Feldstein, M., & Localio, R. (1988). Management and rehabilitation of sexually exploitive therapists. *Hospital and Community Psychiatry, 39,* 1070–1074.

Gartrell, N., Herman, J., Olarte, S., Feldstein, M., & Localio, R. (1989). Prevalence of psychiatrist-patient sexual contact. In G. O. Gabbard (Ed.), *Sexual exploitation in professional relationships* (pp. 4–13). Washington, DC: American Psychiatric Press.

Gibbs, N. (1995, April 3) Romancing the student. *Time,* 58–59.

Glaser, R. D., & Thorpe, J. S. (1986). Unethical intimacy: A survey of sexual contact and advances between psychology educators and female graduate students. *American Psychologist, 41,* 43–51.

Gottlieb, M., Sell, J. M., & Schoenfeld, L. S. (1988). Social/romantic relationships with present and former clients: State licensing board actions. *Professional Psychology: Research and Practice, 19,* 459–462.

Gutheil, T. G. (1989). Borderline personality disorder, boundary violations, and patient-therapist sex: Medicolegal pitfalls. *American Journal of Psychiatry, 146,* 597–602.

Gutheil, T. G., & Gabbard, G. O. (1992). Obstacles to the dynamic understanding of therapist-patient sexual relations. *American Journal of Psychotherapy, 46,* 515–525.

Gutheil, T. C., & Gabbard, G. O. (1993). The concept of boundaries in clinical practice: Theoretical and risk-management dimensions. *American Journal of Psychiatry, 150,* 188–196.

Hall, J. E. (1987). Gender-related ethical dilemmas and ethics education. *Professional Psychology: Research and Practice, 18,* 573–579.

Holroyd, J., & Bouhoutsos, J. C. (1985). Biased reporting of therapist-patient sexual intimacy. *Professional Psychology: Research and Practice, 16,* 701–709.

Holroyd, J. C., & Brodsky, A. M. (1977). Psychologists' attitudes and practices regarding erotic and nonerotic physical contact with patients. *American Psychologist, 32,* 843–849.

Holroyd, J. C., & Brodsky, A. M. (1980). Does touching patients lead to sexual intercourse? *Professional Psychology: Research, Theory and Practice, 11,* 807–811.

Holub, E. A., & Lee, S. S. (1990). Therapists' use of nonerotic physical contact: Ethical concerns. *Professional Psychology: Research and Practice, 21,* 115–117.

Jones, E. (1957). *Life and work of Sigmund Freud* (Vol. 3). New York: Basic Books.

Kardener, S. H. (1974). Sex and the physician-patient relationship. *American Journal of Psychiatry, 131,* 1134–1136.

Kardener, S. H., Fuller, M., & Mensh, I. (1973). A survey of physicians' attitudes and practices regarding erotic and nonerotic contact with patients. *American Journal of Psychiatry, 130,* 1077–1081.

Keith-Spiegel, P., & Koocher, G. P. (1985). *Ethics in psychology: Standards and cases.* New York: Random House.

Keith-Spiegel, P., & Lett, R. (1996). The 2 Year moratorium on sex with ex-clients: How do the psychologists who adopted it interpret it? Ball State University, Unpulished paper.

Keith-Spiegel, P., Tabachnick, B. G., & Allen, M. (1993). Ethics in academia: Students views of professors' actions. *Ethics and Behavior, 3,* 149–162.

Keith-Spiegel, P., Wittig, A. F., Perkins, D. V., Balogh, D. W., & Whitley, B. E. (1993). *The ethics of teaching: A casebook.* Muncie, IN: Ball State University.

Kertay, L., & Reviere, S. L. (1993). The use of touch in psychotherapy: Theoretical and ethical considerations. *Psychotherapy, 30,* 32–40.

Kluft, R. P. (1989). Treating the patient who has been sexually exploited by a previous therapist. *Psychiatric Clinics of North America, 12,* 483–499.

Marmor, J. (1972). Sexual acting-out in psychotherapy. *American Journal of Psychoanalysis, 22,* 3–8.

Masters, W. H., & Johnson, V. E. (1976). Principles of the new sex therapy. *American Journal of Psychiatry, 110,* 3370–3373.

Mooney, C. J. (1993, April 14). U. of Virginia eyes formally banning student-faculty sex. *Chronicle of Higher Education,* A21.

Noel, B., & Watterson, K. (1992). *You must be dreaming.* New York: Poseidon.

Notman, M. T., & Nadelson, C. C. (1994). Psychotherapy with patients who have had sexual relations with a previous therapist. *Journal of Psychotherapy Practice and Research*, 3, 185–193.

Olarte, S. W. (1991). Characteristics of therapists who become involved in sexual boundary violations. *Psychiatric Annals*, 21, 657–660.

Plasil, E. (1985). *Therapist*. New York: St. Martin's/ Marek.

Pope, K. S. (1987). Preventing therapist-patient sexual intimacy: Therapy for a therapist at risk. *Professional Psychology: Research and Practice*, 18, 624–628.

Pope, K. S. (1989a). Therapist-patient sex syndrome: A guide for attorneys and subsequent therapists to assessing damage. In G. Gabbard (Ed.), *Sexual exploitation in professional relationships* (pp. 39–55). Washington, DC: American Psychiatric Press.

Pope, K. S. (1989b). Therapists who become sexually intimate with a patient: Classifications, dynamics, recidivism and rehabilitation. *Independent Practitioner*, 9, 28–34.

Pope, K. S. (1990a). Therapist-patient sex as sex abuse: Six scientific, professional, and practical dilemmas in addressing victimization and rehabilitation. *Professional Psychology: Research and Practice*, 21, 227–239.

Pope, K. S. (1990b). Therapist-patient sexual involvement: A review of the research. *Clinical Psychology Review*, 10, 477–490.

Pope, K. S. (1993). Licensing disciplinary actions for psychologists who have been sexually involved with a client: Some information about offenders. *Professional Psychology: Research and Practice*, 24, 374–377.

Pope, K. S. (1994). *Sexual involvement with therapists: Patient assessment, subsequent therapy, forensics*. Washington, DC: American Psychological Association.

Pope, K. S., & Bouhoutsos, J. C. (1986). *Sexual intimacy between therapists and patients*. New York: Praeger.

Pope, K. S., Keith-Spiegel, P., & Tabachnick, B. G. (1986). Sexual attraction to clients: The human therapist and the (sometimes) inhuman training system. *American Psychologist*, 34, 682–689.

Pope, K. S., Levenson, H., & Schover, L. R. (1979). Sexual intimacy in psychology training. *American Psychologist*, 34, 682–689.

Pope, K. S., Schover, L. R., & Levenson, H. (1980).

Sexual behavior between clinical supervisors and trainees: Implications for professional standards. *Professional Psychology: Research, Theory and Practice*, 11, 157–162.

Pope, K. S., Sonne, J. L., & Holroyd, J. (1993). *Sexual feelings in psychotherapy*. Washington, DC: American Psychological Association.

Pope, K. S., & Tabachnick, B. G. (1993). Therapists' anger, hate, fear, and sexual feelings: National survey of therapist responses, client characteristics, critical events, formal complaints, and training. *Professional Psychology: Research and Practice*, 24, 142–152.

Pope, K. S., Tabachnick, B. G., & Keith-Spiegel, P. (1987). Ethics of practice: The beliefs and behaviors of psychologists as therapists. *American Psychologist*, 42, 993–1006.

Pope, K. S., & Vetter, V. A. (1991). Prior therapist-patient sexual involvement among patients seen by psychologists. *Psychotherapy*, 28, 429–437.

Quatrella, L. A., & Wentworth, K. (1995). Student's perceptions of unequal status dating relationships in academia. *Ethics and Behavior*, 5, 249–258.

Raimo, A. M. (1985). Therapist-patient sex: Legal and ethical implications. *American Journal of Forensic Psychology*, 3, 13–33.

Robinson, W. L., & Reid, P. T. (1985). Sexual intimacies in psychology revisited. *Professional Psychology: Research and Practice*, 16, 512–520.

Scheller, M. D. (1993, Jan.–Feb.). To touch or not to touch? *The California Therapist*, 49–51.

Schoener, G. R., Milgrom, J. H., Gonsiorek, J. C., Leupker, E. T., & Conroe, R. M. (Eds.). (1989). *Psychotherapists' sexual involvement with clients: Intervention and prevention*. Minneapolis, MN: Walk-In Counseling Center.

Schwendinger, J. R., & Schwendinger, H. (1974). Rape myths in legal, theoretical, and everyday practice. *Crime and Social Justice*, 1, 18–26.

Sell, J. M., Gottlieb, M. C., & Schoenfeld, L. (1986). Ethical considerations of social/romantic relationships with present and former clients. *Professional Psychology: Research and Practice*, 17, 504–508.

Simon, R. I. (1991). Psychological injury caused by boundary violation precursors to therapist-patient sex. *Contemporary Psychiatry*, 21, 614–619.

Skinner, L. J., Giles, M. K., Griffith, S. E., Sontag, M. E., Berry, K., & Beck, R. (1995). Academic sexual intimacy violations: Ethicality and occurrence reports from undergraduates. *The Journal of Sex Research, 32*, 131–143.

Slimp, A. O., & Burian, B. K. (1994). Multiple role relationships during internship: Consequences and recommendations. *Professional Psychology: Research and Practice, 25*, 39–45.

Slovenko, R. (1991). Undue familiarity or undue damages? *Psychiatric Annals, 21*, 598–610.

Solursh, D. S., & Solursh, L. P. (1993). Patient-therapist sex: "Just say no" isn't enough. *Medicine and Law, 12*, 431–438.

Sonne, J. L., & Pope, K. S. (1991). Treating victims of therapist-patient sexual involvement. *Psychotherapy, 28*, 174–187.

Stake, J. E., & Oliver, J. (1991). Sexual contact and touching between therapist and client: A survey of psychologists' attitudes and behavior. *Professional Psychology: Research and Practice, 22*, 297–307.

Strasburger, L. H., Jorgenson, L., & Randles, R. (1990). Mandatary reporting of sexually exploitative psychotherapists. *Bulletin of the American Academy of Psychiatry and the Law, 18*, 379–384.

Strasburger, L. H., Jorgenson, L., & Randles, R. (1991). Criminalization of psychotherapist-patient sex. *American Journal of Psychiatry, 148*, 859–863.

Strasburger, L. H., Jorgenson, L., & Sutherland, P. (1992). The prevention of psychotherapist sexual misconduct: Avoiding the slippery slope. *American Journal of Psychotherapy, 46*, 544–555.

Taylor, B. J., & Wagner, N. N. (1976). Sex between therapist and clients: A review and analysis. *Professional Psychology: Research, Theory and Practice, 7*, 593–601.

Thorn, B. E., Shealy, R. C., & Briggs, S. D. (1993). Sexual misconduct in psychotherapy: Reactions to a consumer-oriented brochure. *Professional Psychology: Research and Practice, 24*, 75–82.

Twemlow, S. W., & Gabbard, G. O. (1989). The lovesick therapist. In G. O. Gabbard (Ed.), *Sexual exploitation in professional relationships* (pp. 71–87). Washington, DC: American Psychiatric Press.

Vasquez, M. J. T. (1991). Sexual intimacies with clients after termination: Should a prohibition be explicit? *Ethics and Behavior, 1*, 45–61.

Vinson, J. S. (1987). Use of complaint procedures in cases of therapist-patient sexual contact. *Professional Psychology: Research and Practice, 18*, 159–164.

Walker, E., & Young, P. D. (1986). *A killing cure.* New York: Holt, Rinehart & Winston.

Williams, M. H. (1992). Exploitation and inference: Mapping the damage from therapist-patient sexual involvement. *American Psychologist, 47*, 412–421.

Wilson, J. M. (1982). The value of touch in psychotherapy. *American Journal of Orthopsychiatry, 52*, 65–72.

Wright, R. H. (1985). Who needs enemies. *Psychotherapy in Private Practice, 3*, 111–118.

Zalk, S., Paludi, M., & Dederick, J. (1990). Women students' assessment of consensual relationships with their professors: Ivory power reconsidered. In E. Cole (Ed.), *Sexual harassment on campus* (pp. 103–133). Washington, DC: National Association of College and University Attorneys.

10

Money Matters and Managed Care

When it is a question of money, everyone is of the same religion.

Voltaire

If you have just picked up this book and are reading this chapter first, it is likely that you are (or aspire to be) in independent practice and are perhaps worried about whether such work will be financially rewarding. To make independent or institutional practice viable, careful attention must be paid to a variety of details not generally discussed in graduate school. Because we are a "helping profession," there is occasionally a sense that discussing money is crass or pecuniary (DiBella, 1980). Such attitudes overlook the fact that helpers have bills to pay, too. When finances are brought up in the course of a psychologist's formal training, specific discussion of actual practices involving billing, collection, and third-party reimbursement are rarely mentioned. Perhaps this is one reason why client complaints and ethical difficulties frequently arise in connection with charges for psychologists' services. Often, the problems arise from miscommunications, procedural ignorance, or naiveté, rather than greed or malice.

If you attended graduate school much before

1990, it is likely that you never even heard of financial aspects of psychological practice or the term *managed care* discussed in the classroom. The notion that psychologists might have to account to third parties (i.e., the client and practitioner being the first and second parties) for their therapeutic decisions or prepare treatment plans for external review would have seemed remote and unreasonable. Few newly licensed psychologists prior to 1990 worried about being unable to secure listing on overcrowded rolls of approved insurance program providers. Today and for the foreseeable future, any psychologist who hopes to build a financially viable practice must work with managed care in some form.

Discussion of money matters in this chapter is divided broadly into five main categories: (1) what to charge, (2) fee splitting, (3) third-party relationships, (4) fraud, and (5) bill collecting. Following the discussion of bill collecting, we also address significant ethical issues related to working with so-called managed care programs.

WHAT TO CHARGE?

Determining the customary charges for one's services is a complicated task that mixes issues of economics, business, self-esteem, and a variety of cultural and professional taboos. When it comes to mental health services, the task is complicated by a host of both subtle and obvious psychological and ethical values. Comparison of fees is further complicated by differences in procedures, length of sessions, and other variables. In its 1995 fee survey, *Psychotherapy Finances* noted that a single therapy session might vary by more than 100% over the range of practitioners by region for a single session hourly rate. The East and Midwest seem to be the least expensive regions, with the West having the highest fees and the South falling in between ("Fee, Practice, and Managed Care Survey," 1995).

Fees also vary by training. Some psychiatrists, for example, charge $200 or more per session. Psychologists have the second highest fees, and social workers and other subdoctoral practitioners are tied for third place. Many marriage-family therapists in the East reported charges as low as $60 per session, whereas psychiatrists in the Northeast and West were the most expensive, often charging fees of $130 or more. Only 4% of marriage-family therapists, 5% of "professional counselors," and 2% of social workers charged over $100 per hour, whereas 72% of psychiatrists and 23% of psychologists charged that much nationally ("Fee, Practice, and Managed Care Survey," 1995). Median fees for group therapy sessions ranged from $35 to $60 across the provider groups, with psychiatrists at the high end.

In considering fees, matters are further complicated by the issue of what constitutes a "therapy hour." A "session" could range from a 10-minute medication check by a psychiatrist or psychiatric nurse to a 120-minute or longer "marathon group." Some practitioners offer their clients 60-minute hours, whereas for others a treatment "hour" may be 50, 45, or even fewer minutes. Likewise, group or family therapy sessions might extend 90 minutes or more, making clear comparisons across modalities and practitioners difficult.

Shortening the session may seem to be a way to increase cash flow by degrees; however, the practice is more often an effort to catch up on the hidden demands on the practitioner's time. Paperwork requirements for filing health insurance reimbursement claims, detailed treatment plans, and telephone contacts related to cases have increased significantly over the past few years. In many circumstances, therapists may spend 50 minutes meeting with the client, only to spend another 50 minutes completing the necessary documentation.

Some practitioners may offer a sliding fee scale for clients who cannot afford to pay a customary charge, while others maintain a high "usual and customary rate" and provide an assortment of discounts. For example, a client who has been in treatment for an extended period of time may be paying a lower rate than a new client. Or, an individual who is being seen 3 hours per week may be given a lower hourly rate than a person seen once per week. The actual fee charged for services rendered is not as important from the ethical standpoint as the manner in which it is set, communicated, managed, and collected. By definition, however, many of a psychologist's clients may be regarded as somewhat vulnerable to potential abuse because of emotional dependency, social naiveté, psychosis, or other psychopathological conditions, and it behooves the psychologist not to take advantage of these factors.

Case 10-1: Arnold Avarice, Ph.D., was contacted by Sally Sibyl for treatment of her emotional problems, and he diagnosed her as having a multiple personality disorder. During the first 2 months of treatment, Dr. Avarice claimed to have treated Ms. Sibyl an average of 3 hours per day (some days as many as 5 to 6 hours) at a rate of $150 per hour. Ms. Sibyl's wealthy family was billed approximately $30,000 for services during this time. When Ms. Sibyl's family questioned the bill, Dr. Avarice justified the frequency of his work with the client by noting, "I often had sessions with two or three different personalities the same day. She is a very disturbed woman requiring intensive work." Dr. Avarice offered to consider reducing his fee in exchange for the "exclusive rights to a book on her case story."

Most psychotherapists, including those expert in treating people with a multiple personality disorder, would question the necessity and appropriateness of Dr. Avarice's intervention. When called before an ethics committee, Dr. Avarice was unable to provide a treatment plan or detailed case notes for the many hours of treatment he claimed to have provided. Ms. Sibyl showed little improvement and could not remember when or how often she had seen Dr. Avarice. The ethics committee was also concerned about Dr. Avarice's focus on turning a profit from the bizarre aspects of the case by seeking to gain literary rights as a financial trade-off.

From the outset of a relationship with a new client, the psychologist should take care to explain the nature of services offered, the fees charged, the mode of payment used, and other financial arrangements that might reasonably be expected to influence the potential client's decision. If the psychologist has reason to question the ability of the client to make a responsible decision, this too must be considered in deciding to accept the client or make some specialized referral elsewhere. Of course, parents or legal guardians may grant permission for treatment of minors or adults over whom they have guardianship. Providing informed consent should be regarded as a process rather than a single event. The flow of information and mutual discussion of the treatment process (including costs) should be ongoing as needed throughout the professional relationship. If an estimate of charges is given, it should be honored, unless unforeseen circumstances arise. In the last situation, any changes should be discussed with and agreed to by the client. If it seems that financial difficulties may be an issue, they should be dealt with openly at the very outset of the relationship.

Occasionally, clients complain to ethics committees about pressure to enter treatment at a higher fee than they can afford. Such practices include both "soft-sell" and "hard-sell" pitches by therapists. An example of the low-pressure pitch might be, "If you really want to get better,

you will find a way to finance good therapy. It's an investment in yourself." A more pressured pitch might be, "You can't afford *not* to see me. I have been very successful in solving your sort of problem. Things will only get worse if you don't take care of them now." Aside from the implication of special skill explicit in both these pitches, they subject clients to unethical pressure by playing on their insecurities.

There are many more appropriate ways to address the issue of the client who cannot afford the usual charges for services. Many psychologists are willing to provide a flexible fee schedule that varies as a function of client income. The APA (American Psychological Association) ethics code specifies the aspirational expectation (EP: F) that psychologists render at least some pro bono services (i.e., professional activity undertaken at no charge in the public interest). A variety of surveys have yielded self-reports that suggest most psychologists do provide at least some services at little or no cost. Many psychologists will offer a financially troubled client the opportunity to extend payment over a long period of time, but this is not helpful if the charges being incurred remain beyond the reasonable means of the client. Some psychotherapists tack on interest or "billing charges" to unpaid bills. This practice may also involve substantial administrative difficulties because state and federal laws generally require a special disclosure statement informing clients about such fees in advance.

It is critical that the psychologist consider these issues very early in the professional relationship and raise them openly with the client in a realistic, yet supportive, fashion. If a prospective client is unable to reasonably afford the services of the practitioner in question, the psychologist should be prepared to make a sensitive and appropriate referral. In this vein, it is important for psychologists to be aware of hospitals, clinics, community mental health centers, training programs, and other resources by which more affordable services might be available for those with financial difficulties.

Along these lines, it is also important to consider obligations to the client and community agencies in terms of treatment continuity and limited financial resources in the community. A practice known as "creaming and dumping" is instructive on this point.

Case 10-2: Roberta Poore consulted Phil T. Lucre, Psy.D., for treatment of long-standing difficulties with her parents and coworkers. After only one session, it was clear to Dr. Lucre that Poore would, at minimum, require several months of weekly psychotherapy to begin addressing her relationship problems effectively. Dr. Lucre's usual hourly rate was $80, and he did not have a policy of reducing his fee for clients who could not afford it. Poore had health insurance coverage that provided up to $500 per year in outpatient mental health benefits. Her salary was low, and she could not afford more than $30 per week to pay out of pocket for psychotherapy. Dr. Lucre saw her for 6 sessions. As soon as her insurance coverage was exhausted, he referred her to the local community health center, where she could be seen at a reduced fee.

In this case, the psychologist has skimmed the "cream" (insurance coverage) and then "dumped" the patient in the lap of a community agency. This is a disservice to the patient, whose therapeutic course is disrupted, and it is a disservice to the community agency, which would have benefited from the insurance payments while also providing continuity of care after the coverage was exhausted. When the possibility of such dumping is evident, the psychologist should not take on the case but, rather, make an appropriate referral immediately. If the psychologist considers the treatment or evaluation plan early and discusses it with the client, including all relevant financial aspects, the client would be in a position to express a preference considering the continuity issue as well.

Case 10-2 represents one type of abandonment of the client by the therapist, but what of the more general situation of the client who cannot pay for services rendered? Should the practitioner terminate services in midcourse of treatment, or does that represent abandonment of the client as well? The ethical practitioner will attempt to avoid abandoning clients with two specific strategies. The first is never to con-

tract for services without first clarifying the costs to the client and reaching an agreement that they are affordable. The second is not to mislead the client into thinking that insurance or other such coverage will bear the full cost of services when it seems reasonably clear that benefits may expire before the need for service. When treatment is in progress and a client becomes unemployed or otherwise can no longer pay for continued services, the practitioner should be especially sensitive to the client's needs. If a psychologist cannot realistically help a client under existing reimbursement restrictions and the resulting process might be too disruptive, it is best simply to explain the problem and not take on the prospective client. While it may be necessary to terminate care or transfer the client's care elsewhere over the long term, this should not be done abruptly or in the midst of a crisis period in the client's life.

Increasing fees in the course of service delivery can also pose ethical dilemmas. If a commitment is made to provide consultation or conduct an assessment for a given fee, it should be honored. Likewise, a client who enters psychotherapy at an agreed-upon fee has a reasonable expectation that the fee will not be raised excessively. Once service has begun, the provider has an obligation to the client that must be considered. Aside from financial hardship issues, the psychologist may have special influence with the client that should not be abused.

Case 10-3: Chuck Gelt began psychotherapy with Helen Takem, Ed.D., expecting to pay $80 per session. After several weeks of treatment, Mr. Gelt shared some intense and painful concerns with Dr. Takem. These emotional issues included mixed feelings over relationships with Gelt's deceased parents, from whom he had inherited substantial wealth. Dr. Takem pressed Gelt to contract with her for a minimum of 100 sessions at a cost of $160 per session. She argued that, for this particular affluent client, the fee needed to be high or else he would not perceive the therapy as "valuable." The minimum contract for 100 sessions was needed, Takem reasoned, because Gelt was "ambivalent and tended to lack commitment."

Dr. Takem's proposed contract is clearly unethical as it proposes terms independent of demonstrated client need and without meaningful client participation in the decision-making process. In addition, the client's mixed feelings may inhibit his ability to see the inappropriateness of the dramatic boost in fees. At the same time, the client may be reluctant to go through the emotional pain of sharing his concerns "from the beginning" with a new therapist. The emotional investment made by the client during the first few sessions may contribute to making him less able to act as an informed, reasoning consumer.

When a client has been in treatment for an extended period of time (i.e., 6 months to a year or more) and inflation or other costs of conducting a professional practice have risen, it is not unreasonable to adjust fees upward accordingly. This should, however, be done thoughtfully, reasonably, and with due consideration for each client's economic status and treatment needs. Some practitioners, for example, will raise fees for new clients while maintaining "old clients" at the existing rate. The ethical point to consider is that professionals incur added responsibility because of the power roles they occupy relative to clients.

Similar issues are discussed in chapter 11 with respect to "free sessions" or "special bonus offers" used in advertisements to attract clients. Clients may not realize the subtle emotional pressures that may accompany an initial consultation or "free visit." While there is certainly nothing wrong with not charging a client under some circumstances, this should never be used as a lure to initiate a professional relationship through advertising media.

Some practitioners require clients to pay certain fees in advance of rendering services as a kind of retainer. This is an unusual practice, but is not unethical so long as the contingencies are mutually agreed on. The most common uses of such advance payments involve relationships in which the practitioner is asked to hold time available on short notice for some reasons (as in certain types of corporate consulting) or when certain types of litigation are involved (see discussion in chapter 15). A specific example would be when a psychologist agrees to undertake a child custody evaluation and the two hostile contesting parties (such as the Bicker family in Case 10-11) each agree in advance to pay half of the fee. It is likely that at least one of the parties will be unhappy with the outcome, and in such circumstances the unhappy party may refuse to pay for the services rendered because of displeasure with the findings. In such situations, it is not unusual for the practitioner to request a retainer or escrow payment prior to commencing work.

Payment for missed appointments is another source of occasional inquiries to ethics committees. It is not unethical to charge a client for an appointment that is not kept or that is canceled on short notice. Again, the key issue is giving proper advance information about this practice to the client (ES: 1.25). No one wants to have their schedule disrupted or lose time that might have been used for other useful purposes. In addition, if a practitioner has a waiting list and could well use the vacant appointment time, it is frustrating and costly to have a client cancel on short notice or simply fail to show up for the appointment. If the practitioner intends to charge the client in such instances, however, it is necessary to advise the client of this at the start of the relationship and to make the conditions explicit. When telling clients about such charges, it is important to advise them that insurance companies generally will not pay for missed appointments, as we discuss below in this chapter. In actual practice, it appears that few psychotherapists charge clients for a missed appointment unless the behavior is a recurrent problem.

Case 10-4: Skippy Session saw Harry Biller, Ph.D., for psychotherapy on a weekly basis for 6 weeks. During the first session, Dr. Biller explained his policy of charging clients for appointments canceled less than 24 hours in advance, and Mr. Session accepted those terms. A few hours before the scheduled seventh appointment, Session's father was killed in an automobile accident. Session telephoned Dr. Biller that he would be unable to keep the appointment and would call to reschedule. Dr. Biller did not charge Mr. Session for the canceled appointment out of deference to the unusual circumstances. Several months later, Mr. Session "totally forgot" an appointment with Dr. Biller. When the psychologist charged him for the session, Mr. Session complained, "That's unethical! After all, you never charged me the last time I missed one."

There may be many different reasons that Mr. Session missed his most recent appointment, ranging from "unconscious acting out" to simple forgetting. He was informed about, and did agree to, Dr. Biller's terms at the start of therapy. Dr. Biller's compassionate waiving of his fee the day Mr. Session's father died may have been misinterpreted by Session. Dr. Biller is ethically entitled to charge for the second missed session; however, it probably would be wisest to discuss both the misunderstanding and the meaning of "forgetting" the appointment, postponing the implementation of the missed session fee until the next occurrence.

Fees certainly do have substantial psychological impact on a number of levels and may often become a "therapeutic issue" (see, for example, Lovinger, 1978; Vasile & O'Loughlin, 1977). Lovinger (1978) notes that the fee is all that the client has to give, aside from coming to the psychologist's office. That is, the client does not owe the practitioner gratitude, respect, consensus, or anything other than a fee for services rendered. The fee may in that sense develop some special meaning via transference. This means that the client may come to regard the fee in the same manner as some duty owed in a prior relationship. It may become a means of addressing the anger held in relation to a demanding parent or represent a penance to atone for some imagined wrong to a spouse. Lovinger, like Freud (who, he reports, viewed fees as a frank matter of the therapist's livelihood), suggests that a direct and candid approach is the best means to begin a client-psychologist relationship. Raising the fee exponentially or without a meaningful economic rationale, however, is seldom, if ever, therapeutically defensible.

FEE SPLITTING

Fee splitting refers to a general practice, often termed a "kickback," by which part of a sum received for a product or service is returned or paid out because of a prearranged agreement or coercion. As practiced in medicine or the mental health professions, the client is usually unaware of the arrangement. Traditionally, there was nearly universal agreement among mental health professionals that such practices are unethical, chiefly because they may preclude a truly appropriate referral in the client's best interests, result in delivery of unneeded services, lead to increased costs of services, and generally exploit the relative ignorance of the client. Unfortunately, fee splitting may exist in rather complex and subtle forms that tend to mask the fact that it is occurring. There is a continuum of types of agreements that ranges from reasonable and ethical to clearly inappropriate. At the two extremes are employer-employee relationships (clearly appropriate) and arrangements by which the person making the referral gets money solely for making the referral. In addition, actions by the Federal Trade Commission (FTC) (as discussed in chapter 11) have legitimized some practices that were previously prohibited by professional associations' ethics codes.

Case 10-5: Irving Slynapse, M.D., a prominent neurologist, agrees to refer substantial numbers of his patients to Ester Choline, Ph.D., for neuropsychological assessment. Dr. Choline bills the client or insurance company and pays Slynapse 10% of all the money collected on clients he refers to her. Slynapse characterizes that 10% as a continuing charge for medical coverage and consultation; however, there are no regular appointments scheduled for consultation, and Choline never avails herself of that service.

Case 10-6: Nick Proffit, Ed.D., P.C., has a large professional practice in that he supervises several master's-level psychotherapists and rents office space to other doctoral-level clinicians. His secretary bills all of the clients at a rate of $80 per session. The supervisees are paid 25% of the fees collected, and the renters are paid 40% of the fees collected. The clients are unaware of this distribution plan.

Case 10-7: G. Ima Helper, Psy.D., is well known for her many self-help books and media appearances. Her public visibility results in many self-referrals by clients in the community. Dr. Helper refers such clients to Helper's Haven, her private clinic, where they are seen for $90 per session by master's-level therapists paid $25 per session. The clients are led to believe that their therapists are supervised or receive consultation from Dr. Helper. Actually, they are not even employees (i.e., salaried) but simply earn a fee for each session held and have no contact with Dr. Helper, who has little direct involvement with the clinic.

Each of the cases cited above has a number of unethical features in common. To begin, the client is generally unaware of the proprietary relationship between the service provider and the person making the referral. It is therefore unlikely that the client would realize that motives other than their own best interests were being considered. In each of the cases, one party is also being paid for services not rendered. That is, Drs. Slynapse, Proffit, and Helper are being paid a commission in a manner that is concealed from, and to the detriment of, the client. Clients may assume that referrals to therapists were based on the therapists' special abilities or competence, rather than chiefly for profit. The more responsibility and liability the referrer has for the case, the more reasonable it is to pay that person a fee. None of these clinicians has objectively weighed the needs of the individual client and considered these in making the referral. A key point is the matter of professional responsibility. Some clients may actually be referred and charged for services that they do not really need.

Dr. Proffit's situation is potentially more appropriate than those of Drs. Slynapse and Helper. If Proffit has a long-term contract with the clinicians who rent space from him and provides supervision, consultation, or case oversight, he may be entitled to a percentage of fees collected. On the other hand, if he has no professional relationship with the therapists and no clear responsibility for their clients' welfare, he is not entitled to a fee. The key issue in determining appropriateness of such fees is the rendering of legitimate, reasonably priced services.

The case of Dr. Helper also raises the basic question of what one must disclose to a client about arrangements among practitioners. Helper may also be exploiting the master's-level therapists in her clinic. The issue in the current context is that clients should be told any aspects of the arrangement that might reasonably be expected to influence their decision about whether to use the services. That is, they should be told that Dr. Helper will not participate in their treatment in any way. In all of the cases in which a commission is being paid to someone not rendering service, the client should also be advised. In this instance, we consider a commission to be any payment for a referral, as opposed to a payment for services rendered.

Group Practice

Many practitioners work in group practices or collaborative arrangements in that certain costs such as rent, secretarial services, utilities, answering services, and so on are shared. Many other practitioners also have, or work as, assistants to other psychologists and are paid at less than the full rate billed to the client. Although these types of arrangements are permitted under the newest version of the APA ethics code (ES: 1.27), we are troubled when compensation is paid to some party simply for referring clients or when percentages of gross income are charged against a clinician automatically rather than for services legitimately provided. In such instances, the clients' welfare is too easily ignored.

In the group practice described above, for example, each practitioner might be asked to make a monthly payment, based on actual or reasonably estimated costs and their use of the services, for office expenses. This charge should be independent of the gross income or the number of clients seen and based instead on an "actual use" paradigm. In the case of the assistant, it is more appropriate to pay him or her a salary or to base compensation on actual gross income less actual costs. Costs might include a reasonable charge for supervision (when allowed by law), administration, marketing, consultation, or office services, but these must be based on a mutually agreed-upon set of real expenses and be open to renegotiation as time-demand shifts occur. In all cases, the practitioners must be free to make referrals to the "outside" when this seems in their clients' best interests. No financial rewards or penalties should accrue to any party as the result of an inside versus outside referral.

One of the subtle difficulties involved in group practice arrangements or the use of assistants is the fair determination of costs and service use. There is much opportunity for inflation of expenses or other manipulations. This is especially so when one of the practitioners is in a position of power over others by virtue of being the senior party or licensed doctoral clinician employing individuals unable to obtain independent licensure; these individuals are particularly dependent on the employer. In such situations, it behooves the practitioner to avoid even the appearance of abuse and to be fully open with his or her colleagues.

Case 10-8: Debbie Doubter, Psy.D., has been invited to join a thriving group practice started 20 years ago by Wally Wealthy, Ph.D. She has been offered 40% of the fees collected for her services during her first year and 50% of the fees every year thereafter. Dr. Wealthy explains that he will provide close supervision and some training for her in the first year. In addition, he notes that 50% of the fees collected are his best estimate of the costs of rent, utilities, billing service, answering service, and coverage of her clients while she is on vacation. Finally, Dr. Wealthy notes that his percentage includes some allowance for "return on investment." That is, he believes he is entitled to recover some money based on the years he has invested in building the practice.

In this case, Dr. Doubter must decide for herself whether she is comfortable with Dr. Wealthy's offer. It is not inappropriate on its face because Dr. Wealthy is indeed providing services and accepting a significant degree of professional and clinical responsibility. Given the difficulties many young psychologists face starting practices in today's economic climate, the 50% cut sought by Dr. Wealthy may seem acceptable to some.

Another subtle difficulty is the tendency to

refer clients to practitioners one knows well. This can be a very appropriate and responsible practice as one tries to help each client obtain the most fitting services for her or his needs. It is critical, however, that the person making the referral receive no financial benefit or gain as the result of the referral. If it happens that the most suitable referral may well be to a colleague or employee and some indirect benefit might be a result (e.g., overhead costs in a group practice kept lower by virtue of more patients being seen), this can still be done. The client should be informed, however, of the fact that a relationship exists between the practitioners and the reasons why a referral is being made to that specific practitioner. Another alternative would be to offer the client a choice among practitioners that includes at least one with no linkage to the referring party. (This issue is discussed further in chapter 13.)

Case 10-9: Finda Dockta, M.B.A., founded a psychotherapy referral service, Shrinks-R-Us, to "guide wise consumers to competent, effective, reasonably priced therapists." Psychotherapists pay Ms. Dockta a registration fee, provide proof that they are licensed and carry liability insurance, and provide three letters of reference. The practitioners provide her database with details on their experience, languages spoken, office location, and other relevant data. They also agree to pay her a 5% royalty on all net fees collected from clients she refers to them. Ms. Dockta markets the service heavily. Clients are not charged a fee and are informed that all costs of the service are paid by the practitioners based on their collections.

Some might say that Ms. Dockta's program involves fee splitting, although the FTC would have no difficulty with it. Yes, she is getting a percentage of the fees, but she is also legitimately earning those fees by providing useful referral information to consumers. The fact that providers pay for the service is not concealed. Although a state legislature may have authority to prohibit such activities within its borders (thus avoiding the FTCs' interstate commerce oversight), practitioners participating in such a service would not be subject to disciplinary action by national professional organizations or their state affiliates.

Special Business Agreements

Although technically not fee splitting, there are a variety of special business agreements common in the commercial world that would be considered potentially unethical in the practice of psychology for reasons similar to the issues raised thus far in this chapter. These agreements would include so-called covenants not to compete or contracts with liquidated damages clauses.

Case 10-10: Lester Workman, Ph.D., spent 10 years building a favorable professional reputation and busy private practice in a suburban community. He began to attract more referrals than he could handle, but he was not sure whether the volume would be sufficient to warrant the addition of a colleague as a full-time employee in the practice. Instead, he hired Peter Partner, Ph.D., as a half-time employee at a salary agreeable to both for a 1-year contract. By the end of the year Dr. Partner, who was young and energetic, began to build a strong reputation in the community and wondered if he ought to consider going into practice independently.

In an ideal world, Workman and Partner will sit down and attempt to sort matters out in their clients' best interests. If they are indeed to have separate practices in the same community, the choice of whom to consult should be the client's. Clients in midtreatment with Partner, for example, should reasonably expect to continue their relationship with him. Unfortunately, however, such split-ups often result in considerable acrimony between the practitioners, with clients caught in between. It would have been preferable for Workman to consider this potential outcome as a possibility from the outset should they terminate working together and include some reasonable professional plan in the agreement with Partner to meet clients' needs. This agreement could include some fair allowance for the effort Workman put into building the practice.

Two types of advance agreement for the termination of such relationships cause serious ethical problems. In the first type, Dr. Workman might have attempted to sign Partner to a contract that included a covenant not to compete. Under such a clause, Partner would agree, for example, not to set up an independent practice or work for any other practitioner within a 50-mile radius of Workman's office for a period of time after leaving the practice. Whereas this might meet Workman's needs, it would deny clients their freedom to choose and is clearly unethical. In some jurisdictions, laws actually have been enacted making such agreements among health care professionals illegal as well. The usual legal standard is reasonableness. Although there are obviously many different perspectives on what is reasonable, the paramount ethical perspective would focus on the well-being of the clients. Clear differences exist between the obligations to a client who is psychologically vulnerable and the more usual circumstances in business and industry, in which such covenants are more appropriately used.

The second type of problematic contractual element Workman might have considered would be a liquidated damages clause. Such a clause might have asked that Partner pay Workman financial "damages" for each client he takes with him, either at a flat fee per client rate or as a percentage of future revenues. Paying a flat fee for each client who leaves with Dr. Partner might be ethically acceptable, so long as the cost of this fee is not passed to the client. Paying a percentage of future earnings or a royalty from the fees of the transferred clients is more clearly a fee-splitting situation and could be legally unenforceable in some states, even if Partner had agreed to it initially.

The message inherent in this discussion is threefold. First, these issues need to be raised and clarified prior to beginning the professional association. Second, the choice of therapist should ultimately rest with the client. Finally, professional colleagues must exercise great care, and at times suffer potential economic disadvantage, so as not to abuse the relative position of power and influence they have over the clients they serve. Psychologists should not profit unfairly at the expense of either clients or colleagues.

Selling a professional practice is another kind of special business agreement that raises ethical questions. Suppose Dr. Workman wanted to retire after 30 years in solo private practice. Can he sell his practice? What does the practice include? Furniture, an office, some aging psychological test equipment, the name of the practice or clinic, and a group of clients make up a practice. One can indeed sell the furniture, real estate, and equipment. But, selling the clients, their files, and access to this information raises many significant ethical issues. Practitioners cannot ethically transfer clinical responsibility for clients or confidential client records in a private practice without the clients' consent. Clients have the right to choose practitioners. A full discussion of these issues was published by Pope and Keith-Spiegel in the *APA Monitor* under the title, "Is Selling a Practice Malpractice?" (1986). They note that, in addition to freedom of choice issues, the seller's clients may be heavily influenced by the seller's recommendation that they continue to obtain services from the buyer. The seller is in a complex role with respect to these clients. That is, the clients are in some respects a commodity when they are referred en masse to the buyer. They have the right to expect that the referral to a new practitioner is based on careful professional judgment of their individual needs. A subsequent article described principles for valuing a practice, including ethical issues related to client lists and records (Woody, 1997). If Dr. Workman wanted to maximize his ability to transfer a thriving practice to another professional, the most ethical and effective way to accomplish this feat would be to spread it out over a period of years in what has been termed an *extended transition* model (Myers & Brezler, 1992). Ideally, Dr. Workman could attract a potential partner and forge an agreement (e.g., a legal entity, partnership, or professional corporation) that included a buyout of the practice over time. As Workman's retirement drew near, he could offer clients the opportunity to transfer to his partner or elsewhere in the community. The agreement could call for the partner to maintain and ad-

minister the practice's records for the legally mandated interval (see chapter 6) and might even include a continuing consulting role for Workman on an as-needed basis should special issues with former clients arise. In this way, the selling of the practice actually becomes an evolutionary transfer that allows time, choice, and continuity options for the clients.

THIRD-PARTY RELATIONSHIPS

Mental health services are essentially paid for in one of three ways: (1) directly out of pocket by the client, (2) in whole or in part by a health insurance plan or health maintenance organization (HMO), or (3) other employee benefit plan, or public funds. In any case in which some agency or organization other than the practitioner and client is involved, we have a fiscal third-party relationship. There is no doubt that these third parties, their reimbursement policies, and the regulations that govern these policies have historically had a direct and powerful influence on practice and client care (Chodoff, 1978; Council on Ethical and Judicial Affairs, 1995; Dujovne, 1980; Rodwin, 1993). Though theoretically possible, it is unrealistic for most mental health practitioners to expect that they will be able to earn a living without substantial interactions with such entities. Although many practitioners will have no difficulties in their relationships with these entities, few will consider these contacts an unmitigated blessing (Meltzer, 1975).

Claims have historically been made that including psychotherapy benefits in health insurance coverage represents inequitable service to different income groups (Albee, 1977; Edwards, Greene, Abramowitz, & Davidson, 1979), raises threats to clients' confidentiality (Grossman, 1971; Jagim, Wittman, & Noll, 1978), creates concern about accountability and review criteria (e.g., Sharfstein, Taube, & Goldberg, 1975; Stricker, 1979), and leads to expensive litigation (Kiesler & Pallak, 1980). Access to such coverage has led to many intra- and interprofessional squabbles about who ought to be able to bill third parties for what services. Confidentiality problems were discussed in chapter 6, and we generally defer discussion of what are deemed chiefly political issues in insurance reimbursement in favor of a focus on the ethical problems such third-party relationships raise. Next, the topics of so-called freedom-of-choice (FOC) options and billing for services not covered are discussed as a lead into a major discussion of fraud and the managed care organizations (MCOs).

Freedom of Choice

The FOC issue refers to legislation and regulations that permit the client to choose their provider of services. As used in discussions of psychological services, FOC generally refers to the matter of whether the psychological practitioner is authorized to bill a third party directly for services rendered to a client or whether that practitioner must first obtain the approval or referral of a psychiatrist. At least that was the historical battle. More recently, mental health benefits have come to be administered along with other specialty services so that a primary care physician (e.g., internist or pediatrician) must authorize a referral, whether to a mental health practitioner, allergist, or proctologist.

Psychologists have pressed the FOC concept as a right of the client, noting that certain psychologists are well trained to function as independent health service providers. Other arguments include the claim that the availability of psychologists improves consumer access to qualified care and increases competition among professional provider groups with resulting cost benefits to consumers. Failure to recognize licensed psychologists as independent providers had been viewed by some as an unreasonable restraint of trade. Now that all states have psychology licensing statutes, it has been possible to enact FOC or so-called direct recognition laws in nearly every state. In many locations, psychologists now find themselves on the other side of the issue, arguing against legislation to reimburse counselors with subdoctoral training directly.

The more recent development of concern to practitioners is limitations to access on closed provider panels. Managed care organizations

frequently create a limited roster of practitioners approved to serve their policyholders. At times, psychologists have been excluded or underrepresented on such panels. At other times, medical and mental health care providers have been abruptly dropped from the listing or denied entry for reasons that are unclear or seem unfair to one or another party. Access to membership on such provider panels remains a major professional concern, although not necessarily an ethical issue. Sometimes, however, practitioners find themselves ethically challenged when they fear that doing what is best for a client may compromise their provider status, as we discuss below.

Complaints may also come from specific providers or provider groups against their colleagues. When social workers, family counselors, psychiatric nurses, or unlicensed psychologists have sought entitlement to be independent vendors for third-party payments, they have generally cited the very same arguments advanced by psychologists (i.e., consumer's right to choose, lower fees based on increased competition, etc.). In general, the entitled practitioner groups tend to oppose direct reimbursement of unentitled groups for a variety of economic and political reasons. Quality of care issues and cost containment are oft-cited reasons for limiting the size of the practitioner pool to doctoral-level clinicians. Others occasionally argue that these reasons are merely covers for the desire to reduce competition for a limited supply of clients. This may indeed present some moral or ethical issues, but the complexity of public policy on such matters and the usual absence of clearly malevolent specific individuals makes pursuit of these problems as ethical matters difficult. They are more properly treated as professional standards problems.

Billing for Services Not Covered

A common third-party problem with major ethical and legal implications relates to billing for services that are not covered under the third party's obligations. Most third parties are health insurance companies and as a result limit their coverage to treatments for illness or health-related problems, usually defined in terms of medical necessity. One must invariably assign a diagnosis to the client to secure payment. Some services provided by psychologists are not, strictly speaking, health or mental health services. For example, marriage counseling, educational testing, school consultation, vocational guidance, child custody evaluations, and a whole variety of forensic functions may not be considered health services and as such would not be covered by health insurance.

Some insurance carriers also specify certain types of diagnostic or therapeutic procedures that are not covered services. Such treatments or services might be considered ancillary, experimental, unproven, or simply health promoting (e.g., weight control and smoking cessation), but not treatment for a specific illness. Attempts to conceal the actual nature of the service rendered, or otherwise attempt to obtain compensation in the face of such restrictions, may constitute fraud. In the first section of this chapter, we discussed the practice of billing clients for missed appointments. Because this is essentially a bill for services that have not been rendered, virtually no third-party payer will cover such charges.

Exactly what is covered under any given insurance policy is a matter of the specific contract language. Some psychologists have found themselves in the position of negotiating one fee if the patient is reimbursed by their insurer and another fee if the service is not covered. This practice can lead to client resentment and be in frank violation of certain contracts between providers and insurance companies. One strategy offered by some clinicians is to offer a reduced rate that represents a cash discount for clients who are no longer using third-party coverage. A legally acceptable rationale would be passing on savings realized when the clinician no longer has to submit claims forms and case reports to the third party.

Case 10-11: Becky and Barney Bicker have been separated for 3 months and have filed for divorce. They are contesting for the custody of their two children. Their respective attorneys suggest a psychological consultation to prepare a forensic re-

port for the courts on the best interests of the children and refer them to Bill Lesser, Ph.D. Lesser assures the Bickers that their Blue Shield policy will cover his fee and proceeds with the evaluation. He subsequently files an insurance claim for his services without noting that it was conducted primarily for resolution of a custody dispute. He assigns the diagnosis "childhood adjustment reaction" to their children for billing purposes.

Case 10-12: Sven Gully, Ed.D., is a licensed psychologist skilled in the use of hypnosis and relaxation techniques. He offers a quit smoking program that regularly attracts clients. Clients often ask about costs and whether Gully will accept health insurance coverage for payment of his services. Gully knows that many companies will not cover hypnosis or will not pay for health-promoting programs in the absence of actual illness. He completes billing forms and lists his services simply as "psychotherapy" and assigns "adjustment reaction" diagnoses to his clients.

Both of the psychologists described above may be competent and caring professionals, but both are being unethical and flirting with fraud charges. Perhaps neither has carefully inquired of the third parties in question as to whether the services are indeed covered and are simply trying to expedite claim processing. On the other hand, each should recognize that the specific services rendered in both cases may not be considered mental health related or treatment of an illness. What appears to be expedient and a help to the client (i.e., making services less expensive) may be illegal and tend to increase insurance costs for other policyholders. The more appropriate behavior would be, when in doubt, to check with the third-party for explicit advice and to inform clients accurately early in the relationship whether coverage is indeed applicable. Drs. Lesser and Gully may believe that they are helping their clients, but they are technically engaged in a "white-collar" ethical violation that costs all consumers money. If Dr. Lesser is concerned that his services are not covered and that the Bickers might squabble over paying for his time, he may reasonably consider requesting a retainer before initiating services.

FRAUD

As a legal concept, *fraud* refers to an act of intentional deception that results in harm or injury to another. There are four basic elements to a fraudulent act. First, a false representation is made by one party, who either knows it to be false or is knowingly ignorant of its truth. This may be done by misrepresentation, deception, concealment, or simply nondisclosure of some key fact. Second, the misrepresenter's intent is that another will rely on the false representation. Third, the recipient of the information is unaware of the intended deception. Fourth, the recipient of the information is justified in relying on or expecting the truth from the communicator. The resulting injury may be financial, physical, or emotional.

A variety of unethical acts might be considered fraudulent, including deception in some research paradigms or educational settings, lies about one's training or qualifications, or some types of promotional advertising (see chapter 11). In this chapter, however, the focus will be on fraud as a financial matter. Cases 10-11 and 10-12 highlight one aspect of the problem in that there is no easily identifiable "victim," as is often the case in fraud situations. Because the offense frequently takes place in paper transactions, some offenders tend to regard themselves as less than serious violators.

Case 10-13: Carla Dingle, Psy.D., was indicted for fraud by a grand jury and asked to explain her conduct to an ethics panel. She explained that she consulted at a private proprietary hospital on a fee-for-service basis by which part of each charge went to her and part to the hospital for administrative costs. To "simplify" the billing process, Dr. Dingle signed several dozen blank claim forms and left them for the billing office secretary to fill out. She described herself as absentminded and reported that she simply had not noticed that insurance companies were paying her for services not rendered. She claimed that hospital administrators must have improperly added extra appointments to the billing sheets to inflate their income.

Case 10-14: Ernest Church, Ph.D., worked as a consulting psychologist for a nursing home run by a religious group. He offered his services free to the home as an act of religious devotion and submitted bills for his services to a government agency, turning over all monies collected to the home. He was indicted for fraud when an audit disclosed that he had been paid for several thousand dollars worth of services not rendered. Church had simply added two to five extra visits to the billing for each of the clients he was asked to evaluate. He was apologetic when confronted, but noted that the home was in need of funds and the money did not come out of the pocket of any patients, all of whom had government-sponsored insurance plans.

Neither Dr. Dingle's absentmindedness nor Dr. Church's well-intentioned diversion of federal funds is ethically tolerable. Dingle should not have provided signed blank forms and remains fully responsible for any acts she delegated to others. Her carelessness and failure to monitor her accounts accurately raises serious questions about her competence and awareness of professional practices. Church was clearly guilty of defrauding the government, despite his good intentions and rationalized sense of economic necessity. Perhaps neither seems as culpable as the greedy individual who deliberately swindles a neurotic senior citizen of his or her life savings, but the financial impact of fraud on third-party payers and those who underwrite their services is substantial.

It is wise to retain duplicate copies of all insurance claims completed. Such a practice will go far to prevent problems that result from alterations made on the forms after they leave the psychologist's hands. In some cases, clients have been known to inflate listed charges, especially when insurance company procedures require the client (rather than the practitioner) to turn in the form, and the insurer reimburses the client directly.

Some third parties, especially MCOs, seek to sign a contract with providers before agreeing to pay for their services. Blue Shield is an example of such a provider in many states. In the typical contract, a provider is asked to agree to accept the company's payment as specified in full for the service rendered to the subscriber or client. The provider also promises not to charge a policyholder more for any given service than would be charged to another client. In other words, the provider agrees to accept, from time to time, certain set fees determined by the company and agrees not to treat policyholders differently from nonpolicyholders. In this way, the company attempts to provide good, inexpensive coverage, while attempting to prevent its policyholders from being overcharged or treated in a discriminatory manner. Ideally, the psychologist gains access to a client population, timely payment for services, and the ability to treat covered clients at less expense to them.

Despite prior agreements between practitioners and MCOs, contractual violations are occasionally the basis of complaints, and such violations, if intentional, are generally considered to be illegal and unethical. Three typical types of such contractual violations include the practices of ignoring the copayment, balance billing, and "hiking your profile," which are illustrated in the following cases.

Case 10-15: Some insurance coverage provides that the client must pay a small set portion of the psychologist's fee, known as a copayment. Nell Goodheart, Psy.D., often does not bother to collect $5 copayments from her clients. She believes she is doing them a favor and that "no one will mind." She does not realize that she may be accused of fraud because of misrepresentation of her professional fees.

Dr. Goodheart's failure to make a reasonable effort to collect the copayments has the net effect of misrepresenting her fee to the insurer. Assume, for example, that she bills the third party $80 for a session and is paid $75 on the assumption that she will collect $5 from the client as a copayment. If she does not make a good faith effort to collect the $5, she has effectively lowered her fee to $75 while continuing to tell the insurer that it is $80. This practice might be interpreted as fraudulent misrepresentation. Dr. Goodheart may choose not to press collection of the fee against indigent patients for whom this is a hardship, but she must be prepared to demonstrate that she made good faith efforts to collect it.

Case 10-16: Sam Moore, Ph.D., is treating a client whose Blue Mace/Blue Helmet health insur-

ance policy provides payment of up to $500 per year for outpatient psychotherapy. His usual charge is $80 per hour, but his contract obliges him to accept a $55 payment from the company as full compensation for each session. Once the $500 is exhausted, he may bill the client his usual fee. Dr. Moore decides to bill his client for the $25 net balance between the Blue Mace/Blue Helmet payment and his usual fee for each session.

This is a clear contract violation and unethical act. Some practitioners have been known to attempt to get around this issue by sending a bill marked "optional" or by telling the client, "You don't have to pay the difference, but I want you to know some of my clients do so voluntarily." This may be a subtle contract violation per se and does seem an abuse of the practitioner's relative power position with respect to the client. Other practitioners similar to Dr. Moore have been known to accept the $55 payment until the coverage is exhausted and then increase their charge to $105 (i.e., the fee plus net difference) for a like number of sessions to recoup their "loss." This is also a contract violation because it results in the policyholder being treated differently from the nonpolicyholder. It is clearly of questionable ethical propriety both in terms of contract violation and in terms of a radical fee increase in midtreatment.

Case 10-17: I. B. Hire, Psy.D., knows that he will only be paid $55 per session by Blue Mace/Blue Helmet, and he abides by his obligation not to balance bill or otherwise subvert the client's coverage. He also knows that no matter what fee he lists on the insurance claim form, $55, $80, or $100, he will still be paid only $55, rather than the $80 per hour he usually charges clients who pay out of pocket. Hire also knows that, according to his contract, future increases in reimbursement by the company are based on his "billing profile," his usual charges filled in on claim forms for similar services. He knows that his future rates will be linked to this profile. As a result, he reports his usual hourly rate as $120 per hour on all the claim forms, reasoning that he will eventually get a fairer rate than if he lets the company know his usual fee is only $80.

Hire's behavior presents a more subtle form of contract violation. In some ways, it is actually fraud because he is deliberately lying to the company in hopes of some future gain. Hire would probably rationalize that he is hurting no one because he will never bill the client more than his usual $80 when coverage is exhausted. He is, however, lying to the company and violating his agreement.

If Drs. More and Hire do not like the insurance contract that is offered, they have the option not to sign it. Some clients would be lost, perhaps, but professional disagreements over fee contracts are not subject to individualized attempts at remedies as described above. The acts of More and Hire are both illegal, given their contracts, as well as unethical.

Some MCOs have been known to use their significant market leverage to insist on nonfinancial contract clauses that raise significant ethical and liability issues. Two of the most significant are so-called gag rules and hold harmless clauses. Ethical aspects of these contract elements are discussed in the section, "Becoming a Provider," below.

BILL COLLECTING

It has been claimed that fee disputes are the most frequent basis of legal complaints against psychologists (Bennett, Bryant, VandenBos, & Greenwood, 1990; Woody, 1988), and this is also true in instances of client-initiated ethical complaints. The creditor and debtor relationships are just as much a part of the psychologist-client relationship as in most other purchases of service. Inevitably, some clients will fall behind in paying for services or fail to pay for them at all. Because of the nature of clients' reasons for consulting psychologists and the nature of the relationships that are established, however, psychologists have some special obligations to consider in formulating debt collection strategies.

When a client remains in active treatment while incurring a debt, the matter should be dealt with frankly, including a discussion of the impact of the debt on treatment. In most cases, however, the problems that arise occur after formal service delivery has terminated.

Case 10-18: Cindy Late complained to an ethics committee that her former therapist, Lucy Tort, Ed.D., had taken her to small claims court over $400 in unpaid bills. Ms. Late reported that she had been emotionally stressed and publicly embarrassed by having to appear in court to acknowledge that she had been treated by a psychologist. Dr. Tort advised the committee that Ms. Late had not responded to her bills or offers to work out an extended payment plan, noting that no confidential information was released; the court was only informed that Ms. Late had been a client and owed the money for services rendered.

Some psychologists have argued that disclosure of client status to the court violates a client's right to confidentiality unless specific informed consent is first obtained (Faustman, 1982). While that is an ethically considerate and conservative view, it is probably not unethical to initiate small claims actions in instances such as Dr. Tort's situation. An unpaid bill constitutes a broken contract between the client and practitioner. The psychologist may pursue legal recourse so long as no confidential material, other than the fact that a person was a client, is disclosed. Even such minimal disclosure might prove distressing to some clients because the court action is public and may even be reported in the community newspaper. Ideally, one should give the client ample notice that court action is being considered before it is actually initiated. While recognizing the difference between confidentiality and privileged communication (see chapter 6), Dr. Tort went on to compare the psychologist-client relationship with the attorney-client relationship, noting that the name and address are not privileged. Only the communications between client and practitioner fall in the confidential category.

Collection agencies represent quite a different matter from the small claims court, however, because the collection agent acts as an agent of the psychologist. This mechanism of resolving a debt is more private than using small claims court, but has its own intrinsic hazards. In such instances, the psychologist would be held responsible for the behavior of the collector. While most states regulate the nature and frequency of contacts by collection agencies, the psychologist could be held responsible for any improper, abusive, invasive, or otherwise noxious collection activities initiated in the psychologist's name.

One study found that 61% of the professional psychologists surveyed had used a collection agency, but of those using such agencies, only 49% reported having obtained consent from their clients about this aspect of the limits of confidentiality on that matter (Faustman, 1982). Faustman discusses a variety of collection practices and related problems, wisely noting, "psychologists should use extreme caution in relying on external services for the collection of delinquent accounts" (p. 208). Another reason for special caution is that collection practices often trigger counterclaims and complaints by clients (Pope, 1988).

Psychologists are in a unique position to cause clients emotional pain and should never take advantage of their professional status or relationship to collect a debt. While "ethics" may not be used as an excuse to deprive psychologists of their legal rights, mental health professionals should use caution in exercising those rights vis-à-vis clients.

Case 10-19: Sara Caustic, Ph.D., was annoyed with Nellie Angst, who had terminated treatment and left a bill unpaid for several months. Dr. Caustic continued to bill Ms. Angst monthly and began adding handwritten notes to the statements, such as, "Don't hold me responsible for the resentment you have toward your mother."

In this instance, Dr. Caustic is inappropriately expressing her anger through the pointed use of sensitive material gained in her professional capacity. While it would not necessarily be inappropriate to give a client factual warning that some collection agency or court action might follow if a bill remains unpaid, threats of this sort are unprofessional and not often effective. If emotional damage results from collection practices, a malpractice suit may follow. In this sense, a psychologist may be obligated to assess the clinical risks associated with different debt collection strategies. As in any situation for which psychologists employ other people to work in their practices, a degree of vicarious

liability exists with bill collection activities. Debt collection should be businesslike and totally void of any psychological or clinical content.

Another way in which a psychologist may occasionally attempt to abuse a professional relationship to collect a debt involves the withholding of information.

Case 10-20: Nellie Angst was so distraught by the notes from Dr. Caustic (Case 10-19) that she sought treatment again, but from a new therapist. She signed a release of information, and the new therapist contacted Dr. Caustic to obtain data on the prior treatment. Caustic told the new therapist that she would not discuss the case or provide copies of any reports she had prepared until Angst paid her bill.

In this situation, Dr. Caustic is continuing to exercise her professional leverage irresponsibly. If she were being asked to undertake new work on behalf of Ms. Angst, she certainly would have the right to decline. On the other hand, she may not ethically withhold materials already prepared or refuse to communicate with a colleague about a vulnerable client solely because of her own financial dispute with the client. In this instance, she is actually potentiating the harm to the client and compounding her own unethical behavior.

MANAGED CARE

The MCOs take many forms. Some may be actual health care delivery organizations, such as a free-standing HMO with its own employees serving as health care providers. Others may be networks of independent providers (so-called independent practice associations or IPA models). Still others may be HMOs that act as insurance companies and contract with a group of professionals organized as PPOs (preferred provider organizations) that agree to certain rules and reduced rates of reimbursement in exchange for patient referrals. Some large businesses and municipalities are self-insured. That is, these entities act as their own insurance company with the help of a claims and risk management program, often run by an insurance company or MCO in exchange for a management fee.

In most models, the MCO manages a full spectrum of health care benefits. In other models, a state Medicaid agency or insurance company may "carve out" mental health benefits from overall health insurance packages and assign management of these particular benefits to an MCO organized chiefly as a benefits manager. A brief lesson on the microeconomics of health insurance can be useful in understanding the forces at work here.

The goal of the various MCOs is essentially the same: to control the increasing costs of health care. When health insurance is provided on an indemnity basis (i.e., costs of covered services are paid for or reimbursed up to policy limits regardless of the provider), few controls or incentives exist to limit spending. In such circumstances, economists would say that the moral hazards of insurance are not well controlled.

The Moral Hazards of Insurance

Suppose we were to offer you "individual pregnancy insurance" at a very low price: complete coverage from prenatal care through delivery at a cost of $1 per month or $9 total per covered individual. Would you buy it? If your answer is, "Yes, where do I sign?" you are most likely to be a female who is considering becoming pregnant at some point within the span of coverage. If we decided that the policy would be available only to men, prepubertal girls, and postmenopausal women, do you think we would have many buyers? Likewise, would you buy automobile insurance if you did not own a car or hold a driver's license? These brief examples illustrate a basic moral hazard (Hemenway, 1983, pp. 112–115) of insurance: rational people are unlikely to buy it unless they think there is a chance they will need to use it. If your chance of becoming pregnant is near zero, you are unlikely to buy the insurance regardless of how low the cost. Similarly, a rational person with no access to a motor vehicle is unlikely to purchase automobile insurance regardless of cost. Pregnancy insurance is indeed available,

but it is bundled together in family-rate health insurance policies that take into account the fact that some members of some families will need the benefit, whereas others will not.

People who have insurance behave different from people without it. This is another moral hazard that can be considered on an *ex ante* and *ex post* basis. The *ex ante* model refers to behavior prior to making an insurance claim. Simply stated, it means that people will be less careful in avoiding insured perils than they would without insurance coverage. Using the pregnancy model, a rational person who is capable of becoming pregnant will generally be less careful about contraception than she would be without any access to health insurance to cover pregnancy. In addition, an automobile owner whose insurance has expired might keep the car in the garage to avoid risk of damage until a new policy was in force.

The *ex post* model refers to behavior following the insured event. People with insurance will demand (i.e., consume) more and higher quality services than would an uninsured person. If your automobile's fender is dented, but the car is driveable and you are uninsured, you might choose to drive the damaged car rather than pay for the repair out of pocket. If fully insured, on the other hand, the rational person would most likely seek complete repair from the best body shop in town. If your health insurance provides full pregnancy coverage, you will be more likely to use all of the prenatal care available to you rather than skipping some services to save money.

Insurance companies traditionally attempted to reduce such moral hazards by devising ways to have policyholders share in the risk. Required deductibles, copayments, and variable coverage limits are examples of these strategies. Although the use of such techniques appears to be effective in the case of automobile and home owner's insurance, health insurance costs were not well controlled in this manner. One reason is that health needs often must be dealt with as a survival issue. One may choose not to rush to repair a dented fender or leaky roof or even to live with the damage rather than bear the expense of repair. Cost sharing reduces inappropriate utilization, but appropriate use is also reduced. However, it is not wise to postpone surgery for an inflamed appendix, ignore treatment for diabetes, or prematurely suspend cancer chemotherapy for economic reasons as the resulting harm may be irreparable later. In addition, our relationships with health care providers must be based on trust, confidence, and professionalism at a level of intimacy that is not usually expected from those we hire to patch a leak in our roof or fix a dented automobile fender.

It is in this context and amid demands from large group insurance purchasers (i.e., employers) that MCOs have evolved. In addition to policy limits, deductibles, and copayments, MCOs introduced case reviews, requirements for prior approval, and other steps intended to reduce unnecessary, redundant, or ineffective (but costly) medical care. By doing so, insurance plans are able to reduce the cost of coverage and thereby offer less expensive benefit packages to employers or reduced costs to state government (Inglehart, 1992). In theory, consumers are free to choose their MCO based on performance, quality of service, and other such factors. In reality, the individual consumer has little impact on the system, and the large employers, major purchasers of coverage, often make decisions with bottom-line cost as the prime directive.

Paramount Ethical Dilemmas

The central ethical threat in managed care involves conflicting loyalties. Practitioners working under managed care must balance the needs and best interests of their clients with an array of rewards, sanctions, and other inducements. In its most common form, this conflict results in providing practitioners with financial incentives to limit care. It may be that the limits on care proposed are efficient, appropriate, and promote reasonable economies. On the other hand, limits curtail the freedom of both clients and practitioners. In the worst circumstances, decisions that are adverse from a client's perspective may be orchestrated without the client's knowledge, input, or consent (Council on Ethical and Judicial Affairs, 1995; Inglehart, 1996).

Sicker and Quicker

Many health and mental health practitioners have railed against MCOs, claiming that patients are turned out of hospitals "sicker and quicker" than in the past. Shore and Beigel (1996) note that infringements on professional autonomy also have been a key point of antagonism between MCOs and practitioners. The issue is an emotional one that often is not well understood by mental health practitioners. Karon (1995) observed that, although managed care programs are essentially vehicles intended to save money by eliminating unnecessary services, it is easier to save by simply cutting services. He worries that these are short-term approaches, with little interest in preventive mental health services. It is true that case review can potentially eliminate unnecessary psychiatric hospital admissions or psychotherapy in the same way second opinions can reduce unnecessary surgeries. However, review and decision making in the arena of mental health care are not often as clear-cut as problems in physical medicine. Regulation of MCOs has become a significant public policy issue.

Newman and Bricklin (1991) noted that legislation on managed care programs has been chiefly of the enabling sort (e.g., removing legal and financial barriers) as opposed to regulating potential adverse consequences of cost containment strategies. They trace the progression of legislation to its regulatory stage and relate it to the potential liabilities associated with cost containment. In this context, it is worthwhile to consider the case of *Wickline v. State of California* (1987).

Case 10-21: Ms. Wickline was a California Medicaid recipient who needed surgery for arteriosclerosis. When postsurgical complications arose, her physician requested an 8-day extension to the 10-day admission originally preauthorized. The reviewer authorized only a 4-day extension, and, because the physician did not object and request additional time again, Ms. Wickline was discharged after a total hospitalization of only 14 days. She subsequently developed a blood clot that ultimately required amputation of her right leg. She sued, alleging that failure to grant the extra 4 days of hospital care requested caused her injuries. The trial court found the reviewer negligent and awarded $500,000 in damages. On appeal, however, the decision was reversed on two bases. First, Ms. Wickline's physician had not protested the lack of a full 8-day extension. Second, the court concluded that the blood clot and resulting amputation would have occurred even if she had remained in the hospital.

The discussion of this case by Newman and Bricklin (1991) is worth reviewing carefully because the court also went on to state that third-party payers could be held legally accountable if appeals made on behalf of the patient by the care provider were "arbitrarily ignored or unreasonably disregarded or overridden" (*Wickline*, p. 1645). The message in this case is that third-party payers can be held liable for negligently designed or implemented cost containment strategies. Mental health professionals should actively call that point to the attention of case managers when they believe an inappropriate and potentially harmful denial of service decision has been made.

In the case of *Muse v. Charter Hospital of Winston-Salem, Incorporated* (1995), a North Carolina appeals court held that a hospital was liable for punitive damages because of "wanton and willful" conduct. The hospital discharged a suicidal adolescent, against the advice of the treating physician, when the teenager's insurance coverage expired. The severely depressed 16-year-old committed suicide a few days following the discharge. We expect more litigation of this sort as aggrieved clients and families seek to hold someone accountable for services they deem improperly "managed."

Becoming a Provider and Staying on the Panel: Between a Rock and a Hard Place

The MCOs have many bases for failing to admit applicant providers to their service pools. They may already have enough practitioners in a limited area, or the applicant may have an ethics complaint, licensing board action, or major malpractice claim on his or her record. In most cases, practitioners not admitted or dropped from MCO provider panels have no clear grounds to appeal. As a result, many providers fear that if they "rock the boat" by raising active objections to decisions they believe are adverse to their clients or by speaking out against MCO policies, they may be terminated from the provider panel. Some MCO contracting strategies do little to reassure providers.

Case 10-22: On June 1, Psychotron Mental Services (PMS) mailed renewal contracts to 2,000 practitioners in three states that caused major symptoms of professional distress. Most recipients received the mailing on June 7 and were told that renewal contracts must be returned no later than June 15. The lengthy contracts included a "hold harmless" clause and a "gag rule." Some providers, fearing economic losses, rushed to sign and return the contracts without seeking legal advice or raising objection.

So-called hold harmless clauses specify that the practitioner will not hold the MCO responsible for actions it may take that may result in harm to the practitioner as a result of decisions they make regarding services to a client. For example, if the MCO denies services and the psychologist must continue treating the client without coverage to avoid abandonment, the psychologist would not attempt to recover damages from the MCO. As another example, suppose the MCO denies services, and, as a result, the client commits suicide and the client's family files a wrongful death suit against the psychologist. Such clauses may be legally invalid as being against public policy, just as the *Wickline* case showed that MCOs can be held accountable. However, the psychologist would not be better off refusing to sign such a contractual condition from the outset.

The so-called no disparagement or gag rule prohibits the psychologist provider from making "critical, adverse, or negative" statements about the MCO to clients or in any public forum. Such policies make sense in traditional business practice, but they are out of place when applied to health care. Aside from the blatant abrogation of practitioners' rights to free speech, such a rule might be deemed a limit on client advocacy and an attempt at intimidation. Such restrictions can interfere with the psychologist's ethical obligation to provide patients with information about benefits, risks, and costs of various interventions. Nonetheless, many provider psychologists felt they had little choice but to sign, especially in the face of the time deadline. Fortunately, 18 states had banned such contract provisions outright by 1997, and legislation pending at other states and at the federal level may soon result in the permanent elimination of such contract clauses.

Some MCOs have been highly aggressive and heavy handed in contract offers. Among the problems reported in contracts offered to psychologists by MCOs are clauses stating that the provider will (1) be solely responsible in any legal actions undertaken by any party, (2) take no legal action against the MCO under any circumstances, (3) deal exclusively with the MCO, (4) agree to abide by all of the MCO's utilization review processes and decisions, (5) agree not to bill clients for noncovered services without advance written consent, (6) agree not to bill clients for covered services except for copayment and deductibles, (7) agree to provide services when benefits are exhausted, and (8) even agree to abide by future contract provisions that the psychologist has not yet seen. Although many such provisions are unenforceable, no sane person would want to be the "test case."

Signing a contract with provisions of this sort does a disservice to clients and psychologists alike. In particular, agreeing to such clauses may void coverage in related cases by the practitioners' professional liability insurance and may compromise their ability to defend themselves in the case of a suit. It also represents an effort to shift unreasonable responsibility for MCO actions to the shoulders of unwitting or coerced providers. When you receive such a contract, have it reviewed by an attorney familiar with mental health practice. Often, state psychological associations will be able to suggest such lawyers or refer you to psychologists in your locale familiar with that MCO's contracts. If you are pressed to sign a contract in haste, be wary.

Practical Considerations

Some illustrative examples may help the reader understand the nature of the struggles practitioners must increasingly address on a daily basis.

Case 10-21: Ralph Downer is significantly depressed: his child died of leukemia a few months ago, his marriage is on the rocks, and he has just learned that the company he works for is headed for a "major downsizing." Based on a careful intake evaluation, Opti Mum, Psy.D., has formulated a plan for individual and couples therapy over the next few weeks. Dr. Mum knows that antidepressant medication may also be useful, but he first wants to gauge the client's response to treatment without seeking a medication consult. When Mum contacts the case manager overseeing Mr. Downer's benefits, Mum is thanked for his assessment and is told to refer the client to a specific psychiatrist for a medication consultation. The manager explains that it is company policy to try treatment with generic antidepressant medication before authorizing verbal psychotherapy because, "A lot of patients get better with just a little medicine."

Case 10-22: Polly Substance, age 13, was brought to the office of Toomuch Thinkin, Ph.D. Her mother was concerned that Polly had been caught smoking pot at school. Her father has a history of problems with alcohol and has allegedly been physically threatening to his wife. Polly also has a history of learning disabilities and depression. Dr. Thinkin recommended family therapy at least once per week to begin addressing the multiple problems in the family. Comprehensive Regional Associated Programs (CRAP, corporate motto: "You're not sick until we say you're sick"), the managed care entity overseeing the family's benefits, will allow only four visits each for the mother and child during a 3-month period and will put both on antidepressant drugs.

In both of these cases, the psychologists' best clinical planning has been brushed aside by case managers with another agenda, presumably formulated by management with the intent of reducing costs. The preference of some managed care companies to prescribe medication instead of therapy is well known (Protos, 1996). In both cases, the ideal ethical conduct of the psychologist would be similar. First, firmly but respectfully explain the reasons for the recommended treatment plan. Cite supportive research and other factual data whenever possible. If the case manager does not agree, respectfully ask about the appeals process or to speak with a supervisor. Again, make the case in a thoughtful, rational manner, stressing the potential adverse consequences of not following it (e.g., failure to address the significant family relationship problems will undermine the chances for permanent change and may result in need for hospitalization or more extensive and costly interventions later). If there is still no favorable resolution, practitioners should meet with their clients and present both their recommendations and the response of the benefits management company. Clients should also be told of their own recourse (e.g., complaints directly to the management company, complaints to their employer, or contacts with regulatory agencies) if they wish to pursue such options. The principles involved are (1) holding the best interests of the client paramount, (2) advocating for the client in a professional manner, and (3) involving the client in the decision-making process.

Having stated the "ideal," it is important to recognize the constraints many psychologists feel. It is not unrealistic to fear that getting a reputation as a psychologist who persistently appeals decisions or encourages clients to do so may result in a "no cause termination." That is, the MCO may exercise a standard contract option to drop a provider without giving a specific reason. In addition, when a company is self-insured, employees may be reluctant to pursue legitimate benefits assertively out of fear of retaliation, even when this fear is unjustified. As noted above, some MCOs occasionally attempt to secure contractual provisions intended to prevent practitioners from speaking critically of company practices or advocating too vigorously for clients. There are also significant financial pressures.

Case 10-23: Tom Swift, Psy.D., was very successful in doing focal short-term therapy. Pleased with his work, Giant Health Organization (GHO) sent him many referrals. A few months later, in a letter to all of its providers, GHO informed Dr. Swift that it planned to narrow its provider pool to those who could provide up to 30 hours of service per week. Soon, GHO subscribers became the major portion of Dr. Swift's practice. GHO then began to offer special incentives, including cash bonuses at the end of each calendar quarter, for meeting a certain quota of cases "successfully terminated in fewer than eight sessions."

In this example Dr. Swift has become the victim of an insidious seduction. He has become increasingly dependent on GHO as a source of income and is then propositioned with a bonus plan that places corporate profit goals ahead of client welfare. Even if Dr. Swift is a psychologist of the highest ethical integrity, he will be sorely tempted by the new plan. One must also wonder how vigorous an advocate he might be for a client who needed more services or wished to appeal a GHO decision. After all, Dr. Swift could be obliquely threatened with a no cause termination. We do not wish to infer that all or even the majority of MCOs would engage in such conduct; however, we do advise our colleagues to be prepared and forewarned of such strategies and the resulting risks.

Two of the most common ethical worries raised by psychologists who practice in MCOs are (1) If I go along with a managed care philosophy that only provides coverage for short-term therapy, can my client charge me with incorrect or inappropriate treatment? (2) If the company decides that the treatment I am providing is not medically necessary, it can stop providing payment with little notice. If my client is unwilling to pay out of pocket, am I at risk for abandonment charges?

The answer to both questions has a similar focus: professional responsibility, competence, and planning. Under no circumstances should a psychologist allow his or her care of a client to be dictated by a third-party payer. If an MCO dictates a "one size fits all" (or even "one size fits most") formula for psychotherapy, a psychologist who agrees to that policy is headed for trouble. The policy implies that treatment is framed independent of a careful diagnostic assessment or plan matched to the client's needs. The nature of the treatment contract (see chapter 4) highlights the importance of helping the client to understand and agree to the treatment plan and costs from the outset of the professional relationship. This includes helping clients to find out what mental health coverage their insurance provides. This may include a recognition that out-of-pocket costs are likely at some point.

One can certainly advocate for a client whose need for services is questioned, and it is easiest to do this when clear, competent treatment plans and records are produced. If a third party refuses payment and a client cannot or does not wish to pay out of pocket, the psychologist should attempt a resolution consistent with the client's need (e.g., offering a reduced fee or making a referral to an agency offering more affordable fees). There is no obligation to continue treating such clients indefinitely, although some reasonable interim coverage should be provided, and no client should be abandoned in the middle of a crisis situation.

Emotional Outrage

Unfortunately, the net result of marketplace changes and occasional MCO horror stories is considerable emotional distress in the mental health community. The resulting behavior is not always rationally driven. So intense are the emotions of clinicians regarding managed care that one author, with some positive comments about managed care, felt the need to do so anonymously out of fear of reprisals from colleagues (Anonymous, 1995). It is unclear whether the article was intended as serious scholarly comment or a mischievous lampoon. Nonetheless, the editors agreed to publish it.

The anonymous author cited four "hidden benefits of managed care: (a) technical assistance and education, (b) opportunities for socializing, (c) the promotion of interdisciplinary collaboration, and (d) free supervision" (Anonymous, 1995, p. 235). The author noted an improvement in personal technical skills that focused on having to learn the Global Assessment of Functioning (GAF) scale (American Psychiatric Association, 1994). Feeling lonely in the relative isolation of private practice, the anonymous clinician found the "built-in opportunity to chat" with managed care reviewers "refreshing" (Anonymous, 1995, p. 235). Citing the enigmatic processes of history, the author expressed the belief that managed care is having a unifying effect on the mental health professions that transcends "professional parochialism" (p. 236). Finally, the author notes that beneficent free supervision is provided by "knowledgeable and helpful colleagues" who are managed care case reviewers and cites, without attribution, a quote to the effect that professional ethics requires seeking assistance and guidance.

Although written in sincere (tongue in cheek?) tones, the claims are rather shallow. For example, the GAF is widely regarded as a measure of dubious reliability and clinical validity. Its scores are easily manipulated to suit the needs of the clinician or care manager. Praising the technical assistance needed to help a doctoral-level clinician to master the GAF is comparable to lauding a school child's ability to hop on one leg while chewing gum.

In addition, the paperwork and other communication requirements involved in managed care can be quite significant. Completion of special treatment plans, approval forms, and other documents are time consuming. The need to schedule and participate in telephone case reviews takes additional time. It is not unusual to spend as much time engaged in paperwork and telephone work on a particular case as one spends in face-to-face contact with the client. There is no evidence that this additional effort improves the quality of client care.

Although the anonymous author is accurate in noting that the mental health professions have discovered common cause in their annoyance and frustration with aspects of managed care, the interdisciplinary alliance is an uneasy one. Some managed care plans differentially include or exclude specific professions or profession-linked services (e.g., psychological testing). Psychologists should have no illusions regarding the solidarity of these new alliances should managed care entities begin to offer incentives that offer differential benefits to one or another profession.

Finally, the anonymous author's delight in the free supervision is seriously misplaced. Citing professional ethics as a rationale for seeking expert assistance and guidance is indeed appropriate. However, the value of such advice and guidance evaporates rapidly when the "advisor" may have personal or corporate interests in cost savings at the patients' potential expense. It is true that many managed care reviewers are competent mental health professionals dedicated to giving high-quality clinical input. The case manager's obligation to the patient, however, is different and of more diluted quality than the obligations of the primary clinician. Even the most competent and ethically sensitive case manager must balance accountability to the company with the patients' needs. To the extent that the relationship is based on a capitated model (i.e., in capitation models, the vendor is paid a set fee for covering a number of lives, regardless of actual service delivery), the ethical tension is even more acute. Free supervision in this context is worth exactly what the anonymous author pays for it.

There are indeed some benefits to society in managed care. These include reductions in the cost of services and insurance, lessening the so-called moral hazards of insurance (from the insurance company perspective), and new pressures on practitioners to think carefully regarding all aspects of their treatment planning. None of these potential benefits are hidden. At the same time, there are great risks inherent in a system of health care delivery that potentially provides systematic incentives to withhold care (as in the case of capitation models, in which a set fee is paid to cover all the mental health needs of a set number of insured people regardless of how much service is provided) or raises unreasonable barriers to reasonable care. Ironically, managed care and capitation models introduce a new kind of moral hazard by creating an incentive to provide less service.

At present, there are MCOs in both the nonprofit and for-profit sectors of the industry. On average, for-profit HMOs spend only 70 to 80 cents of the premium dollar on health services, whereas nonprofit HMOs usually spend 90 cents per dollar (Gentry, 1995, p. 11). The competition between nonprofit and for-profit HMOs may force nonprofit HMOs into the for-profit sector. In order to raise cash for expansion and marketing, nonprofit HMOs may have to go public and sell stock (Gentry, 1995). Such a turn of events would most certainly compromise the public interest.

Key Ethical Problems in Dealing with Managed Care Organizations

Managed care evolved as a function of changes in the economic realities of the health care marketplace. At the same time, managed care raises a number of stressful concerns for psychologists; these concerns range from autonomy (i.e., infringements on the tradition of a professional's independent judgment) to zeal (i.e., the energy with which some care managers have attempted to cut costs). Managed care came about in response to dramatically escalating costs of health care services, lack of meaningful economic controls on prices, demand by employers (who contract for employee health insurance), and legislators (who oversee payment under state and federal insurance plans). Not all of the concerns about managed care are ethical issues in the sense that they directly compromise one's ability to conform to professional ethics codes. Similarly, not all MCOs are sinister or malevolent. Many do a good job of controlling costs with reasonable peer review. When buying health care services, employers and subscribers must recognize that you get what you paid for. A low-cost plan will have more limited coverage and possibly less professional management when it comes to case review decision making. In the end, the quality of services provided is dependent on the competence and integrity of the service providers. One should, however, always pay attention to the key ethical problems listed below.

1. With primary emphasis on cost containment, comprehensiveness of service or needs of specific clients may be compromised.
2. Providers may often be placed in conflicting

roles when they try to offer what the client needs versus what is covered. Increasingly, providers (as individuals or groups) will be pressured by third-party payers to agree to capitation schemes. Under such plans, there are clear financial incentives to reduce the amount of care provided, somewhat akin to the agricultural practice of paying some farmers to let land lie fallow. This will ultimately erode patients' trust; even when practitioners are justified in saying "no," they will be suspect.

3. The reduction in clients' free choice is significant. Clients may be forced to accept a provider from a particular pool; this requires them to work with someone who has a previously negotiated arrangement with the MCO to which the patient was not a party.

4. The PPO structures may lead to the creation of provider panels that are short on diversity (e.g., do not adequately include therapists skilled in working with ethnic minorities, people with sensory impairments, etc.).

5. Confidentiality concerns are potentiated (see chapter 6).

6. Restrictive covenants such as gag rules and hold harmless clauses can have far-reaching liability consequences for practitioners.

SUMMARY GUIDELINES

1. Clients should be informed about fees, billing, collection practices, and other financial contingencies as a routine part of initiating the professional relationship. This information should also be repeated later in the relationship if necessary.

2. Psychologists should carefully consider the client's overall ability to afford services early in the relationship and should help the client to make a plan for obtaining services that will be both clinically appropriate and financially feasible. Encouraging clients to incur significant debt is not psychotherapeutic. In that regard, psychologists should be aware of referral sources in the community.

3. Psychologists ideally perform some services at little or no fee as a pro bono service to the public as a routine part of their practice.

4. Relationships involving kickbacks, fee splitting, or payment of commissions for client referrals may be illegal and unethical. Careful attention to the particular circumstances and state laws will be important before agreeing to such arrangements.

5. It is important for psychologists to pay careful attention to all contractual obligations, understand them, and abide by them. Similarly, psychologists should not sign contracts with stipulations that might subsequently place them in ethical jeopardy.

6. Psychologists may be held responsible for financial misrepresentations effected in their name by an employee or agent they have designated (including billing and collection agents). They must, therefore, choose their employees and representatives with care and supervise them closely.

7. In all debt collection situations, psychologists must be aware of the laws that apply in their jurisdiction and make every effort to behave in a cautious, businesslike fashion. They must avoid using their special position or information gained through their professional role to collect debts from clients.

8. In dealing with managed care organizations, psychologists should adhere to the same standards of competence, professionalism, and integrity as in other contexts. Heightened sensitivity should be focused on the potential ethical problems inherent in such service delivery systems.

References

Albee, G. W. (1977). Does including psychotherapy in health insurance represent a subsidy to the rich from the poor? *American Psychologist*, 32, 719–721.

American Psychiatric Association. (1994). Global assessment of functioning. Washington, DC: Author.

Anonymous. (1995). Hidden benefits of managed care. *Professional Psychology: Research and Practice*, 26, 235–237.

Bennett, B. E., Bryant, B. K., VandenBos, G. R., & Greenwood, A. (1990). *Professional liability and risk management*. Washington, DC: American Psychological Association.

Chodoff, P. (1978). Psychiatry and the fiscal third party. *American Journal of Psychiatry, 135,* 1141–1117.

Council on Ethical and Judicial Affairs, American Medical Association. (1995). Ethical issues in managed care. *Journal of the American Medical Association, 273,* 330–335.

DiBella, G. A. W. (1980). Mastering money issues that complicate treatment: The last taboo. *American Journal of Psychotherapy, 24,* 510–522.

Dujovne, B. E. (1980). Third party recognition of psychological services. *Professional Psychology, 11,* 574–581.

Edwards, D. W., Greene, L. R., Abramowitz, S. I., & Davidson, C. V. (1979). National health insurance, psychotherapy, and the poor. *American Psychologist, 35,* 411–419.

Faustman, W. O. (1982). Legal and ethical issues in debt collection strategies of professional psychologists. *Professional Psychology, 13,* 208–214.

Fee, practice, and managed care survey. (1995). *Psychotherapy Finances, 21,* 1–8.

Gentry, C. (1995, July 4). HMOs' cost-cutting frenzy is a pain. *Boston Globe,* p. 11.

Grossman, M. (1971). Insurance reports as a threat to confidentiality. *American Journal of Psychiatry, 128,* 96–100.

Hemenway, D. (1983). *Prices and choices: Microeconomic vignettes* (rev. edition). Cambridge, MA: Ballinger.

Inglehart, J. K. (1992). The American health care system: Managed care. *New England Journal of Medicine, 327,* 742–747.

Inglehart, J. K. (1996). Managed care and mental health. *New England Journal of Medicine, 334,* 131–135.

Jagim, R. D., Wittman, W. D., & Noll, J. O. (1978). Mental health professionals' attitudes toward confidentiality, privilege, and third-party disclosure. *Professional Psychology, 9,* 458–466.

Karon, B. P. (1995). Provision of psychotherapy under managed care: A growing crisis and national nightmare. *Professional Psychology: Research and Practice, 26,* 5–9.

Kiesler, C. A., & Pallak, M. S. (1980). The Virginia blues. *American Psychologist, 35,* 953–954.

Lovinger, R. J. (1978). Obstacles in psychotherapy: Setting a fee in the initial contact. *Professional Psychology, 9,* 350–352.

Meltzer, M. L. (1975). Insurance reimbursement: A mixed blessing. *American Psychologist, 30,* 1150–1164.

Muse v. Charter Hospital of Winston-Salem, Inc., 452 S.E. 2d 589 (N.C. Ct. App. 1995).

Myers, W., & Brezler, M. F. (1992). Selling or buying a practice. *The Independent Practitioner, 12,* 92–93.

Newman, R., & Bricklin, P. M. (1991). Parameters of managed mental health care: Legal, ethical, and professional guidelines. *Professional Psychology: Research and Practice, 22,* 26–35.

Pope, K. S. (1988). Fee policies and procedures: Causes of malpractice suits and ethics complaints. *The Independent Practitioner, 8,* 24–29.

Pope, K. S., & Keith-Spiegel, P. (1986, May). Is selling a practice malpractice? *APA Monitor,* pp. 4, 40.

Protos, J. (1996, March). Ten things your HMO won't tell you. *Smart Money,* 134–144.

Rodwin, M. (1993). *Medicine, money, and morals: Physicians' conflicts of interest.* New York: Oxford University Press.

Sharfstein, S. S., Taube, C. A., & Goldberg, I. D. (1975). Private psychiatry and accountability: A response to the APA Task Force Report on Private Practice. *American Journal of Psychiatry, 132,* 43–47.

Shore, M. F., & Beigel, A. (1996). The challenges posed by managed behavioral health care. *New England Journal of Medicine, 334,* 116–118.

Stricker, G. (1979). Criteria for insurance review of psychological services. *Professional Psychology, 10,* 118–122.

Vasile, R. G., & O'Loughlin, M. (1977). Initiation of fees in a nonpaying group. *Psychiatric Annals, 7,* 77–84.

Wickline v. State of California, 239 Cal. Rptr. 805, 741 P. 2d 613 (1987).

Woody, R. H. (1988). *Protecting your mental health practice: How to minimize legal and financial risk.* San Francisco: Jossey-Bass.

Woody, R. H. (1997). Valuing a psychological practice. *Professional Psychology: Research and Practice, 28,* 77–80.

11

Psychologists in the Marketplace

Advertising may be described as the science of
arresting the human intelligence long enough to
get money from it.

Stephen Butler Leacock

The manner in which psychologists offer their
services to the public has important ethical implications on a variety of fronts. Certainly, some
forms of advertisements or calling attention to
one's services or products are appropriate ways to
educate and inform potential consumers. However, some psychologists have occasionally used
confusing, anxiety-provoking, or frankly deceptive practices in presenting themselves to the
public. In addition, the nature of psychotherapy
is such that it is not easily compared across
vendors in the same way breakfast cereals or used
cars can be. Inappropriate commercial public
statements by psychologists range from the factual to the bizarre, and it is not often possible
to identify specific clients as "victims" of such
infractions. It is often evident, however, that
certain public behaviors reflect quite unfavor-
ably on the profession as a whole. Because the
practice of psychology has commercial or business aspects and because professional regulatory
bodies are arms of state government or tax exempt organizations (e.g., the American Psychological Association, APA), there is also a tension

between maintaining appropriate conduct and
avoiding restraint of trade.

In this chapter, we review the evolution of
today's advertising patterns and attitudes among
the professions and among psychologists in particular. We review both acceptable and unacceptable types of advertisements, touching on a
number of subtle and obvious variations. We
include some issues related to products (e.g.,
books and devices used by psychologists), as well
as services offered to individuals, groups, and
organizations. A variety of related matters, including ethical problems related to referral services and ethics of the "lecture circuit" or "media circuit," are also covered.

HISTORICAL ISSUES

Historically, the professions have considered
advertising of services or direct solicitation of
clients to be déclassé at the very least. The professions have traditionally liked to think of themselves as self-regulating and rejected the notion

that advertising would be meaningful to a client. The usual point cited as justification for this view is that an advertisement is no indicator of skill or competence, and one should instead rely on the referral of a presumably informed and knowing colleague. Certain types of advertising were considered distasteful or even misleading because they traded on public fears or ignorance related to the services being offered.

From the time of psychology's emergence as an autonomous profession following World War II, emulation of existing practices of other older and better established professions tended to be the usual practice. Advertising was to be "professional in tone," which generally meant discrete, formal, terse, and narrow in scope. The preferred form was more an announcement of availability than an active effort to recruit clients. The model provided by medical practitioners was readily imitated.

A set of guidelines for telephone directory listings published by the APA (1969) nearly three decades ago is typical of the attitudes held at the time. The guidelines enjoined psychologists to list only names, highest relevant degree, and some narrow indication of specialization if desired (e.g., "practice limited to children" or "psychological consultant to management"). The psychologist was advised that the size and typeface should be uniform, and boldface fonts should be avoided. Listing of multiple specializations was considered "a form of self-aggrandizement and . . . unwarranted." So-called box ads were to be avoided, as was listing in directories outside the area where one maintained a bona fide office.

If a psychologist were opening a new practice in that era, a tasteful box notice might be inserted in the local newspaper, such as

Ronald J. MacDonald, Ph.D. announces the opening of his office for the practice of clinical psychology at 555 Main Street in Anytown, U.S.A. Office hours by appointment. 555-1212.

This announcement would not have been repeated more than once or twice, although it was also considered reasonable to send a printed notice by mail to colleagues in the community.

At least these were the views that held sway within psychology and many other professions until the Federal Trade Commission (FTC) became involved.

Federal Trade Commission Actions

The FTC is an independent agency of the federal government that consists of two main branches. The Bureau of Competition is the branch focusing on antitrust issues, while the Bureau of Consumer Protection investigates charges of false or deceptive advertising. Stimulated by the work of Ralph Nader and other consumer advocates, as well as much-publicized class action lawsuits against major corporations, a wave of consumer activism became prominent in America during the 1960s and 1970s. This was an important factor in the decision of the FTC and the U.S. Department of Justice to bring about changes in the ways professional associations attempted to regulate their members (Koocher, 1977, 1994).

By the early 1970s, the Bureau of Competition began approaching professional organizations with concerns about association practices that barred the presentation of useful consumer information through advertising. From the perspective of the FTC's Bureau of Competition, there were three prime directives, which might best be summarized as (1) truthful advertising is good, (2) false or deceptive advertising is bad, and (3) blocking truthful advertising is as bad as false and misleading advertising.

In 1972, the FTC and the Antitrust Division of the Justice Department initiated complaints against a variety of professional associations, including the American Institute of Architects, the American Institute of Certified Public Accountants, and the National Society of Professional Engineers. On June 6, 1975, the U.S. Supreme Court unanimously struck down the publication of fee schedules by bar associations, effectively terminating attempts to enforce a minimum fee schedule for lawyers (*Goldfarb v. Virginia State Bar*, 1975). The *Goldfarb* ruling (1975) and a similar case (*Bates et al. v. State Bar of Arizona*, 1977) made it clear that: (1) the professions do not enjoy some special form of antitrust exemption and (2) at least some rules of professional associations that directly eliminate competition may be illegal per se. The FTC actions were specifically concerned with professional ethical codes that prohibited (1) soliciting business by advertising or otherwise, (2) engaging in price competition, and (3) otherwise engaging in competitive practices. In the case of medical societies, enforcing the existing medical ethics code (American Medical Association, 1971) was deemed to create de facto price interference and frustrate the consumer's right to choose services in an unrestrained fashion (Koocher, 1977).

As early as 1976, the APA Ethics Committee decided to act prospectively rather than awaiting a call from the FTC. One member of the committee was asked to address these issues during a committee-sponsored symposium at the annual convention that year and subsequently published an expanded version of that presentation (Koocher, 1977). At about the same time, the APA Ethics Committee was at work on the third major revision of the APA ethics code (APA, 1981) and declined to take action on advertising complaints so long as the advertisements were accurate and provided information that was important or relevant to consumers. Between 1977 and 1981, the APA Council of Representatives made a number of minor adjustments to the APA ethics code. The completed revision (APA, 1981), which remained in force until 1989, directed that advertising in general would be ethically acceptable so long as certain basic tenets (e.g., avoiding misleading claims, eschewing testimonials, avoiding anxiety-inducing advertisements, etc.) were followed. The principal goal of these sections of the code was to protect potential consumers of psychological services from being taken advantage of by virtue of their cognitive or emotional vulnerabilities (ES: 3.03, 3.05, 3.06).

Psychology also mounted strong political support for consumer interests within the FTC. When bills were introduced in Congress during the Reagan administration to exempt the professions (including psychology) from regulation by the FTC, they were actively opposed by organized psychology (Association for the Advancement of Psychology, 1982). That activity was regarded as a strong public interest position, and the APA was widely praised as a leader among the professions in the consumer protection community. American psychology was proactively striving to be a good citizen and proconsumer.

Investigation of the APA by the FTC began shortly after the 1981 code was adopted. In this respect, the APA was approached later than many other professional and scientific associations. According to Attorney Steven Osnowitz,[1] who represented the FTC in parts of the APA case, this was because the APA was "not the most offensive" and because the FTC was "fine tuning" its enforcement of the issues involved via its work with other professions with practices vis-à-vis advertising that were deemed more troubling. Although not a primary reason for looking at the APA's conduct, Osnowitz also noted that the APA staff had allegedly been giving advice to state psychological associations and licensing boards on the interpretation of the code. According to Osnowitz, some psychologists were subjected to local enforcement actions by state psychological association ethics committees or licensing boards that reportedly relied on the APA's advice; these individuals later complained about the APA to the FTC. It is unclear whether the APA staff ever provided comments regarding a specific case being adjudicated at the state level or simply gave general interpretive advice on the code. However, it is clear that the FTC staff was concerned as much about the appearance of inappropriate consultation by a national professional association as it was about actual improper influence.

The authors' recollections of APA Ethics Office operations in the late 1970s and early 1980s (when they served as members of the APA Ethics Committee) is consistent with Onsowitz's comments. For example, it was not uncommon for callers to the APA Ethics Office to be referred

---

1. The comments reported here were made in two telephone interviews the author had with Attorney Osnowitz during July 1993. The material within quotation marks are verbatim comments transcribed during the conversation. Readers will want to be mindful of the fact that the memories and interpretations made by one party to a series of events may differ from the recollections of other parties.

to members of the APA Ethics Committee in their geographic area for advice on interpretation of general aspects of the code. In addition, there was a period of considerable staff turnover in the APA Ethics Office during this time, and the authors recall specific instances of inappropriate advice being given out.[2]

According to Osnowitz, the APA's code was not the most outrageous among the professions with respect to advertising restrictions, and the APA principles were not being enforced egregiously. However, the APA's flat ban on the use of testimonials was "inherently suspect." Similarly, the FTC opposed blanket prohibitions against claims of "uniqueness" because these might conceivably be true in some cases. One nonpsychologist who also complained to the FTC ran a referral service in the state of Maryland. In a manner akin to some urban dating services, prospective clients could browse at their leisure through a set of videotapes made by psychotherapists listed with the referral service. A state psychological association ethics committee began to target psychologists who were "listed" with this service, and, according to Osnowitz, at one point some members of the APA Ethics Committee "went bezerk over the videos." Asked for clarification, Osnowitz explained that the reactions of some psychologists serving on the ethics panel that addressed these cases seemed overly zealous in their sense of outrage from the standpoint of FTC investigators.

The "Emergency" Actions of 1989

On June 2, 1989, the board of directors of the APA declared an emergency and amended the "Ethical Principles of Psychologists" with no advance notice to the membership or governance structure of APA. The board was acting under provisions of the APA bylaws that authorized extraordinary procedures when acting in

the stead of the Council of Representatives when the council was not in session. Although the few hundred members of the APA active in governance received an explanatory memo, this information was not widely circulated. Alert members might have noticed a few brief mentions of the ongoing APA-FTC dialogue in the *APA Monitor* (see the March 1988 and January 1990 issues) or embedded in occasional committee reports published in the *American Psychologist*. However, the newly truncated version of the code first widely published in the *American Psychologist* (APA, 1990) contained no explanations regarding the changes made or the nature of the emergency. Many members of the APA were confused, thinking somehow that the entire ethics code had been globally revised since the modifications made were not highlighted or summarized in this official presentation.

The seven emergency 1990 changes made in the 1981 version of the code removed prohibitions against testimonials from patients; claims of unusual, unique, or one-of-a-kind abilities; appeals to clients' fears if services are not obtained; claims of the comparative desirability of one service over another; or direct solicitation of individual clients. In addition, a sentence that had previously barred psychologists from "giving or receiving any remuneration for referring clients for professional services" was removed. Even though this principle had been intended to prevent fee splitting or kickback arrangements (see chapter 10), it was interpreted by the FTC as having the potential to prohibit participation in legitimate referral service businesses or some types of managed care operations (Koocher, 1994). The goal of the APA in originally including such language was solely to prohibit kickbacks, which compromise client welfare in two respects. First, referral recommendations for psychological services based on such arrangements might be made on the basis of hidden financial relationships rather than

---

2. For example, a complaint was received about an APA member whose name and photograph (identifying him as a psychologist) appeared in a nationally published magazine advertisement endorsing a particular brand of Scotch whiskey. The APA Ethics Committee began an investigation, but closed the case with considerable embarrassment when the psychologist reported that he had requested a prior opinion from the then APA Ethics Officer, who told him that such an endorsement would not violate the existing code. The staff member in question admitted giving the advice without consulting any members of the APA Ethics Committee.

with paramount regard for a client's best interests. Second, the financial exchanges might have the effect of ultimately increasing the cost of services to the client.

Another sentence was also eliminated. It had specified that, "If a person is receiving similar services from another professional, psychologists do not offer their services to such a person." This section had been intended as a kind of noninterference clause to prevent piracy of clients already receiving services elsewhere. In addition, it reflected a belief that clients simultaneously receiving services from different practitioners might receive compromised care as the result of conflicting advice. The specific prohibition the FTC sought to drop was the barrier to offering such services.

The emergency was related to pending negotiations with the FTC on a final consent agreement and the impending publication of the 1990 APA Biographical Directory. That document, published every 3 years, has an extended shelf-life and includes copies of the APA bylaws and ethics code. Publishing the 1990 edition with the old version of the ethics code (APA, 1981) would have been unacceptable and provocative to the FTC. Why the publication of the newly altered code was unaccompanied by an explanation has never been made clear.

Prior to the emergency declaration, considerable lobbying within the APA governance structure had focused on retaining prohibitions of unfair/deceptive advertising, use of testimonials, and advertising that appealed to fear if services are not obtained. Several divisions, APA committees, and the Board of Social and Ethical Responsibility for Psychology (formerly known as BSERP) adopted resolutions asking the APA Board of Directors to pursue these issues in negotiations or even litigation with the FTC. During this period, legal counsel for the APA and the FTC were involved in ongoing intense negotiations. These exchanges were not shared beyond the APA Ethics Committee and the APA Board of Directors, and little or no feedback was provided to the other boards, committees, or individuals who commented on the issues to the APA. One can imagine that limited access to detailed information on the negotiations was required to effectively forge an agreement with

the FTC, but the result was a sense of surprise and dismay by many not privy to the process. The APA Board of Directors' emergency action ended the discussion, and the FTC's Bureau of Competition carefully reviewed the most recent ethics code (APA, 1992) before its adoption (APA Ethics Committee, 1993b).

The authors believe that a significant reason for "giving in" to many of the FTC requirements ("FTC Consent Order," 1993) was the view that resisting the FTC would lead to potential embarrassment and substantial costs, particularly related to the FTC's demand for production of documents under discovery. Interestingly, one of the FTC commissioners wrote a partial dissent to the FTC decision that tended to corroborate this view. Commissioner Mary L. Azcuenaga was supportive of the APA's ban on advertising that appeals to clients' fears. This issue is discussed in detail below, however, she observed "as often happens in cases of this nature, the respondent has substantial financial incentives to accept the settlement rather than litigate" (Azcuenaga, 1990, p. 2).

THE NATURE OF RESTRICTIONS ON ADVERTISEMENTS

If the general goals of the FTC were to make useful information available to the general public, it is understandable that clinging to vestiges of sameness in public statements for the sake of a sense of professionalism would not survive. However, some limits on advertising may well serve legitimate public interests. This is especially true in professions, such as psychology, that may unduly influence consumers because of the consumers' compromised cognitive or emotional status.

State's Interest Doctrine

The FTC has not focused on state licensing boards and would not be likely to act against state boards that take well-reasoned steps to enforce greater restrictions than are allowed professional associations as a matter of a "state's interests." In the case of *Virginia State Board of Pharmacy*, the Supreme Court ruled in part that, "the State is free to require whatever professional standards it wishes of its pharmacists, and may subsidize them or protect them from competition in other ways, but it may not do so by keeping the public in ignorance of the lawful terms that competing pharmacists are offering" (1975, pp. 766–770). The decision struck down a Virginia law that provided that a pharmacist licensed in Virginia would be guilty of unprofessional conduct if he or she "published or advertised any prices, discounts, or rebates in any manner whatsoever for prescription drugs."

At the same time, the court carved out the state's interest exception by noting, "If there is a kind of commercial speech that lacks all First Amendment protection . . . it must be distinguished by its content" (Virginia State Board of Pharmacy, 1975, p. 761). For example, in *Bates* the court noted "peculiar problems associated with advertising claims relating to *quality* of legal services," noting that these are not subject to precise measurement and "under some circumstances, might well be deceptive or misleading to the public, or even false" (1977, p. 366). The bottom line appears to be whether the state is able to document a legitimate governmental interest in protecting its citizens.

It appears likely that state psychology licensing boards, which unlike the ethics committees of state psychological associations are created by statutory actions of a legislature, would be regarded as having authority to implement more restrictive limitations on advertising than are specified in the current. For example, if a statutory licensing authority were to specifically define a state's interest in proscribing "appeals to fear" or testimonial advertising by mental health professionals, it is quite possible that the FTC would not object. APA, however, would be specifically prevented from cooperating with state agencies in the development of such regulations.

Is Commercial Speech Free Speech Too?

Do restraints imposed by professional association restrictions on advertising violate commercial free speech? While not the same as political free speech in the Constitutional sense, the concept is still highly relevant and has often been an issue in efforts to limit advertising by lawyers. Commercial speech is protected under the First and Fourteenth Amendments just as political speech is protected (Virginia State Board of Pharmacy, 1975); however, the courts have ruled that it is still reasonable to demand substantiation in the face of alleged false or deceptive advertising. The FTC's thrust has been to expand access to truthful information in the marketplace, although there are some exceptions, which are discussed below as "in your face" solicitations. A good example of the commercial free speech argument involved an enterprising Kentucky lawyer named Shapero.

Case 11-1: The U.S. Supreme Court dealt with a case involving a young Kentucky lawyer named Shapero, who wanted to solicit business by sending truthful, nondeceptive letters to potential clients known to be confronting certain legal problems, such as property foreclosures. The letter in question was to go to potential clients who had a foreclosure suit filed against them; it advised, "You may be about to lose your home," and that "Federal law may allow you to . . . ORDER your creditor to STOP." Potential clients were invited by Mr. Shapero to "call my office for FREE information. . . . It may surprise you what I may be able to do for you" (Shapero v. Kentucky Bar Association, 1988, p. 1919).

Mr. Shapero had the foresight to ask the Kentucky state bar for an advisory opinion as to whether his proposed letter to people facing foreclosure was acceptable. Although the state bar commissioners ruled that the letter was not misleading, they told Shapero not to use the letter, citing a then-existing Kentucky Supreme Court rule prohibiting the direct solicitation of individuals (i.e., as opposed to members of the general public) as a direct result of some specific event. Shapero appealed to the U.S. Supreme Court and won. The key point in the decision was that the content of his notice was not false or deceptive and held genuine potential interest for the intend recipients, which they could then choose to act on or ignore.

In Your Face Solicitation

What if the nature of the commercial exercise of free speech involves a more intense approach than Shapero's letter or takes advantage of a client in a vulnerable position? Existing case law suggests that so-called in your face solicitation of clients, especially vulnerable ones, will not be tolerated.

Consider the case of an enterprising lawyer named Ohralik from Montville, Ohio (*Ohralik v. Ohio State Bar Association*, 1978).

Case 11-2: On February 13, 1974, attorney Ohralik was picking up his mail at the Montville Post Office and learned in casual conversation with the postmaster's brother that 18-year-old Carol McClintock had been injured in an automobile accident a week and a half earlier. Attorney Ohralik decided to pay a call on Carol's parents; while there, he learned that she and her passenger, Wanda Lou Holbert, were riding together in the McClintock family car when they were struck by an uninsured motorist. Both girls required hospitalization. Since Carol was 18 years old and no longer a minor, attorney Ohralik immediately set out for the hospital, where he found Carol lying in traction. He attempted to sign her up as a client in the hospital room, but she demurred to seek parental advice. He then went to find Wanda Lou Holbert, but she had just been released by the hospital. On his way back to the McClintock home, attorney Ohralik stopped to take photos of the accident scene and concealed a tape recorder under his raincoat. He reviewed the family insurance policy and discovered that both Carol and Wanda Lou could recover up to $12,500 each under an uninsured motorist clause. Ohralik made a variety of different misrepresentations to the girls, who initially were swayed by his arguments, but soon sought to discharge him from representing them in this matter. He sued them for breach of contract, using excerpts from the surreptitiously made tape recordings in an effort to prove that an oral contract existed.

Both girls complained to the county bar association, which passed the action on to the state bar. Attorney Ohralik was found to have violated the Ohio Code of Professional Responsibility despite his claim of First and Fourteenth Amendment protections. In particular, the Ohio Supreme Court found that this direct solicitation of business was inconsistent with the profession's ideal of the attorney-client relationship. Ohralik had claimed that this solicitation was no different than in the *Bates* case (1977), but the U.S. Supreme Court disagreed and ruled that Ohralik's conduct posed "dangers that the state has a right to prevent" (*Ohralik*, p. 449), noting that the "appellant not only foisted himself upon these clients; he acted in gross disregard for their privacy" (*Ohralik*, p. 469). This approach was bolstered in a recent Supreme Court ruling (*Florida Bar v. Went For It, Inc.*, et al., 1995). The ruling supported the Florida Bar, which had prohibited personal injury lawyers from sending targeted direct-mail solicitations to victims and their relatives for 30 days following an accident or disaster. The decision found that the prohibition did not violate the lawyers' First and Fourteenth Amendment rights.

Testimonials

The use of testimonials by "satisfied users" has a kind of inherent "face validity" that appeals to the FTC. Unfortunately, like many forms of face validity, the true predictive potential of a testimonial endorsement is far more complex so far as psychological services are concerned. If psychotherapy research has taught us anything, it is that any given psychotherapist is not equally efficacious with all potential clients.

One ironic inconsistency in the latest version of the APA's most recent ethics code (APA, 1992) is obvious when contrasting the 2-year interval during which sexual intimacies with former psychotherapy clients are absolutely proscribed (ES: 4.07) with the instant availability of the client as a testimonial provider on the moment of terminating therapy. Psychotherapists know very well that their influence in the life of their clients does not end at the close of the last treatment session. The FTC did allow the APA to bar the use of testimonials from "current psychotherapy patients" or from "persons who because of their particular circumstances are vulnerable to undue influence" (APA, 1992). Apparently the FTC does not regard the lingering influence of the transference relationship and its potential consequences as an automatic barrier to testimonial advertising (e.g., potentially unfair and deceptive endorsements provided in the afterglow of a positive transference).

Although most private practitioners know that satisfied clients and the people who referred those clients are their best sources of future referrals, there are few data to suggest that the public will rely on commercially advertised testimonials in selecting medical or psychological care providers. Among all the professions, one notable exception in the merits of testimonial advertising may be among plastic and cosmetic surgeons, for whom the concept of face validity takes on a unique meaning.

Appeals to Fear

Many psychologists wondered why the FTC would object to the APA's ban of advertising that appeals to potential clients' fears. After all, some of our clients are emotionally insecure and may be even more vulnerable to inappropriate duress than Carol McClintock and Wanda Lou Holbert (Case 11-2). From the FTC's perspective, global bans on advertising that "appeals to fear if services are not obtained" were simply unacceptable in general (APA, 1981). A lot of effective advertising appeals to emotions and fears at some level (e.g., fear of tooth decay if you do not brush, fears of accidental injury or death if you ride in a car without seat belts and air bags, or fears of AIDS as a result of not practicing "safe sex"). In fact, social psychology has taught us that an "appeal to fear" coupled with a designated course of action is highly effective in evoking attitude change.

How might an ethics committee have become involved in such complaints? In one instance, actual complaints were filed when consumers objected to advertising by psychologists who ran programs to help people quit smoking. The advertisements powerfully articulated the potentially fatal consequences of smoking-induced lung cancer and other pulmonary diseases. A more troubling example is the coupling

of an appeal to fear with so-called in your face solicitation, such as the case in the *Ohralik* decision, described above. Imagine the following scenario:

Case 11-3: Dinah Saur, Ph.D., arrives unsolicited at the home of a child who witnessed a playground shooting, urging the parents to subscribe to a course of therapy to prevent "inevitable post-traumatic stress syndrome" in their as yet asymptomatic child.

Interestingly, FTC Commissioner Azcuenaga disagreed with her colleagues on this point. She supported the APA's wish to continue a ban on scare advertising, noting that the justification for banning such advertising by psychologists was plausible and that the FTC ought not to substitute its judgment on the matter without having a sound basis to do so. She cited the FTC's lack of expertise concerning psychotherapy and noted that, "nothing, even hypothetically, suggests that the [APA's] justification is either implausible or invalid" (Azcuenaga, 1990, p. 2). She was outvoted.

Fee Splitting

Providing bribes or kickbacks (fee splitting) in exchange for referrals was never an acceptable practice, but from the FTC's perspective, some ethics panels or licensing boards were interpreting prohibitions on this point as forbidding psychologists' participation in health maintenance organizations (HMOs), preferred provider organizations (PPOs), or referral services during the 1980s. The FTC regards referral services as procompetitive, and barring participation in them per se was regarded as a significant problem. Unfortunately, what constitutes a bribe, as opposed to a legitimate fee reduction or membership payment, is open to a wide range of opinion. The FTC consent order does permit the APA to issue "reasonable" principles that require disclosures to consumers regarding fees paid to referral services or similar entities. The key to discriminating between reasonable and inappropriate payment will have to depend on the rationale for the charges or fee reductions and the openness of information on these arrangements to the consumers of the services.

THE 1992 APA ETHICS CODE

The FTC did not intend that psychologists should necessarily adopt the market tactics of used car dealers and carnival barkers, but rather focused on bans on all advertising. Potential harm that could result from hucksterism and advertising abuses was deemed a valid focus of specific tailored restrictions by professional associations. Claims to "professional dignity" and the imagined need for "uniformity" would no longer constitute a legitimate basis for limiting advertising by professionals.

For the reader interested in reviewing the relevant sections of the current version of the APA ethics code (APA, 1992) most directly covered by the FTC order, they are

  ES 1.27, referrals and fees, which prohibits improper payments between professionals based on referrals
  ES 3.01, which defines what is considered a "public statement"
  ES 3.02, which requires reasonable efforts to correct misstatements made about or on behalf of the psychologist by others and prohibits compensation of media personnel to get publicity and the like
  ES 3.03, which deals with avoiding "false or deceptive statements" regarding psychologists' credentials and the scientific bases for claims of efficacy
  ES 3.05, which bars psychologists from soliciting testimonials from current therapy clients or other persons vulnerable to undue influence by virtue of their particular circumstances
  ES 3.06, which bars uninvited in-person solicitation for psychotherapy of persons vulnerable to undue influence (except for collateral contact with significant others of existing patients)
  ES 4.04, which adds specific requirements to be followed when considering whether to provide services to a client already receiving them elsewhere

Indirectly, ES 1.20a and 120c deal with consultation and referral practices (they focus on clients' best interests and obeying the law); ES 1.25a–125d deal with specifying financial, bill-ing, compensation, and fee arrangements, and non-exploitation in that regard is also relevant. Also, ES 4.01, which addresses structuring the therapeutic relationship so far as fee information is concerned, also applies.

Did the FTC/APA interaction lead to an improved ethics code? The authors believe that some improvements resulted from directing the APA and other professional associations concerned with advertising to focus on substance rather than style. On the other hand, the authors also believe that the FTC failed to fully accept the principle that the relationships between mental health professionals and their clients are qualitatively different from those that exist in many other professions. The result will be a greater reluctance on the part of ethics enforcement groups in psychology to tackle complaints in this arena.

ELEMENTS ALLOWED IN ADVERTISING

Citation of APA Membership Status

For many years, the APA prohibited mention in advertising of a psychologist's membership status. The rationale was that the APA is a scientific and professional organization with membership practices that do not include evaluation of individual credentialing functions. As such, mention of APA membership status would be meaningless to the public and might inappropriately imply APA approval of the psychologist in question. Others argued from time to time that APA membership did represent a credential of sorts. Since APA members are obligated to follow the APA ethics code and since these standards are enforced through an ethics committee, membership does indeed represent a special qualification that merits public attention.

In recognition of the last viewpoint, the APA Ethics Committee voted in October 1978 to recommend that, should they wish, members are permitted to list their APA membership status in public advertising. The recommendation was adopted as official policy by the APA Council of Representatives in January 1979. The manner of listing must not, however, suggest that APA membership status implies sponsorship of the psychologist's activities, competence, or specialized qualifications.

In April 1993, the APA Ethics Committee (1993c) issued a policy statement in response to an inquiry about whether it is appropriate to use the designation "FAPA" following one's name and doctoral degree, which indicates APA Fellow status. The committee declined to offer a definitive guideline, simply citing the need to avoid false or deceptive statements. Presumably, it is not inappropriate to note APA Fellow status in public statements or advertising once it is officially attained.

Mention of Other Credentials

A variety of other credentials exist in psychology, including membership in certain APA divisions that have special entry requirements (e.g., the Division of Clinical Psychology), a diploma from a postdoctoral accrediting body (e.g., the American Board of Professional Psychology), a listing in the *National Register of Health Service Providers in Psychology*, and honorary degrees or other titles. There is some controversy as to whether membership or receipt of such recognition even constitutes a credential since it is often granted in recognition of more valid indicators of professional accomplishment (Koocher, 1979). The general rule of thumb should be to list only those credentials that could reasonably be deemed meaningful to the consumer population (e.g., state licensure and earned degrees). Honorary degrees and degrees earned in fields other than psychology should not be listed when presenting oneself as a psychologist. An exception might be degrees acknowledged by the APA to be equivalent to a psychology degree although technically granted in a related field. Degrees earned at institutions not regionally accredited or recognized by the APA also should not be cited as psychology credentials.

Diplomate status presents a problem because of recent controversies related to specialty status within psychology. The American Board of Professional Psychology (ABPP) was incorporated in 1947, prior to the advent of most state licensing laws, and was recognized by the APA. It originally granted advanced diplomas in recog-

nition of "excellence" in the fields of clinical, counseling, school, and industrial and organizational psychology. An advanced degree, several years of postdoctoral experience, submission of a work sample, and a formal oral examination are required to earn the diploma. Subsequently, an American Board of Psychological Hypnosis was formed; it awards similar diplomas in clinical or experimental hypnosis. This board was also recognized by the APA by virtue of listing its diplomates in the official APA directory. More recently, the ABPP began granting diplomas in additional specialty areas, including behavioral psychology, clinical neuropsychology, family psychology, forensic psychology, and health psychology. Without official votes, the APA granted tacit approval to the ABPP and hypnosis specialty diplomates by recognizing them in its directories.

Other organizations unrecognized by the APA have sprung up to grant diplomas in "administrative psychology," "medical psychotherapy," or other so-called specialty or subspecialty fields. The APA has not yet recognized any of these boards officially for several reasons. First, there is some question about what constitutes a valid specialty area in psychology. Second, some of the organizations have had extensive grandparenting periods during which diplomas were granted with minimal review of credentials and questionable examinations, if any. Finally, questions have been raised about some of the organizations' procedures in conducting their activities. It is probably not unethical to cite a specialty diploma from an organization unrecognized by the APA, but one must be factual in explaining its meaning to clients and others.

At the February 1995 meeting of the APA Council of Representatives, an institutional mechanism was established to provide the official recognition of specialties and special proficiencies in psychology. The mechanism will ultimately require that all specialty fields ultimately apply through an elaborate formal mechanism to be "recognized" afresh by the APA. It remains to be seen what impact this process will have on the evolution of the profession; however, it seems likely to slow the creation of self-declared specialty fields.

Citing One's Doctorate

To indicate an earned degree from an accredited educational institution, it is most proper to use initials following the holder's name (i.e., John Jones, Ph.D., or Mary Smith, M.D.). Simply using the title "Doctor" invites confusion since the doctorate may be in psychology, divinity, social work, law, or even medicine. In fact, there are currently APA members who hold all of these degrees in addition to, or in some cases claiming them as equivalent to, a doctorate in psychology. Occasionally, individuals use listings such as "Ph.D. Cand." or "A.B.D.," presumably to indicate that they are Ph.D. candidates or have completed all but the dissertation. This type of listing is deceptive and is considered ethically inappropriate since only earned degrees may be listed and neither admission to candidacy nor "all but . . . " references relate to an earned degree. One certainly should explain the precise nature of professional training and credentials directly to clients, but abbreviations that falsely imply actual degrees should never be used.

Similarly, one must strive for factual accuracy in mentioning any professional licenses. Most states have so-called generic licensing laws, but a few states have different levels of psychology licensure. In a state with generic laws, psychological practitioners are licensed as psychologists. It is therefore inappropriate to list oneself as a licensed clinical psychologist or licensed school psychologist in such states. The best guide is to look carefully at the certificate or license itself and use only the specific title authorized. Some may handle the situation by a listing such as "Mary Roe, Psy.D., Licensed Psychologist, Practice Limited to Clinical Psychology." This would be both factually accurate and ethically appropriate.

Clinical psychology has grown to acquire a degree of status as a specialization within psychology. Many licensed practitioners, whose doctoral degrees were awarded in counseling psychology, school psychology, or other fields, have taken to identifying themselves as clinical psychologists in dealings with the public. The stated rationale of such individuals is that they are licensed by their state to deliver so-called clinical services (by which most seem to mean health services) and/or that their education and training is similar or equivalent to that obtained in clinical psychology doctoral programs. Some such psychologists attempt to distinguish between Clinical Psychology (as a proper noun) and clinical psychology, much as one would between Kleenex® brand and generic facial tissue. Such reasoning places the psychologist on a very slippery slope. It is most appropriate to list oneself only by the proper titles of credentials actually earned rather than those acquired by idiosyncratic or wishful interpretation.

Listing Affiliations

Many psychologists work in more than one agency or practice relationship. For example, it is not uncommon for a psychologist to be employed by a clinic or corporation full time while also conducting a part-time practice or consultation business. Many psychologists serve on boards and committees of corporations, professional organizations, and private agencies. When presenting this information to others, however, it is important that such affiliations are not presented to falsely suggest sponsorship by or approval of that organization or agency. It must also be made clear to clients whether or not the organization mentioned has any role in their relationship with the psychologist. Consider the case of the "all-purpose" psychologist:

Case 11-4: Robert Hartley received a letter from a psychology ethics committee after a neighbor complained of a 6-foot-high sign he had erected on his lawn that announced his practice of psychology in 4-inch letters. He replied to the committee on stationery even more interesting than the sign. The stationery was headed: "Dr. Robert Hartley, Ph.D., Consulting Clinical Psychologist and Sexologist." Three-color printing ran down the side of the page and listed the services Hartley offered. These included

Psychology
  Adults, Adolescents, and Children
  Individuals and Group
  Hypnosis
  Lay Analysis

Psychology Testing
  Neuropsychological Evaluation
  Personality Assessment
  Intellectual Evaluation
  Diagnostic Evaluation
  Vocational Evaluation
Counseling
  Sex and Divorce
  Marriage Enrichment Courses
Management Consulting
  Executive Leadership, Development, and
    Assessment
  Personnel Evaluations

Across the bottom of the page, the following institutions were listed: Mid-America Hypnosis Clinic, XYZ Learning Disabilities Center, Sex Counseling Institute, Affective Education Foundation, and Plainville Marriage Enrichment Center.

To begin, for Hartley to list himself with the prefix "Dr." and the suffix "Ph.D." is redundant and simply in poor taste. The 6-foot sign and the three-color stationery were equally inappropriate. On investigation, moreover, it was learned that Hartley's Ph.D. was in sociology and from a university not regionally accredited. He did hold a valid master's degree in psychology, but the context in which he listed his doctorate was inappropriate. The organizations listed across the stationery turned out to have two things in common: they were all headquartered in his office, and he was the sole employee of each. When asked about his training relative to the services listed, Hartley proudly cited a long chain of briefly held jobs and workshops he had attended, which covered virtually all of the services mentioned. Suffice it to say that the training was actually rather shallow in most of the areas mentioned, creating a very substantial competence question (discussed in detail in chapter 3). Although Hartley's presentation of self was rather cloddish and he was truly ignorant of his infractions, the potential for public deception in his style of performance is obvious.

Case 11-5: Roger Snob, Ed.D., was in full-time private practice, but volunteered a few hours a week to supervise a practicum student at the state university. In exchange for his time, Dr. Snob was given a largely symbolic appointment as an ad-

junct professor at the university. He promptly had new stationery printed that included his new title and used it for all his professional correspondence.

Case 11-6: C. U. Infer, Psy.D., worked at the Northeast Mental Health Institute, a prestigious nationally known facility, on a research project that was to last for 2 years. He was a licensed psychologist and was permitted to see private clients in his office at the institute during hours when he was technically off duty from the project. Many clients assumed that they were being treated by a clinical staff member of the institute under its auspices. When Infer moved away at the end of the project, several of his former clients were surprised to find that the institute had no records of their treatment and could not easily provide continuity of care for them.

Dr. Snob's misrepresentation is one of pride and possibly ignorance. While he cannot be accused of demonstrably harming any individual, he is attempting to trade on the reputation of the university to enhance his own status. In reality, his relationship to the university is rather remote and does not have actual relevance to much of his professional work. Dr. Infer, on the other hand, may mislead clients, to their later detriment. He, too, is trading on the reputation of an agency in which his actual affiliation is quite different from what the clients may be led to believe. Some clients may have chosen to use his services in part because of the presumed coverage, backup, or expertise represented by the institute. It is inappropriate for Infer simply to remain silent. Rather, he is obligated to disabuse others of incorrect impressions or conclusions they may draw.

Testimonials

It is certainly gratifying when a client values services or has praise for professional efforts, but it is not appropriate to cite such laudatory comments in advertisements for professional services. Such statements may be taken out of context or reflect value judgments from which the public cannot reasonably be expected to draw valid generalizations. In addition, they may compromise a client's confidentially or later prove embarrassing in ways that may not be anticipated when they are initially sought. Although the APA ethics code, revised under pressure from the FTC as described in this chapter, permits the use of testimonials from former clients, we strongly advise our colleagues not to use such advertising or public statements.

One type of exception for which advertising testimonials have traditionally been acceptable involves book promotions, for which excerpts from reviews and adoption lists are frequently used. The rationale for permitting specific use of testimonials in this exceptional circumstance is linked to the type of client involved and the presumption that the psychologist who permits the use of such material will do so fairly. Unlike the potential client who seeks the help of a psychologist in a period of emotional distress, it is assumed that the scholarly review of a book can be made in a relatively thoughtful and dispassionate manner. In addition, it is assumed that the psychologist evaluating the book has some competence to evaluate critically. The reader is more likely to evaluate testimonials from a critical standpoint than is the troubled client. The fact that such testimonials are tolerated places an extra burden on the psychologist who uses them. He or she must be assiduously careful not to take the comments out of context or use them in a misleading fashion. Discovery is likely should such quotes be ill-used since the use of the quote will sooner or later come to the attention of its originator. In fact, permission should be sought prior to the use of such quotes.

Product Endorsements

Endorsements by psychologists of products intended for sale to the general public are not generally considered appropriate, particularly when the psychologist is rewarded or compensated in some way for providing the endorsement. The rationale is twofold. First, if the product is psychological in nature (e.g., a relaxation tape, biofeedback apparatus, assessment technique, etc.), its merit should stand on a foundation of empirical research rather than personal testimony. Second, if the product is not psychological in nature (e.g., a brand of toothpaste, pasta, or soft drink), the psychologist is using

his or her professional stature in an irrelevant realm to endorse a product in a way that may be deceptive and misleading to the public. If a psychologist were to have a dual career, performing psychotherapy by day and announcing television commercials in the evening, the circumstances might theoretically be ethically appropriate, as long as the psychologist's role (i.e., by day) was not mentioned or otherwise employed as a means of influencing the public to buy products in the evening.

Product endorsements may be appropriate in the marketing of products of a professional nature to colleagues. These products might include test equipment, computer software, or other items sold chiefly to qualified professionals. The key point, once again, is that the endorsement should be fair and accurate and should not depend on personal or financial gain.

As noted, this principle especially holds true when the psychologist has played a major role in the development of a particular device, book, or other product. Often, one may be blind to difficulties of this sort when personal involvement is substantial. Nonetheless, every effort should be made to ensure that commercial products offered for public sale are presented in a professional, scientifically acceptable, and factually informative manner. The use of due caution and scientific modesty and the avoidance of sensationalism or undocumented claims will go far in preventing careless ethical infractions of this sort. Many illustrations of problems in this realm are also found in the chapter 12 in the discussion of "self-help" books and similar products.

Tackiness

Occasionally, psychologists will engage in advertising practices that, while not clearly unethical, hold the profession up to ridicule or are otherwise in poor taste. Certainly, Dr. Hartley (Case 11-4) showed such tendencies with his tricolor stationery and lawn billboard, but other and more bizarre examples abound.

Case 11-7: In anticipation of a lecture and workshop program by two psychologists who had written a self-help book for mass consumption, their publisher took out a full-page ad in a large metropolitan newspaper. The ad described the psychologists as the "Butch Cassidy and Sundance Kid of psychology" and included a detailed cartoon depicting the two in cowboy outfits, with guns drawn, charging over the "boot hill" of psychology with grave markers inscribed "Freud," "Adler," and "Jung." It is unclear whether the goal of the ad was to portray them as "straight shooters" or psychological "outlaws."

The psychologists were reportedly embarrassed by the ads, claiming that they had not been consulted. On the other hand, they had certainly not exercised much care in monitoring how their names were being used.

Case 11-8: Consider the following newspaper advertisement:

> The Name's Doc Lame
> Psychotherapy's the game
> Call for appointment:
> Jack Lame, Ph.D.
> 555-1212

or this new business card:

> Roger A. Droit
> Ph.D. (c), MAT, C. Ht.
> Health Psychology
> 111-5555

Although the name has been changed, the examples are genuine. When asked to explain the abbreviations on his business card, Mr. Droit noted that Ph.D. (c) meant that he was a "Ph.D. candidate" (albeit from an unaccredited program in "psychology and transpsychology"), the MAT was a Master of Arts in Teaching, and C. Ht. stood for Clinical Hypnotist (a credential based on a correspondence course). Listing of degrees or certificates from programs that are not regionally accredited is ethically unacceptable. Similarly, the designation of degree "candidacy" or "A.B.D." (all but dissertation) status are ethically inappropriate because they are not officially sanctioned earned degrees.

While not unethical per se, Dr. Lame's advertisement is certainly not doing much to maintain a professional image or demonstrate

a sense of responsibility that would reassure clients and colleagues. Such advertisements are likely to imply a lack of sensitivity and awareness of public reaction. Whether the author of such an ad could also be sensitive to the emotions and problems of others remains an open question.

Case 11-9: The epitome of mixing tackiness with slippery product endorsement can be found in the April, 1995 issue of *Playboy* magazine. Barbara Keesling, Ph.D. who "earned a doctorate in psychology" from an unnamed university appears nude on several pages while posing with her three "self-help" books titled "Sexual Healing," "Sexual Pleasure," and "How to Make Love All Night (and Drive a Woman Wild)." Citations for these texts are not provided in the article, which describes how Dr. Keesling found her way into psychology through work as a sex surrogate involved in doing "hands on counseling" (pp. 68–70).

We know of three female psychologists who have posed nude in *Playboy* (October, 1994; April, 1995; and October, 1997; for those readers who wish to undertake original source research). To the best of our knowledge, none are APA members. We are not aware of any male psychologists who have posed nude for national magazines (while citing their profession or otherwise). We regard citing ones' profession as a psychologist while posing nude in such contexts as tacky, but not intrinsically unethical. However, Dr. Keesling's nude marketing of her books causes us to wonder whether she has empirically documented the claim inherent in the titles of her books.

Contents of Acceptable Advertisements

In general, it is appropriate to advertise in the print and broadcast media so long as the tone and content of the advertisement are appropriate. Specific examples of unethical and inappropriate public statements and advertisements are also discussed in this chapter, but here are samples of the acceptable statements.

Case 11-10: The following notice appeared weekly in a metropolitan newspaper:

Harrison Troll, Ph.D.

- Licensed Psychologist
- Ph.D. in Clinical Psychology, granted by Western State University, 1979
- Specializing in the treatment of children and adolescents
- Convenient office hours
- Sliding fee scale
- Health insurance accepted
- Family therapy available
- 24-hour answering service
- Call 555-6666

Case 11-11: The following is the text of a radio announcement aired in a major metropolitan area: "Mary Okay, Ph.D., is a clinical psychologist specializing in marital therapy. She is opening her practice in Centerville at the Glenwood Mall, with ample free parking and convenient evening office hours. If you are having marital problems, she may be able to help. Call 555-2211 for an appointment."

Assuming that the facts are accurate and truthful and that Drs. Troll and Okay are indeed qualified to perform the services they list, there is nothing wrong with these notices. Any information that might be of interest to a consumer, including facility in speaking a foreign language, application of special techniques (e.g., behavioral treatment of obesity, relaxation training, parent consultation, or hypnosis for habit control), convenience of office location, availability of evening hours, or other facts would be permissible. One must be careful not to mix facts that may be misleading, however. In chapter 10, for example, we noted that some psychological services (e.g., child custody evaluations or other forensic services) may not be covered by health insurance. Therefore, if Dr. Troll were to note that his practice involves only forensic work, he should not simultaneously mention that he accepts health insurance. To do so might mislead readers into thinking that his services will be covered by insurance. Likewise, if Dr. Troll has no more room for low-fee clients in his practice, then he should drop the reference to a sliding fee scale. It is true that such matters can be dealt with in a first session or telephone consultation, but to leave a false impression in the

advertisement is inappropriate even if the situation is later remedied with no harm to the client.

If a psychologist does intend to advertise in any way, several precautionary steps should be taken. First, one should consult with colleagues regarding the plan to obtain informal advice about the nature and content of your plan, as well for as a sense of community standards. Second, one should not delegate the details of the advertising to others, especially those with little understanding of psychological ethics. Third, one must proofread or carefully monitor the final product before it is distributed or broadcast. Finally, a psychologist should retain a copy of the advertisement, whether in print, film, or tape. He or she will then have documentation of exactly what was communicated if questions are asked later. This can be especially important if the broadcast media are used. We know of instances in which psychologists, anxious to take advantage of liberalized advertising policies, hired public relations firms. All were unhappy with the flashy packages created for them, but had to pay the high fees anyway.

Yellow Pages Advertisements

Listing oneself in the classified (yellow) pages of the telephone directory presents an interesting subset of problems. In part, these emanate from the fact that the telephone companies are interested in selling space and are relatively unwise in the ways of professional ethics. Little is known by way of scientific data about whether or not telephone directory advertising generates client referrals. After all, if one were searching for a skilled surgeon or trial lawyer and relied solely on a colorful, cutely illustrated box ad in the telephone directory, the consequences might indeed be unfortunate. Still, telephone directories are highly visible and attract the attention—and occasionally the ire—of colleagues, if not clients.

Some general suggestions should be considered when a psychologist does decide to list in the directory. First, the listing should be only under the heading "Psychologists." Occasionally, individuals will want to list themselves under "Counselors," or "Psychotherapists." This is not unethical, but we believe that if one's primary identity is as a psychologist, that should be the sole listing. Some psychologists do have advanced degrees in other disciplines and may be licensed to practice medicine or are members of the bar or certified public accountants. In such cases, they may also list themselves under the appropriate headings in the classified directory. Second, he or she must be qualified to perform the services listed, if any, including holding licenses in the appropriate geographic areas. In some geographic areas, directories are subdivided into metropolitan and suburban volumes, and occasionally state lines are involved (e.g., a psychologist living in Philadelphia, Pennsylvania, may also have an office in southern New Jersey or a Virginia psychologist may also treat clients in Maryland and the District of Columbia). Third, while the psychologist may list in different directories, a bona fide office address should be listed that is reasonably convenient to the area served by the directory. Fourth, the other guidelines discussed above apply equally to telephone directory ads, with a special caution. A directory may have a relatively long shelf life, so any promises made in the advertisement (e.g., specific fees) may have to be honored for an extended period.

There is some controversy about style matters in telephone directory listings. For example, should graphic display advertisements be permitted, or, now that some directories have color capability, should psychologists be permitted to run ads in color? This is more a matter of taste than a clear-cut ethics issue as long as the ad is otherwise appropriate. In a debate among members of the APA Ethics Committee several years ago, one respected psychologist opined that, for the sake of homogeneity, only names, degrees, and telephone numbers should be permitted. A younger colleague replied that if homogeneity were the paramount issue, why not simply require that every psychologist who chooses to advertise in the directory buy full-page space?

Another controversy has dealt with concern in some parts of the country that individuals not licensed as psychologists were listing themselves in directories as psychologists. Dealing with this issue is the duty and responsibility of the statutory state licensing authority, not the telephone company. Providing a copy of the directory entry

will generally be sufficient for the licensing board to order the unlicensed person to cease and desist from such false advertising.

UNACCEPTABLE ADVERTISING

Although the APA Ethics Committee is now largely blocked from addressing advertising complaints, state licensing boards have the authority to do so, as discussed above. We provide the following illustrations of what many state licensing boards might consider unacceptable, including misrepresentation, guarantee or promise of favorable outcome, appeals to client fears or vulnerability, claims of unique or "one-of-a-kind" services, statements critical of competitive providers, and direct solicitation of vulnerable individual clients. Consider the following cases:

Case 11-12: Martha Newly, Psy.D., a recently licensed psychologist, in an attempt to get her private practice off to a brisk start, took out a full-page ad in the local newspaper to announce an "office open house," complete with a visit from "Psycho, the Crazy Clown," free balloons imprinted with her address and phone number, a "first session free" certificate, and a door prize of "20 free sessions for you or the significant other of your choice."

Case 11-13: The New Wave Underground Milita kidnapped a bus full of school children and held them at gunpoint for several hours before the police were able to negotiate the children's release. Tym Lee Buck, Ph.D., drove to a shopping center parking lot where the children were to be reunited with their parents. He passed out handbills describing himself as an expert on hostage psychology. The material included the following: "It is a well-known fact that hostages can suffer serious emotional delayed reactions. Preventive psychotherapy for your child is a must." His address and phone number were also listed.

Case 11-14: The advertisement read:

"You'll just have to live with it!"
Is that what you've been told? It's not true!
New techniques available at the
Southside Psychological Development Center

will help you master your chronic problems,
whatever they may be: bad habits,
chronic pain, or relationship problems.
Don't delay, call today! 555-9999.

All of these cases have a common element that can be termed lack of a professional perspective, poor taste, or simply gross insensitivity. Each also has some rather unique and difficult aspects. Dr. Newly represents a type of colleague who has been categorized as a "green menace" (Keith-Spiegel, 1982). That is to say, she is a relatively inexperienced psychologist in a big hurry, making ethical blunders out of an impulsive effort to get her practice off and running. Fortunately, such colleagues are generally amenable to constructive, educative approaches to their ethical misconduct. Psycho, the Crazy Clown, certainly does little to enhance the image of the profession, while tending to making a mockery of people with emotional problems. In addition, the offer of free treatment sessions via a door prize drawing tends to belie the careful assessment and planning that should accompany any course of competently delivered psychological services. Finally, the first session free coupons create a problem akin to the bait-and-switch routines used by unscrupulous salespeople. In the *bait-and-switch* scam (see Chapter 14), the potential client is drawn to the store or potential sale by an attractive offer, but on showing interest is encouraged to switch to an item or service more profitable to the seller. In psychological service delivery, a first interview is often critical to the formation of a working rapport between psychologist and client. Often, the client will share emotion-laden material and form an attachment to the psychologist, which may predispose the client to continue the relationship. In this sense, the offer of a free first session represents a type of bait, with implications the client will seldom recognize. There is nothing wrong with offering to waive the fee for a session. However, many psychologists will do this if they find it unlikely that they will be able to work with a client after the first session; however, this is quite different from advertising there is no fee for the first session as bait to bring in clients.

Dr. Buck is much more obnoxious in his behavior since he is trading on the fears and vulnerabilities of people. He may be correct in anticipating psychological problems among the hostage children, but his presumption that virtually all will need so-called preventive psychotherapy is out of line, and his style is offensive. He is also soliciting individual clients directly and personally, which is unethical for a psychologist even when appeals to emotionalism are not used. His behavior and the circumstances under which he approached the families actually seems to create a potential for increasing the psychological stress on the strained families.

The advertisement from the Southside Psychological Development Center seems folksy and well meaning, but it also appears to promise or ensure the likelihood of a favorable outcome. Aside from the inherent misleading quality of its tone, the ad implies success with recalcitrant problems and suggests the application of some novel or unique technique not available elsewhere. In fact, the center turned out to be a group practice of well-intentioned, but overzealous, psychologists trained in behavioral techniques. The comparative desirability of their services and the new techniques were more representative of their hopes than of documented scientific claims. The ad has an additional flaw in that it does not name the individuals responsible for the operation. It is desirable that qualified psychologists not hide behind a corporate or group practice title, and it would be preferable (and, in some states, legally required) to have the names of the psychologists listed along with the name of the center. The final problem with this ad is the implication that effective treatment will be available at the Southside Center for virtually any problem. This is the same sort of problem evident in Dr. Hartley's situation (Case 11-4), since it is likely that the range of effective services to be offered at the center is actually more narrow than the public would be led to believe.

Direct Solicitation

Aside from the blatantly intrusive behavior of Dr. Buck in Case 11-13, it is important to recognize why the direct solicitation of individual clients should be avoided. The central issue is the potential vulnerability of the client relative to the psychologist. Vulnerability may include client insecurities, emotional problems, naiveté, lack of information, or simply awe of the professional. The psychologist's special expertise and knowledge are generally accorded a degree of respect or deference that may predispose clients to follow their advice and recommendations, even if this means changing long-standing patterns of behavior. Psychologists must recognize this social influence or power and consider its use carefully. Advice must be presented with due respect to the limitations of our scientific knowledge and the recognition of a client's freedom to choose a lifestyle or course of action. Recommendations must always be tailored to an understanding of the client and his or her unique life situation.

A personal solicitation of the in your face variety (see Case 11-2) may pit the expert's advantage directly against the potential client's insecurities and fears. It may capitalize on a client's ignorance or social naiveté. While there is nothing wrong with a psychologist's announcing general availability to the community through advertising, the direct solicitation of individual clients has considerable potential for abuse and distress to the object of the pitch.

Case 11-15: Max Pusher, M.D., a psychiatrist well known for his syndicated newspaper column, was invited to teach an extension course at Central State University dealing with the topics anxiety, tension, and depression. A huge audience was attracted by his name and reputation. Dr. Pusher was accompanied by several assistants wearing colored armbands, who passed out brochures about Dr. Pusher's private clinic and other private workshops he offered. In addition, some of the assistants approached selected students, saying, "You look troubled. Perhaps you could use an appointment or two."

This approach was clearly upsetting to many of the students approached and certainly would play on the insecurities of others. This seems little more than an appeal to fear as a means to recruit clients in the guise of a public lecture.

As in the case of testimonials, discussed above, there are some tolerable exceptions to the general prohibition on solicitation of individual clients. These generally apply when the client is not an individual, but an agency, business firm, or other organizational entity. Consider the following examples:

Case 11-16: Edward Efficacy, Ph.D., an industrial and organizational psychologist, has developed a well-validated assessment center program (see Bray, 1976, 1977, for an explanation of assessment centers, which are programs designed to evaluate competence through the use of observed simulations) to evaluate pharmacists. He prepares a factually accurate descriptive brochure and mails it to potential employers of pharmacists and colleges of pharmacy, offering his consultative and evaluative services.

Case 11-17: Karen Kinder, Psy.D., is trained as a school psychologist and has developed a kindergarten screening instrument with good reliability and predictive validity. She has appropriate information printed in pamphlet form and mails these with cover letters offering to conduct training workshops to superintendents of schools and directors of special education in school systems throughout her locale.

While the clients approached by Drs. Efficacy and Kinder are indeed being contacted as individuals, they are not in the same relative position of vulnerability as an "unaffiliated" individual. Employers, schools, or other organizations will generally be in a better position to know their needs for such services, and the nature of the services offered is quite different from individual offers of psychotherapy. (For the sake of illustration, we are assuming that the programs and instruments used by Drs. Kinder and Efficacy are properly validated and reasonably useful. Issues related to assessment in general are discussed in chapter 7.) There are some circumstances for which therapeutic services might also be offered in this manner.

Case 11-18: Ethyl Fluid, Ed.D., plans to approach a variety of large corporations to encourage their purchase of alcoholism counseling services for their employees. She will offer to provide a team of properly trained clinicians to staff an in-house clinic at each company's plant. Employees would be seen on a self-referral basis, with appropriate confidentiality safeguards for counseling. Dr. Fluid cites the advantages of the program include convenience for employees and improved conditions of employment, with a possible reduction in alcohol-related work problems and absenteeism. She presents this plan in letters to presidents and personnel directors of the companies.

Assuming that Dr. Fluid observes other ethical obligations related to providing the treatment she proposes, this type of solicitation presents no problem. No outrageous claims are made, and each company is clearly free to evaluate its own need for the program, as well as other alternatives. Client freedom is ensured, and no one is pressured individually.

What Potential Clients Think

Little research has been done to document the impact of psychologists' advertising on potential clients, but the results of one such study on what potential clients think are interesting (Keith-Spiegel, Seegar, & Tomison, 1978). Keith-Spiegel and her colleagues surveyed 164 California college students who had already completed at least one psychology course. The students were presented with 13 sets of 5 brief ads each and asked to imagine that they had a need for psychological services for themselves or someone close to them. They were told to imagine that they were to consult a telephone directory and find the sets of ads in question. Within each set, they were to indicate the rank order of their choices of whom to call first, after reading all five ads in the set. Within each set of ads, a variety of factors were varied. For example, in some the psychologist was listed as Dr. Jones, instead of J. Jones, Ph.D. Some listed professional affiliations (e.g., APA member), others listed all earned degrees (e.g., B.A., M.A., Ph.D.), still others included slogans (e.g., "the psychologist who cares") or offers (e.g., "no charge for first appointment").

In formulating the study, the investigators had been concerned that flashy, hard-sell, or gimmicky ads might be highly rated in contrast to more simple, professionally dignified ones. While the data and analyses are by no means conclusive, the trends were both interesting and somewhat reassuring. Degrees definitely made a difference in the rankings; the ads that used of Ph.D. ranked higher than those ads without it, although the suffix M.A. was rated more impressive than the appellation "Dr." The dual listing of M.A. and Ph.D. was most favored, suggesting that the public believes the more degrees the better and may not realize that most doctoral-level psychologists also have master's degrees or their equivalent.

Certification, licensure, and memberships in professional associations also tended to enhance selection potential. Interestingly, personalized "grabber" lines (e.g., the psychologist who cares) did not do well. Some particular demographic variables also seem influential. The sex, ethnicity of the name, and even the oddness of the psychologist's name were varied. For example, participants identifying themselves as Jewish on the questionnaire seemed more likely to choose a psychologist named Cohen or Goldstein than one named Caldwell or Thomas. Women participants generally ranked women psychologists higher, and an odd-sounding name (e.g., Fabian Tuna) tended to reduce the likelihood of a high ranking.

When fees were specified, a Ph.D. psychologist with a low fee was chosen most often, and an M.A. psychologist with a low fee was chosen over a Ph.D. with a very high fee. On the other hand, a doctoral-level psychologist was generally chosen over a master's-level psychologist when the M.A. person's fee was only slightly lower. Lowest ranking of all was the person listed with no degree, even though the fee was modest. Ads with additional descriptive or factual information tended to be selected over less detailed ads or those ads that seemed to have an emotional appeal line. In general, a conservative ad listing degree, license, specialty, and the phrase "reasonable rates" seemed to do best. Come-on lines such as "money-back guarantee" rated very low.

Ads offering a free consultation were extremely popular, but would be clearly unethical, as explained in this chapter. The ethical issue is not the free service per se, but the promise of free service as an inducement to a professional relationship. Appeals to informality, such as "Hangups are my business," did not go over well, and visual illustrations or promises of effective results were also not very impressive to the college student sample.

Except for the preference for the "free session" ads, the students seemed to select in favor of ethical appropriateness, even though these standards were not presented to the students. Factual detail and informational material had the most striking impact. Interestingly, diplomate status, as mentioned above, did have a favorable impact when listed. No student queried had any idea what diplomate status entailed, but most thought that it "sounded good." It seems as though this segment of the general public has expectations regarding professionals' behavior in the marketplace that are consistent with ethical decorum.

Growth Groups and Educational Programs

One type of psychological service that has often skirted the border between ethical and clearly unethical behavior in terms of marketing issues is the so-called growth or enrichment seminars and workshops. When does a course or workshop become psychotherapy? Is there a difference between a seminar that has a psychotherapeutic impact on an individual and psychotherapy conducted in the form of a seminar? While psychotherapy and related ethical matters are covered chiefly in chapter 4, it is clear that one is not permitted to solicit clients for therapy. May one then solicit clients for a psychotherapeutic course? Consider these examples of more than semantic interest:

Case 11-19: The Happy Karma Institute, under the direction of Harry Creeshna, Psy.D., frequently advertises seminars in "personal power and creative change" and "relaxation systems." Clients are solicited by direct-mail advertising and told that the seminars teach "increasing harmony in interpersonal relationships, self-analysis, Sullivanian analysis, biofeedback, autogenics, deep muscle relaxation, and guided fantasy." Dr. Creeshna is described in the mailings as having been trained in psychological techniques and esoteric disciplines.

Case 11-20: Communication Associates, Incorporated, advertises a seminar entitled, "Introduction to Personal Growth." The format is described as

lecture and experiential group participation, including "psychodrama, confrontation, gestalt, assertive, encounter transactional analysis, and training" techniques. The ad appears weekly in a metropolitan newspaper.

Case 11-21: Psycho-Tron Laboratory Learning Systems, Incorporated, directed by Lester Clone, Ph.D., uses a business card with an optical illusion imprinted on it. Instructions on the card explain that viewing the illusion in a certain way is a sign of an inflexible problem-solving style in need of "cognitive reprogramming," which can be obtained through an individualized course at Psycho-Tron.

While it is one thing to give didactic or explanatory lectures about therapeutic techniques, it is another thing entirely to apply techniques intended to have some psychotherapeutic outcome in the context of a course or seminar. To begin, certain therapeutic techniques, such as group confrontation, can have a harmful impact on some individuals. On other occasions, individuals with serious somatic problems might seek out psychologically based treatments such as relaxation training instead of first obtaining proper medical care. Without appropriate screening and follow-up, the sampling of seminar topics seems more like random indiscriminate episodes of play with therapy techniques. This may be educational, but it is also potentially harmful if targeted at the lay public in a commercial venture. In addition, the promises or claims alluded to, especially in the ads from the Karma Institute and Psycho-Tron Laboratory, are at best inane and at worst blatant misrepresentation. One can hardly be taught Sullivanian analysis in a few weeks of a group seminar, and cognitive reprogramming seems to be a term conjured up by an Orwellian psychologist. Communication Associates mentions training in their ad, but they target it to the lay public. Who are they intending to train for what?

The point to be made here is that those psychologists oriented toward group enhancement of the human potential must fully explore their goals. If these are therapeutic in nature, they should use appropriate professional cautions. If their goals are educative, then the didactic nature of the course or seminar must be stressed, and it must be clear to all concerned that the program is not intended as therapy or therapeutic training.

Referral Services

In some parts of the country, professional associations operate a service by which callers can specify a needed type of psychological consultation or intervention and be given the names of potential providers. In some cases, similar services are offered by for-profit entities, private practitioners, community agencies, or clinics. Consider the following operations:

Case 11-22: The Northeast State Psychological Association offers a referral service to its members for the benefit of the public. It was developed in response to frequent telephone inquiries from the public. Any members of the association who are licensed, carry professional liability insurance, and have no ethical complaints pending against them may be listed. A file containing provider information, including the availability of a sliding fee scale, foreign language skills, specialty training, and the like is maintained. When a person calls seeking a referral, a message is taken and referred to a doctoral-level psychologist hired as the coordinator of the service. The coordinator contacts the caller to establish the nature of the request and provides three names of psychologists whose skills, location, and availability fit the client's needs. No fees are charged either party, and the service is paid for out of general membership dues. Often, the calls are requests for speakers or general information rather than for referral to a practitioner.

Case 11-23: Psychotherapy Assistance is a psychotherapist-finding service run by three psychologists in a large metropolitan area. They attempt to match potential clients with psychotherapists on the basis of many factors, including fees charged, areas of specialization, treatment style, and so forth. Psychologists who wish to receive referrals are interviewed by the service operators regarding their practice. All must be appropriately licensed and carry liability insurance. Clients who phone the service are given a diagnostic interview and

charged the usual and customary rate for that service. They are then given the names of two or more therapists recommended by the service, assuming that psychotherapy is a recommendation. The only fees are those paid by the client.

Case 11-24: Nadia Nerk is an unemployed real estate agent who has opened a storefront service known as "Shrink Finders." Clients pay Nerk a fee and are offered access to a set of videotaped interviews with psychotherapists, recorded in their offices. Clients may look through as many tapes as they wish and will then be given the names and addresses of any therapists whose tapes impress them. The therapists have paid Nerk $100 for making their tape and an additional $10 per session for each client visit based on a referral from her service.

The three referral services listed all have one feature in common: they provide clients with the names of psychologists. Presumably, they also advertise their services in telephone directories, the media, or elsewhere. Certainly, the same advertising obligations that bind psychologists as individual or group practitioners should also bind the operators of such referral services.

The service run by the state psychological association (Case 11-22) does not charge any fees and is intended as a public service. Clients are advised that the service is not endorsing any particular provider, but rather is giving a list of qualified practitioners who seem to meet the client's stated needs. The rationale for listing only members may be supported on the basis that the organization can only enforce consumer ethical complaints about members. Clients unable to pay normal practitioner fees are referred to those who offer a sliding fee scale or to community clinics. The service is paid for out of general association funds for public benefit.

Psychotherapy Assistance (Case 11-23) represents a fee-for-service matching program. A clinical service is rendered in the form of an evaluation, and referral is then made to practitioners presumably known to the referrer. Supposedly, the matching is more individualized and based on clinical judgments of psychologists, which are not possible under the more limited state association system. No fees are charged to the providers, which is appropriate lest the specter of fee splitting (see chapter 10) be raised. Care should be taken, however, to be certain that any advertising or promotion activity undertaken is appropriate and responsible.

The Shrink Finders (Case 11-24) service seems questionable on several fronts. The effort at a "catchy" name for the services and the video interviews raise the potential for some anxiety that superficial data are being promulgated as the basis for important decisions. There seem to be no efforts to tailor the service to client needs or otherwise introduce professional judgment or advice. While no advertising has been presented for the service, one must wonder what form it would take and how appropriate it might be. Most troubling, however, are the financial arrangements. Because the providers pay a commission to Ms. Nerk, this may pose an ethical problem for the practitioners if the financial arrangement is concealed from clients.

While referral services can be helpful to clients and the public at large, their modus operandi determines their ethical propriety. Advertising and financial aspects of the operations may singly or together raise ethical problems. Any psychologist considering involvement with such a service should be quite careful about exploring all of these issues prior to signing on. The legitimate economic needs of the practitioner should never take precedence over client needs.

Other Public Statements

Psychologists will often have the opportunity to be heard in public. Advertising is only one such avenue, another is the media, as addressed in chapter 12. Other opportunities to influence the public occur while teaching, as discussed in chapter 16, or while giving public lectures. Potential opportunities for misrepresentation, striving for personal gain, causing distress, or embarrassing the profession and one's colleagues abound. It is important to consider the impact of any public pronouncements made in the role of psychologist before presenting them.

Case 11-25: Hokey Line is a clever journalist who majored in psychology as an undergraduate. He is very adept at translating research findings into readable newsy tidbits that would make great filler items for community newspapers. He is marketing two products to mental health professionals. The first is a set of such articles that he is willing to sell and permit the buyers to send to local newspapers under their own names. That is, the psychologist-buyers could send the articles to their local newspapers for possible publication in a weekly professional column. Of course, the newspaper would note that the psychologist is a practitioner in the vicinity, and the column (actually written by Line) could serve as a subtle advertisement. Line's second product is a "newsletter" full of such material. He will sell copies of the newsletter imprinted with the practitioner's name and office address so that the buyer can do bulk mailings to the community that give out the free information, along with the impression that the buyer actually wrote it.

In April 1993, the APA Ethics Committee (1993a) issued a policy statement dealing with so-called canned columns or preauthored newsletters. The statement notes that it is unethical to identify oneself as the author of such a publication using the term "by." Associating oneself with such a column can be false and deceptive, violate publication credit standards, and permit others to make deceptive statements on one's behalf.

Presentation of Self

It is always a heady feeling to be flattered or to hear one's expertise celebrated in public, but it is also important to be represented accurately and objectively. Psychologists are trained as professionals with a scientific base of knowledge. It is just as important to be honest and objective about the limitations of one's knowledge as about one's credentials. If introduced incorrectly or in a misleading manner, even if well intentioned, the psychologist has a duty to correct the misinformation promptly.

Case 11-26: Hank Puffery, Psy.D., held an adjunct academic appointment as an assistant professor in a large medical school. Several documents, including a lecture program and a grant application, listed his academic rank as associate professor or professor. His failure to correct these inaccurate listings over several months ultimately led to the loss of his academic appointment on the basis of professional misrepresentation.

We do not know for certain whether Dr. Puffery's inaccurate listings were intentional or inadvertent, but it was clear to his superiors at the medical school that he did not correct the errors despite many opportunities to do so. Many other examples of presentation-of-self problems with respect to the public appear in chapter 12, but encounters with problems may also occur between psychologist and client alone.

Case 11-27: After an evaluation by Roger Fallic, Ed.D., a competently trained sex therapist, the client was informed that he could probably be helped by a treatment plan involving at least 6 months of office visits. This prediction, Fallic said, was based on the normative patterns documented in his treatment of clients with similar problems. When the client balked at the $150 per hour fee, Dr. Fallic commented, "You really ought to come up with it somehow since I'm the only one who can really help you in your current situation."

Perhaps Fallic did have a good treatment plan, which was well validated and potentially quite effective, for his client. The implication that no one else could provide effective treatment, however, is most likely false. The high fee charged and apparent unwillingness of Fallic to reduce it are not unethical per se, but the statement, with its grandiose implications, and Fallic's apparent unwillingness to make a less costly referral represent serious problems.

Embarrassing Others

It is not unethical to be a fool or an abrasive lout, but such behavior becomes embarrassing to the profession when the perpetrator is identified as a psychologist. At the same time, public comments presented in a sarcastic or offensive manner can easily exceed the bounds of ethical propriety. Chapter 13 deals with these issues vis-à-vis individual colleagues, but consider more globally expressed remarks, such as these comments overhead in public lectures or meetings:

"Psychoanalysis really never helps anyone do anything except enhance their own narcissism."

"Social workers really aren't trained to do deep therapy and ought to be supervised by psychologists or psychiatrists for most direct service work."

Remark to a group of students in abnormal psychology: "Okay, what crazies did we read about this week? Any nominations for psychotic of the week based on people you know on campus?"

These overgeneralizations, offensive comments, casual demeaning of people with problems, and similar remarks tend to hurt the entire profession. The following chapter pursues these matters in more detail, using the print and broadcast media as context. It is important to remember that other public forums are important as well. When lecturing, testifying before a legislative or judicial body, or making any statement for public consumption, one must consider the impact of one's words and style carefully, especially when the public is looking at a person identified as a psychologist.

SUMMARY GUIDELINES

1. Advertising by psychologists is clearly acceptable and cannot be banned, although the content of advertisements should ideally focus on facts of meaningful interest to the potential consumer.

2. One must take great care when listing affiliations, degrees, and other data to ensure that the public is not misled, confused, or otherwise deceived. Both intentional deception and inadvertent errors that are not corrected can be prosecuted.

3. Once completely prohibited, soliciting testimonials or quotes from "satisfied users" is now permissible so long as they are not solicited from current psychotherapy clients or others subject to undue influence. The effectiveness of such advertising for psychologists is unknown.

4. The uninvited, direct, in your face solicitation, as opposed to mass solicitation through media advertising, of individuals

as clients is also prohibited to the extent it subjects the potential client to undue influence. However, this does not include barriers to inviting the significant others of current clients for collateral treatment.

5. Psychologists who serve organizational or industrial clients are entitled to broader latitude than those who serve individuals (e.g., current organizational clients could be solicited for endorsements), lay groups, and families; however, they too must observe factual, validity-based criteria and avoid deception in their advertising claims.

6. Fees may be mentioned in advertisements, but must also be reasonably honored for the reasonable life of the announcement.

7. Referral services may ethically charge a fee to clients, therapists, or both, although this should not be secret from the client, and the fee should not be the primary basis for making the specific referral. When portions of fees are paid to other parties, such fees should be in payment for services actually rendered (e.g., referral service, consultation, supervision, office space rental, etc.).

8. Although there is no longer any prohibition to offer treatment to a client who is receiving services from another professional, specific discussions with the client of the potential risks and conflicts is now required. It would also be wise to seek authorization from the client to contact the other professional and to consult with that person.

9. Psychologists must consider their style of presentation of self and public statements carefully in any public context, whether or not advertising per se is involved.

10. States may impose more stringent restrictions on professional advertising than professional associations so long as a legitimate state's interest is documented and as that state's interest does not violate a consumer's access to useful information.

References

American Bar Association. (1976). Legal profession is considering code amendments to permit restricted advertising by lawyers. *American Bar Association Journal*, 62, 53–54.

American Medical Association. (1971). Principles of medical ethics. In *Judicial council opinions and reports*. Chicago: Author.

American Psychological Association. (1969). Guidelines for telephone directory listings. *American Psychologist*, 24, 70–71.

American Psychological Association. (1981). Ethical principles of psychologists. *American Psychologist*, 36, 633–638.

American Psychological Association. (1990). Ethical principles of psychologists (amended June 2, 1989). *American Psychologist*, 45, 390–395.

American Psychological Association. (1992). Ethical principles of psychologists and code of conduct. *American Psychologist*, 47, 1597–1611.

American Psychologial Association Ethics Committee. (1993a, April 20). *Advertisement and canned columns, revised statement*. Washington, DC: Author.

American Psychological Association Ethics Committee. (1993b). Report of the Ethics Committee, 1991 and 1992. *American Psychologist*, 48, 811–820.

American Psychological Association Ethics Committee. (1993c, April 18). *Use of APA Fellow designation (FAPA)*. Washington, DC: Author.

Association for the Advancement of Psychology. (1982). FTC's jurisdiction over professions threatened. *Advance*, 8, 5.

Azcuenaga, M. L. (1990). Separate statement of Commissioner Mary L. Azcuenaga concurring in part and dissenting in part in *American Psychological Association*, file 861-0082. Washington, DC: Federal Trade Commission.

Bray, D. W. (1976). The assessment center method. In R. L. Craig (Ed.), *Training and development handbook*. New York: McGraw-Hill.

Bray, D. W. (1977). Current trends and future possibilities. In J. L. Moses & W. C. Byham (Eds.), *Applying the assessment center method*. New York: Pergamon.

Bates et al. v. State Bar of Arizona, 433 U.S. 350 (1977).

Florida Bar v. Went For It, Inc., et al., docket number 94-226, *The United States Law Week*, 63 LW 4644 (1995).

FTC consent order text is published in its entirety. (1993, March). *APA Monitor*, 8.

Goldfarb v. Virginia State Bar, 421 U.S. 773 (1975).

Keith-Spiegel, P. (1982). *Moral conundrums, shibboleths, and gordian knots: Current issues in ethical standards for psychologists.* Presidential address to the Western Psychological Association, Sacramento, California.

Keith-Spiegel, P., Seegar, P., & Tomison, G. (1978). *What potential clients think of various modes of advertisting.* Paper presented at the 88th annual meeting of the American Psychological Association, Toronto.

Koocher, G. P. (1977). Advertising for psychologists: Pride and prejudice or sense and sensibility? *Professional Psychology, 8,* 149–160.

Koocher, G. P. (1979). Credentialing in psychology: Close encounters with competence? *American Psychologist, 34,* 696–702.

Koocher, G. P. (1994). APA and the FTC: New adventures in consumer protection. *American Psychologist, 49,* 322–328.

Ohralik v. Ohio State Bar Association, 436 U.S. 447 (1978).

Shapero v. Kentucky Bar Association, 486 U.S. 466 (1988).

Virginia State Board of Pharmacy et al. v. Virginia Citizens Consumer Council, Inc., et al., 425 U.S. 747 (1975).

12

Presenting Psychology to the Public

We live in an age of journalism: an age of skimmed surfaces, of facile confidence that reality is whatever can be seen and taped and reported.

George F. Will

PSYCHOLOGY'S FRACTURED PUBLIC IMAGE

The public's image of psychologists and of psychology remains incomplete, fractured, and confused. Factors contributing to this impression include the frequently inferior quality of information about psychology to which the public is exposed, the inherently complex nature of psychology and its many subspecialties, psychology's still-emerging database and recent theoretical paradigm shifts, and psychologists' own lack of success in educating the general public about who they are and what they do. However, methodological difficulties and sampling discrepancies among the public image surveys conducted since the 1940s make empirically based conclusions difficult to interpret with any degree of confidence (Webb, 1989; Wood, Jones, & Benjamin, 1986).

Psychologists, including the leaders in the field, continue to ponder the nature of their discipline. Bevan asserts that psychology is be-

coming balkanized, as is "increasingly manifest in the rapid proliferation of narrowly focussed and compulsively insular camps" (1991, p. 475). Boneau contends that many psychologists participating in his survey are disappointed in the directions in which psychology is moving and muses whether "psychology as a discipline has outlived its usefulness" and perhaps was always a "hybrid conglomeration of only tangentially related processes and approaches with little conceptual glue to hold it together" (1992, p. 1596). Koch (1993) has long argued that psychology can never be a single, coherent discipline and suggests that it be renamed "psychological studies." Likewise, Gibson (1994) is disappointed that psychology has failed to unite itself, but she remains convinced that we should continue to look for unifying theories and principles. Howell asserts that "raising public awareness that psychology is more than just mental health care is our most fundamental challenge" (1994, p. 6). So, although we take the media to task for its role in confusing the public about what psychology is, we readily acknowledge that psychology is a diverse field that does not present a consolidated front.

Another source of public confusion is the considerable overlap between psychology and other disciplines, such as psychiatry, sociology, education, and physiology. Similarities among the services offered by an array of mental health specialists cloud the identity of psychologists even further. Scores of psychotherapies populate the mainstream, and some hang out at the fringes. Survey findings suggest that the public does not differentiate well among clinical psychologists, psychiatrists, and counselors (Wollersheim & Walsh, 1993), although psychologists may be viewed as more "comfortable" to talk to than psychiatrists and other mental health professionals (Murstein & Fontaine, 1993). Television talk shows smear the psychologist's image even thinner with an array of "professional guests" appearing to function as psychologists, but sporting titles such as "aggression specialist," "griefwork expert," and "divorce consultant." The education and training backgrounds (if any) of these people are rarely disclosed.

This chapter considers the ways that psychologists interface with the public at large. Our main focus is on the love-hate relationship between psychology and the print, broadcast, and electronic media. Because interactive media and computer networks are rapidly changing the way people disperse and absorb the knowledge that shapes what and how they think, we also discuss the impact of these more recent innovations. As McGrath has noted, "Electronic information is the currency of the future. If [psychologists] do not participate in that exchange, we lose an unprecedented opportunity to shape the cultural attitudes of the future global village" (1995, p. 5). Ethical risks and pitfalls lurk close by, with many still coming into awareness. We present cases illustrating how psychologists have already been involved in the kinds of "accidents" that dot the shoulders of the information highway.

We note up front that we wholeheartedly concur with George Miller's now-classic counsel to promote human welfare by "giving psychology away" so that people can better help themselves (Miller, 1969). Both traditional and electronic media are readily available conduits. We differentiate the best that psychologists have to contribute (information with a research or strong practice base) from the cliches and "psychobabble" that permeate much of what the public thinks is psychology. At no time do we suggest that any media or other public forum be designated off limits to psychologists for ethical reasons. However, we warn of the risks inherent in various outlets and opportunities for public statements. Thus, it is not whether, but how psychologists involve themselves with the media that raises ethical questions about social responsibility, competence, conflict of interest, and the public image of psychology (see the definition of *public statements* in the 1992 American Psychological Association [APA] code, ES: 3.01).

MASS MEDIA PORTRAYALS OF PSYCHOLOGY AND PSYCHOLOGISTS

Mass media punctuates the awareness of just about every member of our society on a daily basis. Intricate stories or issues are usually stripped bare to fit within narrow borders. Television interviewers routinely cut interviewees off if the answers to their questions exceed 30 seconds, regardless of the scope and complexity of the inquiries. Much of what the general public thinks it is learning about psychology and psychologists is distorted, trivialized, sensationalized, or inaccurate.

Psychologists face a quandary when it comes to the media. On the one hand, it is clearly to the benefit of society for psychologists to be actively involved in widespread dissemination of psychological information. Psychology can help people gain sensible perspectives of societies and the people who populate them. Yet, unfortunately, psychologists may often fail to inform or may even misinform. Misguidance can be offered unwittingly, as when journalists or producers edit an interview with a blunt hatchet or interject their own version of what the data mean. Misinformation can be transmitted purposefully, as when psychologists and their publishers want to sell more books than a sober and reasoned presentation of the facts would generate, or when psychologists want their work to appear profound and, in the process, obscure distinctions between fact and speculation.

Distortions of Psychological Concepts and Psychologists

Television characters that would be diagnosed with homicidal dissociative personality disorders—usually erroneously referred to as "schizophrenics"—populate shows with a frequency that suggests to uninformed viewers that such frightening people are probably standing in line behind them in the supermarket. When the mentally ill are portrayed, it is also likely that they will be characterized as victimized, unemployed, and leading failed lives (Signorielli, 1989). Jokes and casual use of medical terms are also frequently directed toward the mentally disabled, and name-calling and the use of diagnostic terms (or their archaic or popularized derivatives, such as "lunatic" or "schizo") are common. Other overrepresented (and usually inaccurately presented) conditions include amnesia, homicidal mania, hysterical paralysis, and phobic disorders (Schneider, 1987).

A media portrayal of a psychotherapy session is usually boiled down to a few exchanges between "client" and "therapist," sometimes concluding in a remarkable breakthrough that clears up a lifelong search for just the right insight. Whereas many psychologists appear to find Bob Newhart's characterization of a psychologist endearing, more often psychotherapists are portrayed in dramatic entertainment as uncaring exploiters, incompetent boobs, or rogues who have no sense of professional role boundaries. Schneider (1987) reviewed 207 American films depicting psychiatrists, excluding the exploitative horror genre. Of these, 35% fit his "Dr. Dippy" type, the psychiatrist who is crazier than the patients; 22% were classified as "Dr. Wonderfuls," the type that skillfully maneuvers or interprets at precisely the correct moment, effecting a total cure; 22% were classified as "Dr. Evils," who dabble in forbidden, coercive experimentation for personal profit or gratification.

Research psychologists are largely absent from dramatic media fare save for occasional weird portrayals of power-hungry, mind controllers, who seduce unsuspecting victims into their gadget-and-drug-stocked laboratories, or as ancient, quirky scholars, who dabble in the supernatural. Actual research findings, when cited at all, are often selected on the basis of controversy rather than scientific quality. Isolated or minor findings, if intriguing, may be presented to the public in a way that gives the impression that far more was discovered than the actual data warrant. Correlational data are consistently presented as breakthrough discoveries about cause-and-effect relationships. Typically, compact conclusions are presented with no effort to describe the cautions that attend an evaluation of almost any social science investigation. Overblown, overgeneralized, inaccurate, and misleading research findings also circulate quickly, with the next media commentator using the previously stated erroneous conclusions, possibly altering them just a tad more to fit the story. Support for psychology itself suffers as a result of misinformation because policymakers often rely on the media as a source of data on which to base their decisions (Pallak & Kilburg, 1986).

Display of Sullied Linen

Ratings by the public of psychologists tend to be on the positive side (Wood et al., 1986), and the majority of psychologists (96% according to Good, Simon, & Coursey, 1981) do good works away from the limelight, donating some of their time to clinics and other community services. However, socially responsible psychologists do not seem to attract much media interest. Instead, news items about psychologists usually display flagrant violations of responsibilities or the commission of malicious, reprehensible acts. Although these cases involve serious ethical or legal violations that could easily fit elsewhere in this book, a few were selected for presentation here because each attracted considerable media attention.

Case 12-1: Wyde Awake, Ph.D., was referred to an ethics committee by an insurance carrier. The company's audit revealed that Dr. Awake had billed for 120 hours of psychotherapy during a single 7-day period, for an average of 17 hours a day. Although Dr. Awake's clients failed to substantiate that many of the sessions actually took place, Awake insisted that her patients' recollections were in error, and that "she enjoyed doing psychotherapy and did not require much sleep." When Awake was asked by an ethics committee to explain her actions, she threatened to hire the Mafia to kill all of its members unless the charges were dropped immediately.

Case 12-2: Sik Imposter, Ph.D., used the name and qualifications of a psychiatrist from another state and accepted a position as a staff psychiatrist in a mental health clinic. When Dr. Imposter became suspicious that his true identity was on the verge of discovery, he traveled to the authentic psychiatrist's office and attempted to murder him as he exited a taxicab.

Case 12-3: While bathing her daughter shortly after a therapy session, a mother noticed that the child's genitals were reddened. When questioned, the girl replied that it happened during the "secret game" that she always played with her therapist, Phil Pedo, Ph.D. Dr. Pedo would take off the girl's panties and have her sit on his face. The mother called the police.

Case 12-4: Fearful that a wealthy client with whom he had an affair was going to report him to the authorities, Ben Berserk, Ed.D., broke into her home and attempted to strangle her as she slept.

These actual cases create an alarming image of psychologists. Psychologists are, after all, not exempt from the range of pathology and deviance that affect humankind as a whole. To the extent that the public generalizes its attitudes about psychologists from such high-profile accounts, psychologists would be viewed as potentially fraudulent, exploitative, perverted, and even violent. Although thankfully extremely rare, along with the obvious harm to innocent victims, such incidents also take a serious toll on the public image of the profession.

Whether ethics committees should investigate crimes or other highly questionable acts that are unrelated to one's professional identification as a psychologist has been hotly debated in the past. The current code of the APA (1992) limits the scope of the code to work-related and other activities that are psychological in nature (ES: 1.01). Regardless, it is clear that the public image of psychology is compromised when unrelated acts are publicized. The next two news stories are illustrative.

Case 12-5: A young boy was seriously injured by a hit-and-run driver, Hooch Boozer, Ph.D. A heavily intoxicated Boozer was quickly apprehended. Newspaper accounts highlighted Boozer's six previous arrests for drunk driving and also mentioned that he was a psychologist who taught at the local college.

Whether Dr. Boozer's irresponsible drinking and driving behavior compromised his ability to teach and relate to students is not known for sure. However, along with Boozer himself, his college and the discipline of psychology likely suffered some loss in reputation.

Case 12-6: A discovery that a group in the United States arranged for the selling of arms to an unfriendly nation also revealed that Billy Bazooka, Ed.D., a paramilitary militia member, was among them. News accounts prominently featured Dr. Bazooka's profession as a counseling psychologist.

Again, the same question pertains regarding Dr. Bazooka's competence to deliver psychological services: Was it affected by his illegal gunrunning activity? We do know that his nonprofessional escapade cast shame on his professional peers.

Illegal activity is not a necessary ingredient to the decline of public trust. As the next case illustrates, publicized acts of exploitation by a psychologist may not violate any laws, but nevertheless smear the image of psychology.

Case 12-7: Fast Buck, Ph.D., was treating Persona Galore for a dissociative disorder. Dr. Buck discovered more than 60 "personalities" within Miss Galore and persuaded the client to sign over exclusive book and movie rights to her story. Dr. Buck also arranged press conferences for himself and Miss Galore. Galore eventually charged Dr. Buck with exploiting her condition.

Unfortunately, the public trust in psychology and psychologists may be compromised even when the psychologists themselves were totally innocent of any legal or ethical wrongdoing, as the next case illustrates.

Case 12-8: Edna Scholarly, Ph.D., a prominent research psychologist, wrote to an ethics committee expressing concern about an incident brought to her attention. She had received a letter from a distraught mother blaming her for having lost her child in a custody dispute. Further inquiry revealed that the father's attorney had used Dr. Scholarly's work dealing with the effects of working mothers on child development as expert opinion, and that certain comments taken out of context and embellished inappropriately may have been persuasive to the court. Dr. Scholarly believed that her work had been used in an unethical manner and sought counsel for any possible redress.

Psychologists are admonished to do whatever is within their power to ensure that their work or services will not be misused by others, including the media. Such control, however, is often not possible.

Case 12-9: Journalist Quick Whip advocated the use of physical punishment for children's wrongdoings. He cited a number of prominent psychologists' works to bolster his argument that corporal punishment, including use of electric shock devices, is an effective means of eliminating unwanted behaviors. The cited research had been conducted on hospitalized autistic children and was grossly misrepresented. The psychologists credited by Whip were horrified by their unwitting promotion of a technique never intended for use with noninstitutionalized children.

Even though these psychologists wrote a stern letter to the journalist and the newspaper editor, they were never acknowledged, and no retraction ever appeared.

PSYCHOLOGISTS IN THE MEDIA

The current APA ethics code (APA, 1992) is not a very helpful guide when it comes to inter-

facing with the media. Some of the points of the ethics codes issued during the 1980s, warning psychologists to avoid superficiality and flamboyance, have been deleted. Psychologists are to represent qualifications accurately and base their comments on "appropriate psychological literature and practice" (ES: 3.04). What constitutes "appropriate" is not further defined and leaves considerable latitude for debate. Another statement admonishes psychologists not to encourage a recipient of any media-disseminated advice that "a relationship has been established with them personally" (ES: 3.04). This advice is more protective of the psychologist than of consumers because it may assist in precluding a malpractice charge later. In another item that would, effectively, curb most interactions with the media were it to be strictly followed, the code states, "Psychologists do not participate in activities in which it appears likely that their skills or data will be misused by others, unless corrective mechanisms are available" (ES: 1.16). Correcting any errors later is all but impossible because retractions are rare, and when they are printed they are rarely placed where anyone would notice.

We have arranged the common public forums in which psychologists may actively participate into three categories based on the degree of control psychologists have over what the public receives: little or no control, some control, and considerable control. As a rule, the more control psychologists have, the more responsible they are for the media content. However, in our opinion, psychologists should be wary about participating at all when they do not know the journalist or the control they have is virtually nil.

When Psychologists Have Little or No Control Over Their Presentations to the Public

Public Statements Based on Interviews with Journalists

Journalists and media producers form a solid blockade between what psychologists say and what actually gets through to the public. Alterations, usually in the form of selecting a small portion that fits the journalist's needs, are inevitable. Although there are many fine journalists who select elements well, that reinterpretations will be done judiciously without violating the integrity of the interview is largely a matter of faith. The opportunity to review journalists' final copy or script is rarely offered, and a request to do so is rarely honored. Unforgiving deadlines may preclude journalists from doing thorough and accurate work.

Trained science news journalists would be expected to do the best job. However, these journalists are less interested in the social and behavioral sciences than in the so-called harder sciences (Dunwoody, 1980; McCall, 1988). Journalists who do write about psychological topics apparently think they know a lot more about psychology than they actually do (McCall, 1988). For this reason, psychologists who agree to interact under circumstances of minimal editorial control are advised to proceed with caution in an attempt to ensure that their names and their profession will be treated with integrity and dignity.

Horror Stories

It is natural to feel flattered when a reporter, writer, or associate producer calls to express interest in your work or ideas. The outcome can be beneficial all around. One's work is disseminated to an audience, and one's influence, popularity, and demand might increase significantly (Fox & Levin, 1993). However, not all such alliances prove satisfying. During informal discussions with colleagues, we have consistently observed that those who have had several experiences interfacing with the media had at least one dreadful experience or horror story to share.

> I was interviewed for almost 2 hours. The reporter used all my good stuff in a way that suggested that he created it himself and only quoted me on two offhanded jokes I made. He sounded well informed, and I came off as an idiot.

> I couldn't believe what I saw in print. I was quoted out of context in such a way that the effect was to portray me as holding views to which I am diametrically opposed.

My 20-year commitment to basic research has never drawn the attention of a single journalist despite the many articles, papers, and books I have contributed. Then, last year a student and I did a quick survey on cheating behavior on campus, and every paper and radio station in town called. I worry about the criteria used to determine what the public learns about our discipline.

The producer held out the possibility of putting me on a popular television news show. She asked me to gather lots of information for her. In the end, my voluminous notes were made into a brief table, stripped of everything except those findings that supported the show's slant. I was thanked for my help, but not invited to appear on the show. I ended up being a doctoral-level research assistant who worked 10 hours for free!

The man who called, describing himself as a free-lance writer doing a story on life satisfaction, seemed very nice. I did ask him where the story would appear, and he replied that he wasn't sure, but named a variety of top magazines to which he had previously contributed articles. Three weeks later I got a call from my mother informing me that I was quoted in one of those tabloids, right next to a story about a 3-year-old girl who gave birth to four turtles.

I was thrilled about being invited to appear on a major "magazine show." But, during the filming, it became painfully clear that the interviewer was biased against my work. I was blindsided, defending myself throughout the entire interrogation. I considered walking out, but realized that would make me look cowardly, antisocial, and guilty. I stayed and looked pathetic instead.

Occasionally, a piece written by a journalist about a psychologist has been brought to the attention of an ethics committee. In the majority of instances, the psychologists have been able to defend themselves by affixing the blame on irresponsible or incompetent journalism. As the following case indicates, insult is added to injury when psychologists endure collegial criticism and an ethics inquiry procedure.

Case 12-10: An article in a local newspaper quoted psychologist Adolf Blunt, Ph.D., as having said, "No responsible psychologist can deny that minority ethnic heritage is the major cause of violent crime." Dr. Blunt was upset by the story, as well as by subsequent criticisms from colleagues and others on the basis of a misquote. He noted that the quotation was based on an extended conversation with the reporter, during which Blunt presented data showing that acts of violent street crime were proportionately higher in some areas where certain ethnic minority groups were concentrated, and that this fact cannot be denied. Blunt stated that he then discussed numerous possible explanations, none of which had racist connotations.

This is not to say that psychologists themselves cannot be held accountable for inappropriate disclosure to journalists, as we see in the next two cases.

Case 12-11: Groupie Squeal, Ph.D., was interviewed about his celebrity clients in a popular movie magazine. He identified his clients by name and offered additional personal and interpretive comments. His response to an ethics committee inquiry was that his clients would welcome the free publicity.

Case 12-12: Tim Uppie, Ph.D., was so convinced that a commonly used antidepressant medication was essential to mental well-being that he suggested to a reporter, only 15 minutes into the interview, that she try it to alleviate her mild depression. He then invited her to become his client.

An ethics committee found Dr. Squeal professionally irresponsible and strongly admonished him to leave the promotion of his clients to their publicists. Whether Dr. Uppie's enthusiasm for a particular proactive drug is warranted is not debated here, but his quick diagnosis and verbal prescription raises serious questions of competence and ability to render professional judgments. Uppie should have realized that a reporter interviewing him for a story would surely report this outlandish twist in their interaction and should have known that the result would be damaging to the more respectful image of psychologists as discrete professionals who function within their legal limits of competence.

Sometimes, as the next case reveals, psychologists can be faulted merely for trusting too much.

Case 12-13: Jethrow Relaxed, Ph.D., his colleague Kelia Kasual, Ed. D., and a journalist met at a local coffee shop to discuss some of the problems facing the commissioner of the state's Department of Public Health. The affable journalist treated them both to lunch, and everyone exchanged amusing stories. The discussion slowly moved to the topic at hand. The psychologists were, by then, so comfortable with the journalist that they made some offhanded jokes about the commissioner's possible toilet training history and what they imagined to be his behavior in the bedroom. When lunch was over and the interview appeared to be formally under way, the two psychologists offered serious, professional opinions about the Department of Public Health. The next day, the newspaper article quoted from the interview and included the psychologists' speculations about the commissioner's possible potty training failures and sexual inadequacies.

All of us have made remarks about others, especially when the company is amiable, that would result in considerable distress were they to be made public. When acting in the professional role, however, it is especially important to maintain a grip on the situation and the people present. The psychologists in this case faced considerable unflattering publicity from the public and from their colleagues. The commissioner threatened defamation charges and reported them to the state licensing board.

Minimizing the Risk

We offer some hints for ensuring a veridical journey with minimal risk from your mouth to the public ear. First, it is wise to learn the purpose of the story, how the journalist or producer is approaching it, and more detail about any unfamiliar publication or program that requests your involvement. If the story or the outlet seems exploitative, sensational, or superficial, consider waiting for a better opportunity to share yourself with the public. Psychologists must remember that mass media and scholarly publishing have very different purposes. Keeping that in mind may assist in both a decision to participate in a media activity and understanding why the final product often comes out the way it does.

If you decide to participate in an interview, give the journalist a brief (one to two double-spaced pages at most) written statement of your major points. Many psychologists have reported improved results when brief, but clearly stated, summaries are made available. This material is often quoted directly, which greatly reduces error in the final product.

If you are contacted to comment on a topic about which you have insufficient knowledge or experience, we strongly advise that you politely refuse comment or, if you know one, refer the reporter to a better resource. Reporters may push hard because their imminent deadline renders any psychologist's view acceptable. A pushy journalist under pressure should never be allowed to overpower one's personal integrity.

Avoid getting so comfortable with the interviewer that you make offhanded comments, as did Drs. Relaxed and Kasual in Case 12–13. Remember, these people are working to fulfill their own agendas and view you as a means to that end. They are usually very pleasant people, skilled in the art of "opening people up." Today's cynical brand of journalism, however, can involve more than publicizing what you say. We are certainly not suggesting that every journalist conceals his or her true plan, but the contemporary use of hidden cameras, snares, and bait-and-switch tactics prompt us to encourage caution. Also, remember that any bad joke, side comment, or gesture (including groans or sighs and facial expressions) are fair game. A colleague told us that he blew his nose during an interview, and this was reported in print.

Always keep in mind that you cannot speak for the entire profession, nor can you speak for a professional organization unless authorized to do so (ES: 3.03a). Embarrassment and ethics complaints can be avoided by refraining from making generalizations that imply some unanimous endorsement or agreement unless hard data exist to verify such a statement.

Case 12-14: Several psychologists were outraged on reading an article by Sweep Universal, Ph.D.,

in a popular magazine. Dr. Universal made several generalizations that a great many psychologists would not endorse and that were not supported by data. These included: "Psychologists finally agree that women are better suited to jobs that involve structure rather than complex ones that require a tolerance for ambiguity," and "Psychologists now know that it is almost impossible to break a bad habit, such as smoking, on your own."

Psychologists can certainly give their own opinion, even an unpopular or imprudent one. But, to saddle an entire profession is unfair and unscrupulous because such statements are impossible to rebut effectively.

Stories are often built around newsworthy topics with psychological overtones. Psychologists may be contacted to comment about psychological ramifications of national disasters or being held hostage, the veracity of repressed memories, the effects of psychological well-being on physical health, and so on. When no solid data exist on which to base a definitive comment, be modest by suggesting possibilities clearly labeled as tentative. As Cardinal put it, after reviewing his own ordeal with journalists, "Representatives of the news media do not appear to understand that disagreement almost always exists in journals in the social sciences on any given research question. . . . Yet the media frequently want a simple answer, demanding consensus where it doesn't exist" (1994, p. B3).

Sometimes, journalists are interested in "psychological evaluations" of a specific newsworthy individual the psychologist has never met. Commentary in such instances is likely to be irresponsible and probably inaccurate and should therefore be avoided. Or, reporters may be looking for quotations from experts to bolster an already established slant or point of view. Several Boston psychologists faced criticism following the 1988 presidential campaign when they appeared to be offering gratuitous analyses of why Kitty Dukakis, wife of the Democratic contender, abused drugs and alcohol; the analyses included slightly unflattering speculations about her husband's personality and style. The psychologists later claimed that their comments were misapplied and taken out of context by the reporter.

Psychologists must remember that they do not usually have the luxury that most people do of publicly commenting on the psychological well-being of specific others, whether they know them personally or not. It may be possible to talk about the relevant psychological topic in a detached way, but be careful. Journalists may not make that distinction when they write their story.

If a psychologist has had professional contact with a newsworthy individual (including deceased persons), confidentiality becomes a critical issue and should not be compromised (see chapter 6). Even if the noteworthy individual consents or invites you to make public statements, professional judgment may dictate that such information should not be shared with media representatives. A clinical social worker drew considerable criticism for discussing the content of her few sessions with a murder victim in a high-profile case. She made numerous television appearances and later defended her actions as a way to do a public service by raising awareness of domestic abuse. She further justified disclosing the content of a confidential relationship because the victim had told others about what she had told her, thus rendering the information as no longer "privileged." This inaccurate interpretation of the ethics of confidentiality and the right to privacy probably did far more to keep people from seeking help from therapists (who viewers could assume might later talk about what was said in a private session on national television) than could possibly be offset by a handful of public comments about domestic violence (see chapter 3).

Although you may not be able to review your contribution of what will be disseminated to the public, you can make sure that the journalist is keenly aware of the importance you place on the story's accuracy (see ES: 3.02). Invite the journalist to call you back if any questions arise. This is especially important if the topic is controversial or easily misinterpreted. If, after the interview, you realize that you may have made a significant error or neglected to mention something of importance, call the journalist to offer additional comment. Also, request that the journalist send you a copy of the printed article (or at least to inform you when it is published) as

another way of impressing the journalist with your personal interest in the quality of the piece. If you are embarrassed or dissatisfied with the final product, let the journalist know about it. Because recipients can easily dismiss angry messages, frame your remarks in a constructive way that may help educate the journalist. *How to Work with the Media* by Fox and Levin (1993) presents a deeper analysis of risks and rewards and offers many ideas for maximizing successful interactions with media professionals. The APA Office of Public Affairs (n.d.) also disseminates a booklet, *Media Training for Psychologists*, to help psychologists prepare themselves for satisfactory interactions with media representatives.

Finally, we do not want readers to conclude from the troubling incidents we have shared here that the best course of action is to refrain from speaking to journalists altogether. A well-done story can be a genuine contribution to the field. We do, however, encourage careful preparation and due caution.

When Psychologists Have Some Measure of Control Over What Reaches the Public

When psychologists are appearing on "live" television or doing the writing themselves, their level of control increases, as does their level of responsibility.

"Live" Radio and Television Appearances

Psychologists are often interviewed live on radio or television. This format can produce frustrations, such as getting cut off before the point was fully made, fielding stupid or inappropriate questions, or being repeatedly referred to as a psychiatrist. Sometimes, however, the psychologist bears full responsibility, as the following two cases reveal.

Case 12-15: Buff Showit, Ph.D., was interviewed about his book on holistic, age-regression, hot tub, group therapy. He asserted that his technique was more useful in relieving tensions and dissolving "our ghosts" than "all of the rest of psychiatry and psychology combined," and that the technique guaranteed major relief from any emotional disturbance, no matter how serious.

Showit could produce no data to substantiate the excessive claims about his tub therapy. Elevating an unproven technique above all practices of two traditional disciplines is irresponsible at best.

Case 12-16: Flamba Gambit, Ed.D, made regular appearances on local radio programs to discuss various aspects of psychology. Her authoritative manner and choice of words could be easily interpreted as implying knowledge based on scientific findings, although this was rarely the case. One of several complaints against her concerned her assertion that women who were raped "unconsciously wanted it," and that her research indicated that this was due to "a childhood fantasy of being simultaneously loved and punished by Daddy for being a good and bad little girl."

On inquiry, the "research" Gambit cited consisted of no more than her opinion based on interactions with several of her clients who had been raped. Gambit's statements were highly misleading and irresponsible and may have caused some listeners psychological harm.

Sometimes, psychologists do not recognize beforehand that they may be put into a situation that would necessitate a break with professional decorum.

Case 12-17: Rem Voltic, Ph.D., a noted psychologist and expert on sleep disorders, was invited to appear as a guest on a local television show that was devoting a segment to "The Bedroom." Models were there to show the latest fashions in sleep wear, bedtime snacks were to be demonstrated by the resident chef, and a bedroom set was rigged at the studio. When Dr. Voltic arrived at the studio, the production manager asked him to report to wardrobe for a pajama fitting. Dr. Voltic refused to appear on the show under such conditions. He reasoned that he agreed to participate as a representative of his field and should dress as he would when functioning in a professional capacity.

Voltic may have caused havoc on the set, but his decision was entirely appropriate. He had the courage to escape probable criticism by refusing to put the lure of the footlights above his professional identity.

Offering Advice to Individuals on Radio Call-In Shows

Psychologists who host live radio shows, featuring people "calling in" their problems, were far more popular and prevalent in the 1980s than they are today. In their heyday, the ethical dimensions of "radio therapy" were hotly debated. Some believed that this airborne mode of advice giving did more good for psychology than any previous movement because the public received an inkling of what psychotherapy and those who conduct it were really like. Many types of psychological problems and conflicts were, perhaps, demystified. People who may have felt isolated or uniquely troubled or attached a stigma to needing help might have benefited by learning that others have similar conflicts and concerns. Some listeners may even have been motivated to seek direct, needed services. Because of their immense popularity, supporters argued that radio psychologists could more effectively educate the public about psychology than they could in any other medium. And, it cost the public nothing.

Others have decried radio psychologists as "fast food therapy," embarrassing to the profession as a whole, blatantly unprofessional, and possibly even harmful to the "quasi clients" or passive listeners. Despite the potential for educating the public, critics claimed that psychologist media advice givers were hired not for their clinical competence or expertise as educators and scholars, but rather for qualities aligned with media business criteria such as voice, verbal facility, physical appearance, and engaging or charismatic personality characteristics. It was suggested that psychologists who participated put their professional interests well behind their needs for attention. "Show biz" standards pertained in the forms of maintaining a quick turnover of calls, fast-paced and upbeat dialogue, and high interest or entertainment value, achieved largely through encouraging the callers to share sordid details, which were followed by the psychologists' snappy, engrossing commentary.

Critics also noted that callers and listeners alike received drastic misperceptions about the psychotherapeutic process. The advice was viewed as suspicious because it was based on minimal and incomplete information offered by a stranger. Harm could result, particularly for vulnerable or "emotionally brittle" people with no other ongoing support systems, those advised to make some major life changes, those hit with an interpretation they were not prepared to handle, or those who acted on the advice and found that it failed to ameliorate the problem. Audience members and participants may be led to believe that quick answers can solve even serious personal or interpersonal problems.

Despite the many criticisms and concerns about potential harm to callers, the listening audience, and the image of the profession, ethics committees never received many complaints against radio psychologists. However, occasional letters from listeners and callers questioning specific incidents have resulted in ethics committee investigations.

Case 12-18: A caller complained to an ethics committee that Grace Goodtalk, Ed.D., treated her shamefully during an "on-air" advice session. The caller claimed she was berated as "immature and silly" because she called for advice on how to clear up an argument with a friend. When the caller protested that her problem was very serious to her and she wanted help rather than ridicule, she claimed that Dr. Goodtalk abruptly cut her off. The caller claimed that this incident caused her considerable and prolonged mental stress. She stated, "If this is what psychologists do to people who are hurting, I don't understand why anyone would consult one."

On inquiry, Dr. Goodtalk defended her comments as appropriate for that caller and added, "I don't need psychology. Psychology needs me." The ethics committee recommended acceptance of her indignant letter of resignation from the professional organization.

Case 12-19: A concerned listener wrote to an ethics committee expressing concern about the well-being of a repeat caller to *Flap with Dr. Mike Flap*, a psychology talk show. The caller, who was

on the show several times, complained of headaches she believed were due to intense stress. Dr. Flap offered suggestions during each call about to how to learn to relax and minimize contributing environmental factors. About 3 months after the initial call, the woman informed Dr. Flap that a neurologist had located a brain tumor that was the likely cause of the intense headaches. The listener was extremely concerned that Dr. Flap had behaved irresponsibly by encouraging the woman to continue calling in update reports. The listener saw Flap as contributing to the delay in locating the true reason for the woman's headaches, a cause Dr. Flap could not possibly assess himself.

On inquiry, Dr. Flap insisted that it had been verified off air that the woman was under the close supervision of a physician. The ethics committee, however, concluded that the psychologist should have made the listening audience aware of the fact that he had known about and supported medical intervention, and that he should routinely state on air that a radio advice format should never be the sole source of advice about a physical complaint.

Radio psychologists must think fast, and the results can be unfortunate. Witness the following lamentable example involving the media advice giver's lack of knowledge or confusion about the nature of a potent antipsychotic agent:

I think you are overreacting to what the doctor is telling you about your son's problems. He's receiving Mellaril, which is a mild and commonly used mood elevator. Mellaril would not be used for a serious psychiatric disorder. Your son is probably just depressed, and your worrying will just make things worse. Explore your own guilt, then relax.

The once-thunderous debate about dispensing advice over the radio softened to a hush by the 1990s. This is not because any ethical issues have been resolved. However, research has not substantiated widespread discontent among listeners (e.g., Levy, 1989; Raviv, Yunovitz, & Raviv, 1989). Nor has evidence proving harm materialized. Anyone who may have been harmed rarely complained, or, if they did, complained to the broadcast stations but not to ethics committees. We believe, however, that a major reason for the virtual disappearance of the radio psychologist debate is that the influx of call-in programs hosted by loud, brash, nonpsychologist radio personalities—"shock jocks"—have become so bizarre and outrageous that the few remaining mental health professionals on the air seem mellow by comparison. One of the best-known survivors—assumed by most to be a psychologist because she is introduced as a doctoral-level therapist, although her degree is not in psychology—chides her clients mercilessly. Embedded in today's media context, however, she apparently does not come off as a menace to her considerable audience.

The Modern Colosseum

Television talk shows have replaced the radio as a place to find large numbers of psychologists. About two dozen talk show hosts, competing aggressively for ratings, routinely display guests who appear to be highly dysfunctional or embroiled in grotesque or novel life circumstances. Their troubling stories are milked by the celebrity host for most of the hour: "Can you tell us a little more about what your father did to you after your mother went to her night classes?" "What in your family background may have led to your lack of guilt about sleeping with two of your sisters' husbands?" "How were you feeling when you picked up the shovel and swung it at your wife's head?" Emotional confrontations among the lineup of players trapped in the same lamentable situation are actively stimulated by the host and often enthusiastically cheered or jeered by an agitated, hooting audience, much like a modern colosseum. The clashes among the guests often reach a deafening cacophony of allowable profanity and bleeps.

Two recent trends are especially disturbing to us. One common ploy is to ambush the guests by setting up surprise appearances or revelations that will likely embarrass or humiliate them before a nation of viewers. "Don't you have something you want to tell Alvin?" coos the host with inside knowledge. An on-stage confession of adultery or other betrayal is typically responded to by the audience with audible, perverse glee, while the hapless victims burst into rage or take on the stone-cold stare of a trapped animal in

shock. Such a confrontation was apparently the provocation leading to a "lured" guest to murder his secret admirer (another man) several days after the filming of a television talk show (Kaplan, 1995; Peyser, 1995), although the use of this ploy has not subsequently decreased.

The parading of children or vulnerable adolescents, exposing them to intense questioning about their own situation or the ills plaguing their family, is also currently fashionable. The audience wallows in "as if" pain as tearful or terrified children who have been subjected to abuse or traumatic events are encouraged to open up by seemingly caring hosts. Or, poorly behaved youngsters with behavior or "attitude" problems are scorned by a disapproving audience and sometimes by the host as well. A 12-year-old-boy, while offstage, was described as "a menace." As he walked on stage, he was greeted by the audience with loud hoots and boos. In response, he gave them "the finger." The host sprang over and gave him a tongue-lashing. Yet, an audience is rarely admonished for humiliating a child.

No comprehensive study of the impact on guests appearing on television talk shows has been conducted. Because access to the names and addresses of guests is not possible, we will never be able to make accurate generalizations. Several accounts of individual guests, however, have confirmed that they were "whipped into a frenzy" in the greenroom and then abandoned after the show (Zoglin, 1995). Suffering later consequences, such as being easily recognized at home despite the assurance of a disguise (Hundley, 1995), have also been reported. Perhaps the more significant question—more problematical than even longer term consequences for shortsighted guests—is, when the pain and humiliation of others become a popular form of entertainment, what does that say about a society?

What do psychologists have to do with this modern version of a colosseum blood sport, and why can it be an ethical problem? Psychologists and other mental health professionals do have a major role in these shows, ostensibly as intervention providers and educators. After the guests with the problems have been opened up and wrung dry, an expert is brought on stage to solve the complex quandaries that have usually been steeping for years. This late maneuver, often made as few as 10 minutes before the program is over, appears to us often to serve as a quick-and-easy attempt to lend an air of legitimacy and redeeming social value to an otherwise morally bankrupt concept in entertainment. Often, the experts are mere window dressing, fading behind the psychobabbling hosts, who remain in tight control of the analysis and advice.

So, should psychologists participate in this popular brand of entertainment? Are mental health professionals actually aiding and abetting the exploitation of naive, vulnerable people? The answer cannot be a simple "yes" or "no." Sometimes, these programs are well suited to imparting helpful information or exposure, such as segments on transracial adoptions, effective discipline techniques with children, domestic violence, or plights of the homeless. Psychologists and other experts can enlighten and educate. Many of these shows can be credited for informing the public about self-care groups aimed at a variety of audiences, such as children of Holocaust survivors, spouses of alcoholics, and parents of murdered children (Jacobs & Goodman, 1989).

Sometimes, however, the motivations of the psychologists are far less selfless. A book, usually of the self-help variety (discussed in a section below) needs promoting, and no other avenue of publicity can reach more people at no cost. Perhaps some psychologists believe that their appearance will somehow generate more personal business. Or, like many of the guests, they simply cannot pass up an opportunity to appear on TV.

It seems to us that psychologists need to take a hard look at this entertainment format and be far more selective about what they agree to do. Just because the guests have agreed, voluntarily and possibly enthusiastically, to allow their privacy to be invaded on national television is not a sufficient excuse for psychologists to preclude an ethical analysis of their role. Psychologists can anticipate the possible humiliation that will face some guests as a result of their appearance and know that the Groucho Marx glasses and fright wig will not fool anyone who knows these people personally. Psychologists know that the

informed consent procedures are protective of the television station and not of the guests. Psychologists know that when the guests fly back to wherever they came from, the same problems will be waiting for them, and that the program staff will only be looking forward to rounding up the next set of players. McGrath (1995) relates the case of a young woman who, after describing her violent rape, was whisked, sobbing and trembling, to a limousine for the ride alone to the airport.

One psychologist who appears regularly on talk shows asserted that the main reason people agreed to appear on these shows was to get help because it was not available elsewhere. She justified her appearances as "a public service." Is this assertion true? In a survey, 200 undergraduate students were asked if they would appear on national television to reveal the details of their most intimate private secrets. The results give us clues. Whereas only 5% would enthusiastically embrace the opportunity to tell all on a talk show, an additional 62% would be willing to do it. In order of descending frequency, the main reasons were "a good way to express my point of view," "a way to help other people," "a chance to be on TV," "for money," "a way to travel to a big city," "a chance to meet a celebrity host," and "a chance to see how TV shows are made." Almost a quarter of the respondents who would appear on the talk shows would do so as revenge against someone, and 6% would hope to be "discovered" by a producer. But, most interestingly, the survey revealed that a relatively small number (11%) of respondents who would agree to share their deepest secrets on a TV talk show would do so for the purpose of getting some help for themselves with their problems, even though respondents could check as many reasons as applied (Gaither & Keith-Spiegel, 1994).

So, what if you get an opportunity to appear on a talk show? We suggest that you ask the producers and yourself some hard questions before accepting an opportunity to be a TV talk show "expert."

1. What is the purpose of the show and how will the producer structure it?
2. Who are the guests that will be present?

3. What are the guests' circumstances?

4. What is expected of the guests?

5. Are the guests aware of the full purpose and scope of the show?

6. When will you be brought out?

7. How do the producers envision your role?

8. Will there be other experts? If so, who are they, and what are their credentials?

9. Will there be any guests under the age of 18? If so, what is their role?

10. Will the guests be inflicted with any potentially unwelcome surprises?

If the producers are vague or refuse to answer your questions, consider that a red flag on fire. Finally, become familiar with the program's typical format before you agree to appear. Some are routinely more exploitative than others.

Aside from the issue of the propriety of participation is the matter of what psychologists actually say and do once they get on camera, that is, the "ethics of the performance." Typically, the host asks them to make a quick, quasi diagnosis of the problem, get the guests to talk to (or yell at) each other for a couple of minutes, and then offer commentary as to what needs to be done now. The advice is often simplistic. The guests may be unable or unwilling to take it, and we will never know. However, although most guests may suffer no additional harm from the psychologists' brief contribution, and some guests or audience members may even pick up a useful idea or perspective, there have been unfortunate exceptions, as illustrated in the next cases.

Case 12-20: A mental health professional appearing on a national talk show offered a 10-item self-scoring test, which he called an "emotional thermometer," to viewers; it purportedly assessed their level of self-esteem and depression. Viewers were invited to get a pencil and paper. The 10 questions represented the downside of life almost everybody experiences from time to time, such as feeling sad, self-critical, worried, or unattractive. Response categories were 3 ("a lot"), 2 ("moderately"), 1 ("somewhat"), and 0 ("not at all"). The therapist then hawked his book—described as a "self-administered treatment program"—which promised to boost self-esteem in 10 days (Paramount Pictures, 1994).

It was the therapist's interpretation of scores of his quiz that were startling: He asserted that scores of 3 or 4 (of 30 possible) indicate that self-esteem needs a little boost, akin to "an engine that needs an oil change." This means that "somewhat" answers to as few as 3 of the 10 questions describing common, human conditions are cause for some concern. A score of 5 qualifies for "low self-esteem with probable depression." It is difficult to imagine that this "diagnosis" did not cause considerable concern among a large percentage of viewers.

Case 12-21: On a national television talk show, a father who repeatedly physically and sexually abused his wife and 12 children joined the family by satellite. The now-adult children aggressively confronted the father, and the host skillfully drew out harrowing details of their childhood experiences. A mental health professional was introduced for the purpose of "starting the healing process." She first attempted to sweetly cajole the father into opening up, but he was rightly suspicious of her motivations and clammed up. She then loudly referred to the man as "a monster" and added, "He has what seems to me to be, and I have not diagnosed him, but he seems to be what we call a borderline personality." She lambasted him later, calling him "toxic," and "a danger and a menace to society." Although the children were now grown and out of the house, she fiercely assailed the mother, an obviously distraught and limited woman, for not protecting her children: "Why did you stay with this man? Was he great in bed?" (Multimedia Entertainment, Inc., 1994).

The father was hardly a sympathetic character, and negative responses toward him were to be expected. However, the guest therapist was little more than the mob leader. It was an unfortunate loss because earlier the father had admitted to some of the accusations, and the family members and audience alike might have been enlightened by the outcome of a more professional approach to him. The public diagnosis was also inappropriate. And, although the mother's behavior represents a curious and destructive form of marital loyalty, it is common enough to have already generated considerable analysis in the scholarly literature. To attack the mother with a crude question was boorish and hardly reflective of what is expected of a mental health professional.

When Psychologists Have Considerable Control Over What Reaches the Public

Unless the psychologist owns the media company, complete control of public statements cannot be guaranteed. But, several formats do give psychologists considerable power to ensure that what they say and what reaches the public are the same.

Popular Works Written by Psychologists

Books and articles written for the trade or mass markets (as opposed to self-help books, considered separately) pose few ethical concerns when done conscientiously and objectively. (Ethical issues involving scholarly works, such as textbooks and articles contributed to periodicals intended for professional readership, are considered in chapter 17.)

Many of these are excellent contributions that reveal a talent for making complicated psychological concepts and research findings accessible, interesting, and intelligible to the public. Occasionally, charges of misrepresentation that caused embarrassment, usually from colleagues whose work was referenced or who were quoted, will come to an ethics committee.

Case 12-22: Dunn Damage, Ph.D., claimed that a magazine article written by Leonardo Barracuda, Ph.D., caused him considerable humiliation. While presenting Damage's theories on the antecedents of depression, Dr. Barracuda allegedly quoted Damage as saying, "All other theories are incorrect because they are untestable," when Damage claimed he said, "Many theories must be interpreted tentatively because they have not been subjected to careful verification."

Occasionally, more perplexing cases arise.

Case 12-23: Psychologist Gustav Slammen, Ph.D., wrote a popular article for a women's magazine on the psychological effects of being mugged and robbed in the streets. Based on his literature review and interviews with victims, he asserted that people who resisted their attackers had a better chance of foiling the robbery attempts, recovered more quickly from the emotional impact, and maintained more self-esteem compared to those who did not resist. He concluded by encouraging readers to resist assaults vigorously should they ever be placed in such an unfortunate situation. A research psychologist charged Dr. Slammen with irresponsible scholarship. The complainant did not dispute the facts as far as they went. She noted, however, that research also supports the fact that victims who resist run a much greater risk of being hurt or killed than do nonresisters, and that readers should have been made aware of this peril. The researcher claimed that Dr. Slammen was well aware of this fact because her work was lavishly cited in his article.

Barracuda was sloppy, and the effect was unfair to his colleague. Slammen should have informed readers of the risk factors accompanying his advice. Just because works are being written for a less sophisticated audience than our own colleagues does not mean that the rules of conscientious scholarship can be ignored.

What about the psychologist whose goal is to reach a certain audience, but the outlet that will accomplish that goal is highly questionable?

Case 12-24: Grass Roots, Psy.D., wrote an article on rape and published it in *Scumball Magazine*, considered by most to be hard-core pornography. A psychologist complained to an ethics committee that the profession was demeaned, and that the accompanying photographs simulating rape probably titillated more than they educated.

The quality of Dr. Roots' article was not an issue because it was extremely well written and accurate. Roots responded to an ethics committee inquiry that he chose this outlet because the readership would not be likely to get this important information from "more reputable sources." He explained that he contributed the article without pay as proof of his altruistic motivation. Furthermore, the addition of photos by the publishers was done without his knowledge or permission.

Roots was not sanctioned by the ethics committee because its members were impressed with his rationale and sincerity. But, the general issue remains a complicated one. Under some circumstances, the choice of topics, the mode of presentation, and the nature of the publication outlet might raise ethical concerns.

What about public lectures of a nonpsychological nature and other forms of published expression, such as letters to the editor? Psychologists, like all citizens, have a right to free speech, even if it is offensive or embarrassing. However, we believe that it is ethically inappropriate for a psychologist to saddle the entire profession or a professional organization with implied responsibility or condonement of messages that are clearly the personally held opinions of the content's creator. The next case is illustrative:

Case 12-25: Adolf Hitter, Ph.D., launched a vigorous and insolent attack against Jews in an "open letter" appearing in a nationally distributed newsletter. The letter was signed by the psychologist, followed by, "Diplomate in Clinical Psychology, American Board of Professional Psychology."

Several psychologists sent this article into the APA Ethics Committee; the committee agreed that, aside from the intolerant assault, the psychologist brought undeserved shame on his colleagues by using his affiliation in a way that might enhance his credibility and possibly suggest American Board of Professional Psychology (ABPP) sponsorship of the contents in his letter.

Case 12-26: Peppy Wonderbody, Ph.D., a postdoctoral psychology intern, appeared as the nude centerfold in a popular men's magazine as, she stated, "a form of self-expression."

Although professions tend to limit the scope of their ethical codes to professionally relevant activities, some conduct, although perfectly legal, causes us to wince. Public image is important to every psychologist, and such decisions on the part of only one of us may alter that image in unpreferred directions. One might also question Dr. Wonderbody's level of professional identity.

Advice to Individuals Offered in Writing

The nonpsychologist twins, Ann Landers and Abigail Van Buren, are not the first, but are the most famous, of the columnists offering advice to the troubled. Psychologists have also moved into this realm, writing such things as columns for high-circulation national magazines to local flyers containing advertisements and a few short, newsy articles.

A number of the same ethical issues found for call-in radio and live television appearances apply here, primarily those conflicts related to how competent such quick advice could possibly be. Some ethical dilemmas, however, are diminished by this format. The psychologist can take time to respond thoughtfully and to consult relevant literature or others with specialized expertise. The psychologist can focus on educating the readers. Confidentiality can more easily be guaranteed. Occasionally, however, ethics complaints have been leveled specifically at this format, as the next case illustrates.

Case 12-27: A psychologist complained that the advice column in a local paper by Tacky Gross, Ph.D., was used to entertain readers at the expense of troubled correspondents. For example, an elderly woman expressed how frustrating it was to have sexual desires but no sex partner. Dr. Gross suggested that she either hang around the Senior Citizen's Center after bingo, attend funerals whether she knew the dearly departed or not, or plant a cucumber patch.

An ethics committee responded poorly to Dr. Gross' brand of humor. He was reprimanded for demeaning both the correspondent and his profession.

Self-Administered Therapeutic Programs

Among the public's long-standing favorite forms of "mass psychology" are self-help books, audiotapes, and various paraphernalia and contraptions that purport to assist with emotional and physical healing or the enhancement of overall life quality. Starker's (1988b) interesting book,

Oracle at the Supermarket, traces the pervasive and powerful preoccupation with such products from the beginning of our nation's history.

Stressful living conditions, little spare time, tight budgets, concern about the future, attraction to the promise of quick and painless solutions, and the desire for self-reliance perpetuate the considerable success of the American self-help industry. Mahoney describes the allure of self-care products as "the near-universal search of Everyperson for simple, clear, and guaranteed solutions to the perennial problems and challenges of a life in process" (1988, p. 598). And, although the underlying motivations to create material for this huge consumer base are certainly varied, the promise of fame, fortune, and increased clientele are surely compelling motivations that lure some psychologists to participate.

Self-care materials range from diffuse "feel-good" themes to very specific advice regarding narrowly focused conditions. Three common categories of subjects are (1) how to improve (e.g., self-concept, self-confidence, social assertiveness, parenting skills, physical fitness, sexual functioning, memory, and life satisfaction); (2) how to control (e.g., smoking, weight, stress, phobias, anger); and, (3) how to cope (e.g., with depression, guilt, fears and phobias, shyness, insomnia, anxiety, problem children, loss of love, and divorce). In an analysis of promises to effect specific types of cures or improvements stated in 232 self-help paperbacks, Forest found the most frequent to be related to "fear and anxiety, self-awareness, successful life performance, happiness, and human potential" (1988, p. 599).

We restrict our discussion here to books and other media products, such as audiotapes, that are (1) created by legitimately trained psychologists, (2) proposed as an effective alternative to procedures directed by a therapist, (3) totally self-administered by the individual consumer, and (4) readily obtainable (e.g., sold in bookstores or by mail order) without the necessity for contact or consultation with a professional.

Many of these works, including some that have been extremely successful in the marketplace, are written by people with no discernible professional qualifications. Some of the most popular authors are assumed to be psychologists (even, we have observed, by other psychologists!) because of their seeming comfort with psychological terminology in concert with their "Ph.D. degrees," issued by diploma mills or correspondence schools. However, many legitimate psychologists, including some exceptionally prominent ones, have entered the do-it-yourself-therapy market (Rosen, 1987).

Psychologists as Creators of Self-Care Products

Although numerous ethical concerns surround the involvement of psychologists in the creation of self-care programs, the positive potential has also been described (e.g., Ellis, 1993; Rosen, 1993; Starker, 1988a, 1988b). Psychologists are capable of creating readily available self-administered programs that may prove beneficial for some purposes for a fraction of the cost of long-term, professional care. Experts in a given field can offer their knowledge and insights to those with no prospect for direct access to them. As much time and effort required can theoretically be spent creating products that ensure the highest possible quality.

Psychologists are also capable of properly evaluating and validating their programs. Rosen observes:

> By virtue of their training, [most psychologists] are in a unique position to evaluate the clinical efficacy of self-care methods, to assess people's ability to self-diagnose problems, to compare various instructional formats and identify those that are most effective, and to clarify when self-care efforts should be supplemented by therapist-assisted or therapist-directed programs. Psychologists can systematically investigate, clarify, and possibly answer all of these questions, thereby contributing to self-care. (1993, p. 340)

Thus, we will not argue that psychologists should refrain from interjecting higher quality material into an already established self-help market that is gorged with vacuous potboilers filled to the brim with psychobabble. To the extent that it is possible to offer the public sound, economical, effective programs that do not require extensive professional intervention, it would be socially irresponsible to unduly restrict or discourage psychologists from making such contributions.

Despite the positive potential associated with psychologist involvement in the vast self-care market, a number of ethical questions have been raised about what actually happens. Consumers are often given instructions on how to solve difficult problems or manage their lives, but no support system is available to sustain them through the procedure, to correct errors, to clarify misunderstood statements or directions, to caution against contraindications for particular consumers, or to alleviate any negative consequences that result from following (or failing to follow) the program.

These books are typically written and advertised in ways that are geared to sell. The result, from a scientific perspective, is often inappropriate flamboyance, superficiality, and conclusions not warranted by available evidence. Extravagant claims that may cause unrealistic expectations of favorable results are often promoted in the title, text, or the promotional materials supplied by the publishers or their agents. Rosen (1987) asserts, "At times, it appears that psychologists and their publishers are in a contest to create the most exaggerated and absurd claims," (p. 48) and cites an example of a single book that purports to help the reader relax, overcome fears and bad habits, enhance sexual and athletic abilities, make decisions, and cope with pain.

Sometimes, it is discovered that the psychologist was not directly involved in what appeared to be an ethical impropriety. However, psychologists are obligated to take active steps to correct misrepresentations of themselves by others (ES: 1.16b).

Case 12-28: Several psychologists complained that Lionel Banana, Ph.D., a respected expert in sexual dysfunction, had made absurd and outrageous claims of effectiveness on the cover of his book and in advertisements: "Your sex life will be totally fulfilled after reading this book," and "100% guaranteed to make you the lover of the year."

On questioning by an ethics committee, Dr. Banana expressed outrage over the way his book had been promoted. He contended that no such comments were found in the content of the book, and that these indiscretions had been perpetrated by the publisher without his permission or awareness. He supplied a letter he had sent to the publisher expressing his anger and disappointment.

This now-familiar clash between business promotion standards and ethical standards of the profession is one of the areas of particular concern to critics of self-help products. The situation becomes even further exacerbated when the text or promotional materials discourage obtaining live, professional services, suggesting that they are unnecessary or a waste of money. This tactic could preclude consumers for whom the product was not sufficiently beneficial from seeking more appropriate alternatives.

Case 12-29: The promotional advertisement and content of a do-it-yourself psychotherapy book promised to save the reader thousands of dollars because it would make it "unnecessary to consult paid advisors." The book promised "relief within two weeks from guilt, anxiety, and depression" and claims that anyone can follow the easy-to-understand program. No data are presented to support any of the benefits guaranteed to the readers.

Self-care products often profess that they are innovative and unique and promise the reader something brand new. Although claims of newness or uniqueness are tried-and-true marketing techniques, most books are variations on simple behavioral, relaxation, imagery, and self-suggestion principles that have been around for a very long time. Again, the primary ethical issue for psychologists is simple honesty. Psychologists should not label their work as a "breakthrough" when they know (or should know) better.

Observers of the self-help industry are concerned because the creators of these products leave diagnoses up to the consumers (Rosen, 1987, 1993). By purchasing self-care products, consumers have at least tentatively "diagnosed" themselves as needing particular kinds of assistance. Products typically either require a general self-diagnosis, such as "social inadequacy" or "dissatisfaction with life," or more specific self-diagnoses, such as phobia, depression, shyness, or sexual inadequacy. Few self-help products recognize or attempt to caution the consumer to avoid the dangers of misdiagnosis. People may be falsely convinced that they have a particular problem that requires treatment and may perpetuate inappropriate self-labels. Some might say, "Well, we diagnose ourselves all the time when we purchase over-the-counter medications." True, but these have been tested and approved by the Federal Drug Administration and carry a warning to consult a physician if symptoms persist.

Readers may misapply the program, label themselves as failures, and give up altogether. Because the book was written by an "expert," consumers may be more likely to fault themselves than the faulty product. Or, consumers may have a different problem for which a self-help program or any psychological approach is ineffective or even contraindicated (Barrera, Rosen, & Glasgow, 1981). Consider the next case:

Case 12-30: Wanda Weary was told by her best friend that a brief new book on psychic energy, written by a "real doctor," would help energize her. Weary, who had been feeling exceptionally sluggish for several weeks, was delighted to get it. She practiced the breathing and imaging techniques for several more weeks, but continued to feel drained. Weary finally consulted a physician, who quickly diagnosed hypothyroidism and prescribed appropriate hormone replacement.

Wanda Weary was very lucky. Other diseases or psychopathologies can cause more permanent damage if left to linger.

Before selling instructions to people about how to deal with general or specific life problems, a socially and ethically responsible psychologist should have gathered some form of evidence that his or her program or advice is, in fact, beneficial and effective. Recall our earlier statement that most psychologists have been trained in research methodology, at least to the point of understanding how an evaluation procedure could be accomplished. Unfortunately, most totally self-administered materials devised by psychologists have not been subjected to any systematic evaluation prior to being marketed (Rosen, 1993). This is rather like asking the public to take an untested drug and to stay away

from medical doctors. Because psychological self-care products are not regulated, actual harm would be difficult to prove, and First Amendment rights may pertain to the product itself. Nothing, then, stands in the way except the creator's professional and ethical standards.

Even self-care products that claim to be based on already-evaluated programs have often been inappropriately or incompletely evaluated. Others are based on extensive therapist-assisted evaluations (i.e., the clients used the program as it appears in the product, but were simultaneously supervised by a professional). In addition, some tested programs have not been proven effective, and techniques successfully applied by therapists are not necessarily self-administered successfully (Rosen, 1993). Failure of consumers to comply with program requirements, particularly if the time commitment is lengthy, is a common problem. Consumers acting in a totally self-administered context may be purchasing materials that will be ineffective or unlikely to be used at all (Rosen, 1976, 1981).

It *is* possible, prior to marketing to the public, to evaluate self-help products that offer a specific procedure. But, it takes time, considerable hard work, and an up-front expenditure of resources. An adequate evaluation requires the consideration of many variables, such as expectancy for improvement, format and program length, levels of task difficulty, involvement and role of significant others, reading level, long-term gains, and so on (Glasgow & Rosen, 1978, 1979). The feel-good self-care books would be difficult to evaluate for any long-term gains and should, therefore, never make any promises.

On occasion, programs have been evaluated after their publication and have been found to be useless or even to have produced additional negative consequences. In their evaluation of *Toilet Training in Less Than a Day* (Azrin & Foxx, 1974), Matson and Ollendick (1977) found that only one of the five mothers in the self-administration (book only) group successfully trained her child in the manner prescribed. In addition, those mothers who were unsuccessful reported an increase in behavior problems in their children and tension in the mother-child relationship.

In past years, Rosen has offered guidelines

for evaluating the quality of individual self-care products. He has proposed that several questions be addressed. These have been adopted by *Contemporary Psychology*, the journal of book reviews published by the APA. These include

1. Has the author attempted to convey accurate information regarding empirical support for the program?
2. Has the author determined if readers develop accurate expectations?
3. Does the book provide a basis for self-diagnosis?
4. Have the techniques presented in the book received empirical support?
5. Has the book itself been tested for its clinical efficacy? In light of the above, what is the accuracy of any claims made in the title or content of the book? (Rosen, 1981, p. 190)

Rosen declared, during a symposium presentation at the 1977 annual meeting of the APA, that self-help programs proven to be ineffective, harmful, or both after publication should be removed from the market. This extreme action can certainly be defended on ethical grounds. If psychologists learn that their programs do not work or have negative consequences in a large percentage of trials, then they must wrestle with the ethic that admonishes psychologists to accept responsibility for the consequences of their acts and to make every effort to ensure that their services are used appropriately.

Psychologists who may be more interested in serving their own needs, coupled with a public that is apparently not aware of or concerned about thorough evaluations, are unlikely to carry out the demanding task of even attempting to assess the value of their products. It is probably equally overly optimistic to expect that the publishers and promoters of self-care products will seek to improve the quality of what they sell and, instead, will select only those meeting some minimal standard. However, we recommend that, at the very least, psychologists who create untested self-care products add a disclaimer in a place that readers cannot help but notice. It might go something like this:

Fighting the Naysayer's Noise Inside Your Head is based on the author's ideas and experiences with

some of her clients over the past 13 years. She has not conducted research to evaluate whether her advice could be helpful to people reading on their own.

We have seen a few books that outline steps readers might consider if the advice is not helpful or if they have more severe symptoms than those the advice is intended to alleviate. Such disclaimers certainly earn kudos compared to their promise-blaring companions on the bookstore shelf. Honesty, however, could hurt sales (Holtje, 1988). Mahoney believes that his book sold poorly compared to its competitors because he honestly stated that "significant, long-term weight control is a difficult and time-consuming endeavor with no guarantees of success" (1988, p. 598). Ellis adds: "The great majority of [publishers] are much more interested in turning out a shoddy product that sells well than in producing a fine product that sells poorly. Quantity, not quality, is their main goal, and there is at present little chance that they will change this goal in order to pretest and potentially validate self-help materials" (1993, p. 337).

Psychologists as Prescribers of Self-Care Products

Not every consumer who reads a self-help book found it while browsing in bookstores or by talking to friends. According to Starker's (1988a) survey, the majority of his psychologist-respondents "prescribed" self-help books as supplementary treatments for their clients. Of these, almost a quarter did so "often," and almost another quarter did so "regularly." Virtually all of his sample believed that the books were at least somewhat helpful, and reports of harmfulness were virtually nonexistent. Starker concluded that the prescription of self-help books is common, that the mood is optimistic about their efficacy, and that little concern exists regarding their potential for harm (Starker, 1988c).

Starker (1988c) suggests that psychologists need to approach the public's infatuation with self-help books with greater professional objectivity, and that they should read the books, using Rosen's (1981) criteria to evaluate their usefulness (see Rosen's list, above). We believe that books or tapes, while entertaining, may fall short of being useful to a particular client. Works that are clearly gimmicky (e.g., that suggest men and women originated on different planets, coupled with unsubstantiated generalizations about sex differences) may not be helpful in the long run. Even for more substantial self-help books, psychologists should inform their clients about possible shortcomings and encourage them to discuss anything that is troubling or difficult to understand. Psychologists can also issue cautions, even if the authors do not, about how the books came to be. They might tell a client, "This book is not created from a research base or has not been tested for its effectiveness, but I think the author has some good ideas that might be helpful for you to consider." Or, "This book is not a tested therapeutic tool, but the prose is inspirational, and it may make you feel better as you cope with your loss."

Finally, we add a word about prescribing film as a therapeutic adjunct. Some motion pictures can probably motivate people to find new ways of looking at their circumstance. And, even though films are rarely intended to reflect the absolute, research-based truth, viewers already know that. The compliance problem is largely absent because most people are willing to go see a recommended movie. Films that might be enlightening or supportive for clients abound. Hill's (1993) list includes, as examples, *Tucker* and *Dead Poet's Society*, for those struggling to act independently of their surroundings, and *One Flew Over the Cuckoo's Nest* and *The Fisher King* to better understand oppression and our personal complicity in it. Psychologists should understand, however, that when they prescribe a movie, the client will probably take the experience very seriously. Therefore, psychologists should not assign movies that they have not actually seen and are not prepared to follow up with discussion.

Case 12-31: Peter Prudish complained that Bea Greendoor, Ph.D., insisted that he view a movie that he found extremely disturbing. He abruptly terminated therapy and called Dr. Greendoor "a panderer in filthy smut."

Dr. Greendoor was stunned by her client's strong response. She insisted that she meant no harm and had suggested only that the film might be an enjoyable and a safe way to desensitize Prudish's sexual fears. She had not seen it, but a friend told her that it was a "delightful romp."

Use of the Internet

Electronic communication via the internet is, at once, a window to the world from one's home or office, a pathway to communicate with one or thousands of others simultaneously by a "send" command, and a potential trapdoor to serious trouble.

Case 12-32: Web Strew, Ph.D., figured that he could tell the world about his consulting business at no cost. He typed out a lengthy and glowing advertisement and sent it to every unmoderated newsgroup he could locate.

Dr. Strew is "spamming," an increasingly upsetting practice. It has even bred a group of vigilantes, computer users who have figured out how to create cancel messages. There are worries that spammers will increasingly clog the system with unwanted and junky material, and the vigilantes may not always know the difference between dumping electronic litter and censorship (Wilson, 1995).

Dr. Strew is more irritating than dangerous. Other on-line errors are more likely to cause harm. A problem with the capacity to disseminate information from one's office desk to hundreds of people with the use of a few keystrokes is that there is little time for thoughtful reflection. Once the information is sent, it can travel indefinitely as others pass it along. Any psychologist who "surfs the net" on a regular basis cannot help but notice the mean-spirited insults ("flaming") that attend electronic discussions on any controversial topic, such as debates about the existence of repressed memories, psychologists' role in the courts, or professional politics.

Case 12-33: When Bulah Blowout, Ph.D., read a message on a discussion group that was mildly critical of the academic program from which she received her degree, she ripped off a response that raked the critic's graduate department: "It is a 10th-rate program in a pretty building populated with old, White guys and their white rats." Over 700 people read her impulsive and ill-conceived message, and the response was not positive.

Perhaps little harm was done, except to Dr. Blowout's image. But it would not take too much more to approach liability.

Case 12-34: In response to a posted message in a forensic psychology discussion group, a psychologist referred to a female colleague, who had agreed to testify in a high-profile murder case, as "a whore." That message, and numerous others reflecting both support and outrage, spread rapidly. Psychologists who were active frequenters of the Internet reported receiving the same message many times from different sources, which indicated that this particular exchange was widely disseminated. One psychologist wanted to press ethics charges against the name-caller. Another intended to press charges against the person defending the maligned psychologist for defaming the name-caller.

One cannot help but wonder if the originator might have expressed himself a little differently were he to have known how his message was to be received. As O'Neil states, "Electronic communication does seem to inspire excess, hyperbole, and incivility among users to a degree seldom found in print" (1995, p. A68). Although we know of no extremely serious impropriety involving a psychologist, a university student has been arrested by the FBI for posting his sex-torture fiction, which used the real name of a student he knew as the victim (Elmer-Dewitt, 1995).

Other problems arise and come back to haunt the Internet users who are sloppy or not yet very good at negotiating cyberspace (these people are known as "newbies").

Case 12-35: Hana Hurried, Ed.D., wanted a quick consultation about a suicidal client from a colleague who also belonged to the same moderated Internet discussion group. She included iden-

tifying information and a detailed account of the client's personal circumstances. However, she accidentally sent the message to the list server rather than to the colleague's private account.

This mistake is one of many that are easy to make courtesy of the convenient "reply" function. To be on the safe side, we highly recommend that all identifying information be removed when sending confidential material, even when one feels assured that the message will be received by only the recipient. At this point in time, even when communicating with a specific individual on the Internet, privacy is not guaranteed. Clever intruders can gain access to host computers through a technique known as "spoofing" and then access connections from any user on the system. Information can also be retrieved, even after messages on one's account have been deleted, by the owner of the Internet system.

Psychologists and what they have to say are of interest to the public. With more and more public citizens surfing the net, it is important to recognize that every time we contribute our thoughts and identify our profession on line, we may be making a statement to a large public audience even though we are completely alone in our office or a room at home. (For more about on-line ethics, see chapter 13.)

Lax Facsimile Practices

Another form of a nonvigilant stance around more recent technological innovations involves improper or lax use of facsimile (fax) machines.

Case 12-36: Edgar Fudd, Ph.D., decided to send the third billing notice to a slow-to-pay client at her fax number. The client was not in the office that day, and the bill for "psychological services rendered" with "Third Notice—OVERDUE!!" handwritten with a wide marker sat in the office's open-access mail pickup tray all day.

Fudd's behavior was obviously improper, and he should have known better. Even if he was angry at the client for ignoring his bill, he should have figured out that others in a place of business likely have access to the fax machine. Obviously, no private or sensitive material should be sent by fax unless it is known for sure that the recipient is the only one with access to it or a telephone call verifies that the intended party is standing by the machine, ready to retrieve it.

Another danger is the possibility of transmitting confidential information in error. Scores of detailed, confidential medical records are reported to have been faxed to an accountant's office, which had a telephone number very similar to that of the intended recipient. Despite the accountant's numerous attempts to inform the sender so that the situation could be remedied, confidential records continued to arrive at her office (Stanley & Palosky, 1997).

SOCIALLY RESPONSIBLE (AND IRRESPONSIBLE) PUBLIC ACTS

Public Disclosure at a Risk to Oneself

"Going public" for reasons involving the highest sense of integrity can be risky for psychologists. We refer, of course, to "whistle-blowing" (or "ethical resisters," as some prefer), and present a discussion here because the act often involves informing the public, as well as gaining the attention of (or seeking support from) the media.

In its typical and better known form, whistle-blowing is found among those who hold an "insider" position (often of some authority) as a government, agency, business, or institutional employee. Unethical, illegal, or socially deleterious practices within the work setting became cause for concern because of the whistle-blower's conviction that harm has been or will be caused to others or to the environment. Typically, the whistle-blower has unsuccessfully attempted to remediate the situation through established channels within the organization. The employer's stonewalling, delays, excuses, or unresponsiveness eventually lead to sharing information with an outside source in the hope that the practice will be eliminated by external pressure (Nader, Petkas, & Blackwell, 1972).

Incidents of whistle-blowing rarely come to the attention of the public unless the stakes are high. Two recent cases involving psychologists have "made the papers." Both involved the unmasking of funded research fraud. Dr. Robert L. Sprague, a colleague of psychologist Stephen Breuning who conducted research on drug treatment of retarded children and adults, became suspicious when Breuning was producing more uniform data than seemed probable. Sprague investigated on his own until he was convinced that the research contained serious flaws suggestive of fraud. He contacted his program officer at the National Institute of Mental Health (NIMH). Breuning eventually admitted wrongdoing, but what Sprague thought would just amount to making the painful decision to turn in his colleague became a 3-year ordeal. Sprague himself was called into question; he endured threats by an official of Breuning's university; and, although cause and effect have never been proven, he had his long-standing NIMH funding cut by 75% (Committee on Government Operations, 1990; Sprague, 1993).

Psychologist Sandra Scarr and others brought concerns about the methodology utilized by Herbert Needleman (Ernhart, Scarr, & Geneson, 1993; Scarr & Ernhart, 1993). Needleman's research on the effects of lead exposure on children is so widely cited that policy has been created from it. A report was ultimately sent by Scarr and others to the National Institutes of Health (NIH) for investigation because they believed that they had "an affirmative obligation as scientists and as members of the academic community to speak out against improper and deliberately misleading practices in the conduct and reporting of research" (Ernhart et al., 1993, p. 89). Needleman (1993) responded, defending the quality of his data and questioning the motives of critics paid by those who would benefit by having his work discredited.

In an analysis of 10 cases of whistle-blowing in higher education, most whistle-blowers were retaliated against by their universities (Weiss, 1991). Those who were untenured or were being paid by "soft" grant funds usually lost their jobs. Yet, even tenured full professors have suffered indignities, which ranged from slurs directed at them through their children to being moved to an isolated academic office over a grocery store (Ernhart et al., 1993; Sprague, 1993). Many have had to obtain their own legal counsel, sometimes because their behavior was called into question despite no evidence of impropriety. The time spent and anxiety endured can be extensive. Most disconcerting is the possibility that the action itself may ultimately amount to an exercise in futility if the information shared is ignored by the outside contact or suspended indefinitely in bureaucratic red tape. Even in cases in which the accused has been found guilty, the penalties can be paltry. The highly publicized case of Karen Silkwood (Rashke, 1981) suggests that some whistle-blowers may even risk being killed.

Most incidents coming to our attention about psychologists do not involve matters of national or scientific significance, which typify the better known cases involving major corporations, prestigious universities, and high government offices. In the usual case involving psychologists, the rights or welfare of some people were believed to be jeopardized, and the psychologists requested guidance as to how to expose the dubious practices. One psychologist complained that he was instructed to use assessment techniques he considered extremely inappropriate for the purpose at hand that resulted in the misclassification of hundreds of job applicants. Another reported that a death of a mental hospital patient went unreported, and that the deceased was instead listed as "AWOL." Another opposed the hiring practices at his university, which he claimed were blatantly sexist and racist as evidenced by remarks made during closed recruitment meetings. After he complained, a colleague told him to keep quiet or he would end up as "roadkill on the tenure track." Another protested that confidential client records were available for viewing by anyone, including other clients, because they were stored openly on shelves in the busy reception area of a mental health clinic. When he objected to his supervisor, he was told that there was no other space available, and that he would be better off spending his time paying attention to what he was being paid to do.

The inherent risks in even the less publicized forms of whistle-blowing are numerous and include loss of employment or, failing that, demotion or transfer to some undesirable location or position. If the individual remains within the organization, he or she may be "frozen out," even by those thought to be friends. Those known to be potential informants may have difficulty finding other employment, or they may be accused of acting out of vindictiveness or revenge.

A published portrait of a psychologist whistle-blower is presented by Simon (1978). The real names appear in the actual article, but we use contrived names here.

Case 12-37: Jack Provet, Ph.D., was promoted to chief of the Restoration Program, a position usually held by an M.D., at a large Veterans Administration (VA) psychiatric facility in Brentwood, California. The building that housed Dr. Provet's 200 patients was condemned because of structural deficiencies judged to be uncorrectable. Instead of taking some time to relocate the patients, the medical chief of staff ordered Provet to abruptly discharge them to the streets and to advise them to seek relief from welfare agencies. Provet refused the order on the grounds that many patients were not prepared for community living, and, for the others, additional time was necessary to make adequate plans to facilitate their chances for a successful transition. Provet was relieved of his position on the spot, was assigned to low-status duty in a Quonset hut on the periphery of the grounds, and was supervised by a social worker. The patients called the media and staged a protest in support of Dr. Provet. Reporters were also present to witness Provet clearing out his desk. Provet shortly received transfer orders to a small, rural VA facility in Texas, which he refused on grounds that seniority policy had been violated. Provet refused a second transfer order on the same grounds and was fired for refusing it.

Provet fought back in federal court and, 3 years after being separated from service, won reinstatement with full back pay. But, the victory was a painful lesson in loyalties (or lack thereof) that Provet would wish on no one.

So, why do people put themselves at such risk? The main reasons are a strong belief in individual responsibility and a feeling of obligation to the community (Glazer & Glazer, 1986). Unfortunately, there is no surefire source of support for those who upset a powerful organization in the course of upholding professional standards, although whistle-blower protection statutes are emerging at the state and national levels. The APA ethics code may faintly approve of "ethical resistance" in its aspirational (nonenforceable) standards by stating, "Psychologists respect and protect human and civil rights, and do not knowingly participate in or condone unfair discriminatory practices" (EP: Preamble). Yet, one must still expect the worst. Even though federal rules forbid universities from punishing whistle-blowers, witnesses have testified that these rules have been ignored (Burd, 1994).

Nader, Petkas, and Blackwell provide a list of questions to assist a would-be whistle-blower with decision making and strategy:

1. Is my knowledge of the matter complete and accurate?
2. What are the objectionable practices, and what public interest do they harm?
3. How far should and can I go inside the organization with my concern or objection?
4. Will I be violating any rules by contacting outside parties, and, if so, is whistle-blowing nevertheless justified?
5. Will I be violating any laws or ethical duties by not contacting external parties?
6. Once I have decided to act, what is the best way to blow the whistle: anonymously, overtly, by resignation prior to speaking out, or in some other way?
7. What will be the likely responses from various sources, inside and outside the organization, to the whistle-blowing action?
8. What is expected to be achieved by whistle-blowing in this particular situation? (1972, p. 6)

We would add two more:

9. Document your case carefully.
10. Seek out others, if appropriate, who may help plan the action and provide social support.

As long as whistle-blowers remain the heroes that nobody wants to know, our society may remain in harm's way. Whistle-blowing requires a constitution and a sense of ethics that are backed by considerable courage few are likely to possess. For more about whistle-blowing, see Glazer and Glazer (1989), Miceli and Near (1992), and Volume 3 of *Ethics and Behavior* (1993).

Advocating for Consumers in a Public Forum

Possessing information, accidently or through a process of deliberate discovery, that forces us to confront our moral courage and blow the whistle is not an everyday occurrence. However, another opportunity to "correct the record" occurs regularly and, happily, is far less taxing than whistle-blowing: advocating for consumers in a public forum. Unfortunately, psychologists are not known for doing much of it.

Incorrect stereotypes about the subject matters in psychologists' realm of expertise proliferate. One cannot go very far into a week without hearing someone say something about human behavior or capabilities that is not only outlandish, but is likely to degrade or stigmatize some groups of people in the process. As part of the general ethic to promote human welfare, we believe that taking opportunities to educate—both informally and formally—about the current status of psychological knowledge is a primary social responsibility. The mentally disabled remain especially stigmatized. The gains made by other reference groups are immense in comparison. Discriminatory laws reinforce the public's irrational fears (Melton & Garrison, 1987). People with any psychiatric history, particularly if they were ever hospitalized, are met with fear and mistrust (Mayer & Barry, 1992).

Public education requires more than one-shot corrections. A simple "disclaimer" (i.e., "Violence is not characteristic of mentally ill people") at the end of a film portraying a mentally ill serial killer does not measurably alter the impact of the film on viewers' attitudes (Wahl & Lefkowits, 1989). Psychologists should be very concerned about this situation. We are in a legitimate position to replace misinformation with useful, solid data. We can increase collaboration with patient advocacy groups and help monitor negative portrayals of the mentally disabled (Hyler, Gabbard, & Schneider, 1991). It takes a little courage to speak up as slurs occur, but it is our collective responsibility to do so.

SUMMARY GUIDELINES

1. While committing themselves to assisting the public to understand psychological knowledge, psychologists make every attempt to ensure accuracy, maintain due caution and modesty, avoid collusion or the exploitation of others, and exhibit the highest level of professional responsibility. This may mean that invitations to participate in media activities or other public forums might sometimes might better be refused.

2. Exaggeration, superficiality, and sensationalism should be avoided to the greatest extent possible. When signing contracts for commercial books or other products, it is wise to ask to be consulted on all advertising copy.

3. Psychologists must acknowledge and accept their responsibilities to a public that may be accepting of their statements by virtue of the psychologists' presumed expertise.

4. Recognizing the limits of one's knowledge and experience is especially critical in media activities because large numbers of people can be misled or misinformed by incorrect or incomplete public statements.

5. When offering public statements intended to ameliorate particular problems, considerable caution must be exercised. Such advice should, ideally, have a scientifically based foundation. In any event, commentary should not be presented as factual unless a reasonable database exists. Opinions or personal experiences should be clearly identified as such.

6. Psychologists should avoid public statements that purport to speak for the entire profession.

7. It is important to keep in mind that media goals and purposes are likely to be quite different from those of individual psychologists. Such an awareness may help to detect instances for which caution is in order.

8. Public statements by psychologists should never be made for entertainment or self-gratification purposes at the expense of others or the profession.

9. Psychologists should never publicly comment on the "psychological status" of others they do not know.

10. In emerging technological applications, such as E-mail and electronic bulletin boards, psychologists must attempt to forecast which ethical dilemmas could arise. "Snail mail" (the postal service) or the telephone may still be more appropriate forms for transferring information in many circumstances.

11. Psychologists should take opportunities to correct the public statements of others that depict the mentally disabled and other groups in unfair, stereotyped ways.

References

American Psychological Association. (1992). Ethical principles of psychologists and code of conduct. *American Psychologist, 47,* 1597–1611.

American Psychological Association, Public Affairs Office. (n.d.). *Media training for psychologists: A comprehensive guide for interview preparation.* Washington, DC: Author.

Azrin, N. H., & Foxx, R. M. (1974). *Toilet training in less than a day.* New York: Simon & Schuster.

Barrera, M., Rosen, G. M., & Glasgow, R. E. (1981). "Rights," risks and responsibilities in the use of self help psychotherapy. In G. T. Hannah, W. P. Christian, & H. B. Clark (Eds.), *Preservation of client rights* (pp. 204–220). New York: McMillan Free Press.

Bevan, W. (1991). Contemporary psychology: A tour inside the onion. *American Psychologist, 46,* 475–483.

Boneau, C. A. (1992). Observations on psychology's past and future. *American Psychologist, 47,* 1586–1596.

Burd, T. (1994, December 14). Federal panel weighs a whistle blower's bill of rights. *The Chronicle of Higher Education,* A30.

Cardinal, D. (1994, October 12). Researchers and the press: A cautionary tale. *The Chronicle of Higher Education,* B3.

Committee on Government Operations. (1990, September 10). *Are scientific misconduct and conflict of interest hazardous to our health?* Washington, DC: U.S. Government Printing Office.

Dunwoody, S. (1980). The science writing innerclub: A communication link between science and the lay public. *Science, Technology and Human Values, 5,* 14–22.

Ellis, A. (1993). The advantages and disadvantages of self-help therapy materials. *Professional Psychology: Research and Practice, 24,* 335–339.

Elmer-Dewitt, P. (1995, February 20). Snuff porn on the net. *Time,* 69.

Ernhart, C. B., Scarr, S., & Geneson, D. F. (1993). On being a whistleblower: The Needleman case. *Ethics and Behavior, 3,* 73–93.

Forest, J. J. (1988). Self-help books. *American Psychologist, 43,* 599.

Fox, J. A., & Levin, J. (1993). *How to work with the media.* Newbury Park, CA: Sage.

Gaither, M., & Keith-Spiegel, P. (1994). [Would you be a guest on a TV talk show?] Unpublished data. Ball State University.

Gibson, E. J. (1994). Has psychology a future? *Psychological Science, 5,* 69–76.

Glasgow, R. E., & Rosen, G. M. (1978). Behavioral bibliotherapy: A review of self-help behavior therapy manuals. *Psychological Bulletin, 85,* 1–23.

Glasgow, R. E., & Rosen, G. M. (1979). Self help behavior therapy manuals: Recent developments and clinical usage. *Clinical Behavior Therapy Review, 1,* 1–20.

Glazer, M. P., & Glazer, P. M. (1986, August). Whistleblowing. *Psychology Today,* 37–39, 42–43.

Glazer, M. P., & Glazer, P. M. (1989). *The whistleblowers.* New York: Basic Books.

Good, P., Simon, G. C., & Coursey, R. D. (1981). Public interest activities of APA members. *American Psychologist, 36,* 963–971.

Hill, G. (1993, March–April). Movies as therapy. *The California Therapist,* 51.

Holtje, H. F. (1988). Comment on Rosen. *American Psychologist, 43,* 600.

Howell, W. C. (1994). Giving psychology away successfully. *Psychological Science Agenda (APA), 3,* 6.

Hundley, W. (1995, January 1). Talk show alumni share experiences. Cox News Service.

Hyler, S. E., Gabbard, G. O., & Schneider, I. (1991). Homicidal maniacs and narcissistic parasites: Stigmatization of mentally ill persons in the movies. *Hospital and Community Psychiatry, 42,* 1044–1148.

Jacobs, M. K., & Goodman, G. (1989). Psychology and self-help groups: Predictions on a partnership. *American Psychologist, 44,* 536–545.

Kaplan, J. (1995, April 1). Are talk shows out of control? *TV Guide,* 10–15.

Koch, S. (1993). "Psychology" or "psychological studies." *American Psychologist, 48,* 902–904.

Levy, D. A. (1989). Social support and the media: Analysis of responses by radio psychology talk shows. *Professional Psychology: Research and Practice, 20,* 73–78.

Mahoney, M. J. (1988). Beyond self-help polemics. *American Psychologist, 43,* 598–599.

Matson, J. L., & Ollendick, T. H. (1977). Issues in toilet training normal children. *Behavior Therapy, 8,* 549–553.

Mayer, A., & Barry, D. D. (1992). Working with the media to destigmatize mental illness. *Hospital and Community Psychiatry, 43,* 77–78.

McCall, R. B. (1988). Science and the press: Like oil and water? *American Psychologist, 43,* 87–94.

McGrath, E. (1995). Are we trading our souls for a sound bite? *APA Monitor, 24,* 5.

Melton, G. B., & Garrison, E. G. (1987). Fear, prejudice, and neglect: Discrimination against mentally disabled persons. *American Psychologist, 42,* 1007–1026.

Miceli, M. P., & Near, J. P. (1992). *Blowing the whistle.* New York: Lexington.

Miller, G. A. (1969). Psychology as a means of promoting human welfare. *American Psychologist, 24,* 1063–1075.

Multimedia Entertainment, Inc. (1994, May 2). *Sally.*

Murstein, B. L., & Fontaine, P. A. (1993). The public's knowledge about psychologists and other mental health professionals. *American Psychologist, 48,* 839–845.

Nader, R., Petkas, P., & Blackwell, K. (Eds.). (1972). *Whistle blowing.* New York: Bantam, 1972.

Needleman, H. L. (1993). "On being a whistleblower: The Needleman case": Reply to Ernhart, Scarr, and Geneson. *Ethics and Behavior, 3,* 95–101.

O'Neil, R. M. (1995, November 3). Free speech on the electronic frontier. *Chronicle of Higher Education*, A68.

Pallak, M. S., & Kilburg, R. R. (1986). Psychology, public affairs, and public policy: A strategy and review. *American Psychologist*, 9, 933–940.

Paramount Pictures. (1994, August 26). *The Maury Povich Show*. Livingston, NJ: Burrelle's Information Services.

Peyser, M. (1995, March 20). Making a killing on talk TV. *Newsweek*, 30.

Rashke, R. (1981). *The killing of Karen Silkwood*. New York: Houghton Mifflin.

Raviv, A., Yunovitz, R., & Raviv, A. (1989). Radio psychology and psychotherapy: Comparison of client attitudes and expectations. *Professional Psychology: Research and Practice*, 20, 67–72.

Rosen, G. M. (1976). The development and use of nonprescription behavior therapies. *American Psychologist*, 31, 139–141.

Rosen, G. M. (1981). Guidelines for the review of do-it-yourself treatment books. *Contemporary Psychology*, 26, 189–191.

Rosen, G. M. (1987). Self-help treatment books and the commercialization of psychotherapy. *American Psychologist*, 42, 46–51.

Rosen, G. M. (1993). Self-help or hype? Comments on psychology's failure to advance self-care. *Professional Psychology: Research and Practice*, 24, 340–345.

Scarr, S., & Ernhart, C. B. (1993). Of whistleblowers, investigators, and judges. *Ethics and Behavior*, 3, 199–206.

Schneider, I. (1987). The theory and practice of movie psychiatry. *American Journal of Psychiatry*, 144, 996–1002.

Signorielli, N. (1989). The stigma of mental illness on television. *Journal of Broadcasting and Electronic Media*, 33, 325–331.

Simon, G. C. (1978). The psychologist as whistle blower: A case study. *Professional Psychology: Research, Theory and Practice*, 9, 322–340.

Sprague, R. L. (1993). Whistleblowing: A very unpleasant avocation. *Ethics and Behavior*, 3, 103–133.

Stanley, D., & Palosky, C. S. (1997, February 28). Fax drops records in her lap. *Tampa Tribune*, p. B1.

Starker, S. (1988a). Do-it-yourself therapy: The prescription of self-help books by psychologists, *Psychotherapy*, 25, 142–146.

Starker, S. (1988b). *Oracle at the supermarket*. New Brunswick, NJ: Transaction.

Starker, S. (1988c). Self-help treatment books: The rest of the story. *American Psychologist*, 43, 599–600.

Wahl, O. F., & Lefkowits, J. Y. (1989). Impact of a television film on attitudes towards mental illness. *American Journal of Community Psychology*, 17, 521–528.

Webb, A. R. (1989). What's in a question? Three methods for investigating psychology's public image? *Professional Psychology: Research, Theory and Practice*, 20, 301–304.

Weiss, T. (1991, June 26). Too many scientists who "blow the whistle" end up losing their jobs and careers. *The Chronicle of Higher Education*, A36.

Will, G. F. (1982, July 19). *Newsweek*, p. 76.

Wilson, D. L. (1995, January 13). Vigilantes gain quiet approval on networks. *The Chronicle of Higher Education*, A 17–19.

Wollersheim, D. M., & Walsh, J. A. (1993). Clinical psychologists: Professionals without a role. *Professional Psychology: Research and Practice*, 24, 171–175.

Wood, W., Jones, M., & Benjamin, L. T. Jr. (1986). Surveying psychology's public image. *American Psychologist*, 41, 947–953.

Zoglin, R. (1995, January 30). Talking trash. *Time*, 76–78.

13

Relationships with Colleagues, Supervisees, and Employees

"In quarrelling, the truth is almost always lost."

Publilius Syrus

Do psychologists have a special understanding of the complexities of human relationships that enables them to get along better with others? From our vantage point, any benefit that psychologists might muster in some situations can disintegrate in others. Psychologists are people first, some functioning under great stress or inappropriately focused on their own needs. A few have firmly established personal styles that make the work environment unpleasant for those around them.

A substantial percentage of ethics complaints against psychologists comes from their own colleagues, students, or employees. This is not particularly surprising since these are the very people most likely to be aware of ethical standards and, along with psychotherapy clients, to observe psychologists' behavior directly. The truly intriguing feature of such complaints, however, is the intensity—and, occasionally, bitter vindictiveness—with which they are sometimes pursued. In rare instances, the conflict has turned physically violent. The focus of this chapter is

on the dynamics and breakdowns in interprofessional relationships among colleagues, as well as the ethical conduct expected of psychologists with respect to their interactions with supervisees and employees. (More detailed discussions of relationships with students are presented in chapters 8 and 16.)

PEER AND INTERPROFESSIONAL RELATIONSHIPS

A psychologist's relationships with colleagues ideally should be characterized by a climate of cooperation and mutual respect. The ethics code of the American Psychological Association (APA) encourages cooperation with other professionals and consultation with colleagues in regard to the welfare of the clients (ES: 1.20).

The best interests of psychologists and psychology, however, are not necessarily congruent with those of related professions, such as psychiatry or social work. The recognition of valid competencies and consumer interests should prevail in interprofessional relationships, but this does not always happen. Despite a common focus on human behavior and emotional problems, interprofessional relations sometimes manifest themselves as political, economic, and territoriality disputes.

Case 13-1: Horace Pill, Ph.D., is a nationally recognized authority on psychopharmacology. When he began advocating laws that authorize prescription privileges for psychologists, he became the object of blistering attacks by psychiatrists. Editorials that criticized him in pejorative terms appeared in the *National Psychiatric News*, and officers of the Amalgamated Psychiatric Society wrote angry letters about Dr. Pill to his employer. Pill was invited to deliver a lecture at Urban Medical School. During the course of the talk, Pill made critical comments about the Amalgamated Psychiatric Society. Many psychologists in the interdisciplinary audience were distressed by the remarks, believing that they complicated relationships with their psychiatrist colleagues at the medical school.

Within the profession, the goals and views of some psychologists can clash with those of other psychologists. Deeply held differences in theoretical, practical, and methodological approaches abound. Such disputes can create conditions that sometimes erupt beyond the bounds of stimulating debate, as we see throughout this chapter.

We are not proposing that professional disagreements must always be handled with the etiquette expected of guests at a tea party. Whenever psychologists sincerely believe that they or others are being harmed by their colleagues—ideally, after seeking consultation to confirm that perception—it could be inappropriate to muster feelings of respect. But, in virtually every circumstance, maintaining a professional demeanor is likely to create the best climate for amelioration. (See chapter 1 for recommended techniques for confronting an unethical colleague.)

It happens often enough that two once-reasonable people sink into an extended cycle, and the abuse hurled by one elevates the mistreatment perpetrated by the other.

Case 13-2: Drs. Rosemary Spat and Dameon Tiff cannot stand each other. No one at the clinic can recall when it all started. Both Spat and Tiff have created a litany of ethics complaints against the other that ranges from misappropriation of a single postage stamp to mistreating clients. Each routinely stalks and spies on the other. Their offices have been moved to opposite ends of the hallway. The head of the agency has even had to impose a "gag order" for the one not presenting during the group case management discussion.

Everyone working in the agency, including the unaware clients, is disadvantaged by this unfit dynamic duo. There is no excuse for such unprofessional behavior, yet such entrenched, angry relationships are more common than they should be. If the warring parties cannot reach a level of professional maturity, they should at least keep their feud out of the work setting.

This is not to say that colleagues are never free to criticize or disagree with each other, even in a public forum. The next case illustrates how a conflict can be handled in a professional and ethical manner.

Case 13-3: Clarence Farrow, a young attorney, contacts Jack Forensic, Ph.D., for some advice in regard to another psychologist. The psychologist in question, Marvin Turkey, Ph.D., was appearing as an expert witness against one of Farrow's clients and made some statements under oath that Farrow had reason to question. Dr. Forensic researched Dr. Turkey's credentials, using a professional directory, and learned that they did not appear to include the sort of experiences usually associated with the type of expertise claimed. He suggested some questions Farrow could ask Turkey to establish or challenge his credibility. Forensic also provided Farrow with some publications tended to refute the claims asserted by Turkey in his testimony. Dr. Turkey later telephoned Dr. Forensic and angrily claimed that Farrow had embarrassed him in public by using the information Forensic had supplied.

Dr. Forensic owed no specific duty to Dr. Turkey. It seems that Forensic was asked for consultative advice by a third party, Attorney Farrow, and provided him with factual material (e.g., articles and information readily available from professional directories). If the material supplied to Farrow was used to embarrass Dr. Turkey, this was likely justified. That is, if Turkey were competent as claimed, he should not have been upset about answering direct questions about his credentials or about responding to questions raised in the published scientific literature. These are standard procedures used to establish the qualifications of "expert" witnesses. If Forensic offered gossip or a biased presentation of facts, there would be an ethical problem; however, he owed no duty of protection to Turkey.

Cooperation

Psychologists are usually very busy people who cannot be expected to drop everything and attend to a colleague's immediate need. Often, the correct response can be a simple, prompt response that indicates when or if the request can be filled. Timeliness can become an ethical issue, however, when a colleague or professional-in-training is completely ignored for an extended period of time. Sometimes, passive-aggressive behavior can create unnecessary lags and other wrongs to colleagues, but whatever the reason, extended delays can be harmful.

Case 13-4: Gloria Seeker, Ph.D., proposed a research project to be carried out at a state institution near her university. The project first had to be approved by the facility's Institutional Review Board, headed by Tyrone Plod, Ph.D., the chief psychologist. Seeker eventually filed an ethics complaint that alleged that Plod had procrastinated for 8 months in the consideration of her study, despite the fact that it posed no substantial risk to the population involved. She accused Plod of professional jealousy and, hence, inaction. Dr. Plod replied that he was kept very busy by his duties as chief psychologist and could not give high priority to the request from a colleague outside the agency.

Case 13-5: Rodney Freeman terminated psychotherapy with Stefan Witholden, Psy.D., 1 year ago. Mr. Freeman decided to reenter therapy with another practitioner and signed a release-of-information form that authorized the new therapist to contact Dr. Witholden. When no report or records were forthcoming, and after several unsuccessful attempts to contact Witholden, Freeman was finally told, "I don't have any materials that would be useful to you."

Case 13-6: Susan Predoc's dissertation draft sat among the piles of papers and books on Dr. Sloth's desk for 4 months. When Ms. Predoc politely inquired about it, noting that she was anxious to finish her degree and move her family to another city, Sloth said he would get to it as soon as possible. Three more months passed, and still no feedback was forthcoming.

Each of these cases implies a measure of psychologist passivity or lack of prompt cooperation. While it is not clear whether Dr. Plod was intentionally thwarting Dr. Seeker's project, he certainly gave her request a very low priority. At the very least, Seeker was entitled to know approximately when a decision would be forthcoming and what position the committee might take given its official policies and research practices. If Dr. Plod were truly unable to expeditiously perform his assigned committee duties, he should have stepped down from that position in favor of someone who could. If evidence existed to confirm that Plod treated Seeker unfairly, given institutional policy or relative favoritism to others, his behavior would be clearly unethical.

The example involving Dr. Witholden is not uncommon. At times, a former therapist may be angry at a client's decision to see another therapist, even after an appropriate termination. At other times, a practitioner may fail to cooperate because of some disapproval, based on personal or orientational objections, of the new therapist. In any case, Witholden's reluctance to share information with the new therapist at the client's request is potentially harmful to the client and therefore unethical. The 1992 APA ethics code declares that psychologists cannot withhold records because a client still owes money (ES: 5.11). In this case, payment is not at issue, making Withholden's behavior even less defensible.

Case 13-7: When a client decided to drop Philip Customary, Ph.D., in favor of consulting Rosemary Carrot, an unlicensed individual claiming to be a "vegetarian psychic healer," the client requested that a copy of all treatment notes and assessment scores be sent to the new "therapist." Customary reasoned that it would be improper to send records to someone he believes to be "a charlatan."

With all sorts of alternative medical practices gaining popularity in the mainstream, such situations will occur more frequently. One may empathize with Customary's position, but it is one that may well make him vulnerable. Psychologists are probably obligated to send summaries of the treatment records to nonpsychologist practitioners, but could appropriately withhold sending raw test data. Another alternative would be for Dr. Customary to provide the records to the client, allowing the client to decide what to share with Ms. Carrot.

Ms. Predoc's dilemma is particularly troublesome because Dr. Sloth retains considerable power over her life, and she does not have professional clout or potential allies as do other types of complaining parties. How hard should she push? Should she enlist the assistance of one of Sloth's colleagues? Should she report Sloth to the program director? If she angers her dissertation chair, the chair may exact additional and less passive penalties, such as finding fault with any work she submits. Such unresponsive behavior is addressed by the APA ethics code (1992), which admonishes psychologists to establish appropriate feedback processes for students (ES: 6.05a).

Interference with Ongoing Relationships

What about the situation in which the services of a psychologist are offered or sought, but starting the process might damage another ongoing relationship? The two most common concerns raised in this context are (1) agreeing to work with clients or others who initiate the contact but are currently involved in a relationship with another professional in a similar role and (2) active soliciting ("pirating") of psychotherapy clients in treatment elsewhere. In an agreement with the Federal Trade Commission (FTC), the APA has moved away from strong objections to such behavior. Uninvited in-person solicitations remain generally disallowed in one standard (ES: 3.06), but are implicitly allowed in another (ES: 4.04) as long as the psychologist minimizes the risk of confusion and conflict and focuses on the client's welfare (see also chapter 11).

We continue to take the stand, however, that solicitation or acceptance of clients receiving services from another mental health professional should be undertaken with extraordinary caution. The sole focus must be on the client's individual needs and best interests, and these may not be immediately apparent. Issues that relate to the psychologists' competence to evaluate clients become especially relevant.

Case 13-8: Sidney Switch was still in active treatment with a psychologist when he sought an appointment with Roberto Resque, Ph.D. Switch tells Dr. Resque that he believes his current psychologist is not helping him. He would like to start seeing Resque instead.

What are Resque's obligations and duties? We acknowledge that Switch certainly has the right to choose his service provider. In our view, however, it would not be appropriate for Dr. Resque simply to begin treating Switch, ignoring the other active professional relationship. Ideally, Resque would recognize that "negative transference" or misunderstanding can potentially complicate therapy and would suggest that Mr. Switch discuss his dissatisfaction directly with his current therapist. If Switch is unwilling to do that for some reason, Resque should seek his authorization to contact the therapist and confer about the case. If Switch refuses to permit this, it would be wisest for Resque to decline to offer him services. It could be that Switch is attempting to conceal some issues or is simply acting out in some way against his current therapist. Resque might soon find himself embroiled in an uncomfortable situation.

One can argue that a psychologist should not deny treatment to a client in need. But, it is difficult to treat a client adequately who wishes to hide something about an ongoing psychotherapy experience. It is wise for therapists not to become involved unless it is possible to do so in an open manner. On occasion, however, a serious ethical infraction is discovered, but the psychologist who makes the discovery must withhold the information to protect a client. These situations often involve allegations of therapist sexual misconduct.

Case 13-9: Sonia Victim sought psychotherapy with Anita Rule, Ph.D. Ms. Victim told Dr. Rule that she had recently decided to terminate her "psychotherapeutic" relationship with Peter Grossout, Ph.D., who had convinced her that she should engage in a variety of sexual activities with him as a means to "overcome the adverse psychological influence of her father in her life." Ms. Victim told Dr. Rule that she was feeling increasingly depressed and worthless in the wake of her encounters with Dr. Grossout. Rule inquired as to whether Ms. Victim might wish to pursue a formal complaint against Dr. Grossout. The client responded that she wanted only to "forget those repulsive events" and go into treatment with Dr. Rule for other concerns.

This kind of situation may well be an exception to the generally preferred way of accepting new clients without consulting a colleague who had been serving the same client in the recent past. It has been estimated that about 50% of therapists will encounter at least one client who reports being abused by a previous therapist (Pope & Vetter, 1991). Dr. Rule would doubtless like to see Dr. Grossout called to account for the allegations made by Ms. Victim. If Victim's accusations are true, then Grossout's future clients may be at risk for sexual predation. On the other hand, Victim's disclosures were offered in confidence and cannot be disclosed without the client's consent (see also chapter 6). The client's relative vulnerability and the emotional cost of pursuing a complaint against Grossout may well be too high a price for her to pay.

Dr. Rule can and should provide her new client with information in regard to the fact that the behavior described was unethical, unprofessional, and possibly illegal (depending on state law). The client should also be informed that avenues for pressing formal ethics or legal complaints are open to her. Dr. Rule should not, however, attempt to pressure her client to pursue a formal complaint. Rule cannot initiate a complaint herself because to do so would violate her client's confidence. It also would not be surprising if Ms. Victim did not wish Dr. Rule to contact Dr. Grossout about her case. We can only hope that Rule's client will ultimately develop sufficient personal resources to make an appropriate complaint, or that the offending psychologist will come to the attention of a disciplinary panel by some other route (Sonne & Pope, 1991).

Not all ongoing relationships that pose interference issues involve psychotherapy. These other types of professional alliances can also yield troubling dilemmas.

Case 13-10: Tanya Trainee is a psychology intern at a community mental health center where Lorna Doone, Ed.D., supervises her psychotherapy cases. Ms. Trainee disagrees with some of Doone's recommendations, so she approaches her testing supervisor, Mucho Nicer, Psy.D., for his suggestions.

Ms. Trainee appears to be splitting off aspects of her relationship with Dr. Doone that, for some reason, are unsatisfactory to her. Dr. Nicer must realize that he is being approached by Ms. Trainee about matters for which another supervisor has been designated. He should point this out to Ms. Trainee and suggest that she discuss differences directly with her supervisor or with the person designated as director of the training program. For Dr. Nicer to offer supervisory consultation without the knowledge of Dr. Doone would create a potential for substantially more serious collegial anger, even if that was not Ms. Trainee's intent. If Ms. Trainee has serious questions regarding the nature of Dr. Doone's supervision or competence, and if Doone is unresponsive to a direct discussion with her, she could then consult with other colleagues in the setting for advice on how to proceed.

What about the situation when a request for consultation turns into something more? Consider the following case examples.

Case 13-11: Fritz Couch, M.D., is a psychoanalyst who has been treating Hester Prynn in analysis for 3 years. Prynn has been blocking her free associations for several weeks, and Dr. Couch wonders about the possibility of an impending thought disturbance. He refers Ms. Prynn to Ursula Norms, Ph.D., for psychodiagnostic testing. During the course of the psychological assessment, Ms. Prynn tells Dr. Norms that she is increasingly frustrated with the lack of progress she is making in treatment with Dr. Couch and asks whether Norms would be willing to treat her.

Case 13-12: Gladys Prudent, Psy.D., is concerned about her client's persistent mood state. Dr. Prudent believes that perhaps an antidepressant medication would be useful in resolving what appears to be an endogenous depression. She refers Ms. Downer to Ingrid Meds, M.D., for a medication consultation. Ms. Downer is impressed when Dr. Meds expresses the belief that medication should offer her relief and asks Meds to begin managing her case completely, expressing a willingness to terminate with Dr. Prudent.

Both of these cases illustrate a circumstance that is not uncommon, and it is not difficult to understand why. Often enough, ethical therapists recognize the potential limitations in their ability to adequately diagnose or treat a specific problem and seek specific consultations from qualified colleagues (ES: 1.20a). Clients are often having problems that may make them feel frustrated, depressed, or troubled. When both situations collide, the consultants can be imbued with a positive aura by the clients, who then ask the consultants to take over.

Clients have the right to free choice, even if the choice might be counter to their best interests as seen by their current therapists. The idealized consultants, however, may be benefitting only from a contrast effect, and it is likely that neither one knows the client as well as the referring therapist.

In both of the cases presented above, the correct courses of action would be similar. The consultants should refer the clients back to their therapists with the recommendation that they discuss the issue directly. In Ms. Prynn's situation, this might mean working through a negative transference, whereas for Ms. Downer, it might mean discussing the frustrations of a prolonged depressive reaction. Ultimately, the clients may choose to terminate treatment with the therapists and seek treatment from the consultants or elsewhere. But, the consultants should not encourage this, recognizing the unusual nature of their limited relationships with the clients. Assuming the clients have authorized the consultants to communicate with the referring therapists, it might also be wise for Norms and Meds to inform Couch and Prudent, respectively, of their clients' concerns. That, after all, could be considered a part of the consultation that was originally sought, and these concerns may be impeding the progress of treatment.

Making a Referral

The hazards of making consultation referrals are well illustrated in Cases 13-11 and 13-12, but they also exemplify the importance of knowing when to seek advice from a colleague with a different set of competencies. Let us now consider some other types of referrals. What about the client who seeks a referral for a friend in a neighboring state or the colleague who asks for a suggestion in regard to a specialized type of consultant? The person asking for the referral has the right to expect that the psychologist making it will offer the best advice available, regardless of personal or financial interests.

Cases presented in chapter 10 illustrate inappropriate referrals with respect to fee-splitting arrangements. This does not suggest that psychologists should never make referrals to colleagues with whom they are very familiar or have close working relationships. The key factor should be the best interests of the client, including the client's needs, expressed preferences, geographic location, finances, and other relevant considerations.

Case 13-13: Gene Defer, Psy.D., works in a group practice with several other mental health professionals. He conducts an intake interview with a new female client in her mid-30s who requests a female therapist. Two women work with Dr. Defer in the group practice. He describes both women in terms of age and special clinical interests, suggesting that the client might choose to have an appointment with one of them.

Case 13-14: Ronda Refer, Ed.D., is telephoned by a client who asks her to assist in locating a psychologist to evaluate a relative in a distant state. Dr. Refer does not know anyone in that geographic area, but uses a professional directory to provide the client with the names and addresses of some appropriately licensed practitioners in that general vicinity.

The behavior of both psychologists cited above is ethically appropriate. Dr. Defer has no specific financial interest in his referral to another member of the same practice group. While he may derive some diffuse benefit by keeping the client within the group, the client was, after all, the one who approached that group in the first place. Presumably, the client also understands that Dr. Defer and his female colleagues are part of a group that works in close association. Defer is also being responsive to the client's stated preference for a female therapist and has presented some additional data in regard to options within the group, giving the client an additional measure of informed choice.

Ideally, Dr. Refer is able to suggest a colleague or two with whom she is well enough acquainted to be assured of an appropriate match with the client's needs. In this case, she is not familiar with anyone in the area and knows relatively little about the client's specific needs. By using a professional directory to locate licensed or board-certified colleagues, she reasonably assures at least minimal confidence in regard to the practitioners' competence. One must presume that the practitioners receiving such a referral will have the ethical sensitivity to make additional local referrals should the need be for services they are not equipped to offer. Dr. Refer, however, should offer appropriate caveats to her client (e.g., "Please tell your cousin that I do not know these practitioners personally; however, they are listed as fully licensed"). In

some cases, a psychologist might not feel comfortable making such a referral. The inquirer might then be referred to a state psychological association or community agency.

Despite good and pure intentions, a referral can go askance, as the next two incidents reveal.

Case 13-15: A psychologist in Maine called a friend, Dr. Assist, in California, requesting a referral for a client moving to the Los Angeles area. Dr. Assist asked a few questions about the client's situation and suggested Dr. Mismatch, an acquaintance with a good reputation in the community. The client acted on the referral and was very displeased with Dr. Mismatch. The psychologist in Maine contacted Dr. Assist to complain that the former client had called to express anger toward her for passing on a faulty suggestion; in the client's words, Mismatch was "such a dreadful therapist, he made me much worse." The psychologist in Maine also seemed to be irritated with Dr. Assist, implying that Dr. Assist's referral was ill-conceived.

Case 13-16: A student, whose behavior revealed a high level of agitation, asked a psychology professor, Dr. Helpout, for a referral to a psychologist in the community. Dr. Helpout offered the student several names, specifically noting that the last one was also a very close friend. The student returned several weeks later and accused Dr. Helpout of "setting her up so that she could get a financial cut from the friend out of the referral." The student then recited a list of complaints about Dr. Helpout's friend/therapist and, before slamming the office door behind her, advised Dr. Helpout that she would soon be hearing from an ethics committee.

Both therapists who related these true stories to us have also vowed never again to make referrals. This is an unfortunate decision in consideration of the valuable service to consumers that conscientious referrals can provide. Dr. Request was especially trying to be ethical by revealing the nature of her relationship with one of the referral options, but this time such candor backfired.

To help allay the potential for fallout when referrals do not pan out, psychologists should always remember to convey what may be too obvious to do at the time: Even when the referral is personally known to the referral source, professional services are very personal, and no one can guarantee that a professional relationship will work out satisfactorily. Because part of a psychologist's reputation and professional responsibility is carried in any referral made, appropriate caveats should be offered as thoughtfully as the referral itself.

Professional Etiquette

Colleagues both inside and outside psychology deserve to be treated with outward respect and equanimity and in accordance with professional etiquette, even when one has reason to be annoyed with them. Tossing impolite barbs can result in an escalating professional feud. Ethics complaints are occasionally made about issues that should have been resolved informally between the colleagues early in the dispute.

Case 13-17: Horace Night, Ph.D., was asked by a journal editor to review a manuscript by Lester Day, Ph.D., with whom Night has long had substantial theoretical disagreements. Night drafted a scathing review of the paper based chiefly on theoretical disagreements, including such comments as "Dr. Day continues to cling to obsolete ideas in a narrow-minded and idiotic fashion."

Case 13-18: Dr. Night (Case 13-15) also teaches a course at a local university. During the semester, he frequently attacks the work of Dr. Day, describing it as trivial, ill-conceived, and useless.

Certainly, personal motives—including anger, jealousy, competitiveness, and inflated views of one's importance—may contribute to anger toward colleagues. Such passions should not, however, be expressed in an unprofessional manner. In the case of Dr. Night, it appears that the theoretical disagreements with Dr. Day have been inappropriately personalized. If Night is not prepared to offer a critique in a rational and dispassionate manner, he should consider telling the editor: "I am too personally angry with Dr. Day to give this paper a fair reading. You will need to locate another reviewer." The adjectives "narrow-minded" and "idiotic" have no place in an ethically formu-

lated scholarly review. Because the attack was so blatant in this case, the editor will likely recognize this even if Night does not and disregard emotion-based criticisms.

Dr. Night's classroom attacks are also inappropriate. Such public statements are not in keeping with the scientific foundations of psychology. Ideally, Night could outline Day's concepts and then contrast them with his own in a scholarly fashion. In the case of legitimate scholarly or professional differences, the most fitting means of presenting the dispute is through articles and comments in peer-reviewed professional publications in which full citation and documentation of claims are possible under the critical eye of scholarly peers. Night's attacks on Day were again too personalized and lacked the appropriate validation necessary for presentation in an educational format (ES: 6.03a). (See chapter 16 for an additional discussion of the ethics of classroom presentations.)

Case 13-19: Manfred Potz, Ph.D., and his colleague Stefan Blitz, Ph.D., have known each other personally and professionally for many years. After an unfortunate personal dispute leads to a dissolution of their friendship, Potz complains to an ethics committee that Blitz is spreading untrue rumors to a mutual acquaintance that Potz is a Nazi sympathizer and is having an affair with a woman half his age.

The type of dispute between Drs. Potz and Blitz unfortunately occurs all too frequently. Potz's political affiliations and personal life are not fitting topics of gossip in professional settings. Colleagues usually have no way of assessing the validity of such personal criticisms with respect to professional competence, let alone the veracity of Blitz's verbal assault. If Blitz has some factual basis for criticizing Potz (e.g., if he recently discovered that Potz formerly worked as a Nazi concentration camp guard and has lied about this fact), then he should bring this evidence to appropriate authorities. Gossip and rumors, however, violate the spirit of the professional role.

An area of professional etiquette that has been largely ignored is political activity in psychological associations or organizations. Active campaigning for elective office, with colleagues endorsing other colleagues or campaigning on behalf of one another, is not unusual in some professional organizations (Koocher, Sobel, & Hare-Mustin, 1982). But, sometimes, the campaigning can be downright foul.

Case 13-20: Kirby Urban, Ph.D., and Roscoe Rural, Ed.D., actively sought nomination for the same office in a national psychological organization. Both were invited to submit statements for inclusion with the ballots that reflected their qualifications and positions on major issues. Neither had access to the other's statement until the ballots arrived, at which time Dr. Rural became outraged. It seems that Dr. Urban had cited some direct quotations from a paper written by Rural and used these to contrast with his own position. Rural believed that the statements were unfairly taken out of context, and that the purpose of providing statements was to offer a positive basis for selection rather than a unilateral attack. He filed ethics charges for uncollegial behavior against Urban, including a verbal tirade of his own, and sought to void the election, which he had lost.

The ethics committee that received the complaint was troubled by the vindictive claims and counterclaims being pitched about by two respected senior colleagues. There was some truth to each set of claims. Rural had indeed been quoted accurately, yet the context was not one in which he had reason to believe that he would be quoted. He certainly would have framed his statement differently had he anticipated this use of his words. Urban claimed that the difference between him and Rural was distinct on the matters in question, and that he wanted the electorate to make this discrimination clearly. The ethics committee could not sustain an ethics complaint, but closed the case by chiding both senior colleagues to behave with more composure and balance when such competitions occurred in the future.

The Vindictive Colleague

Some additional mention must be made of colleagues who are so angered by real or perceived

wrongs that they either act out in a manner that is clearly unethical or seek redress through ethics committees for problems that are not, strictly speaking, ethical in nature. The vindictive colleague sincerely believes that he or she has been wronged or attacked by another and responds with either an impulsive reaction or (in very rare cases) carefully plotted retaliation. These actions may eventually lead to feelings of remorse, but in the meantime considerable damage has been done. The acts themselves often have a childish quality to them, with the angry colleague viewing an ethics committee as an ally and a parent figure who will swiftly and authoritatively redress the perceived wrong. Unfortunately, because the players are adults acting in a professional capacity, the consequences of their actions cannot always be easily discounted as mere immaturity.

Case 13-21: Rea Venge, Ph.D., gathered strong circumstantial evidence that her colleague and professional rival at Saltine University had stolen the sole copy of her unprocessed raw research data. Dr. Venge was later seen releasing her colleague's research rats in the university's botanical gardens.

Case 13-22: Ralph Romeo, Ed.D., and Jane Juliet, Ph.D., were fellow faculty members at the Farnsworth Institute of Psychology. They developed a sexual relationship from which Romeo contracted genital herpes. He filed an ethics complaint against Juliet, asserting that he had asked specifically whether she had any sexually transmitted diseases prior to their sexual intimacy and had been assured by her that she did not.

Case 13-23: When Charlene Newer, Ph.D., was recruited to Chaos State University as head of the disorderly clinical psychology training program, she undertook a major reorganization. As a result, Jack Oldster, Ph.D., was reassigned from teaching an elective graduate seminar to a less desirable supervisory role. Hurt and angry, Oldster monitored Newer closely and discovered that she had made a critical comment about his attitude to another staff member. Dr. Oldster prepared a detailed complaint of alleged unprofessional conduct by Dr. Newer and filed it with the APA. He filed the same complaint 6 weeks later with the state psychological association and 6 weeks after that with the state licensing board. Because each of these groups investigates complaints independently, Dr. Newer was forced to defend herself in each forum. Although all three complaints were ultimately dismissed, Dr. Newer, much to Dr. Oldster's delight, spent considerable time and resources.

Case 13-24: Drs. Katz and Dawgs were psychologist colleagues with markedly different political views on several sensitive issues. Their arguments were loud and furious, with little regard for their surroundings. Those overhearing the two battle worried about the form any escalation might take. On a subsequent Saturday night, an inebriated Dr. Dawgs was arrested for firing a gun into the front windows of the Katz family home.

In the case of Dr. Venge, we see a possible ethical breach by a colleague, who provoked Venge to commit a clear violation in retaliation. While her ire may be understandable, the resulting act of scattering her colleague's rodents into the bush is also unethical and merely compounds the situation.

The case of Drs. Romeo and Juliet is instructive from several standpoints. First, it illustrates that, underlying an ethics complaint by one colleague about another, there may well be a host of subsurface emotional issues that cannot be resolved through an ethics inquiry. Second, it illustrates the problem of attempting to address personal or interpersonal difficulties in the context of an ethics complaint. The ethics committee contacted Romeo, acknowledged his distress at contracting the disease, but noted that their infectious relationship was not a professional one and was hence beyond the purview of the committee.

Dr. Oldster had other resources at the university to deal most appropriately with any legitimate complaints against his superior. However, it seems apparent that Oldster's primary goal was to complicate Dr. Newer's life, and he did not care what other resources he burdened in the process. The new APA ethics code (1992) specifically warns against filing what the APA judges to be frivolous or nonsensical complaints motivated to harass.

Little comment is necessary regarding Katz and Dawgs, except to assure our readers that this *is* a true story. Fortunately, such acted-out animosity among psychologists is very uncommon. Yet, in a world in which interpersonal problems often impulsively escalate into violence, we are concerned that this phenomenon may become less unusual. (See further discussion of impaired professionals in chapter 3.)

On-Line Wars

A new term in the electronic communication lexicon is *netiquette*, roughly defined as the capacity to remain civil and the ability to maintain some measure of dignity and decorum while communicating over computer networks. We discussed related issues in chapter 12. Here, we offer examples of a personal attack and an intimate faux pas picked up on the Internet.

Case 13-25: A psychologist in an electronic discussion group disagreed with the assertion of Negate Recall, Psy.D., that repressed memory was merely a "cash cow for therapists and that no such phenomenon actually existed." Dr. Recall sent a message describing the psychologist who spoke out against him as being "witless," "dangerous," "impertinent," and "dense." A number of other subscribers came to the defense of the disagreeing psychologist, suggesting that the topic of repressed memories would profit from a two-sided, but restrained and scholarly, debate. Dr. Recall then blasted the entire group of subscribers for their stupidity and wrong-headedness, and announced he was "unsubscribing immediately." The remaining subscribers "gossiped" about Dr. Recall for months afterward. Recall's tirade was also forwarded to scores of other lists.

Case 13-26: Lilly Whoops, Psy.D., noticed that a past lover posted a message in a newsgroup. She was so excited to see his name that she fired off a passionate note, declaring that he was "always better than my husband," and asking, "Am I still better than your wife?" Unfortunately, Dr. Whoops used the reply command instead of the command to send the message to her one-time lover's private E-mail address. The message is known to have been received by more than 1,000 people.

Modern mass communication has created forms of professional relating that some do not handle well. People who have never met face to face can trash each other on line in ways that appear to be far more vitriolic than most "in-person" professional disagreements. The situational context is odd, which may largely account for the phenomenon. Because communicators are actually alone in their rooms interacting with a nonliving mechanical device, the illusion of privacy and safety exists. Passion without apparent danger may blur the fact that hundreds, even thousands, of others may be witnessing the electronic carnage. Practical restraints, such as having to get up the courage to go to an offending colleague's office or the bother of writing and mailing a letter, have disappeared. There is no passage of time that might otherwise invite reconsideration or cool flaming feelings. Everything happens so quickly: Slam the "send" button, and what is done is done.

We recommend that psychologists make an agreement with themselves never to express themselves on line when feeling angry, intense, or impulsive. Their flaming feelings may come home to haunt them. When the anger subsides, the issues can be discussed in ways that maintain professional decorum, with some discussions perhaps better done over the phone or in an old-fashioned letter. In addition, psychologists should remind themselves every time they send a message to a single recipient that it is in a format ready for the recipient to "spread around" to whomever he or she pleases. Finally, there is no absolute freedom of speech in cyberspace. Libel, defamation, and invasion of privacy legal actions have already been won (Branscum, 1995).

RELATIONSHIPS WITH SUPERVISEES AND EMPLOYEES

A psychologist's relationships with supervisees and employees carry similar ethical duties and responsibilities as those to therapy clients (ES: 1.22). The psychologist as a supervisor or employer is usually the more powerful person in the relationship and must recognize the accom-

panying obligations. Supervisees and employees have the same general rights to privacy, respect, dignity, courtesy, and due process accorded those in psychotherapy client roles.

It is difficult to broadly characterize all of the potential problems that can arise while relating to supervisees and employees. We begin by discussing particular ethical problems within each type of relationship. Two special issues relative to supervisees and employees, as well as to students, have been chosen for closer examination: letters of reference and sexual harassment.

Clinical Supervisees

Every clinical or counseling psychologist was once a trainee and was likely influenced in important ways during that critical period of professional development (Pope & Vasquez, 1991). Clinical supervisors have, perhaps rightly, been referred to as "professional parents" (Alonzo, 1985). Vasquez (1992) describes the clinical supervisors' training responsibilities as falling into three broad areas: (1) ethical knowledge and behavior, (2) competency, and (3) personal functioning. Each has relevance to the quality of the interpersonal relationship between supervisor and supervisee.

Supervisory relationships are far more delicate and complicated than the typical educator-student relationship (see chapter 16). The clinical supervisor performs multiple roles: teacher, mentor, evaluator, and facilitator of self-awareness and exploration, all of which contain elements of a therapeutic relationship (Kurpius, Gibson, Lewis, & Corbet, 1991). These inherent roles may not always integrate smoothly, such as the need to be critical while evaluating at some times, and listening empathically at others (Whiston & Emerson, 1989). Further, these roles include third parties—the supervisee's clients—which makes the relationship even more delicate and in need of responsible, ethical management. Finally, clinical supervisors often have access to information about the emotional lives of their trainees just as they have access to information about therapy clients; this knowledge must be held with special care.

Case 13-27: Supervisee Jimbo Tryhard was not satisfied with the progress of his clients and was experiencing considerable self-doubts. Tryhard's supervisor, Dr. Twosides, always reacted in a critical tone whenever Tryhard attempted to disclose his therapeutic errors. Because Twosides's position was to evaluate Tryhard's performance, with a direct impact on his success in the program and his chances of being hired after completing it, Tryhard switched to playing out the supervisory sessions by saying whatever he thought that Dr. Twosides wanted to hear.

Tryhard may have been overly sensitive to Dr. Twosides' criticisms, but the supervisor did fail to establish an adequate relationship with his supervisee. Although it can be difficult, supervisors must seek to create alliances that allow supervisees to admit mistakes without fear. The ultimate competence levels reached by supervisees, as well as the welfare of future clients, depend heavily on the success of this pivotal phase of training. We suggest adapting Bosk's (1979) notion of supervisee errors and communicating this scheme clearly to supervisees because it may help create the framework for an honest relationship between the supervisor and supervisee. In Bosk's view, errors in technique application and flawed clinical judgments are forgivable and inevitable during training. However, Bosk sees normative errors, those that occur when supervisees fail to do what is expected of them or fail to act conscientiously, as moral failures. Covering up a technical or judgmental error leads to a normative error.

Vasquez states, "Professionals concerned with the problems of unethical behavior believe that the strongest weapon against professional misconduct may be the education of trainees" (1992, p. 196). As models of conduct in actual professional settings, supervisors can be either exemplars or agents of poor professional socialization.

Case 13-28: Jane Dumpee eagerly anticipated supervision by Queenie Topdog, Ph.D., a highly respected clinician known for tireless dedication to her profession. At first, Dumpee enjoyed hearing about Topdog's work, even though such discussions took up almost half of the supervisory hour. However, as listening eroded even further into the hour and Topdog's self-revelations became more personal, Dumpee became concerned because her own needs for case review were not being met.

Case 13-29: The minute Melanie Chic arrived for her clinical supervisory session, Dr. Fox would evaluate what she was wearing (e.g., "That color doesn't do anything for you" or "That sweater is absolutely gorgeous"). He often lost track or interrupted the flow of her attempts to focus on her clients' problems with remarks such as, "Speaking of drinking too much, have you gone to the new jazz bar on 4th Street yet?"

Supervisors who use their status and power for their own gratification or entertainment are exploiting those who have entrusted their professional development to them. Even though neither of the above cases may have involved intentional abuse, both supervisors have abandoned their professional roles in favor of their personal agendas. Although we cannot be sure about Dr. Fox's motives, he is flirting with sexual harassment, discussed separtely in this chapter.

Unfortunately, supervisees who are devalued, humiliated, ignored, or criticized in a nonconstructive way may be unlikely to protest, especially if the supervisor is well liked and respected in the work setting (Jacobs, 1991). Both Dumpee and Chic are unlikely to complain because supervisees are professionally and emotionally vulnerable in the context of their supervision. This compounds their disadvantage in advocating for themselves should the boundaries of the relationship further collapse (Jacobs, 1991).

It is disturbing to note that data from anonymous surveys reveal that sexual contact between clinical supervisees and supervisors occurs fairly frequently (Glaser & Thorpe, 1986; Pope, Levenson, & Schover, 1979). In the 1992 revision of the APA ethics code, sexual relations with supervisees in training have been specifically disallowed because such relationships are so likely to impair judgment and be exploitative (ES: 1.19b). (For additional discussion of sexual relations with supervisees, see chapter 9.)

Timely feedback, or lack thereof, is at the root of many ethical complaints that grow out of supervisory relationships. This is especially true when supervisees are abruptly notified that they are to be terminated or given an unfavorable rating.

Case 13-30: Near the end of a 12-month clinical internship, Sheldon Lout was stunned to read an evaluation by his supervisor that described him as insensitive and rude in his relationships with colleagues. He was fearful that these comments would hurt his chances of finding employment and asserted that such comments were unethical since he had heard nothing about them earlier.

Case 13-31: Lennie Carnal was in the final stages of completing his doctorate and approached Marcus Glide, Ph.D., to arrange for special supervision. Carnal wanted to see a few private clients at his home office and contracted with Dr. Glide to supervise him. Glide agreed and was paid by Carnal for several hours of supervision time. Some months later, several women complained that they were sexually molested by Carnal in the guise of therapy. Carnal fled the state, and a negligence lawsuit was subsequently directed toward Dr. Glide for inadequately supervising Carnal. Dr. Glide claimed that Carnal never told him about the sexual activities, the names of the clients involved, or even that he was practicing in his own home.

Routine feedback sessions should be built into all supervisory relationships (ES: 6.05a). When serious criticisms are discussed with supervisees, they should invariably be put in writing and followed or accompanied by a dialogue about expected changes (Harrar, VandeCreek, & Knapp, 1990). The common thread running through both of the previous cases involves the inadequacy of supervision and poor communication of the supervisory relationship to clients. One could argue that Mr. Lout, were he truly insensitive, might not have heeded supervisory criticism. Nonetheless, he was certainly entitled to timely feedback and would be correct in asserting that it is inappropriate to say nothing about a trainee's shortcomings until the final evaluation. This behavior, if true, allowed Lout

no opportunity to attempt to remediate his defects. In addition, had Lout's conduct been severe enough to warrant termination from the program, he could legitimately claim lack of due process.

The case of Mr. Carnal and Dr. Glide illustrates the importance of fully recognizing the responsibility attending the role of supervisor. It seems that Dr. Glide extended more trust than was warranted to Mr. Carnal when agreeing to provide off-site supervision for private clients. While it is possible that Carnal lied or selectively reported material to the supervisor, Glide may have failed to monitor Carnal's work in adequate detail. Under the legal principle of *respondeat superior*, it was argued that Dr. Glide knew or should have known of activities under his supervision and was therefore also liable to be sued for negligence. It is also likely that some regulations were violated if state law or insurance contracts required the physical presence of the supervisor on site during service delivery or prohibited payment for supervision.

When a client is receiving services from a psychologist who is, in turn, being supervised or otherwise in training, the client has the right to know this, as well as the name of the supervisor, as is clearly stated in the ethics code (ES: 4.01). Similarly, the supervisor should know the names, addresses, and other basic data about clients whose cases they are supervising. The client should also be told explicitly that aspects of the case will be shared with the supervisor. Indeed, many clients would be pleased to know that the psychologist serving them has consulted a senior colleague about their cases. This should not come to a client's attention at a sensitive moment, however, and is best presented factually as a part of the initial contract formed between client and psychologist.

Case 13-32: Amy Shy arrived at the mental health center for her usual weekly appointment with the psychology intern and was met by Solomon Foot, Ph.D., the intern's supervisor. Dr. Foot explained that the intern broke her leg skiing the weekend before and would not be back at the clinic for 4 to 6 weeks. He offered to provide interim services for Ms. Shy because he was familiar with her case through his supervision of the intern. Ms. Shy was embarrassed that this stranger seemed to know "personal things" about her.

Dr. Foot appeared to have Amy Shy's best interests at heart, although she was certainly distressed by his awareness of details of her case. It is unclear whether the trainee failed to inform Ms. Shy that a supervisor was involved in her case or whether Dr. Foot's introduction was a bit too abrupt for her to tolerate. This behavior is not necessarily unethical, but it reveals the difficulty a sensitive client may face if supervisory relationships are not carefully articulated.

To help diffuse some of the inherent role entanglements and abuses in clinical supervision, models other than "one on one" have been proposed. These include group supervision, vertical supervision, and the use of multiple supervisors (Minnes, 1987). A concern, however, is that a diffusion in responsibility may also occur if trainees are being fanned out among several sources of supervision. Vertical and multiple supervision models may also be too burdensome on the resources in many settings. And, whereas group supervision may lessen the resource drain, a reduction of individual attention may result, and supervisees may be even less willing to disclose their difficulties. Some combination of these models, however, may help mitigate the deficiencies and risks inherent in the one-on-one model of supervision.

Clear understandings of the contract between supervisees and supervisors regarding the nature of their relationship, mutual expectations, frequency of contact, feedback format and intervals, and other similar contingencies remain essential regardless of the supervision model adopted. While these arrangements need not be formal contracts, they should be explicit and thoughtfully executed. Such arrangements are not only the obligation of the supervisor (Scofield & Scofield, 1978), but are also much desired by the supervisees (Nelson, 1978). We wholeheartedly agree with Sherry's (1991) conclusion that, because supervision has elements similar to therapy and requires multiple roles of its participants, it should be conceived as a psychological intervention that is highly vulnerable to ethical infractions.

What do trainees really want? In a survey of supervisees, Allen, Szollos, and Williams (1986) found that expertise and trustworthiness were the most favored supervisor characteristics. Many supervisees also welcome assistance with personal growth issues more than the teaching of technical skills. Communication of expectations and clear feedback also ranked high. Sexist or authoritarian treatment was seen as especially detrimental to the quality of supervision.

Research Supervisees

Research experience is critical if graduate students are to be competitive applicants for employment in many settings, especially universities. Research experience as an undergraduate is a primary criterion of graduate school selection committees, including most traditional clinical psychology programs (Keith-Spiegel, 1991). Thus, the availability of ethical research mentors remains a priority in the training of students. Research supervision is less complicated than clinical supervision because the role does not typically involve discussion of feelings or personal disclosures. The welfare of third parties—research participants in this case—remains an issue, as does the critical importance of role modeling and the risk of exploiting supervisees. In a critical incident survey about supervision of student research by Goodyear, Crego, and Johnston (1992), an array of ethical problems in research supervision was described. These included supervisor abandonment, unfair authorship practices, incompetent and inadequate supervision, and abusive and exploitative supervision.

Case 13-33: Simi Gradbound enthusiastically agreed to collaborate on a research project with Professor Desert. She very much wanted to list research experience on her resumé. Dr. Desert had also indicated that they could present the paper at a regional professional meeting. Gradbound collected and analyzed the data and turned the material over to Dr. Desert, who, by prior agreement, would draft a manuscript. In the meantime, Dr. Desert received a large grant for another project and was elected president of the academic senate. Each time Gradbound would drop by to ask how

things were going, Desert would apologize pro-
fusely and promise to get around to the project as
soon as he could. The deadline for the regional
meeting passed, and Gradbound graduated without any further action on the project.

Gradbound is perhaps a too common type
of victim of a professor's busy schedule. The
project was obviously of low priority on Desert's
list, but to Gradbound it was of primary significance. Gradbound rightly feels abandoned and
may blame Desert for any difficulties she experiences in gaining admission to a graduate program. Desert should not have taken Gradbound
on as a supervisee unless he was relatively sure of
his ability to keep his word. Even after becoming
aware of the complications in his own schedule,
he should have followed through anyway or at
least facilitated the completion of the project
in some other way.

Case 13-34: Professor Frawd encouraged his research supervisee, Lionel Twist, to eliminate any
outlier cases because they would elevate the error
term. "If we don't get a significant finding, we
won't be able to publish this article. Extremes don't
tell us much about the phenomenon anyway. And
besides, everybody does it."

Mr. Twist is in a terrible position and is being
professionally corrupted. Frawd's attempt to rationalize away a highly unethical act of scientific
misconduct may well be persuasive to an admiring supervisee who also needs a publication to
advance his own future. (See chapters 16 and
17 for more information about collaborative relationships with students and scientific misconduct.)

Employees

As agents of the psychologists who hire them,
employees also have ethical responsibilities. Psychologists are responsible for training and monitoring the behavior of employees with respect
to any duties delegated to them. Psychologists
should not employ persons who cannot conform
to required standards of behavior when dealing
with clients, students, research participants, or
other consumers of psychological services. Employees who handle gradebooks, confidential
records, data sets, or billing, for example, must
understand the ethical issues involved in managing their duties and be trustworthy in carrying
out these functions. They must also be prepared
to deal with a variety of other situations that
might not come up in a more traditional work
setting.

Case 13-35: An anonymous caller to a psychologist's office reached the bookkeeper and explained
that she is afraid that she is about to abuse her
child. The caller refused to give her name, but
wanted to talk to someone. The psychologist was
not available.

Case 13-36: After beginning work as a secretary
to a group of psychologists, a young man discovered that several of his acquaintances from the
same small town are clients of the group. He was
routinely asked to type reports and notes about
people he knows personally.

Both situations demonstrate the care and
training that must go into the selection and
hiring of employees. We have chosen two examples typical of a clinical practice. They hold
equally well for academic, research, or business
settings in terms of both the need to safeguard
confidential materials and to deal with others
appropriately.

If the anonymous caller in Case 13-35 does
not get some professional help, tragedy could
result. The bookkeeper should be prepared to
refer the caller to the local child abuse hotline
(if one exists) or to another agency at which
emergency personnel might be available (e.g.,
community mental health center, hospital emergency room, or crisis center). Abrupt termination or failure to refer such a call could have
unacceptable consequences. The psychologist
should train all employees to handle these situations. In some work settings, or for some therapists specializing in crisis management, crisis
hotline training for the nonprofessional staff
may be indicated as well.

While it is possible to respect the privacy and
confidences of personal acquaintances in many
situations, a psychologist should assess this ability and sensitivity in potential employees prior

to hiring. This is especially important in communities in which social circles are likely to overlap, such as university towns and rural settings. The new secretary in Case 13-36 may be capable of adequately handling the situation, but the psychologists hiring him are ultimately responsible for his behavior and should take special precautions to protect clients' privacy. For example, safeguards might include placing files in secure locations that are unavailable to the staff. There may be rare times when it may simply be inappropriate for psychologists to delegate clerical or other nonpsychological tasks to others.

Case 13-37: Teeneyville is in chaos. Allegations that the city treasury has been raided by several top officials have created headlines in the town's newspaper for weeks. The mayor's wife is in counseling with Dr. Sanctuary because, she alleges, her husband is drinking and threatening to kill himself. He has refused therapy, but his wife calls frequently, asking to speak to Dr. Sanctuary immediately.

This explosive, small-town crisis requires special measures to be taken regarding how messages from this particular party are received, who transcribes the records, and who has access to these sensitive materials. Similar situations can arise for any high-profile clients and their families.

Letters of Reference

Psychologists are often called upon to write endorsement letters that evaluate the qualifications of colleagues, supervisees, students, and employees. These letters are often influential in the selection process (Purdy, Reinehr, & Swartz, 1989). However, serving as a referee—especially if any negative commentary is to be offered—is an increasingly risky business. Complicating matters further is the threat of a recipient suing the referee if a significant shortcoming was known to the referee and remained unmentioned.

Letter Content

Letters of reference ought to be composed with the assumption that they will eventually be seen by the person about whom they are written. Some letters are accompanied by a confidentiality waiver, but the writer can never be assured of this once the letter leaves the office. A second general rule is that the letter ought to contain the sort of information that the writer would want to know about the candidate (i.e., for graduate school admission, employment, promotion, etc.) if the situation were reversed.

Referees face several peculiar ethical dilemmas not of their own making. Research on the reference letter process has revealed some odd circumstances and a serious contamination that works against referees who want to be completely candid. Unless a referee views the candidate in a highly positive light, being truthful carries the risk that the candidate will be summarily rejected (Keith-Spiegel, 1991). Studies have demonstrated that negative evaluations, even if couched in a letter that is predominantly positive, also result in the candidates' rejection. Why? Because most letters are completely positive, creating a sort of "letter inflation" (Hardin, Craddick, & Ellis, 1991; Miller & Van Rybroek, 1988; Siskind, 1966). Therefore, it is probable that a less-than-enthusiastic letter damns by faint praise, and a minor criticism stands out like a ham at a bar mitzvah party.

We are not suggesting that one should always write a positive letter despite any reservations. However, it is important to recognize in advance that the candidate's chances will likely be decreased substantially should unfavorable comments be included. If one cannot in good conscience write a favorable evaluation, we recommend discussing the matter with the candidate. It is always possible to send a factual confirmation letter (e.g., "Dr. Jones was employed at this facility in the role of staff psychologist for 2 years). While the candidate may not be pleased by a refusal to send a note of commendation, the opportunity to find a more favorably disposed referee should be appreciated.

Some may see the points we are making as contradictory. That is, if the candidate in question has personal flaws and you were considering that person for a position, would you not want to know about them? Our answer is, "Yes, but not if the candidate is unaware of your assessment." Some candidates may disagree with particular points in a letter of reference written by a supervisor, employer, or colleague, but will not be able to address them in an interview without having been informed. Rejection without knowing the reason, and having no chance to respond to someone's negative evaluation, seems fundamentally unfair. We are not suggesting that referees must share their letters with candidates, but informing them in advance of "trouble spots" is recommended.

Obviously, it is prudent for those seeking a reference or endorsement to approach their colleagues, supervisors, or employers prior to using their names. Asking whether the potential referees feel they could write a strong letter of reference in relation to a given position is a fair question. If hesitancy or reluctance on the part of a potential referee is sensed, the option to ask someone else remains open.

What about the applicant who wants a letter despite being warned that reservations would be included? How should the negative material be presented?

Case 13-38: Dr. Snuff wrote the following single-sentence letter in regard to a student seeking graduate training: "With regard to Ms. Bonk, save yourself a headache and burn her application."

Case 13-39: Dr. Golightly wrote a generally positive letter, but also described clear examples of Mike Breezebrain's extreme absentmindedness and the trouble it caused other supervisees in the clinic. Once, for example, he misplaced the group appointment book and could not recall where he put it. It surfaced several days later on the bottom shelf of the coffee room refrigerator. Another time, Breezebrain forgot to show up for his morning appointments, thinking they were for the following day. Dr. Golightly concluded his letter with, "Mike is a nice guy, but he couldn't find his rear end with both hands and a full-length mirror."

Case 13-40: Dr. Fact carefully detailed a number of events that strongly suggested that Fred Firestarter probably had an antisocial personality disorder, although Fact never used an actual diagnostic term in the letter. Each entry stressed the applicant's behavior and was anchored in facts that could be verified should it ever become necessary (e.g.,

others had witnessed Firestarter's harassing behavior, and an administrative record existed of an investigation of improper use of university stationery to perpetrate a fraud).

These three letters form a hierarchy from unacceptable to appropriate ways of relaying negative information in a reference letter. Dr. Snuff provides no basis for his terse and lethal assessment. Was Ms. Bonk truly without merit, or might Snuff be the one with a problem? The letter's recipients may never know, but Ms. Bonk is unlikely to survive such a paper bomb in her application file. It was unethical (and probably defamatory) for Snuff to write such a letter because it does not offer the evaluators any factual or interpretable information. Golightly's letter was fine, grounding his concerns in behavioral examples, until the last sentence. Though perhaps intended as a cute wrap-up, he stated a probable untruth and violated professional decorum. Dr. Fact, however, was correct when he did present clear and supportable data, which allowed the recipients of the letter to make their own decisions.

Should one ever agree to write a letter without indicating to the requester that it will contain a fault-finding comment? This question leads us to the complex issue of loyalties. In Mebane's (1983) survey of professors in a position to recommend students to graduate clinical programs, approximately half of the sample expressed a primary allegiance to the student, while the rest viewed their primary obligation as being to the graduate school that would enroll the applicant, to the profession, or to society at large. These data suggest that perhaps as many as half of those who serve as referees believe that it is their duty to signal potential problems to the recipients of their letters, and that informing the applicant in advance is a matter of discretion.

Case 13-41: When Whit Bummer asked Selma Mire, Ed.D., to write a letter supporting his application to a counseling program, she felt torn. Bummer was a fairly good student, but unkind to others, brash, and interested only in making money. He once announced in class that rich, crazy people would be his ticket to the good life. Mire could not in good conscience write a positive letter, and she felt that the graduate programs should be warned.

One hopes that students like Bummer do not find their way into the profession, and the argument can be made that their educators have an obligation to help ensure that. In the end, this becomes an individual moral decision that should never be made lightly. Hardin et al. advise that "one must decide whether it is better to write about these weaknesses to alert one's colleagues, or to write a neutral letter that will give the student a chance to continue training and hopefully improve" (1991, p. 391). Regardless of the final decision, it is critical to keep unfavorable remarks well grounded in fact and concrete, observed behaviors, as opposed to relating suspicions and innuendo.

What if one receives a telephone call asking for an assessment of a student or colleague? Is it safe to be completely honest over the telephone?

Case 13-42: Chuck Chum, Ph.D., calls his old friend Bernie Pal, Ph.D., for a spontaneous assessment of one of Pal's colleagues, who has applied for a position in Chum's department.

This scenario plays out frequently. It is not so easy, however, to know what to do when telephoned by a prospective employer for "informal" comments about an applicant, especially if you have not been consulted in advance by the applicant about the use of your name as a reference. Advanced consultation would permit you to forewarn the applicant if you cannot give a wholehearted endorsement. We would caution that it is unwise to say something about a colleague in private that might ultimately be repeated to the candidate and attributed to you unless you are willing to have the candidate know your opinions.

Fulfilling the Commitment

An ethical abuse that occurs all too commonly is the agreed-upon reference letter that never materializes. The psychologist promised to supply a letter, but never gets around to doing it.

Even the somewhat better intentioned referer who sends the letter 2 weeks late may still ensure the candidate's rejection. Job, postdoctoral, or graduate school applicants may not discover such omissions until it is too late, or they may never know that their bids were unsuccessful because their incomplete files were never reviewed. Keith-Spiegel (1991) surveyed doctoral program directors' secretaries, who reported that about 20% of reference letters, on the average, came in well after the deadline. It was not unusual for these candidates to remain unconsidered.

The unwritten or past due letter is a particularly cruel act. Whereas a dilatory referee may have been too busy to fulfill a pledge to support a student, the would-be recipients may well interpret the nonresponsiveness as a reflection of lack of enthusiasm or worse for the candidate. An initial agreement to help turns into an act of betrayal.

Students and others may be reluctant to nag the faculty member to send the letter, but they also run the risk of missing deadlines if they do not. If in doubt, applicants should check with the potential recipient or alert the letter writer that the deadline is approaching. Referees should remember that they do not have to write a reference letter just because someone asked, and that if they are that absorbed by other commitments or are ambivalent, it would be much kinder to refuse the initial request than to renege later. (Increasing numbers of programs request that students collect sealed letters and include them with the application. One obvious advantage is that students know for sure who wrote letters for them.)

Sexual and Gender Harassment

Although current law protects both men and women from a sexually harassing workplace environment, 95% of all incidents are reported by females claiming victimization (Terpstra & Cook, 1985). Therefore, this section focuses on women as the targets of sexual and gender harassment. As women increasingly achieve positions of authority, however, they are already finding that their own behavior or remarks (even when intended to be playful) increase their vulnerability to charges of sexual or gender harassment.

Not so very long ago, women were expected to passively endure uninvited expressions of sexual interest and suggestive remarks made by the men who occupied positions of power in the workplace or academic institution. Recipients who took poorly to such remarks or behavior risked sanctions that ranged from ostracism to dismissal. Early complaints under Title VII of the Civil Rights Act of 1964, which prohibited employment discrimination on the basis of sex, were often dismissed simply as inharmonious relationships between the sexes, an unfortunate social experience, or a mere consequence of attraction between the sexes (Koen, 1989).

It is clear that sexual harassment and sex discrimination is prevalent; surveys indicate that between 25% and 90% of women have been victimized (Koen, 1989). Still, incidents of sexual harassment are believed to go mostly unreported (Rubin & Borgers, 1990), perhaps partially due to the grievance procedure itself (Riger, 1991). Hamilton, Alagna, King, and Lloyd (1987) write that sexual harassment places women in an impossible situation, forcing them to choose between the frying pan and the fire. Management tends to deny or minimize the events through denial ("It didn't happen"), minimization ("It wasn't intentional" or "She misunderstood"), or blaming the victim ("She was seductive and came on to me"). Nevertheless, as legal sanctions and grievance procedures become increasingly formalized and available, they are also increasingly utilized.

Clearly agreed-upon specifications of what behaviors or verbalizations constitute sexual or gender harassment and the point at which harmfulness occurs are difficult to obtain. Except for the more extreme vituperations or lewd acts, incidents can be viewed differently depending on the motivations of the perpetrator, the interpretation of the recipient, the nature of the relationship between the parties involved, and the context in which the incident occurred. Men and women have substantially different attitudes toward the acceptability of sexual behaviors (Rubin & Borgers, 1990), and men are more accepting of behavior judged to be harassing (Reilly, Lott, & Gallogly, 1986). Most acts of sexual

harassment take place in private, so credibility becomes a complicating issue (Binder, 1992; Feldman-Schorrig & McDonald, 1992). Some vulnerable or damaged victims may come across as hysterical and unreliable, and some smooth perpetrators may be convincing.

Definitions and Current Legal Status

The climate of confusion surrounding sexual harassment and what it is (and is not) prompts us to provide a short history of the evolution of the concept and its current legal status. In 1980, the Equal Employment Opportunity Commission (EEOC) defined sexual harassment and issued guidelines for employers. Sexual harassment consisted of the following: (1) unwelcome sexual advances, (2) requests for sexual favors and other verbal or physical conduct of a sexual nature that force submission as an explicit or implicit condition of employment or academic standing, and (3) and statements or conduct that interfere with an individual's work or academic performance and creates an intimidating, hostile, or offensive work or learning environment. The Supreme Court, in its first case in regard to sexual harassment (*Meritor Savings Bank v. Vinson*, 1986), ruled that an offensive hostile environment constitutes illegal sexual harassment as long as it is sufficiently severe and pervasive and causes an abusive working environment because it was unwelcome (Binder, 1992). Sexual harassment was elevated in the American consciousness in 1991 by Anita Hill's testimony during the Senate hearings to confirm Clarence Thomas to the U.S. Supreme Court (Binder, 1992; Feldman-Schorrig & McDonald, 1992).

Vinson specified two types of sexual harassment, both of which can also be found in the EEOC definition: (1) quid pro quo (explicit or implicit trades of sexual favors, either in exchange for some job benefit such as a promotion or raise or as a way of preventing some job detriment such as demotion or termination) and (2) hostile working environment. Feldman-Schorig and McDonald (1992) suggest splitting the hostile working environment definition further to sexual assault or other criminal behavior and to actions that produce psychological distress such as making sexual propositions, telling dirty jokes, and displaying sexually explicit visual material. This second group of behaviors is the most common type seen in lawsuits and is also the most difficult to adjudicate. *Vinson* also made it clear that the plaintiff was not burdened with proving tangible economic detriment. It only had to be demonstrated that the harassment was "sufficiently severe or pervasive" to create a working environment that was abusive.

Other cases have also applied and defined the "reasonable woman standard" as a way of attempting to determine a representative woman's response to assist the court in deciding whether a claim is frivolous or trivial (Thacker & Gohmann, 1993). This standard shields employers from having to accommodate the idiosyncratic concerns of the rare hypersensitive woman (Feldman-Schorrig & McDonald, 1992). It also provides a means of precluding any trauma that could be caused by a thorough psychological examination of a plaintiff to determine the merits of her allegations (Thacker & Gohmann, 1993). Other changes in federal and state laws allow victims to receive compensatory and punitive damages for substantiated claims of sexual harassment (Feldman-Schorrig & McDonald, 1992).

Sexual and Gender Harassment Perpetrated by Psychologists

Specific reference to sexual harassment and a stern admonition to refrain from initiating it appear for the first time in the 1981 revision of the APA ethics code. The 1992 APA code is expanded to reflect the EEOC and reasonable woman standards, with a caveat that specifies that victims will not be penalized for coming forward with a complaint (ES: 1.11). (Sexually intimate behavior with psychotherapy clients, students, and trainees is discussed in detail in chapter 9.)

Case 13-43: Professor Jerry Built, Ph.D., often told his technical equipment supervisee, Dyna Graph, that the supplies issued as a vital part of her work responsibilities would be doled out only if she were "nice to him." When the supplies were not forthcoming, he would say that they would

be made available "when she treated him nicer." According to Ms. Graph, "being nice" meant complimenting Dr. Built on his appearance and acting mildly flirtatious. She resented feeling forced to perform in this manner as a prerequisite to function in her job.

Case 13-44: Each time he brought his secretary Ann Scribe a task, Sherman Tactile, Ph.D., habitually rested his hand on her lower back for a prolonged period of time. When Ms. Scribe tried to turn her body or stand farther away, Dr. Tactile would either alter his position so that he could resume his touching or would say, "Come back here so I can explain this to you" or "Why are you such a distant and unfriendly person?" Ms. Scribe brought charges against Dr. Tactile when he fired her on grounds of an "uncooperative attitude."

Case 13-45: Dexter Swinish, Psy.D., was known for making suggestive remarks to his female trainees. When he approached Sandra Firm with, "Want to get it on this weekend?" Ms. Firm replied, "Go sit on your thumb." Swinish reportedly avoided her after that and, at the end of the term, entered unflattering and undocumented criticisms into her evaluation file.

These cases illustrate how demands for sexual favors, and reprisals for rejecting them, can interfere with the job and academic status of particular individuals. However, the intimidations can also be more diffuse, as illustrated by the following case.

Case 13-46: Professor Tim Traditional, Ph.D., announced to his classes that he is admittedly a "dirty old man who likes to flirt with the ladies." He then noted that if anyone found his small pleasure a burden, they had better just put up with it or drop his course because he was "too old to keep up with this feminist nonsense."

Here, women students were placed in a separate category and put on notice. The effect was to cite them as potential targets and to deliver the message that they were unworthy of the contemporary mores that favor equality and respect between the sexes. Dr. Traditional's stance has elements of "gender harassment" (ES: 1.12) that need not involve direct references to sexuality. *Gender harassment* is defined as comments or behavior directed at one sex but not the other (Fuller, 1979). Not all gender-related behavior can be reasonably defined as harassing, but it does result when the behavior causes discomfort or humiliation (e.g., referring to all men as "stud muffins") or is used as a means of power containment (e.g., only inviting male students to collaborate on research projects). To those who would declare that Dr. Traditional is simply of an earlier generation and therefore quite harmless, we would ask: "If a woman asked Dr. Traditional to write a letter of recommendation, how powerful do you think it would be?" "Would a female student even feel comfortable asking Dr. Traditional for a letter" "Do you think Traditional would nominate a woman for an outstanding student award?"

Case 13-47: When Zena Freeman asked Macho Mann, Ph.D., for assistance with problems she was having understanding certain concepts in her industrial psychology class, he commented that women did not belong in the course because they were not suited to the field. He refused to respond to her specific questions. Instead, he continued to refer to the general unsuitability of women for work in industrial psychology and cited her difficulties in comprehension as evidence.

Case 13-48: Marsha Torpid experienced difficulty adapting to the new computer technology in the psychology clinic where she worked as the receptionist. The director, Roger Rough, Psy.D., was irritated by her errors and berated her in front of others with such comments as, "Why are all women so moronic when it comes to machines?" and "You act like the damn thing is about to attack you." Ms. Torpid found such comments so intimidating they interfered with her progress in mastering the technology. When Dr. Rough gave her an unsatisfactory performance evaluation, she complained that his harassment was responsible for blocking her potential.

Case 13-49: Flora Bloom complained that Wag Rogue, Ph.D., made jokes at her expense during class. She alleged that he would tease her about such things as her colorful clothing, black finger-nail polish, close-cropped hair, and oversize purse. Professor Rogue was surprised by her formal complaint. He thought her customary shy, giggling responses were indications that she enjoyed his "gentle chiding."

None of the above examples involved direct sexual references, but the effect was to keep the women in a subordinate position through exclusion or ridicule. In all cases, the women's work or academic experiences were made uncomfortable for them, which in turn had implications for their ability to transact their primary roles as employees or students.

Although rarely discussed as such, sexual harassment can occur in psychotherapy, and its expression often has an interface with competency issues.

Case 13-50: Sheldon Blurt, Ph.D., had met with Mr. and Mrs. Wobble for several sessions of marital therapy. Increasingly frustrated by what he regarded as an alternating pattern of seductive and aversive behavior by Mrs. Wobble toward her spouse, Dr. Blurt shouted, during a joint session, "Well aren't you the cock-teasing bitch of the year!"

Psychotherapists must often respond to what they are witnessing on the spot, which puts them at some risk of crossing over a line. Sarcasm and hostility should be avoided because hurtful comments do not help clients, even if such comments might be well deserved under a different set of relationship circumstances.

Fighting Back

The difficulties with definitions, perceptions, and determination of harm and the escalation in sexual harassment complaints are also accompanied by an increase in vigorous defenses in attempts to fight back.

Case 13-51: A professor is alleged to have stated, "All a woman has to do is to lay on her back and spread her legs, and the government rewards her." Two female students complained. Although the professor contended that it was a student who made the remark, he fought back on the principle that such suits stifle a professor's rights to discuss views openly in class, including taking an unpopular stand.

This actual case questions whether the concept of hostile work environment translates to academic settings, the traditional bastion of free speech and open exchange of ideas (Leatherman, 1994). The university recommended that the professor be suspended for a month without pay, seek sensitivity training, and issue an apology to the students. The professor is taking his university to court.

Even attempting to be clever with analogies can result in sexual harassment charges. A graduate assistant, while teaching students in a human sexuality class how to put on condoms, quipped, "Like basketball players, men dribble before they shoot." The complainant argued that, by "objectifying the penis," the graduate assistant had created a hostile learning environment (Leatherman, 1994).

Professional Sensitivity to Gender-Related Biases

The next case illustrates how important it is for people to maintain an ethical sensitivity to professional interactions in the workplace, regardless of how one defines and interprets sexual harassment.

Case 13-52: A slightly nervous Lina Luckout, Ph.D., was called into the executive board meeting of a large mental health organization to present her primary prevention program idea for consideration. Jerome Foreclose, Ph.D., a man Luckout had met on several occasions, was in charge of the meeting. When she entered the room, Foreclose exclaimed, "Hi there, sweet thing. Whatcha got for us today?" Dr. Luckout had prepared a very formal presentation and was rattled by the tone of the introduction. She stumbled often, and her bid to implement the program was denied.

There is no way to prove whether a more professionally respectful greeting might have altered the way Luckout was perceived or the outcome of Luckout's presentation. Because the incident involved the use of a fleeting "term of endearment," it would not meet any legal definition of sexual harassment. Because of the "severe and pervasive" criteria, even a more offensive single incident would rarely qualify (Perry, 1993). But, first impressions count, and in the board's initial perception, Dr. Luckout was probably not seen as a mature professional. In addition, being thrown off stride by the informality of Dr. Foreclose's comment probably made it difficult for her to overcome that impression.

The APA code (1992) protects all persons who have initiated a sexual harassment charge or who are in the process of defending themselves against one by prohibiting other psychologists from participating in any action that would deny the complainants or respondents academic admittance, employment, tenure, or promotion. Perhaps a good rule of thumb in these confusing times is to think twice about whether you would make the same statement or engage in the same behavior if the intended recipient were your supervisor or superior. If you hesitate for even an instant, then it is best to refrain (DeAngelis, 1991).

RISKY SITUATIONS

The potential for uncollegiality is likely to be increased when such factors as competitiveness, limited resources, few opportunities for advancement, low morale, incompetent or ambiguous management styles, real or perceived inequities, or envy pervade the professional work setting. Disputes are especially likely if the perception of bias appears to be operating in any relevant decision-making process.

Failure to live up to obligations made to one's peers is also a potential risk for later complaints of an ethical nature. Unpleasant or inadequate working conditions, such as an intolerable noise level and lack of privacy, excessive case or teaching loads, and even uncomfortable or shabby furnishings, can also contribute to the kind of irritability that propagates squabbles. Unfortunately, these unstable conditions exist in many academic and other institutions and agencies where psychologists are employed.

Evaluating Others

Among the more likely situations that spawn conflict are those that involve performance or credential evaluations. The person being assessed is usually under considerable personal stress. The evaluator's failure to recognize and respond sensitively to this presents a serious hazard. Such situations include doctoral examinations, tenure decisions, supervisory sessions, grievance hearings, annual salary reviews, or even the receipt of an exam or term paper grade.

Case 13-53: Sabrina LeBlanc dropped out of Professor Blunt's class late in the semester, even though this would mean an automatic grade of "F" on her record. She told friends her reason. Dr. Blunt had circled a large section of her assignment in bright red and scrawled "Awful Writing!!!" in the margin. She said, "I was so disgraced that I could not go back to face him."

It is unlikely that Professor Blunt expected such a reaction to what, for him, was probably experienced as a minor, matter-of-fact evaluation scribbled during a late-night session of reading papers. However, people with evaluative power must constantly remember that others view them quite differently from how they see themselves. Regardless of Blunt's lack of intent to evoke such an extreme reaction, all negative evaluations must maintain professional decorum.

Case 13-54: Urlee Abused revealed her childhood struggles with alcoholic parents to her clinical supervisor, Dee Cipher, Ph.D. Thereafter, every time Urlee reported difficulties with a client or the program, Dr. Cipher told Urlee that her current concerns and shortcomings were linked to her childhood trauma.

Dr. Cipher's constant, and probably inappropriate, psychodynamic interpretations undermined the supervisee's confidence and caused Urlee to distance herself from her supervisor. The relationship was contaminated and stunted by Dr. Cipher's lack of sensitivity to Urlee's disclosures.

Poor Communication

Another type of high risk situation occurs when the parties fail to adequately communicate their expectations for role performance. The absence of specific outcome goals and timely feedback frequently characterize these situations. One or both parties will often assume, erroneously, that the other's needs and goals are fully congruent with their own.

Case 13-55: George Faraway, Ph.D., hired Timothy Toil, Ph.D., a recent graduate of his department, to conduct a research project in rural Ecuador over a 12-month period. Communications between the small towns where the data were being collected and the university were difficult. Dr. Faraway visited Ecuador once shortly after Dr. Toil had arrived, and Faraway seemed satisfied with the progress of the project. Near the end of the project, an earthquake damaged some equipment, and Toil became ill for 2 weeks. He returned to the United States without having completed the data collection. Faraway was angry that the work was not completed and refused to pay Toil until he returned to finish data collection. Toil filed an ethics complaint.

Here, a difficult work environment was complicated by poor communication and a misunderstanding of roles and responsibilities. Toil was prepared to do the best he could under the circumstances for 12 months. Faraway expected a completed project, although he was not in regular contact with Toil and was not able to monitor the complex program from his remote university office. When distance and nature intervened, the friendly agreement broke down.

Case 13-56: Bertram Bizzy, Ph.D., was the clinical supervisor for Suzie Slipper, a graduate student placed at Bizzy's home agency 2 days a week for practicum training. Bizzy juggled a thriving multioffice practice that involved frequent out-of-town consultations. Ms. Slipper appeared to be very independent and often believed she was functioning "just fine" without supervision. One month, Bizzy had to cancel one supervision hour because of professional travel and a second hour when he was out with the flu. Then, Ms. Slipper missed supervision the third week to attend a funeral. Slipper's schedule seemed to preclude "make-up" sessions, which was just as well for the preoccupied Dr. Bizzy. When they finally met after a hiatus of nearly 4 weeks, Dr. Bizzy discovered that Ms. Slipper had made some potentially serious errors in managing a case. He submitted a highly unflattering entry into her evaluation record.

Dr. Bizzy bears the brunt of the responsibility (ES: 1.22). Ms. Slipper was unaware of important agency policies that would have been made known with adequate supervisory input. Neophyte professionals are often more self-confident than is actually warranted. Close supervision mitigates against this.

Conflicts Without a Resolution Mechanism

Still another type of high-risk situation is the dispute for which no format for resolution exists. That is, no mechanism was created in advance to process a complaint or resolve a dispute.

Case 13-57: William Bicker, Ed.D., Frank Fracas, Psy.D., and Mildred Decibel, Ph.D., worked together in a group practice arrangement. They shared the cost of office space, utilities, and a receptionist's salary. As time went on, it became clear that each engaged in behavior that annoyed the other two. Dr. Fracas demanded that he should pay less because he used fewer utilities and little receptionist time. Dr. Bicker complained about everything that seemed out of place, such as leaving a dirty coffee cup in the sink. Mildred Decibel played her office radio so loudly that it could be heard throughout the complex, and efforts to tone her radio down resulted in only temporary compliance.

How can three highly educated individuals get themselves into such a predicament? They thought of themselves as very good friends, so contractual contingencies for handling disputes were never drafted. Each is a strong-willed individual, and now they are threatening each other

with ethics charges and legal suits. This sort of problem happens frequently enough for us to suggest that any business arrangement among colleagues should include formal contracts—a "professional prenuptial agreement," if you will—that deals with both operational contingencies and details of dispute resolution (e.g., agreement to use binding arbitration). Even if all parties have been close friends for years, sufficient informal evidence reveals the wisdom of planning for untoward future developments.

RISKY INDIVIDUALS

The troublesome client is discussed in chapter 4 as a special problem. Ideas for confronting colleagues who may have committed an ethical infraction are presented in chapter 1. Here, we focus on the student, employee, or colleague whose behavior or interpersonal relations are troublesome, though not necessarily in violation of specific ethical standards. By recognizing and dealing with hazardous individuals, particularly as they may have an interface with risky situations, ethical problems can often be avoided. To some extent, these issues are touched on in chapter 3 in the context of the troubled colleague, and several of the case examples cited above in this chapter also illustrate the problems with colleagues who are difficult.

Types of Risky Individuals

There are people who are worrisome or hard to get along with simply by virtue of being who they are. Such people, however, may be perfectly happy with themselves, which makes conflict resolution especially difficult. Individuals who are emotionally labile or unstable certainly present some risk. Perhaps arrogance, narcissism, or a critical personality style also contribute to such problems. We could create a long list of unwholesome personality traits—procrastination, impulsivity, hostility, and so on—but, the point is clear. Given the basics of human nature, every risky situation often includes one or more risky individuals.

Case 13-58: Bernice Dweezel, Ph.D., is a distinguished psychologist whose research is world renowned. Unfortunately, she is also rude, egotistical, and demanding. Students who are willing to endure criticism and pontification often benefit from working with her, but not everyone can tolerate her behavior. The faculty respects her scholarly work and appreciates the way her professional reputation enhances the status of their department, although few would choose to socialize with her.

Dr. Dweezel may be an obnoxious individual by many standards and may border on behaving unethically when she is inconsiderate to her students and colleagues. Unfortunately, she may have little insight into the nature of this problem and no motivation to attempt to change her personal style. In any event, an ethics complaint would be an unlikely means of evoking a positive change given her ingrained characterological attributes. The more serious danger will occur if or when Dr. Dweezel encounters a hostile student or colleague more inclined to act out than back off. One might caution others about the hazards of working with her or suggest avoiding her entirely. Others might attempt some collegial consultation, with gentle references to a need for personal change. Regrettably, however, there will always be people like Dr. Dweezel in the world, and ethics codes and committees are of little help in dealing with them.

Dealing with the Difficult Associate

Rules and procedures are the most powerful tools available to deal with the difficult associate in a risky situation. Having an explicit set of guidelines and standards can provide a giant step toward avoiding conflict and reducing stress for all concerned. The use of formal procedures not only enhances communication, but also cools passions by drawing out a decision in a deliberate fashion (Clark, 1974). Due process provides emotional insulation, as well as procedural safeguards.

While one cannot restructure personality to suit circumstances, it is possible to minimize risk in a volatile situation by imposing structure and enhancing communication. Evaluations, for example, should always be presented thoughtfully and emphatically, with the evaluator listening, as well as informing. At the same time, it is often advisable to offer the same material in writing because oral communications may be forgotten or tempered by intervening variables.

These suggestions may seem contrary to the concept of resolving disputes informally by mutual agreement. Indeed, informal mechanisms are preferable; however, if communication is already complicated or difficult, a more formal approach may be needed. The irony is that the ethics complaints that result from such circumstances are rarely ethics matters.

When the difficult associate is a superior or supervisor rather than a peer or subordinate, similar fundamental principles apply in terms of the ideal course of action. Unfortunately, in many situations management will tend to support itself without a full examination of the issues. Raising an objection, however valid, may be regarded as "rocking the boat" or exhibiting disloyalty. Formal written grievance procedures can be helpful, if they exist; however, one must be sensitive to the potential hazards. Less powerful colleagues in an organizational work setting are advised to scout out difficult associates in advance and chart their courses accordingly. If they are snared into a confrontation, they may seek alliances with more powerful colleagues known for their willingness to take a moral stand.

In conclusion, psychologists are just as human as any other group of people, and ethics complaints cannot serve as a means to overhaul irritable personalities, reform the prejudiced, or enforce social agreements between consenting adult colleagues. Still, it behooves us to tolerate our colleagues with as much professionalism as can be mustered.

SUMMARY GUIDELINES

1. Colleagues should always do their best to cooperate with other professionals when the best interests of clients or students are at stake.

2. Although the ultimate choice of where to seek any service or advice belongs to the client, services should not be delivered in

a manner that causes confusion or conflicts with a client's preexisting or ongoing relationships with other professionals.

3. A display of courtesy while relating to other professionals is usually the most appropriate demeanor, even when one has reason to be annoyed with them. In those instances when professional disagreements require a candid airing, the forum should be an appropriate one, and the goal should be focused on upholding professional integrity rather than on personal humiliation or inflicting professional damage on a colleague's reputation. Displays of personal animosity should be kept away from the professional arena.

4. Colleagues should try to resolve disputes informally whenever possible and appropriate and should attempt to prevent disputes by clarifying mutual expectations at the outset of any collaborative arrangement.

5. Supervisees, employees, and students are at an inherent disadvantage in any disagreement with their instructors, supervisors, and employers, respectively. This fact should be recognized with respect to the obligation to treat these individuals with courtesy, fairness, and dignity.

6. A psychologist should exercise caution and diligence in training and monitoring the behavior of employees and supervisees to ensure their conformity with ethical practice.

7. When preparing letters of reference, it is wise to be honest and direct, focusing on behavioral indicators and objective evidence rather than opinion and innuendo. The sort of letter one can write in good conscience should also be discussed in advance with the candidate.

8. Psychologists must familiarize themselves with both subtle and more obvious forms of sexual and gender harassment and avoid engaging in such behaviors. In addition, they should make efforts to educate colleagues regarding the inappropriateness of such behavior when they observe it.

9. When placed in a decision-making role with respect to a supervisee, colleague, or student (e.g., regarding grades, promotion, or tenure), psychologists should recognize the stress on these individuals and afford appropriate consideration and due process.

10. In dealing with an especially difficult or troubling student, employee, or colleague, it is generally best to use standard rules and procedures, while attempting to avoid being caught up in an angry emotional response.

References

Allen, G. J., Szollos, S. J., & Williams, B. E. (1986). Doctoral students' comparative evaluations of best and worst psychotherapy supervision. *Professional Psychology: Research and Practice, 17*, 91–99.

Alonzo, A. (1985). *The quiet profession: Supervisors of psychotherapy.* New York: Macmillan.

American Psychological Association. (1981). Ethical principles of psychologists. *American Psychologist, 36*, 633–638.

American Psychological Association. (1992). Ethical principles of psychologists and code of conduct. *American Psychologist, 47*, 1597–1611.

Binder, R. L. (1992). Sexual harassment: Issues for forensic psychiatrists. *Bulletin of the Academy of Psychiatry Law, 20*, 409–418.

Bosk, C. L. (1979). *Forgive and remember.* Chicago: University of Chicago Press.

Branscum, D. (1995, May). Cyberspace lawsuits. *MacWorld*, 149–150.

Civil Rigths Act of 1964. Title VII, 42 U.S.C. § 2000e-2(a) (1982).

Clark, R. D. (1974). Tenure and the moderation of conflict. In R. H. Peairs (Ed.), *Avoiding conflict in faculty personnel practices* (pp. 17–40). San Francisco: Jossey-Bass.

DeAngelis, T. (1991, December). Sexual harassment common, complex. *APA Monitor*, 29–30.

Equal Employment Opportunity Commission. (1980). Guidelines and discrimination because of sex (Sec. 1604.11). *Federal Register, 45*, 74676–74677.

Equal Employment Opportunity Commission. (1980). Sex discrimination harassment. *Federal Register, 45*, 25024–25025.

Feldman-Schorrig, S. P., & McDonald, J. J. (1992). The role of forensic psychiatry in the defense of sexual harassment cases. *Journal of Psychology and the Law, 20,* 5–33.

Fuller, M. M. (1979). *Sexual harassment—how to recognize and deal with it.* Annapolis, MD: Eastport Litho.

Glaser, R. D., & Thorpe, J. S. (1986). Unethical intimacy: A survey of sexual contact and advances between psychology educators and female graduate students. *American Psychologist, 41,* 43–51.

Goodyear, R. K., Crego, C. A., & Johnston, M. W. (1992). Ethical issues in the supervision of students research: A study of critical incidents. *Professional Psychology: Research and Practice, 23,* 203–210.

Hamilton, J. A., Alagna, S. W., King, L. S., & Lloyd, C. (1987). The emotional consequences of gender-based abuse in the workplace: New counseling programs for sex discrimination. *Women and Therapy, 5,* 155–182.

Hardin, K. N., Craddick, R., & Ellis, J. B. (1991). Letters of recommendation: Perspectives, recommendations, and ethics. *Professional Psychology: Research and Practice, 22,* 389–392.

Harrar, W. R., VandeCreek, L., & Knapp, S. (1990). Ethical and legal aspects of clinical supervision. *Professional Psychology: Research and Practice, 21,* 37–41.

Jacobs, C. (1991). Violations of the supervisory relationship: An ethical and educational blind spot. *Social Work, 36,* 130–135.

Keith-Spiegel, P. (1991). *The complete guide to graduate school admission.* Hillsdale, NJ: Erlbaum.

Koen, C. M. (1989). Sexual harassment: Criteria for defining hostile environment. *Employee Responsibilities and Rights Journal, 2,* 289–301.

Koocher, G. P., Sobel, S. B., & Hare-Mustin, R. T. (1982). Making of the president 1982: On campaigning for office in a learned society. *Clinical Psychologist, 35,* 1–9.

Kurpius, D., Gibson, G., Lewis, J., & Corbet, M. (1991). Ethical issues in supervising counseling practitioners. *Counselor Education and Supervision, 31,* 48–57.

Leatherman, C. (1994, March 16). Fighting back. *Chronicle of Higher Education,* A17–A18.

Mebane, D. L. (1983, April). *Ethical issues in writing recommendation letters.* Paper presented at the annual meeting of the Western Psychological Association, San Francisco.

Meritor Savings Bank, FSB v. Vinson et al., 477 U.S. 57 (1986).

Miller, R. K., & Van Rybroek, G. J. (1988). Internship letters of recommendation: Where are the other 90%? *Professional Psychology: Research and Practice, 19,* 115–117.

Minnes, P. M. (1987). Ethical issues in supervision. *Canadian Psychology, 28,* 285–290.

Nelson, G. L. (1978). Psychotherapy supervision from the trainee's point of view: A survey of preferences. *Professional Psychology: Research and Practice, 9,* 539–550.

Perry, N. W. (1993). Sexual harassment on campus: Are your actions actionable? *Journal of College Student Development, 34,* 406–410.

Pope, K. S., Levenson, H., & Schover, L. R. (1979). Sexual intimacy in psychology training: Results and implications of a national survey. *American Psychologist, 42,* 993–689.

Pope, K. S., & Vasquez, M. J. T. (1991). *Ethics in psychotherapy and counseling.* San Francisco: Jossey-Bass.

Pope, K. S., & Vetter, V. A. (1991). Prior therapist-patient sexual involvement among patients seen by psychologists. *Psychotherapy, 28,* 429–438.

Purdy, J. E., Reinehr, R. C., & Swartz, J. D. (1989). Graduate admissions criteria of leading psychology departments. *American Psychologist, 44,* 960–961.

Reilly, M. E., Lott, B., & Gallogly, S. M. (1986). Sexual harassment of university students. *Sex Roles, 15,* 333–358.

Riger, S. (1991). Gender dilemmas in sexual harassment: Policies and procedures. *American Psychologist, 46,* 497–505.

Rubin, L. J., & Borgers, S. B. (1990). Sexual harassment in universities during the 1980s. *Sex Roles, 23,* 397–411.

Scofield, M. E., & Scofield, B. J. (1978). Ethical concerns in clinical practice supervision. *Journal of Applied Rehabilitation Counseling, 9,* 27–29.

Sherry, P. (1991). Ethical issues in the conduct of supervision. *Counseling Psychologist, 19,* 566–584.

Siskind, G. (1966). Mine eyes have seen a host of angels. *American Psychologist, 21,* 804–806.

Sonne, J. L., & Pope, K. S. (1991). Treating victims of therapist-patient sexual involvement. *Psychotherapy, 28,* 174–187.

Terpstra, D. E., & Cook, S. E. (1985). Complainant

characteristics and reported behaviors and consequences associated with formal sexual harassment charges. *Personnel Psychology*, 38, 559–574.

Thacker, R. A., & Gohmann, S. A. (1993). Male/female differences in perceptions and effects of hostile environment sexual harassment: "reasonable" assumptions? *Public Personnel Management*, 22, 461–472.

Vasquez, M. J. T. (1992). Psychologist as clinical supervisor: Promoting ethical practice. *Professional Psychology: Research and Practice*, 23, 196–202.

Whiston, S. C., & Emerson, S. (1989). Ethical implications for supervisors in counseling of trainees. *Counselor Education and Supervision*, 28, 318–325.

14

Ethical Dilemmas in Specific Work Settings
Juggling Porcupines

Do the right thing.

Spike Lee

The impact of ethical pressures within the workplace may produce responses that range from subtle erosion of professional values to overwhelming emotional distress. Some settings in which psychologists work seem especially likely to evoke ethical quandaries. Examples include the military, government agencies, schools, medical centers, prisons, and independent practice. In each of these workplaces, psychologists may be expected to serve clients with specialized needs under unique constraints. At times, client needs may actually be incongruent with other demands of the agency or institution, automatically placing the psychologist in an ethical predicament. Independent practice also represents a unique type of work setting with its own special pressures, as do academic and psychological research laboratories (although these last two categories are addressed in chapters 16 and 17).

In categorizing the sorts of difficulties that are linked to specialized work settings, there are three distinct areas of focus. First are the nature and demands of the agency, organization, or special context within which psychologists' services are rendered. Second are issues related to the particular nature of the clients and their problems. Third are the special skills or competencies needed by the psychologists who wish to work with these clients. It is important to clarify and conceptualize each of these.

BASIC CONSIDERATIONS

Who Is the Client?

A major monograph with the title, "Who Is the Client?" (Monahan, 1980) grew out of the work of the American Psychological Association's (APA's) Task Force on the Role of Psychology in the Criminal Justice System. Despite the "criminal justice" focus, the edited collection of papers has important an generic value for helping psychologists recognize the complex nature of many different types of client relationships. In particular, the psychologist must always be mindful of who the client is and be prepared to define carefully client relationships with respect to matters of confidentiality, responsibility, and other critical ethical issues.

Many employment situations involve serving varying categories of clients and distinct client need hierarchies. It is critical that the psychologist carefully think through and conceptualize these situations because the needs of the different components may often compete or be mutually exclusive. For example, psychologists employed by a government agency (e.g., the U.S. Justice Department, Bureau of Prisons) could provide services to an individual person (e.g., an inmate at a federal correctional center). In such circumstances, it may be argued that the psychologist owes professional duties to the individual (i.e., inmate), the employing agency (i.e., the Bureau of Prisons), and to society as a whole (i.e., the citizens, who may be victims of crime), although the specific details and clarity of the lines of obligation will obviously have great potential variability. In such situations, the psychologist's obligations are to clarify the nature of the ethical duties due each party; to inform all concerned about the ethical constraints, if any; and to take whatever actions are necessary to ensure appropriate respect for the client(s).

What Skills Are Needed?

The issue of competence assessment and recognition of limitations by psychologists is addressed in chapter 3, along with the difficulties inherent in evaluating competence, especially with respect to new or emerging areas of practice. In this chapter, we stress how important it is to recognize a more subtle issue in assessing one's skills: the ability to perform with appropriate sensitivity and expertise in unique contexts. That is, one may be highly competent at psychodiagnostic assessment and psychotherapy in general practice, but these talents will not necessarily transfer directly to performing treatment in a prison or conducting psychological assessments to aid in the selection of a corporate executive.

The transfer or generalizability of training across situations or populations is highly variable, and the psychologist who fails to recognize and compensate for this fact may encounter serious ethical problems. There are times when

enthusiasm, necessity, or poor judgment may propel a psychologist into a new professional arena, and, without a clear and thoughtful assessment of the situational demands, the risk of an ethical violation is potentiated substantially. Caution is the primary means of avoiding these sorts of problems, but the discussion that follows highlights some of the more subtle aspects of specialized skills needed at certain work sites.

Organizational Demands

Most individual psychologists are accountable for upholding the *Ethical Principles of Psychologists and Code of Conduct* (APA, 1992). Psychologists who are members of the APA, or a state psychological association or who are licensed can be held to the standards of the ethics code. However, nonmember, unlicensed psychologists and organizations are not accountable in the same manner. There are times when a psychologist-employee may be asked or told to behave in an ethically inappropriate manner as a function of the employing organization's needs. Monahan and his colleagues (1980) provide a cogent example by citing the case of a client of a psychologist in independent practice who reveals racist attitudes or behavior in the course of treatment. These may or may not be relevant to the treatment program, but the issue is clearly a confidential matter between client and therapist. What if a psychologist is providing consultation to a law enforcement agency and, in the course of interviewing various employees, discovers a pattern of racist organizational policies or discrimination? The psychologist might be both repulsed and outraged, but is simultaneously ethically obligated to keep that finding confidential from the general public. It would, however, be unethical for the psychologist to cooperate in setting up, maintaining, or implementing such policies. Whistle-blowing behavior may be unethical in such organizational consulting roles. In such situations, the psychologist must balance an obligation to protect the individual and organizational client's confidentiality with the rights of the public or other parties not privy to the inner workings of the agency.

What if the psychologist in the situation described above chose to inform the agency's employer (e.g., the legislative or executive body supervising the agency) about the racist policies? What if the psychologist took the story to the press? As discussed in chapter 6, limited breaches of confidentiality are permissible to the extent needed to protect intended victims from clear and imminent danger. However, racist behavior does not usually meet the imminent danger test. Certainly, there are circumstances when "whistle-blowing" behavior is appropriate ethical behavior, although the matter is not a simple one to sort out. As Monahan and his colleagues note:

> We are not suggesting that psychologists should avoid serving in imperfect organizations, only that the perennial debate concerning whether it is better to work from inside to achieve gradual change or to leave the organization and apply pressure from the outside for reform . . . is common to all organizational structures. (Monahan, 1980, p. 3)

The point to remember is that what is ethically appropriate for a psychologist's work with an individual client may not be ideally suited to the best interests of client organizations or employing agencies, and vice versa. The differentiation of obligations, and the linkage of these obligations to broader issues of human welfare, are important ethical questions that require thoughtful analysis, yet often lack clear answers.

SAMPLE SETTINGS

Government Employment

The government employs psychologists on many levels and in all branches. Psychologists serve at the municipal, state, and federal levels and have roles in the legislative, judicial, and executive branches. Below, we specifically discuss some subsets of governmental agencies (i.e., the military, schools, community agencies, and the criminal justice system) in detail. First, however, it is worth considering government service as a whole. Working for the government involves upholding an important degree of public trust while at the same time being subject to a high degree of political pressure. Functioning as a public servant–psychologist can be both rewarding and frustrating (e.g., Shakow, 1968), especially at the level of integrating professional judgment with policy making (Boling & Dempsey, 1981).

Case 14-1: Sam Uncle, Ph.D., a psychologist working as a clinician at a federally operated hospital, was instructed to provide access to case records in a manner that seemed contrary to the APA ethics code. He expressed his reservations to his nonpsychologist supervisor, who replied, "Those ethical principles do not apply to federal employees at this facility."

Case 14-2: A government agency planned to administer hallucinogenic drugs to unwitting individuals and observe the resulting behavioral changes. Two psychologists were recruited to participate in the project by a clandestine government agency, and they cooperated in the execution of the project.

Case 14-3: A municipal government hired Maxine Datum, Ed.D., to explore the question of whether racist attitudes among certain officials influenced hiring practices. Datum's study and analysis of the personnel system confirmed the presence of active racial discrimination. The officials ordered Dr. Datum to keep these findings confidential and after several months had done nothing to alter the illegal personnel practices.

These three situations illustrate the range and complexity of issues that may occur in government service. In the first case, Dr. Uncle was informed that the agency employees are not bound by the APA ethics code (1992). That is not true (EP: 8.03). All psychologists who pledge to uphold the "Ethical Principles and Code of Conduct" when they join the American Psychological Association or an affiliated state psychological association or seek state licensing are bound by the code in all contexts of their work as psychologists (ES: Introduction). The supervisor in this particular case was actually misinterpreting federal policy; however, situations may arise in which employers will demand that their psychologist-employees behave contrary to the dictates of ethical standards. Each psychologist must consider how best to handle individual situations as they occur, but the basic principles are not waived for any employer, government or otherwise.

In the case of the covert administration of hallucinogenic drugs to uninformed individuals who had not consented to participate in an experiment of this sort, the psychologists were clearly guilty of unethical complicity. The actual events took place in the 1960s and were addressed in complaints filed in the 1970s. The psychologists' assertions that national security was at issue and that they had not personally administered the drugs were not relevant to the ethics panel that investigated the case. By actively participating in the project, the psychologists had condoned serious ethical misconduct. The ethics committee took no action, however, because the time limit for filing complaints had long since passed.

The case of the municipal personnel research adds a new wrinkle to the role of the psychologist. Presumably, the city in question was the client, and the same government officials who hired Dr. Datum have a right to control the data collected on their behalf, much as an individual would have a right of confidentiality. One could argue that the public interest would best be served by making the data public, but would that produce the socially desirable change? Suppose the municipal officials tell Datum that they will use the information to "bring about appropriate change in our own way." Does Datum have a right or a duty to challenge this? Can one draw an analogy to the racist client in therapy, who listens to the therapist interpret the racist behavior but has no desire to change current attitudes? These questions are not easily answered, but they lead to an important issue in understanding appropriate ethical behavior. The psychologist must assume the burden of articulating the nature and expectations of his or her professional role. When the psychologist works for a government agency, it is no less important to explore these issues to assess the degrees of freedom and ethical comfort one may expect to enjoy in the job.

Next, we explore specific ethical issues related to particular components of government: the military, school systems, criminal justice set-tings, and community agencies. We then discuss special considerations that arise in psychologists' work in business and industry, medical institutions, independent practice, and pastoral counseling contexts.

The Armed Services

Given that psychologists are supposed to be dedicated to advancing the cause of human welfare, should they work for the military, the Central Intelligence Agency, or similar governmental units? The question is not as simplistic as it might seem. Military and intelligence services are certainly necessary for national security, and the behavioral sciences have much to contribute to any other complex human organization (Allen, Chatelier, Clark, & Sorenson, 1982). At the same time, many psychologists might feel concern about the contribution of psychology to military activities.

A paper on military psychology published during the Viet Nam era (Crawford, 1970) evoked a stinging response, which claimed that, "The chief goal of military psychology is the transformation of human beings into more efficient murder machines" (Saks, 1970, p. 876). This in turn brought forth a series of rebuttals (Kelley, 1971; Leuba, 1971) and considerable acrimony. While that debate may have been more a function of the political ethos of the times than of ethics issues, some would express similar concerns today on both sides of the issue.

For purposes of this chapter, we delineate two distinct aspects of military psychology. One is the work of the civilian employee or military personnel in research, and the other is the role of military personnel in the delivery of psychological services. Much of the ethical decision making is precisely analogous to that which goes into the work of the research or industrial-organizational psychologist or the clinician in general, but there are special subtleties and matters of relative emphasis that necessitate critical ethical review.

Allen et al. (1982) described a variety of roles psychologists perform for the military in the nonclinical realm. These can be described as personnel functions (e.g., selection, assessment, classification, and retention of military personnel), training (e.g., leadership development, skill acquisition, teaching, and effectiveness enhancement), human performance research (e.g., human factors engineering, job design, information process, and decision-making studies), development of specialized training (e.g., simulators and assessment centers), and health-related research (e.g., sleep deprivation, fatigue, and physical fitness studies). While the goal of such research may be to enhance the ability to destroy an enemy before being destroyed, any moral decision about whether to participate in such programs is chiefly a matter of personal conscience. The constraints on such research or training programs are essentially the same as those in nonmilitary settings (i.e., informed consent of participants, appropriate respect for the rights of the individual, etc.). It is evident that much of the research conducted on behalf of the military will have beneficial civilian applications, such as flight simulators designed for the military can also be adapted to train civilian pilots or physical fitness research done for the military may be generalized for the public at large.

When a military psychologist is functioning as a provider of clinical or counseling services, some special ethical dilemmas do arise from time to time, as illustrated in the following situations.

Case 14-4: Captain Henry B. Trayed filed a complaint with an ethics committee against a military psychologist at his base hospital. The psychologist had informed Captain Trayed's superiors of his extreme depression and other psychopathological symptoms; this resulted in considerable career sanctions. Captain Trayed stated that the psychologist had indicated that information received in the context of treatment would be held in confidence. The psychologist responded to the committee's inquiry by noting that Captain Trayed knew the base hospital treatment setting operated different from those "on the outside."

It is not unethical to disclose confidential information without an individual's consent when the law demands it. However, psychologists must inform their clients of the limits of confidentiality when the professional relation-

ship begins. The obligation to provide such information applies in both military and civilian settings. Federal law allows officials of the U.S. Department of Defense (DoD) access to service members' health care records on a need to know basis; however, these circumstances are vaguely defined (Sleek, 1995). Active duty military psychologists occupy multiple roles as therapist-clinicians and commissioned military officers. Frequently, simultaneous allegiance to professional ethics and military regulations is impossible. Ongoing collaboration between the APA and the DoD has focused on establishing appropriate criteria to manage the resulting difficulties (Johnson, 1995).

Case 14-5: Major Freddy Flakey, a skilled fighter pilot, appeared tense and interpersonally erratic in ways that his squadron commander could not precisely grasp. Flakey refused attempts to discuss these issues, so the commanding officer ordered him to the base hospital for an outpatient evaluation. After Major Flakey had met with a psychologist for several sessions, the commander went to the hospital and confiscated the patient's file for review without consulting the psychologist.

Case 14-6: Mary Militia, Ph.D., serving as a commissioned officer in a branch of the U.S. military, was ordered to report to her superiors any military personnel seeking services at the base hospitals whom she considered to be at risk for decompensation or who were engaging in homosexual activities.

Confidentiality issues are a key source of concern in mental health service delivery to military personnel by military personnel. On the one hand, individuals in sensitive defense-related positions could be especially dangerous when attempting to perform their duties in emotionally troubled states. At the same time, such individuals ought to have the same rights to privacy and confidentiality so important to effective general psychotherapeutic care. One way to deal with the issue, as noted above, is to make certain that clients are informed from the outset of the professional relationship of all limitations placed on their confidentiality.

The military client can be advised in the first session that certain types of problems (e.g., those related to fitness for duty) must be reported. An individual with concerns about privacy might then have the option to seek treatment off base or from civilian personnel, if appropriate. Obviously, such referral is not possible on a ship or in a battle zone. In addition, military personnel can be ordered to submit to evaluation or treatment against their personal wishes. Although it is easy to understand the concerns of Major Flakey's commander, confiscation of the records was inappropriate. The content of the records may not specifically address issues of concern (e.g., fitness for duty), which could be more specifically and comprehensively addressed by the psychologist who assessed and treated Major Flakey. Having given proper warning to Major Flakey, the psychologist can reasonably release information in accord with military regulations.

The matter of whether sexual preference has any bearing on job performance in the military or elsewhere has been the subject of considerable litigation that led to a "Don't ask, don't tell" policy by executive order of President Clinton. A psychologist may find him- or herself in the position of having to help enforce such criteria, while having personal reservations about their validity. The options are essentially two-fold. The psychologist may decide not to participate in the system at all and seek employment elsewhere or may seek to work for change in the system from within. In any case, once again, the client is entitled to advance warning that certain types of disclosures may have specific consequences.

The APA Ethics Committee (1993) issued a special policy statement in regard to military psychologists and confidentiality; it details the applicable aspects of the APA ethics code and recognizes that DoD rules that apparently run counter to ethical principles can often be addressed appropriately within the context of the APA code (EP: 8.03). The key issues are preventive: discussing potential problem areas proactively with the base commander when first arriving on post and providing clients with appropriate warnings as to confidentiality limitations (EP: 5.01b). There may still be times when specific situations force a psychologist to question the appropriateness of certain military rules. In such circumstances, the psychologist has an

affirmative duty to address the conflict, not blindly follow the regulation without first exploring appropriate alternatives. This approach would also be appropriate in any institutional setting, not just the military.

The current decade has seen increased attention to the ethical problems of psychologists in the military. Johnson (1995; Johnson & Wilson, 1993) notes that military psychologists strive to maintain a delicate balance between APA and DoD requirements. An example of cooperation is the recently formalized DoD requirement that all military psychologists must maintain an active state license. Johnson also presents three important cases examples related to confidentiality and multiple role relationships. In an earlier paper, Johnson and Wilson (1993) presented examples of problems unique to psychology internships at military sites. Others have written of the difficulty of being "in service of two masters" (Jeffrey, Rankin, & Jeffrey, 1992) and presented two illustrative case studies on point. In one instance, a military psychologist was reportedly disciplined by the APA for failure to maintain the confidentiality of a service member's care records long after the psychologist had been transferred to another post. In the second case, a psychologist was disciplined by his commanding officer for failure to reveal an alleged violation of the Uniform Code of Military Justice by a third party. Psychologists are not alone in confronting such dilemmas. Camp (1993) has written of the "double agent" status of psychiatrists serving the military in wartime.

Johnson (1995) appropriately calls for a coordinated effort by the APA and the DoD both to study the practical dilemmas faced by military psychologists and to resolve them collaboratively. Special concerns include standards for informed consent, the differention of clinical from forensic roles, and clarification of practical aspects of implementing the DoD need to know policy.

Medication in the Military

The role of psychologists in prescribing medication on military bases has drawn considerable attention because of the DoD's demonstration project, in which a specially selected cadre of psychologists received special training to qualify for that role. However, at least one ethics inquiry about psychologists prescribing medication predated the DoD project, occurring in the early 1980s.

Case 14-7: A psychologist in the community became concerned when he learned that a female client, whose husband was a military officer, was taking psychoactive medication prescribed by another psychologist working at the base hospital. The community-based psychologist feared that the prescription had been fraudulently written.

The psychologist who was accused of prescribing medication without a medical degree had indeed done so, but not unethically. In addition to his psychology degree, this individual was trained as a physician's assistant in mental health and was authorized under military regulations to prescribe medication, under specific circumstances, for military personnel and their dependents under treatment at military facilities. In this instance, the psychologist was practicing within his sphere of competence in full compliance with military regulations appropriate to the care of the client in question. While this particular type of service is unusual for psychologists, who are not generally trained to prescribe medication and are not yet authorized to do so under state laws, it was appropriate to context and provider competence in this instance. The demonstration project undertaken by the DoD in the 1990s has already proven successful in providing sufficient psychopharmacology training to enable psychologists to function successfully in such roles under military authorization.

Espionage

Cases that involve the intelligence or espionage community are by definition not often in the public eye, but occasional cases have called attention to the work of psychologists.

Case 14-8: Carl Covert, Ph.D., worked on the staff of a defense-related federal agency and was assigned to a project that drafted interrogation protocols for enemy prisoners. His job was to assist in applying psychological principles likely to place emotional pressures to divulge information on the subjects of interrogation. In one "experiment," Covert was assigned to monitor the effectiveness of hallucinogenic drugs in breaking down the resistance of an American soldier. Some years later, the soldier would charge that he had never knowingly volunteered for such an experiment and was harmed psychologically by his unwitting participation.

Case 14-9: Cassandra Troy, Ph.D., also works in a defense-related intelligence service. Her job is to study the behavior and writings of world leaders and to prepare personality profiles for secret applications by other branches of government. She attempts to predict how individuals may respond in different sets of circumstances and is often asked to provide confidential briefings to state and defense department negotiators prior to their meetings with these leaders.

Drs. Covert and Troy are in some sense responsible chiefly to their governmental client, although the immediate impact of their work certainly affects other people. One might argue that their work falls into a special category and is in the national interest. To the extent that Covert was actually involved in the experiment as claimed by the soldier, she was guilty of participating in the unethical abuse of a research participant (i.e., an unwilling one). If her work is accurately able to predict behavior, Dr. Troy may be giving her employer some very useful data. Her work is not unethical per se, although she would certainly want to present appropriate scientific caveats in regard to its predictive validity to those who may rely on the briefings to the exclusion of other factors.

School Systems

Schools come in all shapes and sizes: public or private, secular or religious, day or residential. Most American children are required by law to attend school and hence are subject to the powerful influence of the school as a socialization agent. Much of the recent controversy in the practice of school psychology involves issues of competence, credentials, and professional control. Many psychologists who practice in school settings are at the subdoctoral level in academic training, and the APA has often asserted that the doctorate is the entry-level professional degree. Questions of competence and qualifications are discussed in chapter 3; however, the reader may be interested in the specifics of school psychology as uniquely affected in this area of controversy. We shall not rehash regulatory disputes in school psychology here (see Bardon, 1982), but instead focus on more specific types of ethical dilemmas in the schools (see Hansen, Green, & Kutner, 1989; Phillips, 1990).

Important issues of special ethical concern that have been highlighted in school settings (Hansen et al., 1989; Jacob-Timm & Hartshorne, 1994; O'Leary & O'Leary, 1978; Woody, 1989) include (1) informed consent for assessment and intervention, (2) privacy, (3) rights of children with disabilities, (4) determination of classroom goals, (5) legitimacy of rewards and aversive controls in the classroom, and (6) the use of the "time-out" as a potential type of abuse (Gast & Nelson, 1977a, 1977b; Nagle, 1987; Prilleltensky, 1991). The role of the psychologist in privacy and confidentiality matters (Trachtman, 1974) and the role of a psychologist as "whistle-blower" (Bersoff, 1981, 1995) are both important issues that we shall discuss.

There are also special problems for school psychologists at the interface of ethics and the law (EP: 1.02). At times, laws bearing on mental health and educational issues may conflict (Jacob-Timm & Hartshorne, 1994). For example, the Buckley Amendment, Public Law 94-142, and related state laws give parents access to the relevant records, as well as control over whether their child receives evaluations or special services. Suppose that the state also gives minors the right to independent access to drug counseling, venereal disease information, abortion advice, or psychotherapy? Which set of laws does the school psychologist obey? The next four cases raise, in a fashion somewhat exaggerated for emphasis, a sampling of the issues confronted regularly by school psychologists.

Case 14-10: International Psychometric Services was in the process of developing specialized norms for its high-school-level achievement tests for use in classification work by the military. They offered school systems the opportunity to have the senior classes evaluated on the instrument free of charge to establish an improved normative base. They also added some additional questions regarding "attitude toward the military" to the instrument. These included some potentially sensitive questions, such as asking male students, "Have you registered with the selective service?" Schools were offered the service only if they would require all of their high school seniors to take the test. The director of psychological services at the Lakeville Unified School District accepted the offer.

Here, we see the issues of informed consent and privacy with respect to testing. In particular, one wonders whether the answers to questions irrelevant to school functioning (i.e., draft registration information) would be provided to the military along with the student's name. If the student is required to take a test by the school, it would be an invasion of privacy to compel answers to such questions. It appears that the director of psychological services should carefully examine the manner in which the test information will be used before signing up for the program. In addition, the students should not be required to take the examination or otherwise provide personal data without appropriate informed consent relative to the nature of data to be collected, purpose of the program, and information regarding who will have access to it. We would assert that the school is not justified in waiving these important personal rights of the students.

There is not much by way of actual case law on this type of situation, but at least one federal district court decision seems relevant. In the case of *Merriken v. Cressman* (1973), the American Civil Liberties Union represented the mother of a student who objected to an ill-conceived program intended to predict which junior high school students in Norristown, Pennsylvania, might become drug or alcohol abusers. A "consent" form asking whether parents objected to the program was sent home; it was assumed that parental consent was granted if no objections were raised (Bersoff, 1983). Although many constitutional issues were raised by Mrs. Merriken on behalf of her son, the court specifically addressed the invasion of family privacy rights, finding in their favor. The court noted, "the children are never given the opportunity to consent to the invasion of their privacy; only the opportunity to refuse consent by returning a blank questionnaire" (Merrikin v. Cressman, p. 919). The court also criticized the lack of "candor and honesty" on the part of the school system, comparing the so-called consent letter to a Book-of-the-Month Club solicitation (Bersoff, 1983). The question of the child's privacy rights above and beyond those asserted by his parent on his behalf were not clarified in this case; however, we would encourage colleagues to extend respect for privacy to child, as well as adult, clients.

Case 14-11: Jonathan Swift, Ph.D., gave a lecture on the use of time-out interventions to teachers and administrators at the Centerville Public Schools, where he was employed as a school psychologist. Several weeks later, he discovered that a school principal had interpreted his talk as license to lock misbehaving children in a darkened closet for up to an hour at a time.

When Dr. Swift gave his lecture on time-out practices, he never dreamed that it would be so rapidly misinterpreted and abused. While it seems that the school principal was responsible for the problem behavior, it is also clear that Swift should have used warnings and cautions in an effort to avoid being misunderstood. Ideally, Dr. Swift could have helped to formulate a systemwide policy on the use of such techniques and arranged for appropriate training or supervision of those authorized to use isolation or aversive strategies. As the expert presenting the information, Swift had the additional responsibility of presenting appropriate limitations or otherwise alerting the participants at the lecture on appropriate constraints.

Case 14-12: At the Farnsworth Elementary School, teachers have full access to a child's cumulative school record. Material of a personal nature entered in these record occasionally became a topic of conversation in the teacher's lounge. When school psychologist Sylvia Caution learned of this, she decided that she to no longer document any of her clinical observations in the record.

The case of the school record system highlights a variety of issues covered in chapter 4 and considered specifically in the school confidentiality context by Trachtman (1972, 1974). Ms. Caution's response seems a bit overreactive, however. As discussed in chapter 5, it is possible to consider record entries with a balance of utility and the need to know. The teachers may not need to know that Johnny Smith was born prior to his parents' marriage, but it would clearly help Johnny if teachers could be alerted to his tendency to withdraw socially when stressed. The circumstances of Johnny's birth add nothing to assist teachers in the promotion of Johnny's educational progress, but information regarding his tendency toward social withdrawal might help a teacher reach out to him more effectively in the classroom. In any case, the parents should be aware of what information will be provided to the school and have the option to give their consent. Ms. Caution should take some professional initiative in educating her colleagues about more appropriate treatment of confidential information, or she could take steps to limit access to records should that be needed.

Case 14-13: Andrew Rigor, Ed.D., was frequently asked to assess "special needs children" in his role as a psychologist for the South Suburbia school system. When the special education budget began to show signs of strain, Dr. Rigor was instructed by his superintendent to administer shorter evaluations, produce briefer reports, and refrain from recommending additional services or evaluations for the children he assessed. The superintendent explained that these steps were needed to keep costs in line.

The case of Dr. Rigor is especially endemic to school systems, which are increasingly under pressure to control costs, while also obligated under Public Law 94-142 (Education for All Handicapped Children Act) to meet the needs of special students. It is also relevant to other nonschool institutions in which nonpsychologist administrators may attempt to limit or modify professional standards to meet institutional needs. In a case similar in some ways to Dr. Rigor's, although considerably more complex, the APA filed an amicus brief in support of a school psychologist under such pressures (Bersoff, 1981).

Ideally, Dr. Rigor should vigorously resist any attempt to do less than a fully professional job on his assigned cases. He should be willing to consider reasonable administrative requests consistent with professional standards, but should not be willing to compromise his integrity by providing less-than-adequate services (or violate legal obligations to report genuine student needs) to comply with administrative fiat. The difficulty, of course, is sorting out the appropriateness of each position and balancing one's integrity with threats of job loss or other retaliation. There may be some circumstances for which the psychologist will have to choose between a job and his or her conscience, but often a reasoned attempt at accommodation and a careful explanation of professional standards will bring less drastic formulas to bear on a solution.

The Criminal Justice System

We began this chapter with reference to the APA Task Force report on the ethics of psychological intervention in the criminal justice system (Monahan, 1980), and in the next chapter we discuss the role of psychologists in the courtroom. It seems appropriate, however, to dwell at least briefly on the more broad role of psychologists within the criminal justice system, including their work with criminal defendants, prison populations, and police agencies.

In each of these contexts, the critical route to successfully negotiating the complex ethical relationships is through sorting out obligations to clients. This requires that the psychologist give substantial forethought to the matter of who the client is and spend sufficient time and energy clarifying the accompanying obligations, roles, expectations, and work conditions. When ethical duties are explicitly detailed in advance,

a violation is much less likely, in part because the psychologist has anticipated potential problems and in part because the client has been appropriately cautioned.

Weinberger and Sreenivasan (1994) describe the prevailing ideology of correctional administration as one that deemphasizes treatment or "corrections" and focuses attention on punishment, security, and custodial matters. They relate this shift to the failure of psychotherapy to lower recidivism rates significantly (Ochipinti & Boston, 1987), concluding that psychologists who work in correctional settings often serve as "window dressing" (Weinberger & Sreenivasan, 1994, p. 166) and frequently do not provide meaningful clinical services. In support of that contention, they cite a Federal Bureau of Prisons' orientation program for new employees that focuses on correctional concepts, self-defense, and searching for contraband (among other topics). They cite case examples in which psychologists are ordered to perform the duties of a correctional officer during a personnel shortage (i.e., perform contraband or pat-down searches in inmate cells), are asked to undertake psychological testing with a specific goal of finding a reason to prolong incarceration, or are asked to participate in disciplinary hearings. In addition, they describe circumstances in which a psychologist's legitimate therapeutic recommendations may be ignored or trivialized by institutional staff with differing priorities and views. Weinberger and Sreenivasan raise important and valid issues, but also appear to paint all corrections systems with an overly broad brush. The common thread in the situations they describe is the difficulty faced by psychologists who work for departments of correction as opposed to those who work for administratively distinct mental health units.

The key issue from an ethical standpoint is the degree to which a psychologist's ethical standards and professional role are compromised by any given correctional setting. When working in such settings, psychologists are not exempt from their ethical responsibilities. Prior to undertaking such employment, psychologists should carefully examine the expectations placed on them in the new job and raise any apparent conflicts with their superiors from the outset. To the extent that role expectations are inconsistent with appropriate ethical standards, psychologists should make every effort to bring the role into conformity with their ethics code (EP: 1.02, 1.21, 8.03). If that is impossible, the psychologist should not agree to remain in the inappropriate role.

The next three cases represent classic ethical problems for the psychologist in the criminal justice system. They are modified from material presented by Monahan (1980) and Vetter and Rieber (1980).

Case 14-14: Roberta Reason, Ph.D., often participates in the evaluation of criminal defendants as part of court-ordered determinations of their competence to stand trial. Defendants are usually forced to meet with her unaccompanied by their lawyers. When she begins to interview a woman charged with the beating death of an infant, the defendant complains, "If I don't talk to you, they'll say I'm not cooperating, and I'll be in trouble. If I do talk to you, I'll be losing my fifth Amendment rights."

The defendant who confronts Dr. Reason is quite correct in her assumptions about the risks of her cooperation or noncooperation. It is hoped Dr. Reason has thought through her role sufficiently to guide the defendant. Dr. Reason might note, "My job is to help determine whether you are able to understand the charges against you and their potential consequences and that you can cooperate in your own defense. You may choose not to answer some of my questions if you wish, but I shall try to focus them on matters relative to your ability to assist your lawyer at the trial. I do not want to discuss your guilt or innocence." Dr. Reason must clearly delineate for herself and the defendant her role and responsibilities and must do her best to avoid an undue invasion of privacy or placing her client at inappropriate legal risk.

Dr. Reason should also consult carefully with the defense attorney and judge to ensure that proper protective orders are issued that limit access to her reports. Most courts that have considered the problem have held that the Fifth and Sixth Amendments prohibit admitting as evidence information obtained during a competency evaluation. The problem, however, is that a prosecutor might use such information as an investigative lead for delving further into or planning the conduct of the case. That use of Dr. Reason's report would be ethically troubling.

Case 14-15: Andrew Penal, Ed.D., works at the Stateville Prison Colony as a correctional psychologist. During an individual treatment session, a new inmate reports that an escape attempt involving taking hostages is about to take place. Following this revelation, the client begs, "Please don't tell anyone about this. If the other cons find out I snitched, they'll kill me."

Dr. Penal is in a very difficult situation. As noted in chapter 5, he might be obligated to warn certain potential victims, but he must also protect the rights and welfare of his client. Brodsky (1980) reports a full range of conflicting views on what Dr. Penal should do, varying from upholding absolute confidentiality to the opinion that there is no such thing as confidentiality in a prison setting. The prison setting is by definition one in which the clients will often test the therapist, particularly to determine whether trust is possible. There are also wide variations in reasons inmates would seek treatment or consultation; these range from the traditional (e.g., "I need psychological help.") to the pragmatically self-serving (e.g., "It will look good when I come up for a parole hearing to have therapy on my record here."). While we do not know enough about the context to determine what Dr. Penal's real options are, we can outline the steps he should have considered prior to this situation.

Dr. Penal should have clarified with prison authorities what his legal and professional obligations would be relative to their expectations. If they expect him to report all infractions of the rules, for example, he would need to evaluate his willingness to work in that context. When beginning work with inmates, Dr. Penal should also have clarified with each of them the limits of his role and the nature of their relationship. For example, will he honor every confidence?

Which confidences can he not respect? If inmates have the right to ask him not to speak to the parole board or to clear with them in advance, what he would say? These are just a few sample questions that should routinely be raised. The psychologist should never surrender professional integrity and standards to competing pressures of the work site. Each client is entitled to know the special constraints on, or parameters of, the professional relationships prior to entering it.

Case 14-16: George Cops, Psy.D., is a special consultant to the Center City Police Department. He is available on retainer to provide therapeutic intervention to police officers under pressure from job-related stress and especially to assist officers with their feelings after they have been involved in shootings in which a suspect is killed. A new police chief has been appointed recently who asks Dr. Cops to provide comments for the personnel files of the officers he has counseled.

Dr. Cops will hopefully advise the new chief of police that he must respect the confidentiality of the officers he is asked to treat as therapy clients. If the chief wishes personnel selection advice or other consultation, that should not come from the same person expected to provide an uncritical therapeutic role. We have not raised the more complex situation in regard to what Dr. Cops should do if an officer he is counseling appears to be at some nonspecific but real risk for future behavior problems. The point at which Cops becomes responsible to report a "clear and immediate danger" is an important ethical problem he will have to address for himself. Clearly, these are issues that Dr. Cops will ideally have thought through and resolved with the police department prior to accepting the job.

Community Agencies

A community agency for purposes of this discussion may be a state-funded community mental health center, a nonprofit community-run clinic, a municipal hospital, or some similar service delivery system. These facilities are im-portant community service resources and politically reactive organizations by their very nature (Riger, 1989; Serrano-Garcia, 1994). They often depend on funding or regulatory support from local government. Such agencies often have competing demands placed on them by various interests, and psychologists working in these agencies are likewise subject to multiple demands that occasionally conflict (O'Neill, 1989). At times, these conflicts become significant ethical issues.

Joseph and Peele (1975) illustrate the particular problems presented by the fact that professionals in such settings serve both the community and their individual clients. The following two cases are adapted from their presentation.

Case 14-17: Dale is a 14-year-old boy referred to a community agency by his mother and school because of his unmanageable, hostile, and aggressive behavior. The assessment indicated that collateral treatment for both Dale and his mother would be needed if success were to be achieved. Although she initially agreed to the plan, Dale's mother refused to keep appointments. She did not respond to information that Dale would be dropped from the program if she refused to participate. Ultimately, Dale was discharged because his mother would not cooperate in the treatment plan.

Case 14-18: Mrs. Wilder was admitted to the inpatient service of a community mental health center for treatment of severe depression. Because she had abused her children, a protective services agency was also involved in her case. After a few weeks, her depression had improved sufficiently to warrant her discharge to outpatient treatment. Afraid that she would again harm her children, the protective service agency urged the mental health center to delay her discharge.

Joseph and Peele (1975) note that the mental health professionals in both cases are caught between two conflicting sets of duties. In Dale's case, they had begun serving the young client, but soon realized that their treatment plan could not be effective without the support and involvement of his mother. Without maternal involvement, allowing Dale to occupy a treatment slot might result in deprivation of services to another client who might make more effective use of treatment. When Dale's mother broke her initial participation contract, the clinic's obligation to Dale was likewise ended.

In Mrs. Wilder's case, a similar situation existed in terms of the allocation of scarce resources and effective cost control in community agencies. The task of the mental health center was to provide the most effective and least restrictive treatment to their client, Mrs. Wilder. Since she no longer required inpatient care, she should not be kept hospitalized simply to serve the needs or convenience of another social agency, however laudable. The children's protective services should provide necessary care for the children regardless of their mother's hospital status.

While other creative solutions might have been possible in the cases of Dale and Mrs. Wilder, the point made is that professionals may often be caught between their appropriate concern for individual clients and concern for the community. Bureaucratic demands in such social welfare agencies can be overwhelming at times, and legislation intended to improve services may result in unrealistic expectations and frustrations. Sharfstein and Wolfe (1982) cite the example of a community mental health center regulation that required a wide range of services to be operational within a limited amount of time if centers wished continued funding. The rules were relatively inflexible and did not take into consideration startup costs, redundant services in the community, components of desirable services, or adequacy of service levels.

It is not surprising that some self-report studies of agency workers and administrators suggest that the supremacy of agency needs over individual client needs is the norm (Billingsley, 1984). As governmental funds evaporate and managed care constraints are placed on Medicaid reimbursement or other subsidies, clinics and mental health centers will be under continuing pressure to take instructions from the bureaucracy regarding how to contain costs and serve clients. This will place substantial pressure on the value systems of practitioners in community settings. Individual long-term psychotherapy will be rejected as a service option in place of modes of treatment that are judged more readily reimbursable and cost efficient. The only question is the degree to which clients' needs will be subordinated to their detriment (Riger, 1989; Serrano-Garcia, 1994). When the survival of the agency (or one's job) is at stake, considerable intellectualization and rationalization is possible (O'Neill, 1989).

It is clear that community mental health work and service in public social welfare agencies forces psychologists in those settings to examine their values and motivations closely. Perlman (1977) notes that ethical issues that grow from the mental health worker's decisions and actions cannot be avoided. He attempts to elaborate the ethical obligations of psychologists as they apply in the context of community participation, continuity of services, politics, planning, services to minority groups, and other critical issues.

Business and Industry

Psychologists are often involved as participants in, or consultants to, businesses or industries. Their roles might include management consulting, personnel selection, organizational research, human factors applications, program evaluation, training, consumer psychology and advertising applications, public relations services, marketing studies, or even applying clinical skills to enhance the functioning of an organization and its executives. The ethical difficulties psychologists face in such settings derive both from the special demands of their particular role and from the fact that the ethics of psychology and the ethics of business often are not congruent.

Once again, we harken back to the basic question: "Who is the client?" This point is raised over and over again in papers on the ethics of the industrial or organizational psychologist (Carkenord, 1996; Clark & Lattal, 1993; London & Bray, 1980; Mirvis & Seashore, 1979; Purcell et al., 1974). The notion of seduction of the psychologist by the pressures of the industry or the marketplace, with resulting severe role conflicts, is hardly a new issue (e.g., see APA Task Force on the Practice of Psychology in Industry, 1971). Most ethical complaints against psychologists that arise in business settings deal with a psychologist's responsibility to his or her client or assessment, advertising, or marketing issues. Often, one senses that the psychologist in the business world about whom a complaint is received may have become a servant of economic power or may have lost some focus on human values compared to those of productivity and the company.

Case 14-19: Hardy Driver has been a member of the management team at Western Bolt and Wrench Corporation for the past 6 years. He is being considered for promotion to the chief operating officer position in the company and is told that he will be sent to the company psychologist for an evaluation as part of the selection process. Driver knows that he can refuse to take the evaluation but probably would not be considered for the promotion in that case. He is concerned about what sort of personal information revealed in the evaluation might be transmitted to others in the company.

The case involving Mr. Driver is not at all uncommon. Such issues were discussed in detail nearly two decades ago by London and Bray (1980). The psychologist involved will hopefully recognize the vulnerability of Mr. Driver, as well as the legitimate needs and rights of Western Bolt and Wrench. The company has a right to screen its applicants using reliable and valid assessment tools. Driver knows that he has the right to refuse participation, just as the company has the right to pass him over should he do so. One assumes that the psychologist will be willing to discuss these issues with Driver, including the nature of the assessment, type of report to be rendered, and circulation of the report. Driver may, for example, fear that some personality inadequacy may be revealed and broadcast widely, when in fact no personality assessment tools are to be used. Driver also has a right to know in advance whether he will have access to the report, test data, debriefing, and so on. In summary, Driver has the right to full informed consent regarding the nature of the planned evaluation before he decides whether to participate. The psychologist should recognize this and provide Driver with ample information to assist him in making the decision.

Case 14-20: Because of declining sales linked to an economic recession, the Paragon Steel Corporation is planning to lay off several hundred workers. The company wants to attempt a modification of its union contract and base the layoffs on employee productivity rather than seniority, as the union's contract specifies. They ask their corporate psychologist to prepare a detailed memorandum that cites research data to support their position. They are not interested in contrary data and, in fact, would prefer that they not be mentioned if they exist. Headquarters also wants a detailed plan for assessing the productivity of its workers to fit these needs.

The Paragon Steel case raises the use of research as an influence strategy (Purcell et al., 1974), but does so in a manner that implies a one-sided bias. Many business executives firmly believe that "corporate self-interest is inexorably involved in the well-being of the society" or, as Charles Wilson put it, "What's good for GM is good for the country" (Purcell et al., 1974, p. 441). Many businesses find nothing wrong in asserting their best interests using whatever legal means are available; the rationale is that they are ultimately helping society and the economy. Intellectual or scientific honesty is not necessary for economic success, and total scientific honesty might not be good for the company in some instances. If we assume that data do exist to support the company's position that productivity can be validly assessed and that laying off employees who fail on that assessment is desirable, is the psychologist behaving ethically in applying it? The answer is probably yes, so long as meaningful contrary data are not concealed or ignored.

Case 14-21: Bozo Pharmaceutical Industries sells over-the-counter "natural food" diet aids. They have developed a new diet, known as "Kelp Power," based on seaweed extracts. A consumer psychologist is approached as a consultant to assist in devising a marketing survey and advertising plan. The psychologist is offered a substantial fee plus a bonus based on the ultimate effectiveness of the program in boosting sales. When the psychologist asks about data on the product to incorporate in the project, she discovers that there is no evidence that the product is actually helpful in dieting. It is not harmful, but there are no documented benefits.

How about overlooking misleading public statements so long as the lies are benign? That is the question raised by the Bozo Pharmaceutical case. A marketing plan would, at the very least, focus on making the public believe that Kelp Power could help them diet. The psychologist might reason that no one will be hurt or that placebo effects might help some people diet. Is that sufficient as an ethical basis for assisting in the promotion of an ineffective product? We would argue that providing support for this product's marketing is unethical, although this would be difficult to prove as an ethics case. The psychologist would have little public visibility, and an ethics complaint most likely would not occur as an idea to the parties who had firsthand knowledge of the activity.

Case 14-22: Manny Jobs, Psy.D., is an industrial psychologist assigned to work on a job-enrichment program aimed at improving the quality of life, and hence quality of work, among assembly line workers at Amalgamated Motors. After a careful job analysis, many hours of interviews, and considerable effort, Dr. Jobs produced a report with many potentially useful suggestions. Management thanked him and shelved the report, which they regarded as "ahead of its time." Dr. Jobs was frustrated that his efforts and the potential benefits were being ignored and toyed with the idea of leaking the report to union negotiators prior to the next round of contract talks.

The Amalgamated Motors case presents another set of complex conflicting needs. Amalgamated Motors needs information and ideas, but is not necessarily ready to act on them. Dr. Jobs is angry that his work has seemingly been wasted, although he has been paid and his client, the company, seems satisfied. Does he have the right to violate his client's right of confidentiality by revealing information to the unions? Dr. Jobs might argue "society's interests are at stake," but he is obligated to respect the proprietary rights of his employer so long as it is possible to do so and still maintain standards of ethical practice (London & Bray, 1980).

Medical Settings

It will come as no surprise to the thousands of psychologists at work in medical settings that psychologists and physicians do not always speak the same language. A degree of mutual education and, implicitly, a willingness to be educated is required for the psychologist who plans to work in such settings. One must, for example, acquire a new lexicon of terminology (e.g., a "progressive disease" is one that gets worse and "positive findings" are a bad sign when discovered during a physical examination). A knowledge of physical illnesses and their symptoms and treatments and an understanding of how medical hospitals (as distinct from mental hospitals, community mental health centers, or college counseling services) are run is very important. Psychologists in medical settings also must be keenly aware of their expertise and its limitations. Some physicians are too willing to see physical complaints as psychological, and some psychologists are all too eager to go along with them. Although the following case is unusual, it provides an important illustration.

Case 14-23: Teri Slim was referred to a major pediatric teaching hospital for the treatment of anorexia nervosa. She had always been petite and slender, but seemed unusually thin to her father just prior to her 14th birthday. She was medically evaluated at a large hospital near her home and sent to the other hospital for treatment. She was again evaluated, diagnosed as anorexic, and admitted to the "psychosomatic unit" for treatment. It was easy for the hospital staff to identify family stressors that might account for Teri's emotional problems. Her parents were recently divorced, her father was an unemployed business executive, and her mother was reported to be a narcotic addict who lived in another state. At the end of 2 months of treatment, Teri was still malnourished and was making "no progress" in treatment. Intravenous feeding was contemplated in the face of her progressive weight loss, and she was prepared for transfer to another hospital ward so that a venous feeding line could be implanted. It was at that time that a senior pediatrician asked, "Has she ever been evaluated for Crohn's disease?" Several weeks later, Teri was discharged from the hospital minus a segment of her intestine and on anti-inflammatory medication. She continues to do well in response to the treatment for Crohn's disease.

Teri Slim had been worked up twice by physicians outstanding in their field, and her care was continually supervised by physicians who were slow to diagnose her physical illness and had referred her for what was essentially a psychological treatment program. Crohn's disease is not easy to diagnose, but neither are a host of medical problems, ranging from neurological disorders to endocrine problems, that seem to manifest themselves chiefly through symptoms that might mistakenly be regarded as psychological (e.g., hallucinations, aberrant behavior, and mood swings). The point is that a close, collaborative, and collegial relationship is needed in dealing with such patients, including good integration of psychological and medical care.

There are times when psychologists working in medical settings will be employed under the supervision of physicians (e.g., in departments of psychiatry or pediatrics). At other times, they may be administratively organized in a separate department (e.g., medical psychology). Wherever they work, psychologists must be careful not to surrender their professional integrity or standards.

Case 14-24: Bertram Botch, M.D., was the chief of neurology at a pediatric hospital and often chaired interdisciplinary case conferences. Reporting on her assessment of a low-functioning mentally retarded child, Melissa Meek, Ph.D., presented her detailed findings in descriptive terms. Dr. Botch listened to her presentation and asked for the child's IQ. When Dr. Meek replied that the instruments used were developmental indices that did not yield IQ scores, Dr. Botch demanded that she compute a specific IQ score to use in his report.

Case 14-25: After sitting in on some lectures that Ralph Worthy, Psy.D., was giving to a group of medical students in regard to projective testing, the chief of medicine called him in to set up a workshop on the topic for medical residents. The chief told Worthy that he thought it would be a good idea to teach the residents how to use "those tests" and assumed that it could be done in "a half-dozen meetings or so."

It is hoped that Drs. Meek and Worthy will not yield to the pressures described. Meek could politely, but firmly, attempt to educate Dr. Botch with respect to the fact that an IQ score is not appropriate in the given situation. She can perhaps help to identify estimated ranges of scores or find other terms useful and meaningfully appropriate for his report, but she should not be coerced or bullied into contriving the digits he seems to want. Likewise, it is hoped Dr. Worthy will attempt to educate his chief regarding the nature of personality assessment and the inappropriateness of thinking that six lectures will enable anyone to use such techniques competently. He might explain that knowledge of personality theory, abnormal behavior, psychotherapeutic interventions, and psychometrics are all required to use these tools effectively.

These situations may, of course, generalize to any context in which one's employer does not understand psychological theory and practice or a cooperative team effort is required for effective and successful work. The psychologist must take the lead in defining the appropriate role for his or her services. The psychologist must also be prepared to recognize and uphold appropriate professional standards.

Independent Practice Settings

To many, the independent practice of the professional psychologist represents glamor, freedom, and a life of ease. At least that was the fantasy or myth of the independent practitioner's lot prior to the advent of managed care (Lewin, 1974; Taylor, 1978). As one practitioner put it, "the portrayal of our work is as a luxury for the self-indulgent . . . we all 'know' of the psychologist working a 35-hour week at $60 per hour . . . [treating only] . . . movie stars, successful writers, and the wives of corporate executives, with maybe a sprinkling of high level bureaucrats" (Taylor, 1978, p. 70). Rumor has it that such psychologists are "out there," although we never seem to meet them.

The realities of independent practice are far less alluring today than the fantasies of the past might suggest. The $60 rate that seemed impressive in 1978 would translate to well over $100 in 1997 dollars when corrected for inflation (see chapter 10). The vicissitudes of dealing with managed care plans (e.g., access to provider panels, incremental paperwork, reduced payments, etc.) have also made the small-business management of an independent practice far more demanding. In many ways, individual and small-group independent practices are more taxing than the work of psychology at an agency, clinic, or hospital. True, the independent practitioner is his or her own boss, but that must be balanced with overhead costs, employee relations (e.g., with a receptionist, answering service, etc.), backup coverage, billing, and a host of other mundane, but necessary, chores. In addition, a kind of professional loneliness or isolation can afflict the independent practitioner, especially when the practice is a solo one.

Little has been written on the ethical problems faced by the independent practitioner, although a number of the examples cited throughout this volume certainly apply. The greatest problem in the ethical sense is probably related to the fact that the independent practitioner must be both a professional and an entrepreneur in order to survive, roles that are not always congruent. In addition, the absence of peer collaborators may lead to less social comparison of a professional nature and a resulting failure to always think carefully about the manner in which one practices or manages cases.

The independent practitioner may have a secretary or other employees who require careful supervision, generally does not have the luxury of paid vacations or sick days, and is far more susceptible to the case management headaches of working with the emotionally troubled (e.g., the client who does not pay bills or often fails to keep scheduled appointments). The material in this volume that deals with psychotherapy, managed care, advertising of services, and employee relations is all highly relevant to the independent practitioner. There are also some unique ethical problems that may come up from time to time.

Case 14-26: Napoleon Solo, Psy.D., practiced psychotherapy on his own in a private office. An automobile accident disabled him for a period of 3 months. During that time, no coverage was available for any of his clients.

It is hoped Dr. Solo had the foresight to take out adequate disability insurance to cover his personal financial needs during the recovery period. He apparently did not consider any means of providing backup for his clients, however, and was clearly in no position to do this easily from his hospital bed. Depending on the clients' individual needs, this could be a serious ethical oversight.

Case 14-27: A young woman appeared in the office of Robert Taylor, Ph.D. Dr. Taylor noted that she seemed to become increasingly uneasy with the surroundings and the direction of his questions. Finally, she interrupted and made the red-faced confession that she had thought she was at a gynecologist's office.

Dr. Taylor's rather humorous example (Taylor, 1978) illustrates that the independent practitioner never knows precisely what to expect when a prospective client comes through the door. The psychologist must be prepared to evaluate and recognize that he or she may not be the sort of person the client is really looking for or needs and must be prepared to make appropriate referrals as needed.

Pastoral Counseling

Pastoral counseling presents some unique work-setting issues for several reasons. Not the least of these is widely varying training. Some members of the clergy are trained as psychologists, psychiatrists, and social workers. Others receive minimal pastoral counseling training that integrates basic counseling skills with religious and moral philosophy content (Dueck, 1987; Foskett, 1992), but no training in professional ethics for psychological or psychotherapeutic practice (Miller & Atkinson, 1988). Still others have little or no formal training in psychodiagnostics or psychotherapy and focus chiefly on a religious- or spiritually based approach. The problem is well illustrated by a guidebook, intended for "Christian counselors of all sorts," *Counselor's Guide to the Brain and Its Disorders: Knowing the Difference Between Disease and Sin* (Welch, 1991). The volume attempts to explain the functions of the brain, organic and functional psychopathological disorders, and issues of moral responsibility from a framework that is "thoroughly biblical." One chapter discusses "The No. 1 Culprit: Licit and Illicit Drugs." Overall, the general standards and orientation of pastoral counseling, as a field, are far less rigorous than graduate training for psychological practice.

Other issues arise when the client or psychologist fails to clearly delineate roles between the pastoral function and more secular psychodiagnostic or psychotherapeutic needs (Craig, 1991; Miller & Atkinson, 1988). We agree with the viewpoint that clergy who are trained as psychotherapists should not attempt to function in both roles for the same client.

Case 14-28: An ethics committee received a complaint from George Gothic, whose psychotherapist, Reverend Dan Damien, D.Min., was both an ordained minister and a licensed psychologist. Dr. Damien had recommended that Gothic undergo an exorcism to relieve his emotional distress. Gothic had taken offense and described Dr. Damien as "a quack in preacher's clothing." When approached for an explanation by the ethics committee, Dr. Damien explained that he knew Gothic needed such treatment because, "His face contorts in a gargoylelike tic whenever God is mentioned." When questioned further on the validity of his diagnosis, Damien denounced the members of the ethics committee as "a bunch of Godless heretics."

The ethics committee had serious questions about Dr. Damien's competence as a psychotherapist, but was unable to pursue their investigation adequately when he ceased replying to their inquiries. As a result, he was expelled from the organization.

Case 14-29: Simon Shifty, Ph.D., was called before a licensing board for failure to report child abuse as mandated under state law. Dr. Shifty, who was also an ordained minister, had been providing family therapy to a couple who regularly and severely beat their children with leather straps for perceived religious infractions. The case came to public attention when one of the badly beaten children collapsed at school. Dr. Shifty had known about the beatings and about the mandated reporter status of psychologists in his state, but explained to the licensing board that clergy were not covered by that statute because of the Constitutional separation of church and state.

The licensing board was not impressed by Dr. Shifty's Constitutional argument. The board noted that he was functioning as a psychologist, not a member of the clergy, when performing family therapy, as evidenced by his clinical case notes and bills to the family's health insurer. The board noted that he could not be functioning simultaneously with one set of clients as both a spiritual counselor and licensed psychologist.

SUMMARY AND GUIDELINES

Each work setting is unique in some way, although those discussed here present special challenges for the psychologist. The key issue common across settings is the need to be mindful of who the client is. By focusing on the welfare of the most vulnerable parties in a client hierarchy, a psychologist should be able to determine the most appropriate ethical course of action. Some other basic guidelines include

1. Psychologists entering a new work setting for the first time should familiarize themselves with the special needs and demands of the job. This includes consulting with colleagues about the ethical pressures and problems unique to that type of work setting.
2. In complex service delivery or consultation systems, the usual psychologist-client relationship may be blurred. It is appropriate that psychologists take the lead in defining their roles and obligations to each level of client served. In addition, the psychologist should clarify role expectations with all relevant parties from the outset of professional contact.
3. A psychologist is never exempted from any portion of the ethics code by virtue of an employer's dictum (EP: 8.03).
4. The matter of whether to work for reform within an unethical institution or whether

to "blow the whistle" in public is often a matter of personal judgment. A psychologist should not, however, cooperate as a party to unethical behavior. In addition, a psychologist must carefully consider any duty of confidentiality owed to a client (including a client organization) before making public disclosures about that client.

5. When a special work setting demands special qualifications or competencies, psychologists should be exceptionally careful that they meet these standards prior to working in that context. Consultation with colleagues experienced in the specialized setting is often the best way to make that assessment.

6. When psychologists are trained in other professions, they must clearly delineate for themselves and their clients the professional capacity in which they are serving.

References

Allen, J. P., Chatelier, P., Clark, H. J., & Sorenson, R. (1982). Behavioral science in the military: Research trends for the 80s. *Professional Psychology, 13,* 918–929.

American Psychological Association. (1992). Ethical principles of psychologists and code of conduct. *American Psychologist, 47,* 1597–1611.

American Psychological Association Ethics Committee. (1993, April 18). Policy Statement of the APA Ethics Committee Regarding Military Psychologists and Confidentiality. Washington, DC: Author.

American Psychological Association Task Force on the Practice of Psychology in Industry. (1971). Effective practice of psychology in industry. *American Psychologist, 26,* 974–991.

Bardon, J. I. (1982). School psychology's dilemma: A proposal for its resolution. *Professional Psychology, 13,* 955–968.

Bersoff, D. N. (1981). The brief for amici curiae in the matter of *Forrest versus Ambach. Academic Psychology Bulletin, 3,* 133–162.

Bersoff, D. N. (1983). Children as participants in psychoeducational assessment. In G. B. Melton, G. P. Koocher, & M. J. Saks (Eds.), *Children's competence to consent* (pp. 149–178). New York: Plenum.

Bersoff, D. N. (Ed.). (1995). *Ethical conflicts in psychology.* Washington, DC: American Psychological Association.

Billingsley, K. R. (1984). Critical decisions in survey/ feedback designs. *Group and Organizational Studies, 1,* 448–453.

Boling, T. E., & Dempsey, J. (1981). Ethical dilemmas in government: Designing an organizational response. *Public Personnel Management Journal, 11,* 11–19.

Brodsky, S. L. (1980). Ethical issues for psychologists in corrections. In J. Monahan (Ed.), *Who is the client: The ethics of psychological intervention in the criminal justice system.* Washington, DC: American Psychological Association.

Camp, N. M. (1993). The Vietnam War and the ethics of combat psychiatry. *American Journal of Psychiatry, 150,* 1000–1010.

Clark, R. W., & Lattal, A. D. (1993). *Winning the integrity revolution.* Lanham, MD: Rowman & Littlefield.

Craig, J. D. (1991). Preventing dual relationships in pastoral counseling. *Pastoral Psychology, 36,* 49–54.

Crawford, M. P. (1970). Military psychology and general psychology. *American Psychologist, 25,* 328–336.

Dueck, A. (1987). Ethical contexts of healing: Peoplehood and righteousness. *Pastoral Psychology, 35,* 239–253.

Foskett, J. (1992). Ethical issues in counseling and pastoral care. *British Journal of Guidance and Counseling, 20,* 39–50.

Gast, D. L., & Nelson, C. M. (1977a). Legal and ethical considerations for the use of timeout in special education settings. *Journal of Special Education, 11,* 457–467.

Gast, D. L., & Nelson, C. M. (1977b). Time out in the classroom: Implications for special education. *Exceptional Children, 43,* 461–464.

Hansen, J. C., Green, S., & Kutner, K. B. (1989). Ethical issues facing school psychologists working with families. *Professional School Psychology, 4,* 245–255.

Jacob-Timm, S., & Hartshorne, T. S. (1994). *Ethics and law for school psychologists (2nd ed.).* Brandon, VT: Clinical Psychology Publishing.

Jeffrey, T. B., Rankin, R. J., & Jeffrey, L. K. (1992). In service of two masters: The ethical-legal dilemma faced by military psychologists. *Profes-*

sional Psychology: Research and Practice, 23, 91–95.

Johnson, W. B. (1995). Perennial ethical quandaries in military psychology: Toward an American Psychological Association–Department of Defense collaboration. *Professional Psychology: Research and Practice, 26,* 281–287.

Johnson, W. B., & Wilson, K. (1993). The military internship: A retrospective analysis. *Professional Psychology: Research and Practice, 24,* 312–318.

Joseph, D. I., & Peele, R. (1975). Ethical issues in community psychiatry. *Hospital and Community Psychiatry, 26,* 295–299.

Kelley, C. R. (1971). In defense of military psychology. *American Psychologist, 26,* 514–515.

Leuba, C. (1971). Military are essential. *American Psychologist, 26,* 515.

Lewin, M. H. (1974). Diaries of the private practitioner: Secrets revealed. *Professional Psychology, 5,* 234–236.

London, M., & Bray, D. W. (1980). Ethical issues in testing and evaluation for personnel decisions. *American Psychologist, 35,* 890–901.

Merriken v. Cressman, 364 F. Supp. 913 E.D. Pa (1973).

Miller, H. M., & Atkinson, D. R. (1988). The clergy person as counselor: An inherent conflict of interest. *Counseling and Values, 32,* 116–123.

Mirvis, P. H., & Seashore, S. E. (1979). Being ethical in organizational research. *American Psychologist, 34,* 766–780.

Monahan, J. (Ed.). (1980). *Who is the client? The ethics of psychological intervention in the criminal justice system.* Washington, DC: American Psychological Association.

Nagle, R. J. (1987). Ethics training in school psychology. *Professional School Psychology, 2,* 163–171.

Ochipinti, L. A., & Boston, R. (1987). The new man at the top. *Corrections Today, 49,* 16–20.

O'Leary, S. G., & O'Leary, K. D. (1978). Ethical issues of behavior modification research in schools. *Psychology in the Schools, 14,* 299–307.

O'Neill, P. T. (1989). Responsible to whom? Responsible to what? Some ethical issues in community intervention. *American Journal of Community Psychology, 17,* 323–341.

Perlman, B. (1977). Ethical concerns in community mental health. *American Journal of Community Psychology, 5,* 45–57.

Phillips, B. N. (1990). *School psychology at a turning point: Ensuring a bright future for the profession.* San Francisco: Jossey-Bass.

Prilleltensky, I. (1991). The social ethics of school psychology: A priority for the 1990s. *School Psychology Quarterly, 6,* 200–222.

Purcell, T. V., Albright, L. E., Grant, D. L., Lockwood, H. C., Schein, V. E., & Friedlander, F. (1974). What are the social responsibilities for psychologists in industry? A symposium. *Personnel Psychology, 27,* 435–453.

Riger, S. (1989). The politics of community intervention. *American Journal of Community Psychology, 17,* 379–383.

Saks, M. J. (1970). On Meredith Crawford's "Military Psychology . . ." *American Psychologist, 25,* 876.

Serrano-Garcia, I. (1994). The ethics of the powerful and the power of ethics. *American Journal of Community Psychology, 22,* 1–20.

Shakow, D. (1968). On the rewards (and, alas, frustrations) of public service. *American Psychologist, 23,* 87–96.

Sharfstein, S. S., & Wolfe, J. C. (1982). The community mental health centers program: Expectations and realities. *Hospital and Community Psychiatry, 29,* 46–49.

Sleek, S. (1995). Military practice creates ethical squeeze. *APA Monitor, 26,* 30.

Taylor, R. E. (1978). Demythologizing private practice. *Professional Psychology, 9,* 68–70.

Trachtman, G. M. (1972). Pupils, parents, privacy, and the school psychologist. *American Psychologist, 27,* 37–45.

Trachtman, G. M. (1974). Ethical issues in school psychology. *The School Psychology Digest, 3,* 4–15.

Vetter, H. J., & Rieber, R. W. (Eds.). (1980). *The psychological foundations of criminal justice* (Vol. 2). New York: John Jay Press.

Weinberger, L. E., & Sreenivasan, S. (1994). Ethical and professional conflicts in correctional psychology. *Professional Psychology: Research and Practice, 25,* 161–167.

Welch, E. T. (1991). *Counselor's guide to the brain and its disorders: Knowing the difference between disease and sin.* Grand Rapids, MI: Zondervan.

Woody, R. H. (1989). Working with families: A school psychology training perspective. *Professional School Psychology, 4,* 257–260.

15

Psychologists in the Legal System
Tort and Retort

> Whatever their other contributions to our society,
> lawyers could be an important source of protein.
>
> Guindon, the cartoon witch

Psychologists are increasingly finding themselves involved with the legal system as defendants or plaintiffs. Psychologists are also playing an important role as expert witnesses or consultants for many different types of legal matters. This is well illustrated by the growing number of books on psychology and the law, the creation of an APA (American Psychological Association) division on that topic, and the emergence of journals such as *Law and Psychology* and *Law and Public Policy*. The legal arena is also paradigmatic of a special work setting, as described in chapter 14, replete with ethical dilemmas for psychologists (Committee on Ethical Guidelines for Forensic Psychologists, 1991). The reasons for this phenomenon are many, but include (1) the evolving nature of psychological practice, (2) the increasing acceptance and utilization of psychological data in legal proceedings, and (3) the heightened accountability to which psychologists are being held when clients believe they have suffered damages as the result of a psychologist's behavior.

The evolution of psychological practice in

forensic roles is linked to the increasing popularity of forensic psychology as a speciality (Weiner & Hess, 1987). Psychologists have recognized that forensic services are not hampered by the same constraints managed care has imposed on health care services. In addition, psychological research in areas such as competency assessment, child custody outcomes, jury selection, and other areas have had a direct impact on the utility and acceptance of psychological testimony. Sometimes, psychological researchers are surprised to find their published work has been used inappropriately in court without their knowledge (see Case 12-8). With regard to psychologists as defendants, survey research and case reports have proven useful in documenting the damages that some clients suffer due to professional negligence. As a result, the ability of aggrieved clients to seek compensation through legal proceedings has shifted accordingly in the direction of increased litigation.

The role of the psychologist as a plaintiff is not addressed here. Except for special considerations when a psychologist sues a client for nonpayment of professional fees, addressed in chapter 10, psychologists are no different in standing than any other profession when bringing suit against another person. This chapter focuses instead on the role of the psychologist as an expert witness and the issues confronting psychologists as defendants in legal actions. Both circumstances can evoke considerable anxiety for similar reasons. In either instance, the consequences of the psychologist's behavior can be very significant. In addition, the legal system, its procedures, culture, and officialdom are often quite different from those to which the psychologist is usually accustomed. The ethical codes of psychologists and lawyers are also very different in focus and content, which results in frequent misunderstandings.

THE CULTURE GAP BETWEEN PSYCHOLOGISTS AND LAWYERS

Several key differences exist in training and culture between psychologists and lawyers that contribute to confusion between the professions. Psychologists are trained as behavioral scientists to believe that an individual who applies rigorous experimental methods can discover significant truths within ranges of statistical certainty. We seldom give simple dichotomous answers to questions, preferring to use probabilities, ranges, norms, and continua that reflect the complexity of individual differences. Lawyers are educated as advocates to believe that the search for truth is best conducted in a vigorous adversarial cross-examination of the facts. They are taught that the facts must be "tried" or weighed and that clear, precise, unambiguous decisions must result. A criminal defendant must be found guilty or innocent. A civil defendant is either liable for damages or not. When damages are assessed, a specific dollar value is determined, even for such complex concepts as the value of a human life. The law seeks black and white answers and eschews the shades of gray that behavioral scientists relish. One cannot simultaneously be a dispassionate scientist, seeking to explain behavior in objective terms, and a partisan advocate seeking to win the day for one's client.

Psychologists must be especially wary when treading into the legal system. They are in philosophically alien territory and will be exposed to frequent opportunities and enticements to compromise their scientific integrity, overlook their ethical obligations, or otherwise put themselves at risk. Consider the following case examples:

Case 15-1: Wellin Tentioned, Ph.D., is recruited to serve as an expert witness by Prima Facie, attorney-at-law. Ms. Facie is representing a client injured in an automobile accident. She hopes that Dr. Tentioned's research on the effects of alcohol ingestion on reaction time will bolster her client's lawsuit. Facie will portray her injured client in the most sympathetic light possible, pay Dr. Tentioned an hourly rate far in excess of his usual university salary, and press him hard to state his findings in the way that most strongly supports her case.

Case 15-2: Carl Cathexis, Psy.D., treated Phineas Bluster in psychoanalysis five times per week for nearly 2 years. Dr. Cathexis offered Mr. Bluster a clinical interpretation and was taken aback by the rageful transference reaction it precipitated. Bluster stormed out of the office saying, "You'll hear from my lawyer, I'm going to sue." Bluster did not return for further sessions. A few weeks later, Dr. Cathexis receives a letter from an attorney representing Mr. Bluster, who had enclosed a release form and was asking for copies of all case records. Dr. Cathexis makes a note to himself, "Telephone Bluster and suggest he stop this acting out and return to treatment so that we can work through the transference."

In each of these cases, the psychologist is in a highly vulnerable position with a significant chance of slipping into ethical quicksand because of inexperience with the legal system. Dr. Tentioned is at risk of becoming an unwitting partisan in attorney Facie's advocacy plan. If Tentioned is going to consult as an expert witness, he must be prepared to assert and maintain his scholarly and professional integrity. He can feel empathy for the client and is entitled to be reasonably compensated for his professional time, but cannot allow his professional judgment to be swayed by cajoling, sympathy, or monetary considerations. Dr. Cathexis is at risk of allowing his potentially valid theoretical conceptualization of Mr. Bluster's behavior to cloud his judgment in what has clearly become a legal matter, regardless of whether Cathexis chooses to recognize it as such. His planned phone call will almost certainly exacerbate the situation and put him at greater legal risk than is currently the case.

Poythress (1979) describes several curricula for psychologists interested in forensic work, including topical introductions (e.g., philosophical issues, terminology, application of psychological skills to legal problems, and ethical issues); topical seminars (e.g., criminal law, civil law, child/juvenile law); and supervised practica or field placements. Such formal training is obviously a necessity for those who would be forensic "experts." A special issue of the journal, *Ethics and Behavior* (1993, volume 3–4), highlighted the complexity and diversity of the content domain. In the discussion that follows, the hazards of being a psychological expert or defendant are reviewed in detail. The key principle to keep in mind is that psychologists who venture into the legal arena, whether by choice or chance, should not do so without specialized training or expert guidance. When in doubt, consult an attorney who will represent only your interests.

THE FORENSIC EXPERT

As previously noted, the logic of jurisprudence assumes that truth may best be revealed when two parties confront each other with passionate debate on the merits of their respective cases. In contrast, the rules of science assume that a single party employing rigorous scientific methods can test and eliminate erroneous conclusions (Anderten, Staulcup, & Grisso, 1980). Anderten and her colleagues also note that the law requires that decisions based on available evidence be made regardless of residual ambiguities. Science, and psychology in particular, do not require that all problems investigated have a clear conclusion. Scientists must endure ambiguity with nearly infinite patience to avoid conclusions based on inadequate data. These differences highlight key sources of potential ethical conflicts.

Unlike so-called percipient witnesses, who are called to testify as to what they personally perceived (e.g., saw, heard, touched, smelled, or tasted), expert witnesses may give opinions to the court. Experts help the trier of fact (i.e., judge or jury) reach an opinion by providing specialized information not available to the layperson. Experts may report on specialized examinations they conduct, critique or interpret data provided by others, and respond to hypothetical situations or fact patterns proposed by lawyers. In this context, the word *expert* is a legal term established under rules of evidence, not a psychological term. Expert status is based on a judge's ruling after review of information on the training, education, and *voir dire* examination of the witness. Based on the old French term meaning to "speak the truth," the *voir dire* is preliminary questioning of the expert under oath to establish qualifications. The legal system uses breadth, depth, and duration of experience as part of qualifying or credentialing an expert witness. Judges and juries expect expert witnesses to be unbiased educators who help them to understand technical information necessary for their deliberations, despite the fact that one side pays for the service (Ackerman, 1995). Clinicians should be aware, however, that clinical experience by itself is unrelated to the accuracy of diagnostic judgments (Faust, 1994; Garb, 1989, 1992).

In addition to the differences in perspectives between psychologists and lawyers described above, the courtroom setting can be a disarmingly seductive place where a psychologist can too easily forget about professional rigor. Imagine a setting in which you are asked to play a role in assessing truth and justice, central values of American society. Surrounded by the trappings of power (e.g., official buildings, flags, robed judges, and uniformed court officers), you are placed at center stage in the witness box, acknowledged as an expert in the eyes of the court, and carefully questioned about your opinions (a luxury not extended to lay witnesses). All of those present hang on your every word, and a stenographer dutifully records it all for posterity. You are asked about weighty matters, and the fate of others may well turn on what you have to say. Will the temptation to provide crisp answers and have your advice taken cause you to forget, even for a moment, the scientific underpinnings and caveats that necessarily accompany psychological "facts"? How can the skills of the psychologist be most fairly and ethically applied in the courtroom and other legal contexts? Should the psychologist be a dispassionate educator about behavioral science or a fully partisan collaborator on the advocacy team? The questions are clearly rhetorical, but the ethical dilemmas are quite serious. The trappings of expertise cannot be allowed to cloud the judgment or analytical ability of the psychologist. Rather, they should be highly sobering and signal the would-be expert a need to be thoughtful, cautious, nondefensive, and scientifically rigorous in the testimony that is about to occur.

Specialty Guidelines for Forensic Psychologists

The American Psychology-Law Society, also known as Division 41 of the APA, developed a set of practice guidelines (Committee on Ethical Guidelines for Forensic Psychologists, 1991) that were subsequently approved by the group and by the American Academy of Forensic Psychology. Although never submitted to the APA Council of Representatives for adoption as official APA standards, these guidelines provide an important model of practice to which all forensic psychologists should aspire. These guidelines generally elaborate basic aspects of the APA ethics code in force at that time. Elements of the guidelines are addressed throughout this chapter; however, some aspects that bear on the differences between psychologists and lawyers deserve special mention here.

Contingent fees are a useful example of a practice commonly used by lawyers, but very inappropriate for psychologists doing forensic work. Lawyers will frequently take on cases in which the client pays a small percentage of the legal fees and agrees that the lawyer will be entitled to a percentage of any financial award if the case is won. Because the lawyer is expected to function as an advocate for the client, such a contingency is appropriate. However, when a psychologist testifies as an expert whose testimony is to be relied on by a judge or jury trying the facts of the case, agreeing to a fee based on the trial outcome is ethically inappropriate.

Case 15-3: Slimy Grubber, Ph.D., was approached by an attorney representing Eben Fired in an employment discrimination case against Large Multinational Corporation (LMC). LMC is alleging that Mr. Fired had serious personality problems that compromised his work and led to his termination. The attorney believes Mr. Fired's assertion that he was inappropriately fired from his job at LMC for discriminatory reasons and tells Dr. Grubber that there is a good chance of winning triple punitive damages to yield a financial award of $1.5 million or more. Mr. Fired's attorney would like Grubber to evaluate his client with an eye toward rebutting LMC's assertions. Unfortunately, Fired is unemployed and has no money to pay for evaluation service. The attorney offers Grubber 2% of the ultimate financial settlement in exchange for his services.

Were Dr. Grubber to agree to these terms, he would be engaging in significant unethical conduct. To begin, Grubber would essentially be agreeing to support the plaintiff's position before ever evaluating the plaintiff. In addition, Dr. Grubber would have a significant incentive to cast Mr. Fired in a favorable light regardless of the actual facts of the case or psychological data. Even if Dr. Grubber were able to ignore his potential gain and testify objectively, his testimony would be given with the appearance of conflicting interests and would easily be discredited in court.

Role conflicts are also a significant issue for forensic mental health professionals. In many situations there will be invitations to switch roles from therapist to an evaluator or vice versa. The demands of conducting an ethical, objective, expert evaluation often conflict with those required to function as an effective therapist. It may be possible to shift from one role to another under some circumstances, with the full informed consent of the client, but such changes should be undertaken only with extreme caution.

Case 15-4: Dahlia Discord, Ph.D., has been treating Melissa Malfunction for anxiety and mild depression in the aftermath of an automobile accident. Ms. Malfunction has been out of work for 3 months and is collecting disability payments. Her case is scheduled for a disability review, and she has asked Dr. Discord to complete a disability evaluation form and testify as a psychological expert in support of her claim. Dr. Discord would like to be supportive of her psychotherapy client, but is not certain that she can support Ms. Malfunction's claim that she is totally unable to work at any job for emotional reasons.

Psychotherapists are often asked to write letters of various sorts in support of their clients, but must be careful not to compromise their professional integrity. Dr. Discord should not allow herself to be manipulated into making a recommendation or evaluative statement that she cannot support. At the same time, she does not want to disrupt the rapport with her client. One possible solution would be to advise Ms. Malfunction that, although she cares deeply about her welfare, Dr. Discord cannot take on the role of an independent evaluator to determine disability. Dr. Discord could also agree to write a letter, with the client's consent, that documents her work with Ms. Malfunction, the symptoms reported by the client, her diagnostic impressions, and other treatment information. However, the letter should include only accurate information and should avoid commenting specifically on Ms. Malfunction's ability to work or qualification for disability. Those recommendations should be left to other mental health experts who do not have preexisting or ongoing therapeutic relationships with her.

Case 15-5: Ben and Betty Bombast were so angry at each other about their impending divorce that they could not seem to agree about anything. They certainly could not imagine arranging child custody plans for their children, Barney and Bella. When Hugh Kidder, Psy.D., a private practitioner with extensive experience in child custody matters, was appointed to provide family mediation services through the court clinic, they reluctantly agreed to try. The Bombast's were amazed by the way Dr. Kidder was able to establish rapport with

each of them and with the children. He refocused the parents on the children's needs, and they were able to agree on a joint custody plan on their own after several sessions. Dr. Kidder was able to issue a report to the court in support of their decision. A few weeks after the divorce was final, the Bombasts both contacted Dr. Kidder at his private office. Barney was having some school adjustment problems, and both parents agreed that they would like Dr. Kidder to evaluate and counsel him. They expressed considerable mutual confidence in Dr. Kidder because of their previous experience with him.

Assuming that Dr. Kidder's arrangement with the court clinic does not preclude working with former court-referred clients in this way, the Bombast's request may be a reasonable one. However, Dr. Kidder would first have to carefully consider and discuss with the Bombasts the nature of this role transition. Once he agrees to become the therapist for one member of the divorced family, he could not reasonably resume a mediator or evaluator role should the Bombasts again begin to bicker. His primary obligation would be refocused on the best interests of their child. Assuming that all are in agreement and that no other roadblocks are evident, Dr. Kidder could ethically proceed in his new role.

Training Issues

Doctoral training programs have not historically prepared psychologists for participation in the forensic arena (Brodsky, 1991; Melton, 1987; Poythress, 1979). Most psychologists are unfamiliar with the adversary system and with legal tests and concepts such as levels of proof, competence to stand trial, criminal responsibility, or legal definitions of insanity. Well-trained mental health clinicians often confuse psychological concepts (e.g., psychosis) with legal ones (e.g., insanity). Even when the psychologist understands the legal concepts and questions, usual training in psychological assessment is often of little help in answering them (Brodsky, 1991; Poythress, 1979; Shapiro, 1991). Few of the standard instruments used in psychological test batteries have, for example, content or construct validity that bears on competence issues or the prediction of dangerousness.

Case 15-6: Hasty Injuria, Ph.D., was approached by an attorney to do a pretrial evaluation of his client, who had been charged with assault and battery. Injuria administered the WAIS-III (Wechsler Adult Intelligence Scale III), Thematic Apperception Test, Rorschach Inkblots, Minnesota Multiphasic Personality Inventory (MMPI), and the House-Tree-Person drawing. When placed on the witness stand, Dr. Injuria was asked about the defendant's propensity to commit violent acts against others and about his criminal responsibility at the time of the alleged assault. Although Injuria had no information regarding the defendant's history (which was devoid of violent acts) and was unfamiliar with the concept of criminal responsibility, he testified that the defendant was schizophrenic and therefore clearly both dangerous and not responsible.

Not only did Dr. Injuria misunderstand the legal concepts in question, he was also not in a position to address the questions on the basis of solid knowledge. He did not, for example, consider one of the most consistent predictors of dangerous behavior (i.e., prior dangerous behavior) and made the erroneous assumption that being schizophrenic per se absolves one of responsibility for one's acts and indicates dangerousness. In this case, the psychologist made the major mistake of falling back on an old and successful assessment behavior (i.e., his standard clinical test battery) without recognizing his involvement in a special setting with unique requirements and complexities he was not qualified to address (Committee on Ethical Guidelines for Forensic Psychologists, 1991; Grisso & Appelbaum, 1992). In his ignorance, Injuria may well have caused serious problems for his client.

The Quality of Expertise

A more basic question that is being debated among psychologists and attorneys is the question of what kinds of opinions, if any, by mental health professionals are sufficiently reliable and valid to warrant admissibility (see Golding, 1990;

Melton, Petrila, Poythress, & Slobogin, 1987; Morse, 1982; Poythress, 1982; Sales & Shuman, 1993). Beyond the question of whether courts should admit such opinions, is the issue of the limits that ethics must place on the expression of opinions (EP: 7.04). This is especially true when psychologists are called on to give "informed speculation" (Bonnie & Slobogin, 1980; Golding, 1990; McCloskey, Egeth, & McKenna, 1986) on matters defined in law rather than behavioral science. For example, it is clearly unethical to provide an ultimate issue opinion without also giving the caveat that such opinions are legal judgments and are not based on psychological expertise. In a legal case, the ultimate issue is the question to be decided by the trier of fact (i.e., the judge or the jury charged with weighing the evidence).

Case 15-7: Barney Bezerk was to stand trial for the axe murder of his family of four. His attorney was planning to use an insanity defense and hired Cruddy O'Pinion, Psy.D., to conduct an expert psychological evaluation. The evaluation revealed that Mr. Bezerk had a major thought disorder, poor impulse control, considerable unmodulated anger, and considerable paranoid ideation. In particular, Mr. Bezerk's auditory hallucinations had repeatedly warned him that alien beings had taken over the bodies of his family and were about to embark on the conquest of Earth. Dr. O'Pinion cited all these findings and concluded his report with the statement that Mr. Bezerk was clearly insane at the time of the offense.

The ultimate issue of whether a defendant was "insane" at the time of an offense is not a psychological question since the concept of insanity is defined by law, rather than by psychology. Dr. O'Pinion can appropriately describe the defendant's bizarre behavior, confirm his impulsivity and instability with test data, explain how a lack of control might result, link these findings to the facts of the case, and provide other such expert commentary. Based on his knowledge of schizophrenia and his evaluation of Mr. Bezerk, Dr. O'Pinion may also testify about the probability that the symptoms observed were likely to have affected the defendant's behavior on the day of the crime. However, it is up to the judge or jury to decide whether the information presented proves beyond a reasonable doubt that Mr. Bezerk met the legal definition of insanity. Too frequently, psychologists will neglect such cautions in their testimony and may even be encouraged to do so by attorneys and judges (Melton et al., 1987; Sales & Shuman, 1993).

The Use of Research Data

The extent to which psychologists called to testify as expert witnesses can fall back on scientific research data has been a topic of much professional interest (Loftus, 1986; Loftus & Monahan, 1980; McCloskey et al., 1986; Tanke & Tanke, 1979). Whereas expert psychological testimony based on empirical data has been used in cases that deal with jury size, eyewitness identification, prediction of dangerousness, adequacy of warning labels, and child custody, to name a few (Loftus, 1986; Loftus & Monahan, 1980), judges and juries are not always influenced by these presentations. Some interesting questions have been raised regarding the context in which such research is presented. Are the findings valid and generalizable to the situation in question? Are there legitimate differences in interpretation of the data, and, if so, must the psychologist testifying present both sides? How should psychologists testifying deal with the probabilistic nature of some research findings? What role should the psychologist's personal values play in the decision to testify or not in certain cases?

Case 15-8: Helena Scruples, Ph.D., is very knowledgeable in regard to research in eyewitness identification. Her research shows the frequent unreliability of such identifications. She is sought as an expert witness by the defense in a rape case. Dr. Scruples is sympathetic to the woman who was raped and knows that it is difficult to convict men charged with rape. If she agrees to help the defense, she may be reducing the defendant's chance of being convicted.

Case 15-9: Herman Beastly is accused of raping and murdering an adolescent babysitter. Evidence

strongly indicates that he is guilty and can be sentenced to death based on a state law that permits capital punishment for criminals likely to commit repeat violent crimes of this sort. John Qualm, Psy.D., is considered an expert on the prediction of dangerousness and has published reports that highlight the difficulty in making such prediction reliably. He is asked to testify by the defense in the hope that his opinions may save Beastly from execution.

Both of these cases illustrate major clashes in personal value systems. Both Scruples and Qualm may be repulsed by their client's behavior. At the same time, each defendant is entitled to a vigorous legal defense. Although the defendant has a right to present the relevant scientific data, any given psychologist is not ethically obligated to testify in such a case simply because he or she is asked to do so. The expert's beliefs, preferences, and personal values certainly enter into any decision about testifying. In similar situations, Loftus reports reasoning that her testimony could help to prevent the conviction of an innocent person (Loftus & Monahan, 1980). Monahan reports testifying for the defense in a case similar to Dr. Qualm's because, although repulsed by the defendant, he is morally opposed to the death penalty (Loftus & Monahan, 1980).

The extent to which an expert witness is obligated to present both sides when discussing psychological research or theory is also a very complex matter. Wolfgang (1974) and Rivlin (1973), for example, make cases for the legitimacy of the expert scientist as an adversary. That is, they assert that a balanced objective presentation of research or theory is not needed in expert testimony. Loftus and Monahan (1980) point out, on the other hand, that an oath to "tell the whole truth and nothing but the truth" is violated if the "whole truth" is not told. They note also that opposing counsel may always ask the witness: "Do you know of any studies which show the opposite result?" (p. 279). We would not argue in favor of universal discussion of all possible interpretations of a data set, but we strongly agree with the assertion that the whole truth is a necessity for the psychologist acting as an expert witness.

Hypnosis in the Courtroom

Hypnosis presents an excellent prototypical example of how a technique that has been widely used by psychologists can lead to special complications in forensic settings. Hypnosis has been widely used in forensic settings by mental health practitioners and others (Annon, 1989; Spiegel & Spiegel, 1987). Inappropriate applications of hypnotic techniques have, however, occasionally led to significant compromise in the judicial process. In fact, when the 1992 version of the APA ethics code was being adopted, the Council Representative for the Division of Psychological Hypnosis succeeded in inserting a vaguely worded late amendment (ES: 6.04) that stated, "Psychologists do not teach the use of . . . hypnosis . . . to individuals who lack the prerequisite training" (APA, 1992, p. 1607). An article published in *Science* summarized the problem succinctly: "Researchers fear misuse by police and warn that hypnotic state is no guarantor of truth" (Kolata, 1980). While the intense concentration that characterizes hypnosis often enables individuals to recall events or details in striking fashion (Yuille & Kim, 1987), many individuals may respond with embellishments to subtle suggestions of the examiners. Following a hypnotic session, some hypnotic subjects may "confabulate" or inject new elements into their reports of events. These confabulations may be based on conscious or unconscious motivations (Kolata, 1980).

Case 15-10: Theodore Trance, Ed.D., consulted with the police investigating a double homicide. He hypnotized and interrogated a woman who claimed to be an eyewitness to the murders, but recalled little of what happened. During the hypnotic sessions, the woman emotionally recalled being forced by two male companions to shoot the two victims. Her testimony resulted in conviction of the two for murder. Subsequently, it became clear that the two were innocent, and that the woman had substantial motivation to wish them punished for reasons of her own.

It seems that Dr. Trance failed to investigate fully the background and motivation of the woman he was asked to hypnotize. At the time of the trial, there were also allegations that Dr. Trance may have conducted his questioning of the witness in a suggestive manner; however, tapes of his sessions with the woman had somehow been erased. No information was provided to the jury regarding the potential for confabulation by individuals using hypnotic techniques to "enhance" memory for purposes of testimony.

As a result of cases such as this one, many jurisdictions now prohibit from being admitted as evidence at a trial information uncovered through hypnosis. Psychologists have long recognized the fact that hypnosis interacts significantly with suggestibility, and Dr. Trance's role in applying it with few caveats and cautions raises serious ethical problems (Annon, 1989; Spiegel & Spiegel, 1987).

Child Custody

Divorce may affect as many as 40% of children and 50% of newly married couples (Bray & Hetherington, 1993; Castro-Martin & Bumpass, 1989), and parents agree on child custody and visitation 90% of the time (Melton et al., 1987), leaving no dispute for the court to decide. However, in the 10% of cases that are disputed, mental health professionals are increasingly involved as *guardians ad litem*, evaluators, mediators, and psychotherapists. Psychologists may also find themselves unwittingly involved in such cases when the marriage of one of their clients (or child client's parents) begins to dissolve.

Most mental health professionals agree that matters of child custody should be predicated on the best interests of the child. Occasionally, that is their only point of agreement. Some writers on the nature side of the fence have asserted that "Family loyalty is . . . [based] . . . on biological hereditary kinship" (Boszhormenyi-Nagy & Spark, 1973, p. 42). Others, on the nurture side, argue that biological ties are far less important than psychological ones based on "a continuing, day-to-day basis . . . [which] . . . fulfills the child's psychological needs for a parent, as well as the child's physical needs" (Goldstein, Freud, & Solnit, 1979, p. 98). Common criticisms of mental health professionals' work in child custody cases include (1) deficiencies and abuses in professional practice, (2) inadequate familiarity with the legal system and applicable legal standards, (3) inappropriate application of psychological assessment techniques, (4) presentation of opinions based on partial or irrelevant data, (5) overreaching by exceeding the limits of psychological knowledge of expert testimony, (6) offering opinions on matters of law, (7) loss of objectivity through inappropriate engagement in the adversary process, and (8) failure to recognize the boundaries and parameters of confidentiality in the custody context (EP: 7.02–7.06; APA, 1994; Weithorn, 1987).

It is very difficult to predict what will happen as a result of custody decisions. Unfortunately, however, it can be reliably predicted that a contested custody situation will have an adverse effect on the children. Great stresses, both emotional and financial, are applied, and there are prolonged periods of uncertainty and instability in the lives of such children. They are subjected to the whims of the legal system and too often are cast as pawns in the struggle between sets of angry combatants for custody. Into this void rides (or are tossed) too many unwary would-be psychological Solomons ready to share their wisdom with the courts to resolve these agonizing cases, despite the fact that there is no research base on which to support many opinions about custody (Clingempeel & Reppucci, 1982; DeKraai & Sales, 1991; Melton et al., 1987; Weithorn, 1987). Too often, psychologists agree to assist in performing child custody evaluations with little understanding of statutes that govern child custody, adversarial proceedings, data useful for making such decisions (Ackerman, 1995; APA, 1994; Weithorn, 1987), or their own values and attitudes that might contribute to biased outcomes (APA, 1994). At times, these custodial struggles clearly harm a child rather than attend to his or her best interests.

There are times, however, when psychological testimony or participation, even short of actual courtroom appearance, is relevant and constructive (Melton et al., 1987; Woody, 1988). Ideally, the psychologist should function as an advocate for the child or as a neutral expert, preferably appointed by the court to avoid being cast as the advocate of one contesting party or the other (Ackerman, 1995; Weithorn, 1987). This will not always work, however, and at times

full adversarial proceedings, with experts on both sides, result. It is not our purpose to provide a "how to do it" manual here, but rather to highlight some potential ethical problems that can arise and be detrimental to all concerned.

Case 15-11: Helen Tester, Ph.D., agreed to undertake a child custody evaluation. During the course of her assessment, she administered psychological tests, including the MMPI-2 and the Rorschach Inkblots, to both parents. The mother, who was a foreign national, had an elevated L-scale score on the MMPI-2 and was "evasive" on the Rorschach inquiry. As a result, Dr. Tester concluded that she was a "highly defended pathological liar" and recommended against awarding her custody.

Dr. Tester made several serious errors. To begin, she seems to be basing her evaluation on two instruments that have never been validated for use in child custody work (i.e., the Rorschach and MMPI-2). Indeed, she seems to be misinterpreting the actual meaning of the L scale and is taking one score out of context from the overall profile. Her interpretation of an MMPI-2 profile obtained from a foreign national, whose culture and language may differ from the standardization group, raises additional validity questions. Dr. Tester's conclusion, based on two isolated test findings that have many alternative interpretations, is highly suspect. One wonders if Dr. Tester ever bothered to do critically important interviews with the child or observe parent-child interactions.

Case 15-12: Jack Balance, Psy.D., undertook a child custody evaluation at the request of the attorney representing the child's father. The attorney advised Dr. Balance that both parents were interested in cooperating with the evaluation. Balance met with the father and the child for assessment purposes, but the mother subsequently declined to participate. At the trial, Dr. Balance testified only with respect to the child-father relationship, but the mother's attorney attempted to discredit him as an expert because he had not interviewed the child's mother.

Dr. Balance would have been better advised to confirm in advance the willingness of all parties to cooperate. This might have been accomplished through personal contact or by court order, if necessary. He was certainly being ethical in commenting only on his actual contacts (i.e., the adequacy of the child-father relationship) while refraining from any comments about the parent who declined to participate. In addition, Dr. Balance had to pay special attention to note the limitations, based on incomplete data, of any recommendations he might make (APA, 1994). The attempt to discredit his testimony is unfortunate, but not a matter of psychological ethics.

Case 15-13: Sam and Sylvia Splitter were in the midst of a bitter divorce and child custody dispute. Each sought and found a mental health professional willing to advocate on their behalf at the custody hearing. Both professionals testified in support of "their client" based on interviews with the one parent and children. Neither professional had sought contact with the other parent or the other professional prior to the hearing, and each testimony dramatically contradicted the other.

The Splitters have successfully "split" the clinicians they each hired and set up a so-called battle of the shrinks. Nothing does more to discredit the mental health professions in public than adversarial confrontations by experts with only pieces of the data. While the Splitters may have set up this situation, both mental health professionals were foolish to agree to participate. Under ideal circumstances, the professionals would have insisted on (1) functioning as nonpartisan experts, (2) demanding access to all appropriate data, and (3) seeking the right to interview the other spouse as a prerequisite for agreeing to do the evaluation. One cannot help but wonder whether their contradictory testimony grew out of information that their clients kept from them.

Case 15-14: Cynthia Oops, Psy.D., conducted a careful evaluation of both parents and two children involved in a custody dispute. She had been recruited by one parent, but her participation was seemingly agreed to by the other. When Dr. Oops

completed her report prior to the hearing, the parent who was not favored asserted her right of confidentiality and demanded that the report be kept out of court. Dr. Oops had not obtained a signed waiver from the parties.

Dr. Oops had the best of intentions, but she should have spelled out the parameters of her role from the outset. Each of her clients (i.e., the two parents and the children) should have been given a clear understanding of her obligations to each, especially since their needs and wishes were mutually exclusive in some areas. In particular, she should have secured written waivers from all concerned to share her findings with the court. Now, the status of one claim of confidentiality is unclear and will have to be resolved by the judge. It is not possible to predict the outcome based on the information presented, but the problem was avoidable.

While the case of Dr. Oops seems to be a routine confidentiality problem, a slight variation yields a rather commonly noted problem of a more complex nature. Suppose that Dr. Oops had provided marriage counseling to both parents prior to their decision to divorce and is subsequently subpoenaed by one to testify in a child custody dispute. In this situation, a legitimate duty of confidentiality to both parties might exist even if Oops believes that she has some basis on which to offer an opinion to the courts. Ideally, Dr. Oops should avoid such a role by discussing the potential problem early (if it appears a couple in treatment may divorce) or by suggesting that expert testimony be sought from another practitioner who does not have a preexisting relationship with the clients. All of these examples support the overarching premise that no substitute for specialized education and training exists, including sensitivity to special ethical issues inherent in forensic work.

Conducting a Forensic Evaluation

In undertaking any sort of evaluation that is likely to come before the courts, a psychologist should pay special attention to helping the person being examined to understand the purpose of the activity and the people or agencies who will have access to the information. Even when the evaluation is court ordered or paid for by a governmental agency, the psychologist must recognize that the individual being assessed is a client, too.

Consent and confidentiality issues must be treated different from most other psychological work when forensic issues are involved. Before undertaking any forensic evaluation, it is critical that interviewees be notified that any of their statements or findings of the evaluation may become a part of the public record. The APA ethics code (EP: 5.01) requires that clients be notified of the limits of confidentiality from the outset of the professional relationship. In a forensic evaluation, there are often many layers of clients, such as the state, the attorney, and the person being interviewed. Rather than assuring confidentiality, forensic evaluators must fully inform the people they interview that no privilege exists. These individuals should instead be cautioned to avoid saying anything that they prefer not be revealed. In many jurisdictions and circumstances, the written consent of the interviewee is not technically required. We recommend, however, that the psychologist always give notice of the limitations and seek evidence to confirm that the client understood the information. Ideally, this notice should be acknowledged by the client in writing or witnessed by an objective third party. In some criminal cases, expert testimony may be excluded from consideration if such notice was not given.

Case 15-15: Mr. Smith was indicted for murder, and the prosecutor for the state of Texas announced that he would seek the death penalty. Dr. Grigson, a psychiatrist who later came to be nicknamed "Dr. Death" by some, was assigned to evaluate Smith's competence to stand trial. After a single 90-minute interview, Dr. Grigson determined that Smith was competent and so testified. Smith was tried and convicted. A separate penalty-phase proceeding was held for the jury to determine whether to impose the death penalty. One factor the jury had to consider was any propensity for Smith to commit similar acts again. Dr. Grigson was again called by the state to testify about any proclivity of Mr. Smith toward future violence. Based on the same 90-minute interview, Dr. Grigson opined that Smith would be a continuing

danger to society. The jury sentenced Smith to death.

The facts summarized here are the essentials of *Estelle v. Smith* (1981), in which the Supreme Court overturned the death sentence. This case is fully discussed by Bersoff (1995), but the key issue can best be understood as one of consent. Mr. Smith was not advised that he had a right to remain mute when interviewed by Dr. Grigson, and Smith was not told that information he told Grigson might later be used in the death penalty phase of the case. The same principle applies to all forensic evaluations, both civil and criminal. The client has the right to know at the outset the full purpose of the evaluation and the parties who will have access to it. Even when an evaluation is not court ordered, but may ultimately serve some forensic purpose, we recommend clarifying these issues. When conducting a child custody evaluation, for example, it is wise to obtain reciprocating waivers of confidentiality that cover the contesting parties and their counsel. Many divorcing couples who seek consultation from a psychologist on custody matters as they plan their custody agreement never intend to litigate the issue, but change their minds later (Gardner, 1992; Hetherington, 1990; Koocher & Keith-Spiegel, 1992).

Case 15-16: Bob and Harriet Splinter have decided to divorce and want to do what is best for their three young children. They seek therapeutic consultation with Connie Sensus, Ph.D., a family psychologist in the community, about joint custody and visitation options. During their sessions together, Bob acknowledges that Harriet would be better as the custodial parent because he has a drinking problem and was involved in some unsavory delinquent conduct as a youth. They agree that the children will live with Harriet and that Bob will have frequent visitation. Just before finalizing the full divorce agreement, Bob and Harriet have a falling out over financial issues, and Bob states his intent to seek sole custody of the children. Harriet wants to call Dr. Sensus as a witness and plans to use her testimony to get Bob's admitted character flaws on the record. Bob demands that Sensus keep confidential all that he told her.

One may not agree with either Bob's or Harriet's conduct, but Dr. Sensus's lack of forethought has created a problem. In some jurisdictions (e.g., Texas), any rights of confidentiality that Bob or Harriet might assert with respect to their own mental health records would be set aside in the interests of the children. In other states, however, the outcome in terms of legally compelled disclosure would be less clear. If Dr. Sensus had raised this issue at the outset and had obtained consensual waivers from Bob and Harriet, she would be free to testify about any elements of her work with the Splinters that is relevant to the court.

Record keeping and documentation are especially important. Psychologists should keep more precisely detailed records in forensic cases than might be necessary in more routine treatment or assessment work (Vandecreek, 1986). Detailed information of dates, times, durations of appointments, phone calls, sources of information, reviews of records, examination of corroborating information (e.g., police reports), and other points that lead to an opinion should be recorded and cited in any forensic reports. Vagueness may become a source of vulnerability on the witness stand (Brodsky, 1991). Some psychologists take loose notes or make tentative observations and consolidate them into structured notes or reports, but once a formal report or official case note is written, it should not be altered. It is always possible to write and date an addendum or supplementary information to notes, but altering completed reports creates an aura of suspicion. For similar reasons, we recommend keeping only one set of records.

Case 15-17: Melba Meticulous, Ed.D., undertook a court-ordered child custody investigation for the Fragmento family. She conducted nearly 20 hours of interviews with the parties, the children, and collateral sources. Much of the information she gathered was relevant to the matters before the court, but some was extraneous (e.g., Mr. Fragmento wore a poor quality hairpiece; Mrs. Fragmento's great aunt Tillie died 6 years ago, and her husband had the temerity to tell jokes at the wake; Mrs. Fragmento is at least 30 pounds overweight; and the maternal grandmother recently underwent a facelift). The extraneous data made their way

into Dr. Meticulous' files as she did not know which bits would be relevant as she heard them. She will now complete her report, citing all relevant factors, and will then delete all extraneous material.

The procedures employed by Dr. Meticulous are entirely appropriate. If material she gathers proves relevant, it should be a part of the case file and her report. If any of the data collected prove to be irrelevant, they should not become a part of the permanent file.

Preparation for deposition and trial are important obligations of the forensic practitioner. It is important for psychologists to ensure that their knowledge is current in psychological conceptualization, assessment practices, ethical standards, and other relevant professional issues (Brodsky, 1994). For example, if choosing to use psychological tests, one must be sure that the test is validated for the intended purpose (Borum & Grisso, 1995). There is very little normative data available for applying most psychological tests to forensic assessment (Heilbrun, 1992), and some of the techniques used for forensic assessment (e.g., anatomically detailed dolls) do not even qualify as psychological tests (Koocher et al., 1995). Depositions (i.e., questioning under oath outside of court) are used by both sides in a case for purposes of discovery. Depositions help each side to weigh evidence that may lead to settlement discussions. They also allow witnesses to learn lines of inquiry that may be pursued at trial. It is entirely appropriate for psychologists to meet with the attorney who has hired them to review testimony beforehand (Brodsky, 1991). If you do not know the answer to a question, simply say so. Do not speculate beyond your knowledge, competence, or findings (Brodsky, 1994).

Understand the legal context and rules of evidence regarding what is acceptable (see, for example, Melton et al., 1987). Experts are bound by the *Daubert* decision of the U.S. Supreme Court (*Daubert v. Merrell Dow Pharmaceuticals*, 1993) to testify only within the scope of reasonable and accepted scientific knowledge. The *Daubert* decision identified four factors courts can use to assess validity when admitting scientific conclusions under the Federal

Rules of Evidence (Faigman, 1995; Zonana, 1994): (1) falsifiability, (2) error rate, (3) peer review and publication, and (4) general acceptance. Using these standards, expert testimony on eyewitness identification would hold up well under scrutiny for scientific validity, whereas expert testimony regarding so-called repressed memories might not (Ceci & Bruck, 1995; Faigman, 1995). Research results should be used in an impartial manner in the face of adversarial pulls of attorneys. It is not unethical to disagree with other experts about applications of knowledge, but it is unethical to relinquish the role of neutral expert in favor of highly selective gleaning of knowledge (Sales & Shuman, 1993; Sales & Simon, 1993). Do not deny existing information that contradicts your conclusions. Freely and without defensiveness acknowledge and discuss any contradicting information.

Psychologists must be careful to stay within the boundaries of their personal expertise. For example, special training beyond a generic doctoral degree in clinical or counseling psychology is required prior to undertaking forensic assessments that involve children, geriatric patients, or individuals with neuropsychological injuries. Do not be defensive about your credentials. Readily admit all nonaccomplishments matter of factly. Do not be afraid to admit ignorance or to say "I don't know."

Case 15-18: Windy Fluffball, J.D., Ph.D., agreed to serve as an expert witness in a civil lawsuit that involved alleged wrongful termination of a clinical psychology graduate student from a doctoral program. Dr. Fluffball expounded on his years of teaching and membership on the National Psychological Society's Education and Training Oversight Committee. On cross-examination Fluffball was forced to admit (1) his doctorate was in physiological psychology, (2) he never had clinical training, (3) he never taught in a clinical psychology program, (4) he was not licensed as a psychologist, and (5) he was newly appointed to the Education and Training Oversight Committee and had yet to attend a single meeting.

After the jury returned a verdict favoring the other side, the lawyers were allowed to poll the jurors and discovered that Dr. Fluffball's testimony was given very little weight. One must wonder whether the side for which he testified would have fared better using a witness who did less to inflate his qualifications.

PSYCHOLOGISTS AS DEFENDANTS

Rather than simply focus on psychological malpractice, it is more reasonable to think of the broader concept of professional liability as applying to all of one's professional service delivery activities. In a legal sense, there are four elements that must be present before a successful civil liability lawsuit is possible. First, the psychologist must have a professional relationship with the party in question. That is, a psychologist-client relationship must have existed with a resulting duty to the client. Second, there must be some negligence or dereliction of that duty on the part of the psychologist. Third, some harm must have accrued to the client as a direct result of the negligence or dereliction of the duty. Finally, a causal relationship between the negligence and the resulting damages must be shown (Bennett, Bryant, VandenBos, & Greenwood, 1990; Leesfield, 1987). Needless to say, by this definition a successful prosecution for malpractice would necessarily mean that the behavior of the psychologist was unethical by virtue of negligence.

Case 15-19: Luke Acher sought the services of Anna Sthesia, Psy.D., in response to her newspaper announcement of a pain clinic she had opened. Mr. Acher gave a history of low back pain that began several years earlier, and he expressed interest in the application of biofeedback techniques. He told Dr. Sthesia that he had "been to everyone, chiropractors, orthopedists, hypnotists, and even tried acupuncture." The psychologist initiated biofeedback training. Several weeks later, Mr. Acher collapsed at work and was taken to a hospital, where he was discovered to have a malignant tumor of the spine. The disease had metasticized widely and was too advanced for all but palliative care.

Case 15-20: Regina Yahoo met Sonia Specula, Ph.D., at a cocktail party. On learning that Specula was a psychologist who specialized in work with children, Ms. Yahoo began telling her about threats that her 15-year-old daughter was making to run away from home. Dr. Specula casually mentioned that "lots of teenagers say things like that to annoy their parents, but never do it." Two days later, Ms. Yahoo's daughter ran away from home and was hit by a truck and killed while attempting to hitchhike out of town.

Case 15-21: Manual Kant was angry that, after 9 months in psychotherapy with Seymour Suregood, Ph.D., still he could not get women to date him. For some reason, Kant did not understand why few women were willing to go out with him beyond the first date. Several had told him: "You need a lot of help!" Dr. Suregood had agreed to work with Kant on this problem, but as far as Kant could tell, things had not changed much.

All three of these clients attempted to sue the psychologist in question, but only one was successful. If you guessed that was Mr. Acher, then you probably understand the concept of malpractice. Acher was clearly a client of Dr. Sthesia's, and she clearly had an obligation to treat him reasonably. She neglected to check on his physical status or send for reports from the other professionals to whom he alluded, and she began to treat an important physical symptom (i.e., pain) without first ruling out a medical problem. By this negligent act, she contributed to a delay in forcing Mr. Acher to seek other treatment or proper evaluation, giving his cancer time to spread. While it is not clear that Mr. Acher's life could have been saved with early treatment, the psychologist's behavior may have cost him the opportunity to find out.

Dr. Specula was not guilty of malpractice. Perhaps she should have been more cautious in the willing way she gave advice, but it is clear that Ms. Yahoo was never her client. The contact was casual because it took place at a social gathering rather than in an office, no fees were charged or paid, and the relationship between the alleged advice and the injury sustained is by no means clear.

In the case of Dr. Suregood and Mr. Kant, there was indeed a psychologist-client relationship. We have no evidence of negligence, however, and no evidence that harm was sustained by the client. If Dr. Suregood had promised results within a certain time span and these did not occur, he might be accused of misrepresentation or misleading the client. But, we have no evidence that any promises of hard results were made. It is also unclear whether the best psychotherapist in the world would have been of greater help to Mr. Kant.

In some cases, causality becomes an important issue, as in the case of a psychologist named Carmichael, who practiced in Washington, DC.

Case 15-22: Frederica Saunders sought psychological treatment from Dr. Carmichael. During the course of counseling, Carmichael and Saunders engaged in sexual relations, and Carmichael convinced Saunders to divorce her husband. Carmichael and Saunders then married. Saunders later brought a malpractice action against her new husband after he sued for divorce. The trial court found Carmichael liable for malpractice and also granted the divorce. Carmichael appealed, claiming his wife did not prove harm. The appeals court found that Saunders did not present any expert testimony that showed a causal relationship between the malpractice and her injury. Her expert testified about the nature of transference and stated that initiating a sexual relationship during the course of a professional relationship was a fundamental betrayal of a patient's trust. This testimony could establish that Carmichael breached the applicable standard of care, and that Saunders' symptoms, which included depression, distress, and suicidal feelings, were consistent with the effects of a doctor betraying a patient's trust. The witness did not testify "to a reasonable degree of medical certainty" that Carmichael's behavior played a substantial part in causing his wife's injuries. Moreover, the expert admitted under cross-examination that all of Saunders's symptoms could have existed when she first sought treatment from Carmichael (*Carmichael v. Carmichael*, 1991).

The ethical offensiveness of Dr. Carmichael's conduct is clear. Unfortunately for Mrs. Carmichael's (the former patient-wife) effort to recover financial damages, it was not possible to legally link his behavior as the cause of the damages she suffered.

Common Precipitants of Suits Against Psychologists

Although at least 25 different types of suits (causes of action) against practitioners have been conceptualized (Hogan, 1979), most are unlikely hazards for psychologists in the sense that they are low-incidence bases of complaints (e.g., breach of contract, undue influence, alienation of affection, failure to supervise properly, failure to treat, complaints linked to serving on licensing boards or ethics committees, abandonment, false arrest or false imprisonment, abuse of process, assault and battery, and misrepresentation). Interestingly, the greatest number of malpractice or professional liability insurance claims against psychologists arise from complaints about sexual matters, finances, or problematic evaluations, including those associated with child custody and child sexual abuse evaluations; this underscores the need to develop significant expertise before venturing into such work (Bennett et al., 1990; Woody, 1988).

Retrospective review of claims against psychologists (Bennett et al., 1990; Wright, 1981a) reveals that two causes of suits against psychologists were very clear: sex and professional fees. Allegations of sexual misconduct are predictable enough as sources of complaint, but it is also worth noting that suits are also frequently filed when a practitioner takes steps to collect a debt (i.e., engages a collection agency or files suit against the client; see chapter 10). Wright also provides a very readable and useful set of suggestions to follow in the event psychologists are notified that they are about to be sued (1981b); many of these suggestions are incorporated in recommendations below. The good news is that the cumulative risk of a psychologist in the United States being sued is less than 0.5% (Bennet et al., 1990). The bad news is that defending such a suit is time consuming and costly in both financial and emotional terms.

Avoiding the Tort of Defamation

When false or misleading statements (or true statements that cannot be proven in court) damage a person's reputation, a defamation lawsuit may result. Oral defamation or slander may occur whenever comments about clients are made aloud in public settings. It is wise to be cautious in public statements about current or former clients, even when one has their consent. Exercise particular caution if you are inclined to use disguised clinical case materials in teaching or other oral public presentations. Written defamation or libel may occur when material in reports, letters, or other written media are deemed to have wrongly harmed another's reputation. Use care in record keeping, report writing, and use of disguised case materials in books or other published materials. Be especially careful of repeating information provided by angry spouses unless the source is clearly documented.

Specific Prevention Strategies

Aside from being competent and applying sound professional practices, in devising specific prevention strategies it is important to know and respect both your limitations and those of your employees and supervisees. Be aware of your psychological issues and vulnerabilities, including transference and countertransference hazards (APA, 1992). Avoid behaviors that might lead to sexual intimacies with clients (see chapter 9). Seek treatment for any substance abuse or personal emotional problems you may have (see chapter 3). Heed cautions from colleagues; if one of them dares to express concerns, there are probably several others who are thinking the same thing but are afraid to speak up. Avoid grandiose claims or outcome promises. Provide meaningful supervision to your support staff and to trainees whose work you oversee because you can be held responsible for their actions under the doctrine of *respondeat superior*.

Case 15-23: A woman known as Jane Doe sued the Samaritan Counseling Center as *respondeat superior* for the acts of one of its pastoral counselors; the counselor had sexual intercourse with her when she came to seek "emotional and spiritual therapy." During two of Doe's sessions at the agency, the counselor allegedly kissed and fondled her. Sexual intercourse followed outside the center after she had canceled her counseling sessions. A trial court initially dismissed the case, finding that the agency was not responsible for its employee's acts; however, the state supreme court disagreed. The court ruled that the fact that sexual intercourse occurred after Doe canceled therapy did not bar employer liability because the counselor's conduct during the sessions constituted the initiation of a sexual relationship and negligence in handling transference issues (*Doe v. Samaritan Counseling Center*, 1990).

In this case, the supervising agency was held financially responsible for the unethical acts of one of its employees, even though much of the offensive behavior was off site. Problems began while the therapist should have been under agency supervision.

Be especially sensitive when treating high-risk clients and in problematic practice areas. High-risk clients include clients you are not competent to treat, litigious clients, those with volatile psychopathology (e.g., borderline personality disorder, especially with histrionic or paranoid features), people with histories of dangerousness, and clients who develop a rapid or intense transference relationship. High-risk practice areas include child custody or other forensic or "high-scrutiny" arenas and work with some trauma victims (e.g., those seeking to recover memories of abuse). We are not suggesting that psychologists should never treat such clients or provide such services. Rather, we are emphasizing the importance of training and competence when dealing with these populations or providing services that carry an above-average risk component.

Be sure to carry adequate professional liability insurance and understand your coverage. Understand the differences between a "claims made" policy and an "occurrence-based" policy (APA, Insurance Trust, 1995). Only about half of claims against psychologists surface during any given insurance policy year to which they apply. As a result, it is important to maintain continuous coverage. A claims made policy covers acts that occurred during the policy year only if a renewed policy is in force when the complaint is filed. Psychologists who have such policies should buy "tail coverage" in order to cover any cases filed in subsequent years if they switch insurance companies or retire. The "tail" refers to the trailing off likelihood of claims

being filed as years go by. An occurrence policy is more expensive because tail coverage is built in to the price. Such policies provide coverage forever for any incidents that occurred during the policy year. We believe that professional liability insurance is an ethical necessity since it provides a means for clients to recover damages, even when the psychologist in question has few financial resources, in the event of professional errors.

Use consultation. Pay for consultation when needed and treat it as a professional service (APA Insurace Trust, 1995). Keep a list of potential consultants handy for use on short notice and have contingency plans for whom to call if you must consider admitting a client to a hospital, provide a warning about a dangerous client, deal with a suicidal client, or have another risky clinical situation. Use your consultant as soon as you suspect any risky situation. Do not wait for a disastrous event or a lawsuit. Although not absolutely necessary, in many cases it may be best to go to the head of your agency or outside your immediate circle of colleagues. When you do consult, document it and include the date, details, and actions taken. Psychologists who act as consultants will also want to keep careful notes and beware of vicarious liability (i.e., when someone who consults you is sued and you are also named as a defendant).

Develop clear payment and collection policies and follow them (APA, 1992; Pope, 1988). Inform clients of your billing and payment policies. Do not allow large or unexpected bills to accumulate. Keep "affect" out of billing and collection letters (see chapter 10).

When Prevention Fails: What to Do When an "Adverse Incident" Occurs

If no lawsuit has been threatened or filed, but some significant difficulties or adverse events arise (e.g., a client is not benefitting from treatment, is not adhering to key aspects of a treatment program, has become too difficult to work with, or harms a third party), consider the following series of steps.

First, obtain a consultation from a colleague experienced with such clients or issues and take any appropriate actions recommended.

Next, consider whether the circumstances suggest that you should initiate termination of the professional relationship. If you decide that it is appropriate to do so, notify the patient both orally and in writing, specifying the effective date for termination and providing a specific and appropriate reason for terminating the relationship. Agree to continue providing interim services for a reasonable period and recommend other care providers or means of locating them. Offer to provide records to new care providers on receipt of a signed authorization. Document all of these steps in your case records.

We recommend avoiding unilateral termination if the client is in the midst of a mental health crisis or emergency situation or if substitute services will be difficult for the client to obtain (e.g., in a rural area where other practitioners might not be readily available). It would also be unethical to seek to terminate a client if the basis for doing so is unreasonably discriminatory (e.g., terminating psychotherapy with a client after learning of his or her HIV status).

If a high-risk client does not return for a scheduled appointment, follow up by telephone and in writing, documenting these steps in your records. Be especially prompt in doing so if the client seemed depressed or emotionally distressed in the last session.

If a high-risk client complains to you about some aspect of your professional relationship, listen carefully and treat the complaint with serious professional concern. Investigate, if necessary, and respond in as sympathetic and tactful a manner as possible. Try not to be defensive. Apologize, if appropriate. Document in your record all steps taken.

In the event of a client's death, express sincere compassion and sympathy to surviving relatives, but do not discuss any personal feelings of guilt you may be experiencing. Save those feelings for your personal psychotherapist.

If you become aware of the possibility of a suit against you, follow these steps:

1. Notify your insurance carrier immediately.
2. Never interact orally or in writing, "informally" or otherwise, with a client's lawyer once a case is threatened. Once a lawyer representing your client contacts you in any dispute that involves you and that client, get your own attorney or one hired by your liability insurance carrier involved. Cease all further personal contact with that client until you have consulted your attorney. Never try to settle matters yourself.
3. Do not make incriminating statements or discuss the case with anyone other than representatives of the insurance carrier or your lawyer. Do not discuss details of the case with colleagues. These other parties may be subject to subpoena and testimony about what you told them.
4. Compile and organize all of your records, case materials, chronicles of events, and so on to assist in your defense. Do not throw anything away, and do not show anything to anyone except your attorney.
5. When asked to provide information or documents to your legal counsel, send copies and safeguard the originals.
6. In any malpractice or professional liability action, consult a personal attorney (in addition to the one assigned by the insurance carrier), especially if sued for damages in excess of the limits of the policy. Before agreeing to a settlement, consult an attorney whose only interest is you (rather than you and your insurer).
7. Take steps to manage your own anxiety and stress level. Such cases can take a severe emotional toll and require several years to resolve, even though there may be no legitimate basis for the suit. Seeking support from friends and colleagues is a normal reaction; however, discussions of specific details should occur only in privileged contexts.

References

Ackerman, M. (1995). *Clinician's guide to child custody evaluations.* New York: Wiley.

American Psychological Association. (1992). Ethical principles of psychologists and code of conduct. *American Psychologist, 47,* 1597–1611.

American Psychological Association. (1993). Record keeping guidelines. *American Psychologist, 48,* 984–986.

American Psychological Association. (1994). Guidelines for child custody evaluations in divorce proceedings. *American Psychologist, 49,* 677–680.

American Psychological Association Insurance Trust. (1995). *Avoiding malpractice and ethical liability: Risk management in the evolving health care market.* Washington, DC: Author.

Anderten, P., Staulcup, V., & Grisso, T. (1980). On being ethical in legal places. *Professional Psychology, 11,* 764–773.

Annon, J. S. (1989). Use of hypnosis in the forensic setting: A cautionary note. *American Journal of Forensic Psychology, 7,* 37–48.

Bennett, B. E., Bryant, B. K., VandenBos, G. R., & Greenwood, A. (1990). *Professional liability and risk management.* Washington, DC: American Psychological Association.

Bersoff, D. N. (1995). *Ethical conflicts in psychology.* Washington, DC: American Psychological Association.

Bonnie, R., & Slobogin, C. (1980). The role of mental health professionals in the criminal process: The case for "informed speculation." *Virginia Law Review, 66,* 427–522.

Borum, R., & Grisso, T. J. (1995). Psychological test use in criminal forensic evaluations. *Professional Psychology: Research and Practice, 26,* 465–473.

Boszhormenyi-Nagy, I. B., & Spark, G. (1973). *Loyalties.* New York: Harper and Row.

Bray, J. H., & Hetherington, E. M. (1993). Families in transition: Introduction and overview. *Journal of Family Psychology, 7,* 3–8.

Brodsky, S. L. (1991). *Testifying in court: Guidelines and maxims for the expert witness.* Washington, DC: American Psychological Association.

Brodsky, S. L. (1994). Are there sufficient foundations for mental health experts to testify in court? Yes. In S. A. Kirk & S. D. Einbinder (Eds.), *Controversial issues in mental health* (pp. 63–92). Needham Heights, MA: Allyn & Bacon.

Carmichael v. Carmichael, 597 A. 2d 1326 (D.C. Ct. App. 1991).

Castro-Martin, T., & Bumpass, L. (1989). Recent trends and differentials in marital disruption. *Demography, 26,* 37–51.

Ceci, S. J., & Bruck, M. (1995). *Jeopardy in the courtroom: A scientific analysis of children's testimony.* Washington, DC: American Psychological Association.

Clingempeel, W. G., & Reppucci, N. D. (1982). Joint custody after divorce: Major issues and goals for research. *Psychological Bulletin, 91,* 102–127.

Committee on Ethical Guidelines for Forensic Psychologists. (1991). Specialty guidelines for forensic psychologists. *Law and Human Behavior, 15,* 655–665.

Daubert v. Merrill Dow Pharmaceuticals, Inc. USCal 113 Sct. 2786 (1993).

DeKraai, M. B., & Sales, B. D. (1991). Liability in child therapy and research. *Journal of Consulting and Clinical Psychology, 59,* 853–860.

Doe v. Samaritan Counseling Center, 791 P. 2d 344 (Alaska Sup. Ct. 1990).

Estelle v. Smith, 451 U.S. 459 (1981).

Faigman, D. L. (1995). The evidentiary status of social science under Daubert: Is it "scientific," "technical," or "other" knowledge? Special Issue: Witness memory and law. *Psychology, Public Policy, and Law, 1,* 960–979.

Faust, D. (1994). Are there sufficient foundations for mental health experts to testify in court? No. In S. A. Kirk & S. D. Einbinder (Eds.), *Controversial issues in mental health* (pp. 287–299). Needham Heights, MA: Allyn & Bacon.

Garb, H. N. (1989). Clinical judgement, clinical training, and professional experience. *Psychological Bulletin, 105,* 387–396.

Garb, H. N. (1992). The *trained* psychologist as expert witness. *Clinical Psychology Review, 12,* 451–467.

Gardner, R. A. (1992). *The parental alienation syndrome: A guide for mental health and legal professionals.* Cresskill, NJ: Creative Therapeutics.

Golding, S. L. (1990). Mental health professionals in the courts: The ethics of expertise. *International Journal of Law and Psychiatry, 13,* 281–307.

Goldstein, J., Freud, A., & Solnit, A. J. (1979). *Beyond the best interests of the child.* New York: Free Press.

Grisso, T. J., & Appelbaum, P. S. (1992). Is it unethical to offer predictions of future violence? *Law and Human Behavior, 16,* 621–633.

Heilbrun, K. (1992). The role of psychological testing in forensic assessment. Special Issue: Expert evidence. *Law and Human Behavior, 16,* 257–272.

Hetherington, E. M. (1990). Coping with family transitions: Winners, losers, and survivors. *Child Development, 60,* 1–4.

Hogan, D. B. (1979). *The regulation of psychotherapists* (Vol. 1–4). Cambridge, MA: Ballinger.

Kolata, G. B. (1980). Forensic use of hypnosis on the increase. *Science, 208,* 1443–1444.

Koocher, G. P., Goodman, G. S., White, S., Friedrich, W. N., Sivan, A. B., & Reynolds, C. R. (1995). Psychological science and the use of anatomically detailed dolls in child sexual abuse assessments. *Psychological Bulletin, 118,* 199–222.

Koocher, G. P., & Keith-Spiegel, P. C. (1990). *Children, ethics, and the law: Professional issues and cases.* Lincoln, NE: University of Nebraska Press.

Leesfield, I. (1987). Negligence of mental health professionals. *Trial,* 57–61.

Loftus, E. F. (1986). Experimental psychologist as advocate or impartial educator. *Law and Human Behavior, 10,* 63–78.

Loftus, E. F., & Monahan, J. (1980). Trial by data: Psychological research as legal evidence. *American Psychologist, 35,* 270–283.

McCloskey, M., Egeth, H., & McKenna, J. (1986). The experimental psychologist in court: The ethics of expert testimony. *Law and Human Behavior, 10,* 1–13.

Melton, G. B. (1987). Training in psychology and law. In I. B. Weiner & A. K. Hess (Eds.), *Handbook of Forensic Psychology* (pp. 681–697). New York: Wiley.

Melton, G. B., Petrila, J., Poythress, N. G., & Slobogin, C. (1987). *Psychological evaluations for the courts: A handbook for mental health professionals and lawyers.* New York: Guilford.

Morse, S. J. (1982). Reforming expert testimony: An open response from the tower (and the trenches). *Law and Human Behavior, 6,* 45–47.

Pope, K. S. (1988). Fee policies and procedures: Causes of malpractice suits and ethics complaints. *The Independent Practitioner, 8,* 24–29.

Poythress, N. G. (1979). A proposal for training in training in forensic psychology. *American Psychology, 34,* 612–621.

Poythress, N. G. (1982). Concerning reform in expert testimony: An open letter from a practicing psychologist. *Law and Human Behavior, 6,* 39–43.

Rivlin, A. (1973). Forensic social science. *Harvard Educational Review, 43,* 61–75.

Sales, B. D., & Shuman, D. W. (1993). Reclaiming the integrity of science in expert witnessing. *Ethics and Behavior, 3,* 223–229.

Sales, B. D., & Simon, L. (1993). Institutional constraints on the ethics of expert testimony. *Ethics and Behavior, 3,* 231–249.

Shapiro, D. L. (1991). *Forensic psychological assessment: An integrative approach.* Needham Heights, MA: Allyn & Bacon.

Spiegel, D., & Spiegel, H. (1987). Forensic uses of hypnosis. In I. B. Weiner & A. K. Hess (Eds.), *Handbook of forensic psychology* (pp. 343–353). New York: Wiley.

Tanke, E. D., & Tanke, T. J. (1979). Getting off a slippery slope: Social Science in the judical process. *American Psychologist, 34,* 1130–1138.

Vandecreek, L. (1986). Patient records as evidence in malpractice litigation. *The Psychotherapy Bulletin, 21,* 6–8.

Weiner, I. B., & Hess, A. K. (Eds.). (1987). *Handbook of forensic psychology.* New York: Wiley.

Weithorn, L. A. (Ed.). (1987). *Psychology and child custody determinations: Knowledge, roles, and expertise.* Lincoln, NE: University of Nebraska Press.

Wolfgang, M. E. (1974). The social scientist in court. *Journal of Criminial Law and Criminology, 65,* 239–247.

Woody, R. H. (1988). *Protecting your mental health practice: How to minimize legal and financial risk.* San Francisco: Jossey-Bass.

Wright, R. H. (1981a). Psychologists and professional liability (malpractice) insurance: A retrospective review. *American Psychologist, 36,* 1485–1493.

Wright, R. H. (1981b). What to do until the malpractice lawyer comes: A survivor's manual. *American Psychologist, 36,* 1535–1541.

Yuille, J. C., & Kim, C. K. (1987). A field study of the forensic use of hypnosis. Special Issue: Forensic psychology. *Canadian Journal of Behavioural Science, 19,* 418–429.

Zonana, H. (1994). *Daubert v. Merrell Dow Pharmaceuticals:* A new standard for scientific evidence in the courts? *Bulletin of the American Academy of Psychiatry and the Law, 22,* 309–325.

16

Psychologists as Teachers
Classroom Conundrums

To educate a person in mind and not in morals
is to educate a menace to society.

Theodore Roosevelt

Colleges and universities are among the primary sites where productivity, creativity, and excellence thrive. At the same time, an array of ethical problems plague the academy. An unacceptable number of incidents that involve racism, sexual harassment, and academic dishonesty smear the reputation of higher education. Campus scandals, ranging from illegal perks for athletes to scientific misconduct, receive far more public attention than do the positive contributions made by students and faculty. Negative publicity about grade inflation, huge lecture classes, and overreliance on objective examinations and teaching assistants cause the public to wonder what is really going on behind those impressive-looking doors. Once sacred grounds for freedom of expression, institutions of higher education are wrestling with what can and cannot be uttered in a public forum or even in a private conversation. Whether "political correctness" debates will elevate campuses to islands of civility or lead to the imposition of unhealthy restraints on personal expression remains to be seen.

Academic communities, as mirrors of the larger society, are not exempt from the growing tendency to eschew personal responsibility and to blame others for real or perceived shortcomings. Increasingly, colleges and universities are being sued for bizarre reasons. An undergraduate student, while "mooning" those outside by pressing his bare backside against an inside window, fell through and hurtled 30 feet to the ground. He attempted to sue the university for close to a million dollars for his not-too-extensive injuries (which included "deeply bruised buttocks" and "trauma"), alleging a failure to specifically warn students about the dangers of upper story windows (Gose, 1994). In another instance, two students sought monetary damages because a course was too difficult (Shea, 1994). The judge ruled, in small claims court, that the professor was guilty of educational malpractice for making an entry-level course too demanding. Finally, a client, who had already successfully sued her therapist and the clinic employing the therapist, attempted to take legal action against the university at which the therapist was trained for failing to ensure the competence of its graduates (Custer, 1994).

Hard economic times coupled with stagnant or declining university enrollments have led to funding cutbacks for most academic institutions. Shrinking resources invariably lead to competition among faculty for equipment, travel funds, laboratory space, and promotions. Shortages often lead to tension, which may reveal itself in low morale and explosive bickering and dissension among faculty members. Professors who find it difficult, for whatever reason, to conduct research and publish it in scholarly journals put their job status in jeopardy. The ironic result is that energy is diverted from teaching students, while, at the same time, uninspired, shoddy, or trivial work is churned into the knowledge stockpile. "Professor bashing" trade books (e.g., Sykes's *Profscam*, 1988, and Anderson's *Impostors in the Temple*, 1992) give the impression to the public at large that most professors are lazy, selfish, exploitative, and unconcerned about anything except perpetuating themselves through contributions to journals that nobody reads.

The scholarly literature on the ethics of instruction is not large, although the ethical implications of professors' job functions have been gaining some interest in recent years (e.g., Blevins-Knabe, 1992; Cahn, 1986, 1990; Cheny, 1992; Dill, 1982; Hogan & Kimmel, 1992; Kitchener, 1992; Long, 1992; Matthews, 1991; May, 1990; Payne & Charnov, 1987; Tabachnick, Keith-Spiegel, & Pope, 1991; Whicker & Kronenfeld, 1994). The ethics code of the American Psychological Association (APA, 1992) offers very little specific guidance to teaching psychologists compared with that offered to clinicians and researchers (Keith-Spiegel, 1994). A presumption that ethical improprieties are handled within the institution probably accounts for the relatively modest interest in having external sources establish guidelines for academic psychologists. A professor's conduct, however, typically must involve an egregious violation before any formal action will be taken within the academy. Even when institutional channels are functioning in ways that allow for fair hearings and due process, only the most assertive students appear to use them. Students may feel relatively powerless and inadequate, which may hinder them from seeking formal redress for grievances. Also, many students may routinely accept personal blame for their discontent. Finally, an implicit "silent pact" may sometimes exist between students and professors in which professors do less-than-adequate jobs and require less-than-adequate student performance in return, leaving everyone involved free to do something else with their time.

The full array of ethical dilemmas that invade the academy cannot be covered in a single chapter. We have selected the following topics for discussion: (1) advertising and student contracts, including course and program descriptions and course syllabi; (2) competency issues in teaching, including teaching skills and course preparation, lecturing on sensitive or controversial topics, arguable classroom demonstrations, unconventional teaching styles and assignments, educational experiences that require student disclosure, maintaining classroom decorum, oral plagiarism, and impaired psychologists who teach; (3) evaluations of students, including grading students' performances, biases in evaluation, extra credit, and dealing with dishonest students; (4) exploitation of students; (5) telling students' stories; (6) advising and mentoring tangles; and (7) other self-serving issues not directly involving students, including textbook adoption practices, disposing of complimentary textbooks, and moonlighting. Some of the cases presented in this chapter are adapted from a casebook on the ethics of teaching (Keith-Spiegel, Wittig, Perkins, Balogh, & Whitley, 1993). Related issues are also discussed in other sections of this book; for instance, the discussion of confidential case material in the classroom is presented in chapter 6, social and other multiple role relationships with students are included in chapters 8 and 12, letters of recommendation are mentioned in chapter 13, and research collaboration with students is included in chapter 17.

ADVERTISING AND STUDENT CONTRACTS

Course descriptions included in university catalogs or other promotional materials are a type of service advertisement, although we usually do not think of them as such. Once a student enrolls in a course, the syllabus becomes a contract of sorts between the instructor and the student. (Discussions of advertising and client contracts can be found in chapters 11 and 4, respectively.)

Course and Program Descriptions

Complaints about university catalog entries and program descriptions are rarely seen by the ethics committees of professional organizations, probably because such descriptions are usually brief and general, leaving little to debate. Further, an ethics committee is an unlikely choice of redress should a student be dissatisfied. Nevertheless, and perhaps because of the potential for misrepresentation, the most detailed coverage of teaching-related ethics in the APA's ethics code (1992) deals with program and course advertisements (ES: 6.02).

Case 16-1: Doogie Stretch was eager to obtain more hands-on research experience. He enrolled in Psychology 314 because the catalog description stated that the course required the completion of an original research project. However, the syllabus handed out on the first day of classes included only required textbook readings and two brief article review papers. When Doogie inquired about the research project, Professor Switcheroo replied, "Oh, we used to do that, but it got to be too much of a hassle."

Many students base their course selections on the catalog description, especially when the course is unfamiliar or not in their major field of study. When a significant course component is added, shifted, or eliminated, a correction should be made in the next catalog printing. In the meantime, any discrepancies should be communicated in other forums (e.g., electronic mail, bulletin boards, department newsletters) and, most certainly, specifically addressed on the first day of class. It appears that Switcheroo's department had known of the discrepancy for some time, but did nothing about it.

Ethics complaints have been filed by consumers of commercial educational programs, such as weekend continuing education workshops, on the basis of incongruities between the program's promotional descriptions and the actual experiences.

Case 16-2: Dean Smart, Psy.D., paid $250 to attend a 1-day continuing education workshop on diagnosing the borderline personality disorder. The promotional flyer listed the most prominent experts as speakers and specifically promised "brand new and unpublished material." However, two of the five speakers did not appear and were replaced by local therapists. The three experts did not present new material. Instead, they recited directly from their own books and published articles that Smart had already read. Smart requested a refund from Org Deal, Ph.D., the psychologist in charge of arranging the program, but was refused. Dr. Smart then complained to an ethics committee.

Case 16-3: Two women attended the first session of a 6-week program offered to the public on hypnosis. The basis of their decision was the promotional material that listed the course name, "Deep Relaxation Hypnosis Techniques as taught by . . . " followed by a list of three prominent experts. Other information followed, and, on the bottom line, the small print read "Group Leader: Hype Rook, Psy.D." When the women arrived at the hotel conference room, only Dr. Rook was present. When the women complained to Rook after the session, he explained that his ad did not say that the three experts would actually teach the course, but that "as taught by" meant that he, Rook, would use their techniques. The women asked for a refund, received it after a long hassle, and wrote an ethics committee, charging Rook with fraudulent advertising.

After reviewing the two advertisements, ethics committees agreed that the consumers had been given misleading information. Dr. Deal pleaded that the problem was beyond his control because two of the speakers backed out after the promotional materials were mailed, and the other speakers were clearly instructed to include their latest thinking. Although Dr. Deal may have done the best he could, he was reminded that the basis of the decision to buy into his program was disparate from what consumers actually received, and that those who expressed dissatisfaction should receive consideration. Dr. Rook was admonished to cease and desist from using an advertisement that allowed people to easily infer that famous experts would appear in person.

Psychologists who become involved with continuing education programs and workshops must realize that today's busy consumers on a budget (and that includes other psychologists!) expect both their time and money to be well spent. Promotional materials that offer current and complete information, as well as realistic depictions, of what can be expected from the experience will preclude most the problems that could otherwise arise.

The APA ethics code (1992) requires that academic psychology programs be described accurately by spelling out what competencies students can expect to attain and for which credentials students can expect to qualify on completion of the program (ES: 6.01).

Case 16-4: After Pam Sincere completed a semester of her master's-level counseling program at Minus U., she learned that she could not qualify for licensure as a counselor. When she confronted her advisor, he pointed out that the program did offer a legitimate degree in counseling psychology and that no promises were ever made about direct entry into a profession on graduation. He advised her to complete the program and later try to transfer into a doctoral-level program.

Case 16-5: Mark Skinnerman selected the M&M Institute for his doctoral training because of its strong behaviorist orientation. However, soon after he enrolled, it became clear that the program was actually weak in this area. Two of the behaviorists had retired the previous year, and the program was undergoing a major transformation in emphasis.

One may be tempted to fault the students for not asking enough questions of the program representatives prior to seeking enrollment. Certainly, had Sincere and Skinnerman been more inquisitive, they might have saved themselves considerable time, grief, and money. However, the two cases above illustrate instances in which applicants have been misled. Assuming that cor-

rect information and appropriate caveats were not spelled out in the Minus U. program descriptions, Ms. Sincere and the other students were recruited in a manner inconsistent with APA ethical standards. Mr. Skinnerman's plight illustrates another situation that is not uncommon, namely, failing to update program descriptions promptly, especially when the changes are substantial. Mr. Skinnerman was affected more profoundly than was Doogie Stretch (Case 16-1) because an entire program, rather than a single course, was at issue. Program representatives must take whatever extra steps are necessary to ensure that applicants are informed of changes or circumstances that may affect their interest in entering a program. In the actual case involving Mr. Skinnerman, the director claimed that the program changes occurred quite abruptly, and there was not enough time to rewrite all of the program description materials. The program director further contended that Mr. Skinnerman should have known that the psychologists with whom he wanted to study were very old and would have retired soon anyway. Such attempts to rationalize away responsibility and place it on time pressures and the applicants who made major decisions based on presumably correct information is inappropriate and unethical.

The Course Syllabus

Course syllabi deserve comment primarily because they provide the basis of a student's informed consent to commit to a course (Handelsman, Rosen, & Arguello, 1987). When a student recognizes that a catalog description is inconsistent with a syllabus, the student usually has the option of dropping the class. However, if the syllabus does not reflect how the course will actually play itself out, students can be unfairly disadvantaged.

Case 16-6: Heather Active carefully mapped out her semester, allowing sufficient time to study and prepare assignments, as well as to perform her part-time job and student government duties. When Professor Delay glibly announced 2 days before the midterm date listed in the syllabus that the exam would be moved back 2 weeks, Heather's schedule was thrown off. When Heather asked if she could take the exam at the time it was originally scheduled, Delay responded that he had to postpone it because he hadn't written it yet, adding that most students usually welcomed the extra time.

Circumstances beyond professors' control can arise that require deviations from the syllabus plan. For example, new knowledge or opportunities can arise during the course of a semester that could be to the students' advantage, but require syllabus modifications in the process. Or, a genuine emergency can legitimately require a course schedule modification. In such instances, professors should minimize any negative impact. It appears, however, that Professor Delay made his decision based on his own convenience and rationalized this action by invoking an assumption that was not valid for all students.

Professors would be wise to think of their syllabi as representing far more than "first-day handouts." Syllabi are increasingly viewed as contracts with students and can even serve as legal exhibits when disputes arise.

Case 16-7: Les Miserables instigated a grievance procedure against Crisp List, Ph.D. Miserables was graded down for poor class attendance and given a 25% deduction for a late paper. Miserables supplied the single-page syllabus for the course that made no mention of these penalties. Dr. List retorted that announcements about these matters were made three times in class, but Miserables was never there to hear them.

Although Mr. Miserables was hardly a paragon of responsibility, Professor List was open to criticism because the rules that governed student evaluation were not "in writing." To be an effective guide for students, as well as the best possible defense should complaints arise, syllabi should include considerable information about what will be covered in the course. Other information that should be provided from the onset includes learning objectives, required reading, details about assignments and deadlines, test formats, any penalties for nonattendance or late papers, and whatever else will help connect the student to the course (Rubin, 1985).

COMPETENCY ISSUES IN TEACHING

Proficiency requirements for psychology instructors extend beyond mastery of the subject matter being taught. Also relevant are a number of matters that require competent pedagogic judgments and adept management skills, such as how classroom decorum is maintained, the effectiveness of one's teaching style, the quality of assignments, and the handling of sensitive content. Teaching psychologists can provide incompetent services if they are emotionally upset or focused solely on their own needs. (For more details of competency issues, see chapter 3.)

Teaching Skills and Course Preparation

Psychologists are admonished by the APA ethics code to provide services and to use techniques in only those areas for which they are qualified by training and experience (ES: 1.04) and to remain reasonably current in their areas of expertise (ES: 1.05). Although there is no mandate for teaching psychologists to obtain regular continuing education, it is assumed that professors consistently update their knowledge base through self-directed reading, collegial discussions and mentoring, and attendance at professional meetings and teaching conferences.

Most students probably do not realize that psychology professors who are ill-prepared or who exclusively cite older work and theories on a topic (when more recently recognized work and theories are also readily available) are failing to fulfill the ethical requirements of their profession. The accuracy, objectivity, and completeness of the information taught are not qualities that student consumers can easily assess. Usually, by definition, students do not know the topic area well enough to make such judgments. Maintaining competence, then, requires a personal commitment by psychologists who teach (ES: 6.03a). Whereas the complaints received about psychology educators are most often associated with disputed performance evaluations and offensive interpersonal styles, occasional complaints about teaching skill and course preparation have been reported to ethics committees.

Case 16-8: Daze Fluster, Ed.D., was charged with incompetence by an angry student, who doubted the quality of education he was receiving from Dr. Fluster and was upset by the department's apparent unwillingness to remedy the situation. The student claimed that Dr. Fluster always arrived late, spent most of the time flipping through a tangled mass of papers in his briefcase, had no apparent agenda for each class session, and rambled in an unconnected fashion. The student asserted that, because he was spending both money and valuable time pursuing his education, he was entitled to a better classroom experience.

Assuming that Fluster's report is valid, we still cannot tell for sure if Dr. Fluster is competent in his field, but unskilled as a lecturer, or if he has some more serious underlying problem. If Fluster was ill-prepared for class on a regular basis, he is fulfilling neither his professional nor ethical responsibilities.

Case 16-9: Mala Droit, Ph.D., joked on the first day of class that she did not know much about statistics, but was assigned to teach it because no one else was available. Many students were concerned. They approached the department chair and requested a qualified statistics teacher, but were told that they should feel lucky that the class was offered at all. The most tenacious of the group, which consisted of graduate school aspirants, wrote an ethics committee and charged Dr. Droit and the department chair with disregard for their legitimate academic needs.

Dr. Droit should never have been requested to teach a class for which she is not at all qualified. Whereas pinch hitters are a fairly common necessity, they should have sufficient expertise in the area or adequate time to prepare a respectable course. Some courses cannot be offered competently by anyone except a specialist. If the course is a requirement in the major, as statistics most certainly is in most psychology departments, resources should be found to hire an adequate instructor or to locate an acceptable substitute course in another department or at a nearby educational institution.

Ethics committees are not in an advantageous position to resolve directly disputes such as those presented by Drs. Fluster and Droit, even though the allegations, if true, would violate the overall spirit of the ethics code (see especially EP: E). In such instances, ethics committees typically take an "educative" stance by informing the complainant or the respondent of other relevant remedies.

Retreading

Graduate school training does not necessarily represent the skills and interest areas that will endure across an entire career. Sometimes, by choice, psychologists seek proficiency to teach in an area for which they have received no or insufficient formal training. Often enough, and especially at small colleges, professors may be assigned several courses, including some in which they possess only rudimentary backgrounds.

Case 16-10: Matt Mutate, M.A., did not receive graduate-level training in industrial psychology, but wanted to teach the undergraduate course entitled, "Psychology and Business." He spent a summer reading relevant textbooks and a number of primary sources. He interviewed an industrial psychologist for several hours and consulted with two other professors who had taught the course.

Teaching psychologists can usually arrange a course of study that will enable them to teach competently some classes for which they received no graduate training. The nature of an adequate plan can vary from self-directed reading to taking additional course work or obtaining additional supervised experiences. The time and effort required is based on such factors as the course level (lower division survey versus specialized upper division or graduate) and type (text knowledge versus technique application). Whether Mr. Mutate has put together a sufficient undergraduate course is not entirely clear, but there are ways he can reassure himself. Consultation with colleagues who are fully capable of teaching the course should be sought. Locating a colleague who will supervise course progress (i.e., content, exams, and assignments) is also highly desirable. (See a more detailed discussion of "retreading" in chapter 3.)

Lecturing on Sensitive or Controversial Topics

It is impossible for teaching psychologists to be totally objective and value free. With today's widely diverse student population and the inherently delicate or controversial nature of many psychological topics, attempts to remain both sensitive and evenhanded become somewhat of a challenge. We use the terms *controversial* and *sensitive* to refer to topics or theories about which there are strong enough differences in opinion or potential for distressful reactions to warrant caution. Teaching psychologists need to remain aware of their own biases and students' sensitivities. This can prove trying, despite their best efforts.

Case 16-11: Chip Straight complained that Lenny Open, Ph.D., offended him by discussing homosexuality in class and showing a film that depicted people of the same sex embracing. He believed such matters should be "confined to the gutter and not discussed in an institution of higher learning."

Case 16-12: Murray Green, Ph.D., was complained about by Chaim Gold for making derisive statements about Jews. Dr. Green allegedly listed a number of traits sometimes attributed to people of the Jewish religion, such as large noses, pushiness, and ruthlessness in business practices.

These two cases illustrate how a professor might offend a particularly sensitive student. During an inquiry, Dr. Open produced materials that indicated that the topic was relevant to the course content, based on scholarly writings, and balanced in terms of varying views people have about homosexuality. The movie was an educational film, owned by the university. Dr. Green, who noted he was an observant Jew himself and was thus particularly taken aback by Gold's rendition of the class presentation, explained that he was discussing stereotyping in his social psychology course. He used the list of characteristics sometimes attributed to Jews as a way of concretely illustrating stereotypes. After the list was read, a discussion of the dangers, inaccuracies, and functions of stereotyping had ensued.

It is possible to lower the incidence of offensiveness to some students without compromising the rights of professors to express themselves. Students should be informed from the onset if sensitive or controversial material will be covered. Such up-front disclosures allow students to make a voluntary, informed decision about whether to remain in the class. If exceptionally sensitive material will be covered on a particular day, the professor might consider informing the students during the prior meeting and at the very beginning of the class session. Offering other points of view, in as objective a fashion as possible, is encouraged. Explicitly admitting bias is far preferable to omitting that fact. It is best to stick as closely as possible to a scientific database (if one exists) when discussing sensitive or controversial topics. If the information base is rooted only in opinion, present the full range rather than only one side of an argument. A professor can always then state why he or she personally disagrees with other opinions. Students should be allowed an opportunity to express their own views respectfully without penalty, censure, or ridicule and be given opportunities to discuss in private any feelings they might have about the sensitive or controversial material presented in class.

As long as class presentations can be justified on pedagogical grounds and are related to the course, disapproval is less likely to occur. Sometimes, criticism arises because the material was added for "effect" or "shock value" (see case 16-17). Such complaints have even made their way through the legal system (Sherrer & Sherrer, 1972). The American Association of University Professors' *Principles on Academic Freedom and Tenure* (1984) also warns against persistently interjecting into the classroom controversial matter that has no relation to the subject at hand.

The next two cases are problematic because the professor's own value judgments have crept into and contaminated presentations that the students are led to believe are completely factual.

Case 16-13: Libby Now complained that Gude Olboy, M.A., derided women by declaring that sufficient research demonstrated that women's brains, physical bodies, and lack of aggressive tendencies precluded the possibility of success in endeavors currently dominated by men. He cited, as "definitive proof," the observation that, if women had been endowed with attributes similar to those of men, they would have "achieved equality during a much earlier phase of human evolution."

Case 16-14: Connie Right complained that her professor, Rad Left, Ph.D., was highly selective in his choice of topics and data presentation in his course on social issues. Ms. Right claimed that value judgments were imparted as facts, and that students received a highly biased perspective on various topics, such as abortion, child rearing, and politics. She did not dispute Dr. Left's right to offer his perspective. She did object, however, to Left's lack of coverage or derision of opposing views.

These instances reveal how professors' judgments may not only offend students, but also compromise the quality of the educational process (ES: 1.09).

Arguable Classroom Demonstrations

Closely aligned with controversial lectures are problematic or arguable classroom demonstrations, including films.

Case 16-15: Abe Ablation, Ph.D., showed a movie in his undergraduate neuropsychology class that demonstrated graphic brain surgery techniques on a dog and a cat. Two students fled the room in tears, and many others were visibly distressed. When one student asked Dr. Ablation why he didn't give them some warning, he replied, "That's not a requirement. You're supposed to be in class every day. This is a class about the brain, after all."

Films can evoke powerful emotions. Having sat through multiple previous showings, teaching psychologists may lose touch with the reactions to seeing a film for the first time. Contemporary students seem to be either more squeamish or more open than students a couple of decades ago in expressing distress when shown films or demonstrations that involve ani-

mal experimentation (Herzog, 1990). We recommend that teaching psychologists remain alert to what kinds of film experiences may be too intense for some students and excuse them or provide alternative assignments if at all possible. In areas that are legitimately upsetting for many or most undergraduate students, such as animal experimentation, the professor might consider available alternative teaching methods.

Unusual classroom demonstrations can range from exciting and memorable learning experiences to the questionable or inappropriate.

Case 16-16: Wily Sly, Ph.D., came to class a little early and left his briefcase on the desk. While students were still filing in, a young man snatched the briefcase and ran from the room. When Sly returned, he looked confused, then worried, and then boomed out, "Has anyone seen my briefcase? I left it here just a minute ago."

Professor Sly is attempting to bring his about-to-be-delivered lecture on eye witness testimony to life. As long as the students are not embarrassed or upset by such demonstrations in which they are unwitting participants, no ethical issues pertain. However, a number of students indicated that they would be upset by demonstrations that had been published by APA as suggested classroom activities (Harcum & Friedman, 1991). Such demonstrations might be checked out, in advance, on focus groups. This would help to ensure that the intended lesson is received without untoward side effects, such as the student who informed on the "thief" who stole Dr. Wily's briefcase later being scorned as a "snitch." In any event, students should not be deceived for long, and the staged demonstration should be easily defended educationally as sound.

Unconventional Teaching Styles and Assignments

Unconventional or nontraditional teaching styles and assignments may raise questions of an ethical nature. Many professors are deeply involved with innovations geared to motivate students' involvement in the learning process. It is, indeed, a daunting task to try to second-guess all possible sensibilities in an increasingly pluralistic culture. While we neither desire nor intend to regiment teaching style or stunt originality, it is worthwhile to note how ethical controversy can arise. In all of the next three cases, the professors argued that their methods were used to "focus attention" or to "bring a sense of reality to the learning process." However, questions about pedagogical justification were raised in each instance.

Case 16-17: John Nicetalk complained about the teaching style of Flam Boyant, Ph.D. Nicetalk was offended by Boyant's frequent use of profanity in the classroom. He felt that it was not only unprofessional, but served as a poor role model for other students and trivialized the knowledge being imparted. Nicetalk complained about the consistent use of four-letter words to describe just about everything Dr. Boyant talked about.

Just as some comedians are complimented for their ability to be funny without resorting to a barrage of vulgarities, so should professors be able to teach effectively without using language that is offensive to others. An occasional coarse term might best illustrate a point, but consistent irreverence serves neither the profession nor the students well. Profanity may catch attention but it is a quicker "solution" than finding ways to genuinely challenge students to think. Profanity for its own sake is commonplace and only rarely the best communication tool that a creative teacher can muster.

Professors may use off-color language because they think the students will enjoy it. The available data suggest that caution is warranted. A survey by Keith-Spiegel, Tabachnick, and Allen (1993) revealed that, although the majority of students did not view the use of profanity in lectures as an ethical problem, about 27% rated the use of profanity as unethical under "most" or "virtually all" circumstances, indicating that over one in four students may have strong negative reactions. Professors themselves, in an earlier survey (Tabachnick et al., 1991) gave a similar pattern of responses. Students are far more concerned with off-color stories or jokes, with more than half of the students viewing telling them during class as unethical under

"many" or "virtually all" circumstances. Only 12% viewed off-color stories as ethically acceptable in the classroom (Keith-Spiegel, Tabachnick, & Allen, 1993).

What about unusual out-of-class assignments? Teaching psychologists must discriminate between the acceptably nontraditional and the problematical.

Case 16-18: Riley Blatant, Ph.D., faced university sanctions when students complained about required assignments for a course on contemporary lifestyles. These included visiting swinging singles clubs, gay bars, group living compounds such as nudist camps and religious cults, massage parlors, militant political group meetings, and sexual paraphernalia shops.

It would appear that Blatant's assignments did mirror the course topic. However, a number of the students objected to having to do "such strange things" off campus. However, Blatant might have escaped criticism had he included other options that did not demand such intense experiences. Further, Blatant does not seem to realize that, by requiring his students to engage in off-campus experiences that could put them at some risk of emotional and possibly even physical harm, he could be endangering the students and placing the university at legal risk.

Case 16-19: Bob Tail, Ph.D., stunned his students when he showed stills of male and female genitalia in his human sexuality class and then announced that the last slide of the series was a photograph of his own penis.

Professor Tail used terrible judgment and skidded way past the bounds of propriety. It eventually cost him his job. We are not suggesting, however, that all forms of personal disclosure are out of bounds. Teaching psychologists, especially, find that what has occurred in their own lives often closely parallels what they are teaching. Students enjoy stories with a personal touch, especially if the stories are also amusing. But, it is very wise to think twice before getting into personal areas.

Case 16-20: Gerhard Gloom, Ph.D., spoke in great detail about his wife's condition in his abnormal psychology class. She was diagnosed with schizophrenia and believed herself to be an Amazon queen. Whenever Gloom went to see her, she ordered him executed. The class was given a rundown on her condition after each of his visits. Finally, a class representative approached Gloom and expressed considerable sympathy but firmly communicated that Gloom's disclosures provided far more detail about his wife's illness and their marital relationship than the students were comfortable in knowing.

Gloom is a piteous figure and surely requires considerable support. But, his own students are not the appropriate source of it.

Educational Experiences that Require Student Disclosure

The "experiential" group seminar, in which students are encouraged to explore and share their own feelings and conflicts, can pose risks to students (Grauerholz & Copenhaver, 1994). Judging from the paucity of ethics complaints received about them, it is probable that such experiences usually run satisfactorily. But, when complaints arise, they are typically volatile, and the inherent dual role (that is, student/quasi client and professor/quasi therapist) is usually at the root of the dissatisfaction.

Case 16-21: Lettit Hangout always spoke up during her sensitivity training class. She revealed many areas of personal discontent and assumed that by doing so she was being a "good student." She began to notice, however, that the instructor was becoming increasingly distant toward her. The other students began to withdraw as well. Her advising professor began making vague suggestions that she select another line of study. Hangout eventually instituted grievance procedures against the instructor for explicitly encouraging her to reveal personal problems, which resulted in considerable gossip and endangerment of her academic reputation and alienation from her peers and the other faculty.

Case 16-22: Tim Orous complained against Morris Tellall, Ph.D., on receiving a D in Group Experience 463, a required class in his degree program. His grade was a reflection of his silence throughout the quarter, although he told the professor early in the term that he did not feel comfortable participating in the discussions. Orous asserted that it was inappropriate to require students to reveal personal, nonacademic information and then jeopardize their academic status for noncompliance.

It may be valuable to expose students to experiences that could assist them in interacting with people about delicate topics, especially for those aspiring to become service providers to troubled people. Those who may someday do group process work may also benefit from participating in this course model. However, concern has been expressed about the ethical risks of blending elements of therapeutic treatment with academic course work (Sherrer & Sherrer, 1972). The professor should have pulled Ms. Hangout aside the moment it became clear that her vision of achieving success in the course was too candid. Even if Ms. Hangout was highly disturbed and unfit to deliver mental health services, this particular forum was not the appropriate one to expose her lack of suitability. Tim Orous, illustrating the other end of the participatory pole, was punished academically for refusing to disclose strictly personal information. We seriously question the ethicality of requiring this type of class at the undergraduate level. Some students are simply unsuited for this type of experience.

A self-disclosure variation is the written assignment, sometimes in the form of a journal, that requires students to record their personal feelings and share private recollections. This type of assignment has been coming under ethical scrutiny, with claims that it often requires inappropriate self-revelation. An assignment to write about a childhood trauma, for example, may exacerbate feelings of powerlessness and deference to authority figures (Swartzlander, Pace, & Stamler, 1993). Confidentiality and privacy issues are also relevant. Such assignments may result in unintended consequences and, in the process, cause a student genuine harm.

Case 16-23: Clyde Reveal decided to acknowledge for the first time, in an assigned paper on "My Worst Experience and How I Survived It," that an uncle had molested him when he was 6 years old. He wrote passionately. When he received a good grade and a brief notation of sympathy from the instructor, Reveal went to the professor's office to talk more extensively about the traumatic incident, reasoning that the professor would welcome continuing involvement. Instead, the professor seemed ill at ease and suggested that Reveal seek professional counseling. Reveal, who was already emotionally raw, felt embarrassed and abandoned. He decided never to tell anyone else about the molestation.

Despite the professor's error in requiring this assignment, he was correct in refraining from giving counsel because it would have created a dual-role relationship. The professor could have helped Reveal find appropriate counsel. This gesture would reduce Reveal's feelings of abandonment.

Professors may never become aware of any harmful, longer term effects of highly personal disclosures. We suggest that this type of assignment be considered risky and therefore subject to special scrutiny regarding appropriateness. We offer some precautions that may preclude untoward consequences for "affective" learning experiences, particularly for courses that are required as part of a degree program.

1. Students should be informed at the beginning of the course of exactly what will be expected of them, coupled with a candid revelation of some of the possible negative effects that might be experienced.
2. If, after considering the details, a student decides not to continue with the course or assignment, the instructor should assist the student to locate an alternative educational experience. Offering a choice of course assignments, at least one of which does not demand highly personal disclosure, is another way to defuse potential problems.
3. The instructor should make time available on a regular basis for individual discussions with students who may be experiencing difficulties with the class or its assignments.

4. Grading criteria must be carefully established and, to the greatest extent possible, consideration of the nature of the students' problems or willingness to share them should be minimal. Some programs offer such courses on a "credit only," pass/fail, or ungraded basis. Sometimes, faculty grade students only on written the assignments that do not involve personal disclosure.
5. Student-selection criteria and screening are encouraged.
6. Hiring a psychologist from off campus to lead experiential courses has advantages. This arrangement would create a separation from the ongoing training pipeline to an extent that greatly softens any dual-role conflicts that might be experienced by both students and regular, ongoing faculty.

Some programs allow (or even require) students to enter individual psychotherapy for academic credit as part of an applied program. Again, benefits to the students and their future clients may accrue, although questions about how to fund such services and whether they constitute an appropriate "educational experience" can be debated. Nevertheless, using regular faculty members in the program to provide these services is not recommended, even if the students do not pay extra fees for it.

Case 16-24: Ned Fears revealed to his therapist that he was terrified of most animals and children under 3 feet tall. He described the many ingenious ways he attempted to avoid these beings and the apprehension caused by inevitable contacts. The therapist was also Fears's instructor in a personality theory seminar. Fears began to feel so self-conscious in class that he dropped out of the graduate program.

Fears required professional services, but they should not have been delivered by his classroom instructor. Even if Fears and his therapist-instructor were completely comfortable with the arrangement and believed that the two roles could be juggled objectively, it constituted a multiple role relationship and was, therefore, unethical (ES: 1.17) (see also, chapter 8).

Maintaining Classroom Decorum

Not all students in a classroom are enthused about what is going on. Late-arriving, sleeping, whispering, and "eye-rolling" students disrupt the learning environment for everyone. Not all students appreciate the demands of the teaching performance and the heartache professors may feel when carefully crafted lectures appear to fall on indifferent ears. However, overly rigid or uncharitable classroom policies for decorum can be grounds for ethical concern.

Case 16-25: Austin Harsh, Ph.D., deducts grade points from exam scores for students who talk in class or engage in other behaviors he deems disruptive. He defends his practice on the grounds that mature behavior is to be expected of college-level students.

The case of Dr. Harsh (adapted from Keith-Spiegel, Wittig et al., 1993) illustrates the risky business of subtracting points for undesirable classroom behavior that the student earned for academic performances. Whereas Dr. Harsh most certainly has the right and obligation to maintain a classroom environment conducive to learning, already-earned academic credit should remain intact.

Humiliating students can be a swift way to control unwanted classroom behaviors, but this technique is also ethically risky.

Case 16-26: Bringem Down, Ph.D., yells at students who engage in any behavior he finds annoying, chides them if their questions or comments strike him as off target or ill-conceived, and writes "colorful" evaluative comments in the margins of their assignments (e.g., "This is bull." or "Do you call *this* a sentence?").

Dr. Down's class may have been whipped into her notion of proper classroom deportment, but what else his students have been taught is unclear. Students are very sensitive to humiliation or ridicule, and the APA ethics code warns against such behavior (ES: 6.03b). According to the findings of a large survey of undergraduate students, 80% or more of the respondents rated "insulting or ridiculing a student in the student's

presence" and "telling a student during a class discussion 'That was a stupid comment,'" were extremely unethical (Keith-Spiegel, Tabachnick, & Allen, 1993). We believe that shaming tactics undermine the respect that should define relationships between students and their teachers. Sometimes, however, strong measures of some sort are needed, as the next case illustrates.

Case 16-27: Beanie Blowout made loud "raspberry sounds" when the professor turned to the chalkboard, smirked as he asked questions that were purposely irrelevant or inane (e.g., "Was the hippocampus named after a school for large animals?"), and constantly dropped his pen and pencil. The professor was at her wits end and sought to have Blowout removed from the class.

Assuming that the professor attempted unsuccessfully to convince Blowout, in private, that his behavior made it impossible for her to do her job and for other students to learn and also had consulted with the department chair, who could not help, she cannot be faulted for instituting Blowout's removal from the classroom. Most campuses have policies and procedures related to difficult students that allow due process while, at the same time, preserve a climate for learning (Pavela, 1985).

Oral Plagiarism

An underdiscussed ethical issue involves the use of the work and words of others to create lecture presentations (oral plagiarism). Whereas it is obvious that professors craft their lectures with a reliance on the already produced work of others, how does one acknowledge those sources? Is acknowledgment always necessary? After all, as opposed to the printed word, lectures leave no visible tracks. Besides, even if it was possible to credit every source of every point made in a lecture, it would take up valuable class time and probably contribute little of lasting use to the students.

Case 16-28: Cat Copy, Ed.D., duplicated sections from various textbooks that competed with the one she assigned to her students, taped them together, and read them to her students. Students find her lecture style dull and unappealing, but they do assume that she created the material herself.

Case 16-29: Sultan Credit, Ph.D., read two articles about forgetting and created a lecture that drew heavily from both articles. At the beginning of the lecture, Dr. Credit announced, "Most of my lecture material is based on two articles, one by Dexter Noengram and another by Webster Blankbrain. I can give you the full references after class if you would like to delve further into their work."

Professor Copy is a lazy oral plagiarist (ES: 6.22). She lacks inspiration and is stealing others' intellectual property. Professors may consult many books, including competing textbooks, and then create an "original" lecture without having to credit every author. Further, much of the material in basic textbooks would be classified as common knowledge. For lectures, the question is, "Did you find your own voice in interpreting published information?" Professor Copy did not.

Professor Credit's technique is sound. Because Credit focused heavily on the work of two authors, it was proper for him to credit them briefly. Spending great amounts of class time reading lecture references is not necessary. Credit's acknowledgments took less than 20 seconds. Being generous to those who created the material that provides information or inspiration by acknowledging their efforts is always both commendable and appropriate. (For a discussion on written plagiarism, see chapter 17.)

Impaired Psychologists Who Teach

Psychologists who teach can experience impairments ranging from mild to debilitating. First we consider the more common types of personal difficulties that plague almost everybody, including teaching psychologists, at least on occasion. (These cases are adapted from Keith-Spiegel, Wittig et al., 1993.)

Case 16-30: The refrigerator broke down, a friend needed to talk about the problems she was having with her boss, and the cat threw up on the carpet. So much for the evening that Addie Lib, Ph.D., was planning to spend developing tomorrow morning's lecture.

Case 16-31: Wo Izmee, Ph.D., had a terrible fight with his girlfriend, and his son from a previous marriage was just arrested for possession of cocaine. When the alarm went off in the morning, he was so agitated that he called in sick and arranged for a film to be shown instead.

A national survey (Tabachnick et al., 1991) revealed that 92% of a large sample of teaching psychologists admitted to being unprepared for class on occasion, and 66% have taught classes when they were too distressed to be effective. Drs. Adlib and Izmee are likely to rebound fully. In the meantime, can they deal with their misfortune in a way that protects students while still fulfilling their professional responsibilities? Dr. Adlib could have "pulled an all-nighter," just as students force themselves to do sometimes, and put together an adequate presentation. Or, she could have facilitated a useful discussion among the students. Because unanticipated events are so common, it serves to remind us that early preparation is always preferable.

Dr. Izmee's stressors are probably more acute, and he may not be able to perform well enough that day. Arranging for films to be shown instead, or even canceling classes if no other options were available, are ethically acceptable because of his extreme mental anguish. Otherwise, something like the unfortunate scenes in the next case could happen.

Case 16-32: Lucy Lostit, Ed.D., had been feeling depressed after an investment went sour. Last night, her father refused her request to borrow $2000. She was enraged. On entering the departmental office in a huff, she threw a book at the receptionist, who had asked, in jest, "Did you just eat a firecracker?" She then went to her class and angrily announced to the students that not one of them was bright enough to ever make it into a doctoral program.

Dr. Lostit would have spared everyone, most of all herself, had she taken sufficient time out to calm down. Should a distressed state prove to be other than transient, teaching psychologists are ethically responsible to seek professional help and to refrain from teaching altogether if they cannot function competently.

Case 16-33: Once a vibrant, active member of the department, Dave Decline, Ph.D., has steadily backed away from contributions to the college. He is withdrawn, cuts students off, assigns minimal work, and often tells colleagues that he "just doesn't care anymore." He leaves campus as soon as he can to go home and sit or work in his garden.

Professor Decline is burned out (and probably clinically depressed) and does not appear to be attempting a renewal. Although Decline may be experiencing other problems, his students and commitment to the university and its mission have been abandoned.

More rarely, teaching psychologists can be more severely disturbed, at least temporarily, and even be dangerous.

Case 16-34: Millard Fury, Ed.D., became enraged at the incompetent performance of a research assistant and knocked him to the ground with such force that medical attention was required.

Case 16-35: Bob Spurn, Ph.D., had recently been divorced by his wife. When he discovered that he and a graduate student working in his lab were both dating the same woman, he terminated the student's access to lab equipment. Dr. Spurn became increasingly paranoid and subsequently accused the student of turning poisonous spiders loose in his office, although no such spiders were ever found.

Both students and psychotherapy clients can be hurt by vengeful or troubled psychologists who act out in unethical ways (see EP: 1.13). Clients, however, normally have greater freedom because they can "fire" the psychologist and seek therapy elsewhere. Students, however, cannot extricate themselves so easily from a relationship that is inseparable from their academic program, thus running the risk of a poor grade assignment or worse. In some situations, the faculty member might even cause longer range career problems for the student. For example, if Drs. Fury and Spurn were the only professors

teaching in the students' specialty areas, the students' professional future could be seriously endangered. In one of these actual episodes, Spurn's student fortunately was able to find academic shelter in the laboratory of a sympathetic colleague. (For more information about impaired psychologists, see chapter 3.)

Some professors fall short of psychosis, but sport rather nasty temperaments much of the time and even take pleasure in exerting power over students. They appear to feel entitled to yell at students or to treat them with disrespect at the slightest provocation. These outbursts can be traumatic for students, especially when a student is singled out.

Case 16-36: Torr Menter, Ed.D., found a student assistant still in the classroom when he entered the room to teach his class. He yelled at the student to get out of the room immediately. The student apologized and hurried to pick up the papers, but Dr. Menter continued to scream at her. Witnesses told the assistant's supervisor that they were afraid when Menter got so close into the assistant's face that he was going to attack her physically.

Professors whose personal style is combative and assaultive rarely have insight into the harm that they are causing students and the institution. Unfortunately, higher education has not proven effective in managing perpetually grumpy, mean-spirited, or irksome faculty members once they become tenured.

EVALUATIONS OF STUDENTS

Grading Students' Performances

Psychological tests and assessment (see chapter 7) emerge as more relevant for ethics committee scrutiny than do grading students' performances, not because they are more important, but because the "rules" of their construction, administration, and interpretation have been formalized. Academic course assessments are based on information and assignments unique to the educational experience that each teaching psychologist offers to students. These factors, however, do not excuse academic psychologists from their personal and ethical obligations to invest considerable effort in educating and evaluating students fairly based on actual performance and in a timely manner (EP: 6.05b).

Case 16-37: Brittany Brilliant was upset because she received a C in her psychological testing course, and it was the only C on her record. She wrote to the ethics committee, claiming that Dr. Washout's exams were unfair and that his term assignment was not carefully explained in advance.

The ethics committees of professional organizations cannot handle this sort of case. They are virtually always returned to the student with the suggestion to use the grievance procedure within the institution. Only on rare occasions, when a student has documented negligent or prejudicial evaluations (EP: 1.10), have ethics committees intervened. In such instances, the student typically has support from other faculty members and institution officials, who corroborate the student's position. It is common to also find departments that are embroiled in bitter factional disputes or controversies. The grievance mechanisms have broken down, and the student appears to have received insufficient due process.

Case 16-38: Sookey Judge received a negative evaluation from her clinical supervisor, Robert Dilatory, Ph.D., during the last term of the program. She complained that the supervisor could have warned her of any perceived shortcomings and given her an opportunity to remedy them. She also asserted that her attempts to meet with Dr. Dilatory about some of the problems she was experiencing with her internship assignment were met with excuses such as, "I am too busy today; maybe next week."

Dr. Dilatory responded that he had refrained from issuing early evaluations of substandard performance and from meeting with the student because, "It looked like Ms. Judge was improving at the time." However, to withhold feedback for 7 months in areas in which improvement was required was unfair to Ms. Judge and did not fulfill Dilatory's ethical obligation

to facilitate the development of professionals in training.

The fact that formal ethics committees do not address, except under unusual and extreme circumstances, grading and evaluation disputes does not mean that profound ethical issues are not inherent in the evaluation of students. Indeed, academic performance ratings are assumed to differentiate among bright, average, and poor students. Given the significance of such labels in our culture, these blessings and stigmas have major implications for admission to advanced educational programs, job seeking, and even self-concept. In this context, academic psychologists must hold themselves accountable for their judgments. To assess students using hastily developed test questions or nonvalid or biased evaluation criteria constitutes infliction of harm and is therefore unethical.

Biases in Evaluation

Regardless of the many issues associated with grading systems, teaching psychologists are expected to remain objective when evaluating students. Students see the maintenance of a "level playing field" as a primary ethic of the professorate. The majority of the students in the survey by Keith-Spiegel, Tabachnick, and Allen (1993) rated grading students based on how much the professor liked them as unethical under "most" or "virtually all" circumstances. Almost two thirds of teaching psychologists, however, admitted to allowing how much they like (or dislike) a student to influence the grades they give, at least on occasion. However, most of these same respondents also agreed that such biased practices were ethically questionable (Tabachnick et al., 1991).

Case 16-39: From his men's room stall, Professor Uptite overheard his best student, Alfie Slip, refer to him as "an arrogant dork." Uptite made it a point to be particularly critical of Slip's next paper, and assigned it a B minus. When Slip subsequently asked for a letter of reference, Uptite refused.

Case 16-40: At the urging of his vocational rehabilitation counselor, Joe Fleet, a disabled Vietnam veteran, returned to school. Fleet had been volunteering as a counselor for several years at the local junior high school and had received outstanding evaluations. The school principal told Fleet that he would hire him for the position full time once he had earned a master's degree. One of Fleet's professors, Wanna Support, Ed.D., also advocated Fleet and his goal, but was concerned because Fleet's grades were below average. Professor Support was sure that Fleet was capable, but had trouble motivating himself to do, as Fleet called it, "this busy paper work." Professor Support gave Fleet a B in the course even though, using the class curve, he earned a low C.

Professor Uptite is under no obligation to write any student a letter of reference, and Slip's unfortunate characterization cost him dearly. It was unethical, however, for Uptite to bias his grading criteria in retaliation. Professor Support is trying to help a student who needs a credential to enter a profession for which he already has demonstrated skill and suitability. However, Support acted unfairly to other students, who received no special consideration. Other options for advocacy—such as providing detailed letters of recommendation that focus on Fleet's strengths, arranging for some tutoring sessions, or attempting to alter Fleet's attitude about the basics of schoolwork—were appropriate, available options that Support should have considered instead.

If universities are to remain valid credentialing agencies, "blind" assessment of students is mandatory. Advanced courses, especially when the students are performing supervised services, may require evaluations of personality and suitability for delivering psychological services. However, even these judgments should be based on established, behavioral criteria rather than idiosyncratic personal judgments that may say as much about the evaluator as the student.

Extra Credit as an Ethical Issue

Across all disciplines, professors, as a group, are not favorably inclined toward offering students extra credit options (Norcross, Dooley, & Stevenson, 1993; Norcross, Horrocks, & Stevenson, 1989). Psychology professors, however, may offer it more often than do professors in other disciplines (Hill, Palladino, & Eison, 1993). Students generally favor extra credit opportunities. In fact, over half of the students in a large survey believed that offering students no opportunity to do extra work is unethical (Keith-Spiegel, Tabachnick, & Allen, 1993). Better students, however, are less likely to be concerned about extra credit (Wittig, Keith-Spiegel, & Tabachnick, 1994), probably because they do not need it to obtain a high grade.

Ethical issues can arise when extra credit is offered selectively.

Case 16-41: Tiwana Slipup asked Dr. Pushover if she could do something to compensate for her low exam score despite the fact that the syllabus clearly stated "no extra credit will be offered in this class." She pointed out that her other scores were good, but the night before the last exam she and her roommate had a terrible fight. Dr. Pushover allowed her to do a short paper on the topic of the midterm and added, "Don't tell anyone I let you do this."

Dr. Pushover showed compassion, but because it was offered to only one student who had the temerity to request a waiver of Pushover's rules, it was not fair to the other students, who remained respectful of course policy but who may have also benefitted substantially from an opportunity to earn extra credit. Pushover, himself, appears to recognize his own inequitable offer by requesting Tiwana to keep it a secret from her peers. Generally, extra credit opportunities should be described in the syllabus and available to everyone.

The nature of the extra credit assignment can also be grounds for ethical concern, as the next two cases illustrate.

Case 16-42: Professor Shotgun allowed a wide array of extra credit options in his introductory psychology class. Students could write book reports or participate in research projects. Other options included adopting a pet, donating blood, or being present in class on days that Shotgun wore a Star Wars tie.

This case (adapted from Hill et al., 1993), illustrates how professors may dilute the educational mission through the use of inappropriate extra credit options. Even when the activities themselves are morally meritorious or designed to increase student attendance, they dilute the academic component and the importance students may place on it.

Case 16-43: To bolster the treasury of a nonprofit children's mental health fund in which she was active, Birdy Twostones, Ph.D., gave her students one point for every dollar they could raise. Two hundred points were worth the same as one of the four exams.

Professor Twostones was very defensive when requested by university authorities to explain her extra credit scheme. She noted that she gained nothing from the project, and needy children were helped. Further, she reasoned, one of the segments of the course was on children's mental health, making the assignment "quite relevant." It was pointed out by officials that fund-raising is not an appropriate scholarly activity, and that it created legal entanglements for the university. Further, students of means or with affluent contacts were at a distinct advantage because they could essentially buy a better grade. Twostones admitted that she never considered those issues.

Some faculty believe that extra credit encourages irresponsibility, serves primarily to advantage those who do not deserve it, and contributes to grade inflation. Those in favor point out that extra credit options provide a second chance, reward effort, and allow students to explore topics in greater depth (Norcross et al., 1989). Regardless of one's stand on the overall merits of extra credit, if used it should be applied equitably and be directly relevant to the learning goals of the course (Palladino, Hill, & Norcross, 1995).

Dealing with Dishonest Students

Unethical students pose ethical dilemmas for their teachers. Sadly, it appears that increasing numbers of students are more interested in getting a degree and following a course of least resistance than in acquiring a genuine education. It is widely acknowledged that the rate of cheating in our nation's colleges and universities is occurring at unacceptably high rates (Davis, Grover, Becker, & McGregor, 1992; Davis & Ludvigson, 1995; Fass, 1990; McCabe & Bowers, 1994; McCabe & Trevino, 1993). It is also known that many professors are likely to ignore cheating, and that administrators do too little to address academic dishonesty (Correnti, 1986; Kibler, 1992).

Case 16-44: Harry Hesitant, Ph.D., suspected that Peeky Dense was looking at her neighbor's test paper, but was not sure. Dense's term paper also had a "familiar look" and exceeded, in both style and content, the level expected of an undergraduate student. The mere thought of confronting and dealing with the matter made Hesitant feel nauseous. Dr. Hesitant figured that he could never prove that Dense cheated and instead decided not to give her any benefit of a doubt when he assigned the final grade. If, for example, her grade was to fall between a C and a B, he would assign the lower grade as his way of dealing with the matter.

Dr. Hesitant's "solution" to handling a student suspected of cheating is probably widespread. In a survey of teaching psychologists, 77% agreed that dealing with a cheating student was among the most distasteful aspects of the profession. When asked why they thought that many professors ignored strong evidence of cheating, the inability to prove the case conclusively was the major reason given. Other frequently selected reasons were anxiety and stress, onerousness of facing a formal hearing, insufficient time to track down the evidence, lack of courage, and a concern about how the conflict would escalate if the student denied the charges (Keith-Spiegel, Tabachnick, & Washburn, 1997).

Despite the burden of establishing proof and the noxiousness of confronting dishonest students, cheating must be managed effectively as it occurs if the mission of higher education is to remain valid. Ignoring cheating also positively reinforces such behavior and gives a message to students that honest accomplishment is unimportant. As for Dense, if she were innocent, she could be potentially disadvantaged without an opportunity to explain herself. (And, she does not realize that she had better not ask Professor Hesitant for a letter of recommendation.) If Dense is guilty, her dishonest method of handling the rigors of a college education has been fortified. As unsettling as it may be, Hesitant should call Dense in for a private talk, perhaps asking her to explain how she created the paper. Preventive tactics can make this process easier, such as telling students in advance (and in the syllabus) that they may be asked to discuss their papers or exams with the professor, and that academic dishonesty will not be tolerated. Professors may require a meeting with students as they are drafting their papers and ask them many questions at that time. Unfortunately, many preventive techniques, while they discourage cheating, are labor intensive and not feasible for use in very large classes.

EXPLOITATION OF STUDENTS

When professors place their own needs above the welfare of their students, abuse can result. Because students often want to please their professors, they may allow themselves to be mistreated. Or, because students can sometimes benefit from participating in activities that also fill their professors' needs (e.g., research), they may not recognize the point at which a collaborative relationship edges into exploitation. This section provides examples of taking from students with little or nothing given in return. Additional issues involving student exploitation that arise from multiple role relationships are discussed in chapter 8.

Case 16-45: Clinton Clever's term paper contained a detailed design for an ingenious experiment. Professor Purloin fleshed it out a little more, collected data, and published it without reference to Clever's contribution. Clever complained to his advisor, who, in turn, confronted Purloin. Purloin's response was, "Clever expressed no intention of ever running the study. He is just an undergraduate student. If he had asked to be involved, I would have let him help with it. He could never have done it on his own."

Purloin's attitude reflects a lack of sensitivity to others' rights. That Clever is "just an undergraduate student" is not relevant in and of itself. Further, it was not Clever's responsibility to initiate an intention to execute the study to maintain ownership of the design. It may well be true that Clever did not intend to run the study on his own. However, he should have been consulted by Purloin. At that point, Clever could have declined the invitation to get involved and given Purloin permission to go ahead independently. Even here, it would have been very appropriate for Purloin to credit Clever's contribution to the design in a footnote (see ES: 6.23).

What if Clever's work had been less detailed, maybe in the form of a couple of sentences that suggested an idea for a study? We acknowledge that there certainly comes a point at which a student paper or a casual discussion provides but a glimmer of an idea. In such instances, involving the others who may have jump-started an independent creation is not morally mandated, although we maintain that acknowledging students' contributions never hurts the faculty member and can even enhance a positive reputation for mentoring.

We are in an interesting (and sometimes disheartening) time warp in that many of today's young students are considerably more proficient with computers and computer applications than are their middle-age professors. There is nothing inherently wrong with utilizing students to help fill gaps in our own skill bases, but this must be done fairly, giving full credit when due, and without resorting to power plays.

Case 16-46: Giga Byte is a gifted, young computer whiz. Dr. Slowstat hires Byte to be his research assistant. Byte analyzes Slowstat's data and creates tables and interpretative text. When Slowstat publishes the study, Byte is given no acknowledgment for her contribution to the project. Slowstat argues that, as a minimum wage departmental employee, no recognition of her involvement is necessary.

Exploitation is at issue in this case because Byte is doing professional-level work, including the interpretation of results. If Byte selected and creatively applied the statistical analysis and provided extensive interpretive text, an authorship credit should have been extended. Byte is working as a student assistant and is being paid very little for her contribution, but both conditions are irrelevant. After all, Slowstat is also an employee paid for his work, albeit at a better wage. Byte deserves a full acknowledgment of her contribution. (Authorship credits are more fully discussed in chapter 17.)

Research collaboration with students (including undergraduate students) is popular because of the benefits that can accrue to everyone involved. Scholarly output remains the major factor in faculty promotion and retention decisions. Research experience is a primary determinant of graduate school admission, including to science-practitioner clinical programs (Keith-Spiegel, 1991; Keith-Spiegel, Tabachnick, & Spiegel, 1994). Psychologists must be careful, however, to carefully prepare their students with a realistic picture of expectations.

Case 16-47: Professor Gallop's research fascinated Sid Sweat. Gallop warned Sweat that coming on board as a volunteer research assistant would be time consuming. Sweat assumed that he would be actively collecting data as part of a team. But, what started out as a boon for Sweat became a drab and tedious drain on his already busy schedule. Sweat's task was to enter data while sitting alone in a small cubicle for up to 20 hours a week. Sweat felt betrayed and had to squelch urges to enter bogus numbers just to get out early.

Although a plan cannot always be cast in stone, this case illustrates how feelings of exploitation might have been greatly diminished had the student fully understood and voluntarily agreed to all aspects of the commitment in advance. That Dr. Gallop has unknowingly put her own work in serious jeopardy by insufficiently preparing her now-resentful helper illustrates how good lines of communication are also in everyone's best interests. Inexperienced research assistants, in particular, should be monitored carefully, not only for the quality and

accuracy of their work, but also for their satisfaction with the arrangement.

Students should never be used as weapons to fight one's battles because it is also exploitative.

Case 16-48: Tim Anxious, the spokesperson for an entire class of students, complained that part-time instructor Milton Strike, M.A., had withheld grades for the whole class for 5 months after the course had ended. Mr. Strike, a part-time instructor at the private college, claimed that the administration had not paid him his salary. He promised to turn in the grade roster on receipt of a paycheck.

Mr. Strike's desire to be reimbursed for his services is understandable, and he may have been employed by an unethical institution. Holding students' evaluations hostage, however, is inappropriate and unethical.

TELLING STUDENTS' STORIES

Teaching psychologists probably have more opportunities to learn intimate details of students' lives than professors in other disciplines because the subject matter is conducive to discussion of personal issues. Further, psychology instructors are likely viewed as having more counseling expertise. The openness of many students during private office hours, especially when they explain why they did not take an exam or meet a deadline, suggests that they believe that their personal disclosures will be held in strict confidence. That assumption may be a risky one. A large, national survey of teaching psychologists revealed that, at least on occasion, 38% passed along material shared in confidence even though most of those who admitted doing so judged it to be wrong (Tabachnick et al., 1991).

The student-teacher relationship is very different from the client-therapist relationship. Teaching psychologists and students know each other in various ways, making the lines of communication complex and snarly. Although the integration of possibly identifiable information about psychotherapy clients into class lecture notes is discussed in chapter 6, the same concerns can be applied to what students divulge to teaching psychologists.

Case 16-49: A description of a sordid, abusive childhood was relayed in class by Lucy Lips, Ph.D. Although no identities were shared, it strongly resembled something a sorority sister had recently told one of Lip's students in the strictest of confidence. The victim was devastated on learning that her story had been openly relayed to others. The student had confided in Dr. Lips after a lecture on child abuse the previous semester.

Students very much enjoy lectures heavily peppered with interesting case stories. Removing names and other identifying data, however, may not always be sufficient. Therefore, teaching psychologists must adequately disguise material before using someone's private life as a teaching tool (EP: 5.02, 5.08b).

Another type of confidentiality dilemma arises when colleagues relax with each other and "talk shop." Professors are like everyone else with a job. Flushing out frustrations in the presence of sympathetic peers can release work-related stress. However, if the story sessions have a ritualistic or obsessive quality (e.g., the story-telling is a weekly contest to see who can tell the most outrageous student story), the appropriateness and constructiveness of this social tourney must be questioned (Keith-Spiegel, Wittig et al., 1993).

Case 16-50: Six professors in the psychology department enjoy meeting at the faculty club on Friday afternoons to review the week. The usual agenda is to divulge student behavior that was stupid, weird, or suspicious. Several students have become especially fair game because most of the professors know them. "Guess what Nancy Noskill put as the answer of a quiz question?" was the typical way such interactions would start.

Students can be very amusing (even when they do not mean to be). Purposely disgracing students, however, is not an ethical way to release tension, and actual harm is more likely than may be readily evident in the lightness of the moment. In this case (adapted from Keith-

Spiegel, Wittig et al., 1993), Nancy Noskill has little chance of gaining serious support because, by now, her reputation precedes her. In informal settings, unflattering stories that identify the students by name or other means will likely influence the way other professors will see them.

Naming students cannot always be avoided in conversations with colleagues. A professor who is having trouble dealing with a particular student may seek counsel from a colleague known to be wise in such matters or who has previously taught that student. Although such discussions approach the edge of confidentiality mandates (EP: 5.03b), when such consultations take place, they should occur in private and in a professional setting (e.g., university office rather than the local pub). Addressing issues that will advance the student's welfare should be the primary intent of such discussions.

Sometimes an emergency creates an unavoidable confidentiality dilemma for teaching psychologists.

Case 16-51: Bonnie Bruised told her professor, Deema Disclose, Ph.D., that she was afraid for her life. Her boyfriend had beaten her badly when she broke up with him, was currently stalking her, was carrying a loaded revolver, and has threatened her with physical harm. Dr. Disclose advised the student to contact the campus police and the counseling center immediately. The student adamantly refused to interact with either resource. Dr. Disclose contacted them herself to warn them about the potential danger.

Dr. Disclose has been put in a terrible position and must take some action to protect the student and others on campus (EP: 5.05a). For a while, at least, Dr. Disclose must become involved with a student's personal life and, simultaneously, risk alienating her student by divulging information presumably shared in confidence. It may be difficult to rebuild the student-professor relationship with Ms. Bruised. (For more information about confidentiality, including divulging information shared in confidence and the duty to warn, see chapter 6.)

Under emergency conditions, ethical guidelines are not always helpful (see chapter 1). Psychologists can minimize the risk of future censure, however, as long as their actions can later be viewed as attempts to protect others rather than to exploit or harm them.

ADVISING AND MENTORING TANGLES

When it comes to shared interests, professors may be closer to their students than they are to each other. Colleagues' specialty areas typically differ markedly because a department's faculty must represent the fullest possible spectrum of the discipline. Students, on the other hand, can be brought into professors' narrow circles and nurtured to embrace similar interests. Ethical problems can result from advising and mentoring. (See chapter 8 for a discussion of social relationships with students.)

Case 16-52: Angela Sturm, Ph.D., and Portia Drang, Ph.D., were intense rivals at Trenchant University. Drang filed an ethics complaint against Sturm that charged that she had taken on a graduate student and convinced the student to develop a dissertation aimed at discrediting theories and research published by Drang.

Students are free to select their own advisors and dissertation sponsors. Once having done so, students are usually heavily influenced by them. Whereas the freedom to pursue any areas of valid scientific inquiry must always remain open, psychologists should take special care to refrain from pulling students into personal quarrels. In this instance, it is not clear that Sturm was behaving unethically in attempting to interest a student in a dissertation topic, but she may well have been jeopardizing that student's welfare by injecting him into her dispute with Drang. Psychological research should seek scientific truth, and initiating studies primarily designed to discredit rather than to explore lacks integrity.

Sometimes, it is the student who, perhaps unwittingly, starts a troubling ball rolling.

Case 16-53: After taking a seminar from Trance Mesmer, Psy.D., an impressed graduate student decided to change his master's thesis topic to hypnosis. The student had already been working on a master's project for some time with Professor Drop, who had recruited the student the previous year. The student told Mesmer that he wanted to terminate his association with Dr. Drop and start a new project with Dr. Mesmer.

Dr. Mesmer might send the student to Dr. Drop to discuss the situation or might prefer to approach Dr. Drop himself, depending on what is the most comfortable and reasonable given the nature of the relationships involved. The two professors should communicate about the situation at some point to ensure that an equitable understanding has been reached. Responses by major professors to students who expressed a desire to jump ship vary from acceptance (and even relief) to engenderment of considerable resentment toward both the student and the new mentor. How far the student's project had already progressed, the interdependence that had been created, and the level of the advisor's commitment to the student or the student's project are primary factors that determine the original advisor's response. Sometimes, the original advisor already has a poor relationship with the potential new advisor, and the student's departure is viewed as a humiliating mutiny.

In most instances, it is wise for a potential advisor to remain cautious until the student and the original advisor have reached an understanding. Sometimes, it is best simply to refuse to take on a student who is already working for someone else, perhaps noting that other opportunities to work together in the future might arise. Switching advisors from the master's thesis to the doctoral dissertation is not unusual, and Mesmer could suggest that the student discuss the possibility of working together later because the current master's project is already well under way. Mesmer may also want to remind the student that he had, after all, committed to work with Dr. Drop. Just because the student's interests have changed does not automatically absolve a responsibility or erase a commitment.

Professors who are willing to selflessly help their students advance professionally deserve great respect. However, boundary checks can be just as important for the teaching psychologist as for psychotherapists. Sometimes, becoming too involved can even move into exploitation, as the following case (from Keith-Spiegel, Wittig et al., 1993) illustrates.

Case 16-54: Brigitt is a gifted senior who has been collaborating on scholarly projects with Professor Immobile for almost 2 years. She has excellent grades and achieved very high Graduate Record Examination scores. When Brigitt starts to discuss graduate school plans, Immobile convinces her that she should stay with him for another year as a postbaccalaureate student to continue their work. That way, he explains, she could get even more relevant academic experience, and he could write a stronger reference letter.

Some students may be better off forestalling graduation to strengthen their academic record and gain more relevant experience. Brigitt, however, is not one of them. Immobile is serving only himself, at the expense of a student who is fully capable of starting graduate study now (ES: 1.19).

Finally, when does personal advisement of students go beyond an acceptable boundary?

Case 16-55: Virgil Vestal fidgeted in the chair, looking very disturbed. "What is it?" Professor Blunt asked? "I have a girlfriend," said Virgil, "who wants to make love." "So, what's the problem?" asked Blunt. "I'm 22 and haven't ever had sex. I am really afraid of sex, and I wanted to ask you what I should do," replied Virgil. "Go for it," said Professor Blunt with a big grin. "Seize the moment."

Psychology professors may be especially sought for free personal advice on matters that go well beyond a discussion of the literature, school-related matters, and the student's future education or career. Matters relating to sex, family and relationship conflicts, personal fears, and complaints about just about anything are typical conversational staples for approachable professors. However, Blunt treated what may have been a very complex issue as one that he thought required only a little encouragement. His impulsive blessing could have been contraindicated. Blunt would have served the student bet-

ter had he indicated that, although this is an issue Vestal should talk over with somebody, he was not the right person. An offer to help set up an appointment, or even to walk over to the counseling center with the student if he appeared to be in a crisis, are acceptable, benevolent acts.

We advise setting one's training and expertise aside in such situations and asking, "Is this a matter that a caring professor in another discipline might refer to the counseling center or some other type of mental health professional?" If the answer is even "probably," we suggest that such a referral be made.

OTHER SELF-SERVING ISSUES NOT DIRECTLY INVOLVING STUDENTS

Textbook Adoption Practices

Teaching psychologists have the obligation to select required readings with care, and the textbook adoption practices should be based strictly on the merits of the content.

Case 16-56: Minny Racket, Ed.D., told a book sales representative that she would adopt the company's text for her classes if the company agreed to a $1 kickback on each copy purchased by her students.

Case 16-57: Sammy Snooker, Ph.D., agreed to adopt a particular company's book after being offered a relatively large sum of money for providing the company with a 3-page book review.

Such practices engaged in for personal gain are reprehensible. They exploit students, who assume that professors respect their learning interests by selecting resources entirely on the basis of educational merit (see ES: 1.15).

Disposing of Complimentary Textbooks

A tangential issue that has generated debate is the practice of selling still marketable, unsolicited, or unwanted courtesy textbooks (supplied to professors by book publishers) to used textbook vendors who roam the halls with little carts and hard cash. Teaching psychologists vary widely in their views of the appropriateness of such transactions, and most are unsure about its moral dimension. About half of the faculty in one survey do sell complimentary books to vendors (Tabachnick et al., 1991).

Those defending this avenue of disposal as a legitimate way to earn a few extra dollars contend that they have incurred no obligation, and that the unsolicited property is theirs to do with as they please. Those in tune with the increased costs passed to students when a large number of complimentary textbooks are interjected into the text market, and the lack of fairness to authors who receive no royalty for their efforts, decry such resales by professors.

We favor returning unwanted courtesy textbooks to the publisher. (Many now include envelopes for that purpose.) Other acceptable dispositions include donating the books to a worthy institution, a departmental Psi Chi or psychology club library, or a high school psychology teacher.

Moonlighting

Is working off campus during the active school year, in addition to holding a full-time teaching position, an ethical issue? It can be argued that it is unfair to students if a professor is available minimally, or only at odd hours, and often is too tired or distracted to attend to students' legitimate needs.

Case 16-58: Tillie Rushbutt, Ph.D., held a full-time university teaching position and saw 25 private practice clients per week. She also consulted regularly to mental health clinics around the country, which caused her to miss classes several times a semester. Dr. Rushbutt reasoned that her outside employment provided excellent lecture material and kept her current in her field and that her national reputation brought status to the university.

The ethics of moonlighting are difficult to resolve at a macro level. We cannot, for example, establish a meaningful "hour limit" for off-campus employment. People have higher or lower energy levels, require more or less sleep, have no or many family obligations, require considerable or little effort to do their outside job, and so on. These factors affect the impact of outside employment on students, as well as the quality of teaching, advising, and other services to the university that each teaching psychologist is expected to perform as a "good citizen." Surely, however, regardless of a professor's stamina and life circumstance, a point is reached at which students and the university are being shortchanged. Dr. Rushbutt, for example, sees more clients than do most full-time private practitioners.

Some types of moonlighting are more self-serving than others. This is the most extreme case that has come to our attention.

Case 16-59: Buzi Agent, Ed.D., was a tenured professor with a real estate broker's license. He held office hours from 6 to 7 A.M. and taught his classes from 7 A.M. until noon three mornings a week. Students rarely came to his predawn office hours, and Agent would use this time to review his lectures and to create and grade exams. He left promptly at noon and went to his real estate office. He never came to campus on Tuesdays or Thursdays.

Dr. Agent contributed nothing to the university community besides meeting the minimum requirements. It would be difficult to argue convincingly that his ongoing real estate career contributed anything of substance to his teaching of psychology. Many colleges and universities have disclosure policies that limit the extent of outside employment and restrict how many classes can be taught end to end. Regardless, it remains every teaching psychologist's own responsibility to know when extracurricular activities—whether outside employment, an absorbing hobby, or even textbook writing—impair the quality of the paid-for services they have undertaken on behalf of the academic institution and its students.

SUMMARY AND GUIDELINES

1. Descriptions of academic courses or other educational programs should reflect accu-

rately the experiences students will receive and the obligations they will incur.

2. Course materials should be prepared carefully and should include recent, important work relevant to the topic being taught. Teaching psychologists should teach only in those areas in which they have gained sufficient mastery relative to the level of the course.

3. When lecturing on sensitive or controversial topics, teaching psychologists should prepare the students in advance, the presentation should be objective and well balanced, and the choice of content should be pedagogically defensible.

4. Teaching psychologists should not present their own values or opinions in a way that could be mistaken for established fact.

5. Teaching psychologists must grade students fairly and adhere to criteria that apply equally to all students.

6. In interactions with students, teaching psychologists should treat them with respect and maintain appropriate professional boundaries. Teaching psychologists do not exploit students.

7. Except under very unusual circumstances, student confidences should be respected.

8. Teaching psychologists must monitor their own emotional status and take appropriate steps if personal problems are interfering with their ability to teach or to fulfill other responsibilities to the institution.

9. Teaching psychologists should find their own voice when creating lecture presentations and should credit sources from which they adapt extensively.

10. To maintain the quality and meaning of higher education, teaching psychologists must deal with academic dishonesty in a proactive and direct manner.

11. Assignments and textbooks should be selected solely for their pedagogical appropriateness.

12. Teaching psychologists must balance their teaching and other obligations to the institution with other activities in a way that ensures that their responsibilities to the academy are fulfilled.

References

American Association of University Professors. (1984). *Policy documents and reports.* Washington, DC: Author.

American Psychological Association. (1992). Ethical principles of psychologists and code of conduct. *American Psychologist, 47,* 1597–1611.

Anderson, M. (1992). *Impostors in the temple.* New York: Simon & Shuster.

Blevins-Knabe, B. (1992). The ethics of dual relationships in higher education. *Ethics and Behavior, 2,* 151–163.

Cahn, S. (1986). *Saints and scamps: Ethics in academia.* Totowa, NJ: Rowman & Littlefield.

Cahn, S. (Ed.). (1990). *Morality, responsibility, and the university.* Philadelphia: Temple University Press.

Cheny, L. V. (1992). *Telling the truth.* Washington, DC: National Endowment for the Humanities.

Correnti, R. (1986). Introduction. In D. Gehring, E. M. Nuss, & G. Pavela, *Issues and perspectives on academic integrity* (p. 7). Columbus, OH: National Association of Student Personnel Administration.

Custer, G. (1994, November). Can universities be liable for incompetent grads? *APA Monitor,* 7.

Davis, S. F., Grover, C. A., Becker, C. A., & McGregor, L. N. (1992). Academic dishonesty: Prevalence, determinants, techniques, and punishments. *Teaching of Psychology, 19,* 16–20.

Davis, S. F., & Ludvigson, H. W. (1995). Additional data on academic dishonesty and a proposal for remediation. *Teaching of Psychology, 22,* 119–121.

Dill, D. D. (Ed.). (1982). Ethics and the academic profession [Special Issue]. *Journal of Higher Education, 53.*

Fass, R. A. (1990). Cheating and plagiarism. In W. M. May (Ed.), *Ethics in higher education.* New York: American Council on Education and Macmillan.

Gose, B. (1994, April 17). Lawsuit "feeding frenzy." *Chronicle of Higher Education,* A27–A28.

Grauerholz, E., & Copenhaver, S. (1994). When the personal becomes problematic: The ethics of using experiential teaching methods. *Teaching Sociology, 22,* 319–327.

Handelsman, M. M., Rosen, J., & Arguello, A. (1987).

Informed consent of students: How much information is enough? *Teaching of Psychology, 14,* 107–109.

Harcum, E. R., & Friedman, H. (1991). Student's ethics ratings of demonstrations in introductory psychology. *Teaching of Psychology, 19,* 215–218.

Herzog, H. A. (1990). Discussing animal rights and animal research in the classroom. *Teaching of Psychology, 17,* 90–94.

Hill, G. W., Palladino, J. J., & Eison, J. A. (1993). Blood, sweat, and trivia: Faculty ratings of extra credit opportunities. *Teaching of Psychology, 20,* 209–213.

Hogan, P. M., & Kimmel, A. J. (1992). Ethical teaching of psychology: One department's attempts at self-regulation. *Teaching of Psychology, 19,* 205–210.

Keith-Spiegel, P. (1991). *The complete guide to graduate school admission.* Hillsdale, NJ: Lawrence Erlbaum.

Keith-Spiegel, P. (1994). Teaching psychologists and the new APA ethics code: Do we fit in? *Professional Psychology: Research and Practice, 25,* 362–368.

Keith-Spiegel, P., Tabachnick, B. G., & Allen, M. (1993). Ethics in academia: Students' views of professors' actions. *Ethics and Behavior, 3,* 149–162.

Keith-Spiegel, P., Tabachnick, B. G., & Spiegel, G. (1994). When demand exceeds supply: Second order criteria in graduate school selection criteria. *Teaching of Psychology , 21,* 79–85.

Keith-Spiegel, P., Tabachnick, B. G., & Washburn, J. (1997). *Why academic dishonesty is ignored: Professor's opinions.* Unpublished manuscript, Ball State University, Muncie, IN.

Keith-Spiegel, P., Wittig, A. F., Perkins, D. V., Balogh, D. W., & Whitley, B. E. (1993). *The ethics of teaching: A casebook.* Muncie, IN: Ball State University Office of Academic Research and Sponsored Projects.

Kibler, W. L. (1992, November 11). Cheating—Institutions need a comprehensive plan for promoting academic integrity. *Chronicle of Higher Education,* B1–B2.

Kitchener, K. S. (1992). Psychologist as teacher and mentor: Affirming ethical values throughout the curriculum. *Professional Psychology, 23,* 190–195.

Long, E., Jr. (1992). *Higher education as a moral enterprise.* Washington, DC: Georgetown University Press.

Matthews, J. (1991). The teaching of ethics and the ethics of teaching. *Teaching of Psychology, 18,* 80–85.

May, W. (Ed.). (1990). *Ethics and higher education.* New York: Macmillan.

McCabe, D. L., & Bowers, W. J. (1994). Academic dishonesty among males in college: A 30 year perspective. *Journal of College Student Development, 35,* 5–10.

McCabe, D., & Trevino, L. K. (1993). Faculty responses to academic dishonesty. *Research in Higher Education, 34,* 647–658.

Norcross, J. C., Dooley, H. S., & Stevenson, J. F. (1993). Faculty use and justification of extra credit: No middle ground? *Teaching of Psychology, 20,* 240–242.

Norcross, J. C., Horrocks, L. J., & Stevenson, J. F. (1989). Of bar fights and gadflies: Attitudes and practices concerning extra credit in college courses. *Teaching of Psychology, 16,* 199–203.

Palladino, J. J., Hill, G. W., & Norcross, J. C. (1995). The use of extra credit in teaching. *APS Observer, 8,* 34–35, 40.

Pavela, G. (1985). *The dismissal of students with mental disorders: Legal issues, policy considerations and alternative responses.* Asheville, NC: College Administration Publications.

Payne, S., & Charnov, B. (Eds.). (1987). *Ethical dilemmas for academic professionals.* Springfield, IL: Thomas Books.

Rubin, S. (1985, August 7). Professors, students, and the syllabus. *Chronicle of Higher Education,* p. 56.

Shea, C. (1994, July 20). Two students at Pace U. win refund and damages over computer course they say was too hard. *Chronicle of Higher Education,* A-28.

Sherrer, C. W., & Sherrer, M. S. (1972). Professional or legal standards for academic psychologists and counselors. *Journal of Law and Education, 1,* 289–302.

Swartzlander, S., Pace, D., & Stamler, V. L. (1993, February 17). The ethics of requiring students to write about their personal lives. *Chronicle of Higher Education,* B1–B2.

Sykes, C. J. (1988). *Profscam: Professors and the de-*

mise of higher education. Washington, DC: Regnery Gateway.

Tabachnick, B. G., Keith-Spiegel, P., & Pope, K. S. (1991). The ethics of teaching: Beliefs and behaviors of psychologists as educators. *American Psychologist, 46,* 506–515.

Whicker, M. L., & Kronenfeld, J. J. (1994). *Dealing with ethical dilemmas on campus*. Thousand Oaks, CA: Sage.

Wittig, A., Keith-Spiegel, P., & Tabachnick, B. G. (1994, August). *Do the best students hold professors to higher ethical standards?* Poster session presented at the annual meeting of the American Psychological Association, Los Angeles.

17

Scholarly Publication and Research Ethics

Your manuscript is both good and original, but the part that is good is not original, and the part that is original is not good.

Samuel Johnson

Scholarly writers and scientific investigators have traditionally claimed vast freedom to pursue knowledge and to impart discoveries without censure or restriction. However, calls for accountability emerged with the heightened awareness of individual rights, academic scandals that involved reports of scientific misconduct, and a creeping reluctance to accept the pronouncements of "experts" as infallible. Drawing the line between social responsibility and repressive censorship will never be easy, nor should it be. Therefore, psychologists have embraced many ethical standards related to fair publishing and ethical, competent research practices.

SCHOLARLY PUBLISHING ISSUES AND ABUSES

Knowledge is shared and advanced through scholarly publications. Publication is also the currency for recognition in the scientific community. Consequently, writing and publishing are fraught with temptations for ambitious psychologists. This section explores the following: (1) ethical aspects of assigning publication credits, (2) plagiarism and unfair use, (3) ghosted and author-assisted publications, (4) scientific misconduct, and (5) the responsibilities of publishing gatekeepers, especially editors of scholarly journals.

Publication Credit Assignments

Multiple-authored research papers are common, especially as disciplines become increasingly complex and specialized (Garfield, 1978). It may seem like deciding who deserves authorship credit on joint projects and in what order the names should be placed should be a straightforward procedure. The ethics code of the American Psychological Association (APA, 1992a) specifies that authorship credits are to be in proportion to authors' actual contributions. Minor or routine professional contributions or extensive nonprofessional assistance (e.g., typing a complicated manuscript, coding data, or helpful ideas offered by a colleague) may be acknowledged in a footnote or in an introductory statement (ES: 6.23). However, bitter disputes that concern assignments of publication credit are among the most common complaints to ethics committees that arise from the academic-scientific sector of psychology.

Readers may wonder why matters such as whose name appears as first ("senior") author or whether one receives a footnote rather than an authorship are all that important. A complex set of factors apply. These include the need for publication credits to advance one's career (e.g., to gain entrance into graduate school, obtain a job, or earn a promotion), to gain status among one's peers, to become recognized as an expert, and to accord personal satisfaction to compensate for the low or nonexistent monetary rewards associated with writing for strictly scholarly outlets.

Sole or senior authorship of scholarly publications is especially coveted (Fine & Kurdek, 1993), and the drive to achieve top-slot credit clashes with the ethic of collaboration (Cohen, 1995). In collaborative projects, readers assume that the individual listed as the senior author was primarily responsible for the entire project, although, in reality, this is not always the case. Also, once a citation has been noted in a writing with multiple authors, only the senior author's name is listed (followed by "et al.") for subsequent citations, rendering every major contributor except the senior author invisible. "Junior" authors have become very upset when individuals—usually people with the power and authority over them—claim the senior authorship for themselves when they allegedly were less involved in the project than were the others. Sometimes, people complain that they received a footnote credit or no acknowledgment at all when their contributions warranted a junior authorship. Others have asserted that psychologists have bullied their way into junior and sometimes senior authorship positions on work done primarily by others except for minor editorial critique or corrections. Ethics committees have agreed in some cases that more powerful and sometimes exploitative psychologists disadvan-

taged junior-listed authors. At other times, honest differences in the meaning of and value placed on the significance of each others' contributions are at issue.

Complaints that graduate students made several times in the 1970s and early 1980s alleged that dissertation supervisors insisted on being listed as coauthors on any published version of the students' project. Students argued that their supervising professors had the duty to facilitate their professional development, and that assisting them with their projects was a teaching obligation. The supervising professors responded that their contributions to the student projects were of significant magnitude or that the work could have never become publishable without their involvement, thus warranting coauthorship (sometimes senior authorship) credit.

Case 17-1: A major magazine invited Meg Byte, Ph.D., to contribute a brief version of her doctoral dissertation on the impact of regular play with computer games. She would be paid $1,000 for her contribution. Her thesis supervisor, Leonard Grab, Ph.D., insisted on being involved in the write-up and on sharing the income. Dr. Grab claimed that the dissertation would have never been completed without his guidance, so he deserved both credit and payment for this commercial opportunity.

Case 17-2: A student completed her doctoral dissertation under the supervision of Jack Pervasive, Ph.D., within the framework of his programmatic line of inquiry. Dr. Pervasive provided laboratory space, equipment, and research animals. Pervasive approved the design and read drafts of the work as it progressed. After completion, Pervasive insisted that his name appear as the senior author. The student was exasperated because she felt that Dr. Pervasive was primarily interested in getting himself another publication by using a student to do the grunt work and exploiting the dissertation requirement. She asked an ethics committee for an opinion.

An ethics committee decided that Dr. Grab was not automatically entitled to involvement in the popularized version of Byte's dissertation.

Regarding Dr. Pervasive, a committee opined that, assuming the facts of the case were exactly as the student had described, Pervasive appeared to be putting his own career needs above those of his student and his responsibility to promote her professional autonomy. The student wrote a thank you note to the committee, but decided not to pursue the matter further because of the possible consequences to her own professional well-being. This case prompted the ethics committee to create an informal policy designed to thwart such practices (Fields, 1983).

We suspect that the increase of graduate student complaints reflected changes in the assertiveness level of contemporary students and changing perceptions of the professorial role. Perhaps there was a time when professors readily served as mentors to their students and expected no more than an expression of appreciation in the preface and perhaps a footnote in any published version of the work. The respondents to the large national survey of publication credit practices and beliefs generally expressed generosity and responsibility toward students without expectations of authorship credit on students' projects (Spiegel & Keith-Spiegel, 1970). Research support and student assistant funds, however, have steadily withered, while competition for jobs and promotions has increased. These factors may have led to a revised perception of almost fully trained but still subordinate and primarily powerless graduate students as one solution to the disappearing resource problem. The 1992 APA ethics code formally incorporated elements of the earlier informal policy by suggesting that the student should normally be listed as the principal author on work that is based on a doctoral dissertation or master's thesis (ES: 6.23c). And, as Crespi (1994) reminds us, we must not forget that certain students may be sufficiently skilled as researchers and writers to warrant only very minor assistance from their professors.

Let us explore other patterns that arise regarding publication credit disputes: (1) obtaining authorships by virtue of power in the organization, (2) the unfulfilled commitment, and (3) the role of time spent on a project in the assignment of credits.

Case 17-3: Holden Power, Ph.D., insists that all research projects carried out by the psychologists he supervises in his hospital psychology service department bear his name as the last-listed author. He argues that this is appropriate because he is the one who arranges for the staff time to spend on research activity and is administratively in charge of all departmental activities. The psychology staff resented the forced inclusion of a person who contributes nothing substantive to the research and who often does not even read the manuscript prior to submission for publication.

In the Spiegel and Keith-Spiegel (1970) survey, researcher respondents rejected status as a consideration by overwhelmingly agreeing that all contributors, including paid or volunteer personnel at the subdoctoral level, be given equal consideration when authorship credit is assigned. They further agreed that it is unethical to give a coauthorship to someone of higher status in one's organization unless she or he makes a substantial contribution to the project. These notions were formally entered into the 1992 ethics code (ES: 6.23b).

Case 17-4: Chuck Ham, Ph.D., and Marvin Eggs, M.A., fleshed out the outline and half of a very rough draft of a book together. Then, Eggs became busy with other things and did not follow through with his agreed-upon obligations. Ham finished the project and published it as the sole author. Eggs complained to an ethics committee that his partial contribution was more than sufficient to warrant a junior authorship. Ham disagreed by declaring that if he had not completed the unpolished material and had not made it into something publishable, the whole project would have been scrapped.

This case presents a common problem as colleagues get involved with competing obligations and projects. Dr. Ham was not acting unethically in completing the project, assuming that Mr. Eggs was indeed shirking his commitment. But, because some groundwork had been completed, it would have been appropriate for Ham to have acknowledged Eggs' contributions during the earlier stages of the project in a footnote. Offering no acknowledgment of Mr. Eggs' contribution whatsoever does not reflect the final product properly, and, in this sense, Ham was acting unethically.

Case 17-5: Don Tedious, B.A., was hired by Jim Longitudinal, Ph.D., to collect data for a long-term study. Don Tedious worked for 3 years at an agreed-upon hourly rate, testing participants, scoring the measures, and entering the raw data on computer disks. Tedious was upset because he was not listed as an author on the finished manuscript. He argued that he had put in far more time than anyone else had and therefore deserved at least a junior position. Dr. Longitudinal argued that a footnote credit was proper because Tedious was paid to perform supervised, routine procedures.

Dr. Longitudinal acted properly in acknowledging Tedious in a footnote, not because he was paid to do his duties, but because of the nature of the work he performed. Time spent on a project per se is not a significant factor in determining authorship credits.

These last two cases also illustrate the wisdom of reaching agreements about what each person can expect in terms of credit before the research or writing collaboration begins and then keeping communications current and addressing any needs for modifications should changes in the project's status occur. It is our observation that many of the bitter credit disputes might have been avoided had the parties decided ahead of time who would receive what type of credit for doing what.

Plagiarism and Unfair Use

Plagiarism, the act of attempting to pass the work of others off as one's own, comes from the Latin *plagiarus* meaning "kidnapper" (Hawley, 1984). There is something inherently shadowy and sleazy about taking the original work of others and passing it off as one's own. Plagiarism has been described as "quite a rather bad little

crime" (Skom, 1986, p. 3). Mallon observes, "No, it isn't murder. And as larceny goes it's usually more distasteful than grand" (1989, p. xi). In the strictest sense of the definition of plagiarism, the intent is to deceive others; although ignorance is often at issue, especially in instances of improper attribution and citation of secondary sources (Froese, Boswell, Garcia, Koehn, & Nelson, 1995). Plagiarism can range from careless paraphrasing (very common) to intentional copying of an entire work without attributing the original source (Hawley, 1984). If the copying is extensive or if economic disadvantage befalls the original author, serious legal issues pertain through federal copyright infringement statutes (LaFollette, 1992).

Fair use is defined as the freedom to use copyrighted material in a reasonable manner without the consent of the copyright owners. Scholarly writings often quote short sections of works by others (properly cited) without explicit permission from the author or owner of the copyright. This practice is typically acceptable, such as when we quoted exact words written by others at the beginning of this section without asking the authors' permission. However, fair use can be exceeded, even when the material is meticulously attributed.[1]

Case 17-6: Armond Gatherup, Ed.D., self-published a small book on self-esteem. He quoted, with correct attribution, over 80% of the content from eight other sources. One of the authors he cited sent a copy of the book to an ethics committee, complaining that Gatherup had used his and others' work as a means of crediting himself with a book that others, in effect, wrote.

It appears that psychologists are far from the worst offenders when it comes to plagiarism and unfair use (Owens & Hardley, 1985). Complaints have, however, been received by ethics committees; these ranged from presentations of blatant hard evidence to uncertain speculation. Obvious instances of plagiarism, in which large amounts of material were copied verbatim, are

---

1. The most recent conflict regarding copyright and fair use involves electronic publishing and Internet postings. No one debates the desirability of clarifying the rules of use as applied to cyberspace and new teaching technologies, but these are still being argued as of this writing.

easy for ethics committees to adjudicate because the evidence is concrete and overwhelming. Interestingly, the primary source of discovery of major acts of plagiarism is neither by the public nor by psychologists, but by graduate students who are in the process of researching for their projects, as the next case illustrates.

Case 17-7: In the course of accessing the literature for her doctoral dissertation, a graduate student found that the 1995 dissertation of Rep Lica, "Ph.D.," was almost identical in wording and contained the same data and analysis as that of a 1989 doctoral dissertation by Paula Primary. She showed the two documents to her supervisor, who wrote to an ethics committee. Lica could not dispute the facts, but offered the defense that he was under extreme pressure to finish his degree and was receiving no support or assistance from his committee.

The overlap was so substantial that an ethics committee was able to reach a swift decision. The penalties imposed in such cases are usually severe. Lica was dropped from APA membership, his psychology license was revoked, and his degree was withdrawn by the university.

Less clear-cut cases that allege plagiarism or unfair use are based on brief or occasionally similar passages, heavy paraphrasing, or unattributed previously published ideas. These complaints are more difficult, and sometimes impossible, to uphold conclusively.

Case 17-8: Tick Off, Ph.D., complained to an ethics committee that Sam Likeness, M.A., used a number of his previously published ideas, including a few similar sentences, in Likeness' article on signal detection theory without crediting Dr. Off. The committee noted the similarity in ideas and an occasional resemblance in wording. Likeness, however, adamantly denied using or even having read Off's work, provided other articles (which were cited in Likeness' paper) as his primary sources, and asserted that the occasional wording similarities were strictly coincidental.

Writers or researchers working in the same specialty area may cull notions from each other and even similar ways of expressing themselves,

which render cases based on similar, but not identical, written material difficult or impossible to unravel. Remember that ideas per se are not legally protected; although Mr. Likeness probably had access to Dr. Off's already-published work, it cannot be proved that he ever read it. The basic ideas also appeared elsewhere, and these were cited by Likeness. The exact word overlap was minimal and could have been coincidental.

Although ideas per se are not subject to legal protection, ethical issues may well pertain.

Case 17-9: Sammy Snatch, Ph.D., listened to a panel of scientists at a professional meeting speaking informally about their programmatic research. Yanuus Yappy, Ph.D., responded in great detail to a question from the audience about his future research plans, outlining the work that needed to be done and how it should be accomplished, right down to the research design and equipment specifications. Using his notes, Snatch recreated the design and ran the experiment. When the study was submitted for publication, a reviewer who attended the same panel discussion recognized Yappy's design.

Should Snatch be held ethically liable for preempting Yappy's opportunity to follow through with his own carefully stated plan? Or, is a verbally stated idea fair game regardless of the detail? In the actual case, the arguments among the editor, the reviewers (who also suggested one could not trust the data of a "research design thief"), and Snatch shed more heat than light. Although the matter was left unresolved, the story was passed around. Snatch was shunned by his colleagues, and his work has never been published.

Because science has become a proprietary enterprise with economic, career status, and financial consequences for investigators, "who owns what" has become an increasingly visible area of debate, especially when a commercial sponsor and the attendant conflicts of interest are involved (Korenman, 1993). Unfortunately, scientific progress stands to be stunted in the chilling wake of incidents such as that involving Drs. Snatch and Yappy. Yappy was heard to say that he would never again discuss his work in an open forum until the work had been completed. This is unfortunate, if only because Yappy is also precluding collegial feedback that could enhance the quality of his future efforts. (For more about idea and data ownership, see Adler, 1990; Ceci & Walker, 1983; Fields & Price, 1993; Melton, 1988; Sieber, 1991a, 1991b).

Let us consider another, more perplexing case that involved a convoluted set of circumstances between literature access and final publication.

Case 17-10: Ann Tecedent, Ed.D., was shocked to see chunks of her previously published journal article appearing in another journal under the name Jack Next, Ph.D. Dr. Tecedent contacted an ethics committee and charged plagiarism. The investigation revealed a complicated chain of events. Dr. Next had assigned the literature review phase to his graduate assistant, who, in turn, assigned the initial library research to two undergraduate assistants. These assistants copied information, usually verbatim, from the literature and passed the information to the graduate assistant, who, after finding the material "well written," passed the notes virtually unchanged to Dr. Next. Next also found the notes well written and incorporated them directly into his manuscript.

Dr. Next was exonerated from the more serious ethics charge of intentional plagiarism, but was directed to explain the situation to the original author and to the journal staff (which printed an explanation in a subsequent issue). He was reprimanded by the ethics committee for lax supervision and careless scholarship.

The growing stockpile of published material allows malintentioned psychologists to risk a lower probability of plagiarism detection, as well as the possibility for innocent psychologists to publish something that might appear suspiciously similar to another person's work. Publishers of both books and journal articles, faced with their own space and financial limitations, increasingly admonish authors to "write tightly," which often makes it difficult or impossible to cite every source of every idea. But, the rules of thumb remain: Do not copy the work of others and pass it off as your own; and, if you use a small section of someone else's work in your own, credit it properly.

Ghosted and Author-Assisted Textbooks

Pairing psychology scholars with professional journalists for the purpose of creating textbooks or other scholarly books is no longer uncommon. If all authors are fully and saliently credited, no ethical questions arise, leaving purchasers to decide whether the addition of a professional writer enhances or decreases the pedagogical value of the product. At some point along the continuum between original work and unauthorized copying, however, claiming credit for unoriginal work becomes technically legal, but ethically questionable. Ghost-written works, for example, pose no legal problems as long as a valid contract is honored between the "ghost" and the author of record. But, is it ethical for psychologists to let readers believe that they originated a work that, in fact, someone else was paid to create in their name?

Author-assisted or "managed" books are those in which the publisher retains major control of the creation, development, and completion of the manuscript and, in a sense, becomes the primary author (Whitten, 1976). Many individuals (on the staff of the publishing house, freelance writers, junior-level psychologists, or graduate students) are typically involved in accessing material and drafting chapters to fill the master plan devised by the publishing company. The author of record, whose name appears on the book spine, cover, and title page, has varying degrees of writing and editorial involvement. In some cases, this involvement has been extremely minimal, such as serving as a reviewer of a final manuscript written by others.

Case 17-11: Several textbook authors banded together to complain about the scholarship practices of Polly Parrot, Ph.D. They documented how parts of their respective previously published books could be combined together, resulting in the mosaic attributed to Dr. Parrot. Dr. Parrot responded that she did not actually write any of the chapters, but did help with the organization of topics to be covered and the editing of the final drafts. She placed the blame on others over whom she had no control.

The quality of managed textbooks has been questioned as misleading to the consumer (Mc-Keachie, 1976). Most managed texts involve heavy culling of already published textbook formats, focusing on those that have already achieved success in the marketplace, which raises yet additional questions about the quality of scholarship. Indeed, the resemblance has occasionally been so marked that legal actions against the authors of record of the subsequent (and competing) managed text projects have resulted. In one instance, similar to the circumstances of the Dr. Parrot case presented above, the psychology textbook was ordered removed from the market by the courts (Haupt, 1976).

We believe that readers deserve to know how a book was created and who is responsible for its conceptualization and content; the 1992 APA ethics code echoes that theme (ES: 6.22a). Just as practicing psychologists are admonished to represent themselves accurately by taking care not to mislead the consumers about their services and areas of expertise, no less should be expected from psychologist-authors.

Scientific Misconduct

The scientific enterprise is built on the premise that truth-seeking is each investigator's principal motivation. Those who review submitted grants or papers for publication accept, on faith, that investigators subscribe to the highest standards of integrity (Grinnell, 1992). Unfortunately, other motives have prompted some researchers to present tainted findings. The themes that recur in many instances of unmasked data fraud include lax supervision of the data gathering and analysis procedures and perpetrators who are excessively ambitious and competitive and have previous records of prolific writing. Usually present is an intense pressure to produce findings. A researcher who publishes first, thus establishing a discovery, also establishes a priority for allocation of shrinking grant funds. A project that fails to produce significant findings may

not be accepted for publication, which may then weaken the likelihood of additional funding to continue that same line of inquiry.

Five basic varieties of scientific misconduct are (1) "dry lab" or forged data that are simply "invented" rather than actually collected; (2) tampered, "fudged," "doctored," "smoothed," or "cooked" data based on data actually collected, but altered to approach more closely the desired or expected outcome; (3) selected or "trimmed" data, which are actually collected but edited to delete discrepant or unwanted information from the final analysis (also known as "data dropping"; Rosenthal, 1994); (4) carelessness and disregard for accuracy; and (5) setting up an experimental condition so that the collected data are more likely to confirm the hypothesis. These acts may be more likely when the source of financial support has an interest in obtaining certain findings, which creates a conflict of interest in the investigator (National Institutes of Health, 1989). Other acts that qualify as less than honorable occur when investigators rely on secrecy to get ahead (Grinnell, 1992) or refuse to share data (Sieber, 1991a, 1991b). Or, critical information may be withheld or omitted from a paper, with the intended purpose of making it more difficult or impossible for anyone else to successfully engage in that line of inquiry (see ES: 6.25). Invalid findings may also result from a variety of more subtly malintentioned or inadvertent means, such as inappropriate design, poor or biased sampling procedures, and misused or inappropriately applied statistical tests. For example, "data torturing" involves "repeatedly analyzing the same data in different ways until something—anything—statistically significant shows up" (Whitley, 1995, p. 616).

Similar to plagiarism, the creation of fraudulent data is considered among scientists and scholars to be one of the most grievous ethical violations (see ES: 6.21a). The impact of forged data is, however, far more serious than simply duplicating the work of others because the spurious conclusions are absorbed into and contaminate the knowledge base. Application of fraudulent findings may ultimately harm the well-being of others. For example, the ramifications of Sir Cyril Burt's research (described more fully below) extended beyond the realm of academic debate because the British school tier system was largely justified on the basis of Burt's work in fixed intelligence (Diener & Crandall, 1978). Further, science is a process of building on previous work. Time and effort can be wasted when trusting investigators pursue inquiries based on bogus results published by others. Errors in alleged scientific advances, whether based on honest or deceitful practices, are assumed to be eventually self-correcting through replication. However, research funding sources typically do not support replication research.

The discovery of fraudulent data-reporting practices is not confined to recent times. Ptolemy, Galileo, Gregor Mendel, and Isaac Newton are among the historical scientific luminaries now suspected of fudging a little to align reality more closely with their theories. Unfortunately, numerous instances of fraudulent research have scandalized science in more recent times, many uncovered at the most prestigious and respected universities and institutes (Bell, 1992; Broad, 1980, 1982; Golden, 1981; Grinnell, 1992; Haworth, 1996; Hilts, 1981; Hixon, 1976; Jacobs, 1982; Kimmel, 1996; Kohn, 1986; Roark, 1980; Sarasohn, 1993). The Acadia Institute Project on Professional Values and Ethical Issues (Swazey, Anderson, & Lewis, 1993) surveyed doctoral candidates and faculty members from 99 departments. Anonymous responses to questions about knowledge of instances of scientific misconduct revealed that over two thirds of the graduate students and about one half of the faculty had direct knowledge of scientific misconduct, though fewer were willing to confront or report it, usually from fear of reprisal. Thus, unfortunately, such conduct may be neither rare nor ever adequately resolved.

Three highly publicized discoveries in psychology have brought some discredit to our field. Sir Cyril Burt, one of the most distinguished figures in British psychology, has posthumously been exposed for publishing implausible and fictitious data in his classic identical twin research, which supported his theory of the inherited nature of intelligence (Evans, 1976; Kamin, 1974; MacIntosh, 1995; McAskie, 1978; Wade, 1976). Defenders (e.g., Fletcher, 1991; Jensen, 1974; 1978; Joynson, 1989; Rushton, 1995) attempt to discount the discrepancies as mere carelessness, but others (Eysenck, 1980; Hearnshaw, 1979) describe additional incidents that suggest Burt committed more errors in his publications than can be attributed to nonchalance.

The scandal in the early 1970s at the Institute for Parapsychology, headed by the late Joseph B. Rhine, eroded some of the legitimacy the much beleaguered study of extrasensory perception had achieved through the efforts of its sincere and generally respected founder. In a frank article, an obviously shaken Rhine outlined how his chosen successor, a young medical doctor, was discovered by coworkers to have fabricated data for an investigation of precognition in rats (Rhine, 1974a). Ironically, Rhine had published an article just 3 months earlier on the problems of deceptive practices by parapsychology researchers and had outlined safety measures that should be taken (Rhine, 1974b).

More recently, in the late 1980s, the case of Stephen Breuning brought unwelcome notoriety to psychological research. With federal research funds, Breuning reported findings based on data that were never collected. This case is especially disturbing because of the consequences of the application of Breuning's findings while they were still unknown to be bogus (Committee on Government Operations, 1990). As Bell reports;

> Not only had the reports been relied on nationwide in determining drug therapy for institutionalized, severely retarded children, they had advocated the exact opposite treatment from that suggested by *bona fide* research. Although subsequent scientists recommended the use of tranquilizers for severely retarded children, Breuning's fraudulent claims advocated stimulants. (1992, p. 106)

The majority of the highly publicized data scandals have resulted from biomedical research laboratories, perhaps because biology is the most competitive field within the natural sciences (Benditt, 1995). No one knows for sure whether the incidence is higher in this field than in the social and behavioral sciences, or whether it is simply easier to detect fraud in biomedicine. The latter interpretation could, unfortunately, be valid because most research conducted in the social and behavioral sciences (except, perhaps, in such specialties as physiological psychology) do not necessitate chemical analyses, tissue cultures, or similar "hard" documentation. Psychological research data is often in the form of numerical scores from questionnaires, assessments, or performance measures. The research participants[2] are long gone, taking their anonymous identities with them. Such data are relatively easy to generate, fudge, or trim. We can hope that psychology researchers are motivated by the responsible quest for truth, but it is disquieting to note that the same "publish-or-perish" pressures exist in our field, that fame is an ever-present allure in any field, and that the practice of fabricating data may start as students (e.g., Azrin, Holz, Ulrich, & Goldiamond, 1961; Kimmel, 1996).

Experiences of ethics committees are not very helpful in estimating the incidence of fraudulent data publication among psychologists. Most of the cases of clear guilt involve plagiarized data; that is, the psychologist simply copied someone else's statistical findings and took credit for them. The rare charges of falsifying data brought to the attention of ethics committees have been difficult to adjudicate.

Case 17-12: Golda Brick, Ph.D., was accused by a colleague of analyzing and reporting data that were different from those actually gathered in the laboratory. Brick's concerned graduate student had brought the evidence to the colleague and asked for guidance. After viewing the graduate assistant's data sheets and the reported results, it was very apparent that the two did not jibe.

Case 17-13: Hocum Bunk, Ph.D., was charged by several members of his academic department with presenting, at a professional meeting, data findings based on experimental trials never actually run. The colleagues based their suspicions on the fact that an analysis of the student "subject pool" records did not reveal any used by Dr. Bunk during the last year, although he stated that he collected during that time and used undergraduate students as participants. Furthermore, the room,

shared by several faculty members, allegedly used to collect the data showed no signs of use by Dr. Bunk. He never signed up for it, was never seen in it, and his experimental device had "never changed position and was accumulating dust."

Dr. Brick denied any wrongdoing, explaining that she did not use the data that the student assistant had collected, but rather data she collected by herself. Dr. Bunk alleged that he did not use the student research pool because he conscripted students directly and ran them through a similar device he kept in his office. Neither psychologist could produce their original data; both claimed that they threw it away after completing their statistical analysis. Although both defenses were viewed as deficient, neither the complainants nor the committees could conclusively disprove the respondents' stories. The ethics committees did not exonerate Brick or Bunk, but did declare that insufficient evidence precluded further action.

In the light of such incidents, what stock is the public to place in such scientists' work? The public's generalized distrust, which is sure to ensue as the media prominently exposes cases of scientific intrigue, could have disastrous consequences for everyone. Scientists are as dependent on the public for continued support as society is on scientific contributions. Although part of the problem is a system of rewards that implicitly encourages dishonest practices, researchers must remain true to the search for truth.

Responsibilities of Publishing Gatekeepers

As we have already noted, publication quality and integrity are critical to the growth of a discipline, and "getting published" is often essential to one's professional status. As Rogers puts it: "Psychology journals determine not only the substantive directions of psychology but also

---

2. The term *research participants* is largely used in this chapter to replace the more traditional term *subjects*, as suggested by Gillis (1976). Although more cumbersome, this designation of those who provide research data reflects the ideal (though not always achieved) situation by which research investigators and those whom they study are involved in a cooperative venture with mutual responsibilities. The designation of subject suggests submission and enslavement.

shape the careers of individual psychologists, particularly those in academic and research centers (1992, p. 253)."

Psychology has one of the highest rates of manuscript rejection (Rotton, Levitt, & Foos, 1993). It is not surprising, then, that criticisms of decisions by acquisition editors, journal editors, and manuscript referees abound. Some publishers are faulted for emphasizing "big name" authors, production gimmicks, and large adoption markets. Journal editors and reviewers have been accused of accepting poor quality or trivial work, exhibiting favoritism and prejudices toward certain authors, and harboring biases against certain topics or theoretical approaches. Additional criticisms include long delays in giving author feedback, shoddy or deficient evaluations, and inclinations to reject manuscripts that report negative or equivocal findings, replications, or work in an area for which rigorous methodology does not yet exist (Bornstein, 1990; Brackbill & Korten, 1970; Douglas, 1992; Finke, 1990; Franzini, 1987; Gordon, 1977; Hartley, 1987; Houlihan, Hofschulte, Sachau, & Patten, 1992; Kupfersmid, 1988; McKeachie, 1976; Rogers, 1992; N. E. Smith, 1970; Standing & McKelvie, 1986; Sterling, 1959; Walster & Cleary, 1970).

The now classic and controversial article by Peters and Ceci (1982) assessed the capriciousness of the reviewing process of 12 prestigious psychology journals by resubmitting cosmetically altered (including author and affiliation changes), previously published articles to each respective journal. Surprisingly, only three articles were detected as resubmissions, and eight of the nine remaining articles were rejected for publication in the same journals that had published them only a short time earlier. The authors confirmed that the rejection rates and editorial policies of the journals had not been subsequently altered.

Formal ethics complaints against psychologists who serve as publishing gatekeepers are quite rare, possibly because disgruntled or would-be-published authors realize that ethics committees are in a position neither to referee disputes of this nature nor to dictate what gets published. Or, perhaps is it as a colleague whose manuscript was just rejected put it, "If I protest, it will be interpreted as whining." When a formal complaint is lodged, it is usually along the lines illustrated in the following case:

Case 17-14: Dunwent Bust, Ph.D., complained that Simon Noaction, Ph.D., the long-time editor of the *Journal of Behavioral Anomalies*, routinely published all invited addresses delivered at the Behavioral Anomalies society's annual meeting. Dr. Bust submitted the text of an address, but 9 months passed without a response. He wrote Dr. Noaction and promptly received a return letter from Edy New, Ed.D., who informed Bust that she was the new journal editor and had decided not to publish his address. Dr. Bust complained to an ethics committee that Dr. Noaction's lack of responsiveness ruined his opportunity to publish in the journal, and that the long delay may have rendered his paper too "dated" to be accepted for publication elsewhere.

It certainly appears that Dr. Bust was treated poorly by the outgoing editor and may not have received appropriate consideration by the incoming one. Whether an ethical violation occurred is not entirely clear. Nine months is a very long time, but not an unheard of review period. Judgment of the quality of the article itself is an issue, and we do not know if the paper was rejected by the new editor on those grounds. Editors differ as to their preferences and slants. On inquiry, it was discovered that Dr. Noaction had been ill for several months before his term expired. Whereas the transition period should have been handled more sensitively and expeditiously and the committee sympathized with Dr. Bust, no ethical violation was sustained.

Another ethical violation related to publishing scholarly work involves improper use of materials under review. Manuscripts should be handled as confidential, and proprietary rights of the authors are to be respected (ES: 6.26).

Case 17-15: Eileen Pilfer, Ph.D., received a manuscript from a journal in her area of expertise. She wrote a critical review, concluding that the piece not be published. A year later, the author of the rejected manuscript was shocked to see much of his submitted article appearing in a published report by Pilfer.

Such blatant cases of improper acquisition of material, compounded by plagiarism and (apparently) intentional blocking of competing work, are exceedingly rare. However, the trustworthiness of reviewers is critical because there are less easily detectible forms of misappropriating ideas or materials from works under review.

Finally, a complex dilemma exists whenever research findings judged valuable are discovered to have been acquired unethically. Although psychologists are admonished to conduct only ethical research (see ES: 6.06a, 6.07, 6.08), is it acceptable to publish any work that violated that standard? Some scientists and journal editors may contend that important data should not be ignored, regardless of how it was obtained. But, others would argue that journal editors have a moral obligation to refrain from publishing articles based on data gathered without adhering to ethical standards and policy (Burd, 1996). The fact is that journal editors would rarely be able to detect unethical research from the submitted manuscript content alone. A casual browsing of scholarly journals readily reveals the paucity of detailed descriptions of exactly how research participants were conscripted. Authors could be required to submit copies of their consent procedure and descriptions and steps taken to reduce risks, even though this information would not be included in the publication. This might inform the journal editors of any wrongdoing. But, in the absence of any formal requirement to refrain from publishing ill-gotten data (and the unresolved issue of whether journal editors are appropriate censors), this dilemma will not likely be reconciled soon.

RESEARCH ISSUES

Much has been written over the last several decades about the ethics of social and behavioral research, more, in fact, than about the ethics of any other single topic in this book. This great surge of interest did not emerge from the blue. Consciousness was jolted when scientists learned of the Nazis' use of "Jews and other ethnic mi-norities as human sacrifices to a science gone insane" (Pattullo, 1980, p. 2) and then broadened with revelations of questionable and risky procedures used on human beings without their voluntary and informed consent in other countries, including the United States. The federal government began creating and updating guidelines and policies for social and behavioral research in the 1950s. Institutional review boards (IRBs) have been established at each site that anticipates or receives federal research funds to educate scientists and to ensure that research is reviewed for ethical, as well as scientific, soundness. (For more information about ethical challenges for IRBs, see Edgar & Rothman, 1995; Hilgartner, 1990; Rosnow, Rotheram-Borus, Ceci, Blanck, & Koocher, 1993; and Sieber & Baluyot, 1992.)

Research investigators are held to many standards similar to those of service-providing psychologists. However, differences between the two types of professional activities create additional dilemmas for the research psychologist. Psychotherapy clients usually present themselves for care and realize they are receiving psychotherapeutic services. Research participants are usually actively sought and do not always know or understand what is going on or even that they are being studied. Psychotherapists are performing a service, and the process of therapy is, in itself, the purpose of the activity. Data collection, on the other hand, is the means by which an end is to be achieved, namely, the more self-serving goal of completing one's project. In general, then, the psychotherapist holds the interests and welfare of each individual as primary, whereas the research investigator additionally contends with an intense motivation to gather data and other personal needs and agendas.

This section briefly explores some of the major ethical concerns that arise in the course of conducting social and behavioral research, including the following: (1) competency to conduct research, (2) consent to participate, (3) deception and concealment, (4) special research populations such as college students and more vulnerable groups, (5) risk and benefit assessment, (6) special problems with research conducted outside the laboratory, (7) privacy and confidentiality, and (8) research using animals. For more complete analyses of the array of contemporary ethical issues in research, we recommend Kimmell (1996), Sieber (1982d, 1982e, 1992), and Stanley, Sieber, and Melton (1996).

Competency to Conduct Research

Although the majority of researchers have had extensive academic training, their activities are unregulated in the sense that anyone can conduct research and attempt to publish it. Because psychologists conducting research are not required to take a slate of courses, attain certain degrees, pass exams, be licensed, or possess any formal proof of competence to conduct and publish research, personal sensitivity to the relevant ethical issues and peer and self-regulation are especially crucial. Many people collecting data are still undergraduate students, whose actions are the responsibility of the supervising psychologists (ES: 6.07b, 6.07c).

The scientific merit of a research design has been widely acknowledged as a competence issue. But, the possible ethical consequences of flawed research raises additional ethical issues. Because no meaningful information can result from poorly conceived studies or improperly collected or analyzed data, the use of human beings or animals in such studies cannot be justified on any grounds (Edsall, 1969; Mitchell, 1964; Rutstein, 1969). At best, the participants' efforts are wasted, and, at worst, they could be seriously harmed. In addition, the scientific enterprise has been failed when low-quality data is dumped into the scientific literature. Ideally, IRBs and the editors of scholarly journals manage to weed out most incompetent submissions, but shoddy work slips by for a variety of reasons, including authors' attempts to hide or fudge the problem and inadequate or biased reviews. For example, the more important the topic (e.g., heart disease as opposed to heartburn), the more willing evaluators were to overlook or underrate methodological flaws (T. D. Wilson, DePaulo, Mook, & Klaaren, 1993).

Even the most competent investigators face many serious dilemmas when designing their projects. Good science and solid ethical practice typically result in the best outcomes, but scientific merit and ethical considerations are sometimes at odds, which requires some measure of one to be sacrificed to comply with the other. For example, fully informing the participants of the purpose of the study may weaken or distort scientific validity (see discussion of deception below). The privacy of vulnerable people may be invaded in long-term follow-up studies designed to evaluate and improve treatment techniques. Balanced placebo designs may require misinforming participants to reduce the effects of expectancies. Participants in a control group could be denied valuable treatment.

Many seeming conflicts between science and ethics can be resolved or minimized after careful reflection, consultation, and reworking of the original plan. As Sieber has stated:

> The ethics of research is not about etiquette or about protecting hapless subjects at the expense of science; it is about making research "work" for all concerned—creating a mutually respectful, win-win relationship in which valid research is done, subjects are pleased to participate, and the community regards the conclusions as constructive. (1993, p. 59)

Consent to Participate

The obligation to enter into a fair and clear agreement with research participants is a primary ethical requirement. In a sense, the investigator and the participants enter into a contractual understanding that specifies the rights and responsibilities of both (Lawson, 1995). Consent procedures were designed to preclude repetition of a grotesque period in world history. The requirement of consent as a protection for participants first appeared in the Nuremburg code (first published in the United States in the *Journal of the American Medical Association* in 1946; reprinted in Capron, 1989). Adopted as a judicial summary at the war trials of 23 Nazi physicians indicted for crimes against humanity, the code clearly states the concept of consent:

> The voluntary consent of the human subject is absolutely essential. This means that the person involved should have legal capacity to give consent; should be so situated as to be able to exercise free power of choice, without the intervention of

any element of force, fraud, deceit, duress, over-reaching, or other ulterior form of constraint or coercion; and should have sufficient knowledge and comprehension of the elements of the subject matter involved as to enable him [sic] to make an understanding [sic] and enlightened decision. The latter element requires that before the acceptance of an affirmative decision by the experimental subject there should be made known to him the nature, duration, and purpose of the experiment; the method and means by which it is to be conducted; all inconveniences and hazards reasonably to be expected; and the effects upon his health or person which may possibly come from his participation in the experiment. The duty and responsibility for ascertaining the quality of the consent rests upon each individual who initiates, directs, or engages in the experiment. It is a personal duty and responsibility which may not be delegated to another with impunity. (Capron, 1989, pp. 163–164)

Although never used as a legal precedent, the Nuremberg code is the basis from which subsequent codes and policies have been developed (see ES: 6.10, 6.11). The bottom line is that research participants have a right to self-determination and autonomy. Their involvement in research should be entered into voluntarily, knowingly, and intelligently.

Voluntariness

A person's decision to participate in a research project can be manipulated in both subtle and blatant ways. Whereas it may seem simple enough to ensure that consent is obtained without exercising coercion or causing duress, pressure, or undue enticement or influence, many complex factors make it difficult to ensure total voluntariness.

It has been argued that some element of coercion is involved in any transaction between investigators and research participants. The investigator can be influential without conscious intent. Simply being approached with a request by someone perceived as having prestige and authority may be persuasive. Influence is especially likely if the researcher is enthusiastic and likeable or if the potential participant is vulnera-ble, deferent, in need of attention, desperate for a solution to a personal matter that relates to the subject under investigation, or is an inmate, student, or employee of the organization sponsoring the research.

The explicit offer of rewards, monetary or otherwise, is a sensitive matter that can affect a decision to participate. Offering to pay participants a small amount of money to offset inconvenience and transportation costs is unlikely to be considered coercive. The matter becomes more complicated, however, when the reimbursements or rewards for participating are great enough to sway consent decisions.

Case 17-16: Edward Noharm, Ph.D., complained to a university IRB that a research project involved tactics that were excessively enticing. To obtain a control group for a hospitalized experimental treatment group, the investigators approached parents in a low-income neighborhood and offered them several hundred dollars if they would allow their babies to undergo periodical laboratory tests, some of which involved considerable discomfort. Dr. Noharm argued that the control group children could in no way benefit from the study, and that the offer to financially limited parents of such a large sum constituted a persuasion that could override concern for their children's welfare and best interests.

Case 17-17: Mimi Dogood, Psy.D., complained to a state legislature that prisoners were being subjected to poorly designed, dangerous experimentation procedures in return for $3 a day. Ironically, the prisoners objected to her intervention, noting that the money was sufficient to keep them supplied with cigarettes, candy, and other small items that enhanced the quality of their daily lives.

Both cases illustrate how people of limited means or opportunity may accept attractive enticements or rewards that others with greater resources might see as trivial. Yet, the participants themselves may view as insulting and paternalistic any efforts to "protect" them from the opportunity to decide for themselves. The 1992 APA ethics code admonishes psychologists to refrain from offering "excessive or inappropriate financial or other inducements to obtain research participants, particularly when it might tend to coerce participation" (ES: 6.14b). However, in some lines of research, it is so difficult to conscript volunteers that investigators have offered finders fees to those who can bring them participants (Wheeler, 1991).

Ackerman (1989) presents a moral analysis of paying research participants in which he advocates separating reimbursement for incidental expenses (e.g., carfare or lost work time), from wages (which can be in the form of money or services) earned by being a research participant and from compensation for injury. His analysis compares paid research participants to ordinary workers and attempts to apply the ethics of research remuneration to the responsibilities of employers. The results reveal how careful and thoughtful decisions about payment must be made, especially when the "job" carries a risk of harm.

A more subtle form of coercion has been described by Freedman and Fraser (1966) as the "foot-in-the-door" technique. These authors experimentally confirmed that participants were more likely to comply with a larger request if they had previously complied with a smaller one. The case below illustrates this phenomenon.

Case 17-18: Hester Twostep, Ph.D., recruited participants to complete a brief questionnaire on attitudes toward contemporary sexual mores. After completion, Dr. Twostep told the participants that she would appreciate their cooperation in filling out a lengthy questionnaire about their sexual practices. The participants were not informed of the second phase prior to taking the short, less-sensitive questionnaire. Several participants later expressed that they felt both uncomfortable and "trapped."

Another form of subtle coercion involves appeals to the participants' altruism. This type of coercion can range from personal pleas for help to suggestions that cooperation will benefit humankind or advance science. Refusal to participate may be difficult because the participant may fear coming across as selfish or uncaring. To the extent that investigators genuinely need participants and are sincere in their beliefs that

their studies are valuable efforts, some level of altruistic appeal is probably unavoidable and not always inappropriate as long as undue social pressure is not involved (Ferguson, 1978). It has been found that both adults and children are quite capable of refusing strong altruistic appeals to induce participation in research that involves painful or upsetting procedures (Keith-Spiegel & Maas, 1981).

Exerting undue social pressure can be powerful, as the following case illustrates:

Case 17-19: Betty Roundup, Ph.D., asked her students to do her a favor by staying after class for a few minutes to fill out a research questionnaire. She added that this task was voluntary, but when Skip Busy began to leave, she said, "Well, I'm certainly glad that the rest of you are willing to help me out." Busy sat down, but was embarrassed and felt he had jeopardized his standing with the professor.

Dr. Roundup has power over the participants because of her teaching role, and the students probably felt pressured to comply. When Dr. Roundup proceeded to undermine her own statement of the students' rights by publicly humiliating the one who desired to exercise the option to leave, she clearly violated his rights as a research participant (ES: 6.11c).

The researcher must be careful not to create motives or needs artificially through coercive maneuvers such as suggesting that anyone who declines to participate is revealing a weakness or immaturity. Similarly, some participants may discount any potential risks in the hope of securing needed benefits, or they may believe that needed services are contingent on participation in research. Researchers must also be careful not to engage in "hyperclaiming" (Rosenthal, 1994), that is, suggesting to potential participants that the study will meet goals that are, in fact, unlikely to be achieved.

The wise investigator, whose goal is to obtain useful and valid data, will not only refrain from the use of coercion to gain consent, but will remain alert to signs of discomfort and anxiousness during the data collection phase. Despite the disappointments that investigators undoubtedly experience when participants change their minds midcourse (especially if this occurs well into a complicated or longitudinal study), the right to withdraw, with rare exceptions, should be honored. This right to disengage should be made explicit during the initial consent phase. Withdrawal privileges may be overridden in those more unusual cases when participants are legally or mentally incompetent and the experimental interventions may provide significant benefit to their health and welfare, if it is available only in a research context, and if other alternatives have been exhausted or are unavailable (National Commission for the Protection of Human Subjects, 1977). Such conditions arise only rarely in social and behavioral research.

Knowledge and Understanding

For research participants to understand what they are being asked to agree to do, they must have the capacity to comprehend and evaluate the information that is offered to them.

Case 17-20: Sue Nofathom complained to the IRB at her university that a study conducted by Hy Wordlevel, Ph.D., and his students subjected her to an upsetting experience by asking embarrassing questions about her childhood relationships. Wordlevel produced Nofathom's signed consent form as a defense. Nofathom contended, however, that the wording of the form was confusing to her and used terms like "participatory negative junctions" that she did not understand.

Unfortunately, it has been documented that many legally competent adults had minimal understanding of what they agreed to do (Cassileth, 1980; B. H. Gray, 1975; Martin, Arnold, Zimmerman, & Richard, 1968; Resnick & Schwartz, 1973; Taub, Baker, & Sturr, 1986). Many consent forms have been found to be lacking important elements, such as statements of risks or the right to withdraw. Ms. Nofathom might have asked questions (assuming she was invited to do so) or declined to participate in something she did not understand. Nevertheless, investigators are obligated to use language in consent forms that is comprehensible to the population under study (ES: 6.11b) If the information offered is too detailed or technical, however, willingness to participate may decrease (Berscheid, Dermer, & Libman, 1973; Epstein & Lasagna, 1969).

When participants are not legally capable of giving consent, permission must be obtained from an authorized person. Nevertheless, except for infants and the seriously impaired, participants should be offered an explanation of what they are being asked to do, and, if possible, their proactive assent should be sought (ES: 6.22). Even young children are capable of understanding simple descriptions of what it will be like to participate in a study (Melton, Koocher, & Saks, 1983; Stanley, Sieber, & Melton, 1987). It is our position that, even if permission has been obtained, a child who expresses lack of desire or interest in participating should be excused unless there is a very compelling reason, such as a likelihood of therapeutic benefit, to override the child's wishes (Koocher & Keith-Spiegel, 1990).

Is consent ever unnecessary? Yes, according to the 1992 APA ethics code, under certain conditions. Informed consent may not be necessary for some types of data collection "such as anonymous questionnaires, naturalistic observations, or certain kinds of archival research" (ES: 6.10). However, the onus of responsibility is placed on the investigator, other (unspecified) regulations, and IRBs. The examples offered by the APA do not include any research activity that involves experimental manipulation. But, because the list was not inclusive, investigators who use many techniques for which consent is never obtained are assumedly being overseen elsewhere.

Deception

Deception is one of the thorniest ethical dilemmas associated with social and behavioral research on humans. It is often treated as an embarrassing relative within psychology, the "crazy aunt in the cellar" to borrow from Ross Perot's imagery. But, what can you do when it has become an integral part of the family? In surveys by Stricker (1967) and Menges (1973), psychological research intentionally used deception in about one of every five studies. In social psychology, specifically, the rate has fluctuated over the years, peaking during the 1970s, when deception was used in the majority of social psychology research reports (Adair, Dushenko, & Lindsay, 1985; Sieber, Iannuzzo, & Rodriguez, 1995). The rate has decreased in more recent years, most likely due to changes in social psychology theories, research interests, ethical standards, and federal policy (Nicks, Korn, & Mainieri, 1997).

Arguments that favor the continued use of deception often revolve around the assertion that a considerable amount of useful and valid knowledge could never be accumulated if the participants had foreknowledge of the purpose of the study or its procedures (Baron, 1981; C. P. Smith, 1981; Taylor & Shepperd, 1996). Further, despite the potential for harm, participants are apparently rarely harmed or upset by participating in deceptive research (Christensen, 1988; Sharpe, Adair, & Roese, 1992). Critics argue that deception, by definition, compromises the consent agreement and allowing it condones lying. There is a fear that the public increasingly sees social scientists as a manipulative, exploitative, suspicious group. It is alleged that such techniques provide a quick, noncreative, and undesirable shortcut to more careful and clever, and ultimately higher level, moral and scientific experimentation. And, finally, degradation, embarrassment, anger, disillusionment, and other harms and wrongs are ever-present dangers to "duped" participants (see Baumrind, 1976, 1985; Kelman, 1967; Oliansky, 1991; Sieber, 1992; Stricker, 1967; Weinrach & Ivey, 1975).

Deception techniques range markedly from outright lies or concealment of risks to mild or ambiguous misrepresentations or omissions. Types presented by Gross and Flemming (1982), Kimmell (1996), and Sieber (1982a) include:

1. Misinforming participants (offering inaccurate information during the consent phase that might have influenced the decision to participate)
2. Concealing information (leaving out relevant information during the consent phase that might have influenced the decision to participate)
3. Third-person deception (investigator observing someone else misinforming or misleading participants)
4. Use of confederates ("stooges" pose or interact with the participants in some predetermined way)
5. Making false guarantees (failing to maintain confidentiality or not ultimately giving a promised prize)
6. Misrepresenting one's identity (such as referring to oneself falsely as a medical doctor or actor)
7. False feedback (giving participants performance or other evaluations that are untrue)
8. Self-deception (allowing or encouraging participants to maintain their own expectations that the study purpose is different from what it actually is)
9. Use of placebos or other manipulation of expectations
10. Misrepresentation of study scope (such as presenting a single study as two unrelated measures)
11. Concealed observation or recording
12. No informing (not informing participants that they are being assessed or observed for research purposes)

These practices often overlap or are used in conjunction with each other. Each type has its potential for harms and wrongs to participants, although the nature of the actual experiment can be important in determining whether problems will materialize. Sieber (1982b) notes that *which* behavior is being observed and in *what* setting for *what* purpose are critical factors in assessing the acceptability of deception in research. Public behavior in a context in which one expects to be observed (e.g., what one does in daylight on the street) is quite different from behavior carried out in a private or quasi-private setting with the assumption that no one is watching (e.g., what one does in one's office or the lavatory).

Deception may often be unintentional. Despite an investigator's sincere desire to disclose all aspects of a study's purpose, in the process of summarizing the work, some aspects will remain unexplained. It is the intentional use of deceptive techniques that we are most concerned with here. The use of deception is ethically problematical because it precludes obtaining fully informed consent before the onset of data collection or experimental trial. However, various versions of the APA ethics code have explicitly, though cautiously, allowed the use of deception in research. The 1992 APA ethics code admonishes psychologists to ensure that a study involving deception has scientific or applied value and that effective alternatives have been considered but were unfeasible (ES: 6.15a). Further, deceiving participants about *"significant* [emphasis added] aspects of the research that would affect their willingness to participate, such as physical risks, discomfort, or unpleasant emotional experiences" is disallowed (ES: 6.15b). The difficulty with such seemingly clear directives is that key embedded concepts can be interpreted differently by participants and among investigators:

Case 17-21: When participants arrived at Elmo Gotcha's laboratory, they were told that they would be asked to examine some objects carefully and would later be tested on what they saw. Items included a flashlight, several hand tools, a teddy bear, and a suitcase. When students opened the suitcase, they found a very short but energetic garden snake. Gotcha recorded each student's response. He wrote a paper that classified college students' reactions to "unexpected events," deliberately pointing out that the snake was small and totally harmless.

Psychologists probably differ in their judgments of the potential for emotional distress. In this case, the data suggested that many participants' responses to the snake were extreme. Gotcha defended himself by saying that he had no way of knowing in advance that some of his participants would "get hysterical."

Although ethics committees receive very few complaints from research participants, when complaints do surface, they are most likely to involve intensely negative reactions to being purposely misled. The next case is typical.

Case 17-22: Tillie Testy was outraged about a research study unwittingly conducted on her and her classmates by her professor, Henry Sneak, Ed.D. The students had been told they would be taking a multiple-choice test on a given day that would cover certain textbook readings. On exam day, another person entered the room, explained that Dr. Sneak was ill and had been unable to prepare the test, so an essay question would be substituted. The person wrote a question unrelated to the assigned readings on the board. After 10 minutes, Dr. Sneak entered the room and explained that he was doing a study on the effects of confusion and stress and asked the students to fill out a brief questionnaire. He then handed out the real exam and told the students to "carry on." Ms. Testy was upset not only because she was tricked, but also because she was forced to take an exam immediately following what was, for her, an acutely tense 10 minutes.

An ethics committee agreed that expecting students to perform on an exam that would be graded right after a manufactured disruption was unfair to the students. Further concerns were expressed by the ethics committee because the study was judged to be poorly conceived and unlikely to contribute any beneficial knowledge.

Psychologists who utilize deception are obligated to "come clean" with their participants in a timely fashion after data collection (ES: 6.15c). These procedures are known by various names, some distinguished by the nature of the investigatory procedures used, which include "postinvestigation clarification," "dehoaxing," "desensitization," "disabusing," and, most common, "debriefing" (Holmes, 1976; Kimmel, 1996; Marans, 1988). The goal of the postclarification procedure is to correct any misconceptions or supply any information purposely withheld, and done in a sensitive and educational manner so that the participants can understand and accept the reasons offered, including why deception was necessary. Ideally, all anxieties have been alleviated and the participants feel satisfied with the experience. Baumrind (1976), however, speaks of debriefing as "inflicted insight." We know little about its effectiveness, and we may inappropriately rely on it as an ameliorative step (Fisher & Fryberg, 1994; Geller, 1982; Walster, Bercheid, & Abrahams, 1967) when it could actually result in additional adverse reactions (Holmes, 1976; Mills, 1976; Sieber, 1982c; Tesch, 1977). It may cause embarrassment (Fisher & Fryberg, 1994). Or, it may fail to solve the original problem. For example, even if Dr. Gotcha's student participants (Case 17-21) are given some reasonable explanation as to why they had to be surprised by a snake in a suitcase, they can be said to be dehoaxed but not necessarily effectively desensitized. And, we know almost nothing about how children or others of more limited cognitive ability process investigators' attempts at debriefing. They may cause confusion or discomfort rather than enlightenment (Koocher & Keith-Spiegel, 1990).

Methodological, as well as moral considerations, have impelled a search for alternatives to deception (Fisher & Fryberg, 1994). A number of nondeceptive techniques have been proposed, most involving some form of forewarning (e.g., consenting to be deceived), role enactment, simulation, or naturalistic observations (see Baumrind, 1985; Cooper, 1976; Fisher & Fryberg, 1994; Forward, Canter, & Kirsch, 1976; Geller, 1982; Kimmell, 1996; Lawson, 1995; Sieber, Iannuzzo, & Rodriguez, 1995). Dr. Gotcha (Case 17-21) would have likely learned, simply by asking a group of students how they would react if they opened a suitcase and found themselves face to face with a live snake, that many would be upset.

Alternatives, however, are not without their own methodological challenges. If, for example, consent to be deceived is obtained at the onset, can a research participant proceed without the knowledge that "something else is really going on here" constantly on his or her mind? What effect will this mind-set have on the participant's performance? Nevertheless, we do encourage serious consideration of every possible alternative to the use of deception techniques because the ethical pitfalls and potential for wronging or harming participants are always present, particularly if the study invades privacy or involves observing or inducing behavior that may be socially unacceptable.

Vulnerable or Different
Study Populations

Ethical standards related to the conduct of research with human beings are easiest to apply to participants who are fully functioning, competent, free agents with well-developed senses of autonomy and established, reliable personal and financial resources. The researcher's role is to approach these people in good faith for their assistance and, if they agree to participate, to cause them no harm. Many research populations that are of interest or more readily available to social and behavioral scientists, however, are restricted or vulnerable in ways that do not allow large measures of self-determination (Lasagna, 1969).

When research populations are legally incompetent, permission to participate must be granted by someone (a "proxy") along with the participants themselves. Psychotics, a population frequently studied by social and behavioral scientists, require special considerations when it comes to obtaining consent (Stanley & Stanley, 1981). However, minors comprise the population that receives the most attention with regard to proxy consent procedures. Legally, the researcher is required to obtain permission from the parents or legal guardians, but that procedure does not settle the ethical questions. Children, especially older ones, are not without capacity to reason or to know what they want and do not want to do (Keith-Spiegel & Maas, 1981). How much their wishes to participate should be taken into account has been debated, eventually leading to the recommendation that the verbal child's assent be obtained along with parental permission (Keith-Spiegel, 1976; Koocher & Keith-Spiegel, 1990; National Commission for the Protection of Human Subjects, 1977). (For further details on the array of ethical issues in researching minors, see Ferguson, 1978; Fisher, 1993; Fisher & Tryon, 1990; Frankel, 1978; Hoagwood, Jensen, & Fisher, 1996; Keith-Spiegel, 1983; Lowe, 1970; Lowe, Alexander, & Mishkin, 1974; Melton, 1989; Thompson, 1990).

Other populations require special safeguards because they may be vulnerable to exploitation due to their restrictive, unstimulating environments. Competent, but lonely or bored, individuals residing in convalescent homes, may be willing to engage in almost any research project in return for some attention. Considerable concern has been expressed about research that has been conducted on prisoners, a group that cannot be said to have freedom of choice. Attitudes toward this population may not be particularly compassionate and could translate into a justification for relaxing the ethical standards observed for others (Branson, 1977; Capron, 1973; Kimmell, 1996; Mitford, 1973; Rubin, 1976; Swan, 1979).

Some study populations pose additional vulnerabilities because of their mental or emotional condition, such as the seriously depressed (Stanton & New, 1988). Others are vulnerable because of physical illness, with the vulnerability possibly compounded by issues of confidentiality and stigma. Considerable literature has emerged on how to balance research participants' rights against social welfare in AIDS research (see J. N. Gray, 1985; Melton & Gray, 1988; Melton, Levine, Koocher, Rosenthal, & Thompson, 1988; Sieber, 1992).

Conscious or unconscious biases against a study population may affect both the research question and risks to which the participants are exposed. For example, unfair or inaccurate generalizations about the entire study population may be perpetuated or created. A survey of thousands of psychology articles has confirmed that the incidence of sexism in research (using indicators such as sexist language and inappropriate generalizations) has markedly declined since 1970, although is far from absent (Gannon, Luchetta, Rhodes, Pardie, & Segrist, 1992).

To the extent that current researchers, most of whom are white and middle class, see their study target population as "not like me," potential harm to participants exists unless special sensitivities are cultivated and maintained (Allen, Heckel, & Garcia, 1980; S. W. Gray, 1971; Nikelly, 1971; Rainwater & Pittman, 1967). Sometimes, biases that affect the research may result not so much from assigning one's values to the study population, but from ignorance about the cultural values and traditions of the group under investigation (S. W. Gray, 1971; Price-Williams, 1975). A prevalent false belief is to assume that all members of a social group are alike. As a consequence, research designs may fail to consider important factors that differentiate among members within the population. Levine (1982), for example, discussed aging re-

search and the ethical implications of failing to consider social class, ethnicity, race, and sex as critical factors that contribute to the understanding of old people.

A fascinating article by Darou, Hum, and Kurtness (1993) describes the problems faced by psychologists attempting to study the hunting/trapping Crees, a group of about 10,000 native Canadians. Because these particular people were neither easily intimidated nor compliant, they ejected all but one psychologist from their community. Darou and his colleagues noted that patience (even when grant funds are running low) and adaptation to local values are critical, especially reciprocity and honesty. Comparing one's culture with the one under study should be avoided. Experimental methodology (including tests and assessments) may simply be inappropriate in some cultural settings. These were certainly a problem for the Crees. Darou and his colleagues noted that, although the ejected investigators were scrupulously following extant ethics codes, they "were still culturally inappropriate and incapacitated" (p. 328). Examples included investigators who unwittingly put members of the community in conflict with each other or who failed to act within the constraints and protocol of local authorities.

Just as psychotherapists are admonished to understand differences in age, gender, national origin, race, ethnicity, sexual orientation, disability, language, and socioeconomic status that may describe the clients they counsel, researchers venturing outside of their realm of social comfort must do the same (ES: 1.08). Some investigators may require considerable experience, consultation, or additional training before conducting research on the populations that interest them.

Psychology's Human "Fruit Flies"

Over 50 years ago, Quinn McNemar referred to psychology as "largely the science of the behavior of sophomores" (1946, p. 333). College students still comprise the majority of psychology research participants, and large proportions of these are recruited through "subject pools" (Korn & Bram, 1987; Menges, 1973; A. Miller,

1981; Rosenthal & Rosnow, 1969, 1975). Typically, participants are offered course credit in their introductory psychology courses (Sieber & Saks, 1989) and thereby create a convenient, inexpensive study population (Rubenstein, 1982).

The use of college recruits has been debated on grounds of methodological and other biases. For example, research requiring participants to be naive about the purpose or experience is likely to be contaminated because the information is passed around by those who have already participated, even when asked not to talk about the study (Klein & Cheuvront, 1990). Ethical concerns about coercion and related forms of exploitation have also been raised, especially if alternative ways of satisfying course requirements are not offered, if alternatives are noxious or excessively time consuming, if students receive no worthwhile feedback or educational benefit, and if no readily accessible complaint resource is provided (Diener & Crandall, 1978). The 1992 APA ethics code mandates that alternative assignments to research participation be both available and equitable (ES: 6.22d). Alternatives to participation should be reasonably attractive and, ideally, research related, such as allowing students to observe the research process, attend research presentations by faculty or advanced students, or even allowing the student to assist in the research process for a short while (McCord, 1991). Evidence suggests, however, that, although the majority of psychology departments offer alternatives, most are relatively unattractive (Sieber & Saks, 1989).

Coercion of students participating in the subject pool may be subtle and covary with other considerations. For example, if selection bias is lowered by providing minimal information about the study on the sign-up board, participants will not know exactly what they are getting into until they show up at the designated time and place to participate. At that point, they have already set aside the time and made the effort to be there, which heightens the likelihood of staying to do whatever is required of them by the investigators.

Subject pools are justified on the grounds that they provide some educational value for the students, despite the obvious advantages that subject pools provide for advanced students and faculty. Ensuring educational benefits for the participants takes special care and time, and concerns have been expressed that the benefits are either dubious or not effectively enforced (Korn, 1988; C. P. Miller, 1981; Sieber & Saks, 1989). Although the 1992 APA ethics code requires offering research participants a prompt opportunity to obtain information about the study and its results (ES: 6.18b), it is unlikely that a summary posted on the sign-up board will be read or that many students will accept invitations to come by an office at a later date.

Regardless of the problems with subject pools, surveys have generally shown positive ratings of experiences by subject pool participants (Britton, 1979; Leak, 1981), although Coulter (1986) did find that participants, when later questioned more carefully, found the experience to be boring, trivial, or a waste of time. Nimmer and Handelsman (1992) found some support for the hypothesis that students involved in mandatory participation reported less satisfaction toward the learning value than did a semivoluntary group. Many ethical concerns are alleviated if subject pool participation (along with other alternatives) is accorded a small amount of "extra credit," which gives the students the option to enhance their grades rather than jeopardizing them.

Balancing Benefits and Risks

The potential benefits that accrue from research participation are virtually impossible to estimate accurately. By definition, an experimental procedure is conducted to provide answers to heretofore unanswered questions. If a procedure or technique were known to be beneficial to a particular set of participants, it would not be necessary to conduct research on it.

Ironically, despite the inherent impossibility of accurately predicting benefits, the assessment of potential benefit is a critical factor in judging the acceptability of a research proposal, especially if the participants will be placed at any risk as a result of their participation. In general, the level of acceptable risk can be greater if the research is judged to be significant and important work, especially if the participants require some form of intervention only available in the research context.

Benefit assessment for biomedical research is often easier to evaluate than for social and behavioral research, as, for example, when a study sample population is terminally ill and the experimental treatment holds even a remote prospect of benefit. We all would agree that "physically healthy" is better than "sick." In social and behavioral research, however, benefit may exist primarily in the eye of the beholder since perceptions regarding what is "good" or "bad" for people vary according to one's theoretical beliefs or values. For example, a psychologist may study ways to enhance children's assertiveness, figuring that early training in making clear what you want will provide young people with coping skills that will serve them well, increase independence, and elevate self-esteem. A critic might argue that assertive children would be perceived by adults as bratty, selfish, demanding, and disrespectful and that to encourage youngsters to be assertive, given our present expectations for appropriate child behavior, would actually put them at risk in their homes and in the traditional school system.

The benefit test has also been debated regarding who or what is the appropriate recipient of the benefits. Some argue that the benefit test should be applied strictly to the research participants themselves, that is, as a result of their participation, some benefit might reasonably be expected to accrue directly to them. Others would say that it is not necessary to expect that benefits may be experienced by the participants of a given investigation, but that some likelihood exists for the possibility that the results will be, in some way, useful in the conduct of future studies that may eventually provide beneficial findings. Indeed, science is a continuous and evolving process, and important findings can often be traced to the end of a chain of individual studies, with some tributary links leading to dead ends. Finally, there are those who believe that the benefit test is inappropriate altogether since the process of knowledge accumulation is in itself valuable regardless of whether anyone benefits directly or indirectly from it.

Risks are defined as the probability that future unwanted harms will occur (Meslin, 1990).

The potential severity or magnitude, the duration of the research, the possibility of early detection, and the reversibility of harm are other critical determinants in making decisions about allowing research to go forward (Levine, cited in Diener & Crandall, 1978). Certainly, risk minimization should always be explored as a first order of business. A variety of strategies has been proposed, such as subject screening, many of which are implemented during the design phase (Sieber, 1993; Zeisel, 1970).

Fortunately, potential risks in psychological research are trivial most of the time (Reynolds, 1972). These include boredom, inconvenience, and other minor and temporary irritations, including performance anxiety or confusion regarding how to interpret the experimenters' directions. The more serious risks that could materialize include invasion of privacy, breach of confidentiality, longer term stress and discomfort, loss of self-esteem, upsetting reactions to being deceived or debriefed, embarrassment or humiliation, negative effects from being in a no-treatment control group, and reactions to being induced to commit reprehensible acts. Other "collective risks," by which harm to the participants or others may result on publication and interpretation of the findings (Bower & de Gasparis, 1978; Diener & Crandall, 1978), can also occur. Such socially sensitive research is defined by Sieber and Stanley as "studies in which there are potential social consequences or implications, either directly for the participants in the research or for the class of individuals represented in the research" (1988, p. 49). More obvious examples of sensitive research include explorations of gender and race differences, a focus on negative attributes of specific groups that already struggle with stigma (e.g., homosexuals or the police), or any study with results that might lead to or justify an alteration of the lives of others or of attitudes about them.

Predicting risk occurrence is difficult in social and behavioral sciences because of the seemingly infinite variety of ways people respond to psychological phenomena. What one may find frightening or stressful—such as being asked to touch a spider or view pornography—another may experience as exciting or pleasurably novel. Prescreening of potential participants and careful monitoring during the study trials should be used whenever a question exists. The prudent investigator will also prepare for the possibility that the most seemingly benign request may cause discomfort to sensitive participants, as illustrated in the next case.

Case 17-23: The student experimenter asked Cresti Fallen to categorize brief segments of popular music according to the emotional reactions each evoked. When the student experimenter played one particular song, Fallen broke down in uncontrollable tears. The inexperienced experimenter terminated the session and, in an attempt to be helpful, suggested that Fallen go see a psychotherapist because she "needed help badly." This only intensified Fallen's discomfort, and she bolted from the research cubicle. No follow-up intervention was attempted. The following week, Fallen complained to the department chair about the project and the "insulting" comment made by the student researcher. She also explained that her boyfriend had dumped her for another woman the evening before the session, and "their song" was one of the selections, hence her emotional outburst.

There was no way the student researcher could have anticipated his study would elicit such an extreme reaction. However, the student experimenter's handling of the matter was rather crude and only complicated the problem. It is worth noting here that much research is conducted by undergraduates as part of their training. Even though their efforts are unlikely to be published—leading us sometimes to think of such exercises as not being *real* research—human participants are involved and deserve the same treatment and protection provided in any other experimental effort. Ideally, all students who collect data should undergo training in dealing with upset participants, and a supervisor should be close at hand. Even if a student researcher mishandles a participant, despite any benevolent or sincere intentions, any incidents should be reported immediately to the supervisor, and ameliorative intervention steps should be taken.

A final complicating problem relative to risk assessment is that many contemplated techniques or study approaches have not previously been attempted, and pretesting with animals or less vulnerable participants (i.e., free-agent, competent adults) may not be feasible. Here, the degree of risk may simply be unknown. In general, the conservative ethical stance in such instances is to assume the possibility of risk and engage in preliminary risk evaluations, using appropriate guidelines for consent acquisition, prior to undertaking any larger investigation.

Research Outside the Laboratory

The bulk of discussion in this chapter applies best to work conducted in a traditional laboratory setting. A substantial amount of social and behavioral science data are collected "in the streets." Despite the thorny ethical problems inherent in much of the research outside the laboratory, it has been argued that laboratory settings are susceptible to numerous artifacts that reduce the validity of the findings (D. W. Wilson & Donnerstein, 1976), and that many important varieties of behavior are not amenable to observation in laboratory situations. In these instances, some laboratory setting ethics do not translate well to community or field settings, and new ethical dilemmas not relevant to traditional research settings present themselves.

Social psychologists often use what are called "nonreactive methods." Participants are not aware that they are being observed, thus precluding any advance voluntary and informed consent contract. Sometimes, the participants are simply observed in given settings (e.g., a rock concert) without the inclusion of any experimental manipulation. Sometimes, the context is contrived (e.g., observing people's reactions to an unusual object placed on the sidewalk by the experimenters). At other times, the participants are deceived, and their reactions are observed (e.g., a confederate of the experimenter poses as an obnoxious store customer, while another confederate records the salesperson's reaction).

Ethical problems are minimized if nonobtrusive observations of public behavior are made in such a way that the data cannot be linked directly to those being observed. The ethics code does allow waiving the consent requirement for naturalistic research (ES: 6.10). However, technological advances that allow visual and/or audio recordings of people's behavior using portable and easily concealed equipment complicate the ethical problems because a permanent record is created, heightening the potential for identification of the unwitting participants.

When the participants perceive themselves to be in a private or confidential setting, additional ethical issues accrue when experimenters intrude themselves surreptitiously into these environments. As examples, see Koocher's (1977) criticisms of the work by Middlemist, Knowles, and Matter (1976), which involved the impact on micturition of confederate "crowding" in a university lavatory; Warwick's (1973) and Sieber's (1982e) concerns about Humphreys' (1970) classic "tearoom trade" study, which involved the author's observations while serving as a volunteer "watchqueen" of homosexual contacts in public rest rooms; and Cook's (1975) ethical analysis of the West, Gunn, and Chernicky (1975) "ubiquitous Watergate" study, which attempted to induce participants to agree to commit burglary.

Opinions regarding the ethicality and legality of nonreactive methods vary markedly among social scientists, legal scholars, and the public (Nash, 1975; Silverman, 1975; D. W. Wilson & Donnerstein, 1976). Because it is usually impossible to assess whether harm befell any of the participants, whose actual identities are rarely discernible (which precludes follow-up assessment), nonreactive study techniques will likely continue to be debated in regard to their ethical acceptability (see Brandt, 1972; Kimmell, 1996; Sechrest, 1976; Schwartz and Gottlieb, 1980, 1981).

Primary prevention/intervention programming differs from the nonlaboratory-based research discussed above because benefit to the participants in the "treatment" group is always intended. In general, people judged to be at risk for some potential maladjustment are recruited to participate in a program designed to reduce their risk level so that the maladjustment will not ultimately manifest itself. "At risk" populations include children with schizophrenic parents, recently divorced people, preschoolers from disadvantaged homes, parents who fit patterns that indicate that they might be susceptible to abusing their children, and people functioning under high-stress conditions. Educational, psychotherapeutic, coping, and skill-building training are among the interventions frequently used.

Such research activity is often regarded as humanistic because it attempts to discover ways to minimize human suffering by intervening prior to evolvement of full-scale maladjustment or damage. It is also viewed as cost effective and expedient because it conforms to the old saying, "An ounce of prevention is worth a pound of cure." However, several profound ethical issues lurk just below the surface, including confidentiality, denial of service, and equitable allocation of scarce resources (Connor, 1990). Questions of ethics arise from a number of sources, including research ethicists, social activists, and members of the target study populations. For example, political ideologies frequently enter into attempts to define *what* we should try to prevent. Confidentiality is difficult to maintain, especially if the program is of long duration. Problems can arise whenever the values of the researchers are at variance with the cultural values and traditions of the target groups, especially since most target groups are underprivileged or vulnerable in other ways.

Because the participants in primary prevention research have not, by definition, presented diagnosable symptomatology relative to the purpose of the intervention, three additional issues arise. First, risk-level assignment is an imprecise art, and the potential for harm is present whenever those decisions were made inappropriately. Following directly from risk-level assignment is the process of "labeling" participants as at risk for something not yet manifested. That label (such as "predelinquent" or "potential dropout") may carry a stigma or other consequences that may limit participants' access to opportunity and growth (Hobbs, 1975; Stanley & Stanley, 1981). A third dilemma involves intruding into people's private lives to "treat" them for a condition they do not yet have. Finally, primary prevention programming research is more likely than most other types of research to create dependencies. Researchers must be careful not to dump the participants as soon as data are collected, leaving the participants resourceless (or more resourceless) than before.

Privacy and Confidentiality
Issues in Research

The parallels between client-therapist and participant-researcher relationships relative to the maintenance of confidentiality and invasion of privacy are striking enough to share the same relevant principles in the 1992 APA ethics code (ES: 5.01, 5.03, 5.04). Unless otherwise specified and agreed to by the research participants, data are confidential. Confidentiality also serves the investigators because participants are more likely to be open and honest if confidentiality is guaranteed (Blanck, Bellack, Rosnow, Rotheram-Borus, & Schooler, 1992).

Ethics committees occasionally receive complaints related to confidentiality or, as in the case presented below, privacy invasion related to research activity.

Case 17-24: Tab Cross, Ed.D., a psychologist working at a university counseling center, administered a large number of personality inventories to students in the educational psychology department. He requested that the participants write their names, but promised that identities would be held in the strictest confidence and would be destroyed as soon as code numbers were assigned. A colleague wrote an ethics committee, expressing concern that Dr. Cross then accessed the university's counseling center files and separated the inventories into two piles: those who had sought counseling and those who had not. Cross then wrote an article on personality characteristic differences between the two groups. The colleague argued that Cross entered confidential files for a purpose unrelated to the counseling center business, and that participants were not sufficiently informed of the study's purpose and consent was not obtained to access their files.

Despite the fact that individual identities were not disclosed by the investigator to anyone else, the ethics committee agreed with the complainant that Dr. Cross committed an ethical violation by not informing the participants of his intent to access confidential counseling center records and gaining their consent to do so.

Protecting the privacy and maintaining the confidentiality of data are usually routine procedures in social and behavioral research; that is, the investigator takes simple precautions to ensure that no one has access to the identifying information. In most cases, the task of the researcher is far simpler than that of the mental health professional because actual identities are not necessary to keep on file, or they may not be necessary to record at all. Furthermore, the nature of the information obtained is often not inherently intriguing to anyone except the researchers, such as, how a particular person performs on a memory task.

Researchers, however, may often promise confidentiality without a full understanding of disclosures that could possibly occur later. For example, lists of participants can sometimes be accessed by others, and unauthorized follow-up studies or analyses for purposes other than the original one consented to by the participants could be performed. According to the 1992 APA code, if a possibility exists that others could obtain access, now or in the future, to the information they contributed, these facts should be made known in advance (ES: 6.16). Many techniques have been developed to limit the possibility of identification by others (besides the obvious one of recording data anonymously in the first place); these include the use of certificates of confidentiality (Hoagwood, 1994; Melton, 1990) or the elimination of the usefulness of already collected data for other purposes (see Boruch, Dennis, & Cecil, 1996; Knerr, 1982).

Computers and electronic transfer systems allow inexpensive, instant data sharing anywhere in the world with an ease never envisioned a decade ago. Data sharing among scientists holds the potential for hastening the evolution of a line of inquiry, helps to ensure validity and error corrections, and encourages collaborative ventures. Even research participants receive an advantage in the sense that their contributions are maximized (Sieber, 1989). However, concerns about privacy invasion have drastically increased as technological advances allow sophisticated surveillance, as well as links and access among computer storage banks. Psychologists should resist opportunities to contribute information to databanks if confidentiality cannot be safeguarded or if individuals who have access to them are untrained or unmotivated to interpret the information accurately.

Finally, does one share information without the participants' consent when it may be judged that a given participant is in danger to himself or herself? For example, a research participant may indicate that he sells drugs to schoolchildren or intends to commit suicide even if gleaning information about such activities or intentions was not an integral feature of the study purpose. Researchers (who may well not have had any clinical training) may feel especially inadequate to make a decision. As we have already seen in chapter 6, it is difficult to decide what to do when such situations arise in psychotherapy settings. The obligations of research investigators are even more ambiguous. (See additional information about confidentiality and research data in chapter 6.)

Research Using Animals

Millions of animals are used in research every year, either because reasons (including ethical ones) preclude the use of human beings or because understanding the animals themselves is of interest (Kimmel, 1996). Although ethical principles devoted exclusively to animal experimentation were not included in the APA's ethics code until 1981, they were heavily adapted from an APA statement issued in the 1960s that was to be posted in all psychology laboratories using animals. The statement included the name of the appropriate designee to which abuses were to be promptly reported. Another early APA policy (Committee for the Use of Animals, 1972) outlined guidelines for the use of animals in schools.

In recent times, psychologists have embraced guidelines that are far more complete and strict than ever before to ensure the welfare of animals used in research. The *Guidelines for Ethical Conduct in the Care and Use of Animals* (APA, 1992b) admonishes psychologists to ensure that

their work with animals is justified and has reasonable expectations for increasing knowledge of "the processes underlying the evolution, development, maintenance, alteration, control, or biological significance of behavior [and to] increase understanding of the species under study or provide results that benefit the health or welfare of humans or other animals" (p. 1). Numerous requirements for safeguards and special sensitivities are required, making animals no longer a quickly obtained sample of convenience.

The 1992 APA ethics code issues the requirements for research psychologists to ensure the welfare of animals and to treat them humanely; to follow laws and regulations governing the acquisition, treatment, care, housing, and disposal of animals; to maintain competence in their own knowledge of the species involved and to ensure that assistants are also well trained in these regards; to minimize discomfort; and to terminate animals, when that is necessary, rapidly and painlessly. When animals are subjected to pain or privation, the investigator must carefully consider alternatives first and work under the assumption that if the procedure would cause pain in a human being, it is likely that it will also cause pain in the animal (APA, 1992b). If discomfort cannot be avoided, the study goal must be justified by its prospective scientific, educational, or applied value. Surgical procedures must involve appropriate anesthesia, and techniques to avoid infection and to minimize pain must be applied afterward. Risks to animals must be justified and balanced against potential benefits, as with research using human beings (see ES: 6.20). Despite these stringent ethical mandates, the issue of conscripting animals for research experiments remains impassioned and contentious (Gluck & Kubacki, 1991).

Social and behavioral scientists are often targets of groups opposed to animal use in research because their research findings and applications to date are not perceived as being valuable compared to the stunning advances based on biomedical animal research (Kimmel, 1996; Pratt, 1976; Ryder, 1975; Singer, 1975). Perhaps social scientists have done an inadequate job of educating the public about the contributions to understanding neurological aspects of behavior as a result of animal research (Domjan & Purdy, 1995).

The War from Without and Within

Humans have always had intense relationships with animals. Animals have been exploited from the beginning of time for food, clothing, labor, sport, and pleasure. They have also been adored and worshipped, sometimes with a zeal that far exceeds that extended to other humans. Their vulnerable status often arouses sympathy whenever it is believed they are being treated unfairly or abusively, especially if they appear to be experiencing pain.

Students are more frequently confronting their professors with questions about the ethics and usefulness of animals in research (Azar, 1994; Gallup & Beckstead, 1988; Herzog, 1990). Whereas the public has expressed far less concern about human experimentation than have researchers themselves, quite the opposite is true when the research participants are not human. The main criticism is that most animal research is trivial and inhumane (Dewsbury, 1990). Organized groups range from reformers who are not so much "antiresearch" as they are concerned about the quality of care and welfare of laboratory animals to groups that oppose all research conducted on animals, regardless of merit or the potential benefit to humans. These groups have a long history (Dewsbury, 1990) and hold diverse views about priorities and acceptable tactics used to influence opinion and action (Herzog, 1990; Plous, 1991). The more activist groups have participated in stealing animals being used in experimentation and destroying laboratory facilities. Due to legislation that has levied heavier sanctions against raiding laboratories, activists are also increasingly using the courts or political influence (Azar, 1994; Burd, 1994; Johnson, 1990).

More common forms of confrontations involve name calling, put-downs, and emotional arguments from both sides of the fence. Social scientists tend to discount the radical animal activists as misguided and uninformed, and they make much of the contradictions and inconsistencies to be found in the anti-animal research groups' logic and targets, such as focusing on only cute and cuddly animals, ignoring the larger problem of unwanted pets and their lamentable fates, and slighting discoveries that have improved directly or indirectly the quality of both human life and animal life thanks to animal-based research (e.g., N. E. Miller, 1985). However, Ulrich (1991) notes that increasing numbers of scientists are calling into question practices and perspectives of the past. He also wisely notes that we cannot justify the worthwhileness of the study of animals because of the similarities between them and humans while, at the same time, morally justifying it on the basis of differences.

The intensity and furor of the campaign against animal research may be declining somewhat (Herzog, 1995), perhaps due to the positive impact of earlier campaigns, although threats against targeted behavioral science researchers still continue (APA, 1997). Surveys suggest a steady reduction in the use of animals, at least partially caused by the rising costs of procuring, feeding, and housing them (Gallup & Suarez, 1980; Goodman, 1982; Holden, 1982). Some scientists have become fearful or less interested in animal work, and a few even quit using animals in their research for fear of attack (Azar, 1994; Budiansky, 1987). Other investigators may not have responded to outside pressure so much as they have become more sensitized to the issues, have reevaluated their stand on animal use, and have taken more care to ensure that their work is better understood.

Alternatives to the Use of Whole, Live Mammals

The thought of discovering valid alternatives to the use of whole, live animals in laboratory research is appealing. Current alternatives being considered or already available include math models, isolated organs, tissue and cell cultures, mechanical models, computer simulations, online demonstrations, chemical assays, anthropomorphic "dummies," simulated tissue and body fluids, and increased use of lower organisms. Unfortunately, however, the critics of animal research seem to assume that such technologies are currently developed to the point at which whole, live animal research can be abandoned altogether (Gallup & Suarez, 1985). This is hardly the case. Many methodologies are still in their infancy and will not serve as valid substitutes for many years, although these alternatives will probably eventually lead to greater reductions in the use of animals in research (Holden, 1982).

Naturalistic observation or minimally manipulative naturalistic studies are other alternatives to laboratory research (Bowd & Shapiro, 1993). Laboratory studies have been criticized because they deprive animals of opportunities to exercise their true capacities and to engage in their normal, instinctual behavioral repertoires (Drewett & Kani, 1981). When animals are studied under conditions that are, for them, abnormal, the validity of scientific findings about their capacities may be distorted or blatantly in error. Davenport and Davenport (1990) make the intriguing argument that the "home testing" of household pets could be a valuable way to do sound, behavioral research on animals. Pet owners would give or withhold proxy consent, thus protecting the health and well-being of their pet. Naturalistic methods cause the least disturbance to animals, although scientific control may be lost, making cause-and-effect relationships more difficult to ascertain (Gallup & Suarez, 1985). Using fewer numbers of animals in research and for classroom demonstration purposes is another way to reduce animal use. The ready availability of video equipment may be especially useful in classroom teaching, and it is highly recommended for classroom demonstrations whenever an animal is put at some discomfort, such as during a learning sequence that uses aversive conditioning. The tape made of a single animal can be reused for years. Stunning documentary films that show detailed animal behavior in their natural environments are abundant.

The ethics of research that uses animals, particularly in laboratory settings when discomfort is at issue, will remain debatable because decent, intelligent people differ in their philosophical views about animals and in the perceived value of the contributions based on animal research to social and behavioral science. Ulrich (1991), however, asks that we examine these issues from a more pressing perspective and with

"a greater wisdom," as he calls it, by looking for a balance that will ensure that this earth remain life sustaining for all living things.

SUMMARY GUIDELINES

1. Psychologists should take credit in publications only for work they have actually contributed.
2. In collaborative research projects, early discussions of authorship credit expectations and assignments are encouraged to reduce the possibility of later conflict.
3. Psychologists must be careful to attribute material originated by others when used in their published work.
4. Despite pressures to publish in some work settings, psychologists must remain sensitive to their responsibility and to the integrity of science and its methods by reporting data accurately and completely.
5. Psychologists who serve as publishing gatekeepers through editorial or reviewer positions should remain cognizant of their special influence and strive to perform their duties in an unbiased and competent manner.
6. Research psychologists should fully familiarize themselves with the various extant policies that govern research activity. Psychologists must additionally assess the design, procedures, and experiences to which the participants will be subjected, with special attention paid to any value biases that may have an impact on the participants' welfare, the meaningfulness of the data, and the interpretation of results.
7. Concern for research participants' welfare is paramount. Whenever wrongs or harms to participants are likely, research psychologists have special obligations to search for alternative study methods or even to refrain from conducting the research. If participants become upset during the course of collecting data or afterward, it is the psychologists' responsibility to institute ameliorative procedures.
8. Consent from participants should be voluntary and informed. In those cases for

which participants cannot give meaningful or legal consent or when deception is believed to be justified, psychologists are obligated to take special safeguards to protect the welfare of research participants. If deception is used, the participants must be adequately informed of this fact and given the justification for using such methods soon after the experimental trial. Stressing the participants' freedom to withdraw at any time is an important feature of ethical research. In cases when participants remain unaware of being observed, data should be gathered and disseminated in such a way that maintains anonymity.

9. Research psychologists must actively maintain their competencies, including methods of study design and analysis, or seek access to expert consultants.

10. Means of ensuring confidentiality must be implemented. Research psychologists must be aware of any potential access to participant identities and inform them of any such possibilities.

11. When conflicts arise between risks and potential benefits, scientific and ethical considerations, and participants rights and welfare and society's rights or needs to know, research psychologists must carefully assess these dilemmas and proceed in ways that minimize the potential for wrongs or harms to participants.

12. Psychologists must treat their animal research participants with humane care and respect.

References

Ackerman, T. F. (1989). An ethical framework for the practice of paying research subjects. *IRB: A Review of Human Subjects Research, 11,* 1–4.

Adair, J. G., Dushenko, T. W., & Lindsay, R. C. L. (1985). Ethical regulations and their impact on research practice. *American Psychologist, 40,* 59–72.

Adler, T. (1990, July). Researchers agree data sharing is good, but specifics elude them. *APA Monitor,* 9.

Allen, S. A, Heckel, R. V., & Garcia, S. J. (1980). The black researcher: A view from inside the goldfish bowl. *American Psychologist, 35,* 767–771.

American Psychological Association. (1992a). Ethical principles of psychologists and code of conduct. *American Psychologist, 47,* 1597–1610.

American Psychological Association. (1992b). *Guidelines for ethical conduct in the care and use of animals.* Washington, DC: Author.

American Psychological Association. (1997). Animal rights activity increases. *Science Agenda, 10,* 1, 4.

Azar, B. (1994, December). Animal research threatened by activism. *APA Monitor,* 18.

Azrin, N. H., Holz, W., Ulrich, R., & Goldiamond, I. (1961). The control of the content of conversation through reinforcement. *Journal of the Experimental Analysis of Behavior, 4,* 25–30.

Baron, R. A. (1981). The "costs of deception" revisited: An openly optimistic rejoinder. *IRB: A Review of Human Subjects Research, 3,* 8–10.

Baumrind, D. (1976). Nature and definition of informed consent in research involving deception. In *The Belmont report: Ethical principles and guidelines for the protection of human subjects of research* (DHEW Publication No. (OS) 78-0014). Washington, DC: The National Commission for the Protection of Human Subjects of Biomedical and Behavioral Research.

Baumrind, D. (1985). Research using intentional deception. *American Psychologist, 40,* 165–174.

Bell, R. (1992). *Impure science.* New York: Wiley.

Benditt, J. (1995). Conduct in science. *Science, 268,* 1705.

Berscheid, E. R., Dermer, M., & Libman, M. (1973). Anticipating informed consent—An empirical approach. *American Psychologist, 28,* 913–925.

Blanck, P. D., Bellack, A. S., Rosnow, R. L., Rotheram-Borus, M. J., & Schooler, N. R. (1992). *American Psychologist, 47,* 959–965.

Bornstein, R. F. (1990). Manuscript review in psychology: An alternative model. *American Psychologist, 46,* 672–673.

Boruch, R. F., Dennis, M., & Cecil, J. S. (1996). Fifty years of empirical research on privacy and confidentiality in research settings. In B. H. Stanley, J. E. Sieber, & G. B. Melton (Eds.), *Research ethics* (pp. 127–173). Lincoln, NE: University of Nebraska Press.

Bowd, A. D., & Shapiro, K. J. (1993). The case against

laboratory animal research in psychology. *Journal of Social Issues, 49,* 133–142.

Bower, R. T., & de Gasparis, P. (1978). *Ethics in social research.* New York: Praeger.

Brackbill, Y., & Korten, F. (1970). Journal reviewing practices: Authors' and APA members' suggestions for revision. *American Psychologist, 25,* 937–940.

Brandt, R. M. (1972). *Studying behavior in natural settings.* New York: Holt, Rinehart, & Winston.

Branson, R. (1977). Prison research: National commission says "No, unless." *Hastings Center Report, 7,* 15–21.

Britton, B. K. (1979). Ethical and educational aspects of participating as a subject in psychology experiments. *Teaching of Psychology, 6,* 195–198.

Broad, W. J. (1980). Harvard delays in reporting fraud. *Science, 215,* 478–482.

Budiansky, S. (1987, August 31). Winning through intimidation? *U.S. News and World Report,* 48–49.

Burd, S. (1994, August 10). Advocates for animals are divided on how to deal with court setbacks. *Chronicle of Higher Education,* A23.

Burd, S. (1996, February 2). U.S. urged to bar publication of results of unethical studies. *Chronicle of Higher Education,* A24

Capron, A. M. (1973). Medical research in prisons. *Hastings Center Report, 3,* 4–6.

Capron, A. M. (1989). Human experimentation. In R. M. Veatch (Ed.), *Medical ethics* (pp. 125–172). Boston: Jones & Bartlett.

Cassileth, B. R. (1980). Informed consent—why are its goals imperfectly realized? *New England Journal of Medicine, 302,* 896–900.

Ceci, S. J., & Walker, E. (1983). Private archives and public needs. *American Psychologist, 38,* 414–423.

Christensen, L. (1988). Deception in psychological research: When it its use justifiable? *Personality and Social Psychology Bulletin, 14,* 664–675.

Cohen, J. (1995). The culture of credit. *Science, 268,* 1706–1710.

Committee on Government Operations. (1990). *Are scientific misconduct and conflicts of interest hazardous to our health?* (House Report 101-688). Washington, DC: Author.

Committee for the Use of Animals in School Science Behavior Projects. (1972). Guidelines for the use of animals in school science behavior projects. *American Psychologist, 27,* 337.

Connor, R. F. (1990). Ethical issues in evaluating the effectiveness of primary prevention programs. *Prevention-in-Human-Services, 8,* 89–110.

Cook, S. W. (1975). A comment on the ethical issues involved in West, Gunn, and Chernicky's "Ubiquitous Watergate: An attributional analysis." *Journal of Personality and Social Psychology, 32,* 66–68.

Cooper, J. (1976). Deception and role playing: On telling the good guys from the bad guys. *American Psychologist, 31,* 605–610.

Coulter, X. (1986). Academic value of research participation by undergraduates. *American Psychologist, 41,* 317–318.

Crespi, T. D. (1994). Student scholarship: In the best interests of the scholar. *American Psychologist, 49,* 1094–1095.

Darou, W. G., Hum, A., & Kurtness, J. (1993). An investigation of the impact of psychosocial research on a native population. *Professional Psychology: Research and Practice, 24,* 325–329.

Davenport, L. D., & Davenport, J. A. (1990). The laboratory animal dilemma: A solution in our backyards. *Psychological Science, 1,* 21–216.

Dewsbury, D. A. (1990). Early interactions between animals psychologists and animal activists and the founding of the APA Committee on Precautions in Animal Experimentation. *American Psychologist, 45,* 315–327.

Diener, E., & Crandall, R. (1978). *Ethics in Social and Behavioral Research.* Chicago: University of Chicago Press.

Domjan, M., & Purdy, J. E. (1995). Animal research in psychology. *American Psychologist, 50,* 496–503.

Douglas, R. J. (1992). How to write a highly cited article without even trying. *Psychological Bulletin, 112,* 405–408.

Drewett, R., & Kani, W. (1981). Animal experimentation in the behavioral sciences. In D. Sperlinger (Ed.), *Animals in research* (pp. 175–201). New York: Wiley.

Edgar, H., & Rothman, D. J. (1995). The institutional review board and beyond: Future challenges to the ethics of human experimentation. *The Milbank Quarterly, 73,* 489–506.

Edsall, G. A. (1969). Positive approach to the problem of human experimentation. *Daedalus, 98,* 463–479.

Epstein, L. C., & Lasagna, L. (1969). Obtaining informed consent: Form or substance. *Archives of Internal Medicine, 123,* 682–688.

Evans, P. (1976). The Burt affair—Sleuthing in science. *APA Monitor, 7,* pp. 1, 4.

Eysenck, H. J. (1980). Sir Cyril Burt: Prominence versus personality. *Psychological Reports, 46,* 893–894.

Ferguson, L. R. (1978). The competence and freedom of children to make choices regarding participation in research: A statement. *Journal of Social Issues, 34,* 114–121.

Fields, C. M. (1983, September 14). Professors' demands for credit as "co-authors" of students' research projects may be rising. *Chronicle of Higher Education,* pp. 7, 10.

Fields, K. L., & Price, A. R. (1993). Problems in research integrity arising from misconceptions about the ownership of research. *Academic Medicine, 68,* 560–564.

Fine, M. A., & Kurdek, L. A. (1993). Relections on determining authorship credit and authorship order on faculty-student collaborations. *American Psychologist, 48,* 1141–1147.

Finke, R. A. (1990). Recommendations for contemporary editorial practices. *American Psychologist, 45,* 669–670.

Fisher, C. B. (1993). Integrating science and ethics in research with high-risk children and youth. *SRCD Social Policy Report, 7,* 1–27.

Fisher, C. B., & Fryberg, D. (1994). Participant partners: College students weigh the costs and benefits of deceptive research. *American Psychologist, 49,* 417–427.

Fisher, C. B., & Tryon, W. W. (Eds.). (1990). *Ethics in applied developmental psychology: Emerging issues in an emerging field.* Norwood, NJ: Ablex.

Fletcher, R. (1991). *Science, ideology, and the media: The Cyril Burt scandal.* New Brunswick, NJ: Transaction Press.

Forward, J., Canter, R., & Kirsch, N. (1976). Role-enactment and deception methodologies: Alternative paradigms. *American Psychologist, 31,* 595–604.

Frankel, M. S. (1978). Social, legal, and political responses to ethical issues in the use of children as experimental subjects. *Journal of Social Issues, 34,* 101–113.

Franzini, L. R. (1987). Editors are not blind. *American Psychologist, 42,* 104.

Freedman, J. L., & Fraser, S. C. (1966). Compliance without pressure: The foot-in-the-door technique. *Journal of Personality and Social Psychology, 2,* 195–202.

Froese, A. D., Boswell, K. L., Garcia, E. D., Koehn, L. J., & Nelson, J. M. (1995). Citing secondary sources: Can we correct what students so not know? *Teaching of Psychology, 22,* 235–238.

Gallup, G. G., & Beckstead, J. W. (1988). Attitudes toward animal research. *American Psychologist, 44,* 474–475.

Gallup, G. G., & Suarez, S. D. (1980). On the use of animals in psychological research. *Psychological Record, 30,* 211–218.

Gallup, G. G., & Suarez, S. D. (1985). Alternatives to the use of animals in psychological research. *American Psychologist, 40,* 1104–1111.

Gannon, L., Luchetta, T., Rhodes, K., Pardie, L., & Segrist, D. (1992). Sex bias in psychological research: progress or complacency? *American Psychologist, 47,* 389–396.

Garfield, E. (1978). The ethics of scientific publication. *Current Contents, 40,* 5–12.

Geller, D. M. (1982). Alternatives to deception: Why, what, and how? In J. E. Sieber (Ed.), *The Ethics of Social Research: Surveys and Experiments* (pp. 35–55). New York: Springer-Verlag.

Gillis, J. S. (1976). Participants instead of subjects. *American Psychologist, 31,* 95–96.

Gluck, J. P., & Kubacki, S. R. (1991). Animals in biomedical research: The undermining effect of the rhetoric of the besieged. *Ethics and Behavior, 1,* 157–173.

Golden, F. (1981, September 7). Fudging data for fun and profit. *Time Magazine,* 83.

Goodman, W. (1982, August 9). Of mice, monkeys, and men. *Newsweek,* 61.

Gordon, M. (1977, February). Evaluating the evaluators. *New Scientist,* 342–343.

Gray, B. H. (1975). *Human subjects in medical experimentation.* New York: Wiley.

Gray, J. N. (1985). The law and ethics of psychosocial research on AIDS. *Nebraska Law Review, 64,* 637–688.

Gray, S. W. (1971). Ethical issues in research in early childhood intervention. *Children, 18,* 83–89.

Grinnell, F. (1992). *The scientific attitude* (2nd ed.). New York: Guilford Press.

Gross, A. E., & Flemming, L. (1982). Twenty years of deception in social psychology. *Personality and Social Psychology Bulletin, 12,* 82–86.

Hartley, J. (1987). A code of practice for refereeing journal articles. *American Psychologist, 42,* 959.

Haupt, A. (1976, July). Managed books. *APA Monitor,* pp. 7, 13.

Hawley, C. S. (1984). The thieves of academe. *Improving College and University Teaching, 32,* 35–39.

Haworth, K. (1996, November 8). Head of human genome project retracts 5 journal articles. *Chronicle of Higher Education,* A-11–A-12.

Hearnshaw, L. S. (1979). *Cyril Burt, psychologist.* New York: Random House.

Herzog, H. A. (1990). Discussing animal rights and animal research in the classroom. *Teaching of Psychology, 17,* 90–94.

Herzog, H. A. (1995). Has public interest in animal rights peaked? *American Psychologist, 50,* 945–947.

Hilgartner, S. (1990). Research fraud, misconduct, and the IRB. *IRB: A Review of Human Subjects Research, 12,* 1–4.

Hilts, P. J. (1981, March 4). Science confronted with "crime wave" of researchers faking data in experiments. *Los Angeles Times,* 1A, 6–7.

Hixon, J. (1976). *The patchwork mouse.* New York: Doubleday.

Hoagwood, K. (1994). The certificate of confidentiality at the National Institute of Mental Health: Discretionary considerations in its applicability in research on child and adolescent mental disorders. *Ethics and Behavior, 4,* 123–131.

Hoagwood, K., Jensen, P. S., & Fisher, C. B. (1996). *Ethical issues in mental health research with children and adolescents.* Mahwah, NJ: Erlbaum.

Hobbs, N. (1975). *The future of children.* San Francisco: Jossey-Bass.

Holden, C. (1982). New focus on replacing animals in the lab. *Science, 215,* 35–38.

Holmes, D. S. (1976). Debriefing after psychological experiments. *American Psychologist, 31,* 858–875.

Houlihan, D., Hofschulte, L., Sachau, D., & Patten, C. (1992). Critiqing the peer review process: Examining a potential dual role conflict. *American Psychologist, 47,* 1679–1681.

Humphreys, L. (1970). *Tearoom trade: Impersonal sex in public places.* Chicago: Aldine.

Jacobs, P. (1982, March 26). UCLA medical researcher's methods come under fire. *Los Angeles Times,* sec. 2, pp. 1, 6.

Jensen, A. R. (1974). Kinship correlations reported by Sir Cyril Burt. *Behavior Genetics, 4,* 1–8.

Jensen, A. R. (1978). Sir Cyril Burt in perspective. *American Psychologist, 33,* 499–503.

Johnson, D. (1990). Animal rights and human lives: Time for scientists to right the balance. *Psychological Science, 1,* 213–214.

Joynson, R. B. (1989). *The Burt affair.* London: Routledge.

Kamin, L. J. (1974). *The science and politics of IQ.* Potomac, MD: Erlbaum.

Keith-Spiegel, P. (1976). Children's rights as participants in research. In G. P. Koocher (Ed.), *Children's rights and the mental health professions* (pp. 53–81). New York: Wiley.

Keith-Spiegel, P. (1983). Children and consent to participate in research. In G. B. Melton, G. P. Koocher, & M. J. Saks (Eds.), *Children's competence to consent* (pp. 179–211). New York: Plenum.

Keith-Spiegel, P., & Maas, T. (1981, August). *Consent to research: Are there developmental differences?* Paper presented at the annual meetings of the American Psychological Association, Los Angeles.

Kelman, H. C. (1967). Human use of human subjects: The problem of deception in social psychological experiments. *Psychological Bulletin, 67,* 1–11.

Kimmel, A. J. (1996). *Ethical issues in behavioral research.* Cambridge, MA: Blackwell Publishers.

Klein, K., & Cheuvront, B. (1990). The subject-experimenter contract: A reexamination of subject pool contamination. *Teaching of Psychology, 17,* 166–169.

Knerr, C. R. (1982). What to do before and after a subpoena of data arrives. In J. E. Sieber (Ed.), *The ethics of social research: Surveys and experiments* (pp. 191–206). New York: Springer-Verlag.

Kohn, A. (1986). *False prophets.* New York: Basil Blackwell.

Koocher, G. P. (1977). Bathroom behavior and human dignity. *Journal of Personality and Social Psychology, 35,* 120–121.

Koocher, G. P., & Keith-Spiegel, P. (1990). *Children, ethics and the law.* Lincoln, NE: University of Nebraska Press.

Korenman, S. G. (1993). Conflicts of interest and commercialization of research. *Academic Medicine, 68,* S18–S22.

Korn, J. H. (1988). Students' roles, rights, and responsibilities as research participants. *Teaching of Psychology, 15,* 74–78.

Korn, J. H., & Bram, D. R. (1987). What is missing in the method section of APA journal articles? *American Psychologist, 42,* 1091–1092.

Kupfersmid, J. (1988). Improving what is published. *American Psychologist, 43,* 635–642.

LaFollette, M. C. (1992). *Fraud, plagiarism, and misconduct in scientific publishing.* Berkeley, CA: University of California Press.

Lasagna, L. (1969). Special subjects in human experimentation. *Daedalus, 98,* 449–462.

Lawson, C. (1995). Research participation as a contract. *Ethics and Behavior, 5,* 205–215.

Leak, G. K. (1981). Student perception of coercion and value from participation in psychological research. *Teaching of Psychology, 8,* 147–149.

Levine, E. K. (1982). Old people are not all alike: Social class, ethnicity/race, and sex are bases for important differences. In J. E. Sieber (Ed.), *The ethics of social research: Surveys and experiments* (pp. 127–143). New York: Springer-Verlag.

Lowe, C. U. (1970). Pediatrics: Proper utilization of children as research subjects. *Annals of the New York Academy of Sciences, 169,* 337–343.

Lowe, C. U., Alexander, D., & Mishkin, B. (1974). Non-therapeutic research on children: An ethical dilemma. *Pediatrics, 84,* 468–472.

MacIntosh, N. J. (1995). *Cyril Burt: Fraud or framed?* New York, NY: Oxford University Press.

Mallon, T. (1989). *Stolen words.* New York: Ticknor & Fields.

Marans, D. G. (1988). Addressing research practitioner and subject needs: A debriefing-disclosure procedure. *American Psychologist, 43,* 826–828.

Martin, D. C., Arnold, J. D., Zimmerman, T. F., & Richard, R. H. (1968). Human subjects in clinical research—A report on three studies. *New England Journal of Medicine, 279,* 1426–1431.

McAskie, M. (1978). Kinship data: A critique of Jensen's data. *American Psychologist, 33,* 496–498.

McCord, D. M. (1991). Ethics-sensitive management of the university subject pool. *American Psychologist, 46,* 151.

McKeachie, W. J. (1976). Textbooks: Problems of publishers and professors. *Teaching of Psychology, 3,* 29–30.

McNemar, Q. (1946). Opinion-attitude methodology. *Psychological Bulletin, 43,* 289–374.

Melton, G. B. (1988). Must researchers share their data? *Law and Human Behavior, 12,* 159–162.

Melton, G. B. (1989). Ethical and legal issues in research and intervention. *Journal of Adolescent Health Care, 10,* 365–372.

Melton, G. B. (1990). Certificates of confidentiality under the public health service act: Strong protection but not enough. *Violence and Victims, 5,* 67–71.

Melton, G. B., & Gray, J. N. (1988). Ethical dilemmas in AIDS research. *American Psychologist, 43,* 60–64.

Melton, G. B., Koocher, G. P., & Saks, M. J. (1983). *Children's competence to consent.* New York: Plenum.

Melton, G. B., Levine, R. J., Koocher, G. P., Rosenthal, R., & Thompson, W. C. (1988). Community consultation in socially sensitive research. *American Psychologist, 43,* 573–581.

Menges, R. J. (1973). Openness and honesty versus Coercion and deception in psychological research. *American Psychologist, 28,* 1030–1034.

Meslin, E. M. (1990). Protecting human subjects from harm through improved risk judgments. *IRB: A Review of Human Subjects Research, 12,* 7–10.

Middlemist, R. D., Knowles, E. S., & Matter, C. F. (1976). Personal space invasions in the lavatory: Suggestive evidence for arousal. *Journal of Personality and Social Psychology, 33,* 541–546.

Miller, A. (1981). A survey of introductory psychology subject pool practices among leading universities. *Teaching of Psychology, 8,* 211–213.

Miller, N. E. (1985). The value of behavioral research on animals. *American Psychologist, 40,* 423–440.

Mills, J. (1976). A procedure for explaining experiments involving deception. *Personality and Social Psychology Bulletin, 2,* 3–13.

Mitchell, R. G. (1964). The child and experimental medicine. *British Medical Journal, 1,* 722–726.

Mitford, J. (1973, January). Experiments behind bars. *The Atlantic,* pp. 64–73.

Nash, M. M. (1975). "Nonreactic methods and the law": Additional comments on legal liability in behavior research. *American Psychologist, 30,* 777–780.

National Commission for the Protection of Human

Subjects of Biomedical and Behavioral Research. (1977). *Research involving children* (Publication No. 0577-004). Washington, DC: Department of Health, Education, and Welfare.

National Institutes of Health. (1989). Request for comment on proposed guidelines for policies on conflict of interest. *NIH Guide to Grants and Contracts, 18*, 1–5.

Nicks, S. D., Korn, J. H., & Mainieri, T. (1997). The rise and fall of deception in social psychology and personality research. *Ethics and Behavior, 7*, 69–77.

Nikelly, A. C. (1971). Ethical issues in research on student protest. *American Psychologist, 26*, 475–478.

Nimmer, J. G., & Handelsman, M. M. (1992). Effects of subject pool policy on student attitudes toward psychology and psychological research. *Teaching of Psychology, 19*, 141–144.

Oliansky, A. (1991). A confederate's perspective on deception. *Ethics and Behavior, 1*, 253–258.

Owens, R. G., & Hardley, E. M. (1985). Plagiarism in psychology—What can and should be done? *Bulletin of the British Psychological Society, 38*, 331–333.

Pattullo, E. L. (1980). Who risks what in social research? *IRB: A Review of Human Subjects Research, 2*, 1–4.

Peters, D. P., & Ceci, S. J. (1982). Peer review practices of psychological journals: The fate of published articles, submitted again. *The Behavioral and Brain Sciences, 5*, 187–195.

Plous, S. (1991). An attitude survey of animal rights activists. *Psychological Science, 2*, 194–196.

Pratt, D. (1976). *Painful experiments on animals*. New York: Argus Archives.

Price-Williams, D. R. (1975). *Explorations in cross-cultural psychology*. San Francisco, CA: Chandler & Sharp.

Rainwater, L., & Pittman, D. J. (1967). Ethical problems in studying a politically deviant community. *Social Problems, 14*, 357–365.

Resnick, J. H., & Schwartz, T. (1973). Ethical standards as an independent variable in psychological research. *American Psychologist, 28*, 134–139.

Reynolds, P. D. (1972). On the protection of human subjects and social science. *International Social Science Journal, 24*, 693–719.

Rhine, J. B. (1974a). Comments: "A new case of experimenter unreliability." *Journal of Parapsychology, 38*, 215–225.

Rhine, J. B. (1974b). Comments: "Security versus deception in para-psychology." *Journal of Parapsychology, 38*, 99–121.

Roark, A. C. (1980, September 2). Scientists question profession's standards amid accusations of fraudulent research. *Chronicle of Higher Education*, p. 5.

Rogers, R. (1992). Investigating psychology's taboo: The ethics of editing. *Ethics and Behavior, 2*, 253–261.

Rosenthal, R. (1994). Science and ethics in conducting, analyzing, and reporting psychological research. *Psychological Science, 5*, 127–134.

Rosenthal, R., & Rosnow, R. L. (1969). *Artifact in behavioral research*. New York: Academic Press.

Rosenthal, R., & Rosnow, R. L. (Eds.). (1975). *The volunteer subject*. New York: Wiley.

Rosnow, R. L., Rotheram-Borus, M. J., Ceci, S. J., Blanck, P. D., & Koocher, G. P. (1993). The institutional review board as a mirror of scientific and ethical standards. *American Psychologist, 48*, 821–826.

Rotton, J., Levitt, M., & Foos, P. (1993). Citation impact, rejection rates, and journal value. *American Psychologist, 48*, 911–912.

Rubenstein, C. (1982). Psychology's fruit flies. *Psychology Today, 16*, 83–84.

Rubin, J. S. (1976). Breaking into prison: Conducting a medical research project. *American Journal of Psychiatry, 133*, 230–232.

Rushton, J. P. (1995). Cyril Burt as the victim of scientific hoax. In N. J. Pallone & J. J. Hennessy (Eds.), *Fraud and fallible judgment* (pp. 163–171). New Brunswick, NJ: Transaction Publishers.

Rutstein, D. R. (1969). The ethical design of human experiments. *Dedalus, 98*, 523–541.

Ryder, R. (1975). *Victims of science: The use of animals in research*. London: Davis-Poynter.

Sarasohn, J. (1993). *Science on trial*. New York: St. Martin's Press.

Schwartz, S. H., & Gottlieb, A. (1980). Participation in a bystander intervention experiment and subsequent helping: Ethical considerations. *Journal of Experimental Social Psychology, 16*, 161–171.

Schwartz, S. H., & Gottlieb, A. (1981). Participants'

postexperimental reactions and the ethics of by-stander research. *Journal of Experimental Social Psychology, 17,* 396–407.

Sechrest, L. (1976). Another look at unobtrusive measures: An alternate to what? In H. W. Sinaiko & L. H. Broedling (Eds.), *Perspectives on attitudes assessment: Surveys and their alternatives.* Champaign, IL: Pendelton.

Sharpe, D., Adair, J. G., & Roese, N. J. (1992). Twenty years of deception research: A decline in subject's trust? *Personality and Social Psychology Bulletin, 18,* 585–590.

Sieber, J. E. (1982a). Deception in social research I: Kinds of deception and the wrongs they may involve. *IRB: A Review of Human Subjects Research, 4,* 1–6.

Sieber, J. E. (1982b). Deception in social research II: Evaluating the potential for harm and wrong. *IRB: A Review of Human Subjects Research, 5,* 1–6.

Sieber, J. E. (1982c). Deception in social research III: The nature and limits of debriefing. *IRB: A Review of Human Subjects Research, 6,* 1–4.

Sieber, J. E. (1982d). *The ethics of social research: Fieldwork, regulation, and publication.* New York: Springer-Verlag.

Sieber, J. E. (1982e). *The ethics of social research: Surveys and experiments.* New York: Springer-Verlag.

Sieber, J. E. (1989). Ethical and professional dimensions of socially sensitive research. *American Psychologist, 43,* 49–55.

Sieber, J. E. (1991a). Openness in the social sciences: Sharing data. *Ethics and Behavior, 1,* 69–86.

Sieber, J. E. (Ed.). (1991b). *Sharing social science data: Advantages and challenges.* Newbury Park, CA: Sage.

Sieber, J. E. (1992). *Planning ethically responsible research.* Newbury Park, CA: Sage.

Sieber, J. E. (1993). Ethical considerations in planning and conducting research on human subjects. *Academic Medicine, 9,* 59–513.

Sieber, J. E., & Baluyot, R. M. (1992). A survey of IRB concerns about social and behavioral research. *IRB: A Review of Human Subjects Research, 14,* 9–10.

Sieber, J. E., Iannuzzo, R., & Rodriguez, B. (1995). Deception methods in psychology: Have they changed in 23 years? *Ethics and Behavior, 5,* 67–85.

Sieber, J. E., & Saks, M. J. (1989). A census of subject pool characteristics and policies. *American Psychologist, 44,* 1053–1061.

Sieber, J. E., & Stanley, B. (1988). Sharing scientific data I: New problems for IRBs. *IRB: A Review of Human Subjects Research, 11,* 4–7.

Silverman, I. (1975). Nonreactive methods and the law. *American Psychologist, 30,* 764–769.

Singer, P. (1975). *Animal liberation.* New York: Avon.

Skom, E. (1986, October). Plagiarism. *American Association of Higher Education Bulletin,* 3–7.

Smith, C. P. (1981). How (un)acceptable is research involving deception. *IRB: A Review of Human Subjects Research, 3,* 1–4.

Smith, N. E. (1970). Replication study: A neglected aspect of psychological research. *American Psychologist, 25,* 970–975.

Spiegel, D. E., & Keith-Spiegel. P. (1970). Assignment of publication credits. *American Psychologist, 25,* 738–747.

Standing, L. G., & McKelvie, S. J. (1986). Psychology journals: A case for treatment. *Bulletin of the British Psychological Society, 39,* 445–450.

Stanley, B. H., Sieber, J. E., & Melton, G. B. (1987). Empirical studies of ethical issues in research. *American Psychologist, 42,* 735–741.

Stanley, B. H., Sieber, J. E., & Melton, G. B. (Eds.). (1996). *Research ethics.* Lincoln, NE: University of Nebraska Press.

Stanley, B. H., & Stanley, M. (1981). Psychiatric patients in research: Protecting their autonomy. *Comprehensive Psychiatry, 22,* 420–427.

Stanton, A. L., & New, M. J. (1988). Ethical responsibilities to depressed research participants. *Professional Psychology: Research and Practice, 19,* 279–285.

Sterling, T. C. (1959). Publication decisions and their possible effects on interferences drawn from tests of significance—or vice-versa. *Journal of the American Statistical Association, 54,* 30–34.

Stricker, L. J. (1967). The true deceiver. *Psychological Bulletin, 68,* 13–20.

Swan, L. A. (1979). Research and experimentation in prisons. *Journal of Black Psychology, 6,* 47–51.

Swazey, J. P., Anderson, M. S., & Lewis, K. S. (1993). Ethical problems in academic research. *American Scientist, 81,* 542–553.

Taub, H. A., Baker, M., & Sturr, J. F. (1986). Informed consent for research: Effects of readability, patient age, and education. *Law and Public Policy, 34,* 601–606.

Taylor, K. M., & Shepperd, J. A. (1996). Probing suspicion among participants in deception research. *American Psychologist, 51,* 886–887.

Tesch, F. E. (1977). Debriefing research participants: Though this be method there is madness to it. *Journal of Personality and Social Psychology, 35,* 217–224.

Thompson, R. A. (1990). Vulnerability in research: A developmental perspective on research risk. *Child Development, 61,* 1–16.

Ulrich, R. E. (1991). Animal rights, animal wrongs and the question of balance. *Psychological Science, 2,* 197–201.

Wade, N. (1976). IQ and heredity: Suspicion and fraud beclouds classic experiment. *Science, 194,* 916–918.

Walster, E., Bercheid, E., & Abrahams, D. (1967). Effectiveness of debriefing following deception experiments. *Journal of Personality and Social Psychology, 6,* 371–380.

Walster, G. W., & Cleary, T. A. (1970). A proposal for a new editorial policy in the social sciences. *American Statistician, 24,* 16–19.

Warwick, D. P. (1973). Tearoom trade: Means and ends in social research. *Hastings Center Studies, 1,* 27–38.

Weinrach, S. G., & Ivey, A. E. (1975). Science, psy-chology, and deception. *Bulletin of the British Psychological Society, 28,* 263–267.

West, S. G., Gunn, S. P., & Chernicky, P. (1975). Ubiquitous Watergate: An attributional analysis. *Journal of Personality and Social Psychology, 32,* 55–65.

Wheeler, D. L. (1991, August 14). Researchers debate ethics of payment for human subjects. *Chronicle of Higher Education,* A7.

Whitley, B. A., Jr. (1995). *Principles of research in behavioral science.* Mountain View, CA: Mayfield Publishing.

Whitten, P. (1976). *Analysis of the development and interaction of two innovations in educational publishing: The "managed" book and the "structured" book.* Unpublished doctoral dissertation, Harvard University.

Wilson, D. W., & Donnerstein, E. (1976). Legal and ethical aspects of nonreactive social psychological research: An excursion into the public mind. *American Psychologist, 31,* 765–773.

Wilson, T. D., DePaulo, B. M., Mook, D. G., & Klaaren, K. J. (1993). Scientists' evaluations of research: The biasing effects of the importance of the topic. *Psychological Science, 4,* 322–325.

Zeisel, H. (1970). Reducing the hazards of human experiments through modifications in research design. *Annals of the New York Academy of Sciences, 169,* 475–486.

Appendix A

Ethical Principles of Psychologists and Code of Conduct

American Psychological Association

Contents

This version of the APA Ethics Code was adopted by the American Psychological Association's Council of Representatives during its meeting, August 13 and 16, 1992, and is effective beginning December 1, 1992. Inquiries concerning the substance or interpretation of the APA Ethics Code should be addressed to the Director, Office of Ethics, American Psychological Association, 750 First Street, NE, Washington, DC 20002-4242.

This Code will be used to adjudicate complaints brought concerning alleged conduct occurring on or after the effective date. Complaints regarding conduct occurring prior to the effective date will be adjudicated on the basis of the version of the Code that was in effect at the time the conduct occurred, except that no provisions repealed in June 1989, will be enforced even if an earlier version contains the provision. The Ethics Code will undergo continuing review and study for future revisions; comments on the Code may be sent to the above address.

The APA has previously published its Ethical Standards as follows:

American Psychological Association. (1953). *Ethical standards of psychologists.* Washington, DC: Author.
American Psychological Association. (1958). Standards of ethical behavior for psychologists. *American Psychologist, 13,* 268–271.
American Psychological Association. (1963). Ethical standards of psychologists. *American Psychologist, 18,* 56–60.
American Psychological Association. (1968). Ethical standards of psychologists. *American Psychologist, 23,* 357–361.
American Psychological Association. (1977, March). Ethical standards of psychologists. *APA Monitor,* pp. 22–23.
American Psychological Association. (1979). *Ethical standards of psychologists.* Washington, DC: Author.
American Psychological Association. (1981). Ethical principles of psychologists. *American Psychologist, 36,* 633–638.
American Psychological Associaton. (1990). Ethical principles of psychologists (Amended June 2, 1989). *American Psychologist, 45,* 390–395.

Request copies of the APA's Ethical Principles of Psychologists and Code of Conduct from the APA Order Department, 750 First Street, NE, Washington, DC 20002-4242, or phone (202) 336-5510.

INTRODUCTION

The American Psychological Association's (APA's) Ethical Principles of Psychologists and Code of Conduct (hereinafter referred to as the Ethics Code) consists of an Introduction, a Preamble, six General Principles (A–F), and specific Ethical Standards. The Introduction discusses the intent, organization, procedural considerations, and scope of application of the Ethics Code. The Preamble and General Principles are aspirational goals to guide psychologists toward the highest ideals of psychology. Although the Preamble and General Principles are not themselves enforceable rules, they should be considered by psychologists in arriving at an ethical course of action and may be considered by ethics bodies in interpreting the Ethical Standards. The Ethical Standards set forth enforceable rules for conduct as psychologists. Most of the Ethical Standards are written broadly, in order to apply to psychologists in varied roles, although the application of an Ethical Standard may vary depending on the context. The Ethical Standards are not exhaustive. The fact that a given conduct is not specifically addressed by the Ethics Code does not mean that it is necessarily either ethical or unethical.

Membership in the APA commits members to adhere to the APA Ethics Code and to the rules and procedures used to implement it. Psychologists and students, whether or not they are APA members, should be aware that the Ethics Code may be applied to them by state psychology boards, courts, or other public bodies.

This Ethics Code applies only to psychologists' work-related activities, that is, activities that are part of the psychologists' scientific and professional functions or that are psychological in nature. It includes the clinical or counseling practice of psychology, research, teaching, supervision of trainees, development of assessment instruments, conducting assessments, educational counseling, organizational consulting, social intervention, administration, and other activities as well. These work-related activities can be distinguished from the purely private conduct of a psychologist, which ordinarily is not within the purview of the Ethics Code.

The Ethics Code is intended to provide standards of professional conduct that can be applied by the APA and by other bodies that choose to adopt them. Whether or not a psychologist has violated the Ethics Code does not by itself determine whether he or she is legally liable in a court action, whether a contract is enforceable, or whether other legal consequences occur. These results are based on legal rather than ethical rules. However, compliance with or violation of the Ethics Code may be admissible as evidence in some legal proceedings, depending on the circumstances.

In the process of making decisions regarding their professional behavior, psychologists must consider this Ethics Code, in addition to applicable laws and psychology board regulations. If the Ethics Code establishes a higher standard of conduct than is required by law, psychologists must meet the higher ethical standard. If the Ethics Code standard appears to conflict with the requirements of law, then psychologists make known their commitment to the Ethics Code and take steps to resolve the conflict in a responsible manner. If neither law nor the Ethics Code resolves an issue, psychologists should consider other professional materials[1] and the dictates of their own conscience, as well as seek consultation with others within the field when this is practical.

The procedures for filing, investigating, and resolving complaints of unethical conduct are described in the current Rules and Procedures of the APA Ethics Committee. The actions that APA may take for violations of the Ethics Code

---

1. Professional materials that are most helpful in this regard are guidelines and standards that have been adopted or endorsed by professional psychological organizations. Such guidelines and standards, whether adopted by the American Psychological Association (APA) or its Divisions, are not enforceable as such by this Ethics Code, but are of educative value to psychologists, courts, and professional bodies. Such materials include, but are not limited to, the APA's *General Guidelines for Providers of Psychological Services* (1987), *Specialty Guidelines for the Delivery of Services by Clinical Psychologists, Counseling Psychologists, Industrial/Organizational Psychologists, and School Psychologists* (1981), *Guidelines for Computer Based Tests and Interpretations* (1987), *Standards for Educational and Psychological Testing* (1985), *Ethical*

include actions such as reprimand, censure, termination of APA membership, and referral of the matter to other bodies. Complainants who seek remedies such as monetary damages in alleging ethical violations by a psychologist must resort to private negotiation, administrative bodies, or the courts. Actions that violate the Ethics Code may lead to the imposition of sanctions on a psychologist by bodies other than APA, including state psychological associations, other professional groups, psychology boards, other state or federal agencies, and payors for health services. In addition to actions for violation of the Ethics Code, the APA Bylaws provide that APA may take action against a member after his or her conviction of a felony, expulsion or suspension from an affiliated state psychological association, or suspension or loss of licensure.

Preamble

Psychologists work to develop a valid and reliable body of scientific knowledge based on research. They may apply that knowledge to human behavior in a variety of contexts. In doing so, they perform many roles, such as researcher, educator, diagnostician, therapist, supervisor, consultant, administrator, social interventionist, and expert witness. Their goal is to broaden knowledge of behavior and, where appropriate, to apply it pragmatically to improve the condition of both the individual and society. Psychologists respect the central importance of freedom of inquiry and expression in research, teaching, and publication. They also strive to help the public in developing informed judgments and choices concerning human behavior. This Ethics Code provides a common set of values upon which psychologists build their professional and scientific work.

This Code is intended to provide both the general principles and the decision rules to cover most situations encountered by psychologists. It has as its primary goal the welfare and protection of the individuals and groups with whom psychologists work. It is the individual responsibility of each psychologist to aspire to the highest possible standards of conduct. Psychologists respect and protect human and civil rights, and do not knowingly participate in or condone unfair discriminatory practices.

The development of a dynamic set of ethical standards for a psychologist's work-related conduct requires a personal commitment to a lifelong effort to act ethically; to encourage ethical behavior by students, supervisees, employees, and colleagues, as appropriate; and to consult with others, as needed, concerning ethical problems. Each psychologist supplements, but does not violate, the Ethics Code's values and rules on the basis of guidance drawn from personal values, culture, and experience.

GENERAL PRINCIPLES

Principle A: Competence

Psychologists strive to maintain high standards of competence in their work. They recognize the boundaries of their particular competencies and the limitations of their expertise. They provide only those services and use only those techniques for which they are qualified by education, training, or experience. Psychologists are cognizant of the fact that the competencies required in serving, teaching, and/or studying groups of people vary with the distinctive characteristics of those groups. In those areas in which recognized professional standards do not yet exist, psychologists exercise careful judgment and take appropriate precautions to protect the welfare of those with whom they work. They maintain knowledge of relevant scientific and professional information related to the services they render, and they recognize the need

---

Principles in the Conduct of Research With Human Participants (1982), *Guidelines for Ethical Conduct in the Care and Use of Animals* (1986), *Guidelines for Providers of Psychological Services to Ethnic, Linguistic, and Culturally Diverse Populations* (1990), and *Publication Manual of the American Psychological Association* (3rd ed., 1983). Materials not adopted by APA as a whole include the APA Division 41 (Forensic Psychology)/American Psychology–Law Society's *Specialty Guidelines for Forensic Psychologists* (1991).

for ongoing education. Psychologists make appropriate use of scientific, professional, technical, and administrative resources.

Principle B: Integrity

Psychologists seek to promote integrity in the science, teaching, and practice of psychology. In these activities psychologists are honest, fair, and respectful of others. In describing or reporting their qualifications, services, products, fees, research, or teaching, they do not make statements that are false, misleading, or deceptive. Psychologists strive to be aware of their own belief systems, values, needs, and limitations and the effect of these on their work. To the extent feasible, they attempt to clarify for relevant parties the roles they are performing and to function appropriately in accordance with those roles. Psychologists avoid improper and potentially harmful dual relationships.

Principle C: Professional and Scientific Responsibility

Psychologists uphold professional standards of conduct, clarify their professional roles and obligations, accept appropriate responsibility for their behavior, and adapt their methods to the needs of different populations. Psychologists consult with, refer to, or cooperate with other professionals and institutions to the extent needed to serve the best interests of their patients, clients, or other recipients of their services. Psychologists' moral standards and conduct are personal matters to the same degree as is true for any other person, except as psychologists' conduct may compromise their professional responsibilities or reduce the public's trust in psychology and psychologists. Psychologists are concerned about the ethical compliance of their colleagues' scientific and professional conduct. When appropriate, they consult with colleagues in order to prevent or avoid unethical conduct.

Principle D: Respect for People's Rights and Dignity

Psychologists accord appropriate respect to the fundamental rights, dignity, and worth of all people. They respect the rights of individuals to privacy, confidentiality, self-determination, and autonomy, mindful that legal and other obligations may lead to inconsistency and conflict with the exercise of these rights. Psychologists are aware of cultural, individual, and role differences, including those due to age, gender, race, ethnicity, national origin, religion, sexual orientation, disability, language, and socioeconomic status. Psychologists try to eliminate the effect on their work of biases based on those factors, and they do not knowingly participate in or condone unfair discriminatory practices.

Principle E: Concern for Others' Welfare

Psychologists seek to contribute to the welfare of those with whom they interact professionally. In their professional actions, psychologists weigh the welfare and rights of their patients or clients, students, supervisees, human research participants, and other affected persons, and the welfare of animal subjects of research. When conflicts occur among psychologists' obligations or concerns, they attempt to resolve these conflicts and to perform their roles in a responsible fashion that avoids or minimizes harm. Psychologists are sensitive to real and ascribed differences in power between themselves and others, and they do not exploit or mislead other people during or after professional relationships.

Principle F: Social Responsibility

Psychologists are aware of their professional and scientific responsibilities to the community and the society in which they work and live. They apply and make public their knowledge of psychology in order to contribute to human welfare. Psychologists are concerned about and work to mitigate the causes of human suffering. When undertaking research, they strive to advance human welfare and the science of psychology. Psychologists try to avoid misuse of their work. Psychologists comply with the law and encourage the development of law and social policy that serve the interests of their patients and clients and the public. They are encouraged to contribute a portion of their professional time for little or no personal advantage.

ETHICAL STANDARDS

1. General Standards

These General Standards are potentially applicable to the professional and scientific activities of all psychologists.

1.01 Applicability of the Ethics Code

The activity of a psychologist subject to the Ethics Code may be reviewed under these Ethical Standards only if the activity is part of his or her work-related functions or the activity is psychological in nature. Personal activities having no connection to or effect on psychological roles are not subject to the Ethics Code.

1.02 Relationship of Ethics and Law

If psychologists' ethical responsibilities conflict with law, psychologists make known their commitment to the Ethics Code and take steps to resolve the conflict in a responsible manner.

1.03 Professional and Scientific Relationship

Psychologists provide diagnostic, therapeutic, teaching, research, supervisory, consultative, or other psychological services only in the context of a defined professional or scientific relationship or role. (See also Standards 2.01, Evaluation, Diagnosis, and Interventions in Professional Context, and 7.02, Forensic Assessments.)

1.04 Boundaries of Competence

(a) Psychologists provide services, teach, and conduct research only within the boundaries of their competence, based on their education, training, supervised experience, or appropriate professional experience.

(b) Psychologists provide services, teach, or conduct research in new areas or involving new techniques only after first undertaking appropriate study, training, supervision, and/or consultation from persons who are competent in those areas or techniques.

(c) In those emerging areas in which generally recognized standards for preparatory training do not yet exist, psychologists nevertheless take reasonable steps to ensure the competence of their work and to protect patients, clients, students, research participants, and others from harm.

1.05 Maintaining Expertise

Psychologists who engage in assessment, therapy, teaching, research, organizational consulting, or other professional activities maintain a reasonable level of awareness of current scientific and professional information in their fields of activity, and undertake ongoing efforts to maintain competence in the skills they use.

1.06 Basis for Scientific and Professional Judgments

Psychologists rely on scientifically and professionally derived knowledge when making scientific or professional judgments or when engaging in scholarly or professional endeavors.

1.07 Describing the Nature and Results of Psychological Services

(a) When psychologists provide assessment, evaluation, treatment, counseling, supervision, teaching, consultation, research, or other psychological services to an individual, a group, or an organization, they provide, using language that is reasonably understandable to the recipient of those services, appropriate information beforehand about the nature of such services and appropriate information later about results and conclusions. (See also Standard 2.09, Explaining Assessment Results.)

(b) If psychologists will be precluded by law or by organizational roles from providing such information to particular individuals or groups, they so inform those individuals or groups at the outset of the service.

1.08 Human Differences

Where differences of age, gender, race, ethnicity, national origin, religion, sexual orientation, disability, language, or socioeconomic status significantly affect psychologists' work concerning particular individuals or groups, psychologists obtain the training, experience, consultation, or supervision necessary to ensure the competence of their services, or they make appropriate referrals.

1.09 Respecting Others

In their work-related activities, psychologists respect the rights of others to hold values, attitudes, and opinions that differ from their own.

1.10 Nondiscrimination

In their work-related activities, psychologists do not engage in unfair discrimination based on age, gender, race, ethnicity, national origin, religion, sexual orientation, disability, socioeconomic status, or any basis proscribed by law.

1.11 Sexual Harassment

(a) Psychologists do not engage in sexual harassment. Sexual harassment is sexual solicitation, physical advances, or verbal or nonverbal conduct that is sexual in nature, that occurs in connection with the psychologist's activities or roles as a psychologist, and that either: (1) is unwelcome, is offensive, or creates a hostile workplace environment, and the psychologist knows or is told this; or (2) is sufficiently severe or intense to be abusive to a reasonable person in the context. Sexual harassment can consist of a single intense or severe act or of multiple persistent or pervasive acts.

(b) Psychologists accord sexual-harassment complainants and respondents dignity and respect. Psychologists do not participate in denying a person academic admittance or advancement, employment, tenure, or promotion, based solely upon their having made, or their being the subject of, sexual harassment charges. This does not preclude taking action based upon the outcome of such proceedings or consideration of other appropriate information.

1.12 Other Harassment

Psychologists do not knowingly engage in behavior that is harassing or demeaning to persons with whom they interact in their work based on factors such as those persons' age, gender, race, ethnicity, national origin, religion, sexual orientation, disability, language, or socioeconomic status.

1.13 Personal Problems and Conflicts

(a) Psychologists recognize that their personal problems and conflicts may interfere with their effectiveness. Accordingly, they refrain from undertaking an activity when they know or should know that their personal problems are likely to lead to harm to a patient, client, colleague, student, research participant, or other person to whom they may owe a professional or scientific obligation.

(b) In addition, psychologists have an obligation to be alert to signs of, and to obtain assistance for, their personal problems at an early stage, in order to prevent significantly impaired performance.

(c) When psychologists become aware of personal problems that may interfere with their performing work-related duties adequately, they take appropriate measures, such as obtaining professional consultation or assistance, and determine whether they should limit, suspend, or terminate their work-related duties.

1.14 Avoiding Harm

Psychologists take reasonable steps to avoid harming their patients or clients, research participants, students, and others with whom they work, and to minimize harm where it is foreseeable and unavoidable.

1.15 Misuse of Psychologists' Influence

Because psychologists' scientific and professional judgments and actions may affect the lives of others, they are alert to and guard against personal, financial, social, organizational, or political factors that might lead to misuse of their influence.

1.16 Misuse of Psychologists' Work

(a) Psychologists do not participate in activities in which it appears likely that their skills or data will be misused by others, unless corrective mechanisms are available. (See also Standard 7.04, Truthfulness and Candor.)

(b) If psychologists learn of misuse or misrepresentation of their work, they take reasonable steps to correct or minimize the misuse or misrepresentation.

1.17 Multiple Relationships

(a) In many communities and situations, it may not be feasible or reasonable for psychologists to avoid social or other nonprofessional contacts with persons such as patients, clients, students, supervisees, or research participants. Psychologists must always be sensitive to the potential harmful effects of other contacts on their work and on those persons with whom they deal. A psychologist refrains from entering into or promising another personal, scientific, professional, financial, or other relationship with such persons if it appears likely that such a relationship reasonably might impair the psychologist's objectivity or otherwise interfere with the psychologist's effectively performing his or her functions as a psychologist, or might harm or exploit the other party.

(b) Likewise, whenever feasible, a psychologist refrains from taking on professional or scientific obligations when pre-existing relationships would create a risk of such harm.

(c) If a psychologist finds that, due to unforeseen factors, a potentially harmful multiple relationship has arisen, the psychologist attempts to resolve it with due regard for the best interests of the affected person and maximal compliance with the Ethics Code.

1.18 Barter (With Patients or Clients)

Psychologists ordinarily refrain from accepting goods, services, or other nonmonetary remuner-

ation from patients or clients in return for psychological services because such arrangements create inherent potential for conflicts, exploitation, and distortion of the professional relationship. A psychologist may participate in bartering only if (1) it is not clinically contraindicated, and (2) the relationship is not exploitative. (See also Standards 1.17, Multiple Relationships, and 1.25, Fees and Financial Arrangements.)

1.19 Exploitative Relationships

(a) Psychologists do not exploit persons over whom they have supervisory, evaluative, or other authority such as students, supervisees, employees, research participants, and clients or patients. (See also Standards 4.05–4.07 regarding sexual involvement with clients or patients.)

(b) Psychologists do not engage in sexual relationships with students or supervisees in training over whom the psychologist has evaluative or direct authority, because such relationships are so likely to impair judgment or be exploitative.

1.20 Consultations and Referrals

(a) Psychologists arrange for appropriate consultations and referrals based principally on the best interests of their patients or clients, with appropriate consent, and subject to other relevant considerations, including applicable law and contractual obligations. (See also Standards 5.01, Discussing the Limits of Confidentiality, and 5.06, Consultations.)

(b) When indicated and professionally appropriate, psychologists cooperate with other professionals in order to serve their patients or clients effectively and appropriately.

(c) Psychologists' referral practices are consistent with law.

1.21 Third-Party Requests for Services

(a) When a psychologist agrees to provide services to a person or entity at the request of a third party, the psychologist clarifies to the extent feasible, at the outset of the service, the nature of the relationship with each party. This clarification includes the role of the psychologist (such as therapist, organizational consultant, diagnostician, or expert witness), the probable uses of the services provided or the information obtained, and the fact that there may be limits to confidentiality.

(b) If there is a foreseeable risk of the psychologist's being called upon to perform conflicting roles because of the involvement of a third party, the psychologist clarifies the nature and direction of his or her responsibilities, keeps all parties appropriately informed as matters develop, and resolves the situation in accordance with this Ethics Code.

1.22 Delegation to and Supervision of Subordinates

(a) Psychologists delegate to their employees, supervisees, and research assistants only those responsibilities that such persons can reasonably be expected to perform competently, on the basis of their education, training, or experience, either independently or with the level of supervision being provided.

(b) Psychologists provide proper training and supervision to their employees or supervisees and take reasonable steps to see that such persons perform services responsibly, competently, and ethically.

(c) If institutional policies, procedures, or practices prevent fulfillment of this obligation, psychologists attempt to modify their role or to correct the situation to the extent feasible.

1.23 Documentation of Professional and Scientific Work

(a) Psychologists appropriately document their professional and scientific work in order to facilitate provision of services later by them or by other professionals, to ensure accountability, and to meet other requirements of institutions or the law.

(b) When psychologists have reason to believe that records of their professional services will be used in legal proceedings involving recipients of or participants in their work, they have a responsibility to create and maintain documentation in the kind of detail and quality that

would be consistent with reasonable scrutiny in an adjudicative forum. (See also Standard 7.01, Professionalism, under Forensic Activities.)

1.24 Records and Data

Psychologists create, maintain, disseminate, store, retain, and dispose of records and data relating to their research, practice, and other work in accordance with law and in a manner that permits compliance with the requirements of this Ethics Code. (See also Standard 5.04, Maintenance of Records.)

1.25 Fees and Financial Arrangements

(a) As early as is feasible in a professional or scientific relationship, the psychologist and the patient, client, or other appropriate recipient of psychological services reach an agreement specifying the compensation and the billing arrangements.

(b) Psychologists do not exploit recipients of services or payors with respect to fees.

(c) Psychologists' fee practices are consistent with law.

(d) Psychologists do not misrepresent their fees.

(e) If limitations to services can be anticipated because of limitations in financing, this is discussed with the patient, client, or other appropriate recipient of services as early as is feasible. (See also Standard 4.08, Interruption of Services.)

(f) If the patient, client, or other recipient of services does not pay for services as agreed, and if the psychologist wishes to use collection agencies or legal measures to collect the fees, the psychologist first informs the person that such measures will be taken and provides that person an opportunity to make prompt payment. (See also Standard 5.11, Withholding Records for Nonpayment.)

1.26 Accuracy in Reports to Payors and Funding Sources

In their reports to payors for services or sources of research funding, psychologists accurately state the nature of the research or service provided, the fees or charges, and where applicable, the identity of the provider, the findings, and the diagnosis. (See also Standard 5.05, Disclosures.)

1.27 Referrals and Fees

When a psychologist pays, receives payment from, or divides fees with another professional other than in an employer—employee relationship, the payment to each is based on the services (clinical, consultative, administrative, or other) provided and is not based on the referral itself.

2. Evaluation, Assessment, or Intervention

2.01 Evaluation, Diagnosis, and Interventions in Professional Context

(a) Psychologists perform evaluations, diagnostic services, or interventions only within the context of a defined professional relationship. (See also Standards 1.03, Professional and Scientific Relationship.)

(b) Psychologists' assessments, recommendations, reports, and psychological diagnostic or evaluative statements are based on information and techniques (including personal interviews of the individual when appropriate) sufficient to provide appropriate substantiation for their findings. (See also Standard 7.02, Forensic Assessments.)

2.02 Competence and Appropriate Use of Assessments and Interventions

(a) Psychologists who develop, administer, score, interpret, or use psychological assessment techniques, interviews, tests, or instruments do so in a manner and for purposes that are appropriate in light of the research on or evidence of the usefulness and proper application of the techniques.

(b) Psychologists refrain from misuse of assessment techniques, interventions, results, and interpretations and take reasonable steps to prevent others from misusing the information these techniques provide. This includes refraining

from releasing raw test results or raw data to persons, other than to patients or clients as appropriate, who are not qualified to use such information. (See also Standards 1.02, Relationship of Ethics and Law, and 1.04, Boundaries of Competence.)

2.03 Test Construction

Psychologists who develop and conduct research with tests and other assessment techniques use scientific procedures and current professional knowledge for test design, standardization, validation, reduction or elimination of bias, and recommendations for use.

2.04 Use of Assessment in General and With Special Populations

(a) Psychologists who perform interventions or administer, score, interpret, or use assessment techniques are familiar with the reliability, validation, and related standardization or outcome studies of, and proper applications and uses of, the techniques they use.

(b) Psychologists recognize limits to the certainty with which diagnoses, judgments, or predictions can be made about individuals.

(c) Psychologists attempt to identify situations in which particular interventions or assessment techniques or norms may not be applicable or may require adjustment in administration or interpretation because of factors such as individuals' gender, age, race, ethnicity, national origin, religion, sexual orientation, disability, language, or socioeconomic status.

2.05 Interpreting Assessment Results

When interpreting assessment results, including automated interpretations, psychologists take into account the various test factors and characteristics of the person being assessed that might affect psychologists' judgments or reduce the accuracy of their interpretations. They indicate any significant reservations they have about the accuracy or limitations of their interpretations.

2.06 Unqualified Persons

Psychologists do not promote the use of psychological assessment techniques by unqualified persons. (See also Standard 1.22, Delegation to and Supervision of Subordinates.)

2.07 Obsolete Tests and Outdated Test Results

(a) Psychologists do not base their assessment or intervention decisions or recommendations on data or test results that are outdated for the current purpose.

(b) Similarly, psychologists do not base such decisions or recommendations on tests and measures that are obsolete and not useful for the current purpose.

2.08 Test Scoring and Interpretation Services

(a) Psychologists who offer assessment or scoring procedures to other professionals accurately describe the purpose, norms, validity, reliability, and applications of the procedures and any special qualifications applicable to their use.

(b) Psychologists select scoring and interpretation services (including automated services) on the basis of evidence of the validity of the program and procedures as well as on other appropriate considerations.

(c) Psychologists retain appropriate responsibility for the appropriate application, interpretation, and use of assessment instruments, whether they score and interpret such tests themselves or use automated or other services.

2.09 Explaining Assessment Results

Unless the nature of the relationship is clearly explained to the person being assessed in advance and precludes provision of an explanation of results (such as in some organizational consulting, pre-employment or security screenings, and forensic evaluations), psychologists ensure that an explanation of the results is provided using language that is reasonably understandable to the person assessed or to another legally authorized person on behalf of the client. Re-gardless of whether the scoring and interpretation are done by the psychologist, by assistants, or by automated or other outside services, psychologists take reasonable steps to ensure that appropriate explanations of results are given.

2.10 Maintaining Test Security

Psychologists make reasonable efforts to maintain the integrity and security of tests and other assessment techniques consistent with law, contractual obligations, and in a manner that permits compliance with the requirements of this Ethics Code. (See also Standard 1.02, Relationship of Ethics and Law.)

3. Advertising and Other Public Statements

3.01 Definition of Public Statements

Psychologists comply with this Ethics Code in public statements relating to their professional services, products, or publications or to the field of psychology. Public statements include but are not limited to paid or unpaid advertising, brochures, printed matter, directory listings, personal resumes or curriculum vitae, interviews or comments for use in media, statements in legal proceedings, lectures and public oral presentations, and published materials.

3.02 Statements by Others

(a) Psychologists who engage others to create or place public statements that promote their professional practice, products, or activities retain professional responsibility for such statements.

(b) In addition, psychologists make reasonable efforts to prevent others whom they do not control (such as employers, publishers, sponsors, organizational clients, and representatives of the print or broadcast media) from making deceptive statements concerning psychologists' practice or professional or scientific activities.

(c) If psychologists learn of deceptive statements about their work made by others, psychologists make reasonable efforts to correct such statements.

(d) Psychologists do not compensate employees of press, radio, television, or other communication media in return for publicity in a news item.

(e) A paid advertisement relating to the psychologist's activities must be identified as such, unless it is already apparent from the context.

3.03 Avoidance of False or Deceptive Statements

(a) Psychologists do not make public statements that are false, deceptive, misleading, or fraudulent, either because of what they state, convey, or suggest or because of what they omit, concerning their research, practice, or other work activities or those of persons or organizations with which they are affiliated. As examples (and not in limitation) of this standard, psychologists do not make false or deceptive statements concerning (1) their training, experience, or competence; (2) their academic degrees; (3) their credentials; (4) their institutional or association affiliations; (5) their services; (6) the scientific or clinical basis for, or results or degree of success of, their services; (7) their fees; or (8) their publications or research findings. (See also Standards 6.15, Deception in Research, and 6.18, Providing Participants With Information About the Study.)

(b) Psychologists claim as credentials for their psychological work, only degrees that (1) were earned from a regionally accredited educational institution or (2) were the basis for psychology licensure by the state in which they practice.

3.04 Media Presentations

When psychologists provide advice or comment by means of public lectures, demonstrations, radio or television programs, prerecorded tapes, printed articles, mailed material, or other media, they take reasonable precautions to ensure that (1) the statements are based on appropriate psychological literature and practice, (2) the statements are otherwise consistent with this Ethics Code, and (3) the recipients of the information are not encouraged to infer that a relationship has been established with them personally.

3.05 Testimonials

Psychologists do not solicit testimonials from current psychotherapy clients or patients or other persons who because of their particular circumstances are vulnerable to undue influence.

3.06 In-Person Solicitation

Psychologists do not engage, directly or through agents, in uninvited in-person solicitation of business from actual or potential psychotherapy patients or clients or other persons who because of their particular circumstances are vulnerable to undue influence. However, this does not preclude attempting to implement appropriate collateral contacts with significant others for the purpose of benefiting an already engaged therapy patient.

4. Therapy

4.01 Structuring the Relationship

(a) Psychologists discuss with clients or patients as early as is feasible in the therapeutic relationship appropriate issues, such as the nature and anticipated course of therapy, fees, and confidentiality. (See also Standards 1.25, Fees and Financial Arrangements, and 5.01, Discussing the Limits of Confidentiality.)

(b) When the psychologist's work with clients or patients will be supervised, the above discussion includes that fact, and the name of the supervisor, when the supervisor has legal responsibility for the case.

(c) When the therapist is a student intern, the client or patient is informed of that fact.

(d) Psychologists make reasonable efforts to answer patients' questions and to avoid apparent misunderstandings about therapy. Whenever possible, psychologists provide oral and/or written information, using language that is reasonably understandable to the patient or client.

4.02 Informed Consent to Therapy

(a) Psychologists obtain appropriate informed consent to therapy or related procedures, using language that is reasonably understandable to participants. The content of informed consent will vary depending on many circumstances; however, informed consent generally implies that the person (1) has the capacity to consent, (2) has been informed of significant information concerning the procedure, (3) has freely and without undue influence expressed consent, and (4) consent has been appropriately documented.

(b) When persons are legally incapable of giving informed consent, psychologists obtain informed permission from a legally authorized person, if such substitute consent is permitted by law.

(c) In addition, psychologists (1) inform those persons who are legally incapable of giving informed consent about the proposed interventions in a manner commensurate with the persons' psychological capacities, (2) seek their assent to those interventions, and (3) consider such persons' preferences and best interests.

4.03 Couple and Family Relationships

(a) When a psychologist agrees to provide services to several persons who have a relationship (such as husband and wife or parents and children), the psychologist attempts to clarify at the outset (1) which of the individuals are patients or clients and (2) the relationship the psychologist will have with each person. This clarification includes the role of the psychologist and the probable uses of the services provided or the information obtained. (See also Standard 5.01, Discussing the Limits of Confidentiality.)

(b) As soon as it becomes apparent that the psychologist may be called on to perform potentially conflicting roles (such as marital counselor to husband and wife, and then witness for one party in a divorce proceeding), the psychologist attempts to clarify and adjust, or withdraw from, roles appropriately. (See also Standard 7.03, Clarification of Role, under Forensic Activities.)

4.04 Providing Mental Health Services to Those Served by Others

In deciding whether to offer or provide services to those already receiving mental health services elsewhere, psychologists carefully consider the treatment issues and the potential patient's or client's welfare. The psychologist discusses these issues with the patient or client, or another legally authorized person on behalf of the client, in order to minimize the risk of confusion and conflict, consults with the other service providers when appropriate, and proceeds with caution and sensitivity to the therapeutic issues.

4.05 Sexual Intimacies With Current Patients or Clients

Psychologists do not engage in sexual intimacies with current patients or clients.

4.06 Therapy With Former Sexual Partners

Psychologists do not accept as therapy patients or clients persons with whom they have engaged in sexual intimacies.

4.07 Sexual Intimacies With Former Therapy Patients

(a) Psychologists do not engage in sexual intimacies with a former therapy patient or client for at least two years after cessation or termination of professional services.

(b) Because sexual intimacies with a former therapy patient or client are so frequently harmful to the patient or client, and because such intimacies undermine public confidence in the psychology profession and thereby deter the public's use of needed services, psychologists do not engage in sexual intimacies with former therapy patients and clients even after a two-year interval except in the most unusual circumstances. The psychologist who engages in such activity after the two years following cessation or termination of treatment bears the burden of demonstrating that there has been no exploitation, in light of all relevant factors, including (1) the amount of time that has passed since therapy terminated, (2) the nature and duration of the therapy, (3) the circumstances of termination, (4) the patient's or client's personal history, (5) the patient's or client's current mental status, (6) the likelihood of adverse impact on the patient or client and others, and (7) any statements or actions made by the therapist during the course of therapy suggesting or inviting the possibility of a post-termination sexual or romantic relationship with the patient or client. (See also Standard 1.17, Multiple Relationships.)

4.08 Interruption of Services

(a) Psychologists make reasonable efforts to plan for facilitating care in the event that psychological services are interrupted by factors such as the psychologist's illness, death, unavailability, or relocation or by the client's relocation or financial limitations. (See also Standard 5.09, Preserving Records and Data.)

(b) When entering into employment or contractual relationships, psychologists provide for orderly and appropriate resolution of responsibility for patient or client care in the event that the employment or contractual relationship ends, with paramount con sideration given to the welfare of the patient or client.

4.09 Terminating the Professional Relationship

(a) Psychologists do not abandon patients or clients. (See also Standard 1.25e, under Fees and Financial Arrangements.)

(b) Psychologists terminate a professional relationship when it becomes reasonably clear that the patient or client no longer needs the service, is not benefiting, or is being harmed by continued service.

(c) Prior to termination for whatever reason, except where precluded by the patient's or client's conduct, the psychologist discusses the patient's or client's views and needs, provides appropriate pretermination counseling, suggests alternative service providers as appropriate, and takes other reasonable steps to facilitate transfer of responsibility to another provider if the patient or client needs one immediately.

5. Privacy and Confidentiality

These Standards are potentially applicable to the professional and scientific activities of all psychologists.

5.01 Discussing the Limits of Confidentiality

(a) Psychologists discuss with persons and organizations with whom they establish a scientific or professional relationship (including, to the extent feasible, minors and their legal representatives) (1) the relevant limitations on confidentiality, including limitations where applicable in group, marital, and family therapy or in organizational consulting, and (2) the foreseeable uses of the information generated through their services.

(b) Unless it is not feasible or is contraindicated, the discussion of confidentiality occurs at the outset of the relationship and thereafter as new circumstances may warrant.

(c) Permission for electronic recording of interviews is secured from clients and patients.

5.02 Maintaining Confidentiality

Psychologists have a primary obligation and take reasonable precautions to respect the confidentiality rights of those with whom they work or consult, recognizing that confidentiality may be established by law, institutional rules, or professional or scientific relationships. (See also Standard 6.26, Professional Reviewers.)

5.03 Minimizing Intrusions on Privacy

(a) In order to minimize intrusions on privacy, psychologists include in written and oral reports, consultations, and the like, only information germane to the purpose for which the communication is made.

(b) Psychologists discuss confidential information obtained in clinical or consulting relationships, or evaluative data concerning patients, individual or organizational clients, students, research participants, supervisees, and employees, only for appropriate scientific or professional purposes and only with persons clearly concerned with such matters.

5.04 Maintenance of Records

Psychologists maintain appropriate confidentiality in creating, storing, accessing, transferring, and disposing of records under their control, whether these are written, automated, or in any other medium. Psychologists maintain and dispose of records in accordance with law and in a manner that permits compliance with the requirements of this Ethics Code.

5.05 Disclosures

(a) Psychologists disclose confidential information without the consent of the individual only as mandated by law, or where permitted by law for a valid purpose, such as (1) to provide needed professional services to the patient or the individual or organizational client, (2) to obtain appropriate professional consultations, (3) to protect the patient or client or others from harm, or (4) to obtain payment for services, in which instance disclosure is limited to the minimum that is necessary to achieve the purpose.

(b) Psychologists also may disclose confidential information with the appropriate consent of the patient or the individual or organizational client (or of another legally authorized person on behalf of the patient or client), unless prohibited by law.

5.06 Consultations

When consulting with colleagues, (1) psychologists do not share confidential information that reasonably could lead to the identification of a patient, client, research participant, or other person or organization with whom they have a confidential relationship unless they have obtained the prior consent of the person or organization or the disclosure cannot be avoided, and (2) they share information only to the extent necessary to achieve the purposes of the consultation. (See also Standard 5.02, Maintaining Confidentiality.)

5.07 Confidential Information in Databases

(a) If confidential information concerning recipients of psychological services is to be entered into databases or systems of records available to persons whose access has not been consented to by the recipient, then psychologists use coding or other techniques to avoid the inclusion of personal identifiers.

(b) If a research protocol approved by an institutional review board or similar body requires the inclusion of personal identifiers, such identifiers are deleted before the information is made accessible to persons other than those of whom the subject was advised.

(c) If such deletion is not feasible, then before psychologists transfer such data to others or review such data collected by others, they take reasonable steps to determine that appropriate consent of personally identifiable individuals has been obtained.

5.08 Use of Confidential Information for Didactic or Other Purposes

(a) Psychologists do not disclose in their writings, lectures, or other public media, confidential, personally identifiable information concerning their patients, individual or organizational clients, students, research participants, or other recipients of their services that they obtained during the course of their work, unless the person or organization has consented in writing or unless there is other ethical or legal authorization for doing so.

(b) Ordinarily, in such scientific and professional presentations, psychologists disguise confidential information concerning such persons or organizations so that they are not individually identifiable to others and so that discussions do not cause harm to subjects who might identify themselves.

5.09 Preserving Records and Data

A psychologist makes plans in advance so that confidentiality of records and data is protected in the event of the psychologist's death, incapacity, or withdrawal from the position or practice.

5.10 Ownership of Records and Data

Recognizing that ownership of records and data is governed by legal principles, psychologists take reasonable and lawful steps so that records and data remain available to the extent needed to serve the best interests of patients, individual or organizational clients, research participants, or appropriate others.

5.11 Withholding Records for Nonpayment

Psychologists may not withhold records under their control that are requested and imminently needed for a patient's or client's treatment solely because payment has not been received, except as otherwise provided by law.

6. Teaching, Training Supervision, Research, and Publishing

6.01 Design of Education and Training Programs

Psychologists who are responsible for education and training programs seek to ensure that the programs are competently designed, provide the proper experiences, and meet the requirements for licensure, certification, or other goals for which claims are made by the program.

6.02 Descriptions of Education and Training Programs

(a) Psychologists responsible for education and training programs seek to ensure that there is a current and accurate description of the program content, training goals and objectives, and requirements that must be met for satisfactory completion of the program. This information must be made readily available to all interested parties.

(b) Psychologists seek to ensure that statements concerning their course outlines are accurate and not misleading, particularly regarding the subject matter to be covered, bases for evaluating progress, and the nature of course experiences. (See also Standard 3.03, Avoidance of False or Deceptive Statements.)

(c) To the degree to which they exercise control, psychologists responsible for announcements, catalogs, brochures, or advertisements describing workshops, seminars, or other non-degreegranting educational programs ensure that they accurately describe the audience for which the program is intended, the educational objectives, the presenters, and the fees involved.

6.03 Accuracy and Objectivity in Teaching

(a) When engaged in teaching or training, psychologists present psychological information accurately and with a reasonable degree of objectivity.

(b) When engaged in teaching or training, psychologists recognize the power they hold over students or supervisees and therefore make reasonable efforts to avoid engaging in conduct that is personally demeaning to students or supervisees. (See also Standards 1.09, Respecting Others, and 1.12, Other Harassment.)

6.04 Limitation on Teaching

Psychologists do not teach the use of techniques or procedures that require specialized training, licensure, or expertise, including but not limited to hypnosis, biofeedback, and projective techniques, to individuals who lack the prerequisite training, legal scope of practice, or expertise.

6.05 Assessing Student and Supervisee Performance

(a) In academic and supervisory relationships, psychologists establish an appropriate process for providing feedback to students and supervisees.

(b) Psychologists evaluate students and supervisees on the basis of their actual performance on relevant and established program requirements.

6.06 Planning Research

(a) Psychologists design, conduct, and report research in accordance with recognized standards of scientific competence and ethical research.

(b) Psychologists plan their research so as to minimize the possibility that results will be misleading.

(c) In planning research, psychologists consider its ethical acceptability under the Ethics Code. If an ethical issue is unclear, psychologists seek to resolve the issue through consultation with institutional review boards, animal care and use committees, peer consultations, or other proper mechanisms.

(d) Psychologists take reasonable steps to implement appropriate protections for the rights and welfare of human participants, other persons affected by the research, and the welfare of animal subjects.

6.07 Responsibility

(a) Psychologists conduct research competently and with due concern for the dignity and welfare of the participants.

(b) Psychologists are responsible for the ethical conduct of research conducted by them or by others under their supervision or control.

(c) Researchers and assistants are permitted to perform only those tasks for which they are appropriately trained and prepared.

(d) As part of the process of development and implementation of research projects, psychologists consult those with expertise concerning any special population under investigation or most likely to be affected.

6.08 Compliance With Law and Standards

Psychologists plan and conduct research in a manner consistent with federal and state law and regulations, as well as professional standards governing the conduct of research, and particularly those standards governing research with human participants and animal subjects.

6.09 Institutional Approval

Psychologists obtain from host institutions or organizations appropriate approval prior to conducting research, and they provide accurate in-

formation about their research proposals. They conduct the research in accordance with the approved research protocol.

6.10 Research Responsibilities

Prior to conducting research (except research involving only anonymous surveys, naturalistic observations, or similar research), psychologists enter into an agreement with participants that clarifies the nature of the research and the responsibilities of each party.

6.11 Informed Consent to Research

(a) Psychologists use language that is reasonably understandable to research participants in obtaining their appropriate informed consent (except as provided in Standard 6.12, Dispensing with Informed Consent). Such informed consent is appropriately documented.

(b) Using language that is reasonably understandable to participants, psychologists inform participants of the nature of the research; they inform participants that they are free to participate or to decline to participate or to withdraw from the research; they explain the foreseeable consequences of declining or withdrawing; they inform participants of significant factors that may be expected to influence their willingness to participate (such as risks, discomfort, adverse effects, or limitations on confidentiality, except as provided in Standard 6.15, Deception in Research); and they explain other aspects about which the prospective participants inquire.

(c) When psychologists conduct research with individuals such as students or subordinates, psychologists take special care to protect the prospective participants from adverse consequences of declining or withdrawing from participation.

(d) When research participation is a course requirement or opportunity for extra credit, the prospective participant is given the choice of equitable alternative activities.

(e) For persons who are legally incapable of giving informed consent, psychologists nevertheless (1) provide an appropriate explanation, (2) obtain the participant's assent, and (3) obtain appropriate permission from a legally authorized person, if such substitute consent is permitted by law.

6.12 Dispensing With Informed Consent

Before determining that planned research (such as research involving only anonymous questionnaires, naturalistic observations, or certain kinds of archival research) does not require the informed consent of research participants, psychologists consider applicable regulations and institutional review board requirements, and they consult with colleagues as appropriate.

6.13 Informed Consent in Research Filming or Recording

Psychologists obtain informed consent from research participants prior to filming or recording them in any form, unless the research involves simply naturalistic observations in public places and it is not anticipated that the recording will be used in a manner that could cause personal identification or harm.

6.14 Offering Inducements for Research Participants

(a) In offering professional services as an inducement to obtain research participants, psychologists make clear the nature of the services, as well as the risks, obligations, and limitations. (See also Standard 1.18, Barter [With Patients or Clients].)

(b) Psychologists do not offer excessive or inappropriate financial or other inducements to obtain research participants, particularly when it might tend to coerce participation.

6.15 Deception in Research

(a) Psychologists do not conduct a study involving deception unless they have determined that the use of deceptive techniques is justified by the study's prospective scientific, educational, or applied value and that equally effective alternative procedures that do not use deception are not feasible.

(b) Psychologists never deceive research participants about significant aspects that would affect their willingness to participate, such as physical risks, discomfort, or unpleasant emotional experiences.

(c) Any other deception that is an integral feature of the design and conduct of an experiment must be explained to participants as early as is feasible, preferably at the conclusion of their participation, but no later than at the conclusion of the research. (See also Standard 6.18, Providing Participants With Information About the Study.)

6.16 Sharing and Utilizing Data

Psychologists inform research participants of their anticipated sharing or further use of personally identifiable research data and of the possibility of unanticipated future uses.

6.17 Minimizing Invasiveness

In conducting research, psychologists interfere with the participants or milieu from which data are collected only in a manner that is warranted by an appropriate research design and that is consistent with psychologists' roles as scientific investigators.

6.18 Providing Participants With Information About the Study

(a) Psychologists provide a prompt opportunity for participants to obtain appropriate information about the nature, results, and conclusions of the research, and psychologists attempt to correct any misconceptions that participants may have.

(b) If scientific or humane values justify delaying or withholding this information, psychologists take reasonable measures to reduce the risk of harm.

6.19 Honoring Commitments

Psychologists take reasonable measures to honor all commitments they have made to research participants.

6.20 Care and Use of Animals in Research

(a) Psychologists who conduct research involving animals treat them humanely.

(b) Psychologists acquire, care for, use, and dispose of animals in compliance with current federal, state, and local laws and regulations, and with professional standards.

(c) Psychologists trained in research methods and experienced in the care of laboratory animals supervise all procedures involving animals and are responsible for ensuring appropriate consideration of their comfort, health, and humane treatment.

(d) Psychologists ensure that all individuals using animals under their supervision have received instruction in research methods and in the care, maintenance, and handling of the species being used, to the extent appropriate to their role.

(e) Responsibilities and activities of individuals assisting in a research project are consistent with their respective competencies.

(f) Psychologists make reasonable efforts to minimize the discomfort, infection, illness, and pain of animal subjects.

(g) A procedure subjecting animals to pain, stress, or privation is used only when an alternative procedure is unavailable and the goal is justified by its prospective scientific, educational, or applied value.

(h) Surgical procedures are performed under appropriate anesthesia; techniques to avoid infection and minimize pain are followed during and after surgery.

(i) When it is appropriate that the animal's life be terminated, it is done rapidly, with an effort to minimize pain, and in accordance with accepted procedures.

6.21 Reporting of Results

(a) Psychologists do not fabricate data or falsify results in their publications.

(b) If psychologists discover significant errors in their published data, they take reasonable steps to correct such errors in a correction, retraction, erratum, or other appropriate publication means.

6.22 Plagiarism

Psychologists do not present substantial portions or elements of another's work or data as their own, even if the other work or data source is cited occasionally.

6.23 Publication Credit

(a) Psychologists take responsibility and credit, including authorship credit, only for work they have actually performed or to which they have contributed.

(b) Principal authorship and other publication credits accurately reflect the relative scientific or professional contributions of the individuals involved, regardless of their relative status. Mere possession of an institutional position, such as Department Chair, does not justify authorship credit. Minor contributions to the research or to the writing for publications are appropriately acknowledged, such as in footnotes or in an introductory statement.

(c) A student is usually listed as principal author on any multiple-authored article that is substantially based on the student's dissertation or thesis.

6.24 Duplicate Publication of Data

Psychologists do not publish, as original data, data that have been previously published. This does not preclude republishing data when they are accompanied by proper acknowledgment.

6.25 Sharing Data

After research results are published, psychologists do not withhold the data on which their conclusions are based from other competent professionals who seek to verify the substantive claims through reanalysis and who intend to use such data only for that purpose, provided that the confidentiality of the participants can be protected and unless legal rights concerning proprietary data preclude their release.

6.26 Professional Reviewers

Psychologists who review material submitted for publication, grant, or other research proposal review respect the confidentiality of and the proprietary rights in such information of those who submitted it.

7. Forensic Activities

7.01 Professionalism

Psychologists who perform forensic functions, such as assessments, interviews, consultations, reports, or expert testimony, must comply with all other provisions of this Ethics Code to the extent that they apply to such activities. In addition, psychologists base their forensic work on appropriate knowledge of and competence in the areas underlying such work, including specialized knowledge concerning special populations. (See also Standards 1.06, Basis for Scientific and Professional Judgments; 1.08, Human Differences; 1.15, Misuse of Psychologists' Influence; and 1.23, Documentation of Professional and Scientific Work.)

7.02 Forensic Assessments

(a) Psychologists' forensic assessments, recommendations, and reports are based on information and techniques (including personal interviews of the individual, when appropriate) sufficient to provide appropriate substantiation for their findings. (See also Standards 1.03, Professional and Scientific Relationship; 1.23, Documentation of Professional and Scientific Work; 2.01, Evaluation, Diagnosis, and Interventions in Professional Context; and 2.05, Interpreting Assessment Results.)

(b) Except as noted in (c), below, psychologists provide written or oral forensic reports or testimony of the psychological characteristics of an individual only after they have conducted an examination of the individual adequate to support their statements or conclusions.

(c) When, despite reasonable efforts, such an examination is not feasible, psychologists clarify the impact of their limited information on the reliability and validity of their reports and testimony, and they appropriately limit the nature and extent of their conclusions or recommendations.

7.03 Clarification of Role

In most circumstances, psychologists avoid performing multiple and potentially conflicting roles in forensic matters. When psychologists may be called on to serve in more than one role in a legal proceeding—for example, as consultant or expert for one party or for the court and as a fact witness—they clarify role expectations and the extent of confidentiality in advance to the extent feasible, and thereafter as changes occur, in order to avoid compromising their professional judgment and objectivity and in order to avoid misleading others regarding their role.

7.04 Truthfulness and Candor

(a) In forensic testimony and reports, psychologists testify truthfully, honestly, and candidly and, consistent with applicable legal procedures, describe fairly the bases for their testimony and conclusions.

(b) Whenever necessary to avoid misleading, psychologists acknowledge the limits of their data or conclusions.

7.05 Prior Relationships

A prior professional relationship with a party does not preclude psychologists from testifying as fact witnesses or from testifying to their services to the extent permitted by applicable law. Psychologists appropriately take into account ways in which the prior relationship might affect their professional objectivity or opinions and disclose the potential conflict to the relevant parties.

7.06 Compliance With Law and Rules

In performing forensic roles, psychologists are reasonably familiar with the rules governing their roles. Psychologists are aware of the occasionally competing demands placed upon them by these principles and the requirements of the court system, and attempt to resolve these conflicts by making known their commitment to this Ethics Code and taking steps to resolve the conflict in a responsible manner. (See also Standard 1.02, Relationship of Ethics and Law.)

8. Resolving Ethical Issues

8.01 Familiarity With Ethics Code

Psychologists have an obligation to be familiar with this Ethics Code, other applicable ethics codes, and their application to psychologists' work. Lack of awareness or misunderstanding of an ethical standard is not itself a defense to a charge of unethical conduct.

8.02 Confronting Ethical Issues

When a psychologist is uncertain whether a particular situation or course of action would violate this Ethics Code, the psychologist ordinarily consults with other psychologists knowledgeable about ethical issues, with state or national psychology ethics committees, or with other appropriate authorities in order to choose a proper response.

8.03 Conflicts Between Ethics and Organizational Demands

If the demands of an organization with which psychologists are affiliated conflict with this Ethics Code, psychologists clarify the nature of the conflict, make known their commitment to the Ethics Code, and to the extent feasible, seek to resolve the conflict in a way that permits the fullest adherence to the Ethics Code.

8.04 Informal Resolution of Ethical Violations

When psychologists believe that there may have been an ethical violation by another psychologist, they attempt to resolve the issue by bringing it to the attention of that individual if an informal resolution appears appropriate and the intervention does not violate any confidentiality rights that may be involved.

8.05 Reporting Ethical Violations

If an apparent ethical violation is not appropriate for informal resolution under Standard 8.04 or is not resolved properly in that fashion, psychologists take further action appropriate to the situation, unless such action conflicts with confidentiality rights in ways that cannot be resolved. Such action might include referral to state or national committees on professional ethics or to state licensing boards.

8.06 Cooperating With Ethics Committees

Psychologists cooperate in ethics investigations, proceedings, and resulting requirements of the APA or any affiliated state psychological association to which they belong. In doing so, they make reasonable efforts to resolve any issues as to confidentiality. Failure to cooperate is itself an ethics violation.

8.07 Improper Complaints

Psychologists do not file or encourage the filing of ethics complaints that are frivolous and are intended to harm the respondent rather than to protect the public.

Appendix B

Rules and Procedures

Ethics Committee of the American Psychological Association as Published in the American Psychologist *May 1996, pp. 529–548*

Effective June 1, 1996

Contents

OVERVIEW

This brief overview is intended only to help the reader to understand the structure of these Rules and Procedures (Rules). The overview is not binding on the Ethics Committee or participants in the ethics process and is not an independent source of authority.

These Rules are divided into five parts, which are further subdivided by sections and subsections. The table of contents lists the major section headings.

Parts I and II: General Provisions

Part I describes the objectives and authority of the Ethics Committee. Part II states the Committee's general operating rules. These address such areas as confidentiality and disclosures of information concerning ethics cases; maintenance and disposition of Ethics Committee records; the Committee's jurisdiction, including the time limits within which ethics complaints must be filed; requests to reopen a closed case; and descriptions of the various sanctions and directives that may be imposed.

Parts III–V: Processing and Review of Complaints and Other Matters by the Ethics Committee

Membership Matters

The Ethics Committee may review applications or reapplications for membership in APA and may review allegations that membership was obtained based upon false or fraudulent information. These procedures are described in Part III.

Investigations of Unethical Conduct

These Rules describe two types of investigations: show cause proceedings and reviews of alleged unethical conduct. The Committee may choose to deal with a matter according to either procedure and may convert an investigation from one type to another as appropriate. A show cause review is commenced based on an adverse action by another body; a review of alleged unethical conduct is initiated by a complainant or the Committee and charges violation of the Ethics Code.

Show Cause Proceedings

The show cause procedure, addressed in Part IV, can be used when another body—including criminal courts, licensing boards, and state psychological associations—has already taken specified serious adverse action against a member. For example, if a member has been convicted of a felony or equivalent criminal offense; has been expelled or suspended by a state psychological association; or has been decertified, unlicensed, or deregistered or had a certificate, license, or registration revoked or suspended by a state or local board, the Committee may notify the respondent that he or she has 60 days to explain why APA should not expel the respondent from membership on the basis of that prior action. The respondent may show that procedures used were not fair and may argue the merits of the previous action. The Committee recommends to the Board of Directors whether the respondent should be expelled or allowed to resign under stipulated conditions, reprimanded or censured, or cleared of the charges. Time limits for initiating show cause cases are stated in Part II, Section 5.3.4.

Complaints Alleging Violation of the Ethics Code

Investigations detailed in Part V include those brought by members and nonmembers of the Association and those initiated by the Ethics Committee (*sua sponte* complaints). Complaints must be submitted within specified time periods or allege serious misconduct for which a waiver of the time limit may be granted. (See Part II, Section 5.) Even with a waiver of the time limit, the Committee may not find violations for behavior that occurred 10 years or more before the complaint was filed.

Complaints are evaluated initially by the Ethics Office Director, or Investigators acting as the Director's designees, regarding jurisdictional issues such as whether the subject of the complaint, the respondent, is a member, whether the complaint form is correctly completed, and whether the time limits for filing have been met. Then the Chair of the Ethics Committee and Director of the Ethics Office or their designees determine whether there are grounds for action to be taken by the Committee (defined in Part V, Subsection 5.1). If necessary, the Chair and Director conduct a preliminary investigation (described in Part V, Section 5.3) to assist in making these threshold determinations. If the Committee has no jurisdiction or if cause for action does not exist, the complaint is dismissed. If the Committee has jurisdiction and cause for action exists, the Director will open a case, issue a specific charge letter, and conduct an investigation. The respondent is afforded an opportunity to comment on all evidence that will be considered by the Committee and upon which the Committee may rely in its review of the complaint. At the conclusion of the investigation, the case is referred to the Committee for review and resolution.

In resolving a case, the Committee may dismiss it; recommend that it be resolved with a reprimand or censure, with or without supplemental directives; recommend to the Board of Directors that the respondent be expelled from membership; or offer the member the option of resigning subject to stipulated conditions and subject to approval by the Board of Directors.

If the Committee recommends any action other than dismissal or stipulated resignation, the respondent has a right to an independent case review and evaluation or, in the case of a recommendation of expulsion, a formal hearing or an independent adjudication. In an independent adjudication following a recommendation of censure or reprimand, the respondent provides a rationale for nonacceptance of the Committee's recommendation, and a three member panel, selected by the respondent from six members of the Board of Directors' standing Hearing Panel, provides the final adjudication based on the written record. The Director implements the final adjudication, whether based on the panel's decision or the respondent's acceptance of the Committee's recommendation.

A formal hearing is an in person proceeding before a formal hearing committee, which makes an independent recommendation to the Board of Directors. The respondent may elect to have an independent adjudication instead of a formal hearing. The Board reviews the recommendation of the hearing committee, independent adjudication panel, or, if no hearing was requested, the Ethics Committee, and must adopt that recommendation unless specified defects require the matter to be remanded for further actions.

ADOPTION AND APPLICATION

The revised Rules and Procedures of the Ethics Committee of the American Psychological Association, which are set forth below, were approved by the APA Board of Directors on December 9, 1995, with an effective date of June 1, 1996. The Rules will be applied from that date forward to all complaints and cases pending on the effective date, except, as provided in Part II, Subsection 1.2 of the 1992 Rules, "no amendment shall adversely affect the rights of a member of the Association whose conduct is being investigated by the Ethics Committee or against whom the Ethics Committee has filed formal charges" as of the effective date. In the event application of the revised Rules and Procedures would adversely affect such rights, the pertinent provisions of the Rules and Procedures in effect at the time the member came under the scrutiny of the Ethics Committee will be applied. Failure by the Committee or APA to follow these Rules and Procedures shall be cause to set aside action taken under these Rules only in the event such failure has resulted in genuine prejudice to the respondent.

PART I. OBJECTIVES AND AUTHORITY OF THE COMMITTEE

1. Objectives

The fundamental objectives of the Ethics Committee (hereinafter the Committee) shall be to maintain ethical conduct by psychologists at the highest professional level, to educate psychologists concerning ethical standards, to endeavor to protect the public against harmful conduct by psychologists, and to aid the Association in achieving its objectives as reflected in its By-laws.[1]

2. Authority

The Committee is authorized to

2.1 Formulate rules or principles of ethics for adoption by the Association;

2.2 Investigate allegations of unethical conduct of members (to include fellows) and associates (hereinafter members) and, in certain instances, student affiliates and applicants for membership;

2.3 Resolve allegations of unethical conduct and/or recommend such action as is necessary to achieve the objectives of the Association;

2.4 Report on types of complaints investigated with special description of difficult cases;

2.5 Adopt rules and procedures governing the conduct of all the matters within its jurisdiction;

2.6 Take such other actions as are consistent with the Bylaws of the Association, the Association Rules, the Association's Ethics Code, and these Rules and Procedures, and as are necessary and appropriate to achieving the objectives of the Committee;

2.7 Delegate appropriate tasks to subcommittees, ad hoc committees, and task forces of the Ethics Committee; to Committee Associates; or to employees or agents of the Association, as necessary or appropriate. All of these individuals

and groups shall in any such event be fully bound by these Rules and Procedures.

PART II. GENERAL OPERATING RULES

1. General Provisions

1.1 APA Documents[2]

The Committee shall base its actions on applicable governmental laws and regulations, the Bylaws of the Association, the Association Rules, the Association's Ethics Code, and these Rules and Procedures.

1.2 Applicable Ethics Code

Conduct is subject to the Ethics Code in effect at the time the conduct occurred. If a course of conduct continued over a period of time during which more than one Ethics Code was in effect, each Ethics Code will be applicable to conduct that occurred during the time period it was in effect.

1.3 Rules and Procedures

The Committee may adopt rules and procedures governing the conduct of all matters within its jurisdiction, and may amend such rules from time to time upon a two thirds vote of the Committee members, provided that no amendment shall adversely affect the rights of a member of the Association whose conduct is being investigated by the Ethics Committee or against whom the Ethics Committee has recommended expulsion, stipulated resignation, voiding membership, censure, or reprimand at the time of amendment. Changes to the Rules and Procedures must be ratified by the Board of Directors acting for the Council of Representatives.

---

1. The Ethics Committee seeks to protect the public by deterring unethical conduct by psychologists, by taking appropriate action when an ethical violation has been proved according to these Rules and Procedures, and by setting standards to aid psychologists in understanding their ethical obligations. Of course, in no circumstances can or does the Committee or the Association guarantee that unethical behavior will not occur or that members of the public will never be harmed by the actions of individual psychologists.

2. For a copy of the relevant sections of the current Bylaws and Association Rules, contact the APA Ethics Office.

1.4 Compliance With Time Requirements

The APA and the respondent shall use their best efforts to adhere strictly to the time requirements specified in these Rules and Procedures. Failure to do so will not prohibit final resolution unless such failure was unduly prejudicial. Upon request, the Director may extend time limits stated in these Rules for submitting statements or responses if there is good cause to do so. In all cases in which a time limit for submitting a response is stated in these Rules and Procedures, the period specified is the number of days allowed for receipt of the response by the Ethics Office.

1.5 Computation of Time

In computing any period of time stated by these Rules, the day of the act, event, or default from which the designated period of time begins to run shall not be included. The last day of the period shall be included unless it is a Saturday, a Sunday, or a legal holiday, in which event the period runs until the end of the next business day.

2. Meetings and Officers

2.1 Frequency and Quorum

The Committee shall meet at reasonable intervals as needed. A quorum at such meetings shall consist of the majority of the elected members of the Committee.

2.2 Selection of Officers

The Chair and Vice Chair shall be elected annually at a duly constituted meeting.

2.3 Authority

The Vice Chair shall have the authority to perform all the duties of the Chair when the latter is unavailable or unable to perform them and shall perform such other tasks as are delegated by the Chair or by these Rules.

2.4 Majority Rule

Except as otherwise noted in these Rules and Procedures, all decisions shall be by majority vote of those elected members present or, in the case of a vote by mail, a majority of those elected members qualified to vote.

2.5 Designation of Responsibilities

The Chief Executive Officer of the Association shall designate a staff member to serve as Director of the Ethics Office. Whenever they appear in these Rules, "Chair," "Vice Chair," "Director," and "President" shall mean these individuals or their designees.

2.6 Attendance

Attendance at the Ethics Committee's deliberation of cases is restricted to elected members of the Committee, Committee Associates, the Director of the Ethics Office, the Ethics Office staff, members of the Board of Directors, Legal Counsel of the Association, and other duly appointed persons authorized by the Committee to assist it in carrying out its functions, except when the Committee, by two thirds vote, authorizes the presence of other persons.

3. Confidentiality and Notifications

3.1 Requirement of Confidentiality

All information concerning complaints against members shall be confidential, except that the Director may disclose such information when compelled by a valid subpoena, in response to a request from a state or local board or similar entity,[3] when otherwise required by law, or as

---

3. For purposes of these Rules and Procedures, a reference to state or local boards or similar entities shall include state, local, or provincial licensing boards (whether located in the United States or Canada); state, local, or provincial boards of examiners or education in those cases where the pertinent licensing or certification is secured from such entities; or in states or provinces with no licensing authority, nonstatutory boards established for similar purposes (such as registering bodies).

otherwise provided in these Rules and Procedures. Such information may also be released when the Chair and the Director agree that release of that information is necessary to protect the interests of (a) the complainant or respondent; (b) other investigative or adjudicative bodies; (c) the Association; or (d) members of the public, and release will not unduly interfere with the Association's interest in respecting the legitimate confidentiality interests of participants in the ethics process and its interest in safeguarding the confidentiality of internal peer review deliberation.

3.2 Access by Staff, Legal Counsel, and Other Duly Appointed Persons

Information may be shared with Legal Counsel of the Association, with the Chief Executive Officer of the Association, with staff of the Association's Central Office designated by the Chief Executive Officer to assist the Committee with its work, and with other duly appointed persons authorized by the Committee to assist it in carrying out its functions. Subject to the confidentiality provisions in these Rules, these persons are authorized to use this information for the purposes set out in these Rules regardless of whether the person providing the information has executed a release.

3.3 Notification in Connection with Investigation or Final Disposition of Investigation

Where these Rules provide for notification of final disposition of a matter, this notification shall include the ethical standard(s)[4] that were judged to have been violated and, if violation is found, the standards not violated, and the sanction (including a statement that directives were given), if any. In show cause proceedings under Part IV, this notification shall describe the type of underlying action (e.g., loss of license) without reference to the underlying behavior. In matters in which membership is voided under Part III, Subsection 3.3, the notification shall indicate that membership was voided because it was obtained on the basis of false or fraudulent information. In any of these matters, the rationale may also be included (a) if the notification is required by these Rules, at the discretion of the Board or Committee, (b) if the notification is not required, at the discretion of the entity or person (i.e., the Board, the Committee, or the Director) authorizing the notification, or (c) as set forth in a stipulation.

3.3.1 Respondent.   The Director shall inform the respondent of the final disposition in a matter. This notification shall include the rationale for the Association's actions. As used in these Rules and Procedures, the term respondent includes any member, student affiliate, or membership applicant who is under the scrutiny of the Ethics Committee.

3.3.2 Complainant.   The Director shall inform the complainant of the final disposition in a matter. The Director may also at any time, as a matter of discretion, provide such information as is necessary to notify the complainant of the status of a case.

3.3.3 Membership.   The Director shall report annually to the membership the names of members who have lost membership due to unethical behavior and the ethical standard(s) violated or the type of underlying action for a show cause case or that membership was voided because it was obtained on the basis of false or fraudulent information. No report to membership shall be made for stipulated resignations in which such a report was not stipulated.

3.3.4 Council of Representatives.   The Director shall report annually and in confidence to the Council the names of members who have been allowed to resign under stipulated conditions.

---

4. In this document *ethical standard(s)* refers to the ethical standard(s) in the Ethical Principles of Psychologists and Code of Conduct, the ethical principle(s) in the Ethical Principles of Psychologists, or the enforceable provisions of any subsequent ethics code.

3.3.5 Other Entities. When the Board of Directors, the Committee, or the Director (for stipulated resignations as provided in Part IV, Subsection 12.1.2) determines that further notification is necessary for the protection of the Association or the public or to maintain the standards of the Association, the Director shall communicate the final disposition to those groups and/or individuals so identified. Such notification may be made to (a) affiliated state and regional associations,[5] (b) the American Board of Professional Psychology, (c) state or local boards or similar entities, (d) the Association of State and Provincial Psychology Boards, (e) the Council for the National Register of Health Service Providers in Psychology, and/or (f) other appropriate parties.

3.3.6 Other Parties Informed of the Complaint. The Director may inform such other parties as have been informed of any matter reviewed under these Rules of the final disposition of that matter. Parties with knowledge of a matter may have been informed by the Committee, the Director, the respondent, or the complainant.

3.3.7 Notification in Cases That Have Been Converted. In any cases that have been converted under Part II, Subsections 7.3 or 7.4, the complainant and other persons informed of the complaint shall be notified of final disposition, including the fact that there has been a stipulated resignation, as set forth in Part IV, Subsections 12.1.2 and 12.2.1 and Part V, Subsection 7.6.5.

3.3.8 Disclosure of Fact of Investigation. The Director may disclose to any of the entities enumerated in Subsection 3.3.5 (a) (f) of this part the fact that an individual is under ethical investigation in cases deemed to be serious threats to the public welfare (as determined by a two thirds vote of the Committee), but only when to do so before final adjudication appears necessary to protect the public.

3.3.9 Notification of Additional Parties at the Request of Respondent. The Director may notify such additional parties of the final disposition as are requested by the respondent.

3.3.10 Notification of Loss of Membership Upon Written Request. The Director shall inform any person who submits a written inquiry concerning a psychologist that a former member has lost membership due to unethical behavior or that an individual's membership was voided because it was obtained on the basis of false or fraudulent information. The notification will not include actions that were already decided or were under the scrutiny of the Committee prior to June 1, 1996, or stipulated resignations unless so stipulated.

3.4 Initiation of Legal Action Constitutes Waiver

Initiation of a legal action against the Association or any of its agents, officers, directors, employees, or volunteers concerning any matters considered or actions taken by the Ethics Committee or Director shall constitute a waiver by the person initiating such action of any interest in confidentiality recognized in these Rules or other organic documents of the Association with respect to the subject matter of the legal action.

3.5 Communication for Investigation or Other Functions

Nothing in this section shall prevent the Director from communicating any information (including information from the respondent, complainant, or a witness) to the respondent, complainant, witnesses, or other sources of information to the extent necessary to facilitate

---

5. For purposes of these Rules and Procedures, a state association shall include territorial, local, or county psychological associations, and in cases of Canadian members of the Association, provincial psychological associations.

the performance of any functions set forth in these Rules and Procedures.

4. Records

4.1 Confidentiality of Ethics Files

Files of the Committee related to investigation and adjudication of cases shall be confidential, within the limitations of Section 3 of this part, and shall be maintained, consistent with these Rules and Procedures.

4.2 Investigation Files

Investigation records containing personally identifiable information shall be maintained for at least five years after a matter is closed.

4.3 Files Involving Loss of Membership

In cases in which members have lost membership, records shall be maintained indefinitely, except as provided in Subsection 4.4 of this part.

4.4 Readmission or Death of a Member

Records concerning members whom the Association has readmitted to membership or determined to be deceased shall be maintained for at least five years after that determination was made.

4.5 Records for Educative Purposes

Nothing in these Rules and Procedures shall preclude the Committee from maintaining records in a secure place for archival or record keeping purposes, or from using or publishing information concerning ethics matters for educative purposes without identifying individuals involved.

5. Jurisdiction

5.1 Persons

The Committee has jurisdiction over individual members (to include fellows), associate members, and applicants for membership in the American Psychological Association. The Committee shall also have jurisdiction over student affiliates, but only to the extent that the conduct at issue is not under the direct supervision of the student's educational program or of a training site that is officially approved by the program as part of the student's supervised training.[6]

5.2 Subject Matter

The Committee has jurisdiction to achieve its objectives and perform those functions for which it is authorized in these Rules and Procedures and other organic documents of the Association.

5.3 Time Limits for Complaints and Show Cause Notices

5.3.1 Complaints by Members. Except as provided in Subsections 5.3.5 and 5.3.6 of this part, the Committee may consider complaints brought by members of the Association against other members only if the complaint is received less than three years after the alleged conduct either occurred or was discovered by the complainant.

5.3.2 Complaints by Nonmembers and Student Affiliates. Except as provided in Subsections 5.3.5 and 5.3.6 of this part, the Committee may consider complaints brought by nonmembers and student affiliates only if the complaint is received less than five years after the alleged conduct either occurred or was discovered by the complainant.

---

6. Whether an individual is a member of the Association is determined according to the Bylaws, Association Rules, and other pertinent organic documents of the Association. Under the current rules, non-payment of dues results in discontinuation of membership only after two consecutive calendar years during which dues to the Association have remained unpaid. For a copy of the relevant sections of the current Bylaws and Association Rules, contact the APA Ethics Office. For purposes of these Rules and Procedures, high school and foreign affiliates are not members of the Association.

5.3.3 Sua Sponte *Complaints.*   Except as provided in Subsection 7.4 of this part, the Committee may initiate a *sua sponte* complaint under Part V of these Rules and Procedures only if it does so, or has provided the notice specified in Subsection 5.6.2 of this part, less than one year after it discovered the alleged unethical conduct and less than 10 years after the alleged conduct occurred, except that whether or not such periods have expired, the Committee may initiate a *sua sponte* complaint less than one year after it discovered that any of the following actions had become final, and less than 10 years after the alleged conduct occurred: (a) a felony conviction, (b) a finding of malpractice by a duly authorized tribunal, (c) expulsion or suspension from a state association for unethical conduct, or (d) revocation, suspension, or surrender of a license or certificate, or deregistration for ethical violations by a state or local board or similar entity, or while ethical proceedings before such board were pending.

5.3.4 Show Cause Notices.   The Committee may issue a show cause notice under Part IV of these Rules and Procedures only if it does so, or has provided the notice specified in Subsection 5.6.2 of this part, less than one year after the date it discovered that the applicable predicate for use of show cause procedures (i.e., an event described in Part IV, Section 1) had become final and less than 10 years after the alleged conduct occurred, except this latter time limit shall be 20 years in any matter involving an offense against a minor.

5.3.5 Exceptions to Time Limits for Complaints by Members and Nonmembers

5.3.5.1 Threshold Criteria.   Any complaint not received within the time limits set forth in this section shall not be considered unless, with respect to complaints subject to Subsections 5.3.1 and 5.3.2 of this part, the Chair and Director (with the vote of the Vice Chair if agreement is not reached by the Chair and Director) determine that each of the following criteria is met:

5.3.5.1.1   The behavior alleged involved one of the following: sexual misconduct; felony conviction; insurance fraud; plagiarism; noncooperation; blatant, intentional misrepresentation; or other behavior likely to cause substantial harm;

5.3.5.1.2   The complaint was received less than 10 years after the alleged conduct occurred.

5.3.5.2 Determination to Supersede Applicable Time Limit.   Where the Chair and Director have determined (with the vote of the Vice Chair if agreement is not reached by the Chair and Director) that the threshold criteria in Subsection 5.3.5.1 are met, the applicable limit shall be superseded.

5.3.6 Conduct Outside the Time Limits.   The Committee may consider evidence of conduct outside these time limits in connection with the commencement, investigation, review, or disposition of a matter involving conduct that is within the applicable time limits. However, the Committee may impose sanctions only for conduct that occurred within the time limits. In order for a sanction to be imposed for conduct occurring outside the time limits, the Chair and Director must decide to supersede the time limits applicable to that conduct as stated in Subsection 5.3.5 of this part.

5.3.7 Reopened Investigations.   In a matter reopened under Part II, Section 6, the investigation shall be considered within the time limits as long as the complaint in the original matter was received, or the original investigation was initiated, in a timely manner or a decision was made to supersede the time limit under Part II, Subsection 5.3.5. The Committee may not proceed with such an investigation, however, if the new evidence is received more than 10 years after the date the alleged unethical behavior occurred (except that this time limit shall be 20 years in any case that was initiated as or converted to a show cause case and involves an offense against a minor).

5.4 Resignation Barred.   Except as provided in Subsection 11.4 of this part of these Rules, no one under the scrutiny of the Committee will be allowed to resign from the Association either by letter of resignation, by nonpayment of dues, or otherwise.

5.5 Concurrent Litigation

Civil or criminal litigation involving members shall not bar action by the Committee; the Committee may proceed or may stay the ethics process during the course of litigation. Delay in conducting the investigation by the Committee during the pendency of civil or criminal proceedings shall not constitute waiver of jurisdiction.

5.6 Other Concurrent Disciplinary Proceedings

5.6.1 Concurrent Jurisdiction. Disciplinary proceedings or action by another body or tribunal shall not bar action by the Committee; the Committee may proceed or may stay the ethics process during the course of such proceedings. Delay in conducting the investigation by the Committee during the pendency of such proceedings shall not constitute a waiver of jurisdiction. Where the Committee learns that disciplinary action by another authorized tribunal has been stayed, such stay shall neither require nor preclude action by the Committee. When another body or tribunal has investigated the same allegations and found no merit to the allegations, the Ethics Committee may, in its discretion, decide not to open a matter or, if a matter has already been opened, the Ethics Committee may close the matter.

5.6.2 Nonfinal Disciplinary Action by Another Body. The Chair, Vice Chair, and Director may decide not to open a *sua sponte* or show cause case when a state or local board or similar entity has taken disciplinary action against an Association member if the action is either not final or the member has not completed all directives, probation, or other requirements and if the behavior at issue is not likely to result in expulsion from the Association. If this decision is made, the member will be notified that the matter is under the scrutiny of the Committee, that the member will be monitored until completion of actions required by the state or local board or similar entity, that failure to complete the action may result in further action by the Committee, and that completion of such requirements may result in the Committee taking no further action.

5.7 Referral and Retention of Jurisdiction

The Committee may at any time refer a matter to another recognized tribunal for appropriate action. If a case is referred to another tribunal, the Committee may retain jurisdiction and consider the matter independently under these Rules and Procedures.

6. Reopening a Closed Investigaton

If significant new evidence of unethical conduct comes to the attention of the Committee after a matter has been closed, the investigation may be reopened and acted upon under regular procedures. If, in the judgment of the Director, such information is furnished, the new evidence shall be submitted to the Committee, which may reopen the investigation if it agrees that the criteria listed below are satisfied. To be considered under this rule, new evidence must meet each of the following criteria:

6.1 The evidence was brought to the attention of the Committee after the investigation was closed;

6.2 The evidence could not with reasonable diligence have been brought to the attention of the Committee before the investigation was closed;

6.3 The evidence was provided to the Committee in a timely manner following its discovery;

6.4 The evidence would probably produce a different result.

7. Choice and Conversion of Procedures

7.1 Choice of Procedures

Where a case might be adjudicated according to the show cause procedures in Part IV of these Rules and Procedures, the Chair and the Director shall determine whether to proceed under Part IV or Part V of these Rules and Procedures.

7.2 Conversion of Show Cause Action to Sua Sponte Action

The Chair and the Director may convert a proceeding begun by show cause procedures under Part IV to a *sua sponte* action under Part V. In the event of such conversion, the complaint shall be deemed filed in a timely manner if the show cause proceeding was initiated in a timely fashion.

7.3 Conversion to Show Cause Action

Where the predicates for use of show cause procedures stated in Part IV, Section 1 are present, the Chair and the Director may convert a proceeding begun as a *sua sponte*, member, or nonmember complaint under Part V to a show cause proceeding under Part IV if the predicates are based on some or all of the same underlying conduct as was the basis for the original proceeding. In such event, the show cause proceeding shall be deemed initiated in a timely manner as long as the original proceeding was commenced within the time limits applicable to that proceeding or a decision was made to supersede the time limit under Part II, Subsection 5.3.5.

7.4 Conversion of Action Initiated by a Complainant to a Sua Sponte Action

The Chair and the Director may convert a proceeding commenced following a complaint submitted by a member or nonmember (including a proceeding in which the complaint is withdrawn) into a *sua sponte* action under Part V, Subsection 2.2. The action will be deemed filed in a timely manner as long as the member or nonmember complaint was received within the time limits applicable to the initial complaint or a decision was made to supersede the time limit in Part II, Subsection 5.3.5.

8. Correspondence and Documentation

8.1 Use of Correspondence

The Committee shall conduct as much of its business as is practical through correspondence, including telecopied information.

8.2 Personal Response

Although the respondent has the right to consult with an attorney concerning all phases of the ethics process, the respondent must respond to charges and recommendations of the Ethics Committee personally and not through legal counsel or another third party. If the respondent shows good cause as to why he or she cannot respond personally, the Director may waive this requirement.

8.3 Transcription of Audiotapes, Videotapes, and Similar Data Compilations

It shall be the responsibility of the individual or entity submitting to the Committee an audiotape, videotape, or similar data compilation to provide an accurate transcription of the information it contains. The Director may reject any audiotape, videotape, or similar data compilation provided unaccompanied by a transcription as required in this subsection unless and until such transcription is provided.

8.4 Service of Documents

For purposes of notice, service shall be made by delivery to the respondent or the respondent's attorney or by mail or common carrier to the respondent or the respondent's attorney at the respondent's or attorney's last known address. Delivery within this rule means handing the correspondence to the respondent or the attorney or leaving it at the respondent's office or place of abode or the attorney's office with a receptionist, secretary, clerk, or other person in charge thereof, or, if there is no one in charge, leaving it in a mailbox or a conspicuous place at that address. Service by mail is complete upon mailing. Where, after good faith efforts, the Committee has been unable to locate the respondent, it may give notice by publishing in a newspaper of general circulation in the respondent's last known place of domicile a notice to contact the Ethics Office concerning an important matter.

8.5 Material from the Public Domain

The Committee may consult authoritative resources from the public domain (e.g., the Directory of the American Psychological Association and the National Register of Health Service Providers in Psychology) without providing this material to the respondent.

9. Failure to Cooperate With Ethics Process

Members are required to cooperate fully and in a timely fashion with the ethics process. Failure to cooperate shall not prevent continuation of any proceedings and itself constitutes a violation of the Ethics Code that may warrant being expelled from the Association.

10. Board of Directors' Standing Hearing Panel

The President of the Association shall appoint members of the Standing Hearing Panel. Standing Hearing Panel members shall serve a three year renewable term. The Standing Hearing Panel shall consist of at least 30 members at least 5 of whom shall be public members, and the remainder shall be members of the Association in good standing, and shall not include any present members of the Ethics Committee.

11. Available Sanctions

On the basis of circumstances that aggravate or mitigate the culpability of the member, including prior sanctions, directives, or educative letters from the Association or state or local boards

or similar entities, a sanction more or less severe, respectively, than would be warranted on the basis of the factors set forth below, may be appropriate.

11.1 Reprimand

Reprimand is the appropriate sanction if there has been an ethics violation but the violation was not of a kind likely to cause harm to another person or to cause substantial harm to the profession and was not otherwise of sufficient gravity as to warrant a more severe sanction.

11.2 Censure

Censure is the appropriate sanction if there has been an ethics violation and the violation was of a kind likely to cause harm to another person, but the violation was not of a kind likely to cause substantial harm to another person or to the profession and was not otherwise of sufficient gravity as to warrant a more severe sanction.

11.3 Expulsion

Expulsion from membership is the appropriate sanction if there has been an ethics violation and the violation was of a kind likely to cause substantial harm to another person or the profession or was otherwise of sufficient gravity as to warrant such action.

11.4 Stipulated Resignation

Stipulated resignation may be offered by the Committee as follows:

11.4.1 At the time of the respondent's initial response to the show cause notice, contingent upon execution of an acceptable affidavit admitting responsibility for the violations charged, under Part IV, Subsection 12.1;

11.4.2 Following a Committee finding that the respondent has committed a violation of the Ethics Code or failed to show good cause why he or she should not be expelled, contingent on execution of an acceptable affidavit and approval by the Board of Directors, under Part IV, Subsection 12.2, or Part V, Subsection 7.6.

12. Available Directives

12.1 Cease and Desist Order

Such a directive requires the respondent to cease and desist specified unethical behavior(s).

12.2 Other Corrective Actions.

The Committee may require such other corrective actions as may be necessary to remedy a violation, protect the interests of the Association, or protect the public. Such a directive may not include a requirement that the respondent make a monetary payment to the Association or persons injured by the conduct.

12.3 Supervision Requirement

Such a directive requires that the respondent engage in supervision.

12.4 Education, Training, or Tutorial Requirement

Such a directive requires that the respondent engage in education, training, or a tutorial.

12.5 Evaluation and/or Treatment Requirement

Such a directive requires that the respondent be evaluated to determine the possible need for treatment and/or, if dysfunction has been established, obtain treatment appropriate to that dysfunction.

12.6 Probation

Such a directive requires monitoring of the respondent by the Committee to ensure compliance with the Ethics Committee's mandated directives during the period of those directives.

13. Matters Requiring the Concurrence of the Chair of the Committee and Director of the Ethics Office

Whenever matters entrusted by these Rules and Procedures to the Chair and Director require the concurrence of those officers before certain action may be taken, either officer in the event of disagreement may refer the matter to the Vice Chair, who together with the Chair and Director, shall make a final determination by majority vote.

PART III. MEMBERSHIP

1. Applications

1.1 Specific Jurisdiction

The Committee has the authority to investigate the preadmission scientific and professional ethics and conduct of all applicants for membership or student affiliation in the Association and to make recommendations as to whether an individual shall become a member or student affiliate. In addition, the Committee has the authority to consider all applications submitted by individuals who were previously denied admission as a result of unethical behavior and to make recommendations as to whether such an individual shall become a member or student affiliate. The Membership Committee shall transmit all applications on which there is an indication of possible preadmission unethical conduct and all applications from individuals who were previously denied admission as a result of unethical behavior or as a result of a recommendation by the Ethics Committee to the Director of the Ethics Office.

1.2 Procedures for Review

The Director shall transmit to the Committee a copy of the application and any other materials pertinent to the case. The Director shall take such steps, including contacting the applicant or other sources of information, as are necessary and appropriate to making a fair determination.

Upon review, the Committee may recommend to the Membership Committee that the application be granted or to the Board of Directors that the application be denied. If a recommendation is made to deny the application, the applicant shall be informed of the basis for that recommendation and shall have 30 days to submit a written response for consideration by the Board of Directors.

2. Applications for Readmission

2.1 Specific Jurisdiction

The Ethics Committee has the authority to review and make recommendations concerning all applications for readmission by persons who have lost membership as a result of unethical behavior or whose membership was voided because it was obtained on the basis of false or fraudulent information. The Membership Committee shall transmit all such applications for readmission to the Director of the Ethics Office.

2.2 Elapsed Time for Review

Applications for readmission by members who have lost membership due to unethical behavior (including submission of false or fraudulent information in a membership application) shall be considered by the Committee only after five years have elapsed from the date of that action. Applications for readmission by members who have been permitted to resign shall be considered only after the stipulated period or, where no period has been stipulated, three years have elapsed.

2.3 Procedures for Review

The Director shall transmit to the Committee a summary of the application for readmission and the record of the previous case against the former member. In all cases, the ex member must show that he or she is technically and ethically qualified and has satisfied any conditions upon readmission established by the Board. The Committee shall make one of the following recommendations to the Membership Committee and, as it deems appropriate, shall provide the rationale therefor.

2.3.1 Readmit.   Recommend that the former member be readmitted;

2.3.2 Deny Readmission.   Recommend that readmission be denied;

2.3.3 Defer Readmission.   Recommend that the application for readmission be deferred until certain conditions have been met;

2.3.4 Investigate Further.   Charge the Director to investigate issues specified by the Committee and to place the matter before the Committee at a future date.

3. Allegations That Membership Was Obtained Under False or Fraudulent Pretenses

3.1 Specific Jurisdiction

The Committee has the authority to investigate allegations that membership was obtained on the basis of false or fraudulent information and to take appropriate action. The Membership Committee shall transmit all such allegations to the Director of the Ethics Office.

3.2 Procedures for Review

The respondent will be given notice of the allegations that membership was obtained on the basis of false or fraudulent information, a copy of any evidence relating to these allegations that is submitted to the Committee, and an opportunity to respond in writing. The Director may take any other steps, such as contacting other sources of information, that are considered necessary and appropriate to making a fair determination in the circumstances of the case. The Director shall transmit to the Committee a copy of the membership application and any other materials pertinent to the case.

3.3 Committee's Recommendation

Upon completion of this review, the Committee may recommend to the Board of Directors that it void the election to membership in the Association of any person who obtained membership on the basis of false or fraudulent information.

3.4 Procedures Subsequent to Committee's Recommendation to Void Membership

If the respondent does not accept the Committee's recommendation, the respondent shall, within 30 days of receipt of the recommendation, either submit a written response to the Board of Directors, request a formal hearing in writing, or request an independent adjudication in writing and provide a written rationale for nonacceptance. The respondent's failure to respond within 30 days after notification shall be deemed acceptance of the Committee's recommendation and a waiver of the right to a formal hearing or an independent adjudication. If a written response is submitted, the Ethics Committee shall have 30 days to reply in a written statement to the Board. If a formal hearing is requested, it shall be conducted according to the procedures explained in Part V, Subsections 10.2 through 10.3.4 of these Rules and Procedures. If an independent adjudication is requested, it shall be conducted according to the procedures explained in Part V, Subsections 9.2.2 through 9.2.7 and Subsections 10.3 through 10.3.4.

3.5 Action by the Board of Directors

Within 180 days after receiving the record, the Committee's recommendation, any written response and statement described in Subsection 3.4, above, or any recommendation from a Hearing Committee or Independent Adjudication Panel, the Board of Directors shall vote whether to void the respondent's membership or not.

PART IV. SHOW CAUSE PROCEDURES BASED UPON ACTIONS BY OTHER RECOGNIZED TRIBUNALS

1. Predicates for Use of Show Cause Procedures

1.1 Felony or Equivalent Offense

If a member has been convicted of a felony (including any felony as defined by state/provin-cial law and any other criminal offense with a possible term of incarceration exceeding one year) and such conviction is not under appeal, the show cause process may be used, if determined by the Chair and the Director to be appropriate.

1.2 Expulsion, Suspension, Unlicensure, Decertification, or Other Actions

If one of the following actions has been taken and is not under appeal, the show cause process may be used, if determined by the Chair and the Director to be appropriate: (a) a member has been expelled or suspended from an affiliated state or regional psychological association; (b) a member has been denied a license, certificate, or registration, has been unlicensed, decertified, or deregistered, has had a license, certificate, or registration revoked or suspended by a state or local board or similar entity, or has voluntarily surrendered a license or certificate of registration as a result of pending allegations. The show cause procedures may also be used if a state or local board or similar entity has taken any of the actions specified in (a) or (b) above and has then in any way stayed or postponed that action.

2. Notice by the Committee and Response by Respondent

The respondent shall be notified by the Director that he or she has been barred from resigning membership in the Association (subject only to the terms of Section 12 of this part) and, on the basis of Part IV of these Rules and Procedures, will be afforded 60 days in which to show good cause as to why he or she should not be expelled from membership in the Association.

3. Showing by Respondent That Prior Proceeding Lacked Due Process

In addition to a response to the substance of the charges under Section 2 of this part, the respondent may seek within the 60 day period to show that the other recognized tribunal did not follow fair procedure. If the Committee finds merit to this contention, it may exercise its discretion under Part II, Subsection 7.2 of these Rules and convert the matter to a *sua sponte* action under Part V, or it may dismiss the complaint.

4. Investigation

The Committee may conduct a further investigation, including seeking additional information from the respondent or others or requesting that the respondent appear in person. Any evidence not obtained directly from the respondent and relied upon by the Committee in connection with its review and recommendation shall first have been provided to the respondent, who shall have been afforded not less than 15 days to respond thereto in writing.

5. Failure to Respond

If the 60-day period expires without receipt of a response, the respondent shall be notified that unless a response is received within 30 days, the Committee members may review the matter and vote by mail. If no response is received, the Committee may vote by mail to take one of the actions specified in Subsection 6 of this part.

6. Review and Recommendation by the Committee Following a Response

Upon receipt of the respondent's response and upon conclusion of any necessary further investigation, or the expiration of 60 days without response, the case shall be reviewed by the Ethics Committee. Members of the Ethics Committee and Ethics Committee Associates may be assigned to review and summarize the case. Members and Associates may also be assigned to participate on a panel to review the case and make a preliminary recommendation prior to review by the full Ethics Committee. Ethics Committee Associates may also attend and participate in the full Committee meetings, but shall not vote on the full Committee's disposition of a case. When review of a case has been completed, the Committee shall vote to take one of the following actions:

6.1 Remand

6.2 Dismiss the Matter

6.3 Recommend One of the Following Actions to the Board of Directors:

6.3.1 Reprimand or Censure, With or Without Directives. The Committee may recommend that the repondent be reprimanded or censured, with or without one or more directives.

6.3.2 Expulsion. The Committee may recommend that the respondent be expelled from the Association; or, the Committee may recommend the sanction of stipulated resignation, under the procedure in Subsection 12.2 of this part.

7. Notification of Respondent

The Director shall notify the respondent of the Committee's recommendation and shall provide the respondent the opportunity to file a written response with the Board of Directors.

8. Respondent's Response to Recommendation

Within 15 days of receipt of notification of the Committee's recommendation, the respondent may file a written response with the Board of Directors. The response should be mailed to the Ethics Office.

9. Committee's Statement

The Ethics Committee shall have 15 days from the time it receives the respondent's written response, or from the time such response was due, to file a written statement, if any. A copy will be provided to the respondent.

10. Respondent's Final Response

Within 15 days of receipt of the Ethics Committee's statement, if any, the respondent may submit to the Director a written response to that statement.

11. Review by the Board of Directors

Within 180 days after receiving the record, the Committee's recommendation, any written response by the respondent, any written statement by the Committee, and any final response from the respondent, the Board of Directors shall vote whether to accept the Committee's recommended sanction, to issue a different sanction, or to dismiss the case. The Board may select a sanction more or less severe than that recommended by the Committee, or it may remand the matter to the Ethics Committee for further consideration.

12. Stipulated Resignation

12.1 Stipulated Resignation With Admission of Violation in Respondent's Initial Response to the Show Cause Notice

12.1.1 Respondent's Offer of Stipulated Resignation With Admission of Violation.   In his or her initial response to the Committee's notice to show cause under Section 2 of this part, the respondent may offer to resign membership in the Association with admission of violation. Such an offer must include a statement of intent to execute an affidavit acceptable to the Committee (a) admitting the violation underlying the criminal conviction, expulsion, unlicensure, decertification, or deregistration, and (b) resigning membership in the Association.

12.1.2 Director's Response and Proposed Affidavit of Stipulated Resignation.   When the respondent makes such an offer, the Director will forward to the respondent a proposed affidavit of stipulated resignation. Such stipulations shall include the extent to which the stipulated resignation and its basis shall be disclosed and a minimum period of time, after resignation, during which the resigned member shall be ineligible to reapply for membership.

12.1.3 Acceptance by Respondent.   Within 30 days of receipt, the respondent may resign membership in the Association by signing and having notarized the proposed affidavit and re-

turning it to the Committee. Resignation shall be effective upon the Committee's timely receipt of the signed notarized affidavit.

12.1.4 Rejection by Respondent.   If the member fails to sign, have notarized, and return an acceptable affidavit within 30 days or formally notifies the Committee of rejection of the proposed affidavit, the offer of stipulated resignation shall be deemed rejected. The respondent shall be afforded an additional 30 days within which to supplement his or her response to the Committee's show cause notice. The matter shall then be resolved according to the applicable procedures in this part. All materials submitted by the respondent shall be part of the file to be considered by the Committee and/or the Board of Directors in connection with the case.

12.1.5 Availability of Stipulated Resignation With Admission of Violation.   Stipulated resignation with admission of violation is available only at the time and in the manner set forth in this section. Unless stipulated resignation with admission of violation is accomplished at the time and in the manner stated in this section, respondents may not resign while under scrutiny of the Ethics Committee except as stated in Subsection 12.2 of this part.

12.2 Stipulated Resignation After Review and Recommendation by the Committee.

In lieu of the recommendations set forth in Section 6 of this part, with the agreement of the respondent, the Committee may recommend that the respondent be permitted to resign from the Association under stipulations stated by the Committee, according to the following procedure:

12.2.1 Offer of Stipulated Resignation by Committee.   When the Committee finds that another body has taken one of the actions specified in Part IV Section 1 against a member, the Committee may offer, contingent upon approval by the Board of Directors, the respondent the opportunity to resign from the Association under mutually agreed upon stipulations. Such stipulations shall include the extent to which the stipulated resignation and its basis shall be disclosed and a minimum period of time, after resignation, during which the resigned member shall be ineligible to reapply for membership. The Committee may, in its discretion, also vote to recommend to the Board and inform the respondent of an alternative sanction chosen from among Subsections 11.1–11.3 of Part II of these Rules in the event the respondent does not accept the offer of stipulated resignation.

12.2.2 Notification of Respondent.   In such cases, the respondent shall be notified, in writing, of the Committee's offer of stipulated resignation and that he or she may accept the Committee's offer within 30 days of receipt. The respondent shall also be notified of any alternative recommended sanction.

12.2.3 Acceptance by Respondent.   Within 30 days, the respondent may accept the offer of stipulated resignation by signing a notarized affidavit of resignation acceptable to both the respondent and the Committee and forwarding the signed notarized affidavit to the Committee. Such resignation shall become effective only with the approval of the Board, as set forth in this section.

12.2.4 Transmittal to Board of Directors.   If the respondent accepts the stipulated resignation, the Committee shall submit a copy of the affidavit of resignation, with the record in the matter and the rationale for recommending stipulated resignation on the terms set forth in the affidavit, to the Board of Directors.

12.2.5 Action by Board of Directors.   Within 180 days, the Board of Directors shall take one of the following actions:

12.2.5.1 Acceptance of Stipulated Resignation.   The Board of Directors shall accept the respondent's resignation on the terms stated in the affidavit of resignation, unless it is persuaded that to do so would not be in the best interest of the Association and/or of the public. If the

resignation is accepted by the Board, the Director shall so notify the respondent.

12.2.5.2 Reprimand or Censure.   The Board may reject the stipulated resignation and impose a lesser sanction (reprimand or censure with or without directives). If the Board selects this option, the respondent shall be so notified and shall have 30 days to submit a written request seeking reconsideration of the Board's decision. If no such request is submitted, the Board's decision shall become final. If a request for reconsideration is submitted, the Board shall choose from the options set forth in Subsection 12.2.5 (including adherence to its prior decision).

12.2.5.3 Remand to the Committee.   The Board may choose to reject the affidavit of resignation and remand the matter to the Committee for further consideration. If the Board selects this alternative, the Director shall so notify the respondent and the Committee shall then reconsider the matter.

12.2.6 Rejection of Stipulated Resignation by Respondent.   If the respondent fails within 30 days to accept the recommended resolution, or formally notifies the Committee of rejection of the offer of stipulated resignation within the 30-day period, the offer of stipulated resignation shall be deemed rejected. The Committee shall reconsider the matter or, if an alternative recommended sanction has previously been identified by the Committee, such alternative recommended sanction shall automatically become the recommended sanction. The Director shall notify the respondent of the recommendation and of his or her opportunity to file written responses with the Board of Directors, as stated in Section 8 of this part. Sections 8–11 of this part shall also apply.

PART V. COMPLAINTS ALLEGING VIOLATION OF THE ETHICS CODE

1. Initiation of Actions

Ethics proceedings against a member are initiated by the filing of a complaint or, in the case of a *sua sponte* action, by the issuance of a letter notifying the respondent that a *sua sponte* action has been commenced.

2. Complaints

2.1 Complaints Submitted by Members or Nonmembers

Complaints may be submitted by members or nonmembers of the Association.

2.2 Sua Sponte *Action*

When a member appears to have violated the Association's Ethics Code, the Committee may proceed on its own initiative. The Committee may, at any time, exercise its discretion to discontinue a *sua sponte* action. If the Committee does so, the respondent shall be so notified.

2.3 Sua Sponte *Action Based Upon a Member's Filing of a Capricious or Malicious Complaint*

To prevent abuse of the ethics process, the Committee is empowered to bring charges itself against a complainant if the initial complaint is judged by two thirds of Committee members voting to be (a) frivolous and (b) intended to harm the respondent rather than to protect the public. The filing of such a complaint constitutes a violation of the Ethics Code.

2.4 Countercomplaints

The Committee will not consider a complaint from a respondent member against a complainant member during the course of its investigation and resolution of the initial complaint. Rather, the Committee shall study all sides of the matter leading to the first complaint and consider countercharges only after the initial complaint is finally resolved. The Committee may waive this procedure by a vote of at least two thirds of the voting Committee members and consider both complaints simultaneously.

2.5 Anonymous Complaints

The Committee shall not act upon anonymous complaints. If material in the public domain is provided anonymously, the Committee may choose to consider such material in connection with a *sua sponte* matter or other complaint or may initiate a *sua sponte* action but only if the respondent has been provided with a copy of the material and afforded an opportunity to respond to the material.

2.6 Complaints Against Nonmembers

If the complaint does not involve an individual within the jurisdiction of the Committee, the Director shall inform the complainant and may suggest that the complainant contact another agency or association that may have jurisdiction.

2.7 Consecutive Complaints

When a complaint is lodged against a member with respect to whom a case involving similar alleged behavior was previously closed, materials in the prior case may be considered in connection with the new case and may be considered as evidence as long as the Ethics Committee and/or the Board of Directors is informed of the final disposition of the original case.

2.8 Simultaneous Complaints

When more than one complaint is simultaneously pending against the same member, the Committee may choose to combine the cases or to keep them separate. In the event the cases are combined, the Committee shall take reasonable steps to ensure that the legitimate confidentiality interests of any complainant, witness, or respondent are not compromised by combination.

3. Procedures for Filing Complaints

A complaint by a member or nonmember shall be comprised of

3.1 A completed APA Ethics Complaint Form;

3.2 Such releases as are required by the Committee;

3.3 A waiver by the complainant of any right to subpoena from APA or its agents for the purposes of private civil litigation any documents or information concerning the case;[7]

3.4 For purposes of determining time limits, a complaint shall be considered filed with APA as soon as a completed complaint form has been received by the Ethics Office. A deficiency or omission in the preparation of the complaint form may, at the discretion of the Director, be disregarded for purposes of determining compliance with time limits.

4. Preliminary Evaluation of Complaints by the Director

The Director shall review each complaint to determine if jurisdictional criteria are met and if it can be determined whether cause for action exists.

4.1 Lack of Jurisdiction

If jurisdictional criteria are not satisfied, the matter shall be closed and the complainant so notified.

4.2 Information Insufficient to Determine Jurisdiction

4.2.1 Request for Supplementation of Complaint. If the information is not sufficient to determine whether jurisdictional criteria are met, the Director shall so inform the complainant, who will be given 30 days from receipt of the request to supplement the complaint.

4.2.2 Consequences of Failure to Supplement Complaint. If no response is received from the complainant within 30 days from receipt of the request, the matter may be closed. If at a later date the complainant shows good cause for delay and demonstrates that jurisdictional criteria can be met, the supplemented complaint shall be considered.

4.3 Process With Respect to Superseding Applicable Time Limit

4.3.1 Consideration by Chair and Director. If a complaint otherwise within the jurisdiction of the Ethics Committee appears to have been filed outside the applicable time limit, the Chair and the Director will determine whether the criteria set forth in Part II, Subsection 5.3.5 appear to be satisfied. If they agree that the criteria do not appear to be satisfied, the matter will be closed, unless there are other allegations that are filed in a timely manner, in which case processing of the timely allegations continues under Section 5, below. If they agree that the criteria appear to be satisfied, the Director will contact the respondent according to the procedure in Subsection 4.3.2, below. If they are not in agreement on whether or not those criteria appear to be satisfied, the Vice Chair shall review the matter and cast the deciding vote.

4.3.2 Response by Respondent Where Criteria Appear To Be Satisfied. If a determination is made according to Subsection 4.3.1 above that the criteria of Part II, Subsection 5.3.5 appear to be satisfied, the Director shall notify the respondent and provide the respondent with a copy of the complaint and any other materials the Director deems appropriate. The respondent shall have 30 days from receipt of these materials to address whether the criteria of Part II, Subsection 5.3.5 are met.

4.3.3 Determination by Chair and Director. If the respondent does not provide a response under Subsection 4.3.2, above, the decision

---

7. This waiver is required to help assure participants in the APA ethics process, including complainants, that the process will not be inappropriately used to gain an advantage in other litigation.

made under Subsection 4.3.1, above, shall become final. In any case in which the respondent provides a response, the Chair and the Director shall consider whether the criteria set forth in Part II, Subsection 5.3.5 are satisfied, based upon any materials provided by the complainant and respondent, and any other information available to the Chair and the Director. If they agree that the criteria are not satisfied, the matter will be closed, unless there are other allegations that are filed in a timely manner, in which case processing of the timely allegations continues under Section 5, below. If they agree that the criteria are satisfied, processing continues under Section 5, below. If they are not in agreement on whether or not those criteria are satisfied, the Vice Chair shall review the matter and cast the deciding vote.

5. Evaluation of Complaints by Chair and Director

All complaints not closed by the Director under Section 4 of this part shall be reviewed by the Chair and the Director to determine whether cause for action by the Ethics Committee exists.

5.1 Cause for Action Defined

Cause for action shall exist when the respondent's alleged actions and/or omissions, if proved, would in the judgment of the decision maker constitute a breach of ethics. For purposes of determining whether cause for action exists, incredible, speculative, and/or internally inconsistent allegations may be disregarded.

5.2 Information Insufficient to Determine Cause for Action

5.2.1 Request for Supplementation of Complaint. If the information is not sufficient to determine whether a case should be opened, the Director may so inform the complainant, who will be given 30 days from receipt of the request to supplement the complaint. The Chair and Director may additionally, or in the alternative, commence a preliminary investigation under Subsection 5.3 of this part.

5.2.2 Consequences of Failure to Supplement Complaint. If no response is received from the complainant within 30 days, the matter may be closed. If at a later date the complainant shows good cause for delay and responds to the request for supplementation, the supplemented complaint shall be considered.

5.3 Preliminary Investigation Due to Insufficient Information.

If the Chair and Director agree that they lack sufficient information to determine whether a case should be opened, in either a case initiated by a complainant or in a *sua sponte* action, a preliminary investigation may be initiated.

5.3.1 Notification to Respondent. If a preliminary investigation is opened, the Director shall so inform the respondent in writing. The Director will include a copy of all evidence in the file; a copy of the APA Ethics Code; the Committee's Rules and Procedures; and a statement that information submitted by the respondent shall become a part of the record and can be used if further proceedings ensue.

5.3.2 Time for Respondent Response. The respondent shall have 30 days after receipt of the notification of a preliminary investigation to file an initial response.

5.3.3 Information From Other Sources. Additional information may be requested from the complainant, respondent, or any other appropriate source. The Committee will not rely upon information submitted by such sources unless it has been shared with the respondent and the respondent has been afforded an opportunity to respond thereto.

5.3.4 Action if There Continues to Be Insufficient Information. At the conclusion of the preliminary investigation, if the Director and Chair determine that they still lack evidence sufficient to determine whether cause for action exists, the matter shall be closed.

5.4 Determination of Cause for Action

If the Chair and Director agree that cause for action exists, they shall consider whether to open a formal case under Subsection 5.5, below. If the Chair and Director agree that cause for action does not exist, the matter shall be closed. If the Chair and Director disagree on whether or not there is cause for action by the Committee, the matter shall be reviewed by the Vice Chair, who will cast the deciding vote.

5.5 Decision to Open a Case

In any case in which the determination has been made that cause for action exists, the Chair and Director shall consider whether (a) there is a reasonable basis to believe the alleged violation cannot be proved by a preponderance of the evidence and (b) the allegations would constitute only minor or technical violations that would not warrant further action, have already been adequately addressed in another forum, or are likely to be corrected. If they agree that one or more of the conditions are met, the matter shall be closed. Otherwise, the matter shall be opened as a case.

5.6 Educative Letter

If a matter is closed under Sections 4 or 5 of this part, the Chair and Director may, if appropriate, send an educative letter to the respondent.

5.7 Reconsideration of Decision to Open

A matter not opened under either Subsection 5.4 or 5.5, above, may be reconsidered by the Committee only if it does so in accordance with Part II, Section 6.

5.8 Supplementary or Alternative Action

The Chair and Director may recommend that the complainant refer the complaint to an appropriate state psychological association, state board, regulatory agency, subsidiary body of the Association, or other appropriate entity, or they may make such referral on their own initiative. Such referral does not constitute a waiver of jurisdiction over the complaint provided that the Committee opens a formal case within 24 months from the date of referral.

6. Case Investigation

6.1 Issuance of Charge Letter and Response From Respondent

6.1.1 Charge Letter. If a case is opened, the Director shall so inform the respondent in a charge letter. The charge letter shall contain a concise description of the alleged behaviors at issue and identify the specific section(s) of the Ethics Code that the respondent is alleged to have violated. The Director shall enclose a copy of any completed Ethics Complaint Form and any materials submitted to date by the complainant or on the complainant's behalf that will be included in the record before the Committee; a copy of the APA Ethics Code and the Committee's Rules and Procedures; and a statement that information submitted by the respondent shall become a part of the record, and can be used if further proceedings ensue.

6.1.2 Significance of Charge Letter. A charge letter does not constitute or represent a finding that any unethical behavior has taken place, or that any allegations of the complaint are or are not likely to be found to be true.

6.1.3 Issuance of New Charge Letter to Conform to Evidence Discovered During Investigation. At any time prior to final resolution by the Committee, in order to make the charges conform to the evidence developed during the investigation, the Director and Chair may determine that a new charge letter should be issued setting forth ethical standard(s) and/or describing alleged behaviors different from or in addition to those contained in the initial charge letter. In a *sua sponte* case, the date of issuance shall, for purposes of applicable time limits, be deemed to relate back to the date of the initial letter notifying the respondent that a *sua sponte* action has been initiated. The new charge letter shall in all other respects be treated exactly as an initial charge letter issued according to Subsection 6.1.1 of this part.

6.1.4 Time for Respondent's Response.

The respondent shall have 30 days after receipt of the charge letter to file an initial response. Any request to extend the time for responding to the charge letter must be made in writing, within the 30 days, and must show good cause for an extension.

6.1.5 Personal Appearance.

The Chair and Director may request the respondent to appear personally before the Committee. The respondent has no right to such an appearance.

6.2 Information From Other Sources

Additional information may be requested from the complainant, respondent, or any other appropriate source.

6.3 Referral to Committee

When, in the sole judgment of the Chair and Director, the investigation is complete, the case will be referred to the Committee for review and resolution. The Director shall notify the complainant and respondent that the matter has been referred to the Committee.

6.4 Documentation Subsequent to Investigation and Prior to Resolution by the Committee

Within 30 days after receipt of notification that the case is being referred to the Ethics Committee for review and resolution, the complainant and respondent may submit any additional information or documentation. Any materials submitted in a timely manner by the complainant or on the complainant's or respondent's behalf will be forwarded to the respondent. Within 15 days from receipt of those materials, the respondent may submit any additional information or documentation. All such materials submitted within these time limitations shall be included in the file to be reviewed by the Ethics Commit-

tee. Materials submitted outside of the time limit will not be included in the file materials relative to the ethics case and will not be reviewed by the Ethics Committee.

In the sole discretion of the Director, where good cause for noncompliance with these time limits is shown by the complainant or the respondent, the resolution of the case may be postponed until the next scheduled meeting of the Ethics Committee and the information or documentation provided outside of the time limit may be included in the file materials to be reviewed by the Committee at that later time. In the sole discretion of the Director, in the event the respondent fails to comply with these time limits, the information or documentation provided outside of the time limits may be included in the file materials to be reviewed by the Committee and the matter maintained for resolution by the Committee as originally scheduled.

7. Review and Resolution by the Committee

The Ethics Committee may assign a member of the Committee or an Ethics Committee Associate to serve as a case monitor. The monitor may provide assistance to assure that an adequate record is prepared for Ethics Committee review and in such other respects as necessary to further the objectives of these Rules and Procedures. Upon conclusion of the investigation, the case shall be reviewed by the Ethics Committee. Members of the Ethics Committee and Ethics Committee Associates may be assigned to review and summarize the case. Members and Associates may also be assigned to participate on a panel to review and make a preliminary recommendation prior to review by the full Ethics Committee. Ethics Committee Associates may also attend and participate in the full Ethics Committee meetings, but shall not vote on the full Committee's disposition of a case. When review of a case has been completed, the Ethics Committee shall vote to take one of the following actions described below: remand, dismiss the charges, recommend reprimand or censure, recommend expulsion, or recommend stipulated resignation. In addition to any of these actions, the Committee may vote to issue an educative letter. The Committee may choose to dismiss some charges but find violation and take disciplinary action on the basis of other charges in the charge letter. The respondent shall then be notified of the Committee's action, the ethical standard(s) involved, if any, the rationale for the Committee's decision, any sanction, and any directives.

7.1 Remand

The Committee may remand the matter to the Director for continued investigation or issuance of a new charge letter according to Subsection 6.1.3 of this part.

7.2 Dismiss the Charges

7.2.1 No Violation.   The Committee may dismiss a charge if it finds the respondent has not violated the ethical standard as charged.

7.2.2 Violation Would Not Warrant Further Action.   The Committee may dismiss the complaint if it concludes that any violation it might find (a) would constitute only a minor or technical violation that would not warrant further action, (b) has already been adequately addressed in another forum, or (c) is likely to be corrected.

7.2.3 Insufficient Evidence.   The Committee may dismiss a charge if it finds insufficient evidence to support a finding of an ethics violation.

7.3 Educative Letter

Where the Committee deems it appropriate, the Committee may issue an educative letter, to be shared only with the respondent, concerning the behaviors charged or other matters. An educative letter may be issued whether the Committee dismisses the charges or recommends finding violations.

7.4 Recommend Reprimand or Censure

If the Committee finds that the respondent has violated the Ethics Code, but decides that the nature of the respondent's behavior is such that the matter would be most appropriately resolved without recommending loss of membership, the Committee will recommend reprimand or censure of the respondent, with or without one or more available directives. See Part II, Subsections 11.1, 11.2, and Section 12.

7.5 Recommend Expulsion

The Committee may recommend expulsion if it concludes that there has been an ethics violation, that it was of a kind likely to cause substantial harm to another person or the profession, or that it was otherwise of such gravity as to warrant this action.

7.6 Recommend Stipulated Resignation

In lieu of the other resolutions set forth in this section, with the agreement of the respondent, the Committee may recommend to the Board that the respondent be permitted to resign under stipulations set forth by the Committee, according to the following procedure:

7.6.1 Offer of Stipulated Resignation by the Committee.   When the Committee finds that the respondent has committed a violation of the Ethics Code, the Committee may offer to enter into an agreement with the respondent, contingent upon approval by the Board of Directors, that the respondent shall resign from the Association under mutually agreed upon stipulations. Such stipulations shall include the extent to which the stipulated resignation and underlying ethics violation shall be disclosed and a minimum period of time after resignation during which the respondent shall be ineligible to reapply for membership. The Committee may also vote to recommend and inform the member of an alternative sanction chosen from among Subsections 11.1–11.3 of Part II of these Rules in the event the member does not accept the offer of stipulated resignation.

7.6.2 Notification of Respondent.   In such cases, the respondent shall be notified, in writing, of the Committee's recommended sanction of stipulated resignation and that he or she may accept the Committee's recommended sanction within 30 days of receipt. The respondent shall also be notified of any alternative recommended sanction.

7.6.3 Acceptance by Respondent.
Within 30 days, the respondent may accept the recommended sanction of stipulated resignation by executing a notarized affidavit of resignation acceptable both to the respondent and the Committee and forwarding the executed notarized affidavit to the Committee. Such resignation shall become effective only with the approval of the Board, as set forth in Subsection 7.6.5 of this part.

7.6.4 Transmittal to Board of Directors.
If the respondent accepts the recommended sanction of stipulated resignation, the Committee shall submit a copy of the affidavit of resignation, with the record in the matter and the rationale for recommending stipulated resignation on the terms stated in the affidavit, to the Board of Directors.

7.6.5 Action by Board of Directors.
Within 180 days, the Board of Directors shall accept the respondent's resignation on the terms stated in the affidavit of resignation, unless it is persuaded that to do so would not be in the best interest of the Association and/or of the public. If the resignation is accepted by the Board, the Director shall notify the complainant and respondent of the final disposition of the case.

7.6.6 Rejection of Stipulated Resignation by Respondent.
If the respondent fails to accept the determination within 30 days, or formally notifies the Committee of rejection of the offer of stipulated resignation within the 30 day period, the offer of stipulated resignation shall be deemed rejected. The Committee shall reconsider the matter or, if an alternative recommended sanction has previously been identified by the Committee, such alternative recommended resolution shall automatically become the recommended sanction according to Subsection 7.4 or 7.5 of this part.

7.6.7 Rejection of Stipulated Resignation by Board.
If the Board rejects the affidavit of resignation under Subsection 7.6.5 of this part, the Committee shall so notify the respondent and reconsider the matter.

8. Procedures Subsequent to Dismissal by Committee

The Committee may reconsider a case dismissed under Subsection 7.2 of this part only if it does so in accordance with Part II, Section 6.

9. Procedures Subsequent to Committee Recommendation of Reprimand or Censure

If the Committee proceeds under Subsection 7.4 of this part, the following procedures shall govern:

9.1 Acceptance of Reprimand or Censure

If the respondent accepts the Committee's recommended sanction and directives, if any, the right of independent adjudication shall be waived, any directives will be implemented by the Director, and the case will remain open until the directives are met. The respondent's failure to respond within 30 days of notification shall be deemed acceptance of the Committee's recommended sanction and directives.

9.2 Independent Adjudication After Recommended Sanction of Reprimand or Censure

The method of adjudication for a recommended sanction of reprimand or censure is an independent adjudication based on the written record by a three person Independent Adjudication Panel.

9.2.1 Request for Independent Adjudication and Rationale for Nonacceptance.
The respondent may exercise his or her right to independent adjudication by furnishing the Committee, within 30 days after notification of the

Committee's recommendation, a written request for independent adjudication and rationale for nonacceptance of the recommendation.

9.2.2 Statement by Committee. Within 30 days of receipt of the respondent's rationale for nonacceptance, the Committee may prepare a statement and provide a copy to the respondent. No statement by the Committee is required.

9.2.3 Respondent's Final Response. Within 15 days of receipt of the Ethics Committee's statement, if any, the respondent may submit to the Director a written response to that statement.

9.2.4 Selection of Independent Adjudication Panel

9.2.4.1 Provision of Standing Hearing Panel List. Within 60 days of receipt of the request for an independent adjudication, the Director shall provide the respondent with the names and curricula vitae of six members of the Board of Directors' Standing Hearing Panel, of whom at least one shall be a public member. The proposed panel members need not include any member having a particular speciality or representing a particular geographic location. The Director shall make inquiry and ensure that proposed panel members do not have a conflict of interest as defined by applicable law and appear otherwise able to apply fairly the APA Ethics Code based solely on the record in the particular case.

9.2.4.2 Designation of Panel Members. Within 15 days after receipt of the six member list, the respondent shall select three of the six to constitute the Independent Adjudication Panel. The Panel shall include not fewer than two members of the Association. Whenever feasible, the respondent's selection will be honored. If at any time prior to conclusion of the adjudication, any panelist cannot serve on the Independent Adjudication Panel for any reason, the respondent shall be notified promptly and afforded the opportunity within 10 days of receipt of notification to replace that individual from among a list of not fewer than four members of

the Board of Directors' Standing Hearing Panel. In the event the respondent fails to notify the Director of his or her initial or replacement selections in a timely fashion, the right to do so is waived, and the President of the Association shall select the member(s), whose name(s) shall then be made known to the respondent.

9.2.4.3 Designation of Chair of Independent Adjudication Panel. The President shall designate one of the three Panel members to serve as Chair. The Chair of the Panel shall ensure that the Panel fulfills its obligations according to these Rules and Procedures.

9.2.5 Provision of Case File to Independent Adjudication Panel. Within 15 days of selection of the Independent Adjudication Panel, receipt of the Committee's statement according to Subsection 9.2.2 of this part, if any; receipt of the respondent's final response according to Subsection 9.2.3 of this part, if any; or if no statement or response is received, the expiration of the time period for such statement or response, whichever occurs latest, the Director will provide the case file to the members of the Independent Adjudication Panel. The case file shall include the complaint and all correspondence and evidence submitted to the Ethics Committee, the respondent's rationale for nonacceptance of the Committee's recommendation, the Committee's statement, if any, and the respondent's final response, if any.

9.2.6 Consideration and Vote by Independent Adjudication Panel. Within 60 days of receipt of the case file, the members of the Panel shall confer with each other and, solely on the basis of the documentation provided and deliberations among themselves, shall vote to take one of the following actions:

9.2.6.1 Adopt the Committee's Recommended Sanction and Directives

9.2.6.2 Adopt a Lesser Sanction and/or Less Burdensome Directives

9.2.6.3 Dismiss the Case

9.2.7 Decision of the Independent Adjudication Panel. Decisions of the Independent Adjudication Panel will be made by majority vote, and at least two reviewers must agree to written findings, a sanction, if any, and a directive or directives, if any. The Committee bears the burden to prove the charges by a preponderance of the evidence. The panelists' votes and the majority's written decision must be submitted to the Ethics Office within the 60 day period set forth in Subsection 9.2.6 of this part. If no two panelists can agree as to the appropriate outcome or a written decision, the case will be referred back to the Committee for further action.

9.2.8 Finality of Decision by Independent Adjudication Panel. The decision of the Independent Adjudication Panel is unappealable. The decision is binding on the Committee and the respondent except that subsequent to the Panel's decision, the Committee may determine that directives are impractical or unduly burdensome and may choose to reduce or dismiss directives required in the Panel's decision. A decision by the Panel either to impose a sanction and/or directive(s) or to dismiss the case will be implemented by the Director as the final adjudication, unless modified by the Committee.

9.2.9 Notification. The Director shall inform the respondent and complainant, if any, of the final disposition. The respondent shall be provided a copy of the majority's written decision.

10. Procedures Subsequent to Committee Recommendation of Expulsion

If the Committee proceeds under Subsection 7.5 of this part, the following procedures shall govern:

10.1 Acceptance of Recommendation of Expulsion

If the respondent accepts the Committee's recommendation to the Board of Directors that he or she be expelled from membership, the right to a formal hearing shall be waived, and the

Committee shall proceed with its recommendation to the Board of Directors according to Subsection 10.3.5 and other subsections of this part. In such event, the recommendation of the Ethics Committee shall be treated as the equivalent of the recommendation of a Formal Hearing Committee that the respondent be expelled from membership. The respondent's failure to respond within 30 days after notification shall be deemed acceptance of the Committee's recommendation.

10.2 Formal Hearing After Recommendation of Expulsion

The method of adjudication for a recommended sanction of expulsion issued under Subsection 7.5 of this part is a formal hearing before a three member Hearing Committee. Upon request, the respondent will be provided with a copy of the APA Ethics Office "Guidelines for Formal Hearings." These guidelines are for guidance and information purposes only and are not binding on the APA, the Ethics Committee, or hearing participants. The proceedings are governed solely by the Rules and Procedures of the Ethics Committee and the Ethical Principles of Psychologists and Code of Conduct. Alternatively, a respondent may request an independent adjudication to be provided according to the procedures described in Subsections 9.2.2 through 9.2.7 of this part of these Rules in place of the Subsections 10.2.2 through 10.2.6. The Independent Adjudication Panel will make a recommendation that will be subject to review by the Board of Directors as described in Subsection 10.3.

10.2.1 Request for Formal Hearing. The respondent may exercise his or her right to a formal hearing by requesting a hearing in writing within 30 days of notification of the Committee's recommendaton. Alternatively, the respondent may request an independent adjudication by furnishing the Committee a written request for independent adjudication, and a written rationale for nonacceptance of the Committee's recommendation, within 30 days after notification of the Committee's recommendation.

10.2.2 Formal Hearing Date and Hearing Committee

10.2.2.1 Establishment of Hearing Date and Provision of Standing Hearing Panel List.
Within 60 days after the receipt of the respondent's request for a formal hearing, the Director shall establish the date of the hearing and provide the respondent with the date and the names and curricula vitae of six members of the Board of Directors' Standing Hearing Panel. The six identified members of the Board of Directors' Standing Hearing Panel shall include at least one public member. The proposed panel members need not include any member having a particular specialty or representing a particular geographic location. The Director shall make inquiry and ensure that proposed panel members do not have a conflict of interest as defined by applicable law and appear otherwise able to apply fairly the Ethics Code based solely on the record in the particular case.

10.2.2.2 Designation of Hearing Committee Members.
The Hearing Committee shall consist of three individuals, selected from among the six individuals from the Board of Directors' Standing Hearing Panel identified according to Subsection 10.2.2.1 of this part. The Hearing Committee shall include not fewer than two members of the Association. Within 15 days after the receipt of the names and curricula vitae, the respondent shall notify the Director of his or her selections for the Hearing Committee. Whenever feasible, the respondent's selections will be honored. In the event an individual selected by the respondent cannot serve on the Hearing Committee for any reason, the respondent shall be notified and afforded the opportunity within 10 days of receipt of notification to replace that individual from among a list of not fewer than four members of the Board of Directors' Standing Hearing Panel. If the respondent fails to notify the Director of his or her initial or replacement selections in a timely fashion, the right to do so is waived and the President shall select the Hearing Committee member(s), whose name(s) shall then be made known to the respondent.

10.2.2.3 Voir Dire of Designated Hearing Committee Members.
At the time the respondent selects the three designated Hearing Committee members, the respondent may also submit in writing, to the Director, a request to question designated Hearing Committee members with respect to potential conflict of interest. If the President has chosen the three Hearing Committee members, the respondent shall have 15 days after receipt of their names to submit such a request. Upon receipt of such written request, the Director shall convene by telephone conference call, or otherwise, a formal opportunity for such questioning by the respondent or the respondent's attorney. Legal Counsel for the Association shall preside at such voir dire, shall be the sole judge of the propriety and pertinency of questions posed, and shall be the sole judge with respect to the fitness of designated Hearing Committee members to serve. Failure by the respondent to submit a timely request shall constitute a waiver of the privilege to conduct voir dire.

10.2.2.4 Designation of Chair of Hearing Committee.
The President shall designate one of the three Hearing Committee members to serve as Chair. The Chair of the Hearing Committee and Legal Counsel for the Association shall assure proper observance of these Rules and Procedures at the formal hearing.

10.2.3 Documents and Witnesses

10.2.3.1 Committee.
At least 30 days prior to the scheduled date of the formal hearing, the Ethics Committee shall provide the respondent and the Hearing Committee with copies of all documents and other evidence, and the names of all witnesses that may be offered by the Committee in its case in chief.

10.2.3.2 Respondent.
At least 15 days prior to the scheduled date of the formal hearing, the respondent shall provide the Ethics Committee and the Hearing Committee with copies of all documents and other evidence, and the names of all witnesses that may be offered by the respondent.

10.2.3.3 Rebuttal Documents and Witnesses. At least 5 days prior to the scheduled date of the formal hearing, the Committee shall provide the respondent and the Hearing Committee with copies of all documents and other evidence, and the names of all witnesses that may be offered in rebuttal.

10.2.3.4 Audiotapes, Videotapes, and Similar Data Compilations. Audiotapes, videotapes, and similar data compilations are admissible at the formal hearing, provided usable copies of such items, together with a transcription thereof, are provided in a timely fashion according to the provisions of this section.

10.2.3.5 Failure to Provide Documents, Other Evidence, and Names of Witnesses in a Timely Fashion in Advance of the Formal Hearing. Failure to provide copies of a document or other evidence or the name of a witness in a timely fashion and consistent with this section and these Rules and Procedures is grounds for excluding such document, other evidence, or witness from evidence at the formal hearing, unless good cause for the omission and a lack of prejudice to the other side can be shown.

10.2.4 Formal Hearing Procedures

10.2.4.1 Presiding Officers

10.2.4.1.1 The Chair of the Hearing Committee shall preside at the hearing. The General Counsel of the Association shall designate Legal Counsel to assist the Hearing Committee.

10.2.4.1.2 Legal Counsel for the Hearing Committee shall be present to advise on matters of procedure and admission of evidence and shall represent neither the Ethics Committee nor the respondent at the formal hearing.

10.2.4.2 Legal Representation of the Respondent and Committee

10.2.4.2.1 Respondent. The respondent may choose, at the respondent's own expense, to be represented by a licensed attorney.

10.2.4.2.2 Committee. The General Counsel of the Association may designate Legal Counsel to advise the Ethics Committee. The Chair of the Ethics Committee, the Chair's designee, or Legal Counsel to the Committee presents the Committee's case.

10.2.4.3 Rules of Evidence. Formal rules of evidence shall not apply. All evidence that is relevant and reliable, as determined for the Hearing Committee by Legal Counsel for the Hearing Committee, shall be admissible.

10.2.4.4 Rights of the Respondent and the Committee. Consistent with these Rules and Procedures, the respondent and the Committee shall have the right to present witnesses, documents, and other evidence, to cross examine witnesses, and to object to the introduction of evidence.

10.2.4.5 Burden of Proof. The Ethics Committee shall bear the burden to prove the charges by a preponderance of the evidence.

10.2.5 Decision of the Hearing Committee. The decision shall be by a simple majority vote. Within 30 days of the conclusion of the hearing, the Hearing Committee shall submit in writing to the Board of Directors, through the Director, its decision and the rationale for that decision. The Hearing Committee may decide to

10.2.5.1 Adopt the Committee's Recommendation to the Board of Directors

10.2.5.2 Recommend to the Board of Directors a Lesser Sanction With or Without Directives

10.2.5.3 Dismiss the Charges

10.2.6 Notice to the Respondent and the Ethics Committee. Within 15 days of receipt of the Hearing Committee's decision, a copy of the decision and the rationale for the decision shall be provided to the respondent and the Ethics Committee. If the Hearing Committee determines that the charges must be dismissed, the Ethics Committee will implement this as the final adjudication.

10.3 Proceedings Before the Board of Directors

10.3.1 Referral to Board of Directors. If the Hearing Committee or Independent Adjudication Panel recommends that the respondent be expelled from membership or otherwise disciplined, the matter will be referred to the Board of Directors. The Director shall provide the materials of record to the Board, including a copy of the Hearing Committee's or Independent Adjudication Panel's decision; the respondent's timely response, if any, under Subsection 10.3.2 of this part; the Ethics Committee's timely statement, if any, under Subsection 10.3.3 of this part; the respondent's timely final response, if any, under Subsection 10.3.4 of this part; and the record.

10.3.2 Respondent's Response. Within 30 days of receipt of the Hearing Committee's or Independent Adjudication Panel's decision, the respondent may file a written response with the Board of Directors, through the Ethics Office. A copy of the respondent's written response shall be retained by the Chair of the Ethics Committee.

10.3.3 Ethics Committee's Statement. Within 15 days of receipt of the respondent's response or the date such response was due, the Ethics Committee may prepare a written statement and provide a copy to the respondent.

10.3.4 Respondent's Final Response. Within 15 days of receipt of the Ethics Committee's statement, if any, the respondent may file with the Board of Directors, through the Director, a written response to the Ethics Committee's statement. A copy of this response shall be retained by the Chair of the Ethics Committee.

10.3.5 Action by the Board of Directors. Within 180 days of receipt of the recommendation of the Hearing Committee or Independent Adjudication Panel (or of the Ethics Committee if no subsequent adjudication was held), together with any timely responses thereto and the record, the Board of Directors will consider these materials and will take action as follows:

10.3.5.1 Adopt. The Board of Directors shall adopt the recommendation, unless by majority vote it finds grounds for nonacceptance, as set forth in Subsection 10.3.5.2.

10.3.5.2 Not Adopt After Determining Grounds for Nonacceptance. Only the following shall constitute grounds for nonacceptance of the recommendation by the Board:

10.3.5.2.1 Incorrect Application of Ethical Standard(s). The Ethics Code of the Association was incorrectly applied.

10.3.5.2.2 Erroneous Findings of Fact. The findings of fact were clearly erroneous.

10.3.5.2.3 Procedural Errors. The procedures used were in serious and substantial violation of the Bylaws of the Association and/or these Rules and Procedures.

10.3.5.2.4 Excessive Sanction or Directives. The disciplinary sanction or directives recommended are grossly excessive in light of all the circumstances.

10.3.5.3 Consequences of Nonacceptance. If the Board of Directors finds grounds for nonacceptance, it shall refer the case back to the Ethics Committee. In its discretion, the Ethics Committee may return the matter for reconsideration before a newly constituted Hearing Committee or Independent Adjudication Panel or may continue investigation and/or readjudicate the matter at the Committee level.

10.4 Notification

If the Board of Directors does not adopt the recommendation, it shall notify the Ethics Committee in writing why the decision was not accepted, citing the applicable ground(s) for nonacceptance under Subsection 10.3.5.2 of this part.

10.5 Reconsideration

If a reconsideration is instituted, the procedures of relevant subsections of this part shall apply.

Unless any of the following is offered by the respondent, none shall be part of the record before the second Hearing Committee or Independent Adjudication Panel: the original Hearing Committee's or Independent Adjudication Panel's report; the respondent's written responses or Ethics Committee's written statements made under Subsections 10.3.2, 10.3.3, and 10.3.4 of this part; and the Board of Directors' rationale for nonacceptance of the original Hearing Committee's or Independent Adjudication Panel's recommendation. If the respondent offers any portion of any of the foregoing documents as evidence in the reconsideration, the Committee may introduce any portion of any or all of them.

Index